The Art of Multiprocessor Programming

For my parents, David and Patricia Herlihy, and for Liuba, David, and Anna.

For my parents, Noun and Aliza, my beautiful wife Shafi, and my kids, Yonadav and Lior, for their love and their patience, their incredible, unbelievable, and unwavering patience, throughout the writing of this book.

Contents

Acknowledgments

We would like to thank Doug Lea, Michael Scott, Ron Rivest, Tom Corman, Radia Perlman, George Varghese and Michael Sipser for their help in finding the right publication venue for our book.

We thank all the students, colleagues, and friends who read our draft chapters and sent us endless lists of comments and ideas: Yehuda Afek, Shai Ber, Martin Buchholz, Vladimir Budovsky, Christian Cachin, Cliff Click, Yoav Cohen, Dave Dice, Alexandra Fedorova, Pascal Felber, Christof Fetzer, Shafi Goldwasser, Rachid Guerraoui, Tim Harris, Danny Hendler, Maor Hizkiev, Eric Koskinen, Christos Kozyrakis, Edya Ladan, Doug Lea, Oren Lederman, Pierre Leone, Yossi Lev, Wei Lu, Victor Luchangco, Virendra Marathe, Kevin Marth, John Mellor-Crummey, Mark Moir, Dan Nussbaum, Kiran Pamnany, Ben Pere, Torvald Riegel, Vijay Saraswat, Bill Scherer, Warren Schudy, Michael Scott, Ori Shalev, Marc Shapiro, Yotam Soen, Ralf Suckow, Seth Syberg, Alex Weiss, and Zhenyuan Zhao. We apologize for any names inadvertently omitted.

We thank Mark Moir, Steve Heller, and our colleagues in the Scalable Synchronization group at Sun Microsystems for their incredible support during the writing of the book.

Thanks to all who have sent us errata to improve this book, including: Rajeev Alur, Matthew Allen, Karolos Antoniadis, Cristina Basescu, Liran Barsisa, Igor Berman, Konstantin Boudnik, Bjoern Brandenburg, Martin Buchholz, Kyle Cackett, Mario Calha, Michael Champigny, Neill Clift, Eran Cohen, Daniel B. Curtis, Gil Danziger, Venkat Dhinakaran, David Dice, Wan Fokkink, David Fort, Robert P. Goddard, Brian Goetz, Bart Golsteijn, K. Gopinath, Enes Goktas, Jason T. Greene, Dan Grossman, Tim Halloran, Muhammad Amber Hassaan, Matt Hayes, Francis Hools, Ben Horowitz, Barak Itkin, Paulo Janotti, Kyungho Jeon, Ahmed Khademzadeh, Irena Karlinsky, Habib Khan, Omar

Khan, Namhyung Kim, Guy Korland, Sergey Kotov, Doug Lea, Yossi Lev, Adam MacBeth, Kevin Marth, Adam Morrison, Adam Weinstock, Mike Maloney, Tim McIver, Sergejs Melderis, Bartosz Milewski, Mark Moir, Adam Morrison, Victor Luchangco, Jose Pedro Oliveira, Dale Parson, Jonathan Perry, Amir Pnueli, Pat Quillen, Binoy Ravindran, Roei Raviv, Sudarshan Raghunathan, Jean-Paul Rigault, Michael Rueppel, Mohamed M. Saad, Assaf Schuster, Marc Shapiro, Nathar Shah, Huang-Ti Shih, Joseph P. Skudlarek, James Stout, Mark Summerfield, Deqing Sun, Seth Syberg, Fuad Tabba, Binil Thomas, John A Trono, Thomas Weibel, Adam Weinstock, Jaeheon Yi, Zhenyuan Zhao, Ruiwen Zuo, Chong Xing.

This book offers complete code for all the examples, as well as slides, updates, and other useful tools on its companion web page at: *http://store.elsevier.com/product.jsp?isbn=9780123973375*

Preface

This book is intended to serve both as a textbook for a senior-level undergraduate course, and as a reference for practitioners.

Readers should know enough discrete mathematics to understand "big-O" notation, and what it means for a problem to be NP-complete. It is helpful to be familiar with elementary systems constructs such as processors, threads, and caches. A basic understanding of Java is needed to follow the examples. (We explain advanced language features before using them.) Two appendixes summarize what the reader needs to know: Appendix A covers programming language constructs, and Appendix B covers multiprocessor hardware architectures.

The first third covers the *principles* of concurrent programming, showing how to *think* like a concurrent programmer. Like many other skills such as driving a car, cooking a meal, or appreciating caviar, thinking concurrently requires cultivation, but it can be learned with moderate effort. Readers who want to start programming right away may skip most of this section, but should still read Chapters 2 and 3 which cover the basic ideas necessary to understand the rest of the book.

We first look at the classic *mutual exclusion* problem (Chapter 2). This chapter is essential for understanding why concurrent programming is a challenge. It covers basic concepts such as fairness and deadlock. We then ask what it means for a concurrent program to be correct (Chapter 3). We consider several alternative conditions, and the circumstances one might want to use each one. We examine the properties of *shared memory* essential to concurrent computation (Chapter 4), and we look at the kinds of synchronization primitives needed to implement highly concurrent data structures (Chapters 5 and 6).

We think it is essential that anyone who wants to become truly skilled in the art of multiprocessor programming spend time solving the problems presented in the first part of this book. Although these problems are idealized, they distill the kind of thinking necessary to write effective multiprocessor programs. Most important, they distill the style of thinking necessary to avoid the common mistakes committed by nearly all novice programmers when they first encounter concurrency.

The next two-thirds describe the *practice* of concurrent programming. Each chapter has a secondary theme, illustrating either a particular programming pattern or algorithmic technique. At the level of systems and languages, Chapter 7 covers spin locks and contention. This chapter introduces the importance of the underlying architecture, since spin lock performance cannot be understood without understanding the multiprocessor memory hierarchy. Chapter 8 covers monitor locks and waiting, a common synchronization idiom, especially in Java. Chapter 16 covers work-stealing and parallelism, and Chapter 17 describes barriers, all of which are useful for structuring concurrent applications.

Other chapters cover concurrent data structures. All these chapters depend on Chapter 9, and the reader should read this chapter before reading the others. Linked lists illustrate different kinds of synchronization patterns, ranging from coarse-grained locking, to fine-grained locking, to lock-free structures (Chapter 9). The FIFO queues illustrate the ABA synchronization hazard that arises when using atomic synchronization primitives (Chapter 10), Stacks illustrate an important synchronization pattern called *elimination* (Chapter 11), Hash maps show how an algorithm can exploit natural parallelism (Chapter 13), Skip lists illustrate efficient parallel search (Chapter 14), and priority queues illustrate how one can sometimes weaken correctness guarantees to enhance performance (Chapter 15).

Finally, Chapter 18 describes the emerging *transactional* approach to concurrency, which we believe will become increasingly important in the near future.

The importance of concurrency has not always been acknowledged. Here is a quote from a 1989 *New York Times* article on new operating systems for the IBM PC:

> Real concurrency–in which one program actually continues to function while you call up and use another–is more amazing but of small use to the average person. How many programs do you have that take more than a few seconds to perform any task?

Read this book, and decide for yourself.

Suggested Ways to Teach the Art of Multiprocessor Programming

Preface

The following are three possible tracks to teaching a multiprocessor programming course using the material in the book.

The first track is a short course for *practitioners* who are interested in techniques that can be applied directly to problems at hand.

The second track is a longer course for students who are *not Computer Science majors*, but who are interested in learning the basics of multiprocessor programming, as well as techniques likely to be useful in their own areas.

The third track is a semester-long course for *Computer Science majors*, either upper-level undergraduates or graduate students.

Practitioner Track

Cover Chapter 1, emphasizing Amdahl's law and its implications. In Chapter 2, cover sections 2.1, 2.2, 2.3, and 2.6. Mention the *implications* of the impossibility proofs in Section 2.8. In Chapter 3, skip Sections 3.3 and 3.6.

Cover Chapter 7, except for Sections 7.7 and 7.8. Chapter 8, which deals monitors and reentrant locks, may be familiar to some practitioners. Skip Section 8.5 on Semaphores.

Cover Chapters 9, 10, except for 10.7, and Sections 11.1 and 11.2. Skip the material in Sections 11.3 and onwards. Skip Chapter 12.

Cover Chapters 13 and 14. Skip Chapter 15. Cover Chapter 16, except for Section 16.5. In Chapter 17, teach sections 17.1–17.3.

Non-CS Major Track

Cover Chapter 1, emphasizing Amdahl's law and its implications. In Chapter 2, cover sections 2.1, 2.2, 2.3, 2.5, and 2.6. Mention the *implications* of the impossibility proofs in Section 2.8. In Chapter 3 skip Section 3.6.

Cover the material in Sections 4.1 and 4.2, and Chapter 5. Mention the universality of consensus, but skip Chapter 6.

Cover Chapter 7, except for Sections 7.7 and 7.8. Cover Chapter 8.

Cover Chapters 9, 10, except for 10.7, and Chapter 11. Skip Chapter 12.

Cover Chapters 13 and 14. Skip Chapter 15. Cover Chapter 16. In Chapter 17, teach sections 17.1–17.3. Cover Chapter 18.

CS Major Track

The slides on the companion page were developed for a semester-long course

Cover Chapters 1 and 2 (Section 2.7 is optional) and 3. (Section 3.6 is optional). Cover Chapters 4, 5, and 6. Before starting Chapter 7, it may be useful to review basic multiprocessor architecture (Appendix B).

Cover Chapter 7 (Sections 7.7 and 7.8 are optional). Cover Chapter 8 if your students are unfamiliar with Java monitors. Cover Chapters 9 and 10 (Section 10.7 optional). Cover Chapters 11, 12 (Sections 12.7, 12.8, and 12.9 are optional), 13, and 14. Chapter 15 is optional. Cover Chapters 16 and 17. Chapter 18 is optional.

Introduction

The computer industry is undergoing, if not another revolution, certainly a vigorous shaking-up. The major chip manufacturers have, for the time being at least, given up trying to make processors run faster. Moore's Law has not been repealed: each year, more and more transistors fit into the same space, but their clock speed cannot be increased without overheating. Instead, manufacturers are turning to "multicore" architectures, in which multiple processors (cores) communicate directly through shared hardware caches. Multiprocessor chips make computing more effective by exploiting *parallelism*: harnessing multiple processors to work on a single task.

The spread of multiprocessor architectures will have a pervasive effect on how we develop software. Until recently, advances in technology meant advances in clock speed, so software would effectively "speed up" by itself over time. Now, however, this free ride is over. Advances in technology will mean increased parallelism and not increased clock speed, and exploiting such parallelism is one of the outstanding challenges of modern Computer Science.

This book focuses on how to program multiprocessors that communicate via a shared memory. Such systems are often called *shared-memory multiprocessors* or, more recently, *multicores*. Programming challenges arise at all scales of multiprocessor systems—at a very small scale, processors within a single chip need to coordinate access to a shared memory location, and on a large scale, processors in a supercomputer need to coordinate the routing of data. Multiprocessor programming is challenging because modern computer systems are inherently *asynchronous*: activities can be halted or delayed without warning by interrupts, preemption, cache misses, failures, and other events. These delays are inherently unpredictable, and can vary enormously in scale: a cache miss might delay a processor for fewer than ten instructions, a page fault for a few million instructions, and operating system preemption for hundreds of millions of instructions.

We approach multiprocessor programming from two complementary directions: principles and practice. In the *principles* part of this book, we focus on *computability*: figuring out what can be computed in an asynchronous concurrent environment. We use an idealized model of computation in which multiple concurrent *threads* manipulate a set of shared *objects*. The sequence of the thread operations on the objects is called the *concurrent program* or *concurrent algorithm*. This model is essentially the model presented by the Java^{TM}, C#, or C++ thread packages.

Surprisingly, there are easy-to-specify shared objects that cannot be implemented by any concurrent algorithm. It is therefore important to understand what not to try, before proceeding to write multiprocessor programs. Many of the issues that will land multiprocessor programmers in trouble are consequences of fundamental limitations of the computational model, so we view the acquisition of a basic understanding of concurrent shared-memory computability as a necessary step. The chapters dealing with principles take the reader through a quick tour of asynchronous computability, attempting to expose various computability issues, and how they are addressed through the use of hardware and software mechanisms.

An important step in the understanding of computability is the specification and verification of what a given program actually does. This is perhaps best described as *program correctness*. The correctness of multiprocessor programs, by their very nature, is more complex than that of their sequential counterparts, and requires a different set of tools, even for the purpose of "informal reasoning" (which, of course, is what most programmers actually do). Sequential correctness is mostly concerned with safety properties. A *safety* property states that some "bad thing" never happens. For example, a traffic light never displays green in all directions, even if the power fails. Naturally, concurrent correctness is also concerned with safety, but the problem is much, much harder, because safety must be ensured despite the vast number of ways that the steps of concurrent threads can be interleaved. Equally important, concurrent correctness encompasses a variety of *liveness* properties that have no counterparts in the sequential world. A *liveness* property states that a particular good thing will happen. For example, a red traffic light will eventually turn green. A final goal of the part of the book dealing with principles is to introduce a variety of metrologies and approaches for reasoning about concurrent programs, which will later serve us when discussing the correctness of real-world objects and programs.

The second part of the book deals with the *practice* of multiprocessor programming, and focuses on performance. Analyzing the performance of multiprocessor algorithms is also different in flavor from analyzing the performance of sequential programs. Sequential programming is based on a collection of well-established and well-understood abstractions. When we write a sequential program, we usually do not need to be aware that underneath it all, pages are being swapped from disk to memory, and smaller units of memory are being moved in and out of a hierarchy of processor caches. This complex memory hierarchy is essentially invisible, hiding behind a simple programming abstraction.

In the multiprocessor context, this abstraction breaks down, at least from a performance perspective. To achieve adequate performance, the programmer must sometimes "outwit" the underlying memory system, writing programs that would seem bizarre to someone unfamiliar with multiprocessor architectures.

Someday perhaps, concurrent architectures will provide the same degree of efficient abstraction now provided by sequential architectures, but in the meantime, programmers should beware.

The principles part of the book presents a progressive collection of shared objects and programming tools. Every object and tool is interesting in its own right, and we use each one to expose the reader to higher-level issues: spin-locks illustrate contention, linked lists illustrate the role of locking in data structure design, and so on. Each of these issues has important consequences for program performance. The hope is that the reader will understand the issue in a way that will later allow him or her to apply the lessons learned to specific multiprocessor systems. We culminate with a discussion of state-of-the-art technologies such as *transactional memory*.

We would like to include a few words about style. The book uses the Java programming language. There are, of course, other suitable languages which readers would have found equally appealing. We have a long list of reasons for our specific choice, but perhaps it is more suitable to discuss them over a cup of coffee! In the appendix we explain how the concepts expressed in Java are expressed in other popular languages or libraries. We also provide a primer on multiprocessor hardware. Throughout the book, we avoid presenting specific performance numbers for programs and algorithms, and stick to general trends. There is a good reason for this: multiprocessors vary greatly, and unfortunate though it may be, at this point in time, what works well on one machine may be significantly less impressive on another. Sticking to general trends is our way of guaranteeing that the validity of our assertions will be sustained over time.

We provide references at the end of each chapter. The reader will find a bibliographical survey of the material covered, with suggestions for further reading. Each chapter also includes a collection of exercises which readers can use to gauge their comprehension or entertain themselves on Sunday mornings.

1.1 Shared Objects and Synchronization

On the first day of your new job, your boss asks you to find all primes between 1 and 10^{10} (never mind why), using a parallel machine that supports ten concurrent threads. This machine is rented by the minute, so the longer your program takes, the more it costs. You want to make a good impression. What do you do?

As a first attempt, you might consider giving each thread an equal share of the input domain. Each thread might check 10^9 numbers, as shown in Fig. 1.1. This approach fails, for an elementary, but important reason. Equal ranges of inputs do not necessarily produce equal amounts of work. Primes do not occur uniformly: there are more primes between 1 and 10^9 than between $9 \cdot 10^9$ and 10^{10}. To make matters worse, the computation time per prime is not the same in all ranges: it usually takes longer to test whether a large number is prime than a

```
void primePrint {
  int i = ThreadID.get();  // thread IDs are in {0..9}
  int block = power(10, 9);
  for (int j = (i * block) + 1; j <= (i + 1)* block; j++) {
    if (isPrime(j))
      print(j);
  }
}
```

Figure 1.1 Balancing load by dividing up the input domain. Each thread in {0..9} gets an equal subset of the range.

```
Counter counter = new Counter(1);  // shared by all threads
void primePrint {
  long i = 0;
  long limit = power(10, 10);
  while (i < limit) {              // loop until all numbers taken
    i = counter.getAndIncrement(); // take next untaken number
    if (isPrime(i))
      print(i);
  }
}
```

Figure 1.2 Balancing the work load using a shared counter. Each thread gets a dynamically determined number of numbers to test.

small number. In short, there is no reason to believe that the work will be divided equally among the threads, and it is not clear even which threads will have the most work.

A more promising way to split the work among the threads is to assign each thread one integer at a time (Fig. 1.2). When a thread is finished with testing an integer, it asks for another. To this end, we introduce a *shared counter*, an object that encapsulates an integer value, and that provides a `getAndIncrement()` method that increments its value, and returns the counter's prior value to the caller.

Fig. 1.3 shows a naïve implementation of `Counter` in Java. This counter implementation works well when used by a single thread, but it fails when shared by multiple threads. The problem is that the expression

```
return value++;
```

is actually an abbreviation of the following, more complex code:

```
long temp = value;
value = temp + 1;
return temp;
```

In this code fragment, `value` is a field of the `Counter` object, and is shared among all the threads. Each thread, however, has its own local copy of `temp`, which is a local variable to each thread.

```
public class Counter {
  private long value;    // counter starts at one
  public Counter(int i) {    // constructor initializes counter
    value = i;
  }
  public long getAndIncrement() { // increment, returning prior value
    return value++;
  }
}
```

Figure 1.3 An implementation of the shared counter.

Now imagine that threads *A* and *B* both call the counter's `getAndIncrement()` method at about the same time. They might simultaneously read 1 from `value`, set their local `temp` variables to 1, `value` to 2, and both return 1. This behavior is not what we intended: concurrent calls to the counter's `getAndIncrement()` return the same value, but we expect them to return distinct values. In fact, it could get even worse. One thread might read 1 from `value`, but before it sets `value` to 2, another thread would go through the increment loop several times, reading 1 and setting to 2, reading 2 and setting to 3. When the first thread finally completes its operation and sets `value` to 2, it will actually be setting the counter back from 3 to 2.

The heart of the problem is that incrementing the counter's value requires two distinct operations on the shared variable: reading the `value` field into a temporary variable and writing it back to the `Counter` object.

Something similar happens when you try to pass someone approaching you head-on in a corridor. You may find yourself veering right, then left several times to avoid the other person doing exactly the same thing. Sometimes you manage to avoid bumping into them and sometimes you do not, and in fact, as we see in the later chapters, such collisions are provably unavoidable.[1] On an intuitive level, what is going on is that each of you is performing two distinct steps: looking at ("reading") the other's current position, and moving ("writing") to one side or the other. The problem is, when you read the other's position, you have no way of knowing whether they have decided to stay or move. In the same way that you and the annoying stranger must decide who passes on the left and who on the right, threads accessing a shared `Counter` must decide who goes first and who goes second.

As we will see in Chapter 5, modern multiprocessor hardware provides special *read-modify-write* instructions that allow threads to read, modify, and write a value to memory in one *atomic* (i.e., indivisible) hardware step. For the `Counter` object, we can use such hardware to increment the counter atomically.

---

1 A preventive approach such as "always sidestep to the right" does not work because the approaching person may be British.

We can also provide such atomic behavior by guaranteeing in software (using only read and write instructions) that only one thread executes the read-and-write sequence at a time. The problem of making sure that only one thread at a time can execute a particular block of code is called the *mutual exclusion* problem, and is one of the classic coordination problems in multiprocessor programming.

As a practical matter, you are unlikely ever to find yourself having to design your own mutual exclusion algorithm (instead, you would probably call on a library). Nevertheless, understanding how to implement mutual exclusion from the basics is an essential condition for understanding concurrent computation in general. There is no more effective way to learn how to reason about essential and ubiquitous issues such as mutual exclusion, deadlock, bounded fairness, and blocking versus nonblocking synchronization.

1.2 A Fable

Instead of treating coordination problems (such as mutual exclusion) as programming exercises, we prefer to think of concurrent coordination problems as if they were physics problems. We now present a sequence of fables, illustrating some of the basic problems. Like most authors of fables, we retell stories mostly invented by others (see the Chapter Notes at the end of this chapter).

Alice and Bob are neighbors, and they share a yard. Alice owns a cat and Bob owns a dog. Both pets like to run around in the yard, but (naturally) they do not get along. After some unfortunate experiences, Alice and Bob agree that they should coordinate to make sure that both pets are never in the yard at the same time. Of course, we rule out trivial solutions that do not allow any animals into an empty yard.

How should they do it? Alice and Bob need to agree on mutually compatible procedures for deciding what to do. We call such an agreement a *coordination protocol* (or just a *protocol*, for short).

The yard is large, so Alice cannot simply look out of the window to check whether Bob's dog is present. She could perhaps walk over to Bob's house and knock on the door, but that takes a long time, and what if it rains? Alice might lean out the window and shout "Hey Bob! Can I let the cat out?" The problem is that Bob might not hear her. He could be watching TV, visiting his girlfriend, or out shopping for dog food. They could try to coordinate by cell phone, but the same difficulties arise if Bob is in the shower, driving through a tunnel, or recharging his phone's batteries.

Alice has a clever idea. She sets up one or more empty beer cans on Bob's windowsill (Fig. 1.4), ties a string around each one, and runs the string back to her house. Bob does the same. When she wants to send a signal to Bob, she yanks the string to knock over one of the cans. When Bob notices a can has been knocked over, he resets the can.

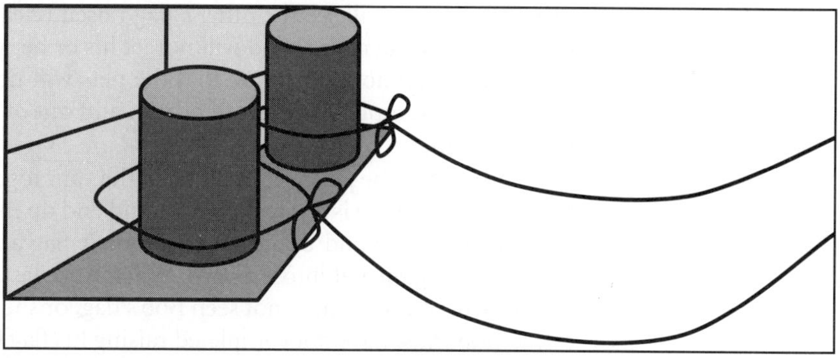

Figure 1.4 Communicating with cans.

Up-ending beer cans by remote control may seem like a creative solution, but it is still deeply flawed. The problem is that Alice can place only a limited number of cans on Bob's windowsill, and sooner or later, she is going to run out of cans to knock over. Granted, Bob resets a can as soon as he notices it has been knocked over, but what if he goes to Cancún for Spring Break? As long as Alice relies on Bob to reset the beer cans, sooner or later, she might run out.

So Alice and Bob try a different approach. Each one sets up a flag pole, easily visible to the other. When Alice wants to release her cat, she does the following:

1. She raises her flag.
2. When Bob's flag is lowered, she unleashes her cat.
3. When her cat comes back, she lowers her flag.

Bob's behavior is a little more complicated.

1. He raises his flag.
2. While Alice's flag is raised
   a) Bob lowers his flag
   b) Bob waits until Alice's flag is lowered
   c) Bob raises his flag
3. As soon as his flag is raised and hers is down, he unleashes his dog.
4. When his dog comes back, he lowers his flag.

This protocol rewards further study as a solution to Alice and Bob's problem. On an intuitive level, it works because of the following *flag principle*. If Alice and Bob each

1. raises his or her own flag, and then
2. looks at the other's flag,

then at least one will see the other's flag raised (clearly, the last one to look will see the other's flag raised) and will not let his or her pet enter the yard. However, this observation does not *prove* that the pets will never be in the yard together. What if, for example, Alice lets her cat in and out of the yard several times while Bob is looking?

To prove that the pets will never be in the yard together, assume by way of contradiction that there is a way the pets could end up in the yard together. Consider the last time Alice and Bob each raised their flag and looked at the other's flag before sending the pet into the yard. When Alice last looked, her flag was already fully raised. She must have not seen Bob's flag, or she would not have released the cat, so Bob must have not completed raising his flag before Alice started looking. It follows that when Bob looked for the last time, after raising his flag, it must have been after Alice started looking, so he must have seen Alice's flag raised and would not have released his dog, a contradiction.

This kind of argument by contradiction shows up over and over again, and it is worthwhile spending some time convincing ourselves why this claim is true. It is important to note that we never assumed that "raising my flag" or the "looking at your flag" happens instantaneously, nor did we make any assumptions about how long such activities take. All we care about is when these activities start or end.

1.2.1 Properties of Mutual Exclusion

To show that the flag protocol is a correct solution to Alice and Bob's problem, we must understand what properties are required of a solution, and then show that they are met by the protocol.

First, we proved that the pets are excluded from being in the yard at the same time, a property we call *mutual exclusion.*

Mutual exclusion is only one of several properties of interest. After all, as we noted earlier, a protocol in which Alice and Bob never release a pet satisfies the mutual exclusion property, but it is unlikely to satisfy their pets. Here is another property of central importance. First, if one pet wants to enter the yard, then it eventually succeeds. Second, if both pets want to enter the yard, then eventually at least one of them succeeds. We consider this *deadlock-freedom* property to be essential.

We claim that Alice and Bob's protocol is deadlock-free. Suppose both pets want to use the yard. Alice and Bob each raise their flags. Bob eventually notices that Alice's flag is raised, and defers to her by lowering his flag, allowing her cat into the yard.

Another property of compelling interest is *starvation-freedom* (sometimes called *lockout-freedom*): if a pet wants to enter the yard, will it eventually succeed? Here, Alice and Bob's protocol performs poorly. Whenever Alice and Bob are in conflict, Bob defers to Alice, so it is possible that Alice's cat can use the yard over and over again, while Bob's dog becomes increasingly uncomfortable. Later on, we will see how to make protocols prevent starvation.

The last property of interest concerns *waiting*. Imagine that Alice raises her flag, and is then suddenly stricken with appendicitis. She (and the cat) are taken to the hospital, and after a successful operation, she spends the next week under observation at the hospital. Although Bob is relieved that Alice is well, his dog cannot use the yard for an entire week until Alice returns. The problem is that the protocol states that Bob (and his dog) must *wait* for Alice to lower her flag. If Alice is delayed (even for a good reason), then Bob is also delayed (for no apparent good reason).

The question of waiting is important as an example of *fault-tolerance*. Normally, we expect Alice and Bob to respond to each other in a reasonable amount of time, but what if they do not do so? The mutual exclusion problem, by its very essence, requires waiting: no mutual exclusion protocol avoids it, no matter how clever. Nevertheless, we see that many other coordination problems can be solved without waiting, sometimes in unexpected ways.

1.2.2 The Moral

Having reviewed both the strengths and weaknesses of Bob and Alice's protocols, we now turn our attention back to Computer Science.

First, we examine why shouting across the yard and placing cell phone calls did not work. Two kinds of communication occur naturally in concurrent systems:

- *Transient* communication requires both parties to participate at the same time. Shouting, gestures, or cell phone calls are examples of transient communication.
- *Persistent* communication allows the sender and receiver to participate at different times. Posting letters, sending email, or leaving notes under rocks are all examples of persistent communication.

Mutual exclusion requires persistent communication. The problem with shouting across the yard or placing cell phone calls is that it may or may not be okay for Bob to unleash his dog, but if Alice is not able to respond to messages, he will never know.

The can-and-string protocol might seem somewhat contrived, but it corresponds accurately to a common communication protocol in concurrent systems: *interrupts*. In modern operating systems, one common way for one thread to get the attention of another is to send it an interrupt. More precisely, thread A interrupts thread B by setting a bit at a location periodically checked by B. Sooner or later, B notices the bit has been set and reacts. After reacting, B typically resets the bit (A cannot reset the bit). Even though interrupts cannot solve the mutual exclusion problem, they can still be very useful. For example, interrupt communication is the basis of the Java language's `wait()` and `notifyAll()` calls.

On a more positive note, the fable shows that mutual exclusion between two threads can be solved (however imperfectly) using only two one-bit variables, each of which can be written by one thread and read by the other.

1.3 The Producer–Consumer Problem

Mutual exclusion is not the only problem worth investigating. Eventually, Alice and Bob fall in love and marry. Eventually, they divorce. (What were they thinking?) The judge gives Alice custody of the pets, and tells Bob to feed them. The pets now get along with one another, but they side with Alice, and attack Bob whenever they see him. As a result, Alice and Bob need to devise a protocol for Bob to deliver food to the pets without Bob and the pets being in the yard together. Moreover, the protocol should not waste anyone's time: Alice does not want to release her pets into the yard unless there is food there, and Bob does not want to enter the yard unless the pets have consumed all the food. This problem is known as the *producer–consumer* problem.

Surprisingly perhaps, the cans-and-string protocol we rejected for mutual exclusion does exactly what we need for the producer–consumer problem. Bob places a can *standing up* on Alice's windowsill, ties one end of his string around the can, and puts the other end of the string in his living room. He then puts food in the yard and knocks the can down. From now on, when Alice wants to release the pets, she does the following:

1. She waits until the can is down.
2. She releases the pets.
3. When the pets return, Alice checks whether they finished the food. If so, she resets the can.

Bob does the following:

1. He waits until the can is up.
2. He puts food in the yard.
3. He pulls the string and knocks the can down.

The state of the can thus reflects the state of the yard. If the can is down, it means there is food and the pets can eat, and if the can is up, it means the food is gone and Bob can put some more out. We check the following three properties:

- *Mutual Exclusion*: Bob and the pets are never in the yard together.
- *Starvation-freedom*: If Bob is always willing to feed, and the pets are always famished, then the pets will eat infinitely often.
- *Producer–Consumer*: The pets will not enter the yard unless there is food, and Bob will never provide more food if there is unconsumed food.

This producer–consumer protocol and the mutual exclusion protocol considered in the last section both ensure that Alice and Bob are never in the yard at the same time. Nevertheless, Alice and Bob cannot use this producer–consumer protocol for mutual exclusion, and it is important to understand why. Mutual exclusion requires deadlock-freedom: anyone must be able to enter the yard infinitely often on their own, even if the other is not there. By contrast, the producer–consumer protocol's starvation-freedom property assumes continuous cooperation from both parties.

Here is how we reason about this protocol:

- *Mutual Exclusion*: We use a slightly different proof style than that used in our earlier mutual exclusion proof: a "state machine"-based proof rather than one by contradiction. We think of the stringed can as a state machine. The can has two states, up and down, and it repeatedly transitions between these states. We argue that mutual exclusion holds since it holds initially and continues to hold when transitioning from any state of the can to the other.

  Initially the can is either up or down. Let us say it was down. Then only the pets can go in, and mutual exclusion holds. In order for the can to be raised by Alice, the pets must first leave, so when the can is raised, the pets are not in the yard and mutual exclusion is maintained since they will not enter again until it is knocked over. In order for the can to be knocked over, Bob must have left the yard, and will not enter until it is raised again, so mutual exclusion is maintained once the can is knocked over. There are no other possible transitions, and so our claim holds.
- *Starvation-freedom*: suppose the claim does not hold: It must be the case that infinitely often Alice's pets are hungry, there is no food, and Bob is trying to provide food but does not succeed. The can cannot be up, as then Bob will provide food and knock over the can, allowing the pets to eat. So it must be that the can is down, and since the pets are hungry, Alice will eventually raise the can, bringing us back to the former case.
- *Producer–Consumer*: The mutual exclusion property implies that the pets and Bob will never be in the yard together. Bob will not enter the yard until Alice raises the can, which she will do only if there is no more food. Similarly, the pets will not enter the yard until Bob lowers the can, which he will do only after placing the food.

Like the mutual exclusion protocol we have already described, this protocol exhibits *waiting*. If Bob deposits food in the yard, and immediately goes on vacation without remembering to reset the can, then the pets may starve, despite the presence of food.

Turning our attention back to Computer Science, the producer–consumer problem appears in almost all parallel and distributed systems. It is the way in which processors place data in communication buffers to be read or transmitted across a network interconnect or shared bus.

1.4 The Readers–Writers Problem

Bob and Alice eventually decide they love their pets so much they need to communicate simple messages about them. Bob puts up a billboard in front of his house. The billboard holds a sequence of large tiles, each tile holding a single letter. Bob, at his leisure, posts a message on the bulletin board by lifting one tile at a time. Alice, at her leisure, reads the message by looking at the billboard through a telescope, one tile at a time.

This may sound like a workable system, but it is not. Imagine that Bob posts the message:

```
sell the cat
```

Alice, looking through her telescope, transcribes the message

```
sell the
```

At this point Bob takes down the tiles and writes out a new message

```
wash the dog
```

Alice, continuing to scan across the billboard transcribes the message

```
sell the dog
```

You can imagine the rest.

There are some straightforward ways to solve the readers–writers problem.

- Alice and Bob can use the mutual exclusion protocol to make sure that Alice reads only complete sentences. She might still miss a sentence, however.
- They can use the can-and-string protocol, where Bob produces sentences and Alice consumes them.

If this problem is so easy to solve, then why do we bring it up? Both the mutual exclusion and producer–consumer protocols require *waiting*: if one participant is subjected to an unexpected delay, so is the other. In the context of shared multiprocessor memory, a solution to the readers–writers problem is a way of allowing a thread to capture an instantaneous view of several memory locations. Capturing such a view without waiting, that is, without preventing other threads from modifying these locations while they are being read, is a powerful tool that can be used for backups, debugging, and in many other situations. Surprisingly, the readers–writers problem does have solutions that do *not* require waiting. We examine several such solutions later on.

1.5 The Harsh Realities of Parallelization

Here is why multiprocessor programming is so much fun. In an ideal world, upgrading from a uniprocessor to an n-way multiprocessor should provide about an n-fold increase in computational power. In practice, sadly, this never happens. The primary reason for this is that most real-world computational problems cannot be effectively parallelized without incurring the costs of inter-processor communication and coordination.

Consider five friends who decide to paint a five-room house. If all the rooms are the same size, then it makes sense to assign each friend to paint one room, and as long as everyone paints at about the same rate, we would get a five-fold speedup over the single-painter case. The task becomes more complicated if the rooms are of different sizes. For example, if one room is twice the size of the others, then the five painters will not achieve a five-fold speedup because the overall completion time is dominated by the one room that takes the longest to paint.

This kind of analysis is very important for concurrent computation. The formula we need is called *Amdahl's Law*. It captures the notion that the extent to which we can speed up any complex job (not just painting) is limited by how much of the job must be executed sequentially.

Define the *speedup* S of a job to be the ratio between the time it takes one processor to complete the job (as measured by a wall clock) versus the time it takes n concurrent processors to complete the same job. *Amdahl's Law* characterizes the maximum speedup S that can be achieved by n processors collaborating on an application, where p is the fraction of the job that can be executed in parallel. Assume, for simplicity, that it takes (normalized) time 1 for a single processor to complete the job. With n concurrent processors, the parallel part takes time p/n and the sequential part takes time $1-p$. Overall, the parallelized computation takes time:

$$1 - p + \frac{p}{n}$$

Amdahl's Law says that the speedup, that is, the ratio between the sequential (single-processor) time and the parallel time, is:

$$S = \frac{1}{1 - p + \frac{p}{n}}$$

To illustrate the implications of Amdahl's Law, consider our room-painting example. Assume that each small room is one unit, and the single large room is two units. Assigning one painter (processor) per room means that five of six units can be painted in parallel, implying that $p = 5/6$, and $1 - p = 1/6$. Amdahl's Law states that the resulting speedup is:

$$S = \frac{1}{1 - p + \frac{p}{n}} = \frac{1}{1/6 + 1/6} = 3$$

Alarmingly, five painters working on five rooms where one room is twice the size of the others yields only a three-fold speedup.

It can get worse. Imagine we have ten rooms and ten painters, where each painter is assigned to a room, but one room (out of ten) is twice the size of the others. Here is the resulting speedup:

$$S = \frac{1}{1/11 + 1/11} = 5.5$$

With even a small imbalance, applying ten painters to a job yields only a five-fold speedup, roughly half of what one might naïvely expect.

The solution therefore, as with our earlier prime printing problem, seems to be that as soon as one painter's work on a room is done, he/she helps others to paint the remaining room. The issue of course is that this shared painting of the room will require coordination among painters, but can we afford to avoid it?

Here is what Amdahl's Law tells us about the utilization of multiprocessor machines. Some computational problems are "embarrassingly parallel": they can easily be divided into components that can be executed concurrently. Such problems sometimes arise in scientific computing or in graphics, but rarely in systems. In general, however, for a given problem and a ten-processor machine, Amdahl's Law says that even if we manage to parallelize 90% of the solution, but not the remaining 10%, then we end up with a five-fold speedup, but not a ten-fold speedup. In other words, the remaining 10% that we did not parallelize cut our utilization of the machine in half. It seems worthwhile to invest an effort to derive as much parallelism from the remaining 10% as possible, even if it is difficult. Typically, it is hard because these additional parallel parts involve substantial communication and coordination. Here is a major focus of this book: understanding the tools and techniques that allow programmers to effectively program the parts of the code that require coordination and synchronization, because the gains made on these parts may have a profound impact on performance.

Returning to the prime number printing program of Fig. 1.2, let us revisit the three main lines of code:

```
i = counter.getAndIncrement(); // take next untaken number
if (isPrime(i))
  print(i);
```

It would have been simpler to have threads perform these three lines atomically, that is, in a single mutually-exclusive block. Instead, only the call to `getAndIncrement()` is atomic. This approach makes sense when we consider the implications of Amdahl's Law: it is important to minimize the granularity of sequential code; in this case, the code accessed using mutual exclusion. Moreover, it is important to implement mutual exclusion in an effective way, since the communication and coordination around the mutually exclusive shared counter can substantially affect the performance of our program as a whole.

1.6 Parallel Programming

For many of the applications you may wish to parallelize, you will find that there are significant parts that can easily be determined as executable in parallel because they do not require any form of coordination or communication. However, at the time this book is being written, there is no cookbook recipe for identifying these parts. This is where the application designer needs to use his or her accumulated understanding of the algorithm being parallelized. Luckily, in many cases it is obvious how to find such parts. The more substantial problem, the one which this book addresses, is how to deal with the remaining parts of the program. As noted earlier, these are the parts that cannot be easily parallelized because the program must access shared data and requires interprocess coordination and communication in an essential way.

The goal of this text is to expose the reader to core ideas behind modern coordination paradigms and concurrent data structures. We present the reader with a unified, comprehensive picture of the elements that are key to effective multiprocessor programming, ranging from basic principles to best-practice engineering techniques.

Multiprocessor programming poses many challenges, ranging from grand intellectual issues to subtle engineering tricks. We tackle these challenges using successive refinement, starting with an idealized model in which mathematical concerns are paramount, and gradually moving on to more pragmatic models, where we increasingly focus on basic engineering principles.

For example, the first problem we consider is mutual exclusion, the oldest and still one of the most basic problems in the field. We begin with a mathematical perspective, analyzing the computability and correctness properties of various algorithms on an idealized architecture. The algorithms themselves, while classical, are not practical for modern architectures. Nevertheless, learning how to reason about such idealized algorithms is a necessary step toward learning how to reason about more realistic (and more complex) algorithms. It is particularly important to learn how to reason about subtle liveness issues such as starvation and deadlock.

Once we understand how to reason about such algorithms in general, we turn our attention to more realistic contexts. We explore a variety of algorithms and data structures using different multiprocessor architectures with the goal of understanding which are effective, and why.

1.7 Chapter Notes

Most of the parable of Alice and Bob is adapted from Leslie Lamport's invited address to the 1984 ACM Symposium on Principles of Distributed Computing [92]. The readers–writers problem is a classical synchronization problem that has received attention in numerous papers over the past twenty years. Amdahl's Law is due to Gene Amdahl, a parallel processing pioneer [9].

1.8 Exercises

Exercise 1. The dining philosophers problem was invented by E. W. Dijkstra, a concurrency pioneer, to clarify the notions of *deadlock* and *starvation* freedom. Imagine five philosophers who spend their lives just thinking and feasting. They sit around a circular table with five chairs. The table has a big plate of rice. However, there are only five chopsticks (in the original formulation forks) available, as shown in Fig. 1.5. Each philosopher thinks. When he gets hungry, he sits down and picks up the two chopsticks that are closest to him. If a philosopher can pick up both chopsticks, he can eat for a while. After a philosopher finishes eating, he puts down the chopsticks and again starts to think.

1. Write a program to simulate the behavior of the philosophers, where each philosopher is a thread and the chopsticks are shared objects. Notice that you must prevent a situation where two philosophers hold the same chopstick at the same time.
2. Amend your program so that it never reaches a state where philosophers are deadlocked, that is, it is never the case that each philosopher holds one chopstick and is stuck waiting for another to get the second chopstick.
3. Amend your program so that no philosopher ever starves.
4. Write a program to provide a starvation-free solution for any number of philosophers n.

Exercise 2. For each of the following, state whether it is a safety or liveness property. Identify the bad or good thing of interest.

1. Patrons are served in the order they arrive.
2. What goes up must come down.

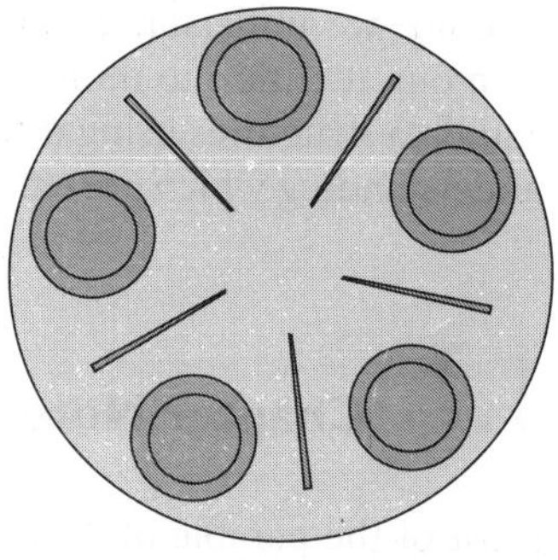

Figure 1.5 Traditional dining table arrangement according to Dijkstra.

3. If two or more processes are waiting to enter their critical sections, at least one succeeds.
4. If an interrupt occurs, then a message is printed within one second.
5. If an interrupt occurs, then a message is printed.
6. The cost of living never decreases.
7. Two things are certain: death and taxes.
8. You can always tell a Harvard man.

Exercise 3. In the producer–consumer fable, we assumed that Bob can see whether the can on Alice's windowsill is up or down. Design a producer–consumer protocol using cans and strings that works even if Bob cannot see the state of Alice's can (this is how real-world interrupt bits work).

Exercise 4. You are one of P recently arrested prisoners. The warden, a deranged computer scientist, makes the following announcement:

> You may meet together today and plan a strategy, but after today you will be in isolated cells and have no communication with one another.
>
> I have set up a "switch room" which contains a light switch, which is either *on* or *off*. The switch is not connected to anything.
>
> Every now and then, I will select one prisoner at random to enter the "switch room." This prisoner may throw the switch (from *on* to *off*, or vice-versa), or may leave the switch unchanged. Nobody else will ever enter this room.
>
> Each prisoner will visit the switch room arbitrarily often. More precisely, for any N, eventually each of you will visit the switch room at least N times.
>
> At any time, any of you may declare: "we have all visited the switch room at least once." If the claim is correct, I will set you free. If the claim is incorrect, I will feed all of you to the crocodiles. Choose wisely!

- Devise a winning strategy when you know that the initial state of the switch is *off*.
- Devise a winning strategy when you do not know whether the initial state of the switch is *on* or *off*.

Hint: not all prisoners need to do the same thing.

Exercise 5. The same warden has a different idea. He orders the prisoners to stand in line, and places red and blue hats on each of their heads. No prisoner knows the color of his own hat, or the color of any hat behind him, but he can see the hats of the prisoners in front. The warden starts at the back of the line and asks each prisoner to guess the color of his own hat. The prisoner can answer only "red" or "blue." If he gives the wrong answer, he is fed to the crocodiles. If he answers correctly, he is freed. Each prisoner can hear the answer of the prisoners behind him, but cannot tell whether that prisoner was correct.

The prisoners are allowed to consult and agree on a strategy beforehand (while the warden listens in) but after being lined up, they cannot communicate any other way besides their answer of "red" or "blue."

Devise a strategy that allows at least $P - 1$ of P prisoners to be freed.

Exercise 6. Use Amdahl's law to answer the following questions:

- Suppose the sequential part of a program accounts for 40% of the program's execution time on a single processor. Find a limit for the overall speedup that can be achieved by running the program on a multiprocessor machine.
- Now suppose the sequential part accounts for 30% of the program's computation time. Let s_n be the program's speedup on n processes, assuming the rest of the program is perfectly parallelizable. Your boss tells you to double this speedup: the revised program should have speedup $s'_n > s_n/2$. You advertise for a programmer to replace the sequential part with an improved version that runs k times faster. What value of k should you require?
- Suppose the sequential part can be sped up three-fold, and when we do so, the modified program takes half the time of the original on n processors. What fraction of the overall execution time did the sequential part account for? Express your answer as a function of n.

Exercise 7. Running your application on two processors yields a speedup of S_2. Use Amdahl's Law to derive a formula for S_n, the speedup on n processors, in terms of n and S_2.

Exercise 8. You have a choice between buying one uniprocessor that executes five zillion instructions per second, or a ten-processor multiprocessor where each processor executes one zillion instructions per second. Using Amdahl's Law, explain how you would decide which to buy for a particular application.

Principles

2 Mutual Exclusion

Mutual exclusion is perhaps the most prevalent form of coordination in multiprocessor programming. This chapter covers classical mutual exclusion algorithms that work by reading and writing shared memory. Although these algorithms are not used in practice, we study them because they provide an ideal introduction to the kinds of algorithmic and correctness issues that arise in every area of synchronization. The chapter also provides an impossibility proof. This proof teaches us the limitations of solutions to mutual exclusion that work by reading and writing shared memory, and will help to motivate the real-world mutual exclusion algorithms that appear in later chapters. This chapter is one of the few that contains proofs of algorithms. Though the reader should feel free to skip these proofs, it is very helpful to understand the kind of reasoning they present, because we can use the same approach to reason about the practical algorithms considered in later chapters.

2.1 Time

Reasoning about concurrent computation is mostly reasoning about time. Sometimes we want things to happen simultaneously, and sometimes we want them to happen at different times. We need to reason about complicated conditions involving how multiple time intervals can overlap, or, sometimes, how they cannot. We need a simple but unambiguous language to talk about events and durations in time. Everyday English is too ambiguous and imprecise. Instead, we introduce a simple vocabulary and notation to describe how concurrent threads behave in time.

In 1689, Isaac Newton stated "absolute, true and mathematical time, of itself and from its own nature, flows equably without relation to anything external." We endorse his notion of time, if not his prose style. Threads share a common time (though not necessarily a common clock). A thread is a *state machine*, and its state transitions are called *events*.

Events are *instantaneous*: they occur at a single instant of time. It is convenient to require that events are never simultaneous: distinct events occur at distinct times. (As a practical matter, if we are unsure about the order of two events that happen very close in time, then any order will do.) A thread A produces a sequence of events $a_0, a_1, \ldots$ Threads typically contain loops, so a single program statement can produce many events. We denote the j-th occurrence of an event a_i by a_i^j. One event a *precedes* another event b, written $a \rightarrow b$, if a occurs at an earlier time. The *precedence* relation "$\rightarrow$" is a total order on events.

Let a_0 and a_1 be events such that $a_0 \rightarrow a_1$. An *interval* (a_0, a_1) is the duration between a_0 and a_1. Interval $I_A = (a_0, a_1)$ *precedes* $I_B = (b_0, b_1)$, written $I_A \rightarrow I_B$, if $a_1 \rightarrow b_0$ (that is, if the final event of I_A precedes the starting event of I_B). More succinctly, the $\rightarrow$ relation is a partial order on intervals. Intervals that are unrelated by $\rightarrow$ are said to be *concurrent*. By analogy with events, we denote the j-th execution of interval I_A by I_A^j.

2.2 Critical Sections

In an earlier chapter, we discussed the `Counter` class implementation shown in Fig. 2.1. We observed that this implementation is correct in a single-thread system, but misbehaves when used by two or more threads. The problem occurs if both threads read the `value` field at the line marked "start of danger zone," and then both update that field at the line marked "end of danger zone."

We can avoid this problem if we transform these two lines into a *critical section*: a block of code that can be executed by only one thread at a time. We call this property *mutual exclusion*. The standard way to approach mutual exclusion is through a `Lock` object satisfying the interface shown in Fig. 2.2.

For brevity, we say a thread *acquires* (alternately *locks*) a lock when it executes a `lock()` method call, and *releases* (alternately *unlocks*) the lock when it executes

```
class Counter {
  private int value;
  public Counter(int c) {          // constructor
    value = c;
  }
  // increment and return prior value
  public int getAndIncrement() {
    int temp = value;              // start of danger zone
    value = temp + 1;              // end of danger zone
    return temp;
  }
}
```

Figure 2.1 The `Counter` class.

```java
public interface Lock {
  public void lock();      // before entering critical section
  public void unlock();    // before leaving critical section
}
```

Figure 2.2 The Lock interface.

```java
public class Counter {
  private long value;
  private Lock lock;                 // to protect critical section

  public long getAndIncrement() {
    lock.lock();                     // enter critical section
    try {
      long temp = value;             // in critical section
      value = temp + 1;              // in critical section
      return temp;
    } finally {
      lock.unlock();                 // leave critical section
    }
  }
}
```

Figure 2.3 Using a lock object.

an `unlock()` method call. Fig. 2.3 shows how to use a `Lock` field to add mutual exclusion to a shared counter implementation. Threads using the `lock()` and `unlock()` methods must follow a specific format. A thread is *well formed* if:

1. each critical section is associated with a unique `Lock` object,
2. the thread calls that object's `lock()` method when it is trying to enter the critical section, and
3. the thread calls the `unlock()` method when it leaves the critical section.

Pragma 2.2.1. In Java, these methods should be used in the following structured way.

```java
mutex.lock();
try {
  ...                 // body
  } finally {
    mutex.unlock();
  }
```

This idiom ensures that the lock is acquired before entering the **try** block, and that the lock is released when control leaves the block, even if some statement in the block throws an unexpected exception.

We now formalize the properties that a good `Lock` algorithm should satisfy. Let CS_A^j be the interval during which A executes the critical section for the j-th time. Let us assume, for simplicity, that each thread repeatedly acquires and releases the lock, with other work taking place in the meantime.

Mutual Exclusion Critical sections of different threads do not overlap. For threads A and B, and integers j and k, either $CS_A^k \rightarrow CS_B^j$ or $CS_B^j \rightarrow CS_A^k$.

Freedom from Deadlock If some thread attempts to acquire the lock, then some thread will succeed in acquiring the lock. If thread A calls `lock()` but never acquires the lock, then other threads must be completing an infinite number of critical sections.

Freedom from Starvation Every thread that attempts to acquire the lock eventually succeeds. Every call to `lock()` eventually returns. This property is sometimes called *lockout freedom.*

Note that starvation freedom implies deadlock freedom.

The mutual exclusion property is clearly essential. Without this property, we cannot guarantee that a computation's results are correct. In the terminology of Chapter 1, mutual exclusion is a safety property. The deadlock-freedom property is important. It implies that the system never "freezes." Individual threads may be stuck forever (called *starvation*), but some thread makes progress. In the terminology of Chapter 1, deadlock-freedom is a liveness property. Note that a program can still deadlock even if each of the locks it uses satisfies the deadlock-freedom property. For example, consider threads A and B that share locks ℓ_0 and ℓ_1. First, A acquires ℓ_0 and B acquires ℓ_1. Next, A tries to acquire ℓ_1 and B tries to acquire ℓ_0. The threads deadlock because each one waits for the other to release its lock.

The starvation-freedom property, while clearly desirable, is the least compelling of the three. Later on, we will see practical mutual exclusion algorithms that fail to be starvation-free. These algorithms are typically deployed in circumstances where starvation is a theoretical possibility, but is unlikely to occur in practice. Nevertheless, the ability to reason about starvation is essential for understanding whether it is a realistic threat.

The starvation-freedom property is also weak in the sense that there is no guarantee for how long a thread waits before it enters the critical section. Later on, we will look at algorithms that place bounds on how long a thread can wait.

2.3 2-Thread Solutions

We begin with two inadequate but interesting `Lock` algorithms.

2.3.1 The LockOne Class

Fig. 2.4 shows the `LockOne` algorithm. Our 2-thread lock algorithms follow the following conventions: the threads have ids 0 and 1, the calling thread has i, and the other $j = 1 - i$. Each thread acquires its index by calling `ThreadID.get()`.

> *Pragma* 2.3.1. In practice, the `Boolean flag` variables in Fig. 2.4, as well as the `victim` and `label` variables in later algorithms must all be declared **`volatile`** to work properly. We explain the reasons in Chapter 1 and Appendix B. We will begin declaring the appropriate variables as volatile in Chapter 7.

We use $\text{write}_A(x = v)$ to denote the event in which A assigns value v to field x, and $\text{read}_A(x == v)$ to denote the event in which A reads v from field x. Sometimes we omit v when the value is unimportant. For example, in Fig. 2.4 the event $\text{write}_A(\texttt{flag}[i] = \textit{true})$ is caused by Line 7 of the `lock()` method.

Lemma 2.3.1. The `LockOne` algorithm satisfies mutual exclusion.

Proof: Suppose not. Then there exist integers j and k such that $CS_A^j \not\rightarrow CS_B^k$ and $CS_B^k \not\rightarrow CS_A^j$. Consider each thread's last execution of the `lock()` method before entering its k-th (j-th) critical section.

Inspecting the code, we see that

$$\text{write}_A(\texttt{flag}[A] = \textit{true}) \rightarrow \text{read}_A(\texttt{flag}[B] == \textit{false}) \rightarrow CS_A \quad (2.3.1)$$

$$\text{write}_B(\texttt{flag}[B] = \textit{true}) \rightarrow \text{read}_B(\texttt{flag}[A] == \textit{false}) \rightarrow CS_B \quad (2.3.2)$$

$$\text{read}_A(\texttt{flag}[B] == \textit{false}) \rightarrow \text{write}_B(\texttt{flag}[B] = \textit{true}) \quad (2.3.3)$$

Note that once `flag[B]` is set to *true* it remains *true*. It follows that Eq. 2.3.3 holds, since otherwise thread A could not have read `flag[B]` as *false*. Eq. 2.3.4 follows from Eqs. 2.3.1–2.3.3, and the transitivity of the precedence order.

```
1  class LockOne implements Lock {
2    private boolean[] flag = new boolean[2];
3    // thread-local index, 0 or 1
4    public void lock() {
5      int i = ThreadID.get();
6      int j = 1 - i;
7      flag[i] = true;
8      while (flag[j]) {}          // wait
9    }
10   public void unlock() {
11     int i = ThreadID.get();
12     flag[i] = false;
13   }
14 }
```

Figure 2.4 The LockOne algorithm.

$$\text{write}_A(\texttt{flag}[A] = \mathit{true}) \rightarrow \text{read}_A(\texttt{flag}[B] == \mathit{false}) \rightarrow \tag{2.3.4}$$

$$\text{write}_B(\texttt{flag}[B] = \mathit{true}) \rightarrow \text{read}_B(\texttt{flag}[A] == \mathit{false})$$

It follows that $\text{write}_A(\texttt{flag}[A] = \mathit{true}) \rightarrow \text{read}_B(\texttt{flag}[A] == \mathit{false})$ without an intervening write to the `flag[]` array, a contradiction. □

The `LockOne` algorithm is inadequate because it deadlocks if thread executions are interleaved. If $\text{write}_A(\texttt{flag}[A] = \mathit{true})$ and $\text{write}_B(\texttt{flag}[B] = \mathit{true})$ events occur before $\text{read}_A(\texttt{flag}[B])$ and $\text{read}_B(\texttt{flag}[A])$ events, then both threads wait forever. Nevertheless, `LockOne` has an interesting property: if one thread runs before the other, no deadlock occurs, and all is well.

2.3.2 The LockTwo Class

Fig. 2.5 shows an alternative lock algorithm, the `LockTwo` class.

Lemma 2.3.2. The `LockTwo` algorithm satisfies mutual exclusion.

Proof: Suppose not. Then there exist integers j and k such that $CS_A^j \not\rightarrow CS_B^k$ and $CS_B^k \not\rightarrow CS_A^j$. Consider as before each thread's last execution of the `lock()` method before entering its k-th (j-th) critical section.

Inspecting the code, we see that

$$\text{write}_A(\texttt{victim} = A) \rightarrow \text{read}_A(\texttt{victim} == B) \rightarrow CS_A \tag{2.3.5}$$

$$\text{write}_B(\texttt{victim} = B) \rightarrow \text{read}_B(\texttt{victim} == A) \rightarrow CS_B \tag{2.3.6}$$

Thread B must assign B to the `victim` field between events $\text{write}_A(\texttt{victim} = A)$ and $\text{read}_A(\texttt{victim} = B)$ (see Eq. 2.3.5). Since this assignment is the last, we have

$$\text{write}_A(\texttt{victim} = A) \rightarrow \text{write}_B(\texttt{victim} = B) \rightarrow \text{read}_A(\texttt{victim} == B). \tag{2.3.7}$$

Once the `victim` field is set to B, it does not change, so any subsequent read returns B, contradicting Eq. 2.3.6. □

```
class LockTwo implements Lock {
  private int victim;
  public void lock() {
    int i = ThreadID.get();
    victim = i;                  // let the other go first
    while (victim == i) {}       // wait
  }
  public void unlock() {}
}
```

Figure 2.5 The `LockTwo` algorithm.

The LockTwo class is inadequate because it deadlocks if one thread runs completely ahead of the other. Nevertheless, LockTwo has an interesting property: if the threads run concurrently, the lock() method succeeds. The LockOne and LockTwo classes complement one another: each succeeds under conditions that cause the other to deadlock.

2.3.3 The Peterson Lock

We now combine the LockOne and LockTwo algorithms to construct a starvation-free Lock algorithm, shown in Fig. 2.6. This algorithm is arguably the most succinct and elegant two-thread mutual exclusion algorithm. It is known as "Peterson's Algorithm," after its inventor.

Lemma 2.3.3. The Peterson lock algorithm satisfies mutual exclusion.

Proof: Suppose not. As before, consider the last executions of the lock() method by threads A and B. Inspecting the code, we see that

$$\text{write}_A(\texttt{flag}[A] = \mathit{true}) \rightarrow \text{write}_A(\texttt{victim} = A) \rightarrow \text{read}_A(\texttt{flag}[B]) \rightarrow \text{read}_A(\texttt{victim}) \rightarrow CS_A \quad (2.3.8)$$

$$\text{write}_B(\texttt{flag}[B] = \mathit{true}) \rightarrow \text{write}_B(\texttt{victim} = B) \rightarrow \text{read}_B(\texttt{flag}[A]) \rightarrow \text{read}_B(\texttt{victim}) \rightarrow CS_B \quad (2.3.9)$$

Assume, without loss of generality, that A was the last thread to write to the victim field.

$$\text{write}_B(\texttt{victim} = B) \rightarrow \text{write}_A(\texttt{victim} = A) \quad (2.3.10)$$

```
class Peterson implements Lock {
  // thread-local index, 0 or 1
  private boolean[] flag = new boolean[2];
  private int victim;
  public void lock() {
    int i = ThreadID.get();
    int j = 1 - i;
    flag[i] = true;                // I'm interested
    victim = i;                    // you go first
    while (flag[j] && victim == i) {}; // wait
  }
  public void unlock() {
    int i = ThreadID.get();
    flag[i] = false;               // I'm not interested
  }
}
```

Figure 2.6 The Peterson lock algorithm.

Equation 2.3.10 implies that A observed `victim` to be A in Eq. 2.3.8. Since A nevertheless entered its critical section, it must have observed `flag[B]` to be *false*, so we have

$$\text{write}_A(\texttt{victim} = A) \rightarrow \text{read}_A(\texttt{flag}[B] == \textit{false}) \tag{2.3.11}$$

Eqs. 2.3.9–2.3.11, together with the transitivity of $\rightarrow$, imply Eq. 2.3.12.

$$\text{write}_B(\texttt{flag}[B] = \textit{true}) \rightarrow \text{write}_B(\texttt{victim} = B) \rightarrow$$
$$\text{write}_A(\texttt{victim} = A) \rightarrow \text{read}_A(\texttt{flag}[B] == \textit{false}) \tag{2.3.12}$$

It follows that $\text{write}_B(\texttt{flag}[B] = \textit{true}) \rightarrow \text{read}_A(\texttt{flag}[B] == \textit{false})$. This observation yields a contradiction because no other write to `flag[B]` was performed before the critical section executions. □

Lemma 2.3.4. The `Peterson` lock algorithm is starvation-free.

Proof: Suppose not. Suppose (without loss of generality) that A runs forever in the `lock()` method. It must be executing the **`while`** statement, waiting until either `flag[B]` becomes *false* or `victim` is set to B.

What is B doing while A fails to make progress? Perhaps B is repeatedly entering and leaving its critical section. If so, however, then B sets `victim` to B as soon as it reenters the critical section. Once `victim` is set to B, it does not change, and A must eventually return from the `lock()` method, a contradiction.

So it must be that B is also stuck in its `lock()` method call, waiting until either `flag[A]` becomes *false* or `victim` is set to A. But `victim` cannot be both A and B, a contradiction. □

***Corollary* 2.3.1.** The `Peterson` lock algorithm is deadlock-free.

2.4 The Filter Lock

We now consider two mutual exclusion protocols that work for n threads, where n is greater than 2. The first solution, the `Filter` lock, is a direct generalization of the `Peterson` lock to multiple threads. The second solution, the `Bakery` lock, is perhaps the simplest and best known n-thread solution.

The `Filter` lock, shown in Fig. 2.7, creates $n-1$ "waiting rooms," called *levels*, that a thread must traverse before acquiring the lock. The levels are depicted in Fig. 2.8. Levels satisfy two important properties:

- At least one thread trying to enter level ℓ succeeds.
- If more than one thread is trying to enter level ℓ, then at least one is blocked (i.e., continues to wait at that level).

```
class Filter implements Lock {
  int[] level;
  int[] victim;
  public Filter(int n) {
    level  = new int[n];
    victim = new int[n]; // use 1..n-1
    for (int i = 0; i < n; i++) {
       level[i] = 0;
    }
  }
  public void lock() {
    int me = ThreadID.get();
    for (int i = 1; i < n; i++) { // attempt level i
      level[me] = i;
      victim[i] = me;
      // spin while conflicts exist
      while ((∃k != me) (level[k] >= i && victim[i] == me)) {};
    }
  }
  public void unlock() {
    int me = ThreadID.get();
    level[me] = 0;
  }
}
```

Figure 2.7 The `Filter` lock algorithm.

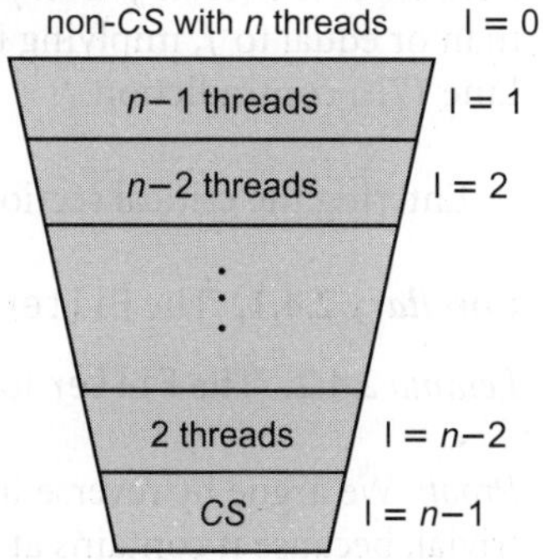

Figure 2.8 There are $n-1$ levels threads pass through, the last of which is the critical section. There are at most n threads that pass concurrently into level 0, $n-1$ into level 1 (a thread in level 1 is already in level 0), $n-2$ into level 2 and so on, so that only one enters the critical section at level $n-1$.

The `Peterson` lock uses a two-element `boolean flag` array to indicate whether a thread is trying to enter the critical section. The `Filter` lock generalizes this notion with an n-element integer `level[]` array, where the value of `level[`A`]` indicates the highest level that thread A is trying to enter. Each thread must pass through $n-1$ levels of "exclusion" to enter its critical section. Each level ℓ has a distinct `victim[`ℓ`]` field used to "filter out" one thread, excluding it from the next level.

Initially a thread A is at *level* 0. We say that A is at *level* j for $j > 0$, when it last completes the waiting loop in Line 17 with `level`$[A] \geqslant j$. (So a thread at level j is also at level $j - 1$, and so on.)

Lemma 2.4.1. For j between 0 and $n - 1$, there are at most $n - j$ threads at level j.

Proof: By induction on j. The base case, where $j = 0$, is trivial. For the induction step, the induction hypothesis implies that there are at most $n - j + 1$ threads at level $j - 1$. To show that at least one thread cannot progress to level j, we argue by contradiction: assume there are $n - j + 1$ threads at level j.

Let A be the last thread at level j to write to `victim`$[j]$. Because A is last, for any other B at level j:

$$\text{write}_B(\texttt{victim}[j]) \rightarrow \text{write}_A(\texttt{victim}[j]).$$

Inspecting the code, we see that B writes `level`$[B]$ before it writes to `victim`$[j]$, so

$$\text{write}_B(\texttt{level}[B] = j) \rightarrow \text{write}_B(\texttt{victim}[j]) \rightarrow \text{write}_A(\texttt{victim}[j]).$$

Inspecting the code, we see that A reads `level`$[B]$ after it writes to `victim`$[j]$, so

$$\text{write}_B(\texttt{level}[B] = j) \rightarrow \text{write}_B(\texttt{victim}[j]) \rightarrow \text{write}_A(\texttt{victim}[j]) \rightarrow \text{read}_A(\texttt{level}[B]).$$

Because B is at level j, every time A reads `level`$[B]$, it observes a value greater than or equal to j, implying that A could not have completed its waiting loop in Line 17, a contradiction. □

Entering the critical section is equivalent to entering level $n - 1$.

***Corollary* 2.4.1.** The `Filter` lock algorithm satisfies mutual exclusion.

Lemma 2.4.2. The `Filter` lock algorithm is starvation-free.

Proof: We argue by reverse induction on the levels. The base case, level $n - 1$, is trivial, because it contains at the most one thread. For the induction hypothesis, assume that every thread that reaches level $j + 1$ or higher, eventually enters (and leaves) its critical section.

Suppose A is stuck at level j. Eventually, by the induction hypothesis, there are no threads at higher levels. Once A sets `level`$[A]$ to j, then any thread at level $j - 1$ that subsequently reads `level`$[A]$ is prevented from entering level j. Eventually, no more threads enter level j from lower levels. All threads stuck at level j are in the waiting loop at Line 17, and the values of the `victim` and `level` fields no longer change.

We now argue by induction on the number of threads stuck at level j. For the base case, if A is the only thread at level j or higher, then clearly it will enter level $j + 1$. For the induction hypothesis, we assume that fewer than k threads cannot be stuck at level j. Suppose threads A and B are stuck at level j. A is stuck as long as it reads victim[j] = A, and B is stuck as long as it reads victim[j] = B. The victim field is unchanging, and it cannot be equal to both A and B, so one of the two threads will enter level $j+1$, reducing the number of stuck threads to $k-1$, contradicting the induction hypothesis. □

***Corollary* 2.4.2.** The Filter lock algorithm is deadlock-free.

2.5 Fairness

The starvation-freedom property guarantees that every thread that calls lock() eventually enters the critical section, but it makes no guarantees about how long this may take. Ideally (and very informally) if A calls lock() before B, then A should enter the critical section before B. Unfortunately, using the tools at hand we cannot determine which thread called lock() first. Instead, we split the lock() method into two sections of code (with corresponding execution intervals):

1. A *doorway* section, whose execution interval D_A consists of a bounded number of steps, and
2. a *waiting* section, whose execution interval W_A may take an unbounded number of steps.

The requirement that the doorway section always finish in a bounded number of steps is a strong requirement. We will call this requirement the *bounded wait-free* progress property. We discuss systematic ways of providing this property in later chapters.

Here is how we define fairness.

***Definition* 2.5.1.** A lock is *first-come-first-served* if, whenever, thread A finishes its doorway before thread B starts its doorway, then A cannot be overtaken by B:

$$\text{If } D_A^j \rightarrow D_B^k, \text{ then } CS_A^j \rightarrow CS_B^k.$$

for threads A and B and integers j and k.

2.6 Lamport's Bakery Algorithm

The Bakery lock algorithm appears in Fig. 2.9. It maintains the *first-come-first-served* property by using a distributed version of the number-dispensing machines often found in bakeries: each thread takes a number in the doorway, and then waits until no thread with an earlier number is trying to enter it.

In the Bakery lock, flag[A] is a Boolean flag indicating whether A wants to enter the critical section, and label[A] is an integer that indicates the thread's relative order when entering the bakery, for each thread A.

```
1  class Bakery implements Lock {
2    boolean[] flag;
3    Label[] label;
4    public Bakery (int n) {
5      flag  = new boolean[n];
6      label = new Label[n];
7      for (int i = 0; i < n; i++) {
8         flag[i] = false; label[i] = 0;
9      }
10   }
11   public void lock() {
12     int i = ThreadID.get();
13     flag[i] = true;
14     label[i] = max(label[0], ...,label[n-1]) + 1;
15     while ((∃k != i)(flag[k] && (label[k],k) << (label[i],i))) {};
16   }
17   public void unlock() {
18     flag[ThreadID.get()] = false;
19   }
20 }
```

Figure 2.9 The Bakery lock algorithm.

Each time a thread acquires a lock, it generates a new `label[]` in two steps. First, it reads all the other threads' labels in any order. Second, it reads all the other threads' labels one after the other (this can be done in some arbitrary order) and generates a label greater by one than the maximal label it read. We call the code from the raising of the flag (Line 13) to the writing of the new `label[]` (Line 14) the *doorway*. It establishes that thread's order with respect to the other threads trying to acquire the lock. If two threads execute their doorways concurrently, they may read the same maximal label and pick the same new label. To break this symmetry, the algorithm uses a lexicographical ordering << on pairs of `label[]` and thread ids:

$$(\texttt{label}[i], i) << (\texttt{label}[j], j))$$

$$\text{if and only if} \tag{2.6.13}$$

$$\texttt{label}[i] < \texttt{label}[j] \quad \text{or} \quad \texttt{label}[i] = \texttt{label}[j] \quad \text{and} \quad i < j.$$

In the waiting part of the Bakery algorithm (Line 15), a thread repeatedly rereads the labels one after the other in some arbitrary order until it determines that no thread with a raised flag has a lexicographically smaller label/id pair.

Since releasing a lock does not reset the `label[]`, it is easy to see that each thread's labels are strictly increasing. Interestingly, in both the doorway and waiting sections, threads read the labels asynchronously and in an arbitrary order, so that the set of labels seen prior to picking a new one may have never existed in memory at the same time. Nevertheless, the algorithm works.

Lemma 2.6.1. The `Bakery` lock algorithm is deadlock-free.

Proof: Some waiting thread A has the unique least (`label`$[A], A)$ pair, and that thread never waits for another thread. □

Lemma 2.6.2. The `Bakery` lock algorithm is first-come-first-served.

Proof: If A's doorway precedes B's, $D_A \rightarrow D_B$, then A's label is smaller since

$$\text{write}_A(\texttt{label}[A]) \rightarrow \text{read}_B(\texttt{label}[A]) \rightarrow \text{write}_B(\texttt{label}[B]) \rightarrow \text{read}_B(\texttt{flag}[A]),$$

so B is locked out while `flag`$[A]$ is *true*. □

Note that any algorithm that is both deadlock-free and *first-come-first-served* is also starvation-free.

Lemma 2.6.3. The `Bakery` algorithm satisfies mutual exclusion.

Proof: Suppose not. Let A and B be two threads concurrently in the critical section. Let labeling_A and labeling_B be the last respective sequences of acquiring new labels prior to entering the critical section. Suppose that (`label`$[A], A) << ($`label`$[B], B)$. When B successfully completed the test in its waiting section, it must have read that `flag`$[A]$ was *false* or that (`label`$[B], B) << ($`label`$[A], A)$. However, for a given thread, its id is fixed and its `label[]` values are strictly increasing, so B must have seen that `flag`$[A]$ was *false*. It follows that

$$\text{labeling}_B \rightarrow \text{read}_B(\text{flag}[A]) \rightarrow \text{write}_A(\text{flag}[A]) \rightarrow \text{labeling}_A$$

which contradicts the assumption that (`label`$[A], A) << ($`label`$[B], B)$. □

2.7 Bounded Timestamps

Notice that the labels of the `Bakery` lock grow without bound, so in a long-lived system we may have to worry about overflow. If a thread's label field silently rolls over from a large number to zero, then the first-come-first-served property no longer holds.

Later on, we will see constructions where counters are used to order threads, or even to produce unique identifiers. How important is the overflow problem in the real world? It is difficult to generalize. Sometimes it matters a great deal. The celebrated "Y2K" bug that captivated the media in the last years of the twentieth century is an example of a genuine overflow problem, even if the consequences were not as dire as predicted. On January 18, 2038, the Unix `time_t` data structure will overflow when the number of seconds since January 1, 1970 exceeds 2^{32}. No one knows whether it will matter. Sometimes, of course, counter overflow is a nonissue. Most applications that use, say, a 64-bit counter are unlikely to last long enough for roll-over to occur. (Let the grandchildren worry!)

In the `Bakery` lock, labels act as *timestamps*: they establish an order among the contending threads. Informally, we need to ensure that if one thread takes a label after another, then the latter has the larger label. Inspecting the code for the `Bakery` lock, we see that a thread needs two abilities:

- to read the other threads' timestamps (*scan*), and
- to assign itself a later timestamp (*label*).

A Java interface to such a timestamping system appears in Fig. 2.10. Since our principal application for a bounded timestamping system is to implement the doorway section of the `Lock` class, the timestamping system must be wait-free. It is possible to construct such a wait-free *concurrent* timestamping system (see the chapter notes), but the construction is long and rather technical. Instead, we focus on a simpler problem, interesting in its own right: constructing a *sequential* timestamping system, in which threads perform *scan*-and-*label* operations one completely after the other, that is, as if each were performed using mutual exclusion. In other words, consider only executions in which a thread can perform a scan of the other threads' labels, or a scan, and then an assignment of a new label, where each such sequence is a single atomic step. The principles underlying a concurrent and sequential timestamping systems are essentially the same, but they differ substantially in detail.

Think of the range of possible timestamps as nodes of a directed graph (called a *precedence graph*). An edge from node a to node b means that a is a later timestamp than b. The timestamp order is *irreflexive*: there is no edge from any node a to itself. The order is also *antisymmetric*: if there is an edge from a to b, then there is no edge from b to a. Notice that we do *not* require that the order be *transitive*: there can be an edge from a to b and from b to c, without necessarily implying there is an edge from a to c.

Think of assigning a timestamp to a thread as placing that thread's token on that timestamp's node. A thread performs a scan by locating the other threads' tokens, and it assigns itself a new timestamp by moving its own token to a node a such that there is an edge from a to every other thread's node.

Pragmatically, we would implement such a system as an array of single-writer multi-reader fields, where array element A represents the graph node where thread A most recently placed its token. The `scan()` method takes a "snapshot" of the array, and the `label()` method for thread A updates the A-th array element.

```java
public interface Timestamp {
  boolean compare(Timestamp);
}
public interface TimestampSystem {
  public Timestamp[] scan();
  public void label(Timestamp timestamp, int i);
}
```

Figure 2.10 A timestamping system interface.

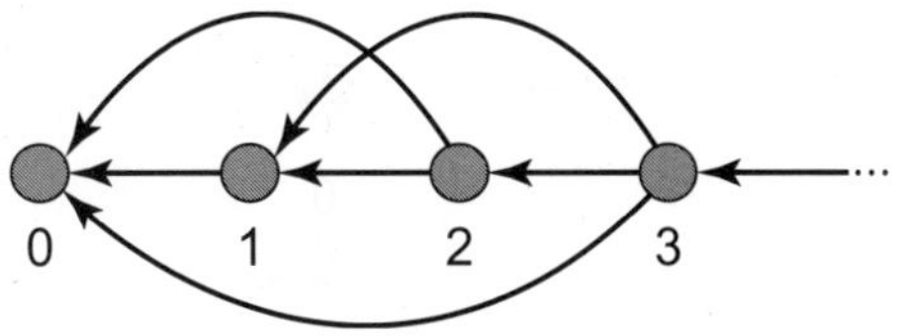

Figure 2.11 The precedence graph for an unbounded timestamping system. The nodes represent the set of all natural numbers and the edges represent the total order among them.

Fig. 2.11 illustrates the precedence graph for the unbounded timestamp system used in the `Bakery` lock. Not surprisingly, the graph is infinite: there is one node for each natural number, with a directed edge from node a to node b whenever $a > b$.

Consider the precedence graph T^2 shown in Fig. 2.12. This graph has three nodes, labeled 0, 1, and 2, and its edges define an ordering relation on the nodes in which 0 is less than 1, 1 is less than 2, and 2 is less than 0. If there are only two threads, then we can use this graph to define a bounded (sequential) timestamping system. The system satisfies the following invariant: the two threads always have tokens located on adjacent nodes, with the direction of the edge indicating their relative order. Suppose A's token is on Node 0, and B's token on Node 1 (so B has the later timestamp). For B, the `label()` method is trivial: it already has the latest timestamp, so it does nothing. For A, the `label()` method "leapfrogs" B's node by jumping from 0 to 2.

Recall that a *cycle*[1] in a directed graph is a set of nodes $n_0, n_1, \ldots, n_k$ such that there is an edge from n_0 to n_1, from n_1 to n_2, and eventually from n_{k-1} to n_k, and back from n_k to n_0.

The only cycle in the graph T^2 has length three, and there are only two threads, so the order among the threads is never ambiguous. To go beyond two threads, we need additional conceptual tools. Let G be a precedence graph, and A and B subgraphs of G (possibly single nodes). We say that *A dominates B* in G if every node of A has edges directed to every node of B. Let *graph multiplication* be the following noncommutative composition operator for graphs (denoted $G \circ H$):

> Replace every node v of G by a copy of H (denoted H_v), and let H_v dominate H_u in $G \circ H$ if v dominates u in G.

Define the graph T^k inductively to be:

1. T^1 is a single node.
2. T^2 is the three-node graph defined earlier.
3. For $k > 2$, $T^k = T^2 \circ T^{k-1}$.

For example, the graph T^3 is illustrated in Fig. 2.12.

---

1 The word "cycle" comes from the same Greek root as "circle."

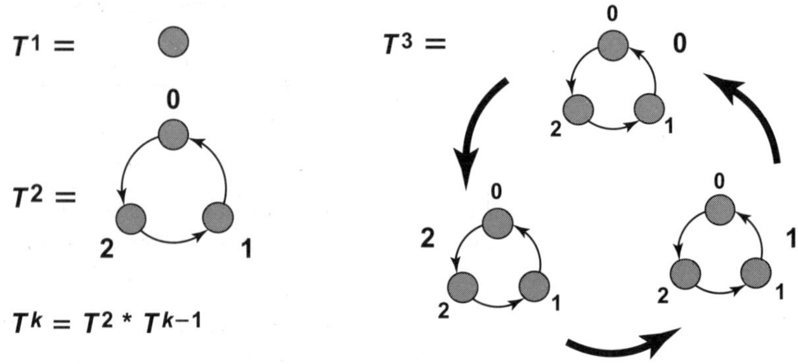

Figure 2.12 The precedence graph for a bounded timestamping system. Consider an initial situation in which there is a token A on Node 12 (Node 2 in subgraph 1) and tokens B and C on Nodes 21 and 22 (Nodes 1 and 2 in subgraph 2) respectively. Token B will move to 20 to dominate the others. Token C will then move to 21 to dominate the others, and B and C can continue to cycle in the T^2 subgraph 2 forever. If A is to move to dominate B and C, it cannot pick a node in subgraph 2 since it is full (any T^k subgraph can accommodate at most k tokens). Instead, token A moves to Node 00. If B now moves, it will choose Node 01, C will choose 10 and so on.

The precedence graph T^n is the basis for an n-thread bounded sequential timestamping system. We can "address" any node in the T^n graph with $n-1$ digits, using ternary notation. For example, the nodes in graph T^2 are addressed by 0, 1, and 2. The nodes in graph T^3 are denoted by $00, 01, \ldots, 22$, where the high-order digit indicates one of the three subgraphs, and the low-order digit indicates one node within that subgraph.

The key to understanding the n-thread labeling algorithm is that the nodes covered by tokens can never form a cycle. As mentioned, two threads can never form a cycle on T^2, because the shortest cycle in T^2 requires three nodes.

How does the `label()` method work for three threads? When A calls `label()`, if both the other threads have tokens on the same T^2 subgraph, then move to a node on the next highest T^2 subgraph, the one whose nodes dominate that T^2 subgraph. For example, consider the graph T^3 as illustrated in Fig. 2.12. We assume an initial acyclic situation in which there is a token A on Node 12 (Node 2 in subgraph 1) and tokens B and C, respectively, on Nodes 21 and 22 (Nodes 1 and 2 in subgraph 2). Token B will move to 20 to dominate all others. Token C will then move to 21 to dominate all others, and B and C can continue to cycle in the T^2 subgraph 2 forever. If A is to move to dominate B and C, it cannot pick a node in subgraph 2 since it is full (any T^k subgraph can accommodate at most k tokens). Token A thus moves to Node 00. If B now moves, it will choose Node 01, C will choose 10 and so on.

2.8 Lower Bounds on the Number of Locations

The `Bakery` lock is succinct, elegant, and fair. So why is it not considered practical? The principal drawback is the need to read and write n distinct locations, where n (which may be very large) is the maximum number of concurrent threads.

Is there a clever `Lock` algorithm based on reading and writing memory that avoids this overhead? We now demonstrate that the answer is *no.* Any deadlock-free `Lock` algorithm requires allocating and then reading or writing at least n distinct locations in the worst case. This result is crucially important, because it motivates us to add to our multiprocessor machines, synchronization operations stronger than read-write, and use them as the basis of our mutual exclusion algorithms.

In this section, we observe why this linear bound is inherent before we discuss practical mutual exclusion algorithms in later chapters. We will observe the following important limitation of memory locations accessed solely by *read* or *write* instructions (in practice these are called *loads* and *stores*): any information written by a thread to a given location could be *overwritten* (stored-to) without any other thread ever seeing it.

Our proof requires us to argue about the state of all memory used by a given multithreaded program. An object's *state* is just the state of its fields. A thread's *local state* is the state of its program counters and local variables. A *global state* or *system state* is the state of all objects, plus the local states of the threads.

***Definition* 2.8.1.** A `Lock` object state s is *inconsistent* in any global state where some thread is in the critical section, but the lock state is compatible with a global state in which no thread is in the critical section or is trying to enter the critical section.

Lemma 2.8.1. No deadlock-free `Lock` algorithm can enter an inconsistent state.

Proof: Suppose the `Lock` object is in an inconsistent state s, where some thread A is in the critical section. If thread B tries to enter the critical section, it must eventually succeed because the algorithm is deadlock-free and B cannot determine that A is in the critical section, a contradiction. □

Any `Lock` algorithm that solves deadlock-free mutual exclusion must have n distinct locations. Here, we consider only the 3-thread case, showing that a deadlock-free `Lock` algorithm accessed by three threads must use three distinct locations.

***Definition* 2.8.2.** A *covering state* for a `Lock` object is one in which there is at least one thread about to write to each shared location, but the `Lock` object's locations "look" like the critical section is empty (i.e., the locations' states appear as if there is no thread either in the critical section or trying to enter the critical section).

In a covering state, we say that each thread *covers* the location it is about to write.

***Theorem* 2.8.1.** Any `Lock` algorithm that, by reading and writing memory, solves deadlock-free mutual exclusion for three threads, must use at least three distinct memory locations.

Proof: Assume by way of contradiction that we have a deadlock-free `Lock` algorithm for three threads with only two locations. Initially, in state s, no thread is in the critical section or trying to enter. If we run any thread by itself, then it must write to at least one location before entering the critical section, as otherwise it creates an inconsistent state.

It follows that every thread must write at least one location before entering. If the shared locations are single-writer locations as in the Bakery lock, then it is immediate that three distinct locations are needed.

Now consider multiwriter locations such as the `victim` location in Peterson's algorithm (Fig. 2.6). Lets assume that we can bring the system to a covering `Lock` state s where A and B respectively cover distinct locations. Consider this possible execution starting from state s as depicted in Fig. 2.13:

> Let C run alone. Because the `Lock` algorithm satisfies the deadlock-free property, C enters the critical section eventually. Then let A and B respectively update their covered locations, leaving the `Lock` object in state s'.

The state s' is inconsistent because no thread can tell whether C is in the critical section, so a lock with two locations is impossible.

It remains to be shown how to maneuver threads A and B into a covering state. Consider an execution in which B runs through the critical section three times. Each time around, it must write some location, so consider the first location it writes when trying to enter the critical section. Since there are only two locations, B must "write first" to the same location twice. Call that location L_B.

Let B run until it is poised to write location L_B for the first time. If A runs now, it would enter the critical section, since B has not written anything. A must write L_A before entering the critical section. Otherwise, if A writes only L_B, then let A enter the critical section, let B write to L_B (obliterating A's last write). The result is an inconsistent state: B cannot tell whether A is in the critical section.

Let A run until it is poised to write L_A. This state is not a covering state, because A could have written something to L_B indicating to thread C that it is trying to enter the critical section. Let B run, obliterating any value A might have

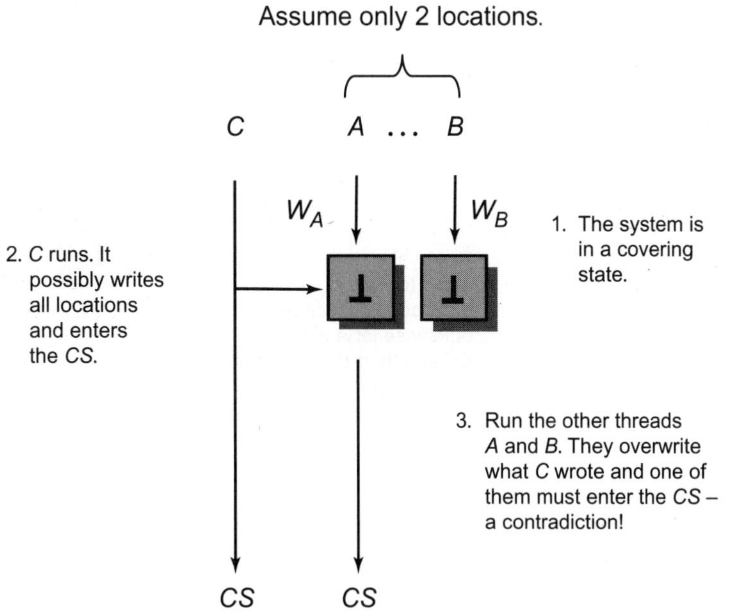

Figure 2.13 Contradiction using a covering state for two locations. Initially both locations have the empty value ⊥.

written to L_B, entering and leaving the critical section at most three times, and halting just before its second write to L_B. Notice that every time B enters and leaves the critical section, whatever it wrote to the locations is no longer relevant.

In this state, A is about to write L_A, B is about to write L_B, and the locations are consistent with no thread trying to enter or in the critical section, as required in a covering state. Fig. 2.14 illustrates this scenario. □

The same line of argument can be extended to show that n-thread deadlock-free mutual exclusion requires n distinct locations. The `Peterson` and `Bakery` locks are thus optimal (within a constant factor). However, as we note, the need to allocate n locations per `Lock` makes them impractical.

This proof shows the inherent limitation of read and write operations: information written by a thread may be overwritten without any other thread ever reading it. We will remember this limitation when we move on to design other algorithms.

In later chapters, we will see that modern machine architectures provide specialized instructions that overcome the "overwriting" limitation of read and write instructions, allowing n-thread `Lock` implementations that use only a constant number of memory locations. We will also see that making effective use of these instructions to solve mutual exclusion is far from trivial.

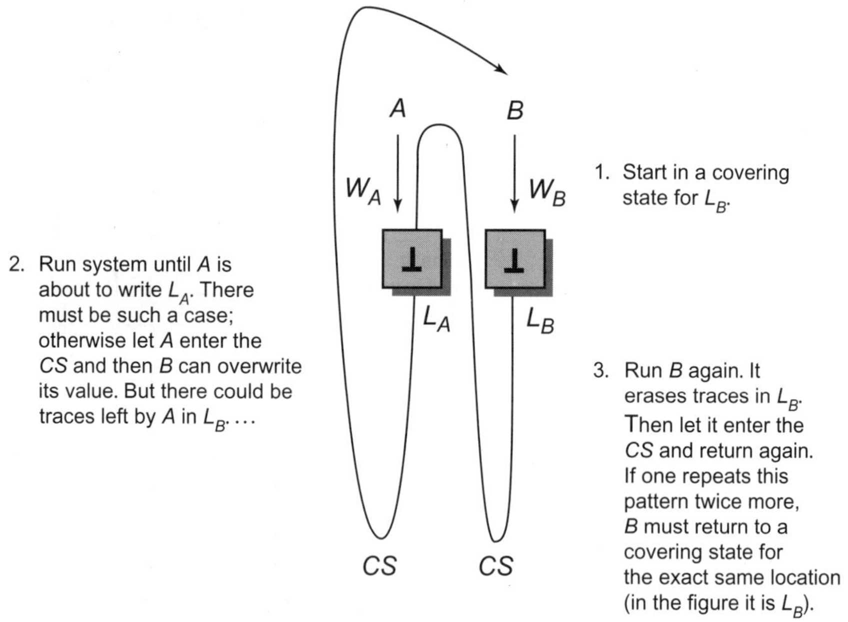

Figure 2.14 Reaching a covering state. In the initial covering state for L_B both locations have the empty value ⊥.

2.9 Chapter Notes

Isaac Newton's ideas about the flow of time appear in his famous *Principia* [121]. The "→" formalism is due to Leslie Lamport [89]. The first three algorithms in this chapter are due to Gary Peterson, who published them in a two-page paper in 1981 [124]. The `Bakery` lock presented here is a simplification of the original Bakery Algorithm due to Leslie Lamport [88]. The sequential time-stamp algorithm is due to Amos Israeli and Ming Li [77], who invented the notion of a bounded timestamping system. Danny Dolev and Nir Shavit [34] invented the first bounded concurrent timestamping system. Other bounded timestamping schemes include Sibsankar Haldar and Paul Vitányi [51], and Cynthia Dwork and Orli Waarts [37]. The lower bound on the number of lock fields is due to Jim Burns and Nancy Lynch [23]. Their proof technique, called a *covering argument*, has since been widely used to prove lower bounds in distributed computing. Readers interested in further reading can find a historical survey of mutual exclusion algorithms in a classic book by Michel Raynal [131].

2.10 Exercises

Exercise 9. Define *r-bounded waiting* for a given mutual exclusion algorithm to mean that if $D_A^j \rightarrow D_B^k$ then $CS_A^j \rightarrow CS_B^{k+r}$. Is there a way to define a doorway for the `Peterson` algorithm such that it provides *r*-bounded waiting for some value of *r*?

Exercise 10. Why do we need to define a *doorway* section, and why cannot we define FCFS in a mutual exclusion algorithm based on the order in which the first instruction in the `lock()` method was executed? Argue your answer in a case-by-case manner based on the nature of the first instruction executed by the `lock()`: a read or a write, to separate locations or the same location.

Exercise 11. Programmers at the Flaky Computer Corporation designed the protocol shown in Fig. 2.15 to achieve *n*-thread mutual exclusion. For each question, either sketch a proof, or display an execution where it fails.

- Does this protocol satisfy mutual exclusion?
- Is this protocol starvation-free?
- is this protocol deadlock-free?

Exercise 12. Show that the `Filter` lock allows some threads to overtake others an arbitrary number of times.

Exercise 13. Another way to generalize the two-thread Peterson lock is to arrange a number of 2-thread Peterson locks in a binary tree. Suppose *n* is a power of two.

```
class Flaky implements Lock {
  private int turn;
  private boolean busy = false;
  public void lock() {
    int me = ThreadID.get();
    do {
      do {
        turn = me;
      } while (busy);
      busy = true;
    } while (turn != me);
  }
  public void unlock() {
    busy = false;
  }
}
```

Figure 2.15 The Flaky lock used in Exercise 11.

Each thread is assigned a leaf lock which it shares with one other thread. Each lock treats one thread as thread 0 and the other as thread 1.

In the tree-lock's acquire method, the thread acquires every two-thread Peterson lock from that thread's leaf to the root. The tree-lock's release method for the tree-lock unlocks each of the 2-thread Peterson locks that thread has acquired, from the root back to its leaf. At any time, a thread can be delayed for a finite duration. (In other words, threads can take naps, or even vacations, but they do not drop dead.) For each property, either sketch a proof that it holds, or describe a (possibly infinite) execution where it is violated.

1. mutual exclusion.
2. freedom from deadlock.
3. freedom from starvation.

Is there an upper bound on the number of times the tree-lock can be acquired and released between the time a thread starts acquiring the tree-lock and when it succeeds?

Exercise 14. The ℓ-exclusion problem is a variant of the starvation-free mutual exclusion problem. We make two changes: as many as ℓ threads may be in the critical section at the same time, and fewer than ℓ threads might fail (by halting) in the critical section.

An implementation must satisfy the following conditions:

ℓ-Exclusion: At any time, at most ℓ threads are in the critical section.

ℓ-Starvation-Freedom: As long as fewer than ℓ threads are in the critical section, then some thread that wants to enter the critical section will eventually succeed (even if some threads in the critical section have halted).

Modify the n-process `Filter` mutual exclusion algorithm to turn it into an ℓ-exclusion algorithm.

Exercise 15. In practice, almost all lock acquisitions are uncontended, so the most practical measure of a lock's performance is the number of steps needed for a thread to acquire a lock when no other thread is concurrently trying to acquire the lock.

Scientists at Cantaloupe-Melon University have devised the following "wrapper" for an arbitrary lock, shown in Fig. 2.16. They claim that if the base `Lock` class provides mutual exclusion and is starvation-free, so does the `FastPath` lock, but it can be acquired in a constant number of steps in the absence of contention. Sketch an argument why they are right, or give a counterexample.

```
class FastPath implements Lock {
  private static ThreadLocal<Integer> myIndex;
  private Lock lock;
  private int x, y = -1;
  public void lock() {
    int i = myIndex.get();
    x = i;                        // I'm here
    while (y != -1) {}            // is the lock free?
    y = i;                        // me again?
    if (x != i)                   // Am I still here?
      lock.lock();                // slow path
  }
  public void unlock() {
    y = -1;
    lock.unlock();
  }
}
```

Figure 2.16 Fast path mutual exclusion algorithm used in Exercise 15.

```
class Bouncer {
  public static final int DOWN = 0;
  public static final int RIGHT = 1;
  public static final int STOP = 2;
  private boolean goRight = false;
  private ThreadLocal<Integer> myIndex; // initialize myIndex
  private int last = -1;
  int visit() {
    int i = myIndex.get();
    last = i;
    if (goRight)
      return RIGHT;
    goRight = true;
    if (last == i)
      return STOP;
    else
      return DOWN;
  }
}
```

Figure 2.17 The Bouncer class implementation.

Exercise 16. Suppose n threads call the `visit()` method of the `Bouncer` class shown in Fig. 2.17. Prove that—

- At most one thread gets the value `STOP`.
- At most $n-1$ threads get the value `DOWN`.
- At most $n-1$ threads get the value `RIGHT`.

Note that the last two proofs are *not* symmetric.

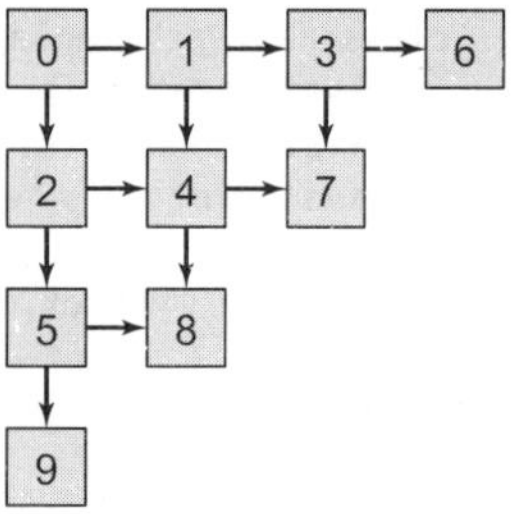

Figure 2.18 Array layout for `Bouncer` objects.

Exercise 17. So far, we have assumed that all n threads have unique, small indexes. Here is one way to assign unique small indexes to threads. Arrange `Bouncer` objects in a triangular matrix, where each `Bouncer` is given an id as shown in Fig. 2.18. Each thread starts by visiting `Bouncer` zero. If it gets `STOP`, it stops. If it gets `RIGHT`, it visits 1, and if it gets `DOWN`, it visits 2. In general, if a thread gets `STOP`, it stops. If it gets `RIGHT`, it visits the next `Bouncer` on that row, and if it gets `DOWN`, it visits the next `Bouncer` in that column. Each thread takes the id of the `Bouncer` object where it stops.

- Prove that each thread eventually stops at some `Bouncer` object.
- How many `Bouncer` objects do you need in the array if you know in advance the total number n of threads?

Exercise 18. Prove, by way of a counterexample, that the sequential time-stamp system T^3, started in a valid state (with no cycles among the labels), does not work for three threads in the concurrent case. Note that it is not a problem to have two identical labels since one can break such ties using thread IDs. The counterexample should display a state of the execution where three labels are not totally ordered.

Exercise 19. The sequential time-stamp system T^3 had a range of $O(3^n)$ different possible label values. Design a sequential time-stamp system that requires only $O(n2^n)$ labels. Note that in a time-stamp system, one may look at all the labels to choose a new label, yet once a label is chosen, it should be comparable to any other label without knowing what the other labels in the system are. Hint: think of the labels in terms of their bit representation.

Exercise 20. Give Java code to implement the `Timestamp` interface of Fig. 2.10 using unbounded labels. Then, show how to replace the pseudocode of the `Bakery` lock of Fig. 2.9 using your `Timestamp` Java code [82].

3 Concurrent Objects

The behavior of concurrent objects is best described through their safety and liveness properties, often referred to as *correctness* and *progress*. In this chapter we examine various ways of specifying correctness and progress.

While all notions of correctness for concurrent objects are based on some notion of equivalence with sequential behavior, different notions are appropriate for different systems. We examine three correctness conditions. *Quiescent consistency* is appropriate for applications that require high performance at the cost of placing relatively weak constraints on object behavior. *Sequential consistency* is a stronger condition, often useful for describing low-level systems such as hardware memory interfaces. *Linearizability*, even stronger, is useful for describing higher-level systems composed from *linearizable* components.

Along a different dimension, different method implementations provide different progress guarantees. Some are *blocking*, where the delay of any one thread can delay others, and some are *nonblocking*, where the delay of a thread cannot delay the others.

3.1 Concurrency and Correctness

What does it mean for a concurrent object to be correct? Fig. 3.1 shows a simple lock-based concurrent FIFO queue. The `enq()` and `deq()` methods synchronize by a mutual exclusion lock of the kind studied in Chapter 2. It is easy to see that this implementation is a correct concurrent FIFO queue. Because each method accesses and updates fields while holding an exclusive lock, the method calls take effect sequentially.

This idea is illustrated in Fig. 3.2, which shows an execution in which A enqueues a, B enqueues b, and C dequeues twice, first throwing `EmptyException`, and second returning b. Overlapping intervals indicate concurrent method calls. All three method calls overlap in time. In this figure, as in others, time moves

```
class LockBasedQueue<T> {
  int head, tail;
  T[] items;
  Lock lock;
  public LockBasedQueue(int capacity) {
    head = 0; tail = 0;
    lock = new ReentrantLock();
    items = (T[])new Object[capacity];
  }
  public void enq(T x) throws FullException {
    lock.lock();
    try {
      if (tail - head == items.length)
        throw new FullException();
      items[tail % items.length] = x;
       tail++;
    } finally {
      lock.unlock();
    }
  }
  public T deq() throws EmptyException {
    lock.lock();
    try {
      if (tail == head)
        throw new EmptyException();
      T x = items[head % items.length];
      head++;
      return x;
    } finally {
      lock.unlock();
    }
  }
}
```

Figure 3.1 A lock-based FIFO queue. The queue's items are kept in an array `items`, where `head` is the index of the next item to dequeue, and `tail` is the index of the first open array slot (modulo the capacity). The `lock` field is a lock that ensures that methods are mutually exclusive. Initially `head` and `tail` are zero, and the queue is empty. If enq() finds the queue is full, i.e., `head` and `tail` differ by the queue size, then it throws an exception. Otherwise, there is room, so enq() stores the item at array entry `tail`, and then increments `tail`. The deq() method works in a symmetric way.

from left to right, and dark lines indicate intervals. The intervals for a single thread are displayed along a single horizontal line. When convenient, the thread name appears on the left. A bar represents an interval with a fixed start and stop time. A bar with dotted lines on the right represents an interval with a fixed start-time and an unknown stop-time. The label "q.enq(x)" means that a thread enqueues item x at object q, while "q.deq(x)" means that the thread dequeues item x from object q.

The timeline shows which thread holds the lock. Here, ***C*** acquires the lock, observes the queue to be empty, releases the lock, and throws an exception. It does not modify the queue. ***B*** acquires the lock, inserts b, and releases the lock. ***A***

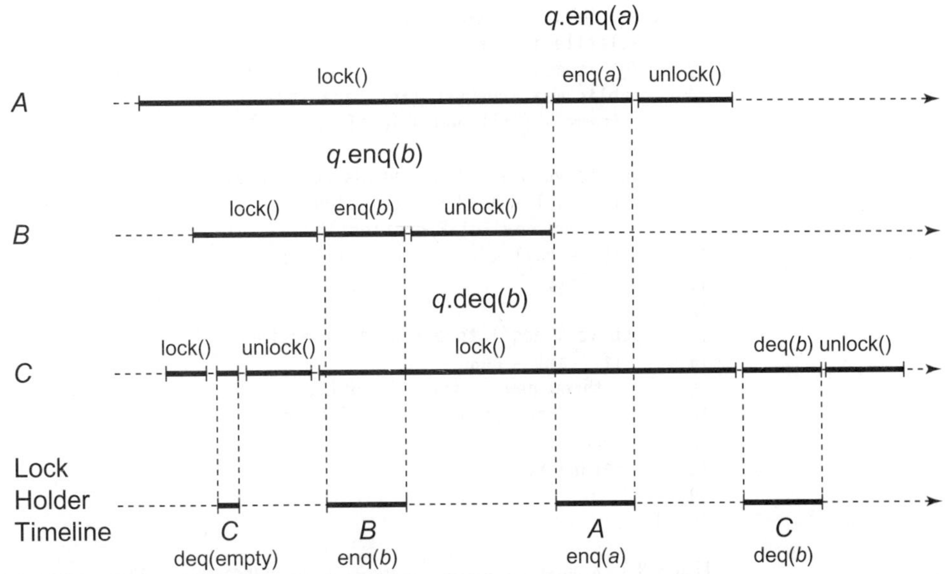

Figure 3.2 Locking queue execution. Here, *C* acquires the lock, observes the queue to be empty, releases the lock, and throws an exception. *B* acquires the lock, inserts *b*, and releases the lock. *A* acquires the lock, inserts *a*, and releases the lock. *C* re-acquires the lock, dequeues *b*, releases the lock, and returns.

acquires the lock, inserts *a*, and releases the lock. *C* reacquires the lock, dequeues *b*, releases the lock, and returns. Each of these calls takes effect sequentially, and we can easily verify that dequeuing *b* before *a* is consistent with our understanding of sequential FIFO queue behavior.

Let us consider, however, the alternative concurrent queue implementation in Fig. 3.3. (This queue is correct only if it is shared by a single enqueuer and a single dequeuer.) It has almost the same internal representation as the lock-based queue of Fig. 3.1. The only difference is the absence of a lock. We claim this is a correct implementation of a single-enqueuer/single-dequeuer FIFO queue, although it is no longer easy to explain why. It may not even be clear what it means for a queue *to be FIFO* when enqueues and dequeues are concurrent.

Unfortunately, it follows from Amdahl's Law (Chapter 1) that concurrent objects whose methods hold exclusive locks, and therefore effectively execute one after the other, are less desirable than ones with finer-grained locking or no locks at all. We therefore need a way to specify the behavior of concurrent objects, and to reason about their implementations, without relying on method-level locking. Nevertheless, the lock-based queue example illustrates a useful principle: it is easier to reason about concurrent objects if we can somehow map their concurrent executions to sequential ones, and limit our reasoning to these sequential executions. This principle is the key to the correctness properties introduced in this chapter.

```
class WaitFreeQueue<T> {
  volatile int head = 0, tail = 0;
  T[] items;
  public WaitFreeQueue(int capacity) {
    items = (T[]) new Object[capacity];
  }
  public void enq(T x) throws FullException {
    if (tail - head == items.length)
      throw new FullException();
    items[tail % items.length] = x;
    tail++;
  }
  public T deq() throws EmptyException {
    if (tail - head == 0)
      throw new EmptyException();
    T x = items[head % items.length];
    head++;
    return x;
  }
}
```

Figure 3.3 A single-enqueuer/single-dequeuer FIFO queue. The structure is identical to that of the lock-based FIFO queue, except that there is no need for the lock to coordinate access.

-has no overlaps (slide 113)

3.2 Sequential Objects

An *object* in languages such as Java and C++ is a container for data. Each object provides a set of *methods* which are the only way to manipulate that object. Each object has a *class*, which defines the object's methods and how they behave. An object has a well-defined *state* (for example, the FIFO queue's current sequence of items). There are many ways to describe how an object's methods behave, ranging from formal specifications to plain English. The application program interface (API) documentation that we use every day lies somewhere in between.

The API documentation typically says something like the following: if the object is in such-and-such a state before you call the method, then the object will be in some other state when the method returns, and the call will return a particular value, or throw a particular exception. This kind of description divides naturally into a *precondition* (describing the object's state before invoking the method) and a *postcondition*, describing, once the method returns, the object's state and return value. A change to an object's state is sometimes called a *side effect*. For example, consider how one might specify a first-in-first-out (FIFO) queue class. The class provides two methods: enq() and deq(). The queue state is just a sequence of items, possibly empty. If the queue state is a sequence q (precondition), then a call to enq(z) leaves the queue in state $q \cdot z$, where "$\cdot$" denotes concatenation. If the queue object is nonempty (precondition), say $a \cdot q$, then the deq() method removes and returns the sequence's first element a

complete history has no loose ends; no responces

(postcondition), leaving the queue in state q (side effect). If, instead, the queue object is empty (precondition), the method throws `EmptyException` and leaves the queue state unchanged (postcondition).

This style of documentation, called a *sequential specification*, is so familiar that it is easy to overlook how elegant and powerful it is. The length of the object's documentation is linear in the number of methods, because each method can be described in isolation. There are a vast number of potential interactions among methods, and all such interactions are characterized succinctly by the methods' side effects on the object state. The object's documentation describes the object state before and after each call, and we can safely ignore any intermediate states that the object may assume while the method call is in progress.

Defining objects in terms of preconditions and postconditions makes perfect sense in a *sequential* model of computation where a single thread manipulates a collection of objects. Unfortunately, for objects shared by multiple threads, this successful and familiar style of documentation falls apart. If an object's methods can be invoked by concurrent threads, then the method calls can overlap in time, and it no longer makes sense to talk about their order. What does it mean, in a multithreaded program, if x and y are enqueued on a FIFO queue during overlapping intervals? Which will be dequeued first? Can we continue to describe methods in isolation, via preconditions and postconditions, or must we provide explicit descriptions of every possible interaction among every possible collection of concurrent method calls?

Even the notion of an object's state becomes confusing. In single-threaded programs, an object must assume a meaningful state only between method calls.[1] For concurrent objects, however, overlapping method calls may be in progress at every instant, so the object may *never* be between method calls. Any method call must be prepared to encounter an object state that reflects the incomplete effects of other concurrent method calls, a problem that simply does not arise in single-threaded programs.

3.3 Quiescent Consistency

One way to develop an intuition about how concurrent objects should behave is to review examples of concurrent computations involving simple objects, and to decide, in each case, whether the behavior agrees with our intuition about how a concurrent object should behave.

Method calls take time. A *method call* is the interval that starts with an *invocation* event and ends with a *response* event. Method calls by concurrent threads may overlap, while method calls by a single thread are always sequential

---

1 There is an exception: care must be taken if one method partially changes an object's state and then calls another method of that same object.

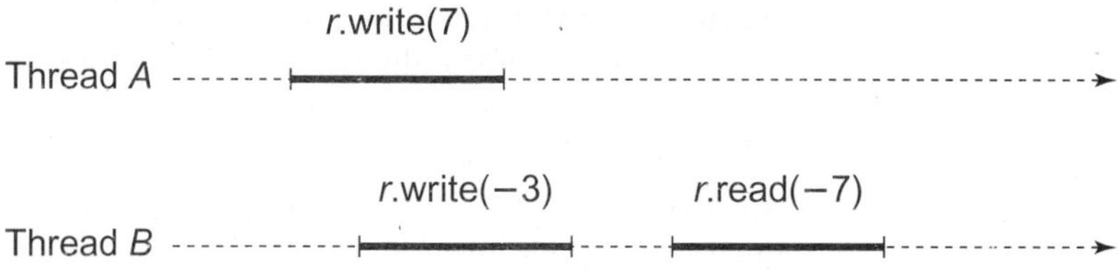

Figure 3.4 Why each method call should appear to take effect instantaneously. Two threads concurrently write −3 and 7 to a shared register r. Later, one thread reads r and returns the value −7. We expect to find either 7 or −3 in the register, not a mixture of both.

(non-overlapping, one-after-the-other). We say a method call is *pending* if its call event has occurred, but not its response event.

For historical reasons, the object version of a read–write memory location is called a *register* (see Chapter 4). In Fig. 3.4, two threads concurrently write −3 and 7 to a shared register r (as before, "r.read(x)" means that a thread reads value x from register object r, and similarly for "r.write(x)."). Later, one thread reads r and returns the value −7. This behavior is clearly not acceptable. We expect to find either 7 or −3 in the register, not a mixture of both. This example suggests the following principle:

***Principle* 3.3.1.** Method calls should appear to happen in a one-at-a-time, sequential order.

By itself, this principle is usually too weak to be useful. For example, it permits reads always to return the object's initial state, even in sequential executions.

Here is a slightly stronger condition. An object is *quiescent* if it has no pending method calls.

***Principle* 3.3.2.** Method calls separated by a period of quiescence should appear to take effect in their real-time order.

For example, suppose A and B concurrently enqueue x and y in a FIFO queue. The queue becomes quiescent, and then C enqueues z. We may not be able to predict the relative order of x and y in the queue, but we know they are ahead of z.

Together, Principles 3.3.1 and 3.3.2 define a correctness property called *quiescent consistency*. Informally, it says that any time an object becomes quiescent, then the execution so far is equivalent to some sequential execution of the completed calls.

As an example of a quiescently consistent object, consider the shared counter from Chapter 1. A quiescently-consistent shared counter would return numbers, not necessarily in the order of the `getAndIncrement()` requests, but always without duplicating or omitting a number. The execution of a quiescently consistent object is somewhat like a musical-chairs game: at any point, the music might stop, that is, the state could become quiescent. At that point, each pending method call must return an index so that all the indexes together meet the specification of a sequential counter, implying no duplicated or omitted numbers. In other words, a quiescently consistent counter is an *index distribution* mechanism, useful as a "loop counter" in programs that do not care about the order in which indexes are issued.

3.3.1 Remarks

How much does quiescent consistency limit concurrency? Specifically, under what circumstances does quiescent consistency require one method call to block waiting for another to complete? Surprisingly, the answer is (essentially), *never*. A method is *total* if it is defined for every object state; otherwise it is *partial*. For example, let us consider the following alternative specification for an unbounded sequential FIFO queue. One can always enqueue another item, but one can dequeue only from a nonempty queue. In the sequential specification of a FIFO queue, `enq()` is total, since its effects are defined in every queue state, but `deq()` is partial, since its effects are defined only for nonempty queues.

In any concurrent execution, for any pending invocation of a total method, there exists a quiescently consistent response. This observation does not mean that it is easy (or even always possible) to figure out what that response is, but only that the correctness condition itself does not stand in the way. We say that quiescent consistency is a *nonblocking* correctness condition. We make this notion more clear in Section 3.6.

A correctness property $\mathcal{P}$ is *compositional* if, whenever each object in the system satisfies $\mathcal{P}$, the system as a whole satisfies $\mathcal{P}$. Compositionality is important in large systems. Any sufficiently complex system must be designed and implemented in a *modular* fashion. Components are designed, implemented, and proved correct independently. Each component makes a clear distinction between its *implementation*, which is hidden, and its *interface*, which precisely characterizes the guarantees it makes to the other components. For example, if a concurrent object's interface states that it is a sequentially consistent FIFO queue, then users of the queue need to know nothing about how the queue is implemented. The result of composing individually correct components that rely only on one anothers' interfaces should itself be a correct system. Can we, in fact, compose a collection of independently implemented quiescently consistent objects to construct a quiescently consistent system? The answer is, *yes*: quiescent consistency is compositional, so quiescently consistent objects can be composed to construct more complex quiescently consistent objects.

every thread. not object

3.4 Sequential Consistency

In Fig. 3.5, a single thread writes 7 and then −3 to a shared register r. Later, it reads r and returns 7. For some applications, this behavior might not be acceptable because the value the thread read is not the last value it wrote. The order

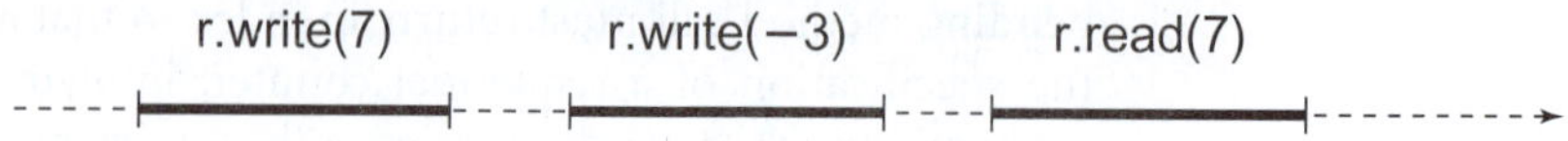

Figure 3.5 Why method calls should appear to take effect in program order. This behavior is not acceptable because the value the thread read is not the last value it wrote.

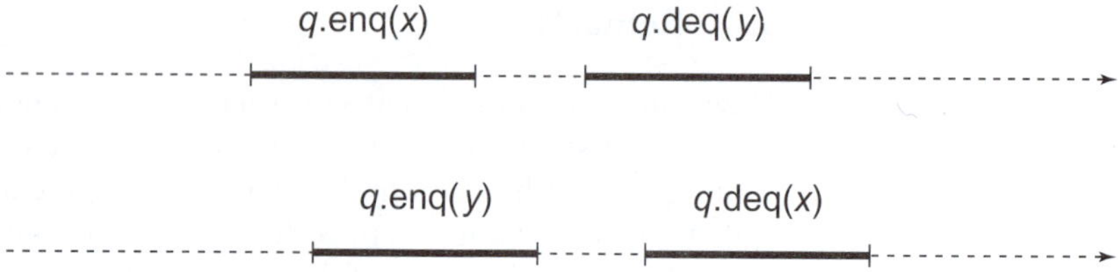

Figure 3.6 There are two possible sequential orders that can justify this execution. Both orders are consistent with the method calls' program order, and either one is enough to show the execution is sequentially consistent.

in which a single thread issues method calls is called its *program order*. (Method calls by different threads are unrelated by program order.)

In this example, we were surprised that operation calls did not take effect in program order. This example suggests an alternative principle:

***Principle* 3.4.1.** Method calls should appear to take effect in program order.

This principle ensures that purely sequential computations behave the way we would expect.

Together, Principles 3.3.1 and 3.4.1 define a correctness property called *sequential consistency*, which is widely used in the literature on multiprocessor synchronization.

Sequential consistency requires that method calls act as if they occurred in a sequential order consistent with program order. That is, in any concurrent execution, there is a way to order the method calls sequentially so that they (1) are consistent with program order, and (2) meet the object's sequential specification. There may be more than one order satisfying this condition. In Fig. 3.6, thread *A* enqueues *x* while *B* enqueues *y*, and then *A* dequeues *y* while *B* dequeues *x*. There are two possible sequential orders that can explain these results: (1) *A* enqueues *x*, *B* enqueues *y*, *B* dequeues *x*, then *A* dequeues *y*, or (2) *B* enqueues *y*, *A* enqueues *x*, *A* dequeues *y*, then *B* dequeues *x*. Both these orders are consistent with the method calls' program order, and either one is enough to show the execution is sequentially consistent.

3.4.1 Remarks

It is worth noting that sequential consistency and quiescent consistency are *incomparable*: there exist sequentially consistent executions that are not quiescently consistent, and vice versa. Quiescent consistency does not necessarily preserve program order, and sequential consistency is unaffected by quiescent periods.

In most modern multiprocessor architectures, memory reads and writes are not sequentially consistent: they can be typically reordered in complex ways. Most of the time no one can tell, because the vast majority of reads–writes are not used for synchronization. In those specific cases where programmers need sequential consistency, they must ask for it explicitly. The architectures provide special instructions (usually called *memory barriers* or *fences*) that instruct the processor to propagate updates to and from memory as needed, to ensure that reads and writes interact correctly. In the end, the architectures do implement sequential consistency, but only on demand. We discuss further issues related to sequential consistency and the Java programming language in detail in Section 3.8.

In Fig. 3.7, thread A enqueues x, and later B enqueues y, and finally A dequeues y. This execution may violate our intuitive notion of how a FIFO queue should behave: the call enqueuing x finishes before the call dequeuing y starts, so although y is enqueued after x, it is dequeued before. Nevertheless, this execution is sequentially consistent. Even though the call that enqueues x happens before the call that enqueues y, these calls are unrelated by program order, so sequential consistency is free to reorder them.

One could argue whether it is acceptable to reorder method calls whose intervals do not overlap, even if they occur in different threads. For example, we might be unhappy if we deposit our paycheck on Monday, but the bank bounces our rent check the following Friday because it reordered our deposit after your withdrawal.

Sequential consistency, like quiescent consistency, is nonblocking: any pending call to a total method can always be completed.

Is sequential consistency compositional? That is, is the result of composing multiple sequentially consistent objects itself sequentially consistent? Here, unfortunately, the answer is *no*. In Fig. 3.8, two threads, A and B, call enqueue and dequeue methods for two queue objects, p and q. It is not hard to see that p and q are each sequentially consistent: the sequence of method calls for p is the same as in the sequentially consistent execution shown in Fig. 3.7, and the behavior of q is symmetric. Nevertheless, the execution as a whole is *not* sequentially consistent.

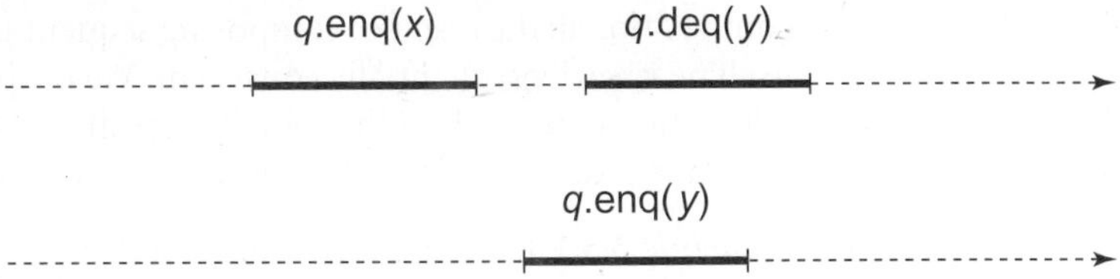

Figure 3.7 Sequential consistency versus real-time order. Thread A enqueues x, and later thread B enqueues y, and finally A dequeues y. This execution may violate our intuitive notion of how a FIFO queue should behave because the method call enqueuing x finishes before the method call dequeuing y starts, so although y is enqueued after x, it is dequeued before. Nevertheless, this execution is sequentially consistent.

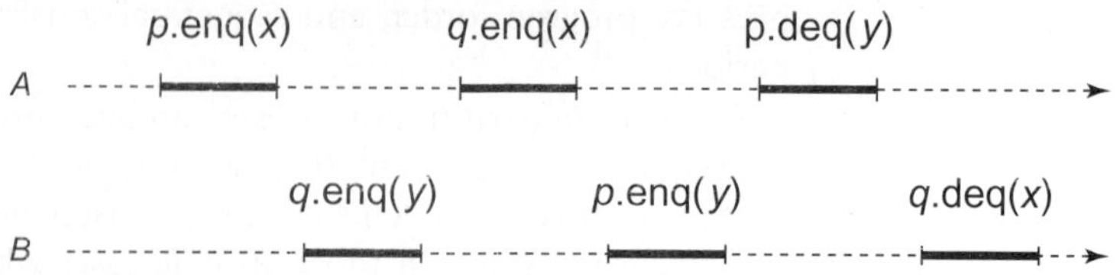

Figure 3.8 Sequential consistency is not compositional. Two threads, *A* and *B*, call enqueue and dequeue methods on two queue objects, *p* and *q*. It is not hard to see that *p* and *q* are each sequentially consistent, yet the execution as a whole is *not* sequentially consistent.

Let us check that there is no correct sequential execution in which these method calls can be ordered in a way consistent with their program order. Let us assume, by way of contradiction, that these method calls can be reordered to form a correct FIFO queue execution, where the order of the method calls is consistent with the program order. We use the following shorthand: $\langle p.enq(x)\ A\rangle \rightarrow \langle p.deq(x)\ B\rangle$ means that any sequential execution must order *A*'s enqueue of *x* at *p* before *B*'s dequeue of *x* at *p*, and so on. Because *p* is FIFO and *A* dequeues *y* from *p*, *y* must have been enqueued before *x*:

$$\langle p.enq(y)\ B\rangle \rightarrow \langle p.enq(x)\ A\rangle$$

Likewise,

$$\langle q.enq(x)\ A\rangle \rightarrow \langle q.enq(y)\ B\rangle.$$

But program order implies that

$$\langle p.enq(x)\ A\rangle \rightarrow \langle q.enq(x)\ A\rangle \quad \text{and} \quad \langle q.enq(y)\ B\rangle \rightarrow \langle p.enq(y)\ B\rangle.$$

Together, these orderings form a cycle.

3.5 Linearizability

We have seen that the principal drawback of sequential consistency is that it is not compositional: the result of composing sequentially consistent components is not itself necessarily sequentially consistent. We propose the following way out of this dilemma. Let us replace the requirement that method calls appear to happen in program order with the following stronger restriction:

***Principle* 3.5.1.** Each method call should appear to take effect instantaneously at some moment between its invocation and response.

This principle states that the real-time behavior of method calls must be preserved. We call this correctness property *linearizability*. Every linearizable execution is sequentially consistent, but not vice versa.

3.5.1 Linearization Points

The usual way to show that a concurrent object implementation is linearizable is to identify for each method a *linearization* point where the method takes effect. For lock-based implementations, each method's critical section can serve as its linearization point. For implementations that do not use locking, the linearization point is typically a single step where the effects of the method call become visible to other method calls.

For example, let us recall the single-enqueuer/single-dequeuer queue of Fig. 3.3. This implementation has no critical sections, and yet we can identify its linearization points. Here, the linearization points depend on the execution. If it returns an item, the `deq()` method has a linearization point when the `head` field is updated (Line 17). If the queue is empty, the `deq()` method has a linearization point when it throws `EmptyException` (Line 15). The `enq()` method is similar.

3.5.2 Remarks

Sequential consistency is a good way to describe standalone systems, such as hardware memories, where composition is not an issue. Linearizability, by contrast, is a good way to describe components of large systems, where components must be implemented and verified independently. Moreover, the techniques we use to implement concurrent objects, are all linearizable. Because we are interested in systems that preserve program order and compose, most (but not all) data structures considered in this book are linearizable.

How much does linearizability limit concurrency? Linearizability, like sequential consistency, is nonblocking. Moreover, like quiescent consistency, but unlike sequential consistency, linearizability is compositional; the result of composing linearizable objects is linearizable.

3.6 Formal Definitions

We now consider more precise definitions. Here, we focus on the formal properties of linearizability, since it is the property most often used in this book. We leave it as an exercise to provide the same kinds of definitions for quiescent consistency and sequential consistency.

Informally, we know that a concurrent object is linearizable if each method call appears to take effect instantaneously at some moment between that method's invocation and return events. This statement is probably enough for most informal reasoning, but a more precise formulation is needed to take care of some tricky cases (such as method calls that have not returned), and for more rigorous styles of argument.

linearizability makes it easy to understand, and ensures sequential

An execution of a concurrent system is modeled by a *history*, a finite sequence of method *invocation* and *response events*. A *subhistory* of a history H is a subsequence of the events of H. We write a method invocation as $\langle x.m(a^*)\ A\rangle$, where x is an object, m a method name, a^* a sequence of arguments, and A a thread. We write a method response as $\langle x : t(r^*)\ A\rangle$ where t is either *Ok* or an exception name, and r^* is a sequence of result values. Sometimes we refer to an event labeled with thread A as a *step* of A.

A response *matches* an invocation if they have the same object and thread. We have been using the term "method call" informally, but here is a more formal definition: a *method call* in a history H is a pair consisting of an invocation and the next matching response in H. We need to distinguish calls that have returned from those that have not: An invocation is *pending* in H if no matching response follows the invocation. An *extension* of H is a history constructed by appending responses to zero or more pending invocations of H. Sometimes, we ignore all pending invocations: *complete*(H) is the subsequence of H consisting of all matching invocations and responses.

In some histories, method calls do not overlap: A history H is *sequential* if the first event of H is an invocation, and each invocation, except possibly the last, is immediately followed by a matching response.

Sometimes we focus on a single thread or object: a *thread subhistory*, $H|A$ ("H at A"), of a history H is the subsequence of all events in H whose thread names are A. An *object subhistory* $H|x$ is similarly defined for an object x. In the end, all that matters is how each thread views what happened: two histories H and H' are *equivalent* if for every thread A, $H|A = H'|A$. Finally, we need to rule out histories that make no sense: A history H is *well formed* if each thread subhistory is sequential. All histories we consider here are well-formed. Notice that thread subhistories of a well-formed history are always sequential, but object subhistories need not be.

How can we tell whether an object is really a FIFO queue? We simply assume that we have some effective way of recognizing whether any sequential object history is or is not a legal history for that object's class. A *sequential specification* for an object is just a set of sequential histories for the object. A sequential history H is *legal* if each object subhistory is legal for that object.

Recall from Chapter 2 that a *partial order* $\rightarrow$ on a set X is a relation that is irreflexive and transitive. That is, it is never true that $x \rightarrow x$, and whenever $x \rightarrow y$ and $y \rightarrow z$, then $x \rightarrow z$. Note that it is possible that there are distinct x and y such that neither $x \rightarrow y$ nor $y \rightarrow x$. A *total order* $<$ on X is a partial order such that for all distinct x and y in X, either $x < y$ or $y < x$.

Any partial order can be extended to a total order:

***Fact* 3.6.1.** If $\rightarrow$ is a partial order on X, then there exists a total order "$<$" on X such that if $x \rightarrow y$, then $x < y$.

We say that a method call m_0 *precedes* a method call m_1 in history H if m_0 finished before m_1 started: that is, m_0's response event occurs before m_1's invocation event. This notion is important enough to introduce some shorthand notation. Given a history H containing method calls m_0 and m_1, we say that $m_0 \rightarrow_H m_1$ if m_0 precedes m_1 in H. We leave it as an exercise to show that $\rightarrow_H$ is a partial order. Notice that if H is sequential, then $\rightarrow_H$ is a total order. Given a history H and an object x, such that $H|x$ contains method calls m_0 and m_1, we say that $m_0 \rightarrow_x m_1$ if m_0 precedes m_1 in $H|x$.

3.6.1 Linearizability

The basic idea behind linearizability is that every concurrent history is equivalent, in the following sense, to some sequential history. The basic rule is that if one method call precedes another, then the earlier call must have taken effect before the later call. By contrast, if two method calls overlap, then their order is ambiguous, and we are free to order them in any convenient way.

More formally,

Definition **3.6.1.** A history H is *linearizable* if it has an extension H' and there is a legal sequential history S such that

L1 *complete*(H') is equivalent to S, and

L2 if method call m_0 precedes method call m_1 in H, then the same is true in S.

We refer to S as a *linearization* of H. (H may have multiple linearizations.)

Informally, extending H to H' captures the idea that some pending invocations may have taken effect, even though their responses have not yet been returned to the caller. Fig. 3.9 illustrates the notion: we must complete the pending enq(x) method call to justify the deq() call that returns x. The second condition says that if one method call precedes another in the original history, then that ordering must be preserved in the linearization.

3.6.2 Compositional Linearizability

Linearizability is compositional:

Theorem **3.6.1.** H is linearizable if, and only if, for each object x, $H|x$ is linearizable.

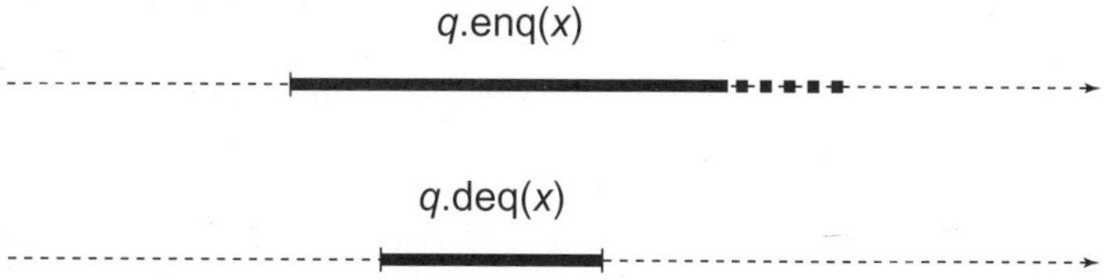

Figure 3.9 The pending enq(x) method call must take effect early to justify the deq() call that returns x.

Proof: The "only if" part is left as an exercise.

For each object x, pick a linearization of $H|x$. Let R_x be the set of responses appended to $H|x$ to construct that linearization, and let $\rightarrow_x$ be the corresponding linearization order. Let H' be the history constructed by appending to H each response in R_x.

We argue by induction on the number of method calls in H'. For the base case, if H' contains only one method call, we are done. Otherwise, assume the claim for every H containing fewer than $k > 1$ method calls. For each object x, consider the last method call in $H'|x$. One of these calls m must be maximal with respect to $\rightarrow_H$: that is, there is no m' such that $m \rightarrow_H m'$. Let G' be the history defined by removing m from H'. Because m is maximal, H' is equivalent to $G' \cdot m$. By the induction hypothesis, G' is linearizable to a sequential history S', and both H' and H are linearizable to $S' \cdot m$. □

Compositionality is important because it allows concurrent systems to be designed and constructed in a modular fashion; linearizable objects can be implemented, verified, and executed independently. A concurrent system based on a noncompositional correctness property must either rely on a centralized scheduler for all objects, or else satisfy additional constraints placed on objects to ensure that they follow compatible scheduling protocols.

3.6.3 The Nonblocking Property

Linearizability is a *nonblocking* property: a pending invocation of a total method is never required to wait for another pending invocation to complete.

***Theorem* 3.6.2.** Let $inv(m)$ be an invocation of a total method. If $\langle x\ inv\ P\rangle$ is a pending invocation in a linearizable history H, then there exists a response $\langle x\ res\ P\rangle$ such that $H \cdot \langle x\ res\ P\rangle$ is linearizable.

Proof: Let S be any linearization of H. If S includes a response $\langle x\ res\ P\rangle$ to $\langle x\ inv\ P\rangle$, we are done, since S is also a linearization of $H \cdot \langle x\ res\ P\rangle$. Otherwise, $\langle x\ inv\ P\rangle$ does not appear in S either, since linearizations, by definition, include no pending invocations. Because the method is total, there exists a response $\langle x\ res\ P\rangle$ such that

$$S' = S \cdot \langle x\ inv\ P\rangle \cdot \langle x\ res\ P\rangle$$

is legal. S', however, is a linearization of $H \cdot \langle x\ res\ P\rangle$, and hence is also a linearization of H. □

This theorem implies that linearizability by itself never forces a thread with a pending invocation of a total method to block. Of course, blocking (or even deadlock) may occur as artifacts of particular implementations of linearizability, but it is not inherent to the correctness property itself. This theorem suggests that linearizability is an appropriate correctness condition for systems where concurrency and real-time response are important.

The nonblocking property does not rule out blocking in situations where it is explicitly intended. For example, it may be sensible for a thread attempting to dequeue from an empty queue to block, waiting until another thread enqueues an item. A queue specification would capture this intention by making the `deq()` method's specification partial, leaving its effect undefined when applied to an empty queue. The most natural concurrent interpretation of a partial sequential specification is simply to wait until the object reaches a state in which the method is defined.

3.7 Progress Conditions

Linearizability's nonblocking property states that any pending invocation has a correct response, but does not talk about how to compute such a response. For example, let us consider the scenario for the lock-based queue shown in Fig. 3.1. Suppose the queue is initially empty. A halts half-way through enqueuing x, and B then invokes `deq()`. The nonblocking property guarantees that B's call to `deq()` has a response: it could either throw an exception or return x. In this implementation, however, B is unable to acquire the lock, and will be delayed as long as A is delayed.

Such an implementation is called *blocking*, because an unexpected delay by one thread can prevent others from making progress. Unexpected thread delays are common in multiprocessors. A cache miss might delay a processor for a hundred cycles, a page fault for a few million cycles, preemption by the operating system for hundreds of millions of cycles. These delays depend on the specifics of the machine and the operating system.

A method is *wait-free* if it guarantees that every call finishes its execution in a finite number of steps. It is *bounded wait-free* if there is a bound on the number of steps a method call can take. This bound may depend on the number of threads. For example, the Bakery algorithm's doorway section studied in Chapter 2 is bounded wait-free, where the bound is the number of threads. A wait-free method whose performance does not depend on the number of active threads is called *population-oblivious*. We say that an object is wait-free if its methods are wait-free, and in an object oriented language, we say that a class is wait-free if all instances of its objects are wait-free. Being wait-free is an example of a *nonblocking* progress condition, meaning that an arbitrary and unexpected delay by one thread (say, the one holding a lock) does not necessarily prevent the others from making progress.

The queue shown in Fig. 3.3 is wait-free. For example, in the scenario where A halts half-way through enqueuing x, and B then invokes `deq()`, then B will either throw `EmptyException` (if A halted before storing the item in the array) or it will return x (if A halted afterward). The lock-based queue is not nonblocking because *B* will take an unbounded number of steps unsuccessfully trying to acquire the lock.

The wait-free property is attractive because it guarantees that every thread that takes steps makes progress. However, wait-free algorithms can be inefficient, and sometimes we are willing to settle for a weaker nonblocking property.

A method is *lock-free* if it guarantees that infinitely often *some* method call finishes in a finite number of steps. Clearly, any wait-free method implementation is also lock-free, but not vice versa. Lock-free algorithms admit the possibility that some threads could starve. As a practical matter, there are many situations in which starvation, while possible, is extremely unlikely, so a fast lock-free algorithm may be more attractive than a slower wait-free algorithm.

3.7.1 Dependent Progress Conditions

The wait-free and lock-free nonblocking progress conditions guarantee that the computation as a whole makes progress, independently of how the system schedules threads.

In Chapter 2 we encountered two progress conditions for blocking implementations: the *deadlock-free* and *starvation-free* properties. These properties are *dependent* progress conditions: progress occurs only if the underlying platform (i.e., the operating system) provides certain guarantees. In principle, the deadlock-free and starvation-free properties are useful when the operating system guarantees that every thread eventually leaves every critical section. In practice, these properties are useful when the operating system guarantees that every thread eventually leaves every critical section *in a timely manner.*

Classes whose methods rely on lock-based synchronization can guarantee, at best, dependent progress properties. Does this observation mean that lock-based algorithms should be avoided? Not necessarily. If preemption in the middle of a critical section is sufficiently rare, then dependent blocking progress conditions are effectively indistinguishable from their nonblocking counterparts. If preemption is common enough to cause concern, or if the cost of preemption-based delay is sufficiently high, then it is sensible to consider nonblocking progress conditions.

There is also a dependent nonblocking progress condition: the *obstruction-free* property. We say that a method call executes *in isolation* if no other threads take steps.

***Definition* 3.7.1.** A method is *obstruction-free* if, from any point after which it executes in isolation, it finishes in a finite number of steps.

Like the other nonblocking progress conditions, the obstruction-free condition ensures that not all threads can be blocked by a sudden delay of one or more other threads. A lock-free algorithm is obstruction-free, but not vice versa.

The obstruction-free algorithm rules out the use of locks but does not guarantee progress when multiple threads execute concurrently. It seems to defy the fair approach of most operating system schedulers by guaranteeing progress only when one thread is unfairly scheduled ahead of the others.

In practice, however, there is no problem. The obstruction-free condition does not require pausing all threads, only those threads that *conflict*, meaning that they call the same shared object's methods. The simplest way to exploit an obstruction-free algorithm is to introduce a *back-off* mechanism: a thread that detects a conflict pauses to give an earlier thread time to finish. Choosing when to back off, and for how long, is a complicated subject discussed in detail in Chapter 7.

Picking a progress condition for a concurrent object implementation depends on both the needs of the application and the characteristics of the underlying platform. The absolute wait-free and lock-free progress properties have good theoretical properties, they work on just about any platform, and they provide real-time guarantees useful to applications such as music, electronic games, and other interactive applications. The dependent obstruction-free, deadlock-free, and starvation-free properties rely on guarantees provided by the underlying platform. Given those guarantees, however, the dependent properties often admit simpler and more efficient implementations.

3.8 The Java Memory Model

The Java programming language does not guarantee linearizability, or even sequential consistency, when reading or writing fields of shared objects. Why not? The principal reason is that strict adherence to sequential consistency would outlaw widely used compiler optimizations, such as register allocation, common subexpression elimination, and redundant read elimination, all of which work by reordering memory reads–writes. In a single-threaded computation, such reorderings are invisible to the optimized program, but in a multithreaded computation, one thread can spy on another and observe out-of-order executions.

The Java memory model satisfies the *Fundamental Property* of relaxed memory models: if a program's sequentially consistent executions follow certain rules, then every execution of that program in the relaxed model will still be sequentially consistent. In this section, we describe rules that guarantee that the Java programs are sequentially consistent. We will not try to cover the complete set of rules, which is rather large and complex. Instead, we focus on a set of straightforward rules that should be enough for most purposes.

Fig. 3.10 shows *double-checked locking*, a once-common programming idiom that falls victim to Java's lack of sequential consistency. Here, the `Singleton` class manages a single instance of a `Singleton` object, accessible through the `getInstance()` method. This method creates the instance the first time it is called. This method must be synchronized to ensure that only one instance is created, even if several threads observe `instance` to be *null*. Once the instance has been created, however, no further synchronization should be necessary. As an optimization, the code in Fig. 3.10 enters the synchronized block only when

```
1 public static Singleton getInstance() {
2   if (instance == null) {
3     synchronized(Singleton.class) {
4       if (instance == null)
5         instance = new Singleton();
6     }
7   }
8   return instance;
9 }
```

Figure 3.10 Double-checked locking.

it observes an `instance` to be *null*. Once it has entered, it *double-checks* that `instance` is still *null* before creating the instance.

This pattern, once common, is incorrect. At Line 5, the constructor call appears to take place before the `instance` field is assigned, but the Java memory model allows these steps to occur out of order, effectively making a partially initialized `Singleton` object visible to other programs.

In the Java memory model, objects reside in a shared memory and each thread has a private working memory that contains cached copies of fields it has read or written. In the absence of explicit synchronization (explained later), a thread that writes to a field might not propagate that update to memory right away, and a thread that reads a field might not update its working memory if the field's copy in memory changes value. Naturally, a Java virtual machine is free to keep such cached copies consistent, and in practice they often do, but they are not required to do so. At this point, we can guarantee only that a thread's own reads–writes appear to that thread to happen in order, and that any field value read by a thread was written to that field (i.e., values do not appear out of thin air).

Certain statements are *synchronization events*. Usually, the term "synchronization" implies some form of atomicity or mutual exclusion. In Java, however, it also implies reconciling a thread's working memory with the shared memory. Some synchronization events cause a thread to write cached changes back to shared memory, making those changes visible to other threads. Other synchronization events cause the thread to invalidate its cached values, forcing it to reread field values from memory, making other threads' changes visible. Synchronization events are linearizable: they are totally ordered, and all threads agree on that ordering. We now look at different kinds of synchronization events.

3.8.1 Locks and Synchronized Blocks

A thread can achieve mutual exclusion either by entering a **`synchronized`** block or method, which acquires an implicit lock, or by acquiring an explicit lock (such as the `ReentrantLock` from the java.util.concurrent.locks package). Both approaches have the same implications for memory behavior.

If all accesses to a particular field are protected by the same lock, then reads–writes to that field are linearizable. Specifically, when a thread releases a lock, modified fields in working memory are written back to shared memory, performing modifications while holding the lock accessible to other threads. When a thread acquires the lock, it invalidates its working memory to ensure fields are reread from shared memory. Together, these conditions ensure that reads–writes to the fields of any object protected by a single lock are linearizable.

3.8.2 Volatile Fields

Volatile fields are linearizable. Reading a volatile field is like acquiring a lock: the working memory is invalidated and the volatile field's current value is reread from memory. Writing a volatile field is like releasing a lock: the volatile field is immediately written back to memory.

Although reading and writing a volatile field has the same effect on memory consistency as acquiring and releasing a lock, multiple reads–writes are not atomic. For example, if x is a volatile variable, the expression x++ will not necessarily increment x if concurrent threads can modify x. Some form of mutual exclusion is needed as well. One common usage pattern for volatile variables occurs when a field is read by multiple threads, but only written by one.

The java.util.concurrent.atomic package includes classes that provide linearizable memory such as AtomicReference<T> or AtomicInteger. The compareAndSet() and set() methods act like volatile writes, and get() acts like a volatile read.

3.8.3 Final Fields

Recall that a field declared to be **final** cannot be modified once it has been initialized. An object's final fields are initialized in its constructor. If the constructor follows certain simple rules, described in the following paragraphs, then the correct value of any final fields will be visible to other threads without synchronization. For example, in the code shown in Fig. 3.11, a thread that calls reader() is

```
class FinalFieldExample {
  final int x; int y;
  static FinalFieldExample f;
  public FinalFieldExample() {
    x = 3;
    y = 4;
  }
  static void writer() {
    f = new FinalFieldExample();
  }
  static void reader() {
    if (f != null) {
      int i = f.x; int j = f.y;
    }
  }
}
```

Figure 3.11 Constructor with final field.

```
public class EventListener {
  final int x;
  public EventListener(EventSource eventSource) {
    eventSource.registerListener(this); // register with event source ...
  }
  public onEvent(Event e) {
   ... // handle the event
  }
}
```

Figure 3.12 Incorrect `EventListener` class.

guaranteed to see x equal to 3, because the x field is final. There is no guarantee that y will be equal to 4, because y is not final.

If a constructor is synchronized incorrectly, however, then final fields may be observed to change value. The rule is simple: the **`this`** reference must not be released from the constructor before the constructor returns.

Fig. 3.12 shows an example of an incorrect constructor in an event-driven system. Here, an `EventListener` class registers itself with an `EventSource` class, making a reference to the listener object accessible to other threads. This code may appear safe, since registration is the last step in the constructor, but it is incorrect, because if another thread calls the event listener's `onEvent()` method before the constructor finishes, then the `onEvent()` method is not guaranteed to see a correct value for `x`.

In summary, reads–writes to fields are linearizable if either the field is volatile, or the field is protected by a unique lock which is acquired by all readers and writers.

3.9 Remarks

What progress condition is right for one's application? Obviously, it depends on the needs of the application and the nature of the system it is intended to run on. However, this is actually a "trick question" since different methods, even ones applied to the same object, can have different progress conditions. A frequently called time-critical method such as a table lookup in a firewall program, should be wait-free, while an infrequent call to update a table entry can be implemented using mutual exclusion. As we will see, it is quite natural to write applications whose methods differ in their progress guarantees.

Which correctness condition is right for one's application? Well, it depends on the needs of the application. A lightly loaded printer server that uses a queue to hold, say print jobs, might be satisfied with a quiescently-consistent queue, since the order in which documents are printed is of little importance. A banking server should execute customer requests in program order (transfer $100 from savings to checking, write a check for $50), so it should use a sequentially consistent queue. A stock-trading server is required to be fair, so orders from different customers must be executed in the order they arrive, so it would require a linearizable queue.

The following joke circulated in Italy in the 1920s. According to Mussolini, the ideal citizen is intelligent, honest, and Fascist. Unfortunately, no one is perfect, which explains why everyone you meet is either intelligent and Fascist but not honest, honest and Fascist but not intelligent, or honest and intelligent but not Fascist.

As programmers, it would be ideal to have linearizable hardware, linearizable data structures, and good performance. Unfortunately, technology is imperfect, and for the time being, hardware that performs well is not even sequentially consistent. As the joke goes, that leaves open the possibility that data structures might still be linearizable while performing well. Nevertheless, there are many challenges to make this vision work, and the remainder of this book is a road map showing how to attain this goal.

Block vs. unlock 'Progress conditions' Slide 189.

3.10 Chapter Notes

The notion of *quiescent consistency* was introduced implicitly by James Aspnes, Maurice Herlihy, and Nir Shavit [16] and more explicitly by Nir Shavit and Asaph Zemach [143]. Leslie Lamport [90] introduced the notion of *sequential consistency*, while Christos Papadimitriou [123] formulated the canonical formal characterization of *serializability*. William Weihl [149] was the first to point out the importance of *compositionality* (which he called *locality*). Maurice Herlihy and Jeannette Wing [69] introduced the notion of *linearizability* in 1990. Leslie Lamport [93, 94] introduced the notion of an *atomic register* in 1986.

To the best of our knowledge, the notion of *wait-freedom* first appeared implicitly in Leslie Lamport's Bakery algorithm [88]. *Lock-freedom* has had several historical meanings and only in recent years has it converged to its current definition. *Obstruction-freedom* was introduced by Maurice Herlihy, Victor Luchangco, and Mark Moir [61]. The notion of *dependent progress* was introduced by Maurice Herlihy and Nir Shavit [63].

Programming languages such as C or C++ were not defined with concurrency in mind, so they do not define a memory model. The actual behavior of a concurrent C or C++ program is the result of a complex combination of the underlying hardware, the compiler, and concurrency library. See Hans Boehm [21] for a more detailed discussion of these issues. The Java memory model proposed here is the *second* memory model proposed for Java. Jeremy Manson, Bill Pugh, and Sarita Adve [111] give a more complete description of the current Java memory.

The 2-thread queue is considered folklore, yet as far as we are aware, it first appeared in print in a paper by Leslie Lamport [91].

3.11 Exercises

Exercise 21. Explain why quiescent consistency is compositional.

Exercise 22. Consider a *memory object* that encompasses two register components. We know that if both registers are quiescently consistent, then so is the memory. Does the converse hold? If the memory is quiescently consistent, are the individual registers quiescently consistent? Outline a proof, or give a counterexample.

Exercise 23. Give an example of an execution that is quiescently consistent but not sequentially consistent, and another that is sequentially consistent but not quiescently consistent.

Exercise 24. For each of the histories shown in Figs. 3.13 and 3.14, are they quiescently consistent? Sequentially consistent? Linearizable? Justify your answer.

Exercise 25. If we drop condition L2 from the linearizability definition, is the resulting property the same as sequential consistency? Explain.

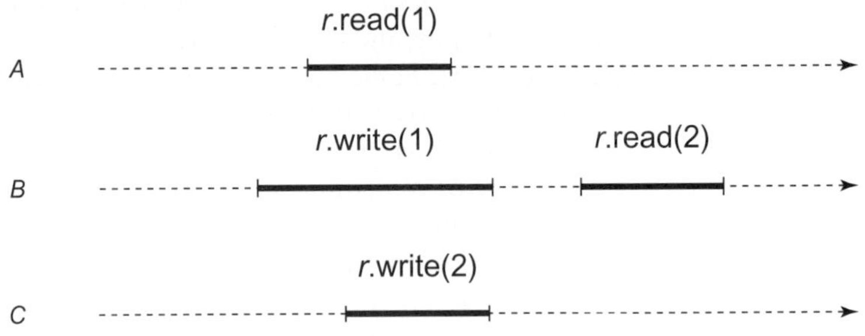

Figure 3.13 First history for Exercise 24.

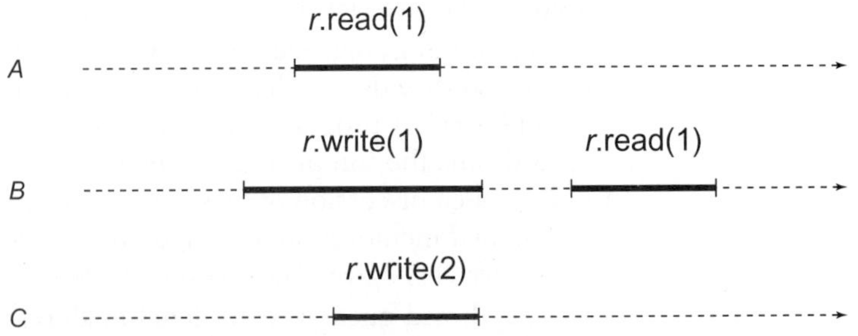

Figure 3.14 Second history for Exercise 24.

Exercise 26. Prove the "only if" part of Theorem 3.6.1

Exercise 27. The `AtomicInteger` class (in the java.util.concurrent.atomic package) is a container for an integer value. One of its methods is

```
boolean compareAndSet(int expect, int update).
```

This method compares the object's current value to `expect`. If the values are equal, then it atomically replaces the object's value with `update` and returns *true*. Otherwise, it leaves the object's value unchanged, and returns *false*. This class also provides

```
int get()
```

which returns the object's actual value.

Consider the FIFO queue implementation shown in Fig. 3.15. It stores its items in an array `items`, which, for simplicity, we will assume has unbounded size. It has two `AtomicInteger` fields: `head` is the index of the next slot from which to remove an item, and `tail` is the index of the next slot in which to place an item. Give an example showing that this implementation is *not* linearizable.

Exercise 28. Consider the class shown in Fig. 3.16. According to what you have been told about the Java memory model, will the *reader* method ever divide by zero?

```
class IQueue<T> {
  AtomicInteger head = new AtomicInteger(0);
  AtomicInteger tail = new AtomicInteger(0);
  T[] items = (T[]) new Object[Integer.MAX_VALUE];
  public void enq(T x) {
    int slot;
    do {
      slot = tail.get();
    } while (! tail.compareAndSet(slot, slot+1));
    items[slot] = x;
  }
  public T deq() throws EmptyException {
    T value;
    int slot;
    do {
      slot = head.get();
      value = items[slot];
      if (value == null)
        throw new EmptyException();
    } while (! head.compareAndSet(slot, slot+1));
    return value;
  }
}
```

Figure 3.15 IQueue implementation.

```
class VolatileExample {
  int x = 0;
  volatile boolean v = false;
  public void writer() {
    x = 42;
    v = true;
  }
  public void reader() {
    if (v == true) {
      int y = 100/x;
    }
  }
}
```

Figure 3.16 Volatile field example from Exercise 28.

Exercise 29. Is the following property equivalent to saying that object x is wait-free?

> For every infinite history H of x, every thread that takes an infinite number of steps in H completes an infinite number of method calls.

Exercise 30. Is the following property equivalent to saying that object x is lock-free?

> For every infinite history H of x, an infinite number of method calls are completed.

Exercise 31. Consider the following rather unusual implementation of a method m. In every history, the ith time a thread calls m, the call returns after 2^i steps. Is this method wait-free, bounded wait-free, or neither?

Exercise 32. This exercise examines a queue implementation (Fig. 3.17) whose `enq()` method does not have a linearization point.

The queue stores its items in an `items` array, which for simplicity we will assume is unbounded. The `tail` field is an `AtomicInteger`, initially zero. The `enq()` method reserves a slot by incrementing `tail`, and then stores the item at that location. Note that these two steps are not atomic: there is an interval after `tail` has been incremented but before the item has been stored in the array.

The `deq()` method reads the value of `tail`, and then traverses the array in ascending order from slot zero to the tail. For each slot, it swaps *null* with the current contents, returning the first non-*null* item it finds. If all slots are *null*, the procedure is restarted.

Give an example execution showing that the linearization point for `enq()` cannot occur at Line 15.

Hint: give an execution where two `enq()` calls are not linearized in the order they execute Line 15.

```
1  public class HWQueue<T> {
2    AtomicReference<T>[] items;
3    AtomicInteger tail;
4    static final int CAPACITY = 1024;
5
6    public HWQueue() {
7      items =(AtomicReference<T>[])Array.newInstance(AtomicReference.class,
8          CAPACITY);
9      for (int i = 0; i < items.length; i++) {
10       items[i] = new AtomicReference<T>(null);
11     }
12     tail = new AtomicInteger(0);
13   }
14   public void enq(T x) {
15     int i = tail.getAndIncrement();
16     items[i].set(x);
17   }
18   public T deq() {
19     while (true) {
20       int range = tail.get();
21       for (int i = 0; i < range; i++) {
22         T value = items[i].getAndSet(null);
23         if (value != null) {
24           return value;
25         }
26       }
27     }
28   }
29 }
```

Figure 3.17 Herlihy/Wing queue.

Give another example execution showing that the linearization point for enq() cannot occur at Line 16.

Since these are the only two memory accesses in enq(), we must conclude that enq() has no single linearization point. Does this mean enq() is not linearizable?

Exercise 33. Prove that sequential consistency is nonblocking.

4 Foundations of Shared Memory

The foundations of sequential computing were established in the 1930s by Alan Turing and Alonzo Church, who independently formulated what has come to be known as the *Church-Turing Thesis*: anything that *can* be computed, can be computed by a Turing Machine (or, equivalently, by Church's Lambda Calculus). Any problem that cannot be solved by a Turing Machine (such as deciding whether a program halts on any input) is universally considered to be unsolvable by any kind of practical computing device. The Turing Thesis is a *thesis*, not a theorem, because the notion of "what is computable" can never be defined in a precise, mathematically rigorous way. Nevertheless, just about everyone believes it.

This chapter describes the foundations of *concurrent shared memory computing*. A shared-memory computation consists of multiple *threads*, each of which is a sequential program in its own right. These threads communicate by calling methods of objects that reside in a shared memory. Threads are *asynchronous*, meaning that they run at different speeds, and any thread can halt for an unpredictable duration at any time. This notion of asynchrony reflects the realities of modern multiprocessor architectures, where thread delays are unpredictable, ranging from microseconds (cache misses), to milliseconds (page faults), to seconds (scheduling interruptions).

The classical theory of sequential computability proceeds in stages. It starts with finite-state automata, moves on to push-down automata, and culminates in Turing Machines. We, too, consider a progression of models for concurrent computing. In this chapter we start with the simplest form of shared-memory computation: concurrent threads apply simple read–write operations to shared-memory locations, called *registers* for historical reasons. We start with very simple registers, and we show how to use them to construct a series of more complex registers.

The classical theory of sequential computability is (for the most part) not concerned with efficiency: to show that a problem is computable, it is enough to show that it can be solved by a Turing Machine. There is little incentive to make such a Turing Machine efficient, because a Turing Machine is not a practical means of computation. In the same way, we make little attempt to make our register constructions efficient. We are interested in understanding whether such constructions exist, and how they work. They are not intended to be a practical model for computation. Instead, we prefer easy-to-understand but inefficient constructions over complicated but efficient ones. In particular, some of our constructions use *timestamps* (counter values) to distinguish older values from newer values.

The problem with timestamps is that they grow without bound, and eventually overflow any fixed-size variable. Bounded solutions (such as the one in Section 2.7 of Chapter 2) are (arguably) more intellectually satisfying, and we encourage readers to investigate them further through the references provided in the chapter notes. Here, however, we focus on simpler, unbounded constructions, because they illustrate fundamental principles of concurrent programming with less danger of becoming distracted by technicalities.

4.1 The Space of Registers

At the hardware level, threads communicate by reading and writing shared memory. A good way to understand inter-thread communication is to abstract away from hardware primitives, and to think about communication as happening through *shared concurrent objects.* Chapter 3 provided a detailed description of shared objects. For now, it suffices to recall the two key properties of their design: safety, defined by consistency conditions, and liveness, defined by progress conditions.

A *read–write register* (or just a *register*), is an object that encapsulates a value that can be observed by a `read()` method and modified by a `write()` method (in real systems these method calls are often called *load* and *store*). Fig. 4.1 illustrates the `Register<T>` interface implemented by all registers. The type `T` of the value is typically either `Boolean`, `Integer`, or a reference to an object. A register that implements the `Register<Boolean>` interface is called a *Boolean* register (we sometimes use 1 and 0 as synonyms for *true* and *false*). A register that implements `Register<Integer>` for a range of M integer values is called an *M-valued register.* We do not explicitly discuss any other kind of register, except to note that any algorithm that implements integer registers can be adapted to implement registers that hold references to other objects, simply by treating those references as integers.

```
public interface Register<T> {
  T read();
  void write(T v);
}
```

Figure 4.1 The `Register<T>` interface.

```
public class SequentialRegister<T> implements Register<T> {
  private T value;
  public T read() {
    return value;
  }
  public void write(T v) {
    value = v;
  }
}
```

Figure 4.2 The `SequentialRegister` class.

If method calls do not overlap, a register implementation should behave as shown in Fig. 4.2. On a multiprocessor, however, we expect method calls to overlap all the time, so we need to specify what the concurrent method calls mean.

One approach is to rely on mutual exclusion: protect each register with a mutex lock acquired by each `read()` and `write()` call. Unfortunately, we cannot use mutual exclusion here. Chapter 2 describes how to accomplish mutual exclusion using registers, so it makes little sense to implement registers using mutual exclusion. Moreover, as we saw in Chapter 3, using mutual exclusion, even if it is deadlock- or starvation-free, would mean that the computation's progress would depend on the operating system scheduler to guarantee that threads never get stuck in critical sections. Since we wish to examine the basic building blocks of concurrent computation using shared objects, it makes little sense to assume the existence of a separate entity to provide one of their key properties: progress.

Here is a different approach. Recall that an object implementation is *wait-free* if each method call finishes in a finite number of steps, independently of how its execution is interleaved with steps of other concurrent method calls. The wait-free condition may seem simple and natural, but it has far-reaching consequences. In particular, it rules out any kind of mutual exclusion, and guarantees independent progress, that is, without relying on an operating system scheduler. We therefore require our register implementations to be wait-free.[1]

An *atomic register* is a linearizable implementation of the sequential register class shown in Fig. 4.2. Informally, an atomic register behaves exactly as we would expect: each read returns the "last" value written. A model in which threads communicate by reading and writing to atomic registers is intuitively appealing, and for a long time was the standard model of concurrent computation.

It is also important to specify how many readers and writers are expected. Not surprisingly, it is easier to implement a register that supports only a single reader and writer than one that supports multiple readers and writers. For brevity, we use SRSW to mean "single-reader, single-writer," MRSW to mean "multi-reader, single-writer," and MRMW to mean "multi-reader, multi-writer."

1 A wait-free implementation is also lock-free.

In this chapter, we address the following fundamental question:

> Can any data structure implemented from the most powerful registers we define also be implemented from the weakest?

We recall from Chapter 1 that any useful form of inter-thread communication must be persistent: the message sent must outlive the active participation of the sender. The weakest form of persistent synchronization is (arguably) the ability to set a single persistent bit in shared memory, and the weakest form of synchronization is (unarguably) none at all: if the act of setting a bit does not overlap the act of reading that bit, then the value read is the same as the value written. Otherwise, a read overlapping a write could return any value.

Different kinds of registers come with different guarantees that make them more or less powerful. For example, we have seen that registers may differ in the range of values they may encapsulate (for example, Boolean vs. M-valued), and in the number of readers and writers they support. Finally, they may differ in the degree of consistency they provide.

A single-writer, multi-reader register implementation is *safe* if—

- A `read()` call that does not overlap a `write()` call returns the value written by the most recent `write()` call.
- Otherwise, if a `read()` call overlaps a `write()` call, then the `read()` call may return any value within the register's allowed range of values (for example, 0 to $M-1$ for an M-valued register).

Be aware that the term "safe" is a historical accident. Because they provide such weak guarantees, "safe" registers are actually quite unsafe.

Consider the history shown in Fig. 4.3. If the register is *safe*, then the three read calls might behave as follows:

- R^1 returns 0, the most recently-written value.
- R^2 and R^3 are concurrent with $W(1)$, so they could return any value in the range of the register.

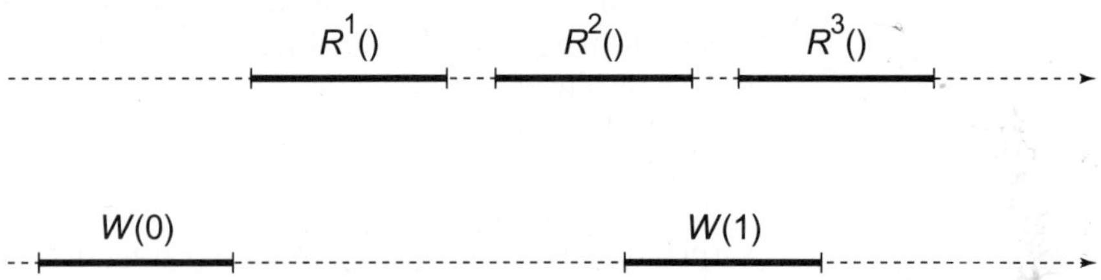

Figure 4.3 A single-reader, single-writer register execution: R^i is the ith read and $W(v)$ is a write of value v. Time flows from left to right. No matter whether the register is *safe*, *regular*, or *atomic*, R^1 must return 0, the most recently written value. If the register is *safe* then because R^2 and R^3 are concurrent with $W(1)$, they can return any value in the range of the register. If the register is *regular*, R^2 and R^3 can each return either 0 or 1. If the register is *atomic* then if R^2 returns 1 then R^3 also returns 1, and if R^2 returns 0 then R^3 could return 0 or 1.

It is convenient to define an intermediate level of consistency between safe and atomic. A *regular* register is a multi-reader, single-writer register where writes do not happen atomically. Instead, while the `write()` call is in progress, the value being read may "flicker" between the old and new value before finally replacing the older value. More precisely:

- A regular register is safe, so any `read()` call that does not overlap a `write()` call returns the most recently written value.
- Suppose a `read()` call overlaps one or more `write()` calls. Let v^0 be the value written by the latest preceding `write()` call, and let $v^1, \ldots, v^k$ be the sequence of values written by overlapping `write()` calls. The `read()` call may return any of the v^i, for any i in the range $0 \ldots k$.

For the execution in Fig. 4.3, a single-reader regular register might behave as follows:

- R^1 returns the old value, 0.
- R^2 and R^3 each return either the old value, 0, or the new value, 1.

Regular registers are quiescently consistent (Chapter 3), but not vice versa. We defined both safe and regular registers to permit only a single writer. Note that a regular register is a quiescently consistent single-writer sequential register.

For a single-reader single-writer atomic register, the execution in Fig. 4.3 might produce the following results:

- R^1 returns the old value, 0.
- If R^2 returns 1 then R^3 also returns 1.
- If R^2 returns 0 then R^3 could return 0 or 1.

Fig. 4.4 shows a schematic view of the range of possible registers as a three-dimensional space: the register size defines one dimension, the number of readers and writers defines another, and the register's consistency property defines the third. This view should not be taken literally: there are several combinations, such as multi-writer safe registers, that are not useful to define.

To reason about algorithms for implementing regular and atomic registers, it is convenient to rephrase our definitions directly in terms of object histories. From now on, we consider only histories in which each `read()` call returns a value written by some `write()` call (regular and atomic registers do not allow reads to make up return values). We assume values read or written are unique.[2]

2 If values are not inherently unique, we can use the standard technique of appending to them auxiliary values invisible to the algorithm itself, used only in our reasoning to distinguish one value from another.

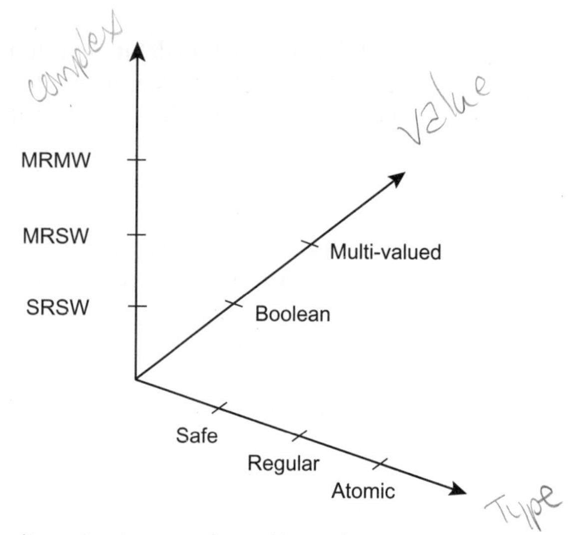

Figure 4.4 The three-dimensional space of possible read–write register-based implementations.

Recall that an object history is a sequence of *invocation* and *response* events, where an invocation event occurs when a thread calls a method, and a matching response event occurs when that call returns. A *method call* (or just a *call*) is the interval between matching invocation and response events. Any history induces a partial $\rightarrow$ order on method calls, defined as follows: if m_0 and m_1 are method calls, $m_0 \rightarrow m_1$ if m_0's response event precedes m_1's call event. (See Chapter 3 for complete definitions.)

Any register implementation (whether safe, regular, or atomic) defines a total order on the `write()` calls called the *write order*, the order in which writes "take effect" in the register. For safe and regular registers, the write order is trivial, because they allow only one writer at a time. For atomic registers, method calls have a linearization order. We use this order to index the write calls: write call W^0 is ordered first, W^1 second, and so on. Note that for SRSW or MRSW safe or regular registers, the write order is exactly the same as the precedence order.

We use R^i to denote any read call that returns v^i, the unique value written by W^i. Remember that a history contains only one W^i call, but it might contain multiple R^i calls.

One can show that the following conditions provide a precise statement of what it means for a register to be regular. First, no read call returns a value from the future:

$$\text{it is never the case that} \quad R^i \rightarrow W^i. \tag{4.1.1}$$

Second, no read call returns a value from the distant past, that is, one that precedes the most recently written non-overlapping value:

$$\text{it is never the case that for some } j \quad W^i \rightarrow W^j \rightarrow R^i. \tag{4.1.2}$$

To prove that a register implementation is regular, we must show that its histories satisfy Conditions 4.1.1 and 4.1.2.

An atomic register satisfies one additional condition:

$$\text{if} \quad R^i \rightarrow R^j \quad \text{then} \quad i \leqslant j. \tag{4.1.3}$$

This condition states that an earlier read cannot return a value later than that returned by a later read. Regular registers are *not* required to satisfy Condition 4.1.3. To show that a register implementation is atomic, we need first to define a write order, and then to show that its histories satisfy Conditions 4.1.1–4.1.3.

4.2 Register Constructions

We now show how to implement a range of surprisingly powerful registers from simple single-reader single-writer Boolean safe registers. These constructions imply that all read–write register types are equivalent, at least in terms of computability. We consider a series of constructions that implement stronger from weaker registers.

The sequence of constructions appears in Fig. 4.5:

Base Class	Implemented Class	Section
SRSW safe	MRSW safe	4.2.1
MRSW Boolean safe	MRSW Boolean regular	4.2.2
MRSW Boolean regular	MRSW regular	4.2.3
MRSW regular	SRSW atomic	4.2.4
SRSW atomic	MRSW atomic	4.2.5
MRSW atomic	MRMW atomic	4.2.6
MRSW atomic	atomic snapshot	4.3

Figure 4.5 The sequence of register constructions.

In the last step, we show how atomic registers (and therefore safe registers) can implement an atomic snapshot: an array of MRSW registers written by different threads, that can be read atomically by any thread. Some of these constructions are more powerful than necessary to complete the sequence of derivations (for example, we do not need to provide the multi-reader property for regular and safe registers to complete the derivation of a SRSW atomic register). We present them anyway because they provide valuable insights.

Our code samples follow these conventions. When we display an algorithm to implement a particular kind of register, say, a safe MRSW Boolean register, we present the algorithm using a form somewhat like this:

```
class SafeMRSWBooleanRegister implements Register<Boolean>
{
...
}
```

While this notation makes clear the properties of the register class being implemented, it becomes cumbersome when we want to use this class to implement other classes. Instead, when describing a class implementation, we use the following conventions to indicate whether a particular field is safe, regular, or atomic. A field otherwise named `mumble` is called `s_mumble` if it is safe, `r_mumble` if it is regular, and `a_mumble` if it is atomic. Other important aspects of the field, such as its type, or whether it supports multiple readers or writers, are noted as comments within the code, and should also be clear from context.

4.2.1 MRSW Safe Registers

Fig. 4.6 shows how to construct a safe MRSW register from safe SRSW registers.

Lemma 4.2.1. The construction in Fig. 4.6 is a *safe MRSW register.*

Proof: If A's `read()` call does not overlap any `write()` call, then the `read()` call returns the value of `s_table`[A], which is the most recently written value. For overlapping method calls, the reader may return any value, because the component registers are safe. □

4.2.2 A Regular Boolean MRSW Register

The next construction in Fig. 4.7 builds a regular Boolean MRSW register from a safe Boolean MRSW register. For Boolean registers, the only difference between safe and regular arises when the newly written value x is the same as the old. A regular register can only return x, while a safe register may return either Boolean value. We circumvent this problem simply by ensuring that a value is written only if it is distinct from the previously written value.

Lemma 4.2.2. The construction in Fig. 4.7 is a regular Boolean MRSW register.

```
public class SafeBooleanMRSWRegister implements Register<Boolean> {
  boolean[] s_table; // array of safe SRSW registers
  public SafeBooleanMRSWRegister(int capacity) {
    s_table = new boolean[capacity];
  }
  public Boolean read() {
    return s_table[ThreadID.get()];
  }
  public void write(Boolean x) {
    for (int i = 0; i < s_table.length; i++)
      s_table[i] = x;
  }
}
```

Figure 4.6 The `SafeBoolMRSWRegister` class: a safe Boolean MRSW register.

```
public class RegBooleanMRSWRegister implements Register<Boolean> {
  ThreadLocal<Boolean> last;
  boolean s_value; // safe MRSW register
  RegBooleanMRSWRegister(int capacity) {
    last = new ThreadLocal<Boolean>() {
      protected Boolean initialValue() { return false; };
    };
  }
  public void write(Boolean x) {
    if (x != last.get()) {
      last.set(x);
      s_value =x;
    }
  }
  public Boolean read() {
    return s_value;
  }
}
```

Figure 4.7 The `RegBoolMRSWRegister` class: a regular Boolean MRSW register constructed from a safe Boolean MRSW register.

Proof: A `read()` call that does not overlap any `write()` call returns the most recently written value. If the calls do overlap, there are two cases to consider.

- If the value being written is the same as the last value written, then the writer avoids writing to the safe register, ensuring that the reader reads the correct value.
- If the value written now is distinct from the last value written, then those values must be *true* and *false* because the register is Boolean. A concurrent read returns some value in the range of the register, namely either *true* or *false*, either of which is correct. □

4.2.3 A Regular *M*-Valued MRSW Register

The jump from Boolean to M-valued registers is simple, if astonishingly inefficient: we represent the value in unary notation. In Fig. 4.7 we implement an M-valued register as an array of M Boolean registers. Initially the register is set to value zero, indicated by the "0"-th bit being set to *true.* A write method of value x writes *true* in location x and then in descending array-index order sets all lower locations to *false.* A reading method reads the locations in ascending index order until the first time it reads the value *true* in some index i. It then returns i. The example in Fig. 4.9 illustrates an *8-valued* register.

Lemma 4.2.3. The `read()` call in the construction in Fig. 4.8 always returns a value corresponding to a bit in $0..M-1$ set by some `write()` call.

Proof: The following property is invariant: if a reading thread is reading `r_bit`[j], then some bit at index j or higher, written by a `write()` call, is set to *true.*

```java
public class RegMRSWRegister implements Register<Byte> {
  private static int RANGE = Byte.MAX_VALUE - Byte.MIN_VALUE + 1;
  boolean[] r_bit = new boolean[RANGE]; // regular boolean MRSW
  public RegMRSWRegister(int capacity) {
    for (int i = 1; i < r_bit.length; i++)
      r_bit[i] = false;
    r_bit[0] = true;
  }
  public void write(Byte x) {
    r_bit[x] = true;
    for (int i = x - 1; i >= 0; i--)
      r_bit[i] = false;
  }
  public Byte read() {
    for (int i = 0; i < RANGE; i++)
      if (r_bit[i]) {
        return i;
      }
    return -1; // impossible
  }
}
```

Figure 4.8 The `RegMRSWRegister` class: a regular *M*-valued MRSW register.

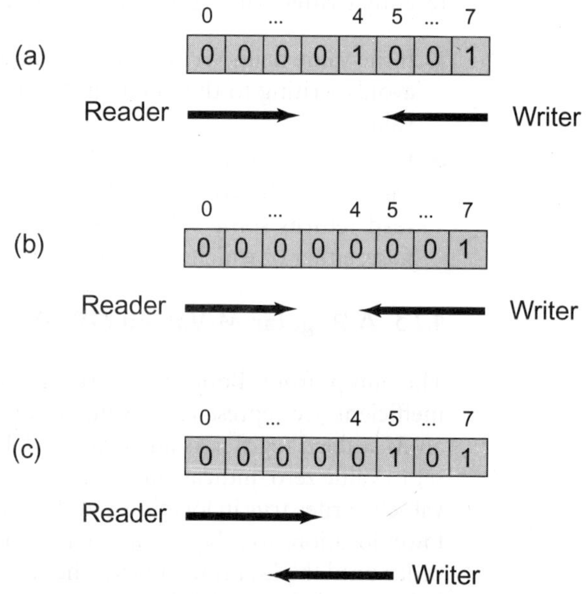

Figure 4.9 The `RegMRSWRegister` class: an execution of a regular *8-valued* MRSW register. The values *true* and *false* are represented by 0 and 1. In Part (a), the value prior to the write was 4, thread *W*'s write of 7 is not read by thread *R* because *R* reaches array entry 4 before *W* overwrites *false* at that location. In Part (b), entry 4 is overwritten by *W* before it is read, so the read returns 7. In Part (c), *W* starts to write 5. Since it wrote array entry 5 before it was read, the reader returns 5 even though entry 7 is also set to *true*.

When the register is initialized, there are no readers, and the constructor (we treat the constructor call as a `write(0)` call) sets `r_bit[0]` to *true*. Assume a reader is reading `r_bit`[j], and that `r_bit`[k] is *true*, for $k \geqslant j$.

- If the reader advances from j to $j + 1$, then `r_bit`[j] is *false*, so $k > j$ (i.e., a bit greater than or equal to $j + 1$ is *true*).
- The writer clears `r_bit`[k] only if it set a higher `r_bit`[ℓ] to *true*, for $\ell > k$. □

Lemma 4.2.4. The construction in Fig. 4.8 is a regular M-valued MRSW register.

Proof: For any read, let x be the value written by the most recent non-overlapping `write()`. At the time the `write()` completed, `a_bit`[x] was set to *true*, and `a_bit`[i] is *false* for $i < x$. By Lemma 4.2.3, if the reader returns a value that is not x, then it observed some `a_bit`[j], $j \neq x$ to be *true*, and that bit must have been set by a concurrent write, proving Conditions 4.1.1 and 4.1.2. □

4.2.4 An Atomic SRSW Register

We first show how to construct an atomic SRSW register from a regular SRSW register. (Note that our construction uses unbounded timestamps.)

A regular register satisfies Conditions 4.1.1 and 4.1.2, while an atomic register must also satisfy Condition 4.1.3. Since an SRSW regular register has no concurrent reads, the only way Condition 4.1.3 can be violated is if two reads that overlap the same write read values out-of-order, the first returning v^i and the latter returning v^j, where $j < i$.

Fig. 4.10 describes a class of values that each have an added tag that contains a timestamp. As illustrated in Fig. 4.11, our implementation of an `AtomicSRSWRegister` will use these tags to order write calls so that they can be ordered properly by concurrent read calls. Each read remembers the latest (highest timestamp) timestamp/value pair ever read, so that it is available to future reads. If a later read then reads an earlier value (one having a lower timestamp), it ignores that value and simply uses the remembered latest value. Similarly, the writer remembers the latest timestamp it wrote, and tags each newly written value with a later timestamp (a timestamp greater by 1).

This algorithm requires the ability to read–write a value and a timestamp as a single unit. In a language such as C, we would treat both the value and the timestamp as uninterpreted bits ("raw seething bits"), and use bit-shifting and logical masking to pack and unpack both values in and out of one or more words. In Java, it is easer to create a `StampedValue<T>` structure that holds a timestamp/value pair, and to store a *reference* to that structure in the register.

```
public class StampedValue<T> {
  public long stamp;
  public T   value;
  // initial value with zero timestamp
  public StampedValue(T init) {
    stamp = 0;
    value = init;
  }
  // later values with timestamp provided
  public StampedValue(long stamp, T value) {
    stamp = stamp;
    value = value;
  }
  public static StampedValue max(StampedValue x, StampedValue y) {
    if (x.stamp > y.stamp) {
      return x;
    } else {
      return y;
    }
  }
  public static StampedValue MIN_VALUE =
    new StampedValue(null);
}
```

Figure 4.10 The StampedValue<T> class: allows a timestamp and a value to be read or written together.

Lemma 4.2.5. The construction in Fig. 4.11 is an atomic SRSW register.

Proof: The register is regular, so Conditions 4.1.1 and 4.1.2 are met. The algorithm satisfies Condition 4.1.3 because writes are totally ordered by their timestamps, and if a read returns a given value, a later read cannot read an earlier written value, since it would have a lower timestamp. □

4.2.5 An Atomic MRSW Register

To understand how to construct an atomic MRSW register from atomic SRSW registers, we first consider a simple algorithm based on direct use of the construction in Section 4.2.1, which took us from SRSW to MRSW safe registers. Let the SRSW registers composing the table array a_table$[0..n-1]$ be atomic instead of safe, with all other calls remaining the same: the writer writes the array locations in increasing index order and then each reader reads and returns its associated array entry. The result is not a multi-reader atomic register. Condition 4.1.3 holds for any single reader because each reader reads from an atomic register, yet it does not hold for distinct readers. Consider, for example, a write that starts by setting the first SRSW register a_table[0], and is delayed before writing the remaining locations a_table$[1..n-1]$. A subsequent read by thread 0 returns the correct new value, but a subsequent read by thread 1 that completely follows the read by thread 0, reads and returns the earlier value because the writer has yet

```
public class AtomicSRSWRegister<T> implements Register<T> {
  ThreadLocal<Long> lastStamp;
  ThreadLocal<StampedValue<T>> lastRead;
  StampedValue<T> r_value;            // regular SRSW timestamp-value pair
  public AtomicSRSWRegister(T init) {
    r_value = new StampedValue<T>(init);
    lastStamp = new ThreadLocal<Long>() {
       protected Long initialValue() { return 0; };
    };
    lastRead = new ThreadLocal<StampedValue<T>>() {
      protected StampedValue<T> initialValue() { return r_value; };
    };
  }
  public T read() {
    StampedValue<T> value = r_value;
    StampedValue<T> last = lastRead.get();
    StampedValue<T> result = StampedValue.max(value, last);
    lastRead.set(result);
    return result.value;
  }
  public void write(T v) {
    long stamp = lastStamp.get() + 1;
    r_value = new StampedValue(stamp, v);
    lastStamp.set(stamp);
  }
}
```

Figure 4.11 The `AtomicSRSWRegister` class: an atomic SRSW register constructed from a regular SRSW register.

to update `a_table`[1..$n-1$]. We address this problem by having earlier reader threads *help out* later threads by telling them which value they read.

This implementation appears in Fig. 4.12. The n threads share an n-by-n array `a_table`[0..$n-1$][0..$n-1$] of stamped values. As in Section 4.2.4, we use timestamped values to allow early reads to tell later reads which of the values read is the latest. The locations along the diagonal, `a_table`[i][i] for all i, correspond to the registers in our failed simple construction mentioned earlier. The writer simply writes the diagonal locations one after the other with a new value and a timestamp that increases from one `write()` call to the next. Each reader A first reads `a_table`[A][A] as in the earlier algorithm. It then uses the remaining SRSW locations `a_table`[A][B], $A \neq B$ for communication between readers A and B. Each reader A, after reading `a_table`[A][A], checks to see if some other reader has read a later value by traversing its corresponding column (`a_table`[B][A] for all B), and checking if it contains a later value (one with a higher timestamp). The reader then lets all later readers know the latest value it read by writing this value to all locations in its corresponding row (`a_table`[A][B] for all B). It thus follows that after a read by A is completed, every later read by a B sees the last value A read (since it reads `a_table`[A][B]). Fig. 4.13 shows an example execution of the algorithm.

```
public class AtomicMRSWRegister<T> implements Register<T> {
  ThreadLocal<Long> lastStamp;
  private StampedValue<T>[][] a_table; // each entry is SRSW atomic
  public AtomicMRSWRegister(T init, int readers) {
    lastStamp = new ThreadLocal<Long>() {
      protected Long initialValue() { return 0; };
    };
    a_table = (StampedValue<T>[][]) new StampedValue[readers][readers];
    StampedValue<T> value = new StampedValue<T>(init);
    for (int i = 0; i < readers; i++) {
      for (int j = 0; j < readers; j++) {
        a_table[i][j] = value;
      }
    }
  }
  public T read() {
    int me = ThreadID.get();
    StampedValue<T> value = a_table[me][me];
    for (int i = 0; i < a_table.length; i++) {
      value = StampedValue.max(value, a_table[i][me]);
    }
    for (int i = 0; i < a_table.length; i++) {
      if (i == me) continue;
      a_table[me][i] = value;
    }
    return value;
  }
  public void write(T v) {
    long stamp = lastStamp.get() + 1;
    lastStamp.set(stamp);
    StampedValue<T> value = new StampedValue<T>(stamp, v);
    for (int i = 0; i < a_table.length; i++) {
      a_table[i][i] = value;
    }
  }
}
```

Figure 4.12 The `AtomicMRSWRegister` class: an atomic MRSW register constructed from atomic SRSW registers.

Lemma 4.2.6. The construction in Fig. 4.12 is a MRSW atomic register.

Proof: First, no reader returns a value from the future, so Condition 4.1.1 is clearly satisfied. By construction, `write()` calls write strictly increasing timestamps. The key to understanding this algorithm is the simple observation that the maximum timestamp along any row or column is also strictly increasing. If *A* writes *v* with timestamp *t*, then any `read()` call by *B*, where *A*'s call completely precedes *B*'s, reads (from the diagonal of `a_table`) a maximum timestamp greater than or equal to *t*, satisfying Condition 4.1.2. Finally, as noted earlier, if a read call by *A* completely precedes a read call by *B*, then *A* writes a stamped value with timestamp *t* to *B*'s row, so *B* chooses a value with a timestamp greater than or equal to *t*, satisfying Condition 4.1.3. □

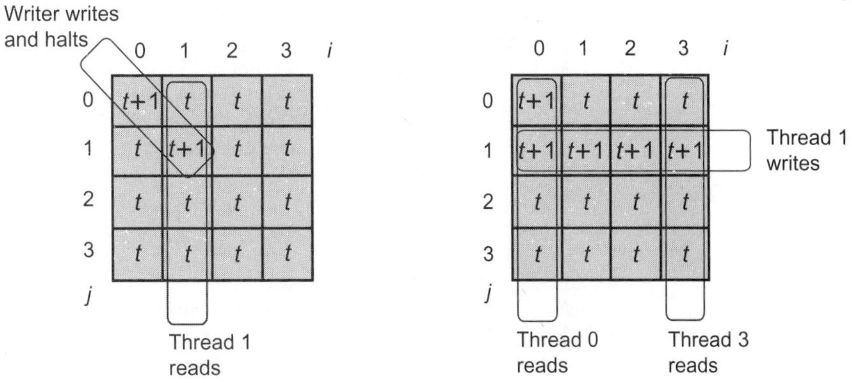

Figure 4.13 An execution of the MRSW atomic register. Each reader thread has an index between 0 and 4, and we refer to each thread by its index. Here, the writer writes a new value with timestamp $t+1$ to locations `a_table[0][0]` and `a_table[1][1]` and then halts. Then, thread 1 reads its corresponding column `a_table[i][1]` for all i, and writes its corresponding row `a_table[1][i]` for all i, returning the new value with timestamp $t+1$. Threads 0 and 3 both read completely after thread 1's read. Thread 0 reads `a_table[0][0]` with value $t+1$. Thread 3 cannot read the new value with timestamp $t+1$ because the writer has yet to write `a_table[3][3]`. Nevertheless, it reads `a_table[1][3]` and returns the correct value with timestamp $t+1$ that was read by the earlier thread 1.

4.2.6 An Atomic MRMW Register

Here is how to construct an atomic MRMW register from an array of atomic MRSW registers, one per thread.

To write to the register, A reads all the array elements, chooses a timestamp higher than any it has observed, and writes a stamped value to array element A. To read the register, a thread reads all the array elements, and returns the one with the highest timestamp. This is exactly the timestamp algorithm used by the Bakery algorithm of Section 2.6. As in the Bakery algorithm, we resolve ties in favor of the thread with the lesser index; in other words, we use a lexicographic order on pairs of timestamp and thread ids.

Lemma 4.2.7. The construction in Fig. 4.14 is an atomic MRMW register.

Proof: Define the write order among `write()` calls based on the lexicographic order of their timestamps and thread ids so that the `write()` call by A with timestamp t_A precedes the `write()` call by B with timestamp t_B if $t_A < t_B$, or if $t_A = t_B$ and $A < B$. We leave as an exercise to the reader to show that this lexicographic order is consistent with $\rightarrow$. As usual, index `write()` calls in write order: $W^0, W^1, \ldots$.

Clearly a `read()` call cannot read a value written in `a_table[]` after it is completed, and any `write()` call completely preceded by the read has a

```
public class AtomicMRMWRegister<T> implements Register<T>{
  private StampedValue<T>[] a_table; // array of atomic MRSW registers
  public AtomicMRMWRegister(int capacity, T init) {
    a_table = (StampedValue<T>[]) new StampedValue[capacity];
    StampedValue<T> value = new StampedValue<T>(init);
    for (int j = 0; j < a_table.length; j++) {
      a_table[j] = value;
    }
  }
  public void write(T value) {
    int me = ThreadID.get();
    StampedValue<T> max = StampedValue.MIN_VALUE;
    for (int i = 0; i < a_table.length; i++) {
      max = StampedValue.max(max, a_table[i]);
    }
    a_table[me] = new StampedValue(max.stamp + 1, value);
  }
  public T read() {
    StampedValue<T> max = StampedValue.MIN_VALUE;
    for (int i = 0; i < a_table.length; i++) {
      max = StampedValue.max(max, a_table[i]);
    }
    return max.value;
  }
}
```

Figure 4.14 Atomic MRMW register.

timestamp higher than all those written before the read is completed, implying Condition 4.1.1.

Consider Condition 4.1.2, which prohibits skipping over the most recent preceding `write()`. Suppose a `write()` call by A preceded a write call by B, which in turn preceded a `read()` by C. If $A = B$, then the later write overwrites `a_table[`A`]` and the `read()` does not return the value of the earlier write. If $A \neq B$, then since A's timestamp is smaller than B's timestamp, any C that sees both returns B's value (or one with higher timestamp), meeting Condition 4.1.2.

Finally, we consider Condition 4.1.3, which prohibits values from being read out of write order. Consider any `read()` call by A completely preceding a `read()` call by B, and any `write()` call by C which is ordered before the `write()` by D in the write order. We must show that if A returned D's value, then B could not return C's value. If $t_C < t_D$, then if A read timestamp t_D from `a_table[`D`]`, B reads t_D or a higher timestamp from `a_table[`D`]`, and does not return the value associated with t_C. If $t_C = t_D$, that is, the writes were concurrent, then from the write order, $C < D$, so if A read timestamp t_D from `a_table[`D`]`, B also reads t_D from `a_table[`D`]`, and returns the value associated with t_D (or higher), even if it reads t_C in `a_table[`C`]`. □

Our series of constructions shows that one can construct a wait-free MRMW multi-valued atomic register from SRSW safe Boolean registers. Naturally, no one wants to write a concurrent algorithm using safe registers, but these constructions show that any algorithm using atomic registers can be implemented on an architecture that supports only safe registers. Later on, when we consider more realistic architectures, we return to the theme of implementing algorithms that assume strong synchronization properties on architectures that directly provide only weak properties.

4.3 Atomic Snapshots

We have seen how a register value can be read and written atomically. What if we want to read multiple register values atomically? We call such an operation an *atomic snapshot*.

An atomic snapshot constructs an instantaneous view of an array of atomic registers. We construct a wait-free snapshot, meaning that a thread can take an instantaneous snapshot of memory without delaying any other thread. Atomic snapshots might be useful for backups or checkpoints.

The `Snapshot` interface (Fig. 4.15) is just an array of atomic MRSW registers, one for each thread. The `update()` method writes a value v to the calling thread's register in that array, while the `scan()` method returns an atomic snapshot of that array.

Our goal is to construct a wait-free implementation that is equivalent (that is, linearizable) to the sequential specification shown in Fig. 4.16. The key property of this sequential implementation is that `scan()` returns a collection of values, each corresponding to the latest preceding `update()`, that is, it returns a collection of register values that existed together in the same system state.

4.3.1 An Obstruction-Free Snapshot

We begin with a `SimpleSnapshot` class for which `update()` is wait-free, but `scan()` is obstruction-free. We then extend this algorithm to make `scan()` wait-free.

Just as for the atomic MRSW register construction, each value includes a `StampedValue<T>` object with `stamp` and `value` fields. Each `update()` call increments the timestamp.

A *collect* is the non atomic act of copying the register values one-by-one into an array. If we perform two collects one after the other, and both collects read the

```
public interface Snapshot<T> {
  public void update(T v);
  public T[] scan();
}
```

Figure 4.15 The `Snapshot` interface.

```
public class SeqSnapshot<T> implements Snapshot<T> {
  T[] a_value;
  public SeqSnapshot(int capacity, T init) {
    a_value = (T[]) new Object[capacity];
    for (int i = 0; i < a_value.length; i++) {
      a_value[i] = init;
    }
  }
  public synchronized void update(T v) {
    a_value[ThreadID.get()] = v;
  }
  public synchronized T[] scan() {
    T[] result = (T[]) new Object[a_value.length];
    for (int i = 0; i < a_value.length; i++)
      result[i] = a_value[i];
    return result;
  }
}
```

Figure 4.16 A sequential snapshot.

same set of timestamps, then we know that there was an interval during which no thread updated its register, so the result of the collect is a snapshot of the system state immediately after the end of the first collect. We call such a pair of collects a *clean double collect.*

In the construction shown in the `SimpleSnapshot<T>` class (Fig. 4.17), each thread repeatedly calls `collect()` (Line 27), and returns as soon as it detects a clean double collect (one in which both sets of timestamps were identical). This construction always returns correct values. The `update()` calls are wait-free, but `scan()` is not because any call can be repeatedly interrupted by `update()`, and may run forever without completing. It is however obstruction-free, since a `scan()` completes if it runs by itself for long enough.

4.3.2 A Wait-Free Snapshot

To make the `scan()` method wait-free, each `update()` call *helps* a `scan()` it may interfere with, by taking a snapshot before modifying its register. A `scan()` that repeatedly fails in taking a double collect can use the snapshot from one of the interfering `update()` calls as its own. The tricky part is that we must make sure the snapshot taken from the helping update is one that can be linearized within the `scan()` call's execution interval.

We say that a thread *moves* if it completes an `update()`. If thread *A* fails to make a clean collect because thread *B* moved, then can *A* simply take *B*'s most recent snapshot as its own? Unfortunately, no. As illustrated in Fig. 4.18, it is possible for *A* to see *B* move when *B*'s snapshot was taken before *A* started its `scan()` call, so the snapshot did not occur within the interval of *A*'s scan.

```
public class SimpleSnapshot<T> implements Snapshot<T> {
  private StampedValue<T>[] a_table; // array of atomic MRSW registers
  public SimpleSnapshot(int capacity, T init) {
    a_table = (StampedValue<T>[]) new StampedValue[capacity];
    for (int i = 0; i < capacity; i++) {
      a_table[i] = new StampedValue<T>(init);
    }
  }
  public void update(T value) {
    int me = ThreadID.get();
    StampedValue<T> oldValue = a_table[me];
    StampedValue<T> newValue =
        new StampedValue<T>((oldValue.stamp)+1, value);
    a_table[me] = newValue;
  }
  private StampedValue<T>[] collect() {
    StampedValue<T>[] copy = (StampedValue<T>[])
        new StampedValue[a_table.length];
    for (int j = 0; j < a_table.length; j++)
      copy[j] = a_table[j];
    return copy;
  }
  public T[] scan() {
    StampedValue<T>[] oldCopy, newCopy;
    oldCopy = collect();
    collect: while (true) {
      newCopy = collect();
      if (! Arrays.equals(oldCopy, newCopy)) {
        oldCopy = newCopy;
        continue collect;
      }
      T[] result = (T[]) new Object[a_table.length];
      for (int j = 0; j < a_table.length; j++)
        result[j] = newCopy[j].value;
      return result;
    }
  }
}
```

Figure 4.17 Simple snapshot object.

The wait-free construction is based on the following observation: if a scanning thread *A* sees a thread *B* move *twice* while it is performing repeated collects, then *B* executed a complete `update()` call within the interval of *A*'s `scan()`, so it is correct for *A* to use *B*'s snapshot.

Figs. 4.19, 4.20, and 4.21 show the wait-free snapshot algorithm. Each `update()` call calls `scan()`, and appends the result of the scan to the value's label. More precisely, each value written to a register has the structure shown in Fig. 4.19: a `stamp` field incremented each time the thread updates its value, a `value` field containing the register's actual value, and a `snap` field containing that thread's most recent scan. The snapshot algorithm is described in Fig. 4.21.

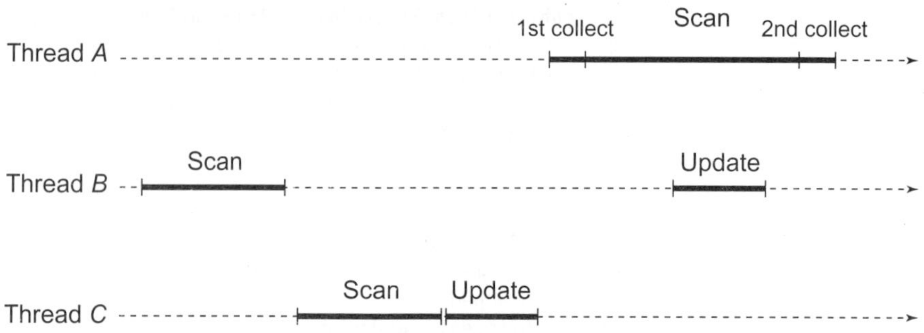

Figure 4.18 Here is why a thread *A* that fails to complete a clean double collect cannot simply take the latest snapshot of a thread *B* that performed an update() during *A*'s second collect. *B*'s snapshot was taken before *A* started its scan(), i.e., *B*'s snapshot did not overlap *A*'s scan. The danger, illustrated here, is that a thread *C* could have called update() after *B*'s scan() and before *A*'s scan(), making it incorrect for *A* to use the results of *B*'s scan().

```
public class StampedSnap<T> {
  public long stamp;
  public T   value;
  public T[] snap;
  public StampedSnap(T value) {
    stamp = 0;
    value = value;
    snap  = null;
  }
  public StampedSnap(long label, T value, T[] snap) {
    stamp = label;
    value = value;
    snap  = snap;
  }
}
```

Figure 4.19 The stamped snapshot class.

A scanning thread creates a Boolean array called moved[] (Line 13), which records which threads have been observed to move in the course of the scan. As before, each thread performs two collects (14 and 16) and tests whether any thread's label has changed. If no thread's label has changed, then the collect is clean, and the scan returns the result of the collect. If any thread's label has changed (Line 18) the scanning thread tests the moved[] array to detect whether this is the second time this thread has moved (Line 19). If so, it returns that thread's scan (Line 20), and otherwise it updates moved[] and resumes the outer loop (Line 21).

4.3.3 Correctness Arguments

In this section, we review the correctness arguments for the wait-free snapshot algorithm a little more carefully.

```java
public class WFSnapshot<T> implements Snapshot<T> {
  private StampedSnap<T>[] a_table; // array of atomic MRSW registers
  public WFSnapshot(int capacity, T init) {
    a_table = (StampedSnap<T>[]) new StampedSnap[capacity];
    for (int i = 0; i < a_table.length; i++) {
      a_table[i] = new StampedSnap<T>(init);
    }
  }

  private StampedSnap<T>[] collect() {
    StampedSnap<T>[] copy = (StampedSnap<T>[])
       new StampedSnap[a_table.length];
    for (int j = 0; j < a_table.length; j++)
      copy[j] = a_table[j];
    return copy;
  }
```

Figure 4.20 The single-writer atomic snapshot class and `collect()` method.

```java
  public void update(T value) {
    int me = ThreadID.get();
    T[] snap = scan();
    StampedSnap<T> oldValue = a_table[me];
    StampedSnap<T> newValue =
      new StampedSnap<T>(oldValue.stamp+1, value, snap);
    a_table[me] = newValue;
  }

  public T[] scan() {
    StampedSnap<T>[] oldCopy;
    StampedSnap<T>[] newCopy;
    boolean[] moved = new boolean[a_table.length];
    oldCopy = collect();
    collect: while (true) {
      newCopy = collect();
      for (int j = 0; j < a_table.length; j++) {
        if (oldCopy[j].stamp != newCopy[j].stamp) {
          if (moved[j]) {
            return newCopy[j].snap;
          } else {
            moved[j] = true;
            oldCopy = newCopy;
            continue collect;
          }
        }
      }
      T[] result = (T[]) new Object[a_table.length];
      for (int j = 0; j < a_table.length; j++)
        result[j] = newCopy[j].value;
      return result;
    }
  }
}
```

Figure 4.21 Single-writer atomic snapshot `update()` and `scan()` methods.

Lemma 4.3.1. If a scanning thread makes a clean double collect, then the values it returns were the values that existed in the registers in some state of the execution.

Proof: Consider the interval between the last read of the first collect, and the first read of the second collect. If any register were updated in that interval, the labels would not match, and the double collect would not be clean. □

Lemma 4.3.2. If a scanning thread A observes changes in another thread B's label during two different double collects, then the value of B's register read during the last collect was written by an `update()` call that began after the first of the four collects started.

Proof: If during a `scan()`, two successive reads by A of B's register return different label values, then at least one write by B occurs between this pair of reads. Thread B writes to its register as the final step of an `update()` call, so some `update()` call by B ended sometime after the first read by A, and the write step of another occurs between the last pair of reads by A. The claim follows because only B writes to its register. □

Lemma 4.3.3. The values returned by a `scan()` were in the registers at some state between the call's invocation and response.

Proof: If the `scan()` call made a clean double collect, then the claim follows from Lemma 4.3.1. If the call took the scan value from another thread B's register, then by Lemma 4.3.2, the scan value found in B's register was obtained by a `scan()` call by B whose interval lies between A's first and second reads of B's register. Either B's `scan()` call had a clean double collect, in which case the result follows from Lemma 4.3.1, or there is an embedded `scan()` call by a thread C occurring within the interval of B's `scan()` call. This argument can be applied inductively, noting that there can be at most $n-1$ nested calls before we run out of threads, where n is the maximum number of threads (see Fig. 4.22). Eventually, some nested `scan()` call must have a clean double collect. □

Lemma 4.3.4. Every `scan()` or `update()` returns after at most $O(n^2)$ reads or writes.

Proof: For a given `scan()`, since there are only $n-1$ other threads, after $n+1$ double collects, either one is clean, or some thread is observed to move twice. It follows that `scan()` calls are wait-free, and so are `update()` calls. □

By Lemma 4.3.3, the values returned by a `scan()` form a snapshot as they are all in the registers in some state during the call: linearize the call at that point. Similarly, linearize `update()` calls at the point the register is written.

***Theorem* 4.3.1.** Figs. 4.20 and 4.21 provide a wait-free snapshot implementation.

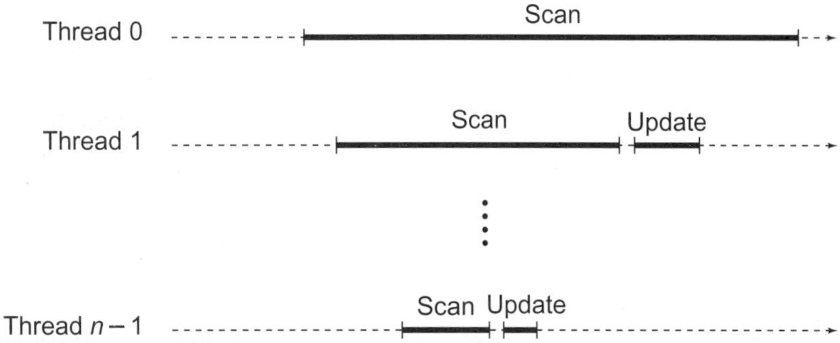

Figure 4.22 There can be at most $n-1$ nested calls of `scan()` before we run out of threads, where n is the maximum number of threads. The `scan()` by thread $n-1$, contained in the intervals of all other `scan()` calls, must have a clean double collect.

4.4 Chapter Notes

Alonzo Church introduced Lambda Calculus around 1934-5 [29]. Alan Turing defined the Turing Machine in a classic paper in 1936-7 [146]. Leslie Lamport first defined the notions of *safe*, *regular*, and *atomic* registers and the register hierarchy, and was the first to show that one could implement non trivial shared memory from safe bits [93, 94]. Gary Peterson first suggested the problem of constructing atomic registers [125]. Jaydev Misra gave an axiomatic treatment of atomic registers [116]. The notion of *linearizability*, which generalizes Leslie Lamport and Jaydev Misra's notions of atomic registers, is due to Herlihy and Wing [69]. Susmita Haldar and Krishnamurthy Vidyasankar gave a bounded MRSW atomic register construction from regular registers [50]. The problem of constructing a multi-reader atomic register from single-reader atomic registers was mentioned as an open problem by Leslie Lamport [93, 94], and by Paul Vitányi and Baruch Awerbuch [148]. Paul Vitányi and Baruch Awerbuch were the first to propose an approach for MRMW atomic register design [148]. The first solution is due to Jim Anderson, Mohamed Gouda, and Ambuj Singh [12, 13]. Other atomic register constructions, to name only a few, were proposed by Jim Burns and Gary Peterson [24], Richard Newman-Wolfe [150], Lefteris Kirousis, Paul Spirakis, and Philippas Tsigas [83], Amos Israeli and Amnon Shaham [78], and Ming Li and John Tromp and Paul Vitányi [104]. The simple timestamp-based atomic MRMW construction we present here is due to Danny Dolev and Nir Shavit [34].

Collect operations were first formalized by Mike Saks, Nir Shavit, and Heather Woll [135]. The first atomic snapshot constructions were discovered concurrently and independently by Jim Anderson [10], and by Yehuda Afek, Hagit Attiya, Danny Dolev, Eli Gafni, Michael Merritt and Nir Shavit [2]. The latter algorithm is the one presented here. Later snapshot algorithms are due to Elizabeth Borowsky and Eli Gafni [22] and Yehuda Afek, Gideon Stupp, and Dan Touitou [4].

The timestamps in all the algorithms mentioned in this chapter can be bounded so that the constructions themselves use registers of bounded size. Bounded timestamp systems were introduced by Amos Israeli and Ming Li [77], and bounded concurrent timestamp systems by Danny Dolev and Nir Shavit [34].

4.5 Exercises

Exercise 34. Consider the safe Boolean MRSW construction shown in Fig. 4.6. True or false: if we replace the safe Boolean SRSW register array with an array of safe M-valued SRSW registers, then the construction yields a safe M-valued MRSW register. Justify your answer.

Exercise 35. Consider the safe Boolean MRSW construction shown in Fig. 4.6. True or false: if we replace the safe Boolean SRSW register array with an array of regular Boolean SRSW registers, then the construction yields a regular Boolean MRSW register. Justify your answer.

Exercise 36. Consider the atomic MRSW construction shown in Fig. 4.12. True or false: if we replace the atomic SRSW registers with regular SRSW registers, then the construction still yields an atomic MRSW register. Justify your answer.

Exercise 37. Give an example of a quiescently-consistent register execution that is not regular.

Exercise 38. Consider the safe Boolean MRSW construction shown in Fig. 4.6. True or false: if we replace the safe Boolean SRSW register array with an array of *regular* M-valued SRSW registers, then the construction yields a regular M-valued MRSW register. Justify your answer.

Exercise 39. Consider the regular Boolean MRSW construction shown in Fig. 4.7. True or false: if we replace the safe Boolean MRSW register with a safe M-valued MRSW register, then the construction yields a regular M-valued MRSW register. Justify your answer.

Exercise 40. Does Peterson's two-thread mutual exclusion algorithm work if the shared atomic `flag` registers are replaced by regular registers?

Exercise 41. Consider the following implementation of a `Register` in a distributed, message-passing system. There are n processors $P_0, \ldots, P_{n-1}$ arranged in a ring, where P_i can send messages only to $P_{i+1 \bmod n}$. Messages are delivered in FIFO order along each link.

Each processor keeps a copy of the shared register.

- To read a register, the processor reads the copy in its local memory.
- A processor P_i starts a `write()` call of value v to register x, by sending the message "P_i: write v to x" to $P_{i+1 \bmod n}$.
- If P_i receives a message "P_j: write v to x," for $i \neq j$, then it writes v to its local copy of x, and forwards the message to $P_{i+1 \bmod n}$.
- If P_i receives a message "P_i: write v to x," then it writes v to its local copy of x, and discards the message. The `write()` call is now complete.

Give a short justification or counterexample.
If `write()` calls never overlap,

- Is this register implementation regular?
- Is it atomic?

If multiple processors call `write()`,

- Is this register implementation safe?

Exercise 42. You learn that your competitor, the Acme Atomic Register Company, has developed a way to use Boolean (single-bit) atomic registers to construct an efficient *write-once* single-reader single-writer atomic register. Through your spies, you acquire the code fragment shown in Fig. 4.23, which is unfortunately missing the code for `read()`. Your job is to devise a `read()` method that works for

```
class AcmeRegister implements Register{
  // N is the length of the register
  // Atomic multi-reader single-writer registers
  private BoolRegister[] b = new BoolMRSWRegister[3 * N];
  public void write(int x) {
    boolean[] v = intToBooleanArray(x);
    // copy v[i] to b[i] in ascending order of i
    for (int i = 0; i < N; i++)
      b[i].write(v[i]);
    // copy v[i] to b[N+i] in ascending order of i
    for (int i = 0; i < N; i++)
      b[N+i].write(v[i]);
    // copy v[i] to b[2N+i] in ascending order of i
    for (int i = 0; i < N; i++)
      b[(2*N)+i].write(v[i]);
  }
  public int read() {
    // missing code
  }
}
```

Figure 4.23 Partial acme register implementation.

this class, and to justify (informally) why it works. (Remember that the register is write-once, meaning that your read will overlap at most one write.)

Exercise 43. Prove that the safe Boolean MRSW register construction from safe Boolean SRSW registers illustrated in Fig. 4.6 is a correct implementation of a regular MRSW register if the component registers are regular SRSW registers.

Exercise 44. A monotonic counter is a data structure $c = c_1 \dots c_m$ (i.e., c is composed of the individual digits c_j, $j > 0$) such that $c^0 \leqslant c^1 \leqslant c^2 \leqslant \dots$, where $c^0, c^1, c^2, \dots$ denote the successive values assumed by c.

If c is not a single digit, then reading and writing c may involve several separate operations. A read of c which is performed concurrently with one or more writes to c may obtain a value different from any of the versions c^j, $j \geqslant 0$. The value obtained may contain traces of several different versions. If a read obtains traces of versions $c^{i_1}, \dots, c^{i_m}$, then we say that it obtained a value of $c^{k,l}$ where k = minimum $(i_1, \dots, i_m)$ and l = maximum $(i_1, \dots, i_m)$, so $0 \leqslant k \leqslant l$. If $k = l$, then $c^{k,l} = c^k$ and the read obtained is a consistent version of c.

Hence, the correctness condition for such a counter simply asserts that if a read obtains the value $c^{k,l}$, then $c^k \leqslant c^{k,l} \leqslant c^l$. The individual digits c_j are also assumed to be atomic digits.

Give an implementation of a monotonic counter, given that the following theorems are true:

***Theorem* 4.5.1.** If $c = c_1 \dots c_m$ is always written from right to left, then a read from left to right obtains a sequence of values $c_1^{k_1,\ell_1}, \dots, c_m^{k_m,\ell_m}$ with $k_1 \leqslant \ell_1 \leqslant k_2 \leqslant \dots \leqslant k_m \leqslant \ell_m$.

***Theorem* 4.5.2.** Let $c = c_1 \dots c_m$ and assume that $c^0 \leqslant c^1 \leqslant \dots$.

1. If $i_1 \leqslant \dots \leqslant i_m \leqslant i$ then $c_1^{i_1} \dots c_m^{i_m} \leqslant c^i$.
2. If $i_1 \geqslant \dots \geqslant i_m \geqslant i$ then $c_1^{i_1} \dots c_m^{i_m} \geqslant c^i$.

***Theorem* 4.5.3.** Let $c = c_1 \dots c_m$ and assume that $c^0 \leqslant c^1 \leqslant \dots$ and the digits c_i are atomic.

1. If c is always written from right to left, then a read from left to right obtains a value $c^{k,l} \leqslant c^l$.
2. If c is always written from left to right, then a read from right to left obtains a value $c^{k,l} \geqslant c^l$.

Note that:
If a read of c obtains traces of version $c^j, j \geqslant 0$, then:

- The beginning of the read preceded the end of the write of c^{j+1}.
- The end of the read followed the beginning of the write of c^j.

Furthermore, we say that a read (write) of c is performed from left to right if for each $j > 0$, the read (write) of c_j is completed before the read (write) of c_{j+1} has begun. Reading or writing from right to left is defined in the analogous way.

Finally, always remember that subscripts refer to individual digits of c while superscripts refer to successive values assumed by c.

Exercise 45. Prove Theorem 4.5.1 of Exercise 44. Note that since $k_j \leqslant \ell_j$, you need only to show that $\ell_j \leqslant k_{j+1}$ if $1 \leqslant j < m$.

(2) Prove Theorem 4.5.3 of Exercise 44, given that the Lemma is true.

Exercise 46. We saw safe and regular registers earlier in this chapter. Define a *wraparound* register that has the property that there is a value v such that adding 1 to v yields 0, not $v + 1$.

If we replace the Bakery algorithm's shared variables with either (a) flickering, (b) safe, (c) or wraparound registers, then does it still satisfy (1) mutual exclusion, (2) first-come-first-served ordering?

You should provide six answers (some may imply others). Justify each claim.

5 The Relative Power of Primitive Synchronization Operations

use registers to implement mutual exclusion.

Imagine you are in charge of designing a new multiprocessor. What kinds of atomic instructions should you include? The literature includes a bewildering array of different choices: *reading* and *writing* to memory, `getAndDecrement()`, `swap()`, `getAndComplement()`, `compareAndSet()`, and many, many others. Supporting them all would be complicated and inefficient, but supporting the wrong ones could make it difficult or even impossible to solve important synchronization problems.

Our goal is to identify a set of primitive synchronization operations powerful enough to solve synchronization problems likely to arise in practice. (Of course, we might want to support other, nonessential synchronization operations for convenience.) To this end, we need some way to evaluate the *power* of various synchronization primitives: what synchronization problems they can solve, and how efficiently they can solve them.

A concurrent object implementation is *wait-free* if each method call finishes in a finite number of steps. A method is *lock-free* if it guarantees that infinitely often *some* method call finishes in a finite number of steps. We have already seen wait-free (and therefore by definition also lock-free) register implementations in Chapter 4. One way to evaluate the power of synchronization instructions is to see how well they support implementations of shared objects such as queues, stacks, trees, and so on. As we explained in Chapter 4, we evaluate solutions that are wait-free or lock-free, that is, guarantee progress without relying on outside support.[1]

We will see that all synchronization instructions are not created equal. If one thinks of primitive synchronization instructions as objects whose exported methods are the instructions themselves (in the literature these objects are often referred to as *synchronization primitives*), one can show that there is an infinite

1 It makes no sense to evaluate solutions that only meet dependent progress conditions. This is because the real power of solutions based on dependent conditions such as obstruction-freedom or deadlock-freedom is masked by the contribution of the operating system they depend on.

hierarchy of synchronization primitives, such that no primitive at one level can be used for a wait-free or lock-free implementation of any primitives at higher levels. The basic idea is simple: each class in the hierarchy has an associated *consensus number*, which is the maximum number of threads for which objects of the class can solve an elementary synchronization problem called *consensus*. We will see that in a system of n or more concurrent threads, it is impossible to construct a wait-free or lock-free implementation of an object with consensus number n from an object with a lower consensus number.

5.1 Consensus Numbers

Consensus is an innocuous-looking, somewhat abstract problem that will have enormous consequences for everything from algorithm design to hardware architecture. A *consensus object* provides a single method `decide()`, as shown in Fig. 5.1. Each thread calls the `decide()` method with its input v *at most once*. The object's `decide()` method will return a value meeting the following conditions:

- *consistent*: all threads decide the same value,
- *valid*: the common decision value is some thread's input.

In other words, a concurrent consensus object is linearizable to a sequential consensus object in which the thread whose value was chosen completes its `decide()` first. Sometimes it is useful to focus on consensus problems where all inputs are either zero or one. We call this specialized problem *binary consensus*. To simplify the presentation, we focus here on binary consensus, but our claims apply verbatim to consensus in general.

We are interested in wait-free solutions to the consensus problem, that is, wait-free concurrent implementations of consensus objects. The reader will notice that since the `decide()` method of a given consensus object is executed only once by each thread, and there are a finite number of threads, by definition a lock-free implementation would also be wait-free and vice versa. Henceforth, we mention only wait-free implementations, and for historical reasons, call any class that implements *consensus* in a wait-free manner a *consensus protocol*.

```
public interface Consensus<T> {
  T decide(T value);
}
```

Figure 5.1 Consensus object interface.

Wait-Free Computation

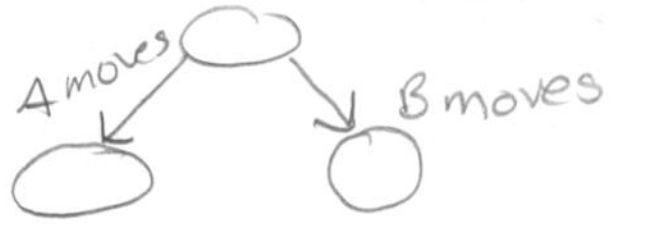

We will restrict ourselves to object classes with deterministic sequential specifications (i.e., ones in which each sequential method call has a single outcome).[2]

We want to understand whether a particular class of objects is powerful enough to solve the consensus problem. How can we make this notion more precise? If we think of such objects as supported by a lower level of the system, perhaps the operating system, or even the hardware, then we care about the properties of the class, not about the number of objects. (If the system can provide one object of this class, it can probably provide more.) Second, it is reasonable to suppose that any modern system can provide a generous amount of read–write memory for bookkeeping. These two observations suggest the following definition.

***Definition* 5.1.1.** A class C *solves* n-thread consensus if there exist a consensus protocol using any number of objects of class C and any number of atomic registers.

***Definition* 5.1.2.** The *consensus number* of a class C is the largest n for which that class solves n-thread consensus. If no largest n exists, we say the consensus number of the class is *infinite.*

***Corollary* 5.1.1.** Suppose one can implement an object of class C from one or more objects of class D, together with some number of atomic registers. If class C solves n-consensus, then so does class D.

5.1.1 States and Valence

Some initial state has to be bivalent.

A good place to start is to think about the simplest interesting case: binary consensus (i.e., inputs 0 or 1) for 2 threads (call them A and B). Each thread makes moves until it decides on a value. Here, a *move* is a method call to a shared object. A *protocol state* consists of the states of the threads and the shared objects. An *initial state* is a protocol state before any thread has moved, and a *final state* is a protocol state after all threads have finished. The *decision value* of any final state is the value decided by all threads in that state.

A wait-free protocol's set of possible states forms a tree, where each node represents a possible protocol state, and each edge represents a possible move by some thread. Fig. 5.2 shows the tree for a 2-thread protocol in which each thread moves twice. An edge for A from node s to node s' means that if A moves in protocol state s, then the new protocol state is s'. We refer to s' as a *successor state* to s. Because the protocol is wait-free, the tree must be finite. Leaf nodes represent final protocol states, and are labeled with their decision values, either 0 or 1.

---

2 We avoid nondeterministic objects since their structure is significantly more complex. See the discussion in the notes at the end of this chapter.

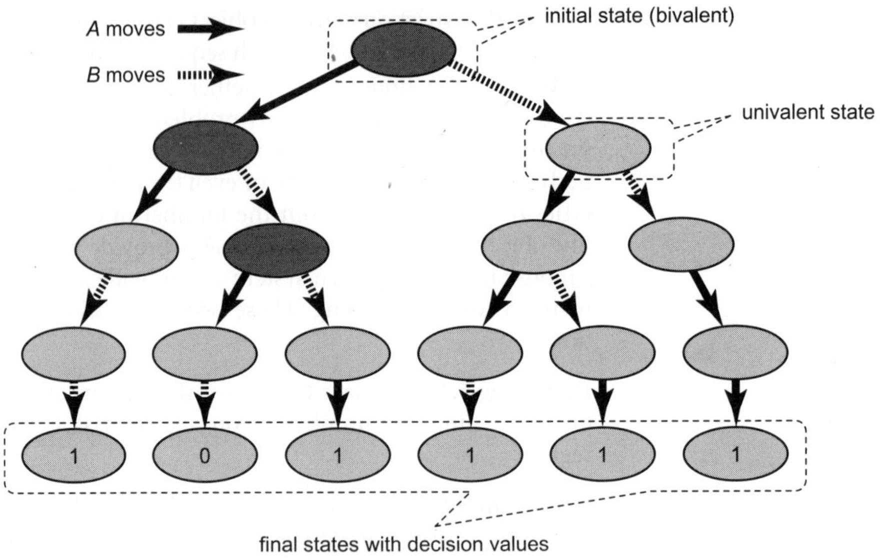

Figure 5.2 An execution tree for two threads *A* and *B*. The dark shaded nodes denote bivalent states, and the lighter ones univalent states.

A protocol state is *bivalent* if the decision value is not yet fixed: there is some execution starting from that state in which the threads decide 0, and one in which they decide 1. By contrast, the protocol state is *univalent* if the outcome is fixed: every execution starting from that state decides the same value. A protocol state is 1-*valent* if it is univalent, and the decision value will be 1, and similarly for 0-*valent*. As illustrated in Fig. 5.2, a bivalent state is a node whose descendants in the tree include both leaves labeled with 0 and leaves labeled with 1, while a univalent state is a node whose descendants include only leaves labeled with a single decision value.

Our next lemma says that an initial bivalent state exists. This observation means that the outcome of the protocol cannot be fixed in advance, but must depend on how `reads` and `writes` are interleaved.

Lemma 5.1.1. Every 2-thread consensus protocol has a bivalent initial state.

Proof: Consider the initial state where *A* has input 0 and *B* has input 1. If *A* finishes the protocol before *B* takes a step, then *A* must decide 0, because it must decide some thread's input, and 0 is the only input it has seen (it cannot decide 1 because it has no way of distinguishing this state from the one in which *B* has input 0). Symmetrically, if *B* finishes the protocol before *A* takes a step, then *B* must decide 1, because it must decide some thread's input, and 1 is the only input it has seen. It follows that the initial state where *A* has input 0 and *B* has input 1 is bivalent. □

Lemma 5.1.2. Every n-thread consensus protocol has a bivalent initial state.

Proof: Left as an exercise. □

A protocol state is *critical* if:

- It is bivalent, and
- if any thread moves, the protocol state becomes univalent.

Lemma 5.1.3. Every wait-free consensus protocol has a critical state.

Proof: Suppose not. By Lemma 5.1.2, the protocol has a bivalent initial state. Start the protocol in this state. As long as there is some thread that can move without making the protocol state univalent, let that thread move. If the protocol runs forever, then it is not wait-free. Otherwise, the protocol eventually enters a state where no such move is possible, which must be a critical state. □

Everything we have proved so far applies to any consensus protocol, no matter what class (or classes) of shared objects it uses. Now we turn our attention to specific classes of objects.

5.2 Atomic Registers

The obvious place to begin is to ask whether we can solve consensus using atomic registers. Surprisingly, perhaps, the answer is no. We will show that there is no binary consensus protocol for two threads. We leave it as an exercise to show that if two threads cannot reach consensus on two values, then n threads cannot reach consensus on k values, where $n > 2$ and $k > 2$.

Often, when we argue about whether or not there exists a protocol that solves a particular problem, we construct a scenario of the form: "if we had such a protocol, it would behave like this under these circumstances …". One particularly useful scenario is to have one thread, say A, run completely by itself until it finishes the protocol. This particular scenario is common enough that we give it its own name: A runs *solo.*

***Theorem* 5.2.1.** Atomic registers have consensus number 1.

Proof: Suppose there exists a binary consensus protocol for two threads A and B. We will reason about the properties of such a protocol and derive a contradiction.

By Lemma 5.1.3, we can run the protocol until it reaches a critical state s. Suppose A's next move carries the protocol to a 0-valent state, and B's next move carries the protocol to a 1-valent state. (If not, then switch thread names.) What

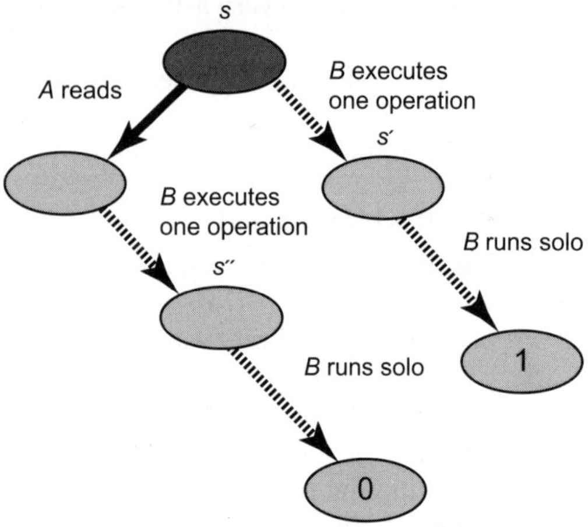

Figure 5.3 Case: *A* reads first. In the first execution scenario, *B* moves first, driving the protocol to a 1-valent state *s*′, and then *B* runs solo and eventually decides 1. In the second execution scenario, *A* moves first, driving the protocol to a 0-valent state *s*″. *B* then runs solo starting in *s*″ and eventually decides 0.

methods could *A* and *B* be about to call? We now consider an exhaustive list of the possibilities: one of them reads from a register, they both write to separate registers, or they both write to the same register.

Suppose *A* is about to read a given register (*B* may be about to either read or write the same register or a different register), as depicted in Fig. 5.3. Consider two possible execution scenarios. In the first scenario, *B* moves first, driving the protocol to a 1-valent state s', and then *B* runs solo and eventually decides 1. In the second execution scenario, *A* moves first, then *B* executes one operation, driving the protocol to a 0-valent state *s*. *B* then runs solo starting in s'' and eventually decides 0. The problem is that the states s' and s'' are indistinguishable to *B* (the read *A* performed could only change its thread-local state which is not visible to *B*), which means that *B* must decide the same value in both scenarios, a contradiction.

Suppose, instead of this scenario, both threads are about to write to different registers, as depicted in Fig. 5.4. *A* is about to write to r_0 and *B* to r_1. Let us consider two possible execution scenarios. In the first, *A* writes to r_0 and then *B* writes to r_1, so the resulting protocol state is 0-valent because *A* went first. In the second, *B* writes to r_1 and then *A* writes to r_0, so the resulting protocol state is 1-valent because *B* went first.

The problem is that both scenarios lead to indistinguishable protocol states. Neither *A* nor *B* can tell which move was first. The resulting state is therefore both 0-valent and 1-valent, a contradiction.

Finally, suppose both threads write to the same register *r*, as depicted in Fig. 5.5. Again, consider two possible execution scenarios. In one scenario *A* writes first, the resulting protocol state s' is 0-valent, *B* then runs solo and decides 0. In

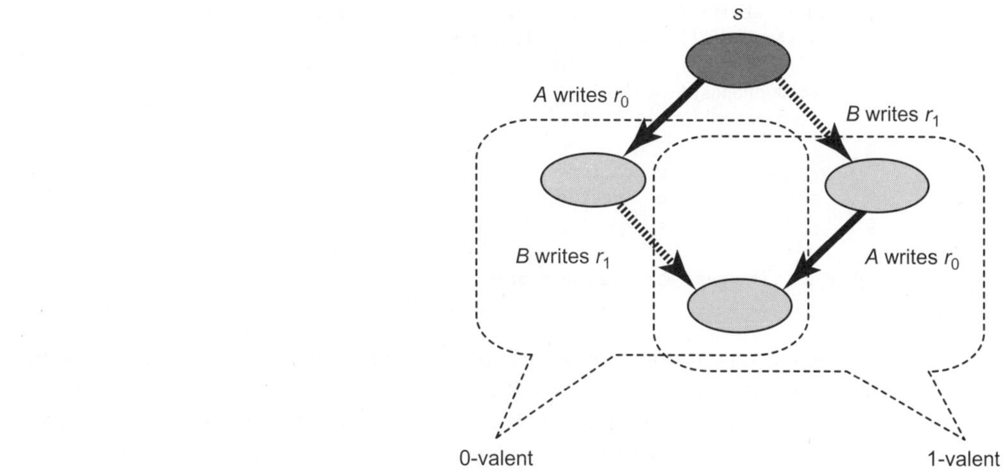

Figure 5.4 Case: *A* and *B* write to different registers.

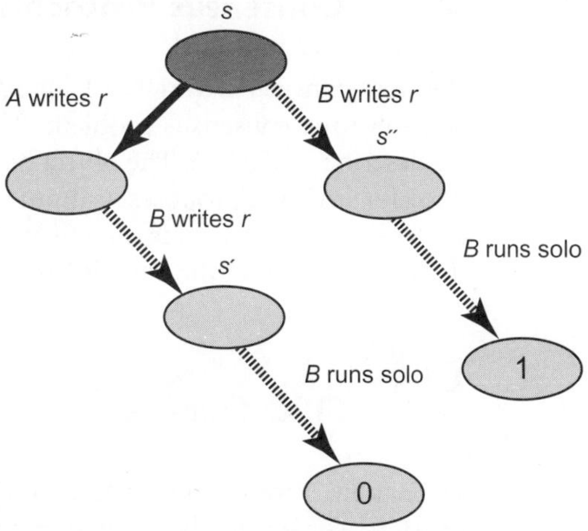

Figure 5.5 Case: *A* and *B* write to the same register.

another scenario, ***B*** writes first, the resulting protocol state s'' is 1-valent, ***B*** then runs solo and decides 1. The problem is that ***B*** cannot tell the difference between s' and s'' (because in both s' and s'' it overwrote the register r and obliterated any trace of A's write) so ***B*** must decide the same value starting from either state, a contradiction. □

***Corollary* 5.2.1.** It is impossible to construct a wait-free implementation of any object with consensus number greater than 1 using atomic registers.

```
public abstract class ConsensusProtocol<T> implements Consensus<T> {
  protected T[] proposed = (T[]) new Object[N];
  // announce my input value to the other threads
  void propose(T value) {
    proposed[ThreadID.get()] = value;
  }
  // figure out which thread was first
  abstract public T decide(T value);
}
```

Figure 5.6 The generic consensus protocol.

The aforementioned corollary is perhaps one of the most striking impossibility results in Computer Science. It explains why, if we want to implement lock-free concurrent data structures on modern multiprocessors, our hardware must provide primitive synchronization operations other than loads and stores (reads–writes).

5.3 Consensus Protocols

We now consider a variety of interesting object classes, asking how well each can solve the consensus problem. These protocols have a generic form, which we describe in Fig. 5.6. The object has an array of atomic registers in which each `decide()` method proposes its input value and then goes on to execute a sequence of steps in order to decide on one of the proposed values. We will devise different implementations of the `decide()` method using various synchronization objects.

5.4 FIFO Queues

In Chapter 3, we saw a wait-free FIFO queue implementation using only atomic registers, subject to the limitation that only one thread could enqueue to the queue, and only one thread could dequeue from the queue. It is natural to ask whether one can provide a wait-free implementation of a FIFO queue that supports multiple enqueuers and dequeuers. For now, let us focus on a more specific problem: can we provide a wait-free implementation of a two-dequeuer FIFO queue using atomic registers?

***Theorem* 5.4.1.** The two-dequeuer FIFO queue class has consensus number at least 2.

Proof: Fig. 5.7 shows a two-thread consensus protocol using a single FIFO queue. Here, the queue stores integers. The queue is initialized by enqueuing the value `WIN` followed by the value `LOSE`. As in all the consensus protocol considered

```
public class QueueConsensus<T> extends ConsensusProtocol<T> {
  private static final int WIN = 0; // first thread
  private static final int LOSE = 1; // second thread
  Queue queue;
  // initialize queue with two items
  public QueueConsensus() {
    queue = new Queue();
    queue.enq(WIN);
    queue.enq(LOSE);
  }
  // figure out which thread was first
  public T decide(T Value) {
    propose(value);
    int status = queue.deq();
    int i = ThreadID.get();
    if (status == WIN)
      return proposed[i];
    else
      return proposed[1-i];
  }
}
```

Figure 5.7 2-thread consensus using a FIFO queue.

here, `decide()` first calls `propose(`v`)`, which stores v in `proposed[]`, a shared array of proposed input values. It then proceeds to dequeue the next item from the queue. If that item is the value `WIN`, then the calling thread was first, and it decides on its own value. If that item is the value `LOSE`, then the other thread was first, so the calling thread returns the other thread's input, as declared in the `proposed[]` array.

The protocol is wait-free, since it contains no loops. If each thread returns its own input, then they must both have dequeued `WIN`, violating the FIFO queue specification. If each returns the other's input, then they must both have dequeued `LOSE`, also violating the queue specification.

The validity condition follows from the observation that the thread that dequeued `WIN` stored its input in the `proposed[]` array before any value was dequeued. □

Trivial variations of this program yield protocols for stacks, priority queues, lists, sets, or any object with methods that return different results if applied in different orders.

***Corollary* 5.4.1.** It is impossible to construct a wait-free implementation of a queue, stack, priority queue, set, or list from a set of atomic registers.

Although FIFO queues solve two-thread consensus, they cannot solve 3-thread consensus.

***Theorem* 5.4.1.** FIFO queues have consensus number 2.

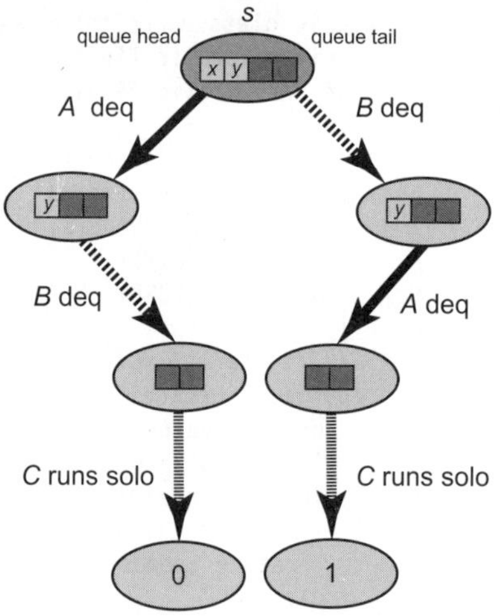

Figure 5.8 Case: A and B both call deq().

Proof: By contradiction. Assume we have a consensus protocol for a thread A, B, and C. By Lemma 5.1.3, the protocol has a critical state s. Without loss of generality, we can assume that A's next move takes the protocol to a 0-valent state, and B's next move takes the protocol to a 1-valent state. The rest, as before, is a case analysis.

First, we know that A and B's pending moves cannot commute, implying that they are both about to call methods of the same object. Second, we know that A and B cannot be about to read or write shared registers. It follows that they are about to call methods of a single queue object.

First, suppose A and B both call deq(), as depicted in Fig. 5.8. Let s' be the protocol state if A dequeues and then B dequeues, and let s'' be the state if the dequeues occur in the opposite order. Since s' is 0-valent, if C runs uninterrupted from s', then it decides 0. Since s'' is 1-valent, if C runs uninterrupted from s'', then it decides 1. But s' and s'' are indistinguishable to C (the same two items were removed from the queue), so C must decide the same value in both states, a contradiction.

Second, suppose A calls enq(a) and B calls deq(). If the queue is nonempty, the contradiction is immediate because the two methods commute (each operates on a different end of the queue): C cannot observe the order in which they occurred. If the queue is empty, then the 1-valent state reached if B executes a dequeue on the empty queue and then A enqueues is indistinguishable to C from the 0-valent state reached if A alone enqueues. Notice that we do not really care what a deq() on an empty queue does, that is, aborts or waits, since this will not affect the state visible to C.

Finally, suppose A calls enq(a) and B calls enq(b), as depicted in Fig. 5.9. Let s' be the state at the end of the following execution:

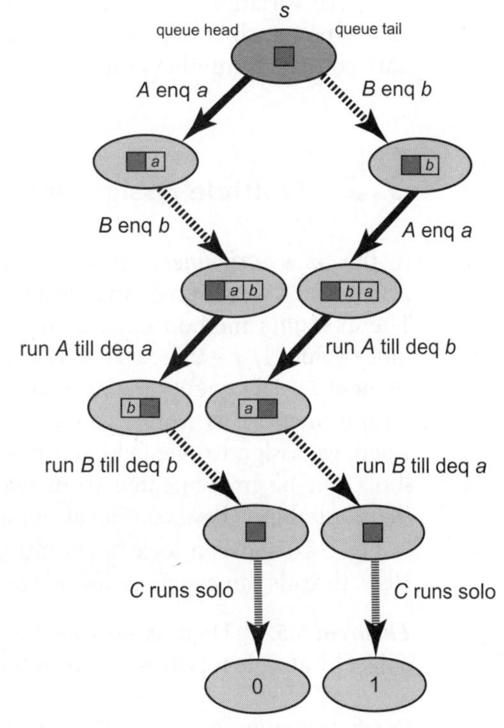

Figure 5.9 Case: *A* calls enq(a) and *B* calls enq(b). Notice that a new item is enqueued by *A* after *A* and *B* enqueued their respective items and before it dequeued (and *B* could have also enqueued items before dequeuing), but that this item is the same in both of the execution scenarios.

1. Let A and B enqueue items a and b in that order.
2. Run A until it dequeues a. (Since the only way to observe the queue's state is via the deq() method, A cannot decide before it observes one of a or b.)
3. Before A takes any further steps, run B until it dequeues b.

Let s'' be the state after the following alternative execution:

1. Let B and A enqueue items b and a in that order.
2. Run A until it dequeues b.
3. Before A takes any further steps, run B until it dequeues a.

Clearly, s' is 0-valent and s'' is 1-valent. Both A's executions are identical until A dequeues a or b. Since A is halted before it can modify any other objects, B's executions are also identical until it dequeues a or b. By a now familiar argument, a contradiction arises because s' and s'' are indistinguishable to C. □

Trivial variations of this argument can be applied to show that many similar data types, such as sets, stacks, double-ended queues, and priority queues, all have consensus number exactly two.

5.5 Multiple Assignment Objects

In the (m, n*-assignment*) problem, for $n \geqslant m > 1$ (sometimes called *multiple assignment*), we are given an object with n fields (sometimes an n-element array). The `assign()` method takes as arguments m values $v_i, i \in 0, \ldots, m-1$, and m index values $i_j, j \in 0, \ldots, m-1, i_j \in 0, \ldots, n-1$. It atomically assigns v_j to array element i_j. The `read()` method takes an index argument, i, and returns the ith array element. This problem is the dual of the *atomic snapshot* object (Chapter 4), where we assign to one field and read multiple fields atomically. Because snapshots can be implemented from read–write registers, Theorem 5.2.1 implies shapshot objects have consensus number 1.

Fig. 5.10 shows a lock-based implementation of a $(2, 3)$-assignment object. Here, threads can assign atomically to any two out of three array entries.

***Theorem* 5.5.1.** There is no wait-free implementation of an (m, n)-assignment object by atomic registers for any $n > m > 1$.

Proof: It is enough to show that we can solve 2-consensus given two threads and a $(2, 3)$-assignment object. (Exercise 75 asks one to justify this claim.) As usual, the `decide()` method must figure out which thread went first. All array entries are initialized with *null* values. Fig. 5.11 shows the protocol. Thread A writes (atomically) to fields 0 and 1, while thread B writes (atomically) to fields 1 and 2. Then they try to determine who went first. From A's point of view, there are three cases, as shown in Fig. 5.12:

```
public class Assign23 {
  int[] r = new int[3];
  public Assign23(int init) {
   for (int i = 0; i < r.length; i++)
     r[i] = init;
  }
  public synchronized void assign(T v0, T v1, int i0, int i1) {
    r[i0] = v0;
    r[i1] = v1;
  }
  public synchronized int read(int i) {
    return r[i];
  }
}
```

Figure 5.10 A lock-based implementation of a (2,3)-assignment object.

- If A's assignment was ordered first, and B's assignment has not happened, then fields 0 and 1 have A's value, and field 2 is *null*. A decides its own input.
- If A's assignment was ordered first, and B's second, then field 0 has A's value, and fields 1 and 2 have B's. A decides its own input.
- If B's assignment was ordered first, and A's second, then fields 0 and 1 have A's value, and 2 has B's. A decides B's input.

A similar analysis holds for B. □

***Theorem* 5.5.2.** Atomic $(n, \frac{n(n+1)}{2})$-register assignment for $n > 1$ has consensus number at least n.

Proof: We design a consensus protocol for n threads $0, \ldots, n-1$. The protocol uses an $(n, \frac{n(n+1)}{2})$-assignment object. For convenience we name the object fields as follows. There are n fields $r_0, \ldots, r_{n-1}$ where thread i writes to register r_i, and $n(n-1)/2$ fields r_{ij}, where $i > j$, where threads i and j both write to field r_{ij}. All fields are initialized to *null*. Each thread i atomically assigns its input value to n fields: its single-writer field r_i and its $n-1$ multi-writer registers r_{ij}. The protocol decides the first value to be assigned.

```
public class MultiConsensus<T> extends ConsensusProtocol<T> {
  private final int NULL = -1;
  Assign23 assign23 = new Assign23(NULL);
  public T decide(T value) {
    propose(value);
    int i = ThreadID.get();
    int j = 1-i;
    // double assignment
    assign23.assign(i, i, i, i+1);
    int other = assign23.read((i+2) % 3);
    if (other == NULL || other == assign23.read(1))
      return proposed[i];        // I win
    else
      return proposed[j];        // I lose
  }
}
```

Figure 5.11 2-thread consensus using (2,3)-multiple assignment.

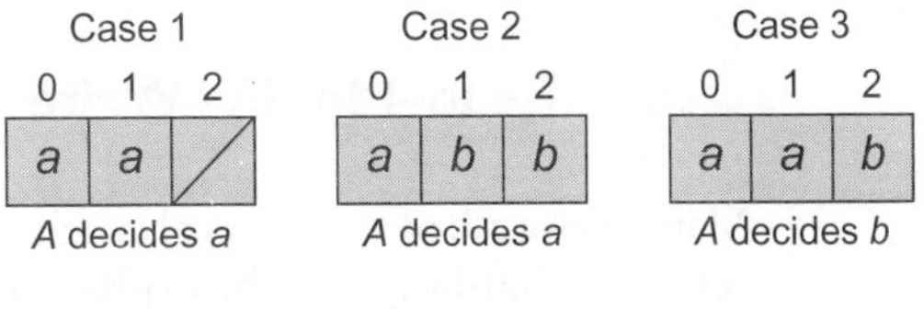

Figure 5.12 Consensus using multiple assignment: possible views.

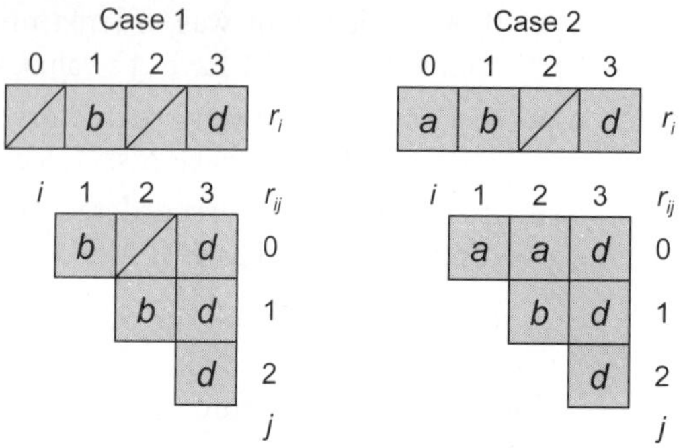

Figure 5.13 Two possible views of (4,10)-assignment solving consensus for 4 threads. In Part 1 only threads *B* and *D* show up. *B* is the first to assign and wins the consensus. In Part 2 there are three threads *A*, *B*, and *D*, and as before, *B* wins by assigning first and *D* assigns last. The order among the threads can be determined by looking at the pairwise order among any two. Because the assignments are atomic, these individual orders are always consistent and define the total order among the calls.

After assigning to its fields, a thread determines the relative ordering of the assignments for every two threads i and j as follows:

- Read r_{ij}. If the value is *null*, then neither assignment has occurred.
- Otherwise, read r_i and r_j. If r_i's value is *null*, then j precedes i, and similarly for r_j.
- If neither r_i nor r_j is *null*, reread r_{ij}. If its value is equal to the value read from r_i, then j precedes i, else vice versa.

Repeating this procedure, a thread can determine which value was written by the earliest assignment. Two example orderings appear in Fig. 5.13. □

Note that multiple assignment solves consensus for any $m > n > 1$ threads while its dual structures and atomic snapshots, have consensus number at most one. Although these two problems may appear similar, we have just shown that writing atomically to multiple memory locations requires more computational power than reading atomically.

5.6 Read–Modify–Write Operations

Many, if not all, of the classical synchronization operations provided by multiprocessors in hardware can be expressed as *read–modify–write* (RMW) operations, or, as they are called in their object form, *read–modify–write registers*. Consider a RMW register that encapsulates integer values, and let $\mathcal{F}$ be a set of functions from integers to integers.[3]

A method is an RMW for the function set $\mathcal{F}$ if it atomically replaces the current register value v with $f(v)$, for some $f \in \mathcal{F}$, and returns the original value v. (Sometimes $\mathcal{F}$ is a singleton set.) We (mostly) follow the Java convention that an RMW method that applies the function **mumble** is called **getAndMumble()**.

For example, the **java.util.concurrent** package provides an `AtomicInteger` class with a rich set of RMW methods.

- The `getAndSet(`v`)` method atomically replaces the register's current value with v and returns the prior value. This method (also called `swap()`) is an RMW method for the set of constant functions of the type $f_v(x) = v$.
- The `getAndIncrement()` method atomically adds 1 to the register's current value and returns the prior value. This method (also called *fetch-and-increment*) is an RMW method for the function $f(x) = x + 1$.
- The `getAndAdd(`k`)` method atomically adds k to the register's current value and returns the prior value. This method (also called *fetch-and-add*) is an RMW method for the set of functions $f_k(x) = x + k$.
- The `compareAndSet()` method takes two values, an *expected* value e, and an *update* value u. If the register value is equal to e, it is atomically replaced with u, and otherwise it is unchanged. Either way, the method returns a Boolean value indicating whether the value was changed. Informally, $f_{e,u}(x) = x$ if $x \neq e$ and u otherwise. Strictly speaking however, `compareAndSet()` is not an RMW method for $f_{e,u}$, because an RMW method would return the register's prior value instead of a Boolean value, but this distinction is a technicality.
- The `get()` method returns the register's value. This method is an RMW method for the identity function $f(v) = v$.

The RMW methods are interesting precisely because they are potential hardware primitives, engraved not in stone, but in silicon. Here, we define RMW registers and their methods in terms of **`synchronized`** Java methods, but, pragmatically, they correspond (exactly or nearly) to many real or proposed hardware synchronization primitives.

An RMW method is *nontrivial* if its set of functions includes at least one function that is not the identity function.

***Theorem* 5.6.1.** Any nontrivial RMW register has consensus number at least 2.

Proof: Fig. 5.14 shows a 2-thread consensus protocol. Since there exists f in $\mathcal{F}$ that is not the identity, there exists a value v such that $f(v) \neq v$. In the `decide()` method, as usual, the `propose(`v`)` method writes the thread's input v to the

3 For brevity, we consider only registers that hold integer values, but they could equally well hold references to other objects.

```
class RMWConsensus extends ConsensusProtocol {
  // initialize to v such that f(v) != v
  private RMWRegister r = new RMWRegister(v);
  public Object decide(Object value) {
    propose(value);
    int i = ThreadID.get();          // my index
    int j = 1-i;                     // other's index
    if (r.rmw() == v)                // I'm first, I win
      return proposed[i];
    else                             // I'm second, I lose
      return proposed[j];
  }
}
```

Figure 5.14 2-thread consensus using RMW.

proposed[] array. Then each thread applies the RMW method to a shared register. If a thread's call returns v, it is linearized first, and it decides its own value. Otherwise, it is linearized second, and it decides the other thread's proposed value. □

***Corollary* 5.6.1.** It is impossible to construct a wait-free implementation of any nontrivial RMW method from atomic registers for two or more threads.

5.7 Common2 RMW Operations

We now identify a class of RMW registers, called *Common2*, that correspond to many of the common synchronization primitives provided by processors in the late Twentieth Century. Although *Common2* registers, like all nontrivial RMW registers, are more powerful than atomic registers, we will show that they have consensus number exactly 2, implying that they have limited synchronization power. Fortunately, these synchronization primitives have by-and-large fallen from favor in contemporary processor architectures.

***Definition* 5.7.1.** A set of functions $\mathcal{F}$ belongs to *Common2* if for all values v and all f_i and f_j in $\mathcal{F}$, either:

- f_i and f_j *commute*: $f_i(f_j(v)) = f_j(f_i(v))$, or
- one function *overwrites* the other: $f_i(f_j(v)) = f_i(v)$ or $f_j(f_i(v)) = f_j(v)$.

***Definition* 5.7.2.** A RMW register belongs to *Common2* if its set of functions $\mathcal{F}$ belongs to *Common2*.

For example, many RMW registers in the literature provide only one nontrivial function. For example, getAndSet() uses a constant function, which overwrites any prior value. The `getAndIncrement()` and `getAndAdd()` methods use functions that commute with one another.

Very informally, here is why RMW registers in *Common2* cannot solve 3-thread consensus. The first thread (the *winner*) can always tell it was first, and each of the second and third threads (the *losers*) can each tell that they were losers. However, because the functions defining the state following operations in *Common2* commute or overwrite, a loser thread cannot tell which of the others went first (was the winner), and because the protocol is wait-free, it cannot wait to find out. Let us make this argument more precise.

***Theorem* 5.7.1.** Any RMW register in *Common2* has consensus number (exactly) 2.

Proof: Theorem 5.6.1 states that any such register has consensus number at least 2. We need only to show that any *Common2* register cannot solve consensus for three threads.

Assume by way of contradiction that a 3-thread protocol exists using only *Common2* registers and read–write registers. Suppose threads A, B, and C reach consensus through *Common2* registers. By Lemma 5.1.3, any such protocol has a critical state s in which the protocol is bivalent, but any method call by any thread will cause the protocol to enter a univalent state.

We now do a case analysis, examining each possible method call. The kind of reasoning used in the proof of Theorem 5.2.1 shows that the pending methods cannot be reads or writes, nor can the threads be about to call methods of different objects. It follows that the threads are about to call RMW methods of a single register r.

Suppose A is about to call a method for function f_A, sending the protocol to a 0-valent state, and B is about to call a method for f_B, sending the protocol to a 1-valent state. There are two possible cases:

1. As depicted in Fig. 5.15, one function overwrites the other: $f_B(f_A(v)) = f_B(v)$. Let s' be the state that results if A applies f_A and then B applies f_B. Because s' is 0-valent, C will decide 0 if it runs alone until it finishes the protocol. Let s'' be the state that results if B alone calls f_B. Because s'' is 1-valent, C will decide 1 if it runs alone until it finishes the protocol. The problem is that the two possible register states $f_B(f_A(v))$ and $f_B(v)$ are the same, so s' and s'' differ only in the internal states of A and B. If we now let thread C execute, since C completes the protocol without communicating with A or B, these two states look identical to C, so it cannot possibly decide different values from the two states.
2. The functions commute: $f_A(f_B(v)) = f_B(f_A(v))$. Let s' be the state that results if A applies f_A and then B applies f_B. Because s' is 0-valent, C will decide 0 if it runs alone until it finishes the protocol. Let s'' be the state that results if A and B perform their calls in the reverse order. Because s'' is 1-valent, C will decide 1 if it runs alone until it finishes the protocol. The problem is that the

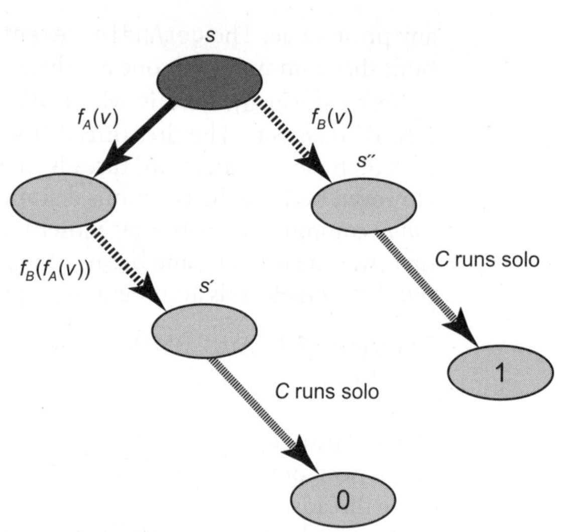

Figure 5.15 Case: two functions that overwrite.

two possible register states $f_A(f_B(v))$ and $f_B(f_A(v))$ are the same, so s' and s'' differ only in the internal states of A and B. Now let thread C execute. Since C completes the protocol without communicating with A or B, these two states look identical to C, so it cannot possibly decide different values from the two states. □

5.8 The compareAndSet() Operation

We consider the `compareAndSet()` operation, a synchronization operation supported by several contemporary architectures. (For example, it is called CMPXCHG on the Intel Pentium™). This method is also known in the literature as *compare-and-swap*. A `compareAndSet()` takes two arguments: an *expected* value and an *update* value. If the current register value is equal to the expected value, then it is replaced by the update value; otherwise the value is left unchanged. The method call returns a Boolean indicating whether the value changed.

***Theorem* 5.8.1.** A register providing `compareAndSet()` and `get()` methods has an infinite consensus number.

Proof: Fig. 5.16 shows a consensus protocol for n threads $0, \ldots, n-1$ using the `AtomicInteger` class's `compareAndSet()` method. The threads share an `AtomicInteger` object, initialized to a constant `FIRST`, distinct from any thread index. Each thread calls `compareAndSet()` with `FIRST` as the expected value, and

```
class CASConsensus extends ConsensusProtocol {
  private final int FIRST = -1;
  private AtomicInteger r = new AtomicInteger(FIRST);
  public Object decide(Object value) {
    propose(value);
    int i = ThreadID.get();
    if (r.compareAndSet(FIRST, i)) // I won
      return proposed[i];
    else                           // I lost
      return proposed[r.get()];
  }
}
```

Figure 5.16 Consensus using compareAndSwap().

its own index as the new value. If thread *A*'s call returns *true*, then that method call was first in the linearization order, so *A* decides its own value. Otherwise, *A* reads the current AtomicInteger value, and takes that thread's input from the proposed[] array. □

We note that having the compareAndSet() register in Theorem 5.8.1 provide a get() method is only a convenience, and so it follows that:

Corollary **5.8.1.** A register providing only compareAndSet() has an infinite consensus number.

As we will see in Chapter 6, machines that provide primitive operations like compareAndSet()[4] are asynchronous computation's equivalents of the Turing Machines of sequential computation: any concurrent object that can be implemented, can be implemented in a wait-free manner on such machines. Thus, in the words of Maurice Sendak, compareAndSet() is the "king of all wild things."

5.9 Chapter Notes

Michael Fischer, Nancy Lynch, and Michael Paterson [40] were the first to prove that consensus is impossible in a message-passing system where a single thread can halt. Their seminal paper introduced the "bivalency" style of impossibility argument widely used in the field of distributed computing. M. Loui and H. Abu-Amara [108] and Herlihy [62] were the first to extend this result to shared memory.

---

4 Some architectures provide a pair of operations similar to get()/compareAndSet() called *load-linked/store-conditional.* In general, the *load-linked* method marks a location as loaded, and the *store-conditional* method fails if another thread modified that location since it was loaded. See Chapter 18 and Appendix B.

Clyde Kruskal, Larry Rudolph, and Marc Snir [133] coined the term *read–modify–write* operation as part of the NYU Ultracomputer project.

Maurice Herlihy [62] introduced the notion of a *consensus number* as a measure of computational power, and was the first to prove most of the impossibility and universality results presented in this chapter and Chapter 6.

The class *Common2* that includes several common primitive synchronization operations was defined by Yehuda Afek and Eytan Weisberger and Hanan Weisman [5]. The "sticky-bit" object used in the exercises is due to Serge Plotkin [126].

The n-bounded `compareAndSet()` object with arbitrary consensus number n in Exercise 5.10 is based on a construction by Prasad Jayanti and Sam Toueg [81]. In the hierarchy used here, we say that X solves consensus if one can construct a wait-free consensus protocol from any number of instances of X and any amount of read–write memory. Prasad Jayanti [79] observed that one could also define resource-bounded hierarchies where one is restricted to using only a fixed number of instances of X, or a fixed amount of memory. The unbounded hierarchy used here seems to be the most natural one, since any other hierarchy is a coarsening of the unbounded one.

Jayanti also raised the question whether the hierarchy is *robust*, that is, whether an object X at level m can be "boosted" to a higher consensus level by combining it with another object Y at the same or lower level. Wai-Kau Lo and Vassos Hadzilacos [106] and Eric Schenk [144] showed that the consensus hierarchy is not robust: certain objects can be boosted. Informally, their constructions went like this: let X be an object with the following curious properties. X solves n-thread consensus but "refuses" to reveal the results unless the caller can prove he or she can solve an intermediate task weaker than n-thread consensus, but stronger than any task solvable by atomic read/write registers. If Y is an object that can be used to solve the intermediate task, Y can boost X by convincing X to reveal the outcome of an n-thread consensus. The objects used in these proofs are nondeterministic.

The Maurice Sendak quote is from *Where the Wild Things Are* [140].

5.10 Exercises

Exercise 47. Prove Lemma 5.1.2.

Exercise 48. Prove that every n-thread consensus protocol has a bivalent initial state.

Exercise 49. Prove that in a critical state, one successor state must be 0-valent, and the other 1-valent.

Exercise 50. Show that if binary consensus using atomic registers is impossible for two threads, then it is also impossible for n threads, where $n > 2$. (Hint: argue by *reduction*: if we had a protocol to solve binary consensus for n threads, then we can transform it into a two-thread protocol.)

Exercise 51. Show that if binary consensus using atomic registers is impossible for n threads, then so is consensus over k values, where $k > 2$.

Exercise 52. Show that with sufficiently many n-thread binary consensus objects and atomic registers one can implement n-thread consensus over n values.

Exercise 53. The `Stack` class provides two methods: `push(x)` pushes a value onto the top of the stack, and `pop()` removes and returns the most recently pushed value. Prove that the `Stack` class has consensus number *exactly* two.

Exercise 54. Suppose we augment the FIFO `Queue` class with a `peek()` method that returns but does not remove the first element in the queue. Show that the augmented queue has infinite consensus number.

Exercise 55. Consider three threads, A, B, and C, each of which has a MRSW register, X_A, X_B, and X_C, that it alone can write and the others can read.

In addition, each pair shares a `RMWRegister` register that provides only a `compareAndSet()` method: A and B share R_{AB}, B and C share R_{BC}, and A and C share R_{AC}. Only the threads that share a register can call that register's `compareAndSet()` method or read its value.

Your mission: either give a consensus protocol and explain why it works, or sketch an impossibility proof.

Exercise 56. Consider the situation described in Exercise 5.55, except that A, B, and C can apply a *double* `compareAndSet()` to both registers at once.

Exercise 57. In the consensus protocol shown in 5.7, what would happen if we announced the thread's value after dequeuing from the queue?

Exercise 58. Objects of the `StickyBit` class have three possible states $\perp, 0, 1$, initially $\perp$. A call to `write(v)`, where v is 0 or 1, has the following effects:

- If the object's state is $\perp$, then it becomes v.
- If the object's state is 0 or 1, then it is unchanged.

A call to `read()` returns the object's current state.

1. Show that such an object can solve wait-free *binary* consensus (that is, all inputs are 0 or 1) for any number of threads.
2. Show that an array of $\log_2 m$ `StickyBit` objects with atomic registers can solve wait-free consensus for any number of threads when there are m possible inputs. (Hint: you need to give each thread one single-writer, multi-reader atomic register.)

Exercise 59. The `SetAgree` class, like the `Consensus` class, provides a `decide()` method whose call returns a value that was the input of some thread's `decide()`

call. However, unlike the `Consensus` class, the values returned by `decide()` calls are not required to agree. Instead, these calls may return no more than k distinct values. (When k is 1, `SetAgree` is the same as consensus.) What is the consensus number of the `SetAgree` class when $k > 1$?

Exercise 60. The two-thread *approximate agreement* class for a given ϵ is defined as follows. Given two threads A and B, each can call `decide`(x_a) and `decide`(x_b) methods, where x_a and x_b are real numbers. These methods return values y_a and y_b respectively, such that y_a and y_b both lie in the closed interval $[\min(x_a, x_b), \max(x_a, x_b)]$, and $|y_a - y_b| \leqslant \epsilon$ for $\epsilon > 0$. Note that this object is nondeterministic.

What is the consensus number of the *approximate agreement* object?

Exercise 61. Consider a distributed system where threads communicate by message-passing. A *type A* broadcast guarantees:

1. every nonfaulty thread eventually gets each message,
2. if P broadcasts M_1 then M_2, then every thread receives M_1 before M_2, but
3. messages broadcast by different threads may be received in different orders at different threads.

A *type B* broadcast guarantees:

1. every nonfaulty thread eventually gets each message,
2. if P broadcasts M_1 and Q broadcasts M_2, then every thread receives M_1 and M_2 in the same order.

For each kind of broadcast,

- give a consensus protocol if possible,
- and otherwise sketch an impossibility proof.

Exercise 62. Consider the following 2-thread `QuasiConsensus` problem:

Two threads, A and B, are each given a binary input. If both have input v, then both must decide v. If they have mixed inputs, then either they must agree, or B may decide 0 and A may decide 1 (but not vice versa).

Here are three possible exercises (only one of which works). (1) Give a 2-thread consensus protocol using `QuasiConsensus` showing it has consensus number 2, or (2) give a critical-state proof that this object's consensus number is 1, or (3) give a read–write implementation of `QuasiConsensus`, thereby showing it has consensus number 1.

Exercise 63. Explain why the critical-state proof of the impossibility of consensus fails if the shared object is, in fact, a `Consensus` object.

Exercise 64. In this chapter we showed that there is a bivalent initial state for 2-thread consensus. Give a proof that there is a bivalent initial state for n thread consensus.

Exercise 65. A *team consensus* object provides the same `decide()` method as consensus. A team consensus object solves consensus as long as no more than *two* distinct values are ever proposed. (If more than two are proposed, the results are undefined.)

Show how to solve n-thread consensus, with up to n distinct input values, from a supply of team consensus objects.

Exercise 66. A *trinary* register holds values $\perp, 0, 1$, and provides `compareAndSet()` and `get()` methods with the usual meaning. Each such register is initially $\perp$. Give a protocol that uses one such register to solve n-thread consensus if the inputs of the threads are *binary*, that is, either 0 or 1.

Can you use multiple such registers (perhaps with atomic read–write registers) to solve n-thread consensus even if the threads' inputs are in the range $0 \ldots 2^K - 1$, for $K > 1$. (You may assume an input fits in an atomic register.) *Important:* remember that a consensus protocol must be wait-free.

- Devise a solution that uses at most $O(n)$ trinary registers.
- Devise a solution that uses $O(K)$ trinary registers.

Feel free to use all the atomic registers you want (they are cheap).

Exercise 67. Earlier we defined lock-freedom. Prove that there is no lock-free implementation of consensus using read–write registers for two or more threads.

Exercise 68. Fig. 5.17 shows a FIFO queue implemented with read, write, `getAndSet()` (that is, swap) and `getAndIncrement()` methods. You may assume

```
class Queue {
  AtomicInteger head = new AtomicInteger(0);
  AtomicReference items[] =
    new AtomicReference[Integer.MAX_VALUE];
  void enq(Object x){
    int slot = head.getAndIncrement();
    items[slot] = x;
  }
  Object deq() {
    while (true) {
      int limit = head.get();
      for (int i = 0; i < limit; i++) {
        Object y = items[i].getAndSet(); // swap
        if (y != null)
          return y;
      }
    }
  }
}
```

Figure 5.17 Queue implementation.

this queue is linearizable, and wait-free as long as deq() is never applied to an empty queue. Consider the following sequence of statements.

- Both getAndSet() and getAndIncrement() methods have consensus number 2.
- We can add a peek() simply by taking a snapshot of the queue (using the methods studied earlier in the course) and returning the item at the head of the queue.
- Using the protocol devised for Exercise 54, we can use the resulting queue to solve n-consensus for any n.

We have just constructed an n-thread consensus protocol using only objects with consensus number 2. Identify the faulty step in this chain of reasoning, and explain what went wrong.

Exercise 69. Recall that in our definition of compareAndSet() we noted that strictly speaking, compareAndSet() is not a RMW method for $f_{e,u}$, because a RMW method would return the register's prior value instead of a Boolean value. Use an object that supports compareAndSet() and get() to provide a new object with a linearizable NewCompareAndSet() method that returns the register's current value instead of a Boolean.

Exercise 70. Define an *n-bounded compareAndSet()* object as follows. It provides a compareAndSet() method that takes two values, an *expected* value e, and an *update* value u. For the first n times compareAndSet() is called, it behaves like a conventional compareAndSet() register: if the register value is equal to e, it is atomically replaced with u, and otherwise it is unchanged, and returns a Boolean value indicating whether the change occurred. After compareAndSet() has been called n times, however, the object enters a *faulty* state, and all subsequent method calls return $\perp$.

Show that an n-bounded compareAndSet() object has consensus number exactly n.

Exercise 71. Provide a wait-free implementation of a two-thread three-location Assign23 multiple assignment object from three compareAndSet() objects (that is, objects supporting the operations compareAndSet() and get()).

Exercise 72. In the proof of Theorem 5.5.1, we claimed that it is enough to show that we can solve 2-consensus given two threads and an $(2, 3)$-assignment object. Justify this claim.

Exercise 73. Prove Corollary 5.8.1.

Exercise 74. We can treat the scheduler as an *adversary* who uses the knowledge of our protocols and input values to frustrate our attempts at reaching consensus. One way to outwit an adversary is through randomization. Assume there are two threads that want to reach consensus, each can flip an unbiased coin, and the adversary cannot control future coin flips.

```
Object prefer[2] = {null, null};

Object decide(Object input) {
  int i = Thread.getID();
  int j = 1-i;
  prefer[i] = input;
  while (true) {
    if (prefer[j] == null) {
      return prefer[i];
    } else if (prefer[i] == prefer[j]) {
      return prefer[i];
    } else {
      if (flip()) {
       prefer[i] = prefer[j];
      }
    }
  }
}
```

Figure 5.18 Is this a randomized consensus protocol?

Assume the adversary scheduler can observe the result of each coin flip and each value read or written. It can stop a thread before or after a coin flip or a read or write to a shared register.

A *randomized consensus protocol* terminates with probability one against an adversary scheduler. Fig. 5.18 shows a plausible-looking randomized consensus protocol. Give an example showing that this protocol is incorrect.

Exercise 75. One can implement a consensus object using read–write registers by implementing a deadlock- or starvation-free mutual exclusion lock. However, this implementation provides only dependent progress, and the operating system must make sure that threads do not get stuck in the critical section so that the computation as a whole progresses.

- Is the same true for obstruction-freedom, the nonblocking dependent progress condition? Show an obstruction-free implementation of a consensus object using only atomic registers.
- What is the role of the operating system in the obstruction-free solution to consensus? Explain where the critical-state-based proof of the impossibility of consensus breaks down if we repeatedly allow an oracle to halt threads so as to allow others to make progress.

(Hint, think of how you could restrict the set of allowed executions.)

6 Universality of Consensus

6.1 Introduction

In Chapter 5, we considered a simple technique for proving statements of the form "there is no wait-free implementation of X by Y." We considered object classes with deterministic sequential specifications.[1] We derived a hierarchy in which no object from one level can implement an object at a higher level (see Fig. 6.1). Recall that each object has an associated *consensus number*, which is the maximum number of threads for which the object can solve the consensus problem. In a system of n or more concurrent threads, it is impossible to construct a wait-free implementation of an object with consensus number n from an object with a lower consensus number. The same result holds for lock-free implementations, and henceforth unless we explicitly state otherwise, it will be implied that a result that holds for wait-free implementations holds for lock-free ones.

The impossibility results of Chapter 5 do not by any means imply that wait-free synchronization is impossible or infeasible. In this chapter, we show that there exist classes of objects that are *universal*: given sufficiently many of them, one can construct a wait-free linearizable implementation of *any* concurrent object.

A class is universal in a system of n threads if, and only if it has a consensus number greater than or equal to n. In Fig. 6.1, each class at level n is universal for a system of n threads. A machine architecture or programming language is computationally powerful enough to support arbitrary wait-free synchronization if, and only if it provides objects of a universal class as primitives. For example, modern multiprocessor machines that provide a `compareAndSet()` operation are universal for any number of threads: they can implement any concurrent object in a wait-free manner.

This chapter describes how to use consensus objects to build a *universal construction* that implements any concurrent object. The chapter does *not* describe

1 The situation with nondeterministic objects is significantly more complicated.

Consensus Number	Object
1	*atomic registers*
2	`getAndSet()`, `getAndAdd()`, `Queue`, `Stack`
⋮	⋮
m	$(m, m(m+1)/2)$-*register assignment*
⋮	⋮
∞	*memory-to-memory move*, `compareAndSet()`, *Load-Linked/StoreConditional*[2]

Figure 6.1 Concurrent computability and the universality hierarchy of synchronization operations.

practical techniques for implementing wait-free objects. Like classical computability theory, understanding the universal construction and its implications will allow us to avoid the naïve mistake of trying to solve unsolvable problems. Once we understand *why* consensus is powerful enough to implement any kind of object, we will be better prepared to undertake the engineering effort needed to make such constructions efficient.

6.2 Universality

A class C is *universal* if one can construct a wait-free implementation of any object from some number of objects of C and some number of read–write registers. Our construction uses multiple objects of class C because we are ultimately interested in understanding the synchronization power of machine instructions, and most machines allow their instructions to be applied to multiple memory locations. We allow an implementation to use multiple read–write registers because it is convenient for bookkeeping, and memory is usually in plentiful supply on modern architectures. To avoid distraction, we use an unlimited number of read–write registers and consensus objects, leaving the question of recycling memory as an exercise. We begin by presenting a lock-free implementation, later extending it to a slightly more complex wait-free one.

6.3 A Lock-Free Universal Construction

Fig. 6.2 shows a *generic* definition for a sequential object, based on the invocation–response formulation of Chapter 3. Each object is created in a fixed initial

2 See Appendix B for details.

```java
public interface SeqObject {
  public abstract Response apply(Invoc invoc);
}
```

Figure 6.2 A Generic sequential object: the `apply()` method applies the invocation and returns a response.

```java
public class Node {
  public Invoc invoc;                  // method name and args
  public Consensus<Node> decideNext;   // decide next Node in list
  public Node next;                    // the next node
  public int seq;                      // sequence number
  public Node(Invoc invoc) {
    invoc = invoc;
    decideNext = new Consensus<Node>()
    seq = 0;
  }
  public static Node max(Node[] array) {
    Node max = array[0];
    for (int i = 1; i < array.length; i++)
      if (max.seq < array[i].seq)
        max = array[i];
    return max;
  }
}
```

Figure 6.3 The Node class.

state. The `apply()` method takes as argument an *invocation* which describes the method being called and its arguments, and returns a *response*, containing the call's termination condition (normal or exceptional) and the return value, if any. For example, a stack invocation might be `push()` with an argument, and the corresponding response would be normal and *void.*

Figs. 6.3 and 6.4 show a universal construction that transforms any sequential object into a lock-free linearizable concurrent object. This construction assumes that sequential objects are *deterministic*: if we apply a method to an object in a particular state, then there is only one possible response, and one possible new object state. We can represent any object as a combination of a sequential object in its initial state and a *log*: a linked list of nodes representing the sequence of method calls applied to the object (and hence the object's sequence of state transitions). A thread executes a method call by adding the new call to the head of the list. It then traverses the list, from tail to head, applying the method calls to a private copy of the object. The thread finally returns the result of applying its own operation. It is important to understand that only the head of the log is mutable: the initial state and nodes preceding the head never change.

How do we make this log-based construction concurrent, that is, allow threads to make concurrent calls to `apply()`? A thread attempting to call `apply()` creates a node to hold its invocation. The threads then compete to append their

```
public class LFUniversal {
  private Node[] head;
  private Node tail;
  public Universal() {
    tail = new Node();
    tail.seq = 1;
    for (int i = 0; i < n; i++)
      head[i] = tail
  }
  public Response apply(Invoc invoc) {
    int i = ThreadID.get();
    Node prefer = new Node(invoc);
    while (prefer.seq == 0) {
      Node before = Node.max(head);
      Node after = before.decideNext.decide(prefer);
      before.next = after;
      after.seq = before.seq + 1;
      head[i] = after;
    }
    SeqObject myObject = new SeqObject();
    Node current = tail.next;
    while (current != prefer){
      myObject.apply(current.invoc);
      current = current.next;
    }
    return myObject.apply(current.invoc);
  }
}
```

Figure 6.4 The lock-free universal algorithm.

respective nodes to the head of the log by running an n-thread consensus protocol to agree which node was appended to the log. The inputs to this consensus are references to the threads' nodes, and the result is the unique winning node.

The winner can then proceed to compute its response. It does so by creating a local copy of the sequential object and traversing the log, following `next` references from tail to head, applying the operations in the log to its copy, finally returning the response associated with its own invocation. This algorithm works even when `apply()` calls are concurrent, because the prefix of the log up to the thread's own node never changes. The losing threads, which were not chosen by the consensus object, must try again to set the node currently at the head of the log (which changes between attempts) to point to them.

We now consider this construction in detail. The code for the lock-free universal construction appears in Fig. 6.4. A sample execution appears in Fig. 6.5. The object state is defined by a linked list of nodes, each one containing an invocation. The code for a node appears in Fig. 6.3. The node's `decideNext` field is a consensus object used to decide which node is appended next in the list, and `next` is the field in which the outcome of that consensus, the reference to the next node, is recorded. The `seq` field is the node's sequence number in the list. This field is zero while the node is not yet threaded onto the list, and positive otherwise. Sequence

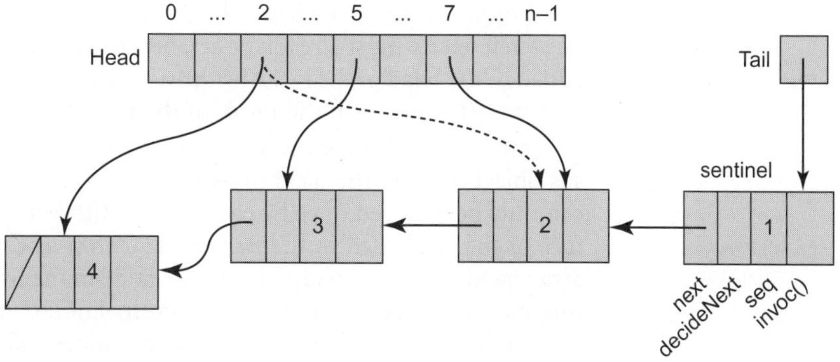

Figure 6.5 Execution of the lock-free universal construction. Thread 2 appends the second node in the log winning consensus on `decideNext` in the sentinel node. It then sets the node's sequence number from 0 to 2, and refers to it from its entry in the `head[]` array. Thread 7 loses the `decideNext` consensus at the sentinel node, sets the `next` reference and sequence number of the decided successor node to 2 (they were already set to the same values by thread 2), and refers to the node from its entry in the `head[]` array. Thread 5 appends the third node, updates its sequence number to 3 and updates its entry in the `head[]` array to this node. Finally, thread 2 appends the fourth node, sets its sequence number to 4, and refers to it from its entry in the `head[]` array. The maximal value in the head array keeps track of the head of the log.

numbers for successive nodes in the list increase by one. Initially, the log consists of a unique sentinel node with sequence number 1.

The hard part about designing the concurrent lock-free universal construction is that consensus objects can be used only once.[3]

In our lock-free algorithm in Fig. 6.4, each thread allocates a node holding its invocation, and repeatedly tries to append that node to the head of the log. Each node has a `decideNext` field, which is a consensus object. A thread tries to append its node by proposing as input to a consensus protocol on the head's `decideNext` field. Because threads that do not participate in this consensus may need to traverse the list, the result of this consensus is stored in the node's `next` field. Multiple threads may update this field simultaneously, but they all write the same value. When the thread's node is appended, it sets the node's sequence number.

Once a thread's node is part of the log, it computes the response to its invocation by traversing the log from the tail to the newly added node. It applies each of the invocations to a private copy of the object, and returns the response from its own

---

3 Creating a reusable consensus object, or even one whose decision is readable, is not a simple task. It is essentially the same problem as the universal construction we are about to design. For example, consider the queue-based consensus protocol in Chapter 5. It is not obvious how to use a `Queue` to allow repeated reading of the consensus object state after it is decided.

invocation. Notice that when a thread computes its response, all its predecessors' `next` references must already be set, because these nodes have already have been added to the head of the list. Any thread that added a node to the list has updated its `next` reference with the result of the `decideNext` consensus.

How do we locate the head of the log? We cannot track the head with a consensus object because the head must be updated repeatedly, and consensus objects can only be accessed once by each thread. Instead, we create a per-thread structure of the kind used in the Bakery algorithm of Chapter 2. We use an n-entry array `head[]`, where `head[`i`]` is the last node in the list that thread i has observed. Initially all entries refer to the `tail` sentinel node. The head is the node with the maximum sequence number among the nodes referenced in the `head[]` array. The `max()` method in Fig. 6.3 performs a collect, reading the `head[]` entries and returning the node with the highest sequence number.

The construction is a linearizable implementation of the sequential object. Each `apply()` call can be linearized at the point of the consensus call adding the node to the log.

Why is this construction lock-free? The head of the log, the latest node appended, is added to the `head[]` array within a finite number of steps. The node's predecessor must appear in the head array, so any node repeatedly attempting to add a new node will repeatedly run the `max()` function on the head array. It detects this predecessor, applies consensus on its `decideNext` field, and then updates the winning node's fields, and including its sequence number. Finally, it stores the decided node in that thread's head array entry. The new head node always eventually appears in `head[]`. It follows that the only way a thread can repeatedly fail to add its own node to the log is if other threads repeatedly succeed in appending their own nodes to the log. Thus, a node can starve only if other nodes are continually completing their invocations, implying that the construction is lock-free.

6.4 A Wait-Free Universal Construction

How do we make a lock-free algorithm wait-free? The full wait-free algorithm appears in Fig. 6.6. We must guarantee that every thread completes an `apply()` call within a finite number of steps, that is, no thread starves. To guarantee this property, threads making progress must help less fortunate threads to complete their calls. This *helping* pattern will show up later in a specialized form in other wait-free algorithms.

To allow helping, each thread must share with other threads the `apply()` call that it is trying to complete. We add an n-element `announce[]` array, where `announce[`i`]` is the node thread i is currently trying to append to the list. Initially, all entries refer to the sentinel node, which has a sequence number 1. A thread i *announces* a node when it stores the node in `announce[`i`]`.

To execute `apply()`, a thread first announces its new node. This step ensures that if the thread itself does not succeed in appending its node onto the list,

```
1  public class Universal {
2    private Node[] announce; // array added to coordinate helping
3    private Node[] head;
4    private Node tail = new node(); tail.seq = 1;
5    for (int j=0; j < n; j++){head[j] = tail; announce[j] = tail};
6    public Response apply(Invoc invoc) {
7      int i = ThreadID.get();
8      announce[i] = new Node(invoc);
9      head[i] = Node.max(head);
10     while (announce[i].seq == 0) {
11       Node before = head[i];
12       Node help = announce[(before.seq + 1) % n];
13       if (help.seq == 0)
14         prefer = help;
15       else
16         prefer = announce[i];
17       Node after = before.decideNext.decide(prefer);
18       before.next = after;
19       after.seq = before.seq + 1;
20       head[i] = after;
21     }
22     SeqObject MyObject = new SeqObject();
23     Node current = tail.next;
24     while (current != announce[i]){
25       MyObject.apply(current.invoc);
26       current = current.next;
27     }
28    head[i] = announce[i];
29    return MyObject.apply(current.invoc);
30   }
31 }
```

Figure 6.6 The wait-free universal algorithm.

some other thread will append that node on its behalf. It then proceeds as before, attempting to append the node into the log. To do so, it reads the head[] array only once (Line 9), and then enters the main loop of the algorithm, which it executes until its own node has been threaded onto the list (detected when its sequence number becomes non zero in Line 10). Here is a change from the lock-free algorithm. A thread first checks to see if there is a node that needs help ahead of it in the announce[] array (Line 12). The node to be helped must be determined dynamically because nodes are continually added to the log. A thread attempts to help nodes in the announce[] array in increasing order, determined by the sequence number modulo the width n of the announce[] array. We will prove that this approach guarantees that any node that does not make progress on its own will eventually be helped by others once its owner thread's index matches the maximal sequence number modulo n. If this helping step were omitted, then an individual thread could be overtaken an arbitrary number of times. If the node selected for help does not require help (its sequence number is non zero in Line 13), then each thread attempts to append its own node (Line 16).

(All `announce[]` array entries are initialized to the sentinel node which has a non zero sequence number.) The rest of the algorithm is almost the same as in the lock-free algorithm. A node is appended when its sequence number becomes non zero. In this case, the thread proceeds as before to compute its result based on the immutable segment of the log from the tail to its own node.

Fig. 6.7 shows an execution of the wait-free universal construction in which, starting from the initial state, thread 5 announces its new node and appends it to the log, and pauses before adding the node to `head[]`. Thread 7 then takes steps. The value of (`before.seq` + 1) mod n is 3, so thread 7 tries to help thread 2. Thread 7 loses the consensus on the sentinel node's `decideNext` reference since thread 5 already won it, and thus completes the operations of thread 5, setting the node's sequence number to 2 and adding thread 5's node to the `head[]` array. Now imagine that thread 3 immediately announces

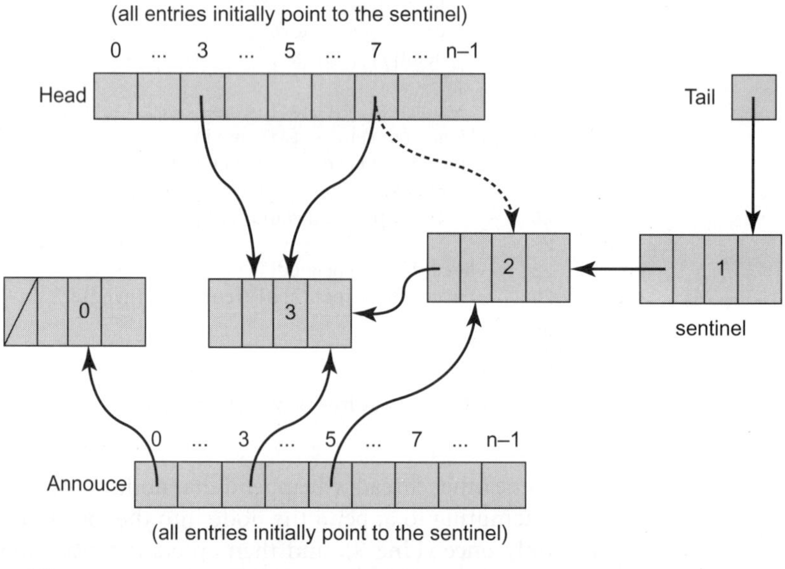

Figure 6.7 Execution of the wait-free universal construction. Thread 5 announces its new node and appends it to the log, but halts before adding the node to the `head[]` array. Another thread 7 will not see thread 5's node in the `head[]` array, and will attempt to help thread (`before.seq + 1 mod n`), which is equal to 3. When attempting to help thread 3, thread 7 loses the consensus on the sentinel node's `decideNext` reference since thread 5 already won. Thread 7 therefore completes updating the fields of thread 5's node, setting the node's sequence number to 2, and adding the node to the `head[]` array. Notice that thread 5's own entry in the `head[]` array is not yet set to its announced node. Next, thread 2 announces its node and thread 7 succeeds in appending thread 3's node, setting thread 3's node's sequence number to 3. Now thread 3 wakes up. It will not enter the main loop because its node's sequence number is non zero, but will continue to update the `head[]` array and compute its output value using a copy of the sequential object.

its node. Then thread 7 succeeds in appending thread 3's node, but again pauses immediately after setting thread 3's node's sequence number to 3, but before adding it to `head[]`. Now thread 3 wakes up. It will not enter the main loop because its node's sequence number is non zero, but will continue to update `head[]` at Line 28 and compute its output value using a copy of the sequential object.

There is a delicate point to understand about these modifications to the lock-free algorithm. Since more than one thread can attempt to append a particular node to the log, we must make sure that no node is appended twice. One thread might append the node, and set the node's sequence number, at the same time that another thread appended the same node and set its sequence number. The algorithm avoids this error because of the order in which threads read the maximum `head[]` array value and the sequence number of a node in the `announce[]` array. Let a be a node created by thread A and appended by threads A and B. It must be added at least once to `head[]` before the second append. Notice, however, that the `before` node read from `head[`A`]` by B (Line 11) must be a itself, or a successor of a in the log. Moreover, before any node is added to `head[]` (either in Line 20 or in Line 28), its sequence number is made non zero (Line 19). The order of operations ensures that B sets its `head[`B`]` entry (the entry based on which B's `before` variable will be set, resulting in an erroneous append) in Lines 9 or 20, and only then validates that the sequence number of a is non zero in Lines 10 or 13 (depending whether A or another thread performs the operation). It follows that the validation of the erroneous second append will fail because the sequence number of node a will already be non zero, and it will not be added to the log a second time.

Linearizability follows because no node is ever added twice, and the order in which nodes are appended to the log is clearly compatible with the natural partial order of the corresponding method calls.

To prove that the algorithm is wait-free, we need to show that the helping mechanism will guarantee that any node that is announced is eventually added to the `head[]` array (implying that it is in the log) and the announcing thread can complete computation of its outcome. To assist in the proof, it is convenient to define some notation. Let max(`head[]`) be the node with the largest sequence number in the `head[]` array, and let "c ∈`head[]`" denote the assertion that node c has been assigned to `head[`i`]`, for some i.

An *auxiliary* variable (sometimes called a *ghost* variable) is one that does not appear explicitly in the code, does not alter the program's behavior in any way, yet helps us reason about the behavior of the algorithm. We use the following auxiliary variables:

- *concur*(A) is the set of nodes that have been stored in the `head[]` array since thread A's last announcement.
- *start*(A) is the sequence number of max(`head[]`) when thread A last announced.

The code reflecting the auxiliary variables and how they are updated appears in Fig. 6.8. For example, the statement

$$(\forall j) concur(j) = concur(j) \cup after$$

means that the node *after* is added to $concur(j)$ for all threads j. The code statements within the angled brackets are considered to be executed atomically. This atomicity can be assumed because auxiliary variables do not affect the computation in any way. For brevity let us slightly abuse the notation by letting the function max() applied to a node or array of nodes return the maximal among their sequence numbers.

Notice that the following property is invariant throughout the execution of the universal algorithm:

$$|concur(A)| + start(A) = \max(\texttt{head[]}). \tag{6.4.1}$$

```
public class Universal {
  private Node[] announce;
  private Node[] head;
  private Node tail = new node(); tail.seq = 1;
  for (int j=0; j < n; j++){head[j] = tail; announce[j] = tail};
  public Response apply(Invoc invoc) {
    int i = ThreadID.get();
    <announce[i] = new Node(invoc); start(i) = max(head);>
    head[i] = Node.max(head);
    while (announce[i].seq == 0) {
      Node before = head[i];
      Node help =  announce[(before.seq + 1) % n];
      if (help.seq == 0)
        prefer = help;
      else
        prefer = announce[i];
      Node after = before.decideNext.decide(prefer);
      before.next = after;
      after.seq = before.seq + 1;
      <head[i] = after; (∀j) (concur(j) = concur(j)∪{after})>
    }
    SeqObject MyObject = new SeqObject();
    Node current = tail.next;
    while (current != announce[i]){
      MyObject.apply(current.invoc);
      current = current.next;
    }
   <head[i] = announce[i]; (∀j) (concur(j) = concur(j)∪{after})>
   return MyObject.apply(current.invoc);
  }
}
```

Figure 6.8 The wait-free universal algorithm with auxiliary variables. Operations in angled brackets are assumed to happen atomically.

Lemma 6.4.1. For all threads A, the following claim is always true:

$$|concur(A)| > n \Rightarrow \texttt{announce}[A] \in \texttt{head}[].$$

Proof: If $|concur(A)| > n$, then $concur(A)$ includes successive nodes b and c (appended to the log by threads B and C) whose respective sequence numbers plus one modulo n are equal to $A - 1$ and A (note that b and c are the nodes thread B and C added to the log, not necessarily the ones they announced). Thread C will, based on the code of Lines 12 through 16, append to the log a node located in A's entry in the announce[] array. We need to show that when it does so, announce[A] was already announced, so c appends announce[A], or announce[A] was already appended. Later, when c is added to head[] and $|concur(A)| > n$, announce[A] will be in head[] as the Lemma requires.

To see why announce[A] was already announced when C reached Lines 12 through 16, notice that (1) because C appended its node c to b, it must have read b as the *before* node in Line 11, implying that B appended b before it was read from head[] by C in Line 11, and (2) because b is in $concur(A)$, A announced before b was added to head[]. From (1) and (2) by transitivity it follows that A announced before C executed Lines 12 through 16, and the claim follows. □

Lemma 6.4.1 places a bound on the number of nodes that can be appended while a method call is in progress. We now give a sequence of lemmas showing that when A finishes scanning the head[] array, either announce[A] is appended, or head[A] lies within $n + 1$ nodes of the end of the list.

Lemma 6.4.2. The following property always holds:

$$\max(\texttt{head}[]) \geqslant start(A).$$

Proof: The sequence number for each head[i] is nondecreasing. □

Lemma 6.4.3. The following is a loop invariant for Line 13 of Fig. 6.3 (i.e., it holds during each iteration of the loop):

$$\max(\texttt{head}[A], \texttt{head}[j], \ldots, \texttt{head}[n] - 1) \geqslant start(A).$$

where j is the loop index.

In other words, the maximum sequence number of head[A] and all head[] entries from the current value of j to the end of the loop never become smaller than the maximum value in the array when A announced.

Proof: When j is 0, the assertion is implied by Lemma 6.4.2. The truth of the assertion is preserved at each iteration, when head[A] is replaced by the node with the sequence number max(head[A], head[j]). □

Lemma 6.4.4. The following assertion holds just before Line 10:

$$\texttt{head}[A].seq \geqslant start(A).$$

Proof: Notice that head$[A]$ is set to point to A's last appended node either in Line 20 or Line 28. Thus, after the call to *Node.max*() at Line 9, max(head$[A]$, head$[0]$,...,head$[n-1]$) is just head$[A]$.seq, and the result follows from Lemma 6.4.3. □

Lemma 6.4.5. The following property always holds:

$$|concur(A)| \geqslant \texttt{head}[A].seq - start(A) \geqslant 0.$$

Proof: The lower bound follows from Lemma 6.4.4, and the upper bound follows from Eq. 6.4.1. □

***Theorem* 6.4.1.** The algorithm in Fig. 6.6 is correct and wait-free.

Proof: To see that the algorithm is wait-free, notice that A can execute the main loop no more than $n+1$ times. At each successful iteration, head$[A]$. *seq* increases by one. After $n+1$ iterations, Lemma 6.4.5 implies that

$$|concur(A)| \geqslant \texttt{head}[A].seq - start(A) \geqslant n.$$

Lemma 6.4.1 implies that announce$[A]$ must have been added to head[]. □

6.5 Chapter Notes

The universal construction described here is adapted from Maurice Herlihy's 1991 paper [62]. An alternative lock-free universal construction using *load-linked–store-conditional* appears in [60]. The complexity of this construction can be improved in several ways. Yehuda Afek, Dalia Dauber, and Dan Touitou [3] show how to improve the time complexity to depend on the number of concurrent threads, not the maximum possible number of threads. Mark Moir [118] shows how to design lock-free and wait-free constructions that do not require copying the entire object. James Anderson and Mark Moir [11] extend the construction to allow multiple objects to be updated. Prasad Jayanti [80] shows that any universal construction has worst-case $\Omega(n)$ complexity, where n is the maximal number of threads. Tushar Chandra, Prasad Jayanti, and King Tan [26] identify a large class of objects for which a more efficient universal construction exists.

6.6 Exercises

Exercise 76. Give an example showing how the universal construction can fail for objects with nondeterministic sequential specifications.

Exercise 77. Propose a way to fix the universal construction of Figure 6.8 to work for objects with nondeterministic sequential specifications.

Exercise 78. In both the lock-free and wait-free universal constructions, the sequence number of the sentinel node at the `tail` of the list is initially set to 1. Which of these algorithms, if any, would cease to work correctly if the sentinel node's sequence number was initially set to 0?

Exercise 79. Suppose, instead of a universal construction, you simply want to use consensus to implement a wait-free linearizable register with `read()` and `compareAndSet()` methods. Show how you would adapt this algorithm to do so.

Exercise 80. In the construction shown here, each thread first looks for another thread to help, and then tries to to append its own node.

Suppose instead, each thread first tries to append its own node, and then tries to help the other thread. Explain whether this alternative approach works. Justify your answer.

Exercise 81. In the construction in Fig. 6.4 we use a "distributed" implementation of a "head" reference (to the node whose `decideNext` field it will try to modify) to avoid having to create an object that allows repeated consensus. Replace this implementation with one that has no head reference at all, and finds the next "head" by traversing down the log from the start until it reaches a node with a sequence number of 0 or with the highest non zero sequence.

Exercise 82. A small addition we made to the wait-free protocol was to have a thread add its newly appended node to the *head* array in Line 28 even though it may have already added it in Line 20. This is necessary because, unlike in the lock-free protocol, it could be that the thread's node was added by another thread in Line 20, and that "helping" thread stopped at Line 20 right after updating the node's sequence number but before updating the *head* array.

1. Explain how removing Line 28 would violate Lemma 6.4.4.
2. Would the algorithm still work correctly?

Exercise 83. Propose a way to fix the universal construction to work with a bounded amount of memory, that is, a bounded number of consensus objects and a bounded number of read–write registers.

Hint: add a `before` field to the nodes and build a memory recycling scheme into the code.

Exercise 84. Implement a consensus object that is accessed more than once by each thread using `read()` and `compareAndSet()` methods, creating a "multiple access" consensus object. Do not use the universal construction.

II Practice

7 Spin Locks and Contention

When writing programs for uniprocessors, it is usually safe to ignore the underlying system's architectural details. Unfortunately, multiprocessor programming has yet to reach that state, and for the time being, it is crucial to understand the underlying machine architecture. The goal of this chapter is to understand how architecture affects performance, and how to exploit this knowledge to write efficient concurrent programs. We revisit the familiar mutual exclusion problem, this time with the aim of devising mutual exclusion protocols that work well with today's multiprocessors.

Any mutual exclusion protocol poses the question: what do you do if you cannot acquire the lock? There are two alternatives. If you keep trying, the lock is called a *spin lock*, and repeatedly testing the lock is called *spinning*, or *busy–waiting*. The `Filter` and `Bakery` algorithms are spin locks. Spinning is sensible when you expect the lock delay to be short. For obvious reasons, spinning makes sense only on multiprocessors. The alternative is to suspend yourself and ask the operating system's scheduler to schedule another thread on your processor, which is sometimes called *blocking*. Because switching from one thread to another is expensive, blocking makes sense only if you expect the lock delay to be long. Many operating systems mix both strategies, spinning for a short time and then blocking. Both spinning and blocking are important techniques. In this chapter, we turn our attention to locks that use spinning.

7.1 Welcome to the Real World

We approach real-world mutual exclusion using the `Lock` interface from the java.util.concurrent.locks package. For now, we consider only the two principal methods: `lock()` and `unlock()`. In most cases, these methods should be used in the following structured way:

```
1  Lock mutex = new LockImpl(...); // lock implementation
2  ...
3  mutex.lock();
4  try {
5    ...            // body
6    } finally {
7      mutex.unlock();
8    }
```

We create a new `Lock` object called `mutex` (Line 1). Because `Lock` is an interface and not a class, we cannot create `Lock` objects directly. Instead, we create an object that *implements* the `Lock` interface. (The java.util.concurrent.locks package includes a number of classes that implement `Lock`, and we provide others in this chapter.) Next, we acquire the lock (Line 3), and enter the critical section, a **`try`** block (Line 4). The **`finally`** block (Line 6) ensures that no matter what, the lock is released when control leaves the critical section. Do not put the `lock()` call inside the **`try`** block, because the `lock()` call might throw an exception before acquiring the lock, causing the **`finally`** block to call `unlock()` when the lock has not actually been acquired.

If we want to implement an efficient `Lock`, why not use one of the algorithms we studied in Chapter 2, such as `Filter` or `Bakery`? One problem with this approach is clear from the space lower bound we proved in Chapter 2: no matter what we do, mutual exclusion using `reads` and `writes` requires space linear in n, the number of threads that may potentially access the location. It gets worse.

Consider, for example, the 2-thread `Peterson` lock algorithm of Chapter 2, presented again in Fig. 7.1. There are two threads, A and B, with IDs either 0 or 1. When thread A wants to acquire the lock, it sets `flag`$[A]$ to *true*, sets `victim` to A, and tests `victim` and `flag`$[1-A]$. As long as the test fails, the thread spins, repeating the test. Once it succeeds, it enters the critical section, lowering `flag`$[A]$ to *false* as it leaves. We know, from Chapter 2, that the `Peterson` lock provides starvation-free mutual exclusion.

```
1  class Peterson implements Lock {
2    private boolean[] flag = new boolean[2];
3    private int victim;
4    public void lock() {
5      int i = ThreadID.get(); // either 0 or 1
6      int j = 1-i;
7      flag[i] = true;
8      victim = i;
9      while (flag[j] && victim == i) {}; // spin
10   }
11 }
```

Figure 7.1 The `Peterson` class (Chapter 2): the order of reads–writes in Lines 7, 8, and 9 is crucial to providing mutual exclusion.

Suppose we write a simple concurrent program in which each of the two threads repeatedly acquires the `Peterson` lock, increments a shared counter, and then releases the lock. We run it on a multiprocessor, where each thread executes this acquire–increment–release cycle, say, half a million times. On most modern architectures, the threads finish quickly. Alarmingly, however, we may discover that the counter's final value may be slightly off from the expected million mark. Proportionally, the error is probably tiny, but why is there any error at all? Somehow, it must be that both threads are occasionally in the critical section at the same time, even though we have proved that this cannot happen. To quote Sherlock Holmes

> How often have I said to you that when you have eliminated the impossible, whatever remains, however improbable, must be the truth?

It must be that our proof fails, not because there is anything wrong with our logic, but because our assumptions about the real world are mistaken.

When programming our multiprocessor, we naturally assumed that read–write operations are atomic, that is, they are linearizable to some sequential execution, or at the very least, that they are sequentially consistent. (Recall that linearizability implies sequential consistency.) As we saw in Chapter 3, sequential consistency implies that there is some global order on all operations in which each thread's operations take effect as ordered by its program. Without calling attention to it at the time, we relied on the assumption that memory is sequentially consistent when proving the `Peterson` lock correct. In particular, mutual exclusion depends on the order of the steps in Lines 7, 8, and 9 of Fig. 7.1. Our proof that the `Peterson` lock provided mutual exclusion implicitly relied on the assumption that any two memory accesses by the same thread, even to separate variables, take effect in program order. (Specifically, it was crucial that *B*'s write to `flag[`*B*`]` take effect before its write to `victim` (Eq. 2.3.9) and that *A*'s write to `victim` take effect before its read of `flag[`*B*`]` (Eq. 2.3.11).)

Unfortunately, modern multiprocessors typically do not provide sequentially consistent memory, nor do they necessarily guarantee program order among reads–writes by a given thread.

Why not? The first culprits are compilers that reorder instructions to enhance performance. Most programming languages preserve program order for each individual variable, but not across multiple variables. It is therefore possible that the order of writes of `flag[`*B*`]` and `victim` by thread *B* will be reversed by the compiler, invalidating Eq. 2.3.9. A second culprit is the multiprocessor hardware itself. (Appendix B has a much more complete discussion of the multiprocessor architecture issues raised in this chapter.) Hardware vendors make no secret of the fact that writes to multiprocessor memory do not necessarily take effect when they are issued, because in most programs the vast majority of writes do not *need* to take effect in shared memory right away. Thus, on many multiprocessor architectures, writes to shared memory are buffered in a special *write buffer* (sometimes called a *store buffer*), to be written to memory only when needed. If thread *A*'s write to `victim` is delayed in a write buffer, it may arrive in memory only after *A* reads `flag[`*B*`]`, invalidating Eq. 2.3.11.

How then does one program multiprocessors given such weak memory consistency guarantees? To prevent the reordering of operations resulting from write buffering, modern architectures provide a special *memory barrier* instruction (sometimes called a *memory fence*) that forces outstanding operations to take effect. It is the programmer's responsibility to know where to insert a memory barrier (e.g., the `Peterson` lock can be fixed by placing a barrier right before each read). Not surprisingly, memory barriers are expensive, about as expensive as an atomic `compareAndSet()` instruction, so we want to minimize their use. In fact, *synchronization instructions* such as `getAndSet()` or `compareAndSet()` described in earlier chapters include a memory barrier on many architectures, as do `reads` and `writes` to **`volatile`** fields.

Given that barriers cost about as much as synchronization instructions, it may be sensible to design mutual exclusion algorithms directly to use operations such as `getAndSet()` or `compareAndSet()`. These operations have higher consensus numbers than `reads` and `writes`, and they can be used in a straightforward way to reach a kind of consensus on who can and cannot enter the critical section.

7.2 Test-And-Set Locks

The `testAndSet()` operation, with consensus number two, was the principal synchronization instruction provided by many early multiprocessor architectures. This instruction operates on a single memory word (or byte). That word holds a binary value, *true* or *false*. The `testAndSet()` instruction atomically stores *true* in the word, and returns that word's previous value, *swapping* the value *true* for the word's current value. At first glance, this instruction seems ideal for implementing a spin lock. The lock is free when the word's value is *false*, and busy when it is *true*. The `lock()` method repeatedly applies `testAndSet()` to the location until that instruction returns *false* (i.e., until the lock is free). The `unlock()` method simply writes the value *false* to it.

The **java.util.concurrent** package includes an `AtomicBoolean` class that stores a Boolean value. It provides a `set(`*b*`)` method to replace the stored value with value *b*, and a `getAndSet(`*b*`)` that atomically replaces the current value with *b*, and returns the previous value. The archaic `testAndSet()` instruction is the same as a call to `getAndSet(`*true*`)`. We use the term *test-and-set* in prose to remain compatible with common usage, but we use the expression `getAndSet(`*true*`)` in our code examples to remain compatible with Java. The `TASLock` class shown in Fig. 7.2 shows a lock algorithm based on the `testAndSet()` instruction.

Now consider the alternative to the `TASLock` algorithm illustrated in Fig. 7.3. Instead of performing the `testAndSet()` directly, the thread repeatedly reads the lock until it appears to be free (i.e., until `get()` returns *false*). Only after the lock appears to be free does the thread apply `testAndSet()`. This technique is called *test-and-test-and-set* and the lock a `TTASLock`.

```java
public class TASLock implements Lock {
  AtomicBoolean state = new AtomicBoolean(false);
  public void lock() {
    while (state.getAndSet(true)) {}
  }
  public void unlock() {
    state.set(false);
  }
}
```

Figure 7.2 The TASLock class.

```java
public class TTASLock implements Lock {
  AtomicBoolean state = new AtomicBoolean(false);
  public void lock() {
    while (true) {
      while (state.get()) {};
      if (!state.getAndSet(true))
        return;
    }
  }
  public void unlock() {
    state.set(false);
  }
}
```

Figure 7.3 The TTASLock class.

Clearly, the TASLock and TTASLock algorithms are equivalent from the point of view of correctness: each one guarantees deadlock-free mutual exclusion. Under the simple model we have been using so far, there should be no difference between these two algorithms.

How do they compare on a real multiprocessor? Experiments that measure the elapsed time for n threads to execute a short critical section invariably yield the results shown schematically in Fig. 7.4. Each data point represents the same amount of work, so in the absence of contention effects, all curves would be flat. The top curve is the TASLock, the middle curve is the TTASLock, and the bottom curve shows the time that would be needed if the threads did not interfere at all. The difference is dramatic: the TASLock performs very poorly, and the TTASLock performance, while substantially better, still falls far short of the ideal.

These differences can be explained in terms of modern multiprocessor architectures. First, a word of caution. Modern multiprocessors encompass a variety of architectures, so we must be careful about overgeneralizing. Nevertheless, (almost) all modern architectures have similar issues concerning caching and locality. The details differ, but the principles remain the same.

For simplicity, we consider a typical multiprocessor architecture in which processors communicate by a shared broadcast medium called a *bus* (like a tiny Ethernet). Both the processors and the memory controller can broadcast on the bus,

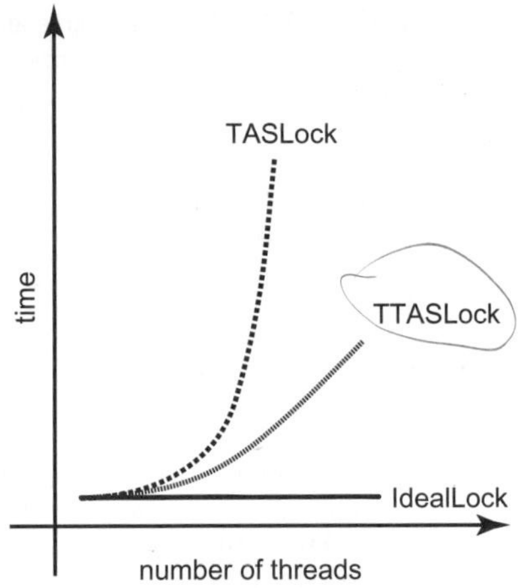

Figure 7.4 Schematic performance of a TASLock, a TTASLock, and an ideal lock with no overhead.

but only one processor (or memory) can broadcast on the bus at a time. All processors (and memory) can listen. Today, bus-based architectures are common because they are easy to build, although they scale poorly to large numbers of processors.

Each processor has a *cache*, a small high-speed memory where the processor keeps data likely to be of interest. A memory access typically requires orders of magnitude more machine cycles than a cache access. Technology trends are not helping: it is unlikely that memory access times will catch up with processor cycle times in the near future, so cache performance is critical to the overall performance of a multiprocessor architecture.

When a processor reads from an address in memory, it first checks whether that address and its contents are present in its cache. If so, then the processor has a *cache hit*, and can load the value immediately. If not, then the processor has a *cache miss*, and must find the data either in the memory, or in another processor's cache. The processor then broadcasts the address on the bus. The other processors *snoop* on the bus. If one processor has that address in its cache, then it responds by broadcasting the address and value. If no processor has that address, then the memory itself responds with the value at that address.

7.3 TAS-Based Spin Locks Revisited

We now consider how the simple `TASLock` algorithm performs on a shared-bus architecture. Each `getAndSet()` call is broadcast on the bus. Because all threads must use the bus to communicate with memory, these `getAndSet()` calls delay all threads, even those not waiting for the lock. Even worse, the `getAndSet()` call forces other processors to discard their own cached copies of the lock, so every spinning thread encounters a cache miss almost every time, and must use the bus to fetch the new, but unchanged value. Adding insult to injury, when the thread holding the lock tries to release it, it may be delayed because the bus is monopolized by the spinners. We now understand why the `TASLock` performs so poorly.

Now consider the behavior of the `TTASLock` algorithm while the lock is held by a thread A. The first time thread B reads the lock it takes a cache miss, forcing B to block while the value is loaded into B's cache. As long as A holds the lock, B repeatedly rereads the value, but hits in the cache every time. B thus produces no bus traffic, and does not slow down other threads' memory accesses. Moreover, a thread that releases a lock is not delayed by threads spinning on that lock.

The situation deteriorates, however, when the lock is released. The lock holder releases the lock by writing *false* to the lock variable, which immediately invalidates the spinners' cached copies. Each one takes a cache miss, rereads the new value, and they all (more-or-less simultaneously) call `getAndSet()` to acquire the lock. The first to succeed invalidates the others, who must then reread the value, causing a storm of bus traffic. Eventually, the threads settle down once again to local spinning.

This notion of *local spinning*, where threads repeatedly reread cached values instead of repeatedly using the bus, is an important principle critical to the design of efficient spin locks.

7.4 Exponential Backoff

We now consider how to refine the `TTASLock` algorithm. First, some terminology: *contention* occurs when multiple threads try to acquire a lock at the same time. *High contention* means there are many such threads, and *low contention* means the opposite.

Recall that in the `TTASLock` class, the `lock()` method takes two steps: it repeatedly reads the lock, and when the lock appears to be free, it attempts to acquire the lock by calling `getAndSet(`*true*`)`. Here is a key observation: if some other thread acquires the lock between the first and second step, then, most likely, there is high contention for that lock. Clearly, it is a bad idea to try to acquire a lock for which there is high contention. Such an attempt contributes to bus traffic (making the traffic jam worse), at a time when the thread's chances of acquiring the lock are slim. Instead, it is more effective for the thread to *back off* for some duration, giving competing threads a chance to finish.

For how long should the thread back off before retrying? A good rule of thumb is that the larger the number of unsuccessful tries, the higher the likely contention, and the longer the thread should back off. Here is a simple approach. Whenever the thread sees the lock has become free but fails to acquire it, it backs off before retrying. To ensure that concurrent conflicting threads do not fall into lock-step, all trying to acquire the lock at the same time, the thread backs off for a random duration. Each time the thread tries and fails to get the lock, it doubles the expected back-off time, up to a fixed maximum.

Because backing off is common to several locking algorithms, we encapsulate this logic in a simple `Backoff` class, shown in Fig. 7.5. The constructor takes these arguments: `minDelay` is the initial minimum delay (it makes no sense for the thread to back off for too short a duration), and `maxDelay` is the final maximum delay (a final limit is necessary to prevent unlucky threads from backing off for much too long). The `limit` field controls the current delay limit. The `backoff()` method computes a random delay between zero and the current limit, and blocks the thread for that duration before returning. It doubles the limit for the next back-off, up to `maxDelay`.

Fig. 7.6 illustrates the `BackoffLock` class. It uses a `Backoff` object whose minimum and maximum back-off durations are governed by the constants chosen for `minDelay` and `maxDelay`. It is important to note that the thread backs off only when it fails to acquire a lock that it had immediately before observed to be free. Observing that the lock is held by another thread says nothing about the level of contention.

The `BackoffLock` is easy to implement, and typically performs significantly better than `TASLock` on many architectures. Unfortunately, its performance is sensitive to the choice of `minDelay` and `maxDelay` values. To deploy this lock on a particular architecture, it is easy to experiment with different values, and to choose the ones that work best. Experience shows, however, that these optimal values are sensitive to the number of processors and their speed, so it is not

```
public class Backoff {
  final int minDelay, maxDelay;
  int limit;
  final Random random;
  public Backoff(int min, int max) {
    minDelay = min;
    maxDelay = max;
    limit = minDelay;
    random = new Random();
  }
  public void backoff() throws InterruptedException {
    int delay = random.nextInt(limit);
    limit = Math.min(maxDelay, 2 * limit);
    Thread.sleep(delay);
  }
}
```

Figure 7.5 The `Backoff` class: adaptive backoff logic. To ensure that concurrently contending threads do not repeatedly try to acquire the lock at the same time, threads back off for a random duration. Each time the thread tries and fails to get the lock, it doubles the expected time to back off, up to a fixed maximum.

```java
public class BackoffLock implements Lock {
  private AtomicBoolean state = new AtomicBoolean(false);
  private static final int MIN_DELAY = ...;
  private static final int MAX_DELAY = ...;
  public void lock() {
    Backoff backoff = new Backoff(MIN_DELAY, MAX_DELAY);
    while (true) {
      while (state.get()) {};
      if (!state.getAndSet(true)) {
        return;
      } else {
        backoff.backoff();
      }
    }
  }
  public void unlock() {
    state.set(false);
  }
  ...
}
```

Figure 7.6 The Exponential Backoff lock. Whenever the thread fails to acquire a lock that became free, it backs off before retrying.

easy to tune the `BackoffLock` class to be portable across a range of different machines.

7.5 Queue Locks

We now explore a different approach to implementing scalable spin locks, one that is slightly more complicated than backoff locks, but inherently more portable. There are two problems with the `BackoffLock` algorithm.

- *Cache-coherence Traffic*: All threads spin on the same shared location causing cache-coherence traffic on every successful lock access (though less than with the `TASLock`).
- *Critical Section Underutilization*: Threads delay longer than necessary, causing the critical section to be underutilized.

One can overcome these drawbacks by having threads form a *queue*. In a queue, each thread can learn if its turn has arrived by checking whether its predecessor has finished. Cache-coherence traffic is reduced by having each thread spin on a different location. A queue also allows for better utilization of the critical section, since there is no need to guess when to attempt to access it: each thread is notified directly by its predecessor in the queue. Finally, a queue provides first-come-first-served fairness, the same high level of fairness achieved by the `Bakery` algorithm. We now explore different ways to implement *queue locks*, a family of locking algorithms that exploit these insights.

7.5.1 Array-Based Locks

Figs. 7.7 and 7.8 show the `ALock`,[1] a simple array-based queue lock. The threads share an `AtomicInteger tail` field, initially zero. To acquire the lock, each thread atomically increments `tail` (Line 17). Call the resulting value the thread's *slot*. The slot is used as an index into a Boolean `flag` array. If `flag`[j] is *true*, then the thread with slot j has permission to acquire the lock. Initially, `flag[0]` is *true*. To acquire the lock, a thread spins until the flag at its slot becomes *true* (Line 19). To release the lock, the thread sets the flag at its slot to *false* (Line 23), and sets the flag at the next slot to *true* (Line 24). All arithmetic is modulo n, where n is at least as large as the maximum number of concurrent threads.

In the `ALock` algorithm, `mySlotIndex` is a *thread-local* variable (see Appendix A). Thread-local variables differ from their regular counterparts in that each thread has its own, independently initialized copy of each variable. Thread-local variables need not be stored in shared memory, do not require synchronization, and

```
1  public class ALock implements Lock {
2    ThreadLocal<Integer> mySlotIndex = new ThreadLocal<Integer> (){
3      protected Integer initialValue() {
4        return 0;
5      }
6    };
7    AtomicInteger tail;
8    volatile boolean[] flag;
9    int size;
10   public ALock(int capacity) {
11     size = capacity;
12     tail = new AtomicInteger(0);
13     flag = new boolean[capacity];
14     flag[0] = true;
15   }
16   public void lock() {
17     int slot = tail.getAndIncrement() % size;
18     mySlotIndex.set(slot);
19     while (! flag[slot]) {};
20   }
21   public void unlock() {
22     int slot = mySlotIndex.get();
23     flag[slot] = false;
24     flag[(slot + 1) % size] = true;
25   }
26 }
```

Figure 7.7 Array-based Queue Lock.

1 Most of our lock classes use the initials of their inventors, as explained in Section 7.10.

do not generate any coherence traffic since they are accessed by only one thread. The value of a thread-local variable is accessed by `get()` and `set()` methods.

The `flag[]` array, on the other hand, is shared[2]. However, contention on the array locations is minimized since each thread, at any given time, spins on its locally cached copy of a single array location, greatly reducing invalidation traffic.

Note that contention may still occur because of a phenomenon called *false sharing*, which occurs when adjacent data items (such as array elements) share a single cache line. A write to one item invalidates that item's cache line, which causes invalidation traffic to processors that are spinning on unchanged but near items that happen to fall in the same cache line. In the example in Fig. 7.8, threads accessing the 8 `ALock` locations may suffer unnecessary invalidations because the locations were all cached in the same two 4-word lines. One way to avoid false sharing is to *pad* array elements so that distinct elements are mapped to distinct cache lines. Padding is easier in low-level languages like C or C++ where the programmer has a direct control over the layout of objects in memory. In the example in Fig. 7.8, we pad the eight original `ALock` locations by increasing the lock array size fourfold, and placing the locations four words apart so that no two locations can fall in the same cache line. (We increment from one location i to the next by computing $4(i + 1) \bmod 32$ instead of $i + 1 \bmod 8$).

7.5.2 The CLH Queue Lock

The `ALock` improves on `BackoffLock` because it reduces invalidations to a minimum, and minimizes the interval between when a lock is freed by one thread and when it is acquired by another. Unlike the `TASLock` and `BackoffLock`, this algorithm guarantees that no starvation occurs, and provides first-come-first-served fairness.

Unfortunately, the `ALock` lock is not space-efficient. It requires a known bound n on the maximum number of concurrent threads, and it allocates an array of that size per lock. Thus, synchronizing L distinct objects requires $O(Ln)$ space, even if a thread accesses only one lock at a time.

We now turn our attention to a different style of queue lock. Fig. 7.9 shows the `CLHLock` class's fields and constructor. This class records each thread's status in a `QNode` object, which has a Boolean `locked` field. If that field is *true*, then the corresponding thread has either acquired the lock, or is waiting for the lock. If that field is *false*, then the thread has released the lock. The lock itself is represented as a virtual linked list of `QNode` objects. We use the term "virtual" because the list is implicit: each thread refers to its predecessor through a thread-local `pred` variable. The public `tail` field is an `AtomicReference<QNode>` to the node most recently added to the queue.

As shown in Fig. 7.10, to acquire the lock, a thread sets the `locked` field of its `QNode` to *true*, indicating that the thread is not ready to release the lock. The thread

2 The role of a volatile statement here is not to introduce a memory barrier but rather to prevent the compiler from applying any optimizations to the loop in Line 19.

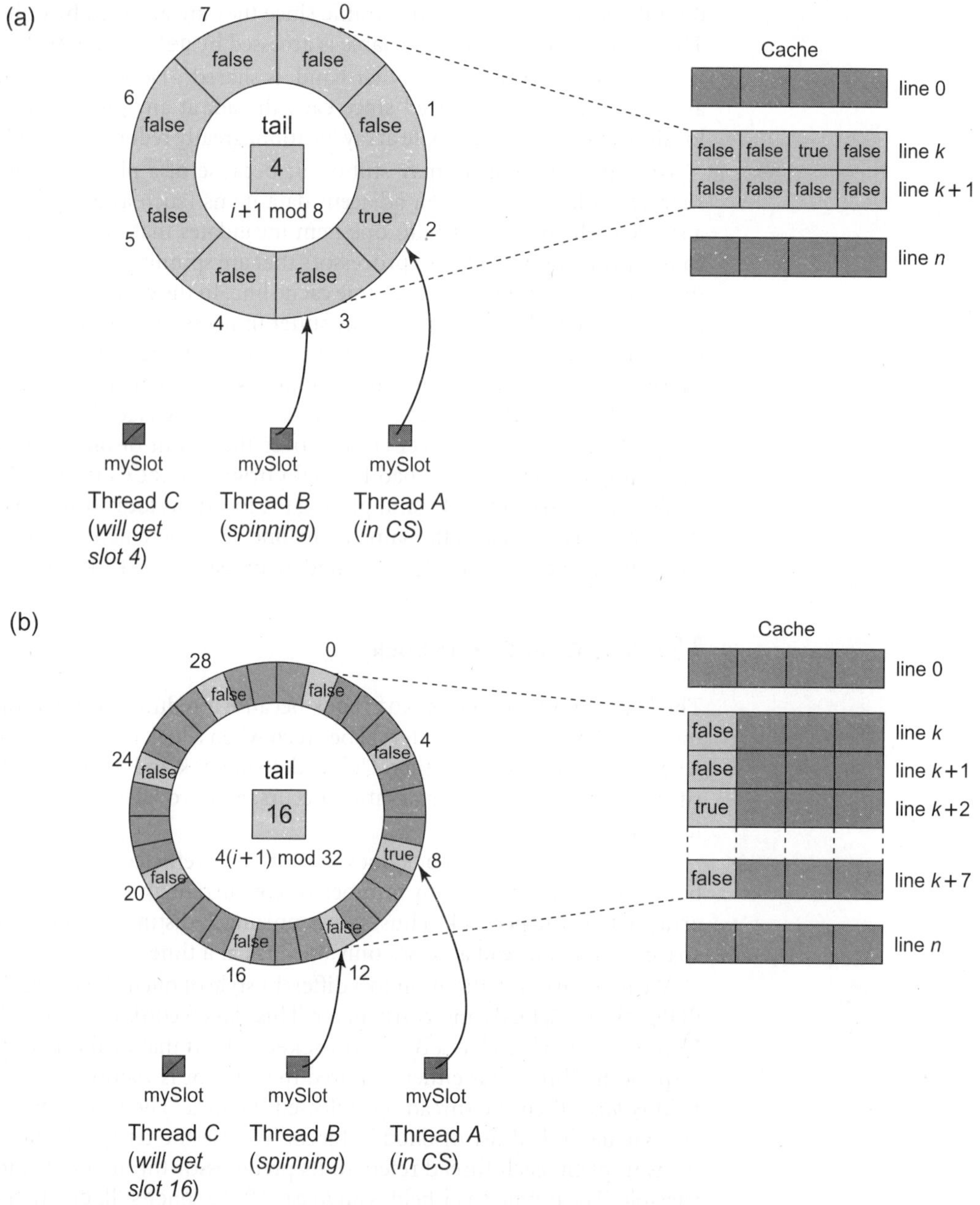

Figure 7.8 The ALock with padding to avoid false sharing. In Part (a) the ALock has 8 slots which are accessed via a modulo 8 counter. Array entries are typically mapped into cache lines consecutively. As can be seen, when thread *A* changes the status of its entry, thread *B* whose entry is mapped to the same cache line *k* incurs a false invalidation. In Part (b) each location is padded so it is 4 apart from the others with a modulo 32 counter. Even if array entries are mapped consecutively, the entry for *B* is mapped to a different cache line from that of *A*, so if *A* invalidates its entry this does not cause *B* to be invalidated.

```
public class CLHLock implements Lock {
  AtomicReference<Qnode> tail;
  ThreadLocal<QNode> myPred;
  ThreadLocal<QNode> myNode;
  public CLHLock() {
  tail = new AtomicReference<QNode>(null);
    myNode = new ThreadLocal<QNode>() {
      protected QNode initialValue() {
        return new QNode();
      }
    };
    myPred = new ThreadLocal<QNode>() {
      protected QNode initialValue() {
        return null;
      }
    };
  }
  ...
}
```

Figure 7.9 The CLHLock class: fields and constructor.

```
  public void lock() {
    QNode qnode = myNode.get();
    qnode.locked = true;
    QNode pred = tail.getAndSet(qnode);
    myPred.set(pred);
    while (pred.locked) {}
  }
  public void unlock() {
    QNode qnode = myNode.get();
    qnode.locked = false;
    myNode.set(myPred.get());
  }
}
```

Figure 7.10 The CLHLock class: lock() and unlock() methods.

applies getAndSet() to the tail field to make its own node the tail of the queue, simultaneously acquiring a reference to its predecessor's QNode. The thread then spins on the predecessor's locked field until the predecessor releases the lock. To release the lock, the thread sets its node's locked field to *false*. It then reuses its predecessor's QNode as its new node for future lock accesses. It can do so because at this point the thread's predecessor's QNode is no longer used by the predecessor, and the thread's old QNode could be referenced both by the thread's successor and by the tail.[3] Although we do not do so in our examples, it is possible to recycle

3 It is not necessary for correctness to reuse nodes in garbage-collected languages such as Java or C#, but reuse would be needed in languages such as C++ or C.

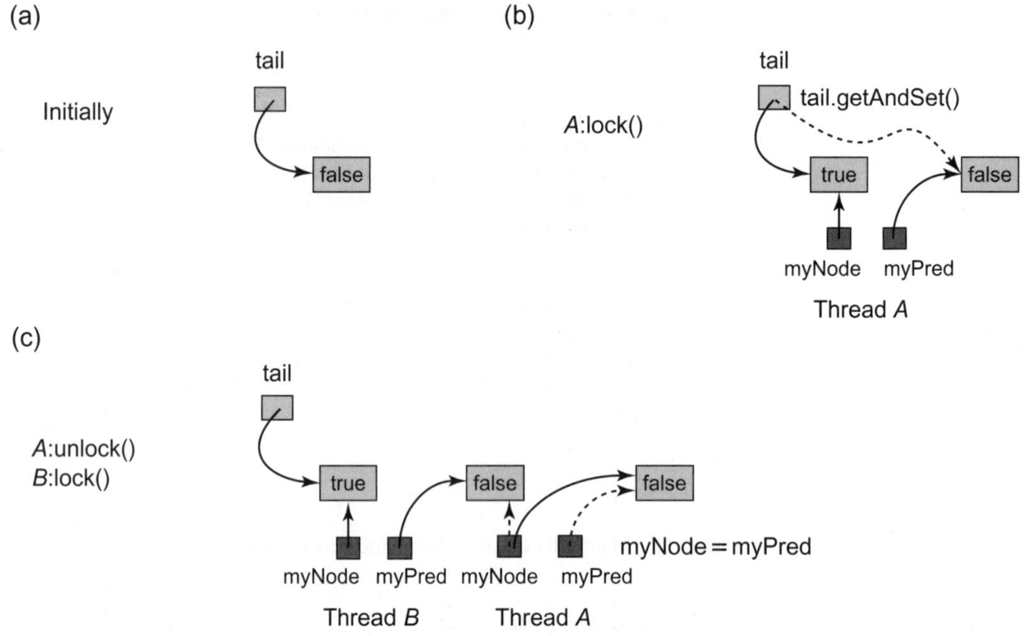

Figure 7.11 CLHLock class: lock acquisition and release. Initially the `tail` field refers to a `QNode` whose `locked` field is false. Thread *A* then applies `getAndSet()` to the `tail` field to insert its `QNode` at the tail of the queue, simultaneously acquiring a reference to its predecessor's `QNode`. Next, *B* does the same to insert its `QNode` at the tail of the queue. *A* then releases the lock by setting its node's `locked` field to false. It then recycles the `QNode` referenced by `pred` for future lock accesses.

nodes so that if there are L locks, and each thread accesses at most one lock at a time, then the `CLHLock` class needs only $O(L+n)$ space, as compared to $O(Ln)$ for the `ALock` class. Fig. 7.11 shows a typical `CLHLock` execution.

Like the `ALock`, this algorithm has each thread spin on a distinct location, so when one thread releases its lock, it invalidates only its successor's cache. This algorithm requires much less space than the `ALock` class, and does not require knowledge of the number of threads that might access the lock. Like the `ALock` class, it provides first-come-first-served fairness.

Perhaps the only disadvantage of this lock algorithm is that it performs poorly on cache-less NUMA architectures. Each thread spins waiting for its predecessor's node's `locked` field to become *false*. If this memory location is remote, then performance suffers. On cache-coherent architectures, however, this approach should work well.

7.5.3 The MCS Queue Lock

Fig. 7.12 shows the fields and constructor for the `MCSLock` class. Here, too, the lock is represented as a linked list of `QNode` objects, where each `QNode` represents

```
1  public class MCSLock implements Lock {
2    AtomicReference<QNode> tail;
3    ThreadLocal<QNode> myNode;
4    public MCSLock() {
5      tail = new AtomicReference<QNode>(null);
6      myNode = new ThreadLocal<QNode>() {
7        protected QNode initialValue() {
8          return new QNode();
9        }
10     };
11   }
12   ...
13   class QNode {
14     boolean locked = false;
15     QNode   next = null;
16   }
17 }
```

Figure 7.12 MCSLock class: fields, constructor and QNode class.

```
18   public void lock() {
19     QNode qnode = myNode.get();
20     QNode pred = tail.getAndSet(qnode);
21     if (pred != null) {
22       qnode.locked = true;
23       pred.next = qnode;
24       // wait until predecessor gives up the lock
25       while (qnode.locked) {}
26     }
27   }
28   public void unlock() {
29     QNode qnode = myNode.get();
30     if (qnode.next == null) {
31       if (tail.compareAndSet(qnode, null))
32         return;
33       // wait until successor fills in the next field
34       while (qnode.next == null) {}
35     }
36     qnode.next.locked = false;
37     qnode.next = null;
38   }
```

Figure 7.13 MCSLock class: lock() and unlock() methods.

either a lock holder or a thread waiting to acquire the lock. Unlike the CLHLock class, the list is explicit, not virtual: instead of embodying the list in thread-local variables, it is embodied in the (globally accessible) QNode objects, via their next fields.

Fig. 7.13 shows the MCSLock class's lock() and unlock() methods. To acquire the lock, a thread appends its own QNode at the tail of the list (Line 20). If the queue was not previously empty, it sets the predecessor's `QNode`'s `next` field to refer to its own `QNode`. The thread then spins on a (local) `locked` field in its own `QNode` waiting until its predecessor sets this field to *false* (Lines 21–26).

The `unlock()` method checks whether the node's `next` field is *null* (Line 30). If so, then either no other thread is contending for the lock, or there is another thread, but it is slow. Let q be the thread's current node. To distinguish between these cases, the method applies `compareAndSet(`q, *null*`)` to the `tail` field. If the call succeeds, then no other thread is trying to acquire the lock, `tail` is set to *null*, and the method returns. Otherwise, another (slow) thread is trying to acquire the lock, so the method spins waiting for it to finish (Line 34). In either case, once the successor has appeared, the `unlock()` method sets its successor's `locked` field to *false*, indicating that the lock is now free. At this point, no other thread can access this `QNode`, and so it can be reused. Fig. 7.14 shows an example execution of the `MCSLock`.

This lock shares the advantages of the `CLHLock`, in particular, the property that each lock release invalidates only the successor's cache entry. It is better suited to cache-less NUMA architectures because each thread controls the location on which it spins. Like the `CLHLock`, nodes can be recycled so that this lock

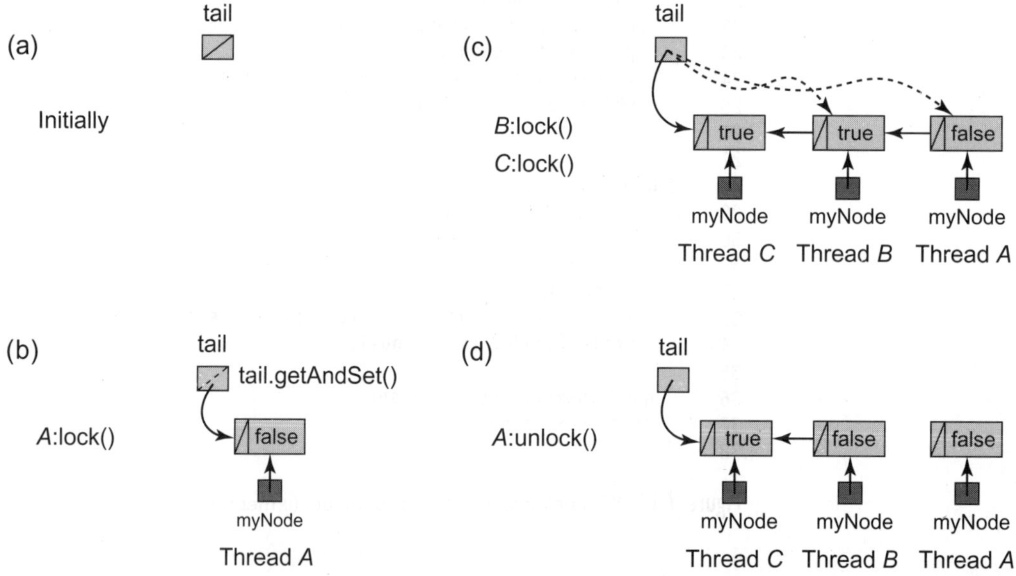

Figure 7.14 A lock acquisition and release in an `MCSLock`. (a) Initially the `tail` is null. (b) To acquire the lock, thread *A* places its own `QNode` at the tail of the list and since it has no predecessor it enters the critical section. (c) thread *B* enqueues its own `QNode` at the tail of the list and modifies its predecessor's `QNode` to refer back to its own. Thread *B* then spins on its `locked` field waiting until *A*, its predecessor, sets this field from true to false. Thread *C* repeats this sequence. (d) To release the lock, *A* follows its `next` field to its successor *B* and sets *B*'s `locked` field to *false*. It can now reuse its `QNode`.

has space complexity $O(L+n)$. One drawback of the `MCSLock` algorithm is that releasing a lock requires spinning. Another is that it requires more reads, writes, and `compareAndSet()` calls than the `CLHLock` algorithm.

7.6 A Queue Lock with Timeouts

The Java `Lock` interface includes a `tryLock()` method that allows the caller to specify a *timeout*: a maximum duration the caller is willing to wait to acquire the lock. If the timeout expires before the caller acquires the lock, the attempt is abandoned. A Boolean return value indicates whether the lock attempt succeeded. (For an explanation why these methods throw `InterruptedException`, see Pragma 8.2.2 in Chapter 8.)

Abandoning a `BackoffLock` request is trivial, because a thread can simply return from the `tryLock()` call. Timing out is wait-free, requiring only a constant number of steps. By contrast, timing out any of the queue lock algorithms is far from trivial: if a thread simply returns, the threads queued up behind it will starve.

Here is a bird's-eye view of a queue lock with timeouts. As in the `CLHLock`, the lock is a virtual queue of nodes, and each thread spins on its predecessor's node waiting for the lock to be released. As noted, when a thread times out, it cannot simply abandon its queue node, because its successor will never notice when the lock is released. On the other hand, it seems extremely difficult to unlink a queue node without disrupting concurrent lock releases. Instead, we take a *lazy* approach: when a thread times out, it marks its node as abandoned. Its successor in the queue, if there is one, notices that the node on which it is spinning has been abandoned, and starts spinning on the abandoned node's predecessor. This approach has the added advantage that the successor can recycle the abandoned node.

Fig. 7.15 shows the fields, constructor, and `QNode` class for the `TOLock` (timeout lock) class, a queue lock based on the `CLHLock` class that supports wait-free time-out even for threads in the middle of the list of nodes waiting for the lock.

When a `QNode`'s `pred` field is *null*, the associated thread has either not acquired the lock or has not released it yet. When a `QNode`'s `pred` field refers to a distinguished, static `QNode` called `AVAILABLE`, the associated thread has released the lock. Finally, if the `pred` field refers to some other `QNode`, the associated thread has abandoned the lock request, so the thread owning the successor node should wait on the abandoned node's predecessor.

Fig. 7.16 shows the `TOLock` class's `tryLock()` and `unlock()` methods. The `tryLock()` method creates a new `QNode` with a *null* `pred` field and appends it to the list as in the `CLHLock` class (Lines 5–8). If the lock was free (Line 9), the thread enters the critical section. Otherwise, it spins waiting for its predecessor's `QNode`'s `pred` field to change (Lines 12–19). If the predecessor thread times out, it sets the `pred` field to its own predecessor, and the thread spins instead on the new

```java
public class TOLock implements Lock{
  static QNode AVAILABLE = new QNode();
  AtomicReference<QNode> tail;
  ThreadLocal<QNode> myNode;
  public TOLock() {
    tail = new AtomicReference<QNode>(null);
    myNode = new ThreadLocal<QNode>() {
      protected QNode initialValue() {
        return new QNode();
      }
    };
  }
  ...
  static class QNode {
    public QNode pred = null;
  }
}
```

Figure 7.15 TOLock class: fields, constructor, and QNode class.

```java
  public boolean tryLock(long time, TimeUnit unit)
      throws InterruptedException {
    long startTime = System.currentTimeMillis();
    long patience = TimeUnit.MILLISECONDS.convert(time, unit);
    QNode qnode = new QNode();
    myNode.set(qnode);
    qnode.pred = null;
    QNode myPred = tail.getAndSet(qnode);
    if (myPred == null || myPred.pred == AVAILABLE) {
      return true;
    }
    while (System.currentTimeMillis() - startTime < patience) {
      QNode predPred = myPred.pred;
      if (predPred == AVAILABLE) {
        return true;
      } else if (predPred != null) {
        myPred = predPred;
      }
    }
    if (!tail.compareAndSet(qnode, myPred))
      qnode.pred = myPred;
    return false;
  }
  public void unlock() {
    QNode qnode = myNode.get();
    if (!tail.compareAndSet(qnode, null))
      qnode.pred = AVAILABLE;
  }
}
```

Figure 7.16 TOLock class: tryLock() and unlock() methods.

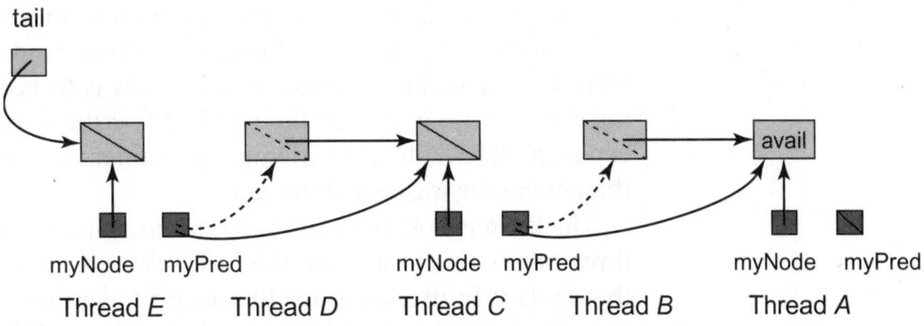

Figure 7.17 Timed-out nodes that must be skipped to acquire the `TOLock`. Threads *B* and *D* have timed out, redirecting their `pred` fields to their predecessors in the list. Thread *C* notices that *B*'s field is directed at *A* and so it starts spinning on *A*. Similarly thread *E* spins waiting for *C*. When *A* completes and sets its `pred` to `AVAILABLE`, *C* will access the critical section and upon leaving it will set its `pred` to `AVAILABLE`, releasing *E*.

predecessor. An example of such a sequence appears in Fig. 7.17. Finally, if the thread itself times out (Line 20), it attempts to remove its `QNode` from the list by applying `compareAndSet()` to the `tail` field. If the `compareAndSet()` call fails, indicating that the thread has a successor, the thread sets its `QNode`'s `pred` field, previously *null*, to its predecessor's `QNode`, indicating that it has abandoned the queue.

In the `unlock()` method, a thread checks, using `compareAndSet()`, whether it has a successor (Line 26), and if so sets its `pred` field to `AVAILABLE`. Note that it is not safe to recycle a thread's old node at this point, since the node may be referenced by its immediate successor, or by a chain of such references. The nodes in such a chain can be recycled as soon as a thread skips over the timed-out nodes and enters the critical section.

The `TOLock` has many of the advantages of the original `CLHLock`: local spinning on a cached location and quick detection that the lock is free. It also has the wait-free timeout property of the `BackoffLock`. However, it has some drawbacks, among them the need to allocate a new node per lock access, and the fact that a thread spinning on the lock may have to go up a chain of timed-out nodes before it can access the critical section.

7.7 A Composite Lock

Spin-lock algorithms impose trade-offs. Queue locks provide first-come-first-served fairness, fast lock release, and low contention, but require nontrivial protocols for recycling abandoned nodes. By contrast, backoff locks support trivial timeout protocols, but are inherently not scalable, and may have slow lock release if timeout parameters are not well-tuned. In this section, we consider an advanced lock algorithm that combines the best of both approaches.

Consider the following simple observation: in a queue lock, only the threads at the front of the queue need to perform lock handoffs. One way to balance the merits of queue locks versus backoff locks is to keep a small number of waiting threads in a queue on the way to the critical section, and have the rest use exponential backoff while attempting to enter this short queue. It is trivial for the threads employing backoff to quit.

The `CompositeLock` class keeps a short, fixed-size array of lock nodes. Each thread that tries to acquire the lock selects a node in the array at random. If that node is in use, the thread backs off (adaptively), and tries again. Once the thread acquires a node, it enqueues that node in a `TOLock`-style queue. The thread spins on the preceding node, and when that node's owner signals it is done, the thread enters the critical section. When it leaves, either because it completed or timed-out, it releases ownership of the node, and another backed-off thread may acquire it. The tricky part of course, is how to recycle the freed nodes of the array while multiple threads attempt to acquire control over them.

The `CompositeLock`'s fields, constructor, and `unlock()` method appear in Fig. 7.18. The `waiting` field is a constant-size `QNode` array, and the `tail` field is an `AtomicStampedReference<QNode>` that combines a reference to the queue tail with a version number needed to avoid the *ABA* problem on updates (see Pragma 10.6.1 of Chapter 10 for a more detailed explanation of the

```
public class CompositeLock implements Lock{
  private static final int SIZE = ...;
  private static final int MIN_BACKOFF = ...;
  private static final int MAX_BACKOFF = ...;
  AtomicStampedReference<QNode> tail;
  QNode[] waiting;
  Random random;
  ThreadLocal<QNode> myNode = new ThreadLocal<QNode>() {
    protected QNode initialValue() { return null; };
  };
  public CompositeLock() {
    tail = new AtomicStampedReference<QNode>(null,0);
    waiting = new QNode[SIZE];
    for (int i = 0; i < waiting.length; i++) {
      waiting[i] = new QNode();
    }
    random = new Random();
  }
  public void unlock() {
    QNode acqNode = myNode.get();
    acqNode.state.set(State.RELEASED);
    myNode.set(null);
  }
  ...
}
```

Figure 7.18 The `CompositeLock` class: fields, constructor, and `unlock()` method.

```
enum State {FREE, WAITING, RELEASED, ABORTED};
class QNode {
  AtomicReference<State> state;
  QNode pred;
  public QNode() {
    state = new AtomicReference<State>(State.FREE);
  }
}
```

Figure 7.19 The CompositeLock class: the QNode class.

```
1   public boolean tryLock(long time, TimeUnit unit)
2       throws InterruptedException {
3     long patience = TimeUnit.MILLISECONDS.convert(time, unit);
4     long startTime = System.currentTimeMillis();
5     Backoff backoff = new Backoff(MIN_BACKOFF, MAX_BACKOFF);
6     try {
7       QNode node = acquireQNode(backoff, startTime, patience);
8       QNode pred = spliceQNode(node, startTime, patience);
9       waitForPredecessor(pred, node, startTime, patience);
10      return true;
11    } catch (TimeoutException e) {
12      return false;
13    }
14  }
```

Figure 7.20 The CompositeLock class: the tryLock() method.

AtomicStampedReference<T> class, and Chapter 11 for a more complete discussion of the ABA problem[4]). The tail field is either *null* or refers to the last node inserted in the queue. Fig. 7.19 shows the QNode class. Each QNode includes a State field and a reference to the predecessor node in the queue.

A QNode has four possible states: WAITING, RELEASED, ABORTED, or FREE. A WAITING node is linked into the queue, and the owning thread is either in the critical section, or waiting to enter. A node becomes RELEASED when its owner leaves the critical section and releases the lock. The other two states occur when a thread abandons its attempt to acquire the lock. If the quitting thread has acquired a node but not enqueued it, then it marks the thread as FREE. If the node is enqueued, then it is marked as ABORTED.

Fig. 7.20 shows the tryLock() method. A thread acquires the lock in three steps. First, it *acquires* a node in the waiting array (Line 7), then it enqueues that node in the queue (Line 8), and finally it waits until that node is at the head of the queue (Line 9).

4 ABA is typically a problem only when using dynamically allocated memory in non garbage collected languages. We encounter it here because we are implementing a dynamic linked list using an array.

```
1  private QNode acquireQNode(Backoff backoff, long startTime,
2                             long patience)
3   throws TimeoutException, InterruptedException {
4    QNode node = waiting[random.nextInt(SIZE)];
5    QNode currTail;
6    while (true) {
7      if (node.state.compareAndSet(State.FREE, State.WAITING)) {
8        return node;
9      }
10     currTail = tail.get(currStamp);
11     State state = node.state.get();
12     if (state == State.ABORTED || state == State.RELEASED) {
13       if (node == currTail) {
14         QNode myPred = null;
15         if (state == State.ABORTED) {
16           myPred = node.pred;
17         }
18         if (tail.compareAndSet(currTail, myPred,
19             currStamp[0], currStamp[0]+1)) {
20           node.state.set(State.WAITING);
21           return node;
22         }
23       }
24     }
25     backoff.backoff();
26     if (timeout(patience, startTime)) {
27       throw new TimeoutException();
28     }
29   }
30 }
```

Figure 7.21 The `CompositeLock` class: the `acquireQNode()` method.

The algorithm for acquiring a node in the `waiting` array appears in Fig. 7.21. The thread selects a node at random and tries to acquire the node by changing that node's state from `FREE` to `WAITING` (Line 7). If it fails, it examines the node's status. If the node is `ABORTED` or `RELEASED` (Line 12), the thread may "clean up" the node. To avoid synchronization conflicts with other threads, a node can be cleaned up only if it is the last queue node (that is, the value of `tail`). If the tail node is `ABORTED`, `tail` is redirected to that node's predecessor; otherwise `tail` is set to *null*. If, instead, the allocated node is `WAITING`, then the thread backs off and retries. If the thread times out before acquiring its node, it throws `TimeoutException` (Line 27).

Once the thread acquires a node, the `spliceQNode()` method, shown in Fig. 7.22, splices that node into the queue. The thread repeatedly tries to set `tail` to the allocated node. If it times out, it marks the allocated node as `FREE` and throws `TimeoutException`. If it succeeds, it returns the prior value of `tail`, acquired by the node's predecessor in the queue.

```
private QNode spliceQNode(QNode node, long startTime, long patience)
 throws TimeoutException {
  QNode currTail;
  do {
    currTail = tail.get(currStamp);
    if (timeout(startTime, patience)) {
      node.state.set(State.FREE);
      throw new TimeoutException();
    }
  } while (!tail.compareAndSet(currTail, node,
      currStamp[0], currStamp[0]+1));
  return currTail;
}
```

Figure 7.22 The `CompositeLock` class: the `spliceQNode()` method.

```
private void waitForPredecessor(QNode pred, QNode node, long startTime,
                                long patience)
 throws TimeoutException {
  int[] stamp = {0};
  if (pred == null) {
    myNode.set(node);
    return;
  }
  State predState = pred.state.get();
  while (predState != State.RELEASED) {
    if (predState == State.ABORTED) {
      QNode temp = pred;
      pred = pred.pred;
      temp.state.set(State.FREE);
    }
    if (timeout(patience, startTime)) {
      node.pred = pred;
      node.state.set(State.ABORTED);
      throw new TimeoutException();
    }
    predState = pred.state.get();
  }
  pred.state.set(State.FREE);
  myNode.set(node);
  return;
}
```

Figure 7.23 The `CompositeLock` class: the `waitForPredecessor()` method.

Finally, once the node has been enqueued, the thread must wait its turn by calling `waitForPredecessor()` (Fig. 7.23). If the predecessor is *null*, then the thread's node is first in the queue, so the thread saves the node in the thread-local `myNode` field (for later use by `unlock()`), and enters the critical section. If the predecessor node is not `RELEASED`, the thread checks whether it is `ABORTED`

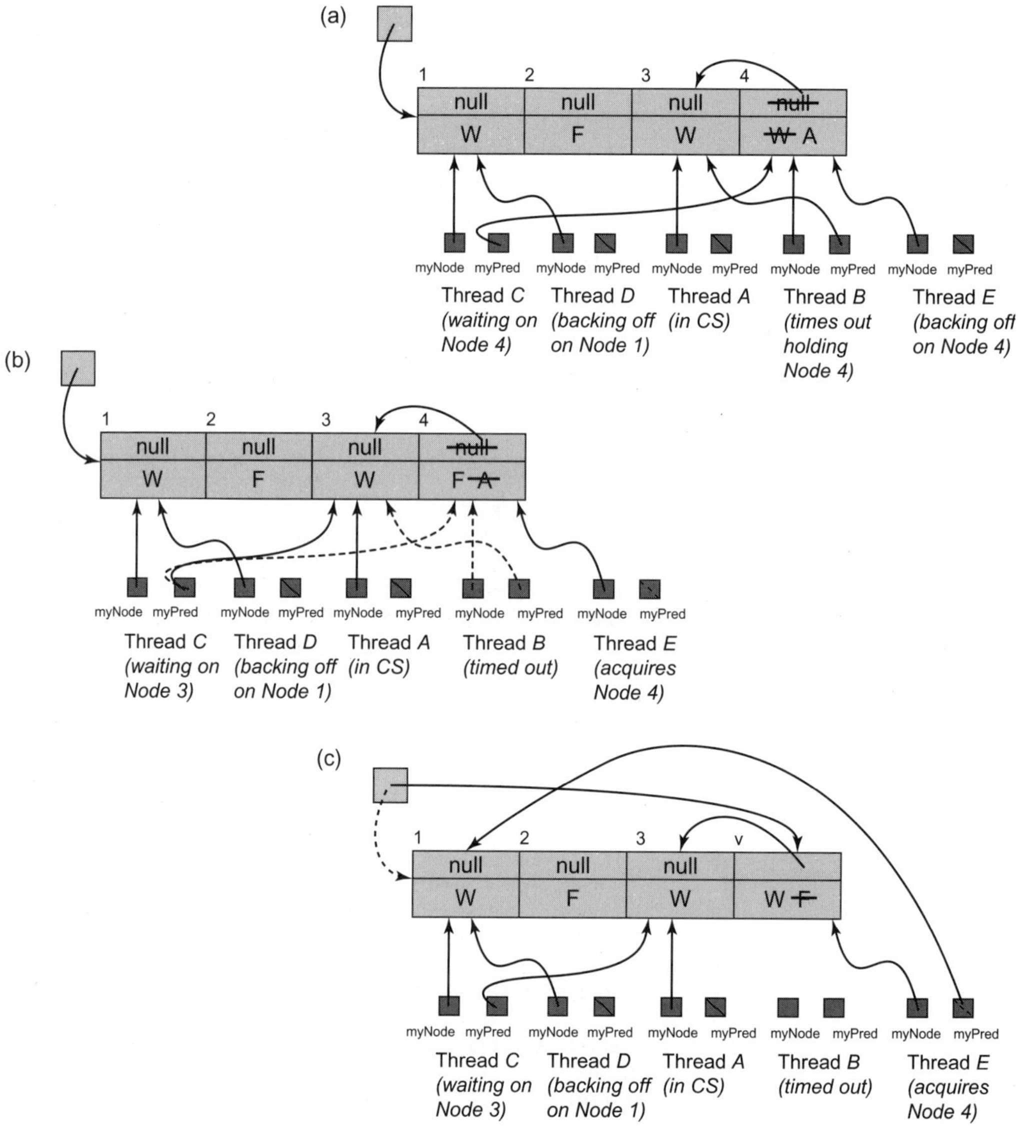

Figure 7.24 The `CompositeLock` class: an execution. In Part (a) thread *A* (which acquired Node 3) is in the critical section. Thread *B* (Node 4) is waiting for *A* to release the critical section and thread *C* (Node 1) is in turn waiting for *B*. Threads *D* and *E* are backing off, waiting to acquire a node. Node 2 is free. The `tail` field refers to Node 1, the last node to be inserted into the queue. At this point *B* times out, inserting an explicit reference to its predecessor, and changing Node 4's state from `WAITING` (denoted by *W*), to `ABORTED` (denoted by *A*). In Part (b), thread *C* cleans up the `ABORTED` Node 4, setting its state to `FREE` and following the explicit reference from 4 to 3 (by redirecting its local `myPred` field). It then starts waiting for *A* (Node 3) to leave the critical section. In Part (c) *E* acquires the `FREE` Node 4, using `compareAndSet()` to set its state to `WAITING`. Thread *E* then inserts Node 4 into the queue, using `compareAndSet()` to swap Node 4 into the tail, then waiting on Node 1, which was previously referred to the tail.

(Line 11). If so, the thread marks the node FREE and waits on the aborted node's predecessor. If the thread times out, then it marks its own node as ABORTED and throws TimeoutException. Otherwise, when the predecessor node becomes RELEASED the thread marks it FREE, records its own node in the thread-local myNode field, and enters the critical section.

The unlock() method (Fig. 7.18) simply retrieves its node from myNode and marks it RELEASED.

The CompositeLock has a number of interesting properties. When threads back off, they access different locations, reducing contention. Lock hand-off is fast, just as in the CLHLock and TOLock algorithms. Abandoning a lock request is trivial for threads in the backoff stage, and relatively straightforward for threads that have acquired queue nodes. For L locks and n threads, the CompositeLock class, requires only $O(L)$ space in the worst case, as compared to the TOLock class's $O(L \cdot n)$. There is one drawback: the CompositeLock class does not guarantee first-come-first-served access.

7.7.1 A Fast-Path Composite Lock

Although the CompositeLock is designed to perform well under contention, performance in the absence of concurrency is also important. Ideally, for a thread running alone, acquiring a lock should be as simple as acquiring an uncontended TASLock. Unfortunately, in the CompositeLock algorithm, a thread running alone must redirect the tail field away from a released node, claim the node, and then splice it into the queue.

A *fast path* is a shortcut through a complex algorithm taken by a thread running alone. We can extend the CompositeLock algorithm to encompass a fast path in which a solitary thread acquires an idle lock without acquiring a node and splicing it into the queue.

Here is a bird's-eye view. We add an extra state, distinguishing between a lock held by an ordinary thread and a lock held by a fast-path thread. If a thread discovers the lock is free, it tries a fast-path acquire. If it succeeds, then it has acquired the lock in a single atomic step. If it fails, then it enqueues itself just as before.

We now examine the algorithm in detail. To reduce code duplication, we define the CompositeFastPathLock class to be a subclass of CompositeLock (see Fig. 7.25).

We use a FASTPATH flag to indicate that a thread has acquired the lock through the fast path. Because we need to manipulate this flag together with the tail field's reference, we "steal" a high-order bit from the tail field's integer stamp (Line 2). The private fastPathLock() method checks whether the tail field's stamp has a clear FASTPATH flag and a *null* reference. If so, it tries to acquire the lock simply by applying compareAndSet() to set the FASTPATH flag to *true*, ensuring that the reference remains *null*. An uncontended lock acquisition thus requires a single atomic operation. The fastPathLock() method returns *true* if it succeeds, and *false* otherwise.

```
public class CompositeFastPathLock extends CompositeLock {
  private static final int FASTPATH = ...;
  private boolean fastPathLock() {
    int oldStamp, newStamp;
    int stamp[] = {0};
    QNode qnode;
    qnode = tail.get(stamp);
    oldStamp = stamp[0];
    if (qnode != null) {
      return false;
    }
    if ((oldStamp & FASTPATH) != 0) {
      return false;
    }
    newStamp = (oldStamp + 1) | FASTPATH;
    return tail.compareAndSet(qnode, null, oldStamp, newStamp);
  }
  public boolean tryLock(long time, TimeUnit unit)
    throws InterruptedException {
    if (fastPathLock()) {
      return true;
    }
    if (super.tryLock(time, unit)) {
      while ((tail.getStamp() & FASTPATH ) != 0){};
      return true;
    }
    return false;
  }
```

Figure 7.25 `CompositeFastPathLock` class: the private `fastPathLock()` method returns true if it succeeds in acquiring the lock through the fast path.

```
  private boolean fastPathUnlock() {
    int oldStamp, newStamp;
    oldStamp = tail.getStamp();
    if ((oldStamp & FASTPATH) == 0) {
      return false;
    }   int[] stamp = {0};
    QNode qnode;
    do {
      qnode = tail.get(stamp);
      oldStamp = stamp[0];
      newStamp = oldStamp & (~FASTPATH);
    } while (!tail.compareAndSet(qnode, qnode, oldStamp, newStamp));
    return true;
  }
  public void unlock() {
    if (!fastPathUnlock()) {
      super.unlock();
    };
  }
```

Figure 7.26 `CompositeFastPathLock` class: `fastPathLock()` and `unlock()` methods.

The tryLock() method (Lines 18–28) first tries the fast path by calling fastPathLock(). If it fails, then it pursues the slow path by calling the CompositeLock class's tryLock() method. Before it can return from the slow path, however, it must ensure that no other thread holds the fast-path lock by waiting until the FASTPATH flag is clear (Line 24).

The fastPathUnlock() method returns *false* if the fast-path flag is not set (Line 4). Otherwise, it repeatedly tries to clear the flag, leaving the reference component unchanged (Lines 8–12), returning *true* when it succeeds.

The CompositeFastPathLock class's unlock() method first calls fastPathUnlock() (Line 16). If that call fails to release the lock, it then calls the CompositeLock's unlock() method (Line 17).

7.8 Hierarchical Locks

Many of today's cache-coherent architectures organize processors in *clusters*, where communication within a cluster is significantly faster than communication between clusters. For example, a cluster might correspond to a group of processors that share memory through a fast interconnect, or it might correspond to the threads running on a single core in a multicore architecture. We would like to design locks that are sensitive to these differences in locality. Such locks are called *hierarchical* because they take into account the architecture's memory hierarchy and access costs.

Architectures can easily have two, three, or more levels of memory hierarchy, but to keep things simple, we assume there are two. We consider an architecture consisting of clusters of processors, where processors in the same cluster communicate efficiently through a shared cache. Inter-cluster communication is significantly more expensive than intra-cluster communication.

We assume that each cluster has a unique *cluster id* known to each thread in the cluster, available via ThreadID.getCluster(). Threads do not migrate between clusters.

7.8.1 A Hierarchical Backoff Lock

A test–and–test–and–set lock can easily be adapted to exploit clustering. Suppose the lock is held by thread A. If threads from A's cluster have shorter backoff times, then when the lock is released, local threads are more likely to acquire the lock than remote threads, reducing the overall time needed to switch lock ownership. Fig. 7.27 shows the HBOLock class, a hierarchical backoff lock based on this principle.

One drawback of the HBOLock is that it may be *too* successful in exploiting locality. There is a danger that threads from the same cluster will repeatedly transfer the lock among themselves while threads from other clusters starve. Moreover, acquiring and releasing the lock invalidates remotely cached copies of the lock field, which can be expensive on cache-coherent NUMA architectures.

```
public class HBOLock implements Lock {
  private static final int LOCAL_MIN_DELAY = ...;
  private static final int LOCAL_MAX_DELAY = ...;
  private static final int REMOTE_MIN_DELAY = ...;
  private static final int REMOTE_MAX_DELAY = ...;
  private static final int FREE = -1;
  AtomicInteger state;
  public HBOLock() {
    state = new AtomicInteger(FREE);
  }
  public void lock() {
    int myCluster = ThreadID.getCluster();
    Backoff localBackoff =
        new Backoff(LOCAL_MIN_DELAY, LOCAL_MAX_DELAY);
    Backoff remoteBackoff =
        new Backoff(REMOTE_MIN_DELAY, REMOTE_MAX_DELAY);
    while (true) {
      if (state.compareAndSet(FREE, myCluster)) {
        return;
      }
      int lockState = state.get();
      if (lockState == myCluster) {
        localBackoff.backoff();
      } else {
        remoteBackoff.backoff();
      }
    }
  }
  public void unlock() {
    state.set(FREE);
  }
}
```

Figure 7.27 The `HBOLock` class: a hierarchical backoff lock.

7.8.2 A Hierarchical CLH Queue Lock

To provide a more balanced way to exploit clustering, we now consider the design of a hierarchical queue lock. The challenge is to reconcile conflicting fairness requirements. We would like to favor transferring locks within the same cluster to avoid high communication costs, but we also want to ensure some degree of fairness, so that remote lock requests are not excessively postponed in favor of local requests. We balance these demands by scheduling *sequences* of requests from the same cluster together.

The `HCLHLock` queue lock (Fig. 7.28) consists of a collection of *local queues*, one per cluster, and a single *global queue*. Each queue is a linked list of nodes, where the links are implicit, in the sense that they are held in thread-local fields, `myQNode` and `myPred`.

We say that a thread *owns* its `myQNode` node. For any node in a queue (other than at the head), its predecessor is its owner's `myPred` node. Fig. 7.30

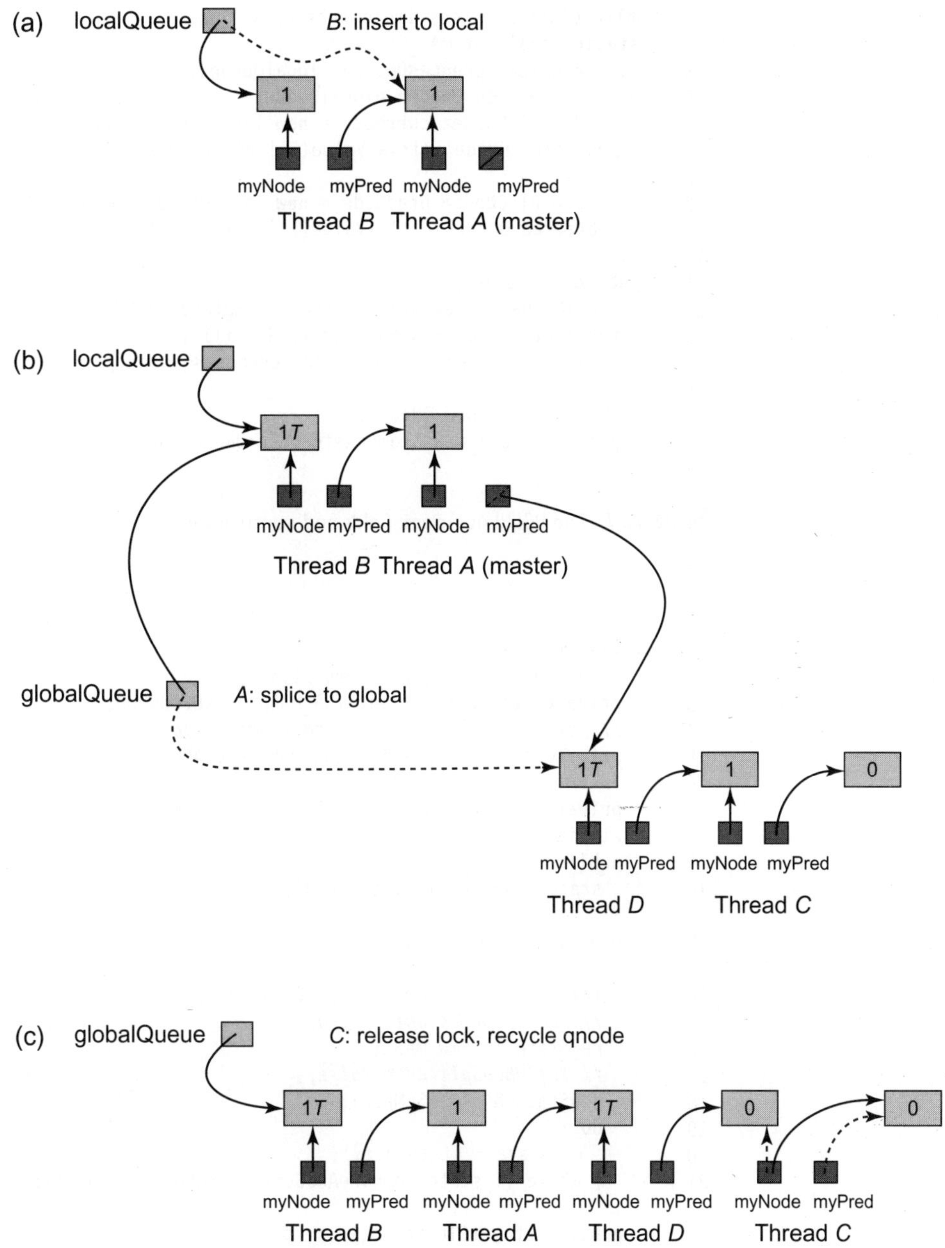

Figure 7.28 Lock acquisition and release in a `HCLHLock`. The `successorMustWait` field is marked in the nodes by a 0 (for false) or a 1 (for true). A node is marked as a local tail when it is being spliced by adding the symbol *T*. In Part (a), *B* inserts its node into the local queue. In Part (b), *A* splices the local queue containing *A* and *B*'s nodes onto the global queue, which already contains *C* and *D*'s nodes. In Part (c), *C* releases the lock by setting its node's `successorMustWait` flag to false, and then setting `myQNode` to the predecessor node.

```
public class HCLHLock implements Lock {
  static final int MAX_CLUSTERS = ...;
  List<AtomicReference<QNode>> localQueues;
  AtomicReference<QNode> globalQueue;
  ThreadLocal<QNode> currNode = new ThreadLocal<QNode>() {
    protected QNode initialValue() { return new QNode(); };
  };
  ThreadLocal<QNode> predNode = new ThreadLocal<QNode>() {
    protected QNode initialValue() { return null; };
  };
  public HCLHLock() {
    localQueues = new ArrayList<AtomicReference<QNode>>(MAX_CLUSTERS);
    for (int i = 0; i < MAX_CLUSTERS; i++) {
      localQueues.add(new AtomicReference <QNode>());
    }
    QNode head = new QNode();
    globalQueue = new AtomicReference<QNode>(head);
  }
```

Figure 7.29 The HCLHLock class: fields and constructor.

```
  class QNode {
    // private boolean tailWhenSpliced;
    private static final int TWS_MASK = 0x80000000;
    // private boolean successorMustWait = false;
    private static final int SMW_MASK = 0x40000000;
    // private int clusterID;
    private static final int CLUSTER_MASK = 0x3FFFFFFF;
    AtomicInteger state;
    public QNode() {
      state = new AtomicInteger(0);
    }
    public void unlock() {
      int oldState = 0;
      int newState = ThreadID.getCluster();
      // successorMustWait = true;
      newState |= SMW_MASK;
      // tailWhenSpliced = false;
      newState &= (~TWS_MASK);
      do {
        oldState = state.get();
      } while (! state.compareAndSet(oldState, newState));
    }
    public int getClusterID() {
      return state.get() & CLUSTER_MASK;
    }
    // other getters and setters omitted.
  }
```

Figure 7.30 The HCLHLock class: the inner QNode class.

shows the `QNode` class. Each node has three virtual fields: the current (or most recent) owner's `ClusterId`, and two Boolean fields, `successorMustWait` and `tailWhenSpliced`. These fields are virtual in the sense that they need to be updated atomically, so we represent them as bit-fields in an `AtomicInteger` field, using simple masking and shifting operations to extract their values. The `tailWhenSpliced` field indicates whether the node is the last node in the sequence currently being spliced onto the global queue. The `successorMustWait` field is the same as in the original CLH algorithm: it is set to *true* before being enqueued, and set to *false* by the node's owner on releasing the lock. Thus, a thread waiting to acquire the lock may proceed when its predecessor's `successorMustWait` field becomes *false*. Because we need to update these fields atomically, they are private, accessed indirectly through synchronized methods.

Fig. 7.28 illustrates how the `HCLHLock` class acquires and releases a lock. The `lock()` method first adds the thread's node to the local queue, and then waits until either the thread can enter the critical section or its node is at the head of the local queue. In the latter case, we say the thread is the *cluster master*, and it is responsible for splicing the local queue onto the global queue.

The code for the `lock()` method appears in Fig. 7.31. The thread's node has been initialized so that `successorMustWait` is *true*, `tailWhenSpliced` is *false*, and the `ClusterId` field is the caller's cluster. The thread then adds its node to the end (tail) of its local cluster's queue, using `compareAndSet()` to change the tail to its node (Line 9). Upon success, the thread sets its `myPred` to the node it replaced as the tail. We call this node the *predecessor*.

The thread then calls `waitForGrantOrClusterMaster()` (Line 11), which causes the thread to spin until one of the following conditions is true:

1. the predecessor node is from the same cluster, and `tailWhenSpliced` and `successorMustWait` are both *false*, or
2. the predecessor node is from a different cluster or the predecessor's flag `tailWhenSpliced` is *true*.

In the first case, the thread's node is at the head of the global queue, so it enters the critical section and returns (Line 14). In the second case, as explained here, the thread's node is at the head of the local queue, so the thread is the cluster master, making it responsible for splicing the local queue onto the global queue. (If there is no predecessor, that is, if the local queue's tail is *null*, then the thread becomes the cluster master immediately.) Most of the spinning required by `waitForGrantOrClusterMaster()` is local and incurs little or no communication cost.

Otherwise, either the predecessor's cluster is different from the thread's, or the predecessor's `tailWhenSpliced` flag is *true*. If the predecessor belongs to a different cluster, then it cannot be in this thread's local queue. The predecessor must have already been moved to the global queue and recycled to a thread in a different cluster. On the other hand, if the predecessor's `tailWhenSpliced` flag

```
1  public void lock() {
2    QNode myNode = currNode.get();
3    AtomicReference<QNode> localQueue = localQueues.get
4                                          (ThreadID.getCluster());
5    // splice my QNode into local queue
6    QNode myPred = null;
7    do {
8      myPred = localQueue.get();
9    } while (!localQueue.compareAndSet(myPred, myNode));
10   if (myPred != null) {
11     boolean iOwnLock = myPred.waitForGrantOrClusterMaster();
12     if (iOwnLock) {
13       predNode.set(myPred);
14       return;
15     }
16   }
17   // I am the cluster master: splice local queue into global queue.
18   QNode localTail = null;
19   do {
20     myPred = globalQueue.get();
21     localTail = localQueue.get();
22   } while(!globalQueue.compareAndSet(myPred, localTail));
23   // inform successor it is the new master
24   localTail.setTailWhenSpliced(true);
25   while (myPred.isSuccessorMustWait()) {};
26   predNode.set(myPred);
27   return;
28 }
```

Figure 7.31 The `HCLHLock` class: `lock()` method. As in the `CLHLock`, `lock()` saves the predecessor's recently released node to be used for next lock acquisition attempt.

is *true*, then the predecessor node was the last that moved to the global queue, and therefore the thread's node is now at the head of the local queue. It cannot have been moved to the global queue because only the cluster master, the thread whose node is at the head of the local queue, moves nodes onto the global queue.

As cluster master, a thread's role is to splice the nodes accumulated in the local queue onto the global queue. The threads in the local queue spin, each on its predecessor's node. The cluster master reads the local queue's tail and calls `compareAndSet()` to change the global queue's tail to the node it saw at the tail of its local queue (Line 22). When it succeeds, `myPred` is the tail of the global queue that it replaced (Line 20). It then sets to *true* the `tailWhenSpliced` flag of the last node it spliced onto the global queue (Line 24), indicating to that node's (local) successor that it is now the head of the local queue. This sequence of operations transfers the local nodes (up to the local tail) into the CLH-style global queue in the same order as in the local queue.

```
29    public void unlock() {
30      QNode myNode = currNode.get();
31      myNode.setSuccessorMustWait(false);
32      QNode node = predNode.get();
33      node.unlock();
34      currNode.set(node);
35    }
```

Figure 7.32 The HCLHLock class: unlock() method. This method promotes the node saved by the lock() operation and initializes the QNode to be used in the next lock acquisition attempt.

Once in the global queue, the cluster master acts as though it were in an ordinary `CLHLock` queue, entering the critical section when its (new) predecessor's `successorMustWait` field is *false* (Line 25). The other threads whose nodes were spliced in are not aware that anything has changed, so they continue spinning as before. Each will enter the critical section when its predecessor's `successorMustWait` field becomes *false*.

As in the original `CLHLock` algorithm, a thread releases the lock by setting its node's `successorMustWait` field to *false* (Fig. 7.32). When unlocking, the thread saves its predecessor's node to be used in its next lock acquisition attempt (Line 34).

The `HCLHLock` lock favors sequences of local threads, one waiting for the other, within the waiting list in the global queue. As with the `CLHLock` lock, the use of implicit references minimizes cache misses, and threads spin on locally cached copies of their successor's node state.

7.9 One Lock To Rule Them All

In this chapter, we have seen a variety of spin locks that vary in characteristics and performance. Such a variety is useful, because no single algorithm is ideal for all applications. For some applications, complex algorithms work best, and for others, simple algorithms are preferable. The best choice usually depends on specific aspects of the application and the target architecture.

7.10 Chapter Notes

The `TTASLock` is due to Larry Rudolph and Zary Segall [133]. Exponential back off is a well-known technique used in Ethernet routing, presented in the context of multiprocessor mutual exclusion by Anant Agarwal and Mathews Cherian [6].

Tom Anderson [14] invented the ALock algorithm and was one of the first to empirically study the performance of spin locks in shared memory multiprocessors. The MCSLock, due to John Mellor-Crummey and Michael Scott [113], is perhaps the best-known queue lock algorithm. Today's Java Virtual Machines use object synchronization based on simplified monitor algorithms such as the *Thinlock* of David Bacon, Ravi Konuru, Chet Murthy, and Mauricio Serrano [17], the *Metalock* of Ole Agesen, Dave Detlefs, Alex Garthwaite, Ross Knippel, Y. S. Ramakrishna and Derek White [7], or the *RelaxedLock* of Dave Dice [31]. All these algorithms are variations of the MCSLock lock.

The CLHLock lock is due to Travis Craig, Erik Hagersten, and Anders Landin [30, 110]. The TOLock with nonblocking timeout is due to Bill Scherer and Michael Scott [138, 139]. The CompositeLock and its variations are due to Virendra Marathe, Mark Moir, and Nir Shavit [120]. The notion of using a fast-path in a mutual exclusion algorithm is due to Leslie Lamport [95]. Hierarchical locks were invented by Zoran Radović and Erik Hagersten. The HBOLock is a variant of their original algorithm [130] and the particular HCLHLock presented here is due to Victor Luchangco, Daniel Nussbaum, and Nir Shavit [109].

Danny Hendler, Faith Fich, and Nir Shavit [39] have extended the work of Jim Burns and Nancy Lynch to show that any starvation-free mutual exclusion algorithm requires $\Omega(n)$ space, even if strong operations such as getAndSet() or compareAndSet() are used, implying that all the queue-lock algorithms considered here are space-optimal.

The schematic performance graph in this chapter is loosely based on empirical studies by Tom Anderson [14], as well as on data collected by the authors on various modern machines. We chose to use schematics rather than actual data because of the great variation in machine architectures and their significant effect on lock performance.

The Sherlock Holmes quote is from *The Sign of Four* [36].

7.11 Exercises

Exercise 85. Fig. 7.33 shows an alternative implementation of CLHLock in which a thread reuses its own node instead of its predecessor node. Explain how this implementation can go wrong.

Exercise 86. Imagine n threads, each of which executes method foo() followed by method bar(). Suppose we want to make sure that no thread star bar() until all threads have finished foo(). For this kind of synchronization, we place a *barrier* between foo() and bar().

First barrier implementation: We have a counter protected by a test–and–test–and–set lock. Each thread locks the counter, increments it, releases the lock, and spins, rereading the counter until it reaches n.

```
public class BadCLHLock implements Lock {
  // most recent lock holder
  AtomicReference<Qnode> tail = new Qnode();
  // thread-local variable
  ThreadLocal<Qnode> myNode;
  public void lock() {
    Qnode qnode = myNode.get();
    qnode.locked = true;      // I'm not done
    // Make me the new tail, and find my predecessor
    Qnode pred = tail.getAndSet(qnode);
    // spin while predecessor holds lock
    while (pred.locked) {}
  }
  public void unlock() {
    // reuse my node next time
    myNode.get().locked = false;
  }
  static class Qnode { // Queue node inner class
    public boolean locked = false;
  }
}
```

Figure 7.33 An incorrect attempt to implement a CLHLock.

Second barrier implementation: We have an n-element array b[0..$n-1$], all 0. Thread zero sets b[0] to 1. Every thread i, for $0 < i < n-1$, spins until b[$i-1$] is 1, sets b[i] to 1, and waits until b[$i+1$] becomes 2, at which point it proceeds to leave the barrier. Thread $n-1$, upon detecting that b[$n-2$] is 1, sets b[$n-1$] to 2 and leaves the barrier.

Compare (in ten lines) the behavior of these two implementations on a bus-based cache-coherent architecture. Explain which approach you expect will perform better under low load and high load.

Exercise 87. Prove that the CompositeFastPathLock implementation guarantees mutual exclusion, but is not starvation-free.

Exercise 88. In the HCLHLock lock, for a given cluster master thread, in the interval between setting the global tail reference and raising the tailWhenSpliced flag of the last spliced node, the nodes spliced onto the global queue are in both its local queue and the global queue. Explain why the algorithm is still correct.

Exercise 89. Notice that, in the HCLHLock lock, what will happen if the time between becoming cluster master and successfully splicing the local queue into the global queue is too small? Suggest a remedy to this problem.

Exercise 90. Why is it important that the fields of the State object accessed by the HCLHLock lock's waitForGrantOrClusterMaster() method be read and modified atomically? Provide the code for the HCLHLock lock's waitForGrantOrClusterMaster() method. Does your implementation require the use of a `compareAndSet()`, and if so, can it be implemented efficiently without it?

Exercise 91. Design an `isLocked()` method that tests whether any thread is holding a lock (but does not acquire the lock). Give implementations for

- Any `testAndSet()` spin lock
- The CLH queue lock, and
- The MCS queue lock.

Exercise 92. (Hard) Where does the $\Omega(n)$ space complexity lower bound proof for deadlock-free mutual exclusion of Chapter 2 break when locks are allowed to use read–modify–write operations?

8 Monitors and Blocking Synchronization

8.1 Introduction

Monitors are a structured way of combining synchronization and data. A class encapsulates both data and methods in the same way that a monitor combines data, methods, and synchronization in a single modular package.

Here is why modular synchronization is important. Let us imagine our application has two threads, a producer and a consumer, that communicate through a shared FIFO queue. We could have the threads share two objects: an unsynchronized queue, and a lock to protect the queue. The producer looks something like this:

```
mutex.lock();
try {
  queue.enq(x)
} finally {
  mutex.unlock();
}
```

This is no way to run a railroad. Suppose the queue is bounded, meaning that an attempt to add an item to a full queue cannot proceed until the queue has room. Here, the decision whether to block the call or to let it proceed depends on the queue's internal state, which is (and should be) inaccessible to the caller. Even worse, suppose the application grows to have multiple producers, consumers, or both. Each such thread must keep track of both the lock and the queue objects, and the application will be correct only if each thread follows the same locking conventions.

A more sensible approach is to allow each queue to manage its own synchronization. The queue itself has its own internal lock, acquired by each method when it is called and released when it returns. There is no need to ensure that every thread that uses the queue follows a cumbersome synchronization protocol. If a thread tries to enqueue an item to a queue that is already full, then the `enq()` method itself can detect the problem, suspend the caller, and resume the caller when the queue has room.

8.2 Monitor Locks and Conditions

Just as in Chapters 2 and 7, a `Lock` is the basic mechanism for ensuring mutual exclusion. Only one thread at a time can *hold* a lock. A thread *acquires* a lock when it first starts to hold the lock. A thread *releases* a lock when it stops holding the lock. A monitor exports a collection of methods, each of which acquires the lock when it is called, and releases it when it returns.

If a thread cannot immediately acquire a lock, it can either *spin*, repeatedly testing whether the desired event has happened, or it can *block*, giving up the processor for a while to allow another thread to run.[1] Spinning makes sense on a multiprocessor if we expect to wait for a short time, because blocking a thread requires an expensive call to the operating system. On the other hand, blocking makes sense if we expect to wait for a long time, because a spinning thread keeps a processor busy without doing any work.

For example, a thread waiting for another thread to release a lock should spin if that particular lock is held briefly, while a consumer thread waiting to dequeue an item from an empty buffer should block, since there is usually no way to predict how long it may have to wait. Often, it makes sense to combine spinning and blocking: a thread waiting to dequeue an item might spin for a brief duration, and then switch to blocking if the delay appears to be long. Blocking works on both multiprocessors and uniprocessors, while spinning works only on multiprocessors.

Pragma 8.2.1. Most of the locks in this book follow the interface shown in Fig. 8.1. Here is an explanation of the `Lock` interface's methods:

- The `lock()` method blocks the caller until it acquires the lock.
- The `lockInterruptibly()` method acts like `lock()`, but throws an exception if the thread is interrupted while it is waiting. (See Pragma 8.2.2.)
- The `unlock()` method releases the lock.
- The `newCondition()` method is a *factory* that creates and returns a `Condition` object associated with the lock (explained below.)
- The `tryLock()` method acquires the lock if it is free, and immediately returns a Boolean indicating whether it acquired the lock. This method can also be called with a timeout.

1 Elsewhere we make a distinction between blocking and nonblocking synchronization algorithms. There, we mean something entirely different: a blocking algorithm is one where a delay by one thread can cause a delay in another.

```
public interface Lock {
  void lock();
  void lockInterruptibly() throws InterruptedException;
  boolean tryLock();
  boolean tryLock(long time, TimeUnit unit);
  Condition newCondition();
  void unlock();
}
```

Figure 8.1 The Lock Interface.

8.2.1 Conditions

While a thread is waiting for something to happen, say, for another thread to place an item in a queue, it is a very good idea to release the lock on the queue, because otherwise the other thread will never be able to enqueue the anticipated item. After the waiting thread has released the lock, it needs a way to be notified when to reacquire the lock and try again.

In the Java concurrency package (and in related packages such as Pthreads), the ability to release a lock temporarily is provided by a `Condition` object associated with a lock. Fig. 8.2 shows the use of the `Condition` interface provided in the java.util.concurrent.locks library. A condition is associated with a lock, and is created by calling that lock's `newCondition()` method. If the thread holding that lock calls the associated condition's `await()` method, it releases that lock and suspends itself, giving another thread the opportunity to acquire the lock. When the calling thread awakens, it reacquires the lock, perhaps competing with other threads.

Pragma 8.2.2. Threads in Java can be *interrupted* by other threads. If a thread is interrupted during a call to a `Condition`'s `await()` method, then the call throws `InterruptedException`. The proper response to an interrupt is application-dependent. (It is not good programming practice simply to ignore interrupts).
Fig. 8.2 shows a schematic example

```
Condition condition = mutex.newCondition();
...
mutex.lock()
try {
  while (!property) { // not happy
     condition.await(); // wait for property
  }   catch (InterruptedException e) {
        ... // application-dependent response
        }
  ... // happy: property must hold
}
```

Figure 8.2 How to use `Condition` objects.

> To avoid clutter, we usually omit `InterruptedException` handlers from example code, even though they would be required in actual code.

Like locks, `Condition` objects must be used in a stylized way. Suppose a thread wants to wait until a certain property holds. The thread tests the property while holding the lock. If the property does not hold, then the thread calls `await()` to release the lock and sleep until it is awakened by another thread. Here is the key point: there is no guarantee that the property will hold at the time the thread awakens. The `await()` method can return spuriously (i.e., for no reason), or the thread that signaled the condition may have awakened too many sleeping threads. Whatever the reason, the thread must retest the property, and if it finds the property still does not hold, it must call `await()` again.

The `Condition` interface in Fig. 8.3 provides several variations of this call, some of which provide the ability to specify a maximum time the caller can be suspended, or whether the thread can be interrupted while it is waiting. When the queue changes, the thread that made the change can notify other threads waiting on a condition. Calling `signal()` wakes up one thread waiting on a condition, while calling `signalAll()` wakes up all waiting threads. Fig. 8.4 describes a schematic execution of a monitor lock.

Fig. 8.5 shows how to implement a bounded FIFO queue using explicit locks and conditions. The `lock` field is a lock that must be acquired by all methods. We must initialize it to hold an instance of a class that implements the `Lock` interface. Here, we choose `ReentrantLock`, a useful lock type provided by the java.util.concurrent.locks package. As discussed in Section 8.4, this lock is *reentrant*: a thread that is holding the lock can acquire it again without blocking.

There are two condition objects: `notEmpty` notifies waiting dequeuers when the queue goes from being empty to nonempty, and `notFull` for the opposite direction. Using two conditions instead of one is more efficient, since fewer threads are woken up unnecessarily, but it is more complex.

```java
public interface Condition {
  void await() throws InterruptedException;
  boolean await(long time, TimeUnit unit)
    throws InterruptedException;
  boolean awaitUntil(Date deadline)
    throws InterruptedException;
  long awaitNanos(long nanosTimeout)
    throws InterruptedException;
  void awaitUninterruptibly();
  void signal();      // wake up one waiting thread
  void signalAll();   // wake up all waiting threads
}
```

Figure 8.3 The `Condition` interface: `await()` and its variants release the lock, give up the processor, and later awaken and reacquire the lock. The `signal()` and `signalAll()` methods awaken one or more waiting threads.

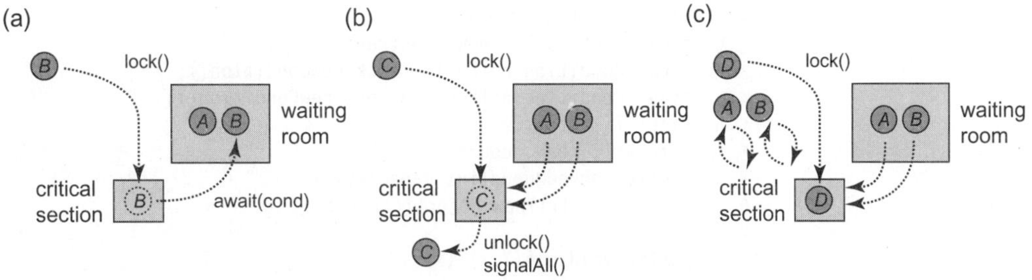

Figure 8.4 A schematic representation of a monitor execution. In Part (a) thread *A* has acquired the monitor lock, called `await()` on a condition, released the lock, and is now in the waiting room. Thread *B* then goes through the same sequence of steps, entering the critical section, calling `await()` on the condition, relinquishing the lock and entering the waiting room. In Part (b) both *A* and *B* leave the waiting room after thread *C* exits the critical section and calls `signalAll()`. *A* and *B* then attempt to reacquire the monitor lock. However, thread *D* manages to acquire the critical section lock first, and so both *A* and *B* spin until *D* leaves the critical section. Notice that if *C* would have issued a `signal()` instead of a `signalAll()`, only one of *A* or *B* would have left the waiting room, and the other would have continued to wait.

This combination of methods, mutual exclusion locks, and condition objects is called a *monitor*.

8.2.2 The Lost-Wakeup Problem

Just as locks are inherently vulnerable to deadlock, `Condition` objects are inherently vulnerable to *lost wakeups*, in which one or more threads wait forever without realizing that the condition for which they are waiting has become true.

Lost wakeups can occur in subtle ways. Fig. 8.6 shows an ill-considered optimization of the `Queue<T>` class. Instead of signaling the `notEmpty` condition each time `enq()` enqueues an item, would it not be more efficient to signal the condition only when the queue actually transitions from empty to non-empty? This optimization works as intended if there is only one producer and one consumer, but it is incorrect if there are multiple producers or consumers. Consider the following scenario: consumers A and B both try to dequeue an item from an empty queue, both detect the queue is empty, and both block on the `notEmpty` condition. Producer C enqueues an item in the buffer, and signals `notEmpty`, waking A. Before A can acquire the lock, however, another producer D puts a second item in the queue, and because the queue is not empty, it does not signal `notEmpty`. Then A acquires the lock, removes the first item, but B, victim of a lost wakeup, waits forever even though there is an item in the buffer to be consumed.

Although there is no substitute for reasoning carefully about our program, there are simple programming practices that will minimize vulnerability to lost wakeups.

- Always signal *all* processes waiting on a condition, not just one.
- Specify a timeout when waiting.

```
class LockedQueue<T> {
  final Lock lock = new ReentrantLock();
  final Condition notFull = lock.newCondition();
  final Condition notEmpty = lock.newCondition();
  final T[] items;
  int tail, head, count;
  public LockedQueue(int capacity) {
    items = (T[])new Object[capacity];
  }
  public void enq(T x) {
    lock.lock();
    try {
      while (count == items.length)
        notFull.await();
      items[tail] = x;
      if (++tail == items.length)
        tail = 0;
      ++count;
      notEmpty.signal();
    } finally {
      lock.unlock();
    }
  }
  public T deq() {
    lock.lock();
    try {
      while (count == 0)
        notEmpty.await();
      T x = items[head];
      if (++head == items.length)
        head = 0;
      --count;
      notFull.signal();
      return x;
    } finally {
      lock.unlock();
    }
  }
}
```

Figure 8.5 The `LockedQueue` class: a FIFO queue using locks and conditions. There are two condition fields, one to detect when the queue becomes nonempty, and one to detect when it becomes nonfull.

Either of these two practices would fix the bounded buffer error we just described. Each has a small performance penalty, but negligible compared to the cost of a lost wakeup.

Java provides built-in support for monitors in the form of **`synchronized`** blocks and methods, as well as built-in `wait()`, `notify()`, and `notifyAll()` methods. (See Appendix A.)

```
public void enq(T x) {
  lock.lock();
  try {
    while (count == items.length)
      notFull.await();
    items[tail] = x;
    if (++tail == items.length)
      tail = 0;
    ++count;
    if (count == 1) {  // Wrong!
      notEmpty.signal();
    }
  } finally {
    lock.unlock();
  }
}
```

Figure 8.6 This example is *incorrect.* It suffers from lost wakeups. The enq() method signals notEmpty only if it is the first to place an item in an empty buffer. A lost wakeup occurs if multiple consumers are waiting, but only the first is awakened to consume an item.

8.3 Readers–Writers Locks

Many shared objects have the property that most method calls, called *readers*, return information about the object's state without modifying the object, while only a small number of calls, called *writers*, actually modify the object.

There is no need for readers to synchronize with one another; it is perfectly safe for them to access the object concurrently. Writers, on the other hand, must lock out readers as well as other writers. A *readers–writers* lock allows multiple readers or a single writer to enter the critical section concurrently. We use the following interface:

```
public interface ReadWriteLock {
  Lock readLock();
  Lock writeLock();
}
```

This interface exports two lock objects: the *read lock* and the *write lock.* They satisfy the following safety properties:

- No thread can acquire the write lock while any thread holds either the write lock or the read lock.
- No thread can acquire the read lock while any thread holds the write lock.

Naturally, multiple threads may hold the read lock at the same time.

8.3.1 Simple Readers–Writers Lock

We consider a sequence of increasingly sophisticated reader–writer lock implementations. The SimpleReadWriteLock class appears in Figs. 8.7– 8.9. This class uses a counter to keep track of the number of readers that have acquired the lock,

```
public class SimpleReadWriteLock implements ReadWriteLock {
  int readers;
  boolean writer;
  Lock lock;
  Condition condition;
  Lock readLock, writeLock;
  public SimpleReadWriteLock() {
    writer = false;
    readers = 0;
    lock = new ReentrantLock();
    readLock = new ReadLock();
    writeLock = new WriteLock();
    condition = lock.newCondition();
  }
  public Lock readLock() {
    return readLock;
  }
  public Lock writeLock() {
    return writeLock;
  }
```

Figure 8.7 The SimpleReadWriteLock class: fields and public methods.

```
  class ReadLock implements Lock {
    public void lock() {
      lock.lock();
      try {
        while (writer) {
          condition.await();
        }
        readers++;
      } finally {
        lock.unlock();
      }
    }
    public void unlock() {
      lock.lock();
      try {
        readers--;
        if (readers == 0)
          condition.signalAll();
      } finally {
        lock.unlock();
      }
    }
  }
```

Figure 8.8 The SimpleReadWriteLock class: the inner read lock.

```
  protected class WriteLock implements Lock {
    public void lock() {
      lock.lock();
      try {
        while (readers > 0 || writer) {
          condition.await();
        }
        writer = true;
      } finally {
        lock.unlock();
      }
    }
    public void unlock() {
      lock.lock();
      try {
       writer = false;
       condition.signalAll();
      } finally {
        lock.unlock();
      }
    }
  }
}
```

Figure 8.9 The `SimpleReadWriteLock` class: inner write lock.

and a Boolean field indicating whether a writer has acquired the lock. To define the associated read–write locks, this code uses *inner classes*, a Java feature that allows one object (the `SimpleReadWriteLock` lock) to create other objects (the read–write locks) that share the first object's private fields. Both the `readLock()` and the `writeLock()` methods return objects that implement the `Lock` interface. These objects communicate via the `writeLock()` object's fields. Because the read–write lock methods must synchronize with one another, they both synchronize on the `Lock` and `condition` fields of their common `SimpleReadWriteLock` object.

8.3.2 Fair Readers–Writers Lock

Even though the `SimpleReadWriteLock` algorithm is correct, it is still not quite satisfactory. If readers are much more frequent than writers, as is usually the case, then writers could be locked out for a long time by a continual stream of readers. The `FifoReadWriteLock` class, shown in Figs. 8.10–8.12, shows one way to give writers priority. This class ensures that once a writer calls the write lock's `lock()` method, then no more readers will be able to acquire the read lock until the writer has acquired and released the write lock. Eventually, the readers holding the read lock will drain out without letting any more readers in, and the writer will acquire the write lock.

The `readAcquires` field counts the total number of read lock acquisitions, and the `readReleases` field counts the total number of read lock releases. When these quantities match, no thread is holding the read lock. (We are, of course, ignoring potential integer overflow and wraparound problems.) The class has

```java
public class FifoReadWriteLock implements ReadWriteLock {
  int readAcquires, readReleases;
  boolean writer;
  Lock lock;
  Condition condition;
  Lock readLock, writeLock;
  public FifoReadWriteLock() {
    readAcquires = readReleases = 0;
    writer   = false;
    lock = new ReentrantLock(true);
    condition = lock.newCondition();
    readLock = new ReadLock();
    writeLock = new WriteLock();
  }
  public Lock readLock() {
    return readLock;
  }
  public Lock writeLock() {
    return writeLock;
  }
  ...
}
```

Figure 8.10 The `FifoReadWriteLock` class: fields and public methods.

```java
  private class ReadLock implements Lock {
    public void lock() {
      lock.lock();
      try {
        while (writer) {
          condition.await();
        }
        readAcquires++;
      } finally {
        lock.unlock();
      }
    }
    public void unlock() {
      lock.lock();
      try {
        readReleases++;
        if (readAcquires == readReleases)
          condition.signalAll();
      } finally {
        lock.unlock();
      }
    }
  }
```

Figure 8.11 The `FifoReadWriteLock` class: inner read lock class.

```
  private class WriteLock implements Lock {
    public void lock() {
      lock.lock();
      try {
        while (writer) {
          condition.await();
        }
        writer = true;
        while (readAcquires != readReleases) {
          condition.await();
        }
      } finally {
        lock.unlock();
      }
    }
    public void unlock() {
      writer = false;
      condition.signalAll();
    }
  }
```

Figure 8.12 The `FifoReadWriteLock` class: inner write lock class.

a private `lock` field, held by readers for short durations: they acquire the lock, increment the `readAcquires` field, and release the lock. Writers hold this lock from the time they try to acquire the write lock to the time they release it. This locking protocol ensures that once a writer has acquired the `lock`, no additional reader can increment `readAcquires`, so no additional reader can acquire the read lock, and eventually all readers currently holding the read lock will release it, allowing the writer to proceed.

How are waiting writers notified when the last reader releases its lock? When a writer tries to acquire the write lock, it acquires the `FifoReadWriteLock` object's `lock`. A reader releasing the read lock also acquires that `lock`, and calls the associated condition's `signal()` method if all readers have released their locks.

8.4 Our Own Reentrant Lock

Using the locks described in Chapters 2 and 7, a thread that attempts to reacquire a lock it already holds will deadlock with itself. This situation can arise if a method that acquires a lock makes a nested call to another method that acquires the same lock.

A lock is *reentrant* if it can be acquired multiple times by the same thread. We now examine how to create a reentrant lock from a non-reentrant lock. This exercise is intended to illustrate how to use locks and conditions. In practice, the java.util.concurrent.locks package provides reentrant lock classes, so there is no need to write our own.

Fig. 8.13 shows the `SimpleReentrantLock` class. The `owner` field holds the ID of the last thread to acquire the lock, and the `holdCount` field is incremented each

```java
public class SimpleReentrantLock implements Lock{
  Lock lock;
  Condition condition;
  int owner, holdCount;
  public SimpleReentrantLock() {
    lock = new SimpleLock();
    condition = lock.newCondition();
    owner = 0;
    holdCount = 0;
  }
  public void lock() {
    int me = ThreadID.get();
    lock.lock();
    try {
      if (owner == me) {
        holdCount++;
        return;
      }
      while (holdCount != 0) {
       condition.await();
      }
      owner = me;
      holdCount = 1;
   } finally {
     lock.unlock();
   }
  }
  public void unlock() {
    lock.lock();
    try {
      if (holdCount == 0 || owner != ThreadID.get())
        throw new IllegalMonitorStateException();
      holdCount--;
      if (holdCount == 0) {
        condition.signal();
      }
    } finally {
      lock.unlock();
    }
  }

  public Condition newCondition() {
    throw new UnsupportedOperationException("Not supported yet.");
  }
 ...
}
```

Figure 8.13 The SimpleReentrantLock class: lock() and unlock() methods.

time the lock is acquired, and decremented each time it is released. The lock is free when the holdCount value is zero. Because these two fields are manipulated atomically, we need an internal, short-term lock. The lock field is a lock used by lock() and unlock() to manipulate the fields, and the condition field is used by threads waiting for the lock to become free. In Fig. 8.13, we initialize the internal `lock` field to an object of a (fictitious) `SimpleLock` class which is presumably not reentrant (Line 6).

The `lock()` method acquires the internal lock (Line 13). If the current thread is already the owner, it increments the hold count and returns (Line 15). Otherwise, if the hold count is not zero, the lock is held by another thread, and the caller releases the lock and waits until the condition is signaled (Line 20). When the caller awakens, it must still check that the hold count is zero. When the hold count is established to be zero, the calling thread makes itself the owner and sets the hold count to 1.

The `unlock()` method acquires the internal lock (Line 29). It throws an exception if either the lock is free, or the caller is not the owner (Line 31). Otherwise, it decrements the hold count. If the hold count is zero, then the lock is free, so the caller signals the condition to wake up a waiting thread (Line 35).

8.5 Semaphores

As we have seen, a mutual exclusion lock guarantees that only one thread at a time can enter a critical section. If another thread wants to enter the critical section while it is occupied, then it blocks, suspending itself until another thread notifies it to try again. A `Semaphore` is a generalization of mutual exclusion locks. Each `Semaphore` has a *capacity*, denoted by c for brevity. Instead of allowing only one thread at a time into the critical section, a `Semaphore` allows at most c threads, where the capacity c is determined when the `Semaphore` is initialized. As discussed in the chapter notes, semaphores were one of the earliest forms of synchronization.

The `Semaphore` class of Fig. 8.14 provides two methods: a thread calls `acquire()` to request permission to enter the critical section, and `release()` to announce that it is leaving the critical section. The `Semaphore` itself is just a counter: it keeps track of the number of threads that have been granted permission to enter. If a new `acquire()` call is about to exceed the capacity c, the calling thread is suspended until there is room. When a thread leaves the critical section, it calls `release()` to notify a waiting thread that there is now room.

8.6 Chapter Notes

Monitors were invented by Per Brinch-Hansen [52] and Tony Hoare [71]. Semaphores were invented by Edsger Dijkstra [33]. McKenney [112] surveys different kinds of locking protocols.

```
public class Semaphore {
  final int capacity;
  int state;
  Lock lock;
  Condition condition;
  public Semaphore(int c) {
    capacity = c;
    state = 0;
    lock = new ReentrantLock();
    condition = lock.newCondition();
  }
  public void acquire() {
    lock.lock();
    try {
      while (state == capacity) {
        condition.await();
      }
      state++;
    } finally {
      lock.unlock();
    }
  }
  public void release() {
    lock.lock();
    try {
      state--;
      condition.signalAll();
    } finally {
      lock.unlock();
    }
  }
}
```

Figure 8.14 Semaphore implementation.

8.7 Exercises

Exercise 93. Reimplement the `SimpleReadWriteLock` class using Java **`synchronized`**, `wait()`, `notify()`, and `notifyAll()` constructs in place of explict locks and conditions.

Hint: you must figure out how methods of the inner read–write lock classes can lock the outer `SimpleReadWriteLock` object.

Exercise 94. The `ReentrantReadWriteLock` class provided by the java.util.concurrent.locks package does not allow a thread holding the lock in read mode to then access that lock in write mode (the thread will block). Justify this design decision by sketching what it would take to permit such lock upgrades.

Exercise 95. A *savings account* object holds a nonnegative balance, and provides deposit(k) and withdraw(k) methods, where deposit(k) adds k to the balance, and withdraw(k) subtracts k, if the balance is at least k, and otherwise blocks until the balance becomes k or greater.

1. Implement this savings account using locks and conditions.
2. Now suppose there are two kinds of withdrawals: *ordinary* and *preferred.* Devise an implementation that ensures that no ordinary withdrawal occurs if there is a preferred withdrawal waiting to occur.
3. Now let us add a transfer() method that transfers a sum from one account to another:

```
void transfer(int k, Account reserve) {
  lock.lock();
  try {
    reserve.withdraw(k);
    deposit(k);
  } finally {lock.unlock();}
}
```

   We are given a set of 10 accounts, whose balances are unknown. At 1:00, each of n threads tries to transfer \$100 from another account into its own account. At 2:00, a Boss thread deposits \$1000 to each account. Is every transfer method called at 1:00 certain to return?

Exercise 96. In the *shared bathroom problem,* there are two classes of threads, called *male* and *female.* There is a single *bathroom* resource that must be used in the following way:

1. Mutual exclusion: persons of opposite sex may not occupy the bathroom simultaneously,
2. Starvation-freedom: everyone who needs to use the bathroom eventually enters.

The protocol is implemented via the following four procedures: enterMale() delays the caller until it is ok for a male to enter the bathroom, leaveMale() is called when a male leaves the bathroom, while enterFemale() and leaveFemale() do the same for females. For example,

```
enterMale();
teeth.brush(toothpaste);
leaveMale();
```

1. Implement this class using locks and condition variables.
2. Implement this class using **synchronized**, wait(), notify(), and notifyAll().

For each implementation, explain why it satisfies mutual exclusion and starvation-freedom.

Exercise 97. The Rooms class manages a collection of *rooms*, indexed from 0 to m (where m is an argument to the constructor). Threads can enter or exit any room in that range. Each room can hold an arbitrary number of threads simultaneously, but only one room can be occupied at a time. For example, if there are two rooms, indexed 0 and 1, then any number of threads might enter the room 0, but no thread can enter the room 1 while room 0 is occupied. Fig. 8.15 shows an outline of the Rooms class.

Each room can be assigned an *exit handler*: calling setHandler(i, h) sets the exit handler for room i to handler h. The exit handler is called by the last thread to

```
public class Rooms {
  public interface Handler {
    void onEmpty();
  }
  public Rooms(int m) { ... };
  void enter(int i) { ... };
  boolean exit() { ... };
  public void setExitHandler(int i, Rooms.Handler h) { ... };
}
```

Figure 8.15 The Rooms class.

```
class Driver {
  void main() {
    CountDownLatch startSignal = new CountDownLatch(1);
    CountDownLatch doneSignal = new CountDownLatch(n);
    for (int i = 0; i < n; ++i) // start threads
      new Thread(new Worker(startSignal, doneSignal)).start();
    doSomethingElse();          // get ready for threads
    startSignal.countDown();    // unleash threads
    doSomethingElse();          // biding my time ...
    doneSignal.await();         // wait for threads to finish
  }
  class Worker implements Runnable {
    private final CountDownLatch startSignal, doneSignal;
    Worker(CountDownLatch myStartSignal, CountDownLatch myDoneSignal) {
      startSignal = myStartSignal;
      doneSignal = myDoneSignal;
    }
    public void run() {
      startSignal.await();      // wait for driver's OK to start
      doWork();
      doneSignal.countDown(); // notify driver we're done
    }
    ...
  }
}
```

Figure 8.16 The CountDownLatch class: an example usage.

leave a room, but before any threads subsequently enter any room. This method is called once and while it is running, no threads are in any rooms.

Implement the `Rooms` class. Make sure that:

- If some thread is in room i, then no thread is in room $j \neq i$.
- The last thread to leave a room calls the room's exit handler, and no threads are in any room while that handler is running.
- Your implementation must be *fair*: any thread that tries to enter a room eventually succeeds. Naturally, you may assume that every thread that enters a room eventually leaves.

Exercise 98. Consider an application with distinct sets of *active* and *passive* threads, where we want to block the passive threads until all active threads give permission for the passive threads to proceed.

A `CountDownLatch` encapsulates a counter, initialized to be n, the number of active threads. When an active method is ready for the passive threads to run, it calls `countDown()`, which decrements the counter. Each passive thread calls `await()`, which blocks the thread until the counter reaches zero. (See Fig. 8.16.)

Provide a `CountDownLatch` implementation. Do not worry about reusing the `CountDownLatch` object.

Exercise 99. This exercise is a follow-up to Exercise 98. Provide a `CountDownLatch` implementation where the `CountDownLatch` object can be reused.

9 Linked Lists: The Role of Locking

9.1 Introduction

In Chapter 7 we saw how to build scalable spin locks that provide mutual exclusion efficiently, even when they are heavily used. We might think that it is now a simple matter to construct scalable concurrent data structures: take a sequential implementation of the class, add a scalable lock field, and ensure that each method call acquires and releases that lock. We call this approach *coarse-grained synchronization.*

Often, coarse-grained synchronization works well, but there are important cases where it does not. The problem is that a class that uses a single lock to mediate all its method calls is not always scalable, even if the lock itself is scalable. Coarse-grained synchronization works well when levels of concurrency are low, but if too many threads try to access the object at the same time, then the object becomes a sequential bottleneck, forcing threads to wait in line for access.

This chapter introduces several useful techniques that go beyond coarse-grained locking to allow multiple threads to access a single object at the same time.

- *Fine-grained synchronization:* Instead of using a single lock to synchronize every access to an object, we split the object into independently synchronized components, ensuring that method calls interfere only when trying to access the same component at the same time.
- *Optimistic synchronization:* Many objects, such as trees or lists, consist of multiple components linked together by references. Some methods search for a particular component (e.g., a list or tree node containing a particular key). One way to reduce the cost of fine-grained locking is to search without acquiring any locks at all. If the method finds the sought-after component, it locks that component, and then checks that the component has not changed in the interval between when it was inspected and when it was locked. This technique is worthwhile only if it succeeds more often than not, which is why we call it optimistic.

```
public interface Set<T> {
  boolean add(T x);
  boolean remove(T x);
  boolean contains(T x);
}
```

Figure 9.1 The `Set` interface: `add()` adds an item to the set (no effect if that item is already present), `remove()` removes it (if present), and `contains()` returns a Boolean indicating whether the item is present.

- *Lazy synchronization:* Sometimes it makes sense to postpone hard work. For example, the task of removing a component from a data structure can be split into two phases: the component is *logically removed* simply by setting a tag bit, and later, the component can be *physically removed* by unlinking it from the rest of the data structure.
- *Nonblocking synchronization:* Sometimes we can eliminate locks entirely, relying on built-in atomic operations such as `compareAndSet()` for synchronization.

Each of these techniques can be applied (with appropriate customization) to a variety of common data structures. In this chapter we consider how to use linked lists to implement a *set*, a collection of *items* that contains no duplicate elements.

For our purposes, as illustrated in Fig. 9.1, a *set* provides the following three methods:

- The `add`(x) method adds x to the set, returning *true* if, and only if x was not already there.
- The `remove`(x) method removes x from the set, returning *true* if, and only if x was there.
- The `contains`(x) returns *true* if, and only if the set contains x.

For each method, we say that a call is *successful* if it returns *true*, and *unsuccessful* otherwise. It is typical that in applications using sets, there are significantly more `contains()` calls than `add()` or `remove()` calls.

9.2 List-Based Sets

This chapter presents a range of concurrent set algorithms, all based on the same basic idea. A set is implemented as a linked list of nodes. As shown in Fig. 9.2, the `Node<T>` class has three fields.[1] The `item` field is the actual item of interest. The `key` field is the item's hash code. Nodes are sorted in `key` order, providing an efficient way to detect when an item is absent. The `next` field is a reference to

1 To be consistent with the Java memory model these fields and their modifications later in the text will need to be volatile, though we ignore this issue here for the sake of brevity.

```
private class Node {
  T item;
  int key;
  Node next;
}
```

Figure 9.2 The `Node<T>` class: this internal class keeps track of the item, the item's key, and the next node in the list. Some algorithms require technical changes to this class.

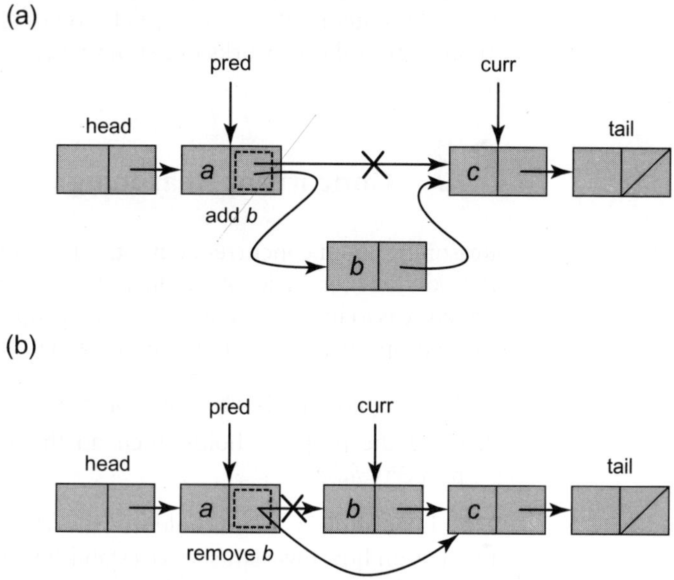

Figure 9.3 A seqential `Set` implementation: adding and removing nodes. In Part (a), a thread adding a node *b* uses two variables: `curr` is the current node, and `pred` is its predecessor. The thread moves down the list comparing the keys for `curr` and *b*. If a match is found, the item is already present, so it returns false. If `curr` reaches a node with a higher key, the item is not in the set so Set *b*'s `next` field to `curr`, and `pred`'s `next` field to *b*. In Part (b), to delete `curr`, the thread sets `pred`'s `next` field to `curr`'s `next` field.

the next node in the list. (Some of the algorithms we consider require technical changes to this class, such as adding new fields, or changing the types of existing fields.) For simplicity, we assume that each item's hash code is unique (relaxing this assumption is left as an exercise). We associate an item with the same node and key throughout any given example, which allows us to abuse notation and use the same symbol to refer to a node, its key, and its item. That is, node *a* may have key *a* and item *a*, and so on.

The list has two kinds of nodes. In addition to *regular* nodes that hold items in the set, we use two *sentinel* nodes, called `head` and `tail`, as the first and last list elements. Sentinel nodes are never added, removed, or searched for, and their keys are the minimum and maximum integer values.[2] Ignoring synchronization for the moment, the top part of Fig. 9.3 schematically describes how an item is added to the set. Each thread A has two local variables used to traverse the list: $\texttt{curr}_A$ is the current node and $\texttt{pred}_A$ is its predecessor. To add an item to the set, thread A sets local variables $\texttt{pred}_A$ and $\texttt{curr}_A$ to `head`, and moves down the list, comparing $\texttt{curr}_A$'s key to the key of the item being added. If they match, the item is already present in the set, so the call returns *false*. If $\texttt{pred}_A$ precedes $\texttt{curr}_A$ in the list, then $\texttt{pred}_A$'s key is lower than that of the inserted item, and $\texttt{curr}_A$'s key is higher, so the item is not present in the list. The method creates a new node b to hold the item, sets b's $\texttt{next}_A$ field to $\texttt{curr}_A$, then sets $\texttt{pred}_A$ to b. Removing an item from the set works in a similar way.

9.3 Concurrent Reasoning

Reasoning about concurrent data structures may seem impossibly difficult, but it is a skill that can be learned. Often, the key to understanding a concurrent data structure is to understand its *invariants*: properties that always hold. We can show that a property is invariant by showing that:

1. The property holds when the object is created, and
2. Once the property holds, then no thread can take a step that makes the property *false*.

Most interesting invariants hold trivially when the list is created, so it makes sense to focus on how invariants, once established, are preserved.

Specifically, we can check that each invariant is preserved by each invocation of `insert()`, `remove()`, and `contains()` methods. This approach works only if we can assume that these methods are the *only* ones that modify nodes, a property sometimes called *freedom from interference*. In the list algorithms considered here, nodes are internal to the list implementation, so freedom from interference is guaranteed because users of the list have no opportunity to modify its internal nodes.

We require freedom from interference even for nodes that have been removed from the list, since some of our algorithms permit a thread to unlink a node while it is being traversed by others. Fortunately, we do not attempt to reuse list nodes that have been removed from the list, relying instead on a garbage collector to recycle that memory. The algorithms described here work in languages without garbage collection, but sometimes require nontrivial modifications that are beyond the scope of this chapter.

---

2 All algorithms presented here work for any ordered set of keys that have maximum and minimum values and that are well-founded, that is, there are only finitely many keys smaller than any given key. For simplicity, we assume here that keys are integers.

When reasoning about concurrent object implementations, it is important to understand the distinction between an object's *abstract value* (here, a set of items), and its *concrete representation* (here, a list of nodes).

Not every list of nodes is a meaningful representation for a set. An algorithm's *representation invariant* characterizes which representations make sense as abstract values. If a and b are nodes, we say that *a points to b* if a's `next` field is a reference to b. We say that b is *reachable* if there is a sequence of nodes, starting at `head`, and ending at b, where each node in the sequence points to its successor.

The set algorithms in this chapter require the following invariants (some require more, as explained later). First, sentinels are neither added nor removed. Second, nodes are sorted by key, and keys are unique.

Let us think of the representation invariant as a contract among the object's methods. Each method call preserves the invariant, and also relies on the other methods to preserve the invariant. In this way, we can reason about each method in isolation, without having to consider all the possible ways they might interact.

Given a list satisfying the representation invariant, which set does it represent? The meaning of such a list is given by an *abstraction map* carrying lists that satisfy the representation invariant to sets. Here, the abstraction map is simple: an item is in the set if and only if it is reachable from `head`.

What safety and liveness properties do we need? Our safety property is *linearizability*. As we saw in Chapter 3, to show that a concurrent data structure is a linearizable implementation of a sequentially specified object, it is enough to identify a *linearization point*, a single atomic step where the method call "takes effect." This step can be a read, a write, or a more complex atomic operation. Looking at any execution history of a list-based set, it must be the case that if the abstraction map is applied to the representation at the linearization points, the resulting sequence of states and method calls defines a valid sequential set execution. Here, `add`(a) adds a to the abstract set, `remove`(a) removes a from the abstract set, and `contains`(a) returns *true* or *false*, depending on whether a was already in the set.

Different list algorithms make different progress guarantees. Some use locks, and care is required to ensure they are deadlock- and starvation-free. Some *nonblocking* list algorithms do not use locks at all, while others restrict locking to certain methods. Here is a brief summary, from Chapter 3, of the nonblocking properties we use[3]:

- A method is *wait-free* if it guarantees that every call finishes in a finite number of steps.
- A method is *lock-free* if it guarantees that *some* call always finishes in a finite number of steps.

We are now ready to consider a range of list-based set algorithms. We start with algorithms that use coarse-grained synchronization, and successively refine them

---

3 Chapter 3 introduces an even weaker nonblocking property called *obstruction-freedom*.

to reduce granularity of locking. Formal proofs of correctness lie beyond the scope of this book. Instead, we focus on informal reasoning useful in everyday problem-solving.

As mentioned, in each of these algorithms, methods scan through the list using two local variables: curr is the current node and pred is its predecessor. These variables are thread-local,[4] so we use pred$_A$ and curr$_A$ to denote the instances used by thread A.

9.4 Coarse-Grained Synchronization

We start with a simple algorithm using coarse-grained synchronization. Figs. 9.4 and 9.5 show the add() and remove() methods for this coarse-grained algorithm. (The contains() method works in much the same way, and is left as an exercise.) The list itself has a single lock which every method call must acquire. The principal

```
public class CoarseList<T> {
  private Node head;
  private Lock lock = new ReentrantLock();
  public CoarseList() {
    head = new Node(Integer.MIN_VALUE);
    head.next = new Node(Integer.MAX_VALUE);
  }
  public boolean add(T item) {
    Node pred, curr;
    int key = item.hashCode();
    lock.lock();
    try {
      pred = head;
      curr = pred.next;
      while (curr.key < key) {
        pred = curr;
        curr = curr.next;
      }
      if (key == curr.key) {
        return false;
      } else {
        Node node = new Node(item);
        node.next = curr;
        pred.next = node;
        return true;
      }
    } finally {
      lock.unlock();
    }
  }
```

Figure 9.4 The CoarseList class: the add() method.

4 Appendix A describes how thread-local variables work in Java.

```
public boolean remove(T item) {
  Node pred, curr;
  int key = item.hashCode();
  lock.lock();
  try {
    pred = head;
    curr = pred.next;
    while (curr.key < key) {
      pred = curr;
      curr = curr.next;
    }
    if (key == curr.key) {
      pred.next = curr.next;
      return true;
    } else {
      return false;
    }
  } finally {
    lock.unlock();
  }
}
```

Figure 9.5 The `CoarseList` class: the `remove()` method. All methods acquire a single lock, which is released on exit by the **`finally`** block.

advantage of this algorithm, which should not be discounted, is that it is obviously correct. All methods act on the list only while holding the lock, so the execution is essentially sequential. To simplify matters, we follow the convention (for now) that the linearization point for any method call that acquires a lock is the instant the lock is acquired.

The `CoarseList` class satisfies the same progress condition as its lock: if the `Lock` is starvation-free, so is our implementation. If contention is very low, this algorithm is an excellent way to implement a list. If, however, there is contention, then even if the lock itself performs well, threads will still be delayed waiting for one another.

9.5 Fine-Grained Synchronization

We can improve concurrency by locking individual nodes, rather than locking the list as a whole. Instead of placing a lock on the entire list, let us add a `Lock` to each node, along with `lock()` and `unlock()` methods. As a thread traverses the list, it locks each node when it first visits, and sometime later releases it. Such *fine-grained* locking permits concurrent threads to traverse the list together in a pipelined fashion.

Let us consider two nodes a and b where a points to b. It is not safe to unlock a before locking b because another thread could remove b from the list in the interval between unlocking a and locking b. Instead, thread A must acquire locks in a kind of "hand-over-hand" order: except for the initial `head` sentinel node, acquire the lock for a node only while holding the lock for its predecessor. This locking protocol is sometimes called *lock coupling*. (Notice that there is no obvious way to implement lock coupling using Java's **synchronized** methods.)

Fig. 9.6 shows the FineList algorithm's add() method, and Fig. 9.7 its remove() method. Just as in the coarse-grained list, remove() makes curr$_A$ unreachable by setting pred$_A$'s next field to curr$_A$'s successor. To be safe, remove() must lock both pred$_A$ and curr$_A$. To see why, let us consider the following scenario, illustrated in Fig. 9.8. Thread *A* is about to remove node *a*, the first node in the list, while thread *B* is about to remove node *b*, where *a* points to *b*. Suppose *A* locks head, and *B* locks *a*. *A* then sets head.next to *b*, while *B* sets a.next to *c*. The net effect is to remove *a*, but not *b*. The problem is that there is no overlap between the locks held by the two remove() calls. Fig. 9.9 illustrates how this "hand-over-hand" locking avoids this problem.

To guarantee progress, it is important that all methods acquire locks in the same order, starting at the head and following next references toward the tail. As Fig. 9.10 shows, a deadlock could occur if different method calls were to acquire locks in different orders. In this example, thread *A*, trying to add *a*, has

```
public boolean add(T item) {
  int key = item.hashCode();
  head.lock();
  Node pred = head;
  try {
    Node curr = pred.next;
    curr.lock();
    try {
      while (curr.key < key) {
        pred.unlock();
        pred = curr;
        curr = curr.next;
        curr.lock();
      }
      if (curr.key == key) {
        return false;
      }
      Node newNode = new Node(item);
      newNode.next = curr;
      pred.next = newNode;
      return true;
    } finally {
      curr.unlock();
    }
  } finally {
    pred.unlock();
  }
}
```

Figure 9.6 The FineList class: the add() method uses hand-over-hand locking to traverse the list. The **finally** blocks release locks before returning.

```
public boolean remove(T item) {
  Node pred = null, curr = null;
  int key = item.hashCode();
  head.lock();
  try {
    pred = head;
    curr = pred.next;
    curr.lock();
    try {
      while (curr.key < key) {
        pred.unlock();
        pred = curr;
        curr = curr.next;
        curr.lock();
      }
      if (curr.key == key) {
        pred.next = curr.next;
        return true;
      }
      return false;
    } finally {
      curr.unlock();
    }
  } finally {
    pred.unlock();
  }
}
```

Figure 9.7 The `FineList` class: the `remove()` method locks both the node to be removed and its predecessor before removing that node.

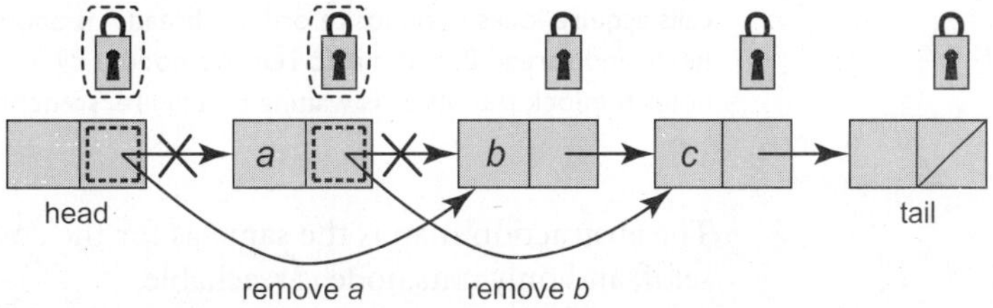

Figure 9.8 The `FineList` class: why `remove()` must acquire two locks. Thread *A* is about to remove *a*, the first node in the list, while thread *B* is about to remove *b*, where *a* points to *b*. Suppose *A* locks `head`, and *B* locks *a*. Thread *A* then sets `head.next` to *b*, while *B* sets *a*'s `next` field to *c*. The net effect is to remove *a*, but not *b*.

locked *b* and is attempting to lock `head`, while *B*, trying to remove *b*, has locked `head` and is trying to lock *b*. Clearly, these method calls will never finish. Avoiding deadlocks is one of the principal challenges of programming with locks.

The `FineList` algorithm maintains the representation invariant: sentinels are never added or removed, and nodes are sorted by key value without duplicates.

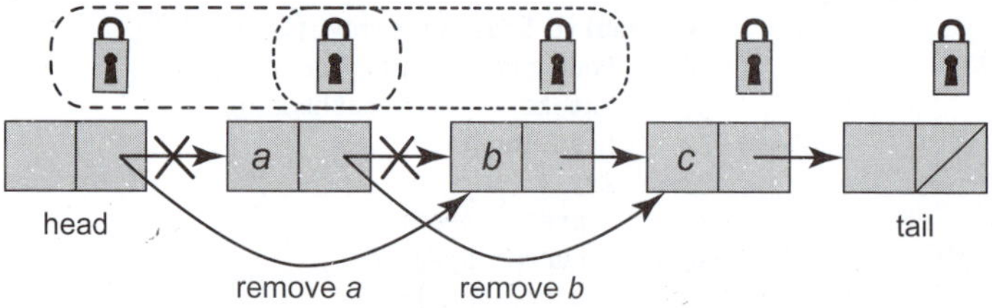

Figure 9.9 The FineList class: Hand-over-hand locking ensures that if concurrent remove() calls try to remove adjacent nodes, then they acquire conflicting locks. Thread *A* is about to remove node *a*, the first node in the list, while thread *B* is about to remove node *b*, where *a* points to *b*. Because *A* must lock both head and *a*, and *B* must lock both *a* and *b*, they are guaranteed to conflict on *a*, forcing one call to wait for the other.

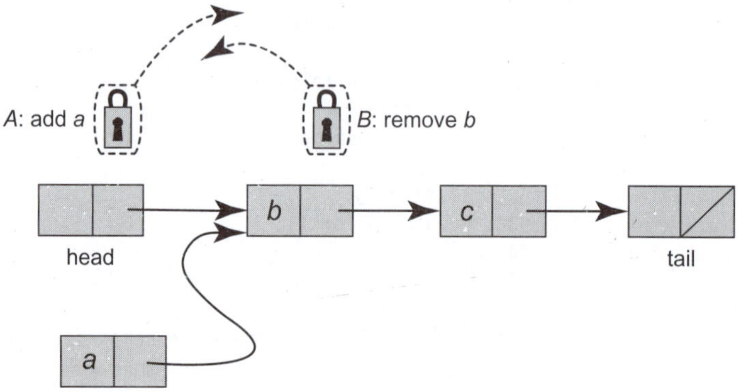

Figure 9.10 The FineList class: a deadlock can occur if, for example, remove() and add() calls acquire locks in opposite order. Thread *A* is about to insert *a* by locking first *b* and then head, and thread *B* is about to remove node *b* by locking first head and then *b*. Each thread holds the lock the other is waiting to acquire, so neither makes progress.

The abstraction map is the same as for the course-grained list: an item is in the set if, and only if its node is reachable.

The linearization point for an add(*a*) call depends on whether the call was successful (i.e., whether *a* was already present). A successful call (*a* absent) is linearized when the node with the next higher key is locked (either Line 7 or 13).

The same distinctions apply to remove(*a*) calls. An unsuccessful call (*a* present) is linearized when the predecessor node is locked (Lines 36 or 42). An unsuccessful call (*a* absent) is linearized when the node containing the next higher key is locked (Lines 36 or 42).

Determining linearization points for contains() is left as an exercise.

The FineList algorithm is starvation-free, but arguing this property is harder than in the coarse-grained case. We assume that all individual locks are starvation-free. Because all methods acquire locks in the same down-the-list order, deadlock is impossible. If thread A attempts to lock `head`, eventually it succeeds. From that point on, because there are no deadlocks, eventually all locks held by threads ahead of A in the list will be released, and A will succeed in locking $\texttt{pred}_A$ and $\texttt{curr}_A$.

9.6 Optimistic Synchronization

Although fine-grained locking is an improvement over a single, coarse-grained lock, it still imposes a potentially long sequence of lock acquisitions and releases. Moreover, threads accessing disjoint parts of the list may still block one another. For example, a thread removing the second item in the list blocks all concurrent threads searching for later nodes.

One way to reduce synchronization costs is to take a chance: search without acquiring locks, lock the nodes found, and then confirm that the locked nodes are correct. If a synchronization conflict causes the wrong nodes to be locked, then release the locks and start over. Normally, this kind of conflict is rare, which is why we call this technique *optimistic synchronization.*

In Fig. 9.11, thread A makes an optimistic `add`(a). It traverses the list without acquiring any locks (Lines 6 through 8). In fact, it ignores the locks completely. It stops the traversal when $\texttt{curr}_A$'s key is greater than, or equal to a's. It then locks $\texttt{pred}_A$ and $\texttt{curr}_A$, and calls `validate()` to check that $\texttt{pred}_A$ is reachable and its `next` field still refers to $\texttt{curr}_A$. If validation succeeds, then thread A proceeds as before: if $\texttt{curr}_A$'s key is greater than a, thread A adds a new node with item a between $\texttt{pred}_A$ and $\texttt{curr}_A$, and returns *true*. Otherwise it returns *false*. The `remove()` and `contains()` methods (Figs. 9.12 and 9.13) operate similarly, traversing the list without locking, then locking the target nodes and validating they are still in the list. To be consistent with the Java memory model, the *next* fields in the nodes need to be declared volatile.

The code of `validate()` appears in Fig. 9.14. We are reminded of the following story:

> A tourist takes a taxi in a foreign town. The taxi driver speeds through a red light. The tourist, frightened, asks "What are you are doing?" The driver answers: "Do not worry, I am an expert." He speeds through more red lights, and the tourist, on the verge of hysteria, complains again, more urgently. The driver replies, "Relax, relax, you are in the hands of an expert." Suddenly, the light turns green, the driver slams on the brakes, and the taxi skids to a halt. The tourist picks himself off the floor of the taxi and asks "For crying out loud, why stop now that the light is finally green?" The driver answers "Too dangerous, could be another expert crossing."

Traversing any dynamically changing lock-based data structure while ignoring locks requires careful thought (there are other expert threads out there). We must make sure to use some form of *validation* and guarantee freedom from *interference*.

```
public boolean add(T item) {
  int key = item.hashCode();
  while (true) {
    Node pred = head;
    Node curr = pred.next;
    while (curr.key < key) {
      pred = curr; curr = curr.next;
    }
    pred.lock(); curr.lock();
    try {
      if (validate(pred, curr)) {
        if (curr.key == key) {
          return false;
        } else {
          Node node = new Node(item);
          node.next = curr;
          pred.next = node;
          return true;
        }
      }
    } finally {
      pred.unlock(); curr.unlock();
    }
  }
}
```

Figure 9.11 The `OptimisticList` class: the `add()` method traverses the list ignoring locks, acquires locks, and validates before adding the new node.

```
public boolean remove(T item) {
  int key = item.hashCode();
  while (true) {
    Node pred = head;
    Node curr = pred.next;
    while (curr.key < key) {
      pred = curr; curr = curr.next;
    }
    pred.lock(); curr.lock();
    try {
      if (validate(pred, curr)) {
        if (curr.key == key) {
          pred.next = curr.next;
          return true;
        } else {
          return false;
        }
      }
    } finally {
      pred.unlock(); curr.unlock();
    }
  }
}
```

Figure 9.12 The `OptimisticList` class: the `remove()` method traverses ignoring locks, acquires locks, and validates before removing the node.

```
public boolean contains(T item) {
  int key = item.hashCode();
  while (true) {
   Node pred = this.head; // sentinel node;
   Node curr = pred.next;
   while (curr.key < key) {
    pred = curr; curr = curr.next;
    }
   pred.lock(); curr.lock();
   try {
     if (validate(pred, curr)) {
       return (curr.key == key);
     }
   } finally {                       // always unlock
     pred.unlock(); curr.unlock();
   }
  }
}
```

Figure 9.13 The `OptimisticList` class: the `contains()` method searches, ignoring locks, then it acquires locks, and validates to determine if the node is in the list.

```
  private boolean validate(Node pred, Node curr) {
     Node node = head;
     while (node.key <= pred.key) {
       if (node == pred)
         return pred.next == curr;
       node = node.next;
     }
     return false;
   }
```

Figure 9.14 The `OptimisticList`: validation checks that $\mathtt{pred}_A$ points to $\mathtt{curr}_A$ and is reachable from `head`.

As Fig. 9.15 shows, validation is necessary because the trail of references leading to $\mathtt{pred}_A$ or the reference from $\mathtt{pred}_A$ to $\mathtt{curr}_A$ could have changed between when they were last read by A and when A acquired the locks. In particular, a thread could be traversing parts of the list that have already been removed. For example, the node $\mathtt{curr}_A$ and all nodes between $\mathtt{curr}_A$ and a (including a) may be removed while A is still traversing $\mathtt{curr}_A$. Thread A discovers that $\mathtt{curr}_A$ points to a, and, without validation, "successfully" removes a, even though a is no longer in the list. A `validate()` call detects that a is no longer in the list, and the caller restarts the method.

Because we are ignoring the locks that protect concurrent modifications, each of the method calls may traverse nodes that have been removed from the list. Nevertheless, absence of interference implies that once a node has been unlinked from the list, the value of its `next` field does not change, so following a sequence of such links eventually leads back to the list. Absence of interference, in turn, relies on garbage collection to ensure that no node is recycled while it is being traversed.

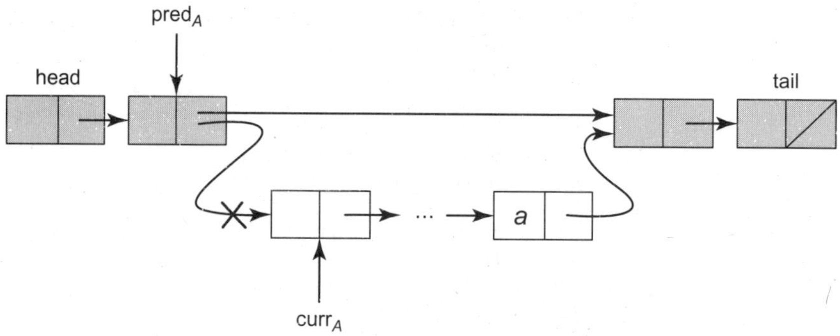

Figure 9.15 The `OptimisticList` class: why validation is needed. Thread *A* is attempting to remove a node *a*. While traversing the list, $curr_A$ and all nodes between $curr_A$ and *a* (including *a*) might be removed (denoted by a lighter node color). In such a case, thread *A* would proceed to the point where $curr_A$ points to *a*, and, without validation, would successfully remove *a*, even though it is no longer in the list. Validation is required to determine that *a* is no longer reachable from `head`.

The `OptimisticList` algorithm is not starvation-free, even if all node locks are individually starvation-free. A thread might be delayed forever if new nodes are repeatedly added and removed (see Exercise 107). Nevertheless, we would expect this algorithm to do well in practice, since starvation is rare.

9.7 Lazy Synchronization

The `OptimisticList` implementation works best if the cost of traversing the list twice without locking is significantly less than the cost of traversing the list once with locking. One drawback of this particular algorithm is that `contains()` acquires locks, which is unattractive since `contains()` calls are likely to be much more common than calls to other methods.

The next step is to refine this algorithm so that `contains()` calls are wait-free, and `add()` and `remove()` methods, while still blocking, traverse the list only once (in the absence of contention). We add to each node a Boolean `marked` field indicating whether that node is in the set. Now, traversals do not need to lock the target node, and there is no need to validate that the node is reachable by retraversing the whole list. Instead, the algorithm maintains the invariant that every unmarked node is reachable. If a traversing thread does not find a node, or finds it marked, then that item is not in the set. As a result, `contains()` needs only one wait-free traversal. To add an element to the list, `add()` traverses the list, locks the target's predecessor, and inserts the node. The `remove()` method is lazy, taking two steps: first, mark the target node, *logically* removing it, and second, redirect its predecessor's `next` field, *physically* removing it.

In more detail, all methods traverse the list (possibly traversing logically and physically removed nodes) ignoring the locks. The add() and remove() methods lock the pred$_A$ and curr$_A$ nodes as before (Figs. 9.17 and 9.18), but validation does not retraverse the entire list (Fig. 9.16) to determine whether a node is in the set. Instead, because a node must be marked before being physically removed, validation need only check that curr$_A$ has not been marked. However, as Fig. 9.20 shows, for insertion and deletion, since pred$_A$ is the one being modified, one must also check that pred$_A$ itself is not marked, and that it points to curr$_A$. Logical removals require a small change to the abstraction map: an item is in the set if, and only if it is referred to by an *unmarked* reachable node. Notice

```
private boolean validate(Node pred, Node curr) {
  return !pred.marked && !curr.marked && pred.next == curr;
}
```

Figure 9.16 The LazyList class: validation checks that neither the pred nor the curr node has been logically deleted, and that pred points to curr.

```
public boolean add(T item) {
 int key = item.hashCode();
 while (true) {
    Node pred = head;
    Node curr = head.next;
    while (curr.key < key) {
     pred = curr; curr = curr.next;
    }
    pred.lock();
    try {
      curr.lock();
      try {
        if (validate(pred, curr)) {
          if (curr.key == key) {
            return false;
          } else {
            Node node = new Node(item);
            node.next = curr;
            pred.next = node;
            return true;
          }
        }
      } finally {
        curr.unlock();
      }
    } finally {
      pred.unlock();
    }
  }
}
```

Figure 9.17 The LazyList class: add() method.

```
public boolean remove(T item) {
  int key = item.hashCode();
  while (true) {
   Node pred = head;
   Node curr = head.next;
   while (curr.key < key) {
    pred = curr; curr = curr.next;
    }
   pred.lock();
   try {
     curr.lock();
     try {
       if (validate(pred, curr)) {
         if (curr.key != key) {
           return false;
         } else {
           curr.marked = true;
           pred.next = curr.next;
           return true;
         }
       }
     } finally {
       curr.unlock();
     }
   } finally {
     pred.unlock();
   }
  }
}
```

Figure 9.18 The LazyList class: the remove() method removes nodes in two steps, logical and physical.

```
public boolean contains(T item) {
  int key = item.hashCode();
  Node curr = head;
  while (curr.key < key)
    curr = curr.next;
  return curr.key == key && !curr.marked;
}
```

Figure 9.19 The LazyList class: the contains() method.

that the path along which the node is reachable may contain marked nodes. The reader should check that any unmarked reachable node remains reachable, even if its predecessor is logically or physically deleted. As in the OptimisticList algorithm, add() and remove() are not starvation-free, because list traversals may be arbitrarily delayed by ongoing modifications.

The contains() method (Fig. 9.19) traverses the list once ignoring locks and returns *true* if the node it was searching for is present and unmarked, and *false*

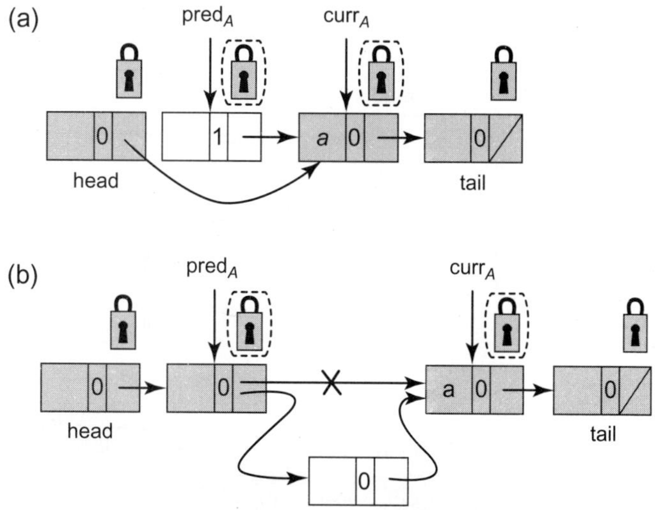

Figure 9.20 The `LazyList` class: why validation is needed. In Part (a) of the figure, thread A is attempting to remove node a. After it reaches the point where $\mathtt{pred}_A$ refers to $\mathtt{curr}_A$, and before it acquires locks on these nodes, the node $\mathtt{pred}_A$ is logically and physically removed. After A acquires the locks, validation will detect the problem. In Part (b) of the figure, A is attempting to remove node a. After it reaches the point where $\mathtt{pred}_A$ refers to $\mathtt{curr}_A$, and before it acquires locks on these nodes, a new node is added between $\mathtt{pred}_A$ and $\mathtt{curr}_A$. After A acquires the locks, even though neither $\mathtt{pred}_A$ or $\mathtt{curr}_A$ are marked, validation detects that $\mathtt{pred}_A$ is not the same as $\mathtt{curr}_A$, and A's call to `remove()` will be restarted.

otherwise. It is thus wait-free.[5] A marked node's value is ignored. Each time the traversal moves to a new node, the new node has a larger key than the previous one, even if the node is logically deleted.

The linearization points for `LazyList` `add()` and unsuccessful `remove()` calls are the same as for the `OptimisticList`. A successful `remove()` call is linearized when the mark is set (Line 17), and a successful `contains()` call is linearized when an unmarked matching node is found.

To understand how to linearize an unsuccessful `contains()`, let us consider the scenario depicted in Fig. 9.21. In Part (a), node a is marked as removed (its `marked` field is set) and thread A is attempting to find the node matching a's key. While A is traversing the list, $\mathtt{curr}_A$ and all nodes between $\mathtt{curr}_A$ and a including a are removed, both logically and physically. Thread A would still proceed to the point where $\mathtt{curr}_A$ points to a, and would detect that a is marked and no longer in the abstract set. The call could be linearized at this point.

Now let us consider the scenario depicted in Part (b). While A is traversing the removed section of the list leading to a, and before it reaches the removed

5 Notice that the list ahead of a given traversing thread cannot grow forever due to newly inserted keys, since the key size is finite.

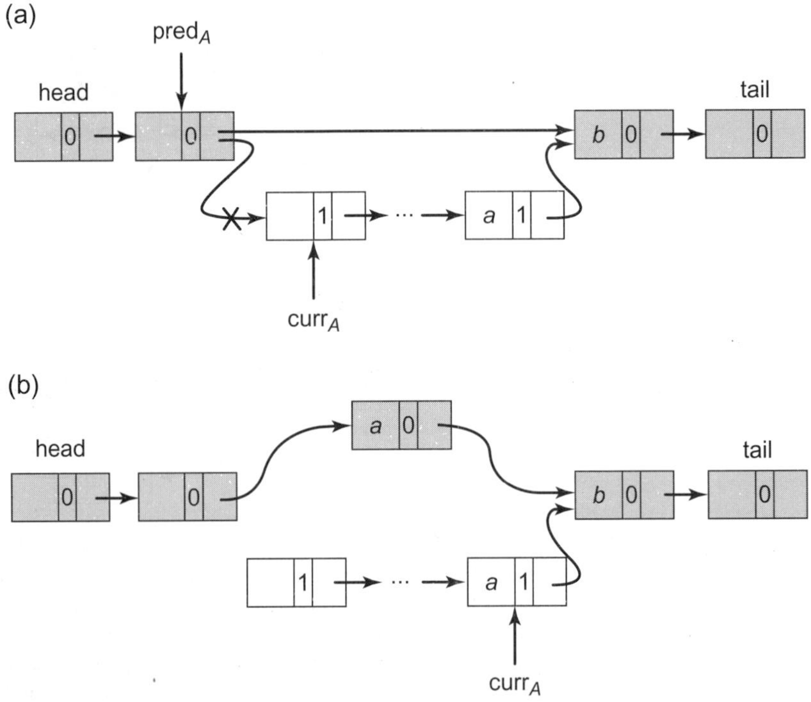

Figure 9.21 The `LazyList` class: linearizing an unsuccessful `contains()` call. Dark nodes are physically in the list and white nodes are physically removed. In Part (a), while thread *A* is traversing the list, a concurrent `remove()` call disconnects the sublist referred to by `curr`. Notice that nodes with items *a* and *b* are still reachable, so whether an item is actually in the list depends only on whether it is marked. Thread *A*'s call is linearized at the point when it sees that *a* is marked and is no longer in the abstract set. Alternatively, let us consider the scenario depicted in Part (b). While thread *A* is traversing the list leading to marked node *a*, another thread adds a new node with key *a*. It would be wrong to linearize thread *A*'s unsuccessful `contains()` call to when it found the marked node *a*, since this point occurs after the insertion of the new node with key *a* to the list.

node *a*, another thread adds a new node with a key *a* to the reachable part of the list. Linearizing thread *A*'s unsuccessful `contains()` method at the point it finds the marked node *a* would be wrong, since this point occurs *after* the insertion of the new node with key *a* to the list. We therefore linearize an unsuccessful `contains()` method call within its execution interval at the earlier of the following points: (1) the point where a removed matching node, or a node with a key greater than the one being searched for is found, and (2) the point immediately before a new matching node is added to the list. Notice that the second is guaranteed to be within the execution interval because the insertion of the new node with the same key must have happened after the start of the `contains()` method, or the `contains()` method would have found that item. As can be seen, the linearization point of the unsuccessful `contains()` is determined by the ordering of events in the execution, and is not a predetermined point in the method's code.

One benefit of lazy synchronization is that we can separate unobtrusive logical steps such as setting a flag, from disruptive physical changes to the structure, such as disconnecting a node. The example presented here is simple because we disconnect one node at a time. In general, however, delayed operations can be batched and performed lazily at a convenient time, reducing the overall disruptiveness of physical modifications to the structure.

The principal disadvantage of the `LazyList` algorithm is that `add()` and `remove()` calls are blocking: if one thread is delayed, then others may also be delayed.

9.8 Non-Blocking Synchronization

We have seen that it is sometimes a good idea to mark nodes as logically removed before physically removing them from the list. We now show how to extend this idea to eliminate locks altogether, allowing all three methods, `add()`, `remove()`, and `contains()`, to be nonblocking. (The first two methods are lock-free and the last wait-free). A naïve approach would be to use `compareAndSet()` to change the `next` fields. Unfortunately, this idea does not work. In Fig. 9.22, part (a) shows a thread *A* attempting to remove a node *a* while thread *B* is adding a node *b*. Suppose *A* applies `compareAndSet()` to `head.next`, while *B* applies `compareAndSet()` to `a.next`. The net effect is that *a* is correctly deleted but *b* is not added to the list. In part (b) of the figure, *A* attempts to remove *a*, the first node in the list, while *B* is about to remove *b*, where a points to *b*. Suppose *A* applies `compareAndSet()` to `head.next`, while *B* applies `compareAndSet()` to `a.next`. The net effect is to remove *a*, but not *b*.

If *B* wants to remove $\texttt{curr}_B$ from the list, it might call `compareAndSet()` to set $\texttt{pred}_B$'s next field to $\texttt{curr}_B$'s successor. It is not hard to see that if these two threads try to remove these adjacent nodes concurrently, the list will end up with b not being removed. A similar situation for a pair of concurrent `add()` and `remove()` methods is depicted in the upper part of Fig. 9.22.

Clearly, we need a way to ensure that a node's fields cannot be updated, after that node has been logically or physically removed from the list. Our approach is to treat the node's `next` and `marked` fields as a single atomic unit: any attempt to update the `next` field when the `marked` field is *true* will fail.

> *Pragma* 9.8.1. An `AtomicMarkableReference<T>` is an object from the java.util.concurrent.atomic package that encapsulates both a reference to an object of type T and a Boolean `mark`. These fields can be updated atomically, either together or individually. For example, the `compareAndSet()` method

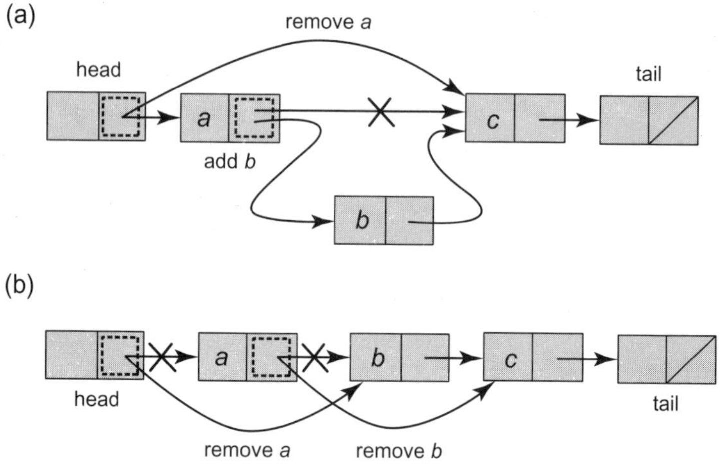

Figure 9.22 The `LockFreeList` class: why mark and reference fields must be modified atomically. In Part (a) of the figure, thread *A* is about to remove *a*, the first node in the list, while *B* is about to add *b*. Suppose *A* applies `compareAndSet()` to `head.next`, while *B* applies `compareAndSet()` to `a.next`. The net effect is that *a* is correctly deleted but *b* is not added to the list. In Part (b) of the figure, thread *A* is about to remove *a*, the first node in the list, while *B* is about to remove *b*, where *a* points to *b*. Suppose *A* applies `compareAndSet()` to `head.next`, while *B* applies `compareAndSet()` to `a.next`. The net effect is to remove *a*, but not *b*.

tests the expected reference and mark values, and if both tests succeed, replaces them with updated reference and mark values. As shorthand, the `attemptMark()` method tests an expected reference value and if the test succeeds, replaces it with a new mark value. The `get()` method has an unusual interface: it returns the object's reference value and stores the mark value in a Boolean array argument. Fig. 9.23 illustrates the interfaces of these methods.

```
public boolean compareAndSet(T expectedReference,
                             T newReference,
                             boolean expectedMark,
                             boolean newMark);
public boolean attemptMark(T expectedReference,
                           boolean newMark);
public T get(boolean[] marked);
```

Figure 9.23 Some `AtomicMarkableReference<T>` methods: the `compareAndSet()` method tests and updates both the mark and reference fields, while the `attemptMark()` method updates the mark if the reference field has the expected value. The `get()` method returns the encapsulated reference and stores the mark at position 0 in the argument array.

In C or C++, one could provide this functionality efficiently by "stealing" a bit from a pointer, using bit-wise operators to extract the mark and the pointer from a single word. In Java, of course, one cannot manipulate pointers directly, so this functionality must be provided by a library.

As described in detail in Pragma 9.8.1, an `AtomicMarkableReference<T>` object encapsulates both a reference to an object of type `T` and a Boolean `mark`. These fields can be atomically updated, either together or individually.

We make each node's `next` field an `AtomicMarkableReference<Node>`. Thread *A* logically removes $\texttt{curr}_A$ by setting the mark bit in the node's `next` field, and shares the physical removal with other threads performing `add()` or `remove()`: as each thread traverses the list, it cleans up the list by physically removing (using `compareAndSet()`) any marked nodes it encounters. In other words, threads performing `add()` and `remove()` do not traverse marked nodes, they remove them before continuing. The `contains()` method remains the same as in the `LazyList` algorithm, traversing all nodes whether they are marked or not, and testing if an item is in the list based on its key and mark.

It is worth pausing to consider a design decision that differentiates the `LockFreeList` algorithm from the `LazyList` algorithm. Why do threads that add or remove nodes never traverse marked nodes, and instead physically remove all marked nodes they encounter? Suppose that thread *A* were to traverse marked nodes without physically removing them, and after logically removing $\texttt{curr}_A$, were to attempt to physically remove it as well. It could do so by calling `compareAndSet()` to try to redirect $\texttt{pred}_A$'s `next` field, simultaneously verifying that $\texttt{pred}_A$ is not marked and that it refers to $\texttt{curr}_A$. The difficulty is that because *A* is not holding locks on $\texttt{pred}_A$ and $\texttt{curr}_A$, other threads could insert new nodes or remove $\texttt{pred}_A$ before the `compareAndSet()` call.

Consider a scenario in which another thread marks $\texttt{pred}_A$. As illustrated in Fig. 9.22, we cannot safely redirect the `next` field of a marked node, so *A* would have to restart the physical removal by retraversing the list. This time, however, *A* would have to physically remove $\texttt{pred}_A$ before it could remove $\texttt{curr}_A$. Even worse, if there is a sequence of logically removed nodes leading to $\texttt{pred}_A$, *A* must remove them all, one after the other, before it can remove $\texttt{curr}_A$ itself.

This example illustrates why `add()` and `remove()` calls do not traverse marked nodes: when they arrive at the node to be modified, they may be forced to retraverse the list to remove previous marked nodes. Instead, we choose to have both `add()` and `remove()` physically remove any marked nodes on the path to their target node. The `contains()` method, by contrast, performs no modification, and therefore need not participate in the cleanup of logically removed nodes, allowing it, as in the `LazyList`, to traverse both marked and unmarked nodes.

In presenting our LockFreeList algorithm, we factor out functionality common to the add() and remove() methods by creating an inner Window class to help navigation. As shown in Fig. 9.24, a Window object is a structure with pred and curr fields. The find() method takes a head node and a key a, and traverses the list, seeking to set pred to the node with the largest key less than a, and curr to the node with the least key greater than or equal to a. As thread A traverses the list, each time it advances $\mathtt{curr}_A$, it checks whether that node is marked (Line 16). If so, it calls compareAndSet() to attempt to physically remove the node by setting $\mathtt{pred}_A$'s next field to $\mathtt{curr}_A$'s next field. This call tests both the field's reference and Boolean mark values, and fails if either value has changed. A concurrent thread could change the mark value by logically removing $\mathtt{pred}_A$, or it could change the reference value by physically removing $\mathtt{curr}_A$. If the call fails, A restarts the traversal from the head of the list; otherwise the traversal continues.

The LockFreeList algorithm uses the same abstraction map as the LazyList algorithm: an item is in the set if, and only if it is in an *unmarked* reachable node.

```
1   class Window {
2     public Node pred, curr;
3     Window(Node myPred, Node myCurr) {
4       pred = myPred; curr = myCurr;
5     }
6   }
7   public Window find(Node head, int key) {
8     Node pred = null, curr = null, succ = null;
9     boolean[] marked = {false};
10    boolean snip;
11    retry: while (true) {
12      pred = head;
13      curr = pred.next.getReference();
14      while (true) {
15        succ = curr.next.get(marked);
16        while (marked[0]) {
17          snip = pred.next.compareAndSet(curr, succ, false, false);
18          if (!snip) continue retry;
19          curr = succ;
20          succ = curr.next.get(marked);
21        }
22        if (curr.key >= key)
23          return new Window(pred, curr);
24        pred = curr;
25        curr = succ;
26      }
27    }
28  }
```

Figure 9.24 The Window class: the find() method returns a structure containing the nodes on either side of the key. It removes marked nodes when it encounters them.

The compareAndSet() call at Line 17 of the find() method is an example of a *benevolent side effect*: it changes the concrete list without changing the abstract set, because removing a marked node does not change the value of the abstraction map.

Fig. 9.25 shows the LockFreeList class's add() method. Suppose thread *A* calls add(*a*). *A* uses find() to locate pred$_A$ and curr$_A$. If curr$_A$'s key is equal to *a*'s, the call returns *false*. Otherwise, add() initializes a new node *a* to hold *a*, and sets *a* to refer to curr$_A$. It then calls compareAndSet() (Line 11) to set pred$_A$ to *a*. Because the compareAndSet() tests both the mark and the reference, it succeeds only if pred$_A$ is unmarked and refers to curr$_A$. If the compareAndSet() is successful, the method returns *true*, and otherwise it starts over.

Fig. 9.26 shows the LockFreeList algorithm's remove() method. When *A* calls remove() to remove item *a*, it uses find() to locate pred$_A$ and curr$_A$. If curr$_A$'s key fails to match *a*'s, the call returns *false*. Otherwise, remove() uses a compareAndSet() to attempt to mark curr$_A$ as logically removed (Line 27). This call succeeds only if no other thread has set the mark first. If it succeeds, the call returns *true*. A single attempt is made to physically remove the node, but there is no need to try again because the node will be removed by the next thread to traverse that region of the list. If the compareAndSet() call fails, remove() starts over.

The LockFreeList algorithm's contains() method is virtually the same as that of the LazyList (Fig. 9.27). There is one small change: to test if curr is marked we must apply curr.next.get(marked) and check that marked[0] is *true*.

```
1  public boolean add(T item) {
2     int key = item.hashCode();
3     while (true) {
4      Window window = find(head, key);
5      Node pred = window.pred, curr = window.curr;
6      if (curr.key == key) {
7          return false;
8        } else {
9          Node node = new Node(item);
10         node.next = new AtomicMarkableReference(curr, false);
11         if (pred.next.compareAndSet(curr, node, false, false)) {
12           return true;
13         }
14       }
15     }
16   }
```

Figure 9.25 The LockFreeList class: the add() method calls find() to locate pred$_A$ and curr$_A$. It adds a new node only if pred$_A$ is unmarked and refers to curr$_A$.

```
  public boolean remove(T item) {
    int key = item.hashCode();
    boolean snip;
    while (true) {
     Window window = find(head, key);
     Node pred = window.pred, curr = window.curr;
     if (curr.key != key) {
       return false;
     } else {
       Node succ = curr.next.getReference();
       snip = curr.next.compareAndSet(succ, succ, false, true);
       if (!snip)
         continue;
       pred.next.compareAndSet(curr, succ, false, false);
       return true;
     }
    }
  }
```

Figure 9.26 The `LockFreeList` class: the remove() method calls `find()` to locate `pred`$_A$ and `curr`$_A$, and atomically marks the node for removal.

```
  public boolean contains(T item) {
    boolean[] marked = false;
    int key = item.hashCode();
    Node curr = head;
    while (curr.key < key) {
     curr = curr.next.getReference();
     Node succ = curr.next.get(marked);
    }
    return (curr.key == key && !marked[0])
  }
```

Figure 9.27 The `LockFreeList` class: the wait-free `contains()` method is almost the same as in the `LazyList` class. There is one small difference: it calls `curr.next.get(marked)` to test whether `curr` is marked.

9.9 Discussion

We have seen a progression of list-based lock implementations in which the granularity and frequency of locking was gradually reduced, eventually reaching a fully nonblocking list. The final transition from the `LazyList` to the `LockFreeList` exposes some of the design decisions that face concurrent programmers. As we will see, approaches such as optimistic and lazy synchronization will appear time and again when designing more complex data structures.

On the one hand, the `LockFreeList` algorithm guarantees progress in the face of arbitrary delays. However, there is a price for this strong progress guarantee:

- The need to support atomic modification of a reference and a Boolean mark has an added performance cost.[6]
- As `add()` and `remove()` traverse the list, they must engage in concurrent cleanup of removed nodes, introducing the possibility of contention among threads, sometimes forcing threads to restart traversals, even if there was no change near the node each was trying to modify.

On the other hand, the lazy lock-based list does not guarantee progress in the face of arbitrary delays: its `add()` and `remove()` methods are blocking. However, unlike the lock-free algorithm, it does not require each node to include an atomically markable reference. It also does not require traversals to clean up logically removed nodes; they progress down the list, ignoring marked nodes.

Which approach is preferable depends on the application. In the end, the balance of factors such as the potential for arbitrary thread delays, the relative frequency of calls to the `add()` and `remove()` methods, the overhead of implementing an atomically markable reference, and so on determine the choice of whether to lock, and if so, at what granularity.

9.10 Chapter Notes

Lock coupling was invented by Rudolf Bayer and Mario Schkolnick [19]. The first designs of lock-free linked-list algorithms are credited to John Valois [147]. The Lock-free list implementation shown here is a variation on the lists of Maged Michael [114], who based his work on earlier linked-list algorithms by Tim Harris [53]. This algorithm is referred to by many as the Harris-Michael algorithm. The Harris-Michael algorithm is the one used in the Java Concurrency Package. The `OptimisticList` algorithm was invented for this chapter, and the lazy algorithm is credited to Steven Heller, Maurice Herlihy, Victor Luchangco, Mark Moir, Nir Shavit, and Bill Scherer [55].

9.11 Exercises

Exercise 100. Describe how to modify each of the linked list algorithms if object hash codes are not guaranteed to be unique.

---

6 In the Java Concurrency Package, for example, this cost is somewhat reduced by using a reference to an intermediate dummy node to signify that the `marked` bit is set.

Exercise 101. Explain why the fine-grained locking algorithm is not subject to deadlock.

Exercise 102. Explain why the fine-grained list's `add()` method is linearizable.

Exercise 103. Explain why the optimistic and lazy locking algorithms are not subject to deadlock.

Exercise 104. Show a scenario in the optimistic algorithm where a thread is forever attempting to delete a node.

Hint: since we assume that all the individual node locks are starvation-free, the livelock is not on any individual lock, and a bad execution must repeatedly add and remove nodes from the list.

Exercise 105. Provide the code for the `contains()` method missing from the fine-grained algorithm. Explain why your implementation is correct.

Exercise 106. Is the optimistic list implementation still correct if we switch the order in which `add()` locks the `pred` and `curr` entries?

Exercise 107. Show that in the optimistic list algorithm, if $\texttt{pred}_A$ is not *null*, then `tail` is reachable from $\texttt{pred}_A$, even if $\texttt{pred}_A$ itself is not reachable.

Exercise 108. Show that in the optimistic algorithm, the `add()` method needs to lock only `pred`.

Exercise 109. In the optimistic algorithm, the `contains()` method locks two entries before deciding whether a key is present. Suppose, instead, it locks no entries, returning *true* if it observes the value, and *false* otherwise.

Either explain why this alternative is linearizable, or give a counterexample showing it is not.

Exercise 110. Would the lazy algorithm still work if we marked a node as removed simply by setting its `next` field to *null*? Why or why not? What about the lock-free algorithm?

Exercise 111. In the lazy algorithm, can $\texttt{pred}_A$ ever be unreachable? Justify your answer.

Exercise 112. Your new employee claims that the lazy list's validation method (Fig. 9.16) can be simplified by dropping the check that `pred.next` is equal to `curr`. After all, the code always sets `pred` to the old value of `curr`, and before `pred.next` can be changed, the new value of `curr` must be marked, causing the validation to fail. Explain the error in this reasoning.

Exercise 113. Can you modify the lazy algorithm's `remove()` so it locks only one node?

Exercise 114. In the lock-free algorithm, argue the benefits and drawbacks of having the `contains()` method help in the cleanup of logically removed entries.

Exercise 115. In the lock-free algorithm, if an `add()` method call fails because `pred` does not point to `curr`, but `pred` is not marked, do we need to traverse the list again from `head` in order to attempt to complete the call?

Exercise 116. Would the `contains()` method of the lazy and lock-free algorithms still be correct if logically removed entries were not guaranteed to be sorted?

Exercise 117. The `add()` method of the lock-free algorithm never finds a marked node with the same key. Can one modify the algorithm so that it will simply insert its new added object into the existing marked node with same key if such a node exists in the list, thus saving the need to insert a new node?

Exercise 118. Explain why the following cannot happen in the `LockFreeList` algorithm. A node with item x is logically but not yet physically removed by some thread, then the same item x is added into the list by another thread, and finally a `contains()` call by a third thread traverses the list, finding the logically removed node, and returning *false*, even though the linearization order of the `remove()` and `add()` implies that x is in the set.

10 Concurrent Queues and the ABA Problem

10.1 Introduction

In the subsequent chapters, we look at a broad class of objects known as *pools*. A pool is similar to the `Set` class studied in Chapter 9, with two main differences: a pool does not necessarily provide a `contains()` method to test membership, and it allows the same item to appear more than once. The `Pool` has `get()` and `set()` methods as in Fig. 10.1. Pools show up in many places in concurrent systems. For example, in many applications, one or more *producer* threads produce items to be consumed by one or more *consumer* threads. These items may be jobs to perform, keystrokes to interpret, purchase orders to execute, or packets to decode. Sometimes, producers are *bursty*, suddenly and briefly producing items faster than consumers can consume them. To allow consumers to keep up, we can place a *buffer* between the producers and the consumers. Items produced faster than they can be consumed accumulate in the buffer, from which they are consumed as quickly as possible. Often, pools act as producer–consumer buffers.

Pools come in several varieties.

- A pool can be *bounded* or *unbounded*. A bounded pool holds a limited number of items. This limit is called its *capacity*. By contrast, an unbounded pool can hold any number of items. Bounded pools are useful when we want to keep producer and consumer threads loosely synchronized, ensuring that producers do not get too far ahead of consumers. Bounded pools may also be simpler to implement than unbounded pools. On the other hand, unbounded pools are useful when there is no need to set a fixed limit on how far producers can outstrip consumers.
- Pool methods may be *total*, *partial*, or *synchronous*.
  - A method is *total* if calls do not wait for certain conditions to become true. For example, a `get()` call that tries to remove an item from an empty pool immediately returns a failure code or throws an exception. If the pool is bounded, a total `set()` that tries to add an item to a full pool immediately

```
public interface Pool<T> {
  void set(T item);
  T get();
}
```

Figure 10.1 The `Pool<T>` interface.

returns a failure code or an exception. A total interface makes sense when the producer (or consumer) thread has something better to do than wait for the method call to take effect.

- — A method is *partial* if calls may wait for conditions to hold. For example, a partial `get()` call that tries to remove an item from an empty pool blocks until an item is available to return. If the pool is bounded, a partial `set()` call that tries to add an item to a full pool blocks until an empty slot is available to fill. A partial interface makes sense when the producer (or consumer) has nothing better to do than to wait for the pool to become nonfull (or nonempty).
- — A method is *synchronous* if it waits for another method to overlap its call interval. For example, in a synchronous pool, a method call that adds an item to the pool is blocked until that item is removed by another method call. Symmetrically, a method call that removes an item from the pool is blocked until another method call makes an item available to be removed. (Such methods are partial.) Synchronous pools are used for communication in programming languages such as CSP and Ada in which threads *rendezvous* to exchange information.

- Pools provide different *fairness* guarantees. They can be first-in-first-out (a queue), last-in-first-out (a stack), or other, weaker properties. The importance of fairness when buffering using a pool is clear to anyone who has ever called a bank or a technical support line, only to be placed in a pool of waiting calls. The longer you wait, the more consolation you draw from the recorded message asserting that calls are answered in the order they arrive. Perhaps.

10.2 Queues

In this chapter we consider a kind of pool that provides *first-in-first-out* (FIFO) fairness. A sequential `Queue<T>` is an ordered sequence of items (of type `T`). It provides an `enq`(x) method that puts item x at one end of the queue, called the *tail*, and a `deq`() method that removes and returns the item at the other end of the queue, called the *head.* A concurrent queue is linearizable to a sequential queue. Queues are pools, where `enq`() implements `set`(), and `deq`() implements `get`(). We use queue implementations to illustrate a number of important principles. In later chapters we consider pools that provide other fairness guarantees.

10.3 A Bounded Partial Queue

For simplicity, we assume it is illegal to add a *null* value to a queue. Of course, there may be circumstances where it makes sense to add and remove *null* values, but we leave it as an exercise to adapt our algorithms to accommodate *null* values.

How much concurrency can we expect a bounded queue implementation with multiple concurrent enqueuers and dequeuers to provide? Very informally, the `enq()` and `deq()` methods operate on opposite ends of the queue, so as long as the queue is neither full nor empty, an `enq()` call and a `deq()` call should, in principle, be able to proceed without interference. For the same reason, concurrent `enq()` calls probably will interfere, and the same holds for `deq()` calls. This informal reasoning may sound convincing, and it is in fact mostly correct, but realizing this level of concurrency is not trivial.

Here, we implement a bounded queue as a linked list. (We could also have used an array.) Fig. 10.2 shows the queue's fields and constructor, Figs. 10.3 and 10.4 show the `enq()` and `deq()` methods, and Fig. 10.5 shows a queue node. Like the lists studied in Chapter 9, a queue node has `value` and `next` fields.

As seen in Fig. 10.6, the queue itself has `head` and `tail` fields that respectively refer to the first and last nodes in the queue. The queue always contains a *sentinel* node acting as a place-holder. Like the sentinel nodes in Chapter 9, it marks a position in the queue, though its value is meaningless. Unlike the list algorithms in Chapter 9, in which the same nodes always act as sentinels, the queue repeatedly replaces the sentinel node. We use two distinct locks, `enqLock` and `deqLock`, to ensure that at most one enqueuer, and at most one dequeuer at a time can manipulate the queue object's fields. Using two locks instead of one ensures that an enqueuer does not lock out a dequeuer unnecessarily, and vice versa. Each lock has an associated *condition* field. The `enqLock` is associated with

```
public class BoundedQueue<T> {
  ReentrantLock enqLock, deqLock;
  Condition notEmptyCondition, notFullCondition;
  AtomicInteger size;
  volatile Node head, tail;
  int capacity;
  public BoundedQueue(int _capacity) {
    capacity = _capacity;
    head = new Node(null);
    tail = head;
    size = new AtomicInteger(0);
    enqLock = new ReentrantLock();
    notFullCondition = enqLock.newCondition();
    deqLock = new ReentrantLock();
    notEmptyCondition = deqLock.newCondition();
  }
```

Figure 10.2 The BoundedQueue class: fields and constructor.

```
public void enq(T x) {
  boolean mustWakeDequeuers = false;
  enqLock.lock();
  try {
    while (size.get() == capacity)
      notFullCondition.await();
    Node e = new Node(x);
    tail.next = tail; tail = e;
    if (size.getAndIncrement() == 0)
      mustWakeDequeuers = true;
  } finally {
    enqLock.unlock();
  }
  if (mustWakeDequeuers) {
    deqLock.lock();
    try {
      notEmptyCondition.signalAll();
    } finally {
      deqLock.unlock();
    }
  }
}
```

Figure 10.3 The BoundedQueue class: the enq() method.

```
public T deq() {
  T result;
  boolean mustWakeEnqueuers = false;
  deqLock.lock();
  try {
    while (size.get() == 0)
      notEmptyCondition.await();
    result = head.next.value;
    head = head.next;
    if (size.getAndDecrement() == capacity) {
      mustWakeEnqueuers = true;
    }
  } finally {
    deqLock.unlock();
  }
  if (mustWakeEnqueuers) {
    enqLock.lock();
    try {
      notFullCondition.signalAll();
    } finally {
      enqLock.unlock();
    }
  }
  return result;
}
```

Figure 10.4 The BoundedQueue class: the deq() method.

```
  protected class Node {
    public T value;
    public volatile Node next;
    public Node(T x) {
      value = x;
      next = null;
    }
  }
}
```

Figure 10.5 BoundedQueue class: List Node.

the `notFullCondition` condition, used to notify waiting dequeuers when the queue is no longer full. The `deqLock` is associated with `notEmptyCondition`, used to notify waiting enqueuers when the queue is no longer empty.

Since the queue is bounded, we must keep track of the number of empty slots. The `size` field is an `AtomicInteger` that tracks the number of objects currently in the queue. This field is decremented by `deq()` calls and incremented by `enq()` calls.

The `enq()` method (Fig. 10.3) works as follows. A thread acquires the `enqLock` (Line 19), and reads the `size` field (Line 21). While that field is equal to the capacity, the queue is full, and the enqueuer must wait until a dequeuer makes room. The enqueuer waits on the `notFullCondition` field (Line 22), releasing the enqueue lock temporarily, and blocking until that condition is signaled. Each time the thread awakens (Line 22), it checks whether there is room, and if not, goes back to sleep.

Once the number of empty slots exceeds zero, however, the enqueuer may proceed. We note that once the enqueuer observes an empty slot, while the enqueue is in progress no other thread can fill the queue, because all the other enqueuers are locked out, and a concurrent dequeuer can only increase the number of empty slots. (Synchronization for the `enq()` method is symmetric.)

We must carefully check that this implementation does not suffer from the kind of "lost-wakeup" bug described in Chapter 8. Care is needed because an enqueuer encounters a full queue in two steps: first, it sees that `size` is the queue capacity, and second, it waits on `notFullCondition` until there is room in the queue. When a dequeuer changes the queue from full to not-full, it acquires `enqLock` and signals `notFullCondition`. Even though the `size` field is not protected by the `enqLock`, the dequeuer acquires the `enqLock` before it signals the condition, so the dequeuer cannot signal between the enqueuer's two steps.

The `deq()` method proceeds as follows. It reads the size field to check whether the queue is empty. If so, the dequeuer must wait until an item is enqueued. Like the `enq()` method, the dequeuer waits on `notEmptyCondition`, which temporarily releases `deqLock`, and blocks until the condition is signaled. Each time the thread awakens, it checks whether the queue is empty, and if so, goes back to sleep.

It is important to understand that the abstract queue's head and tail items are not always the same as those referenced by `head` and `tail`. An item is logically added to the queue as soon as the last node's `next` field is redirected to the

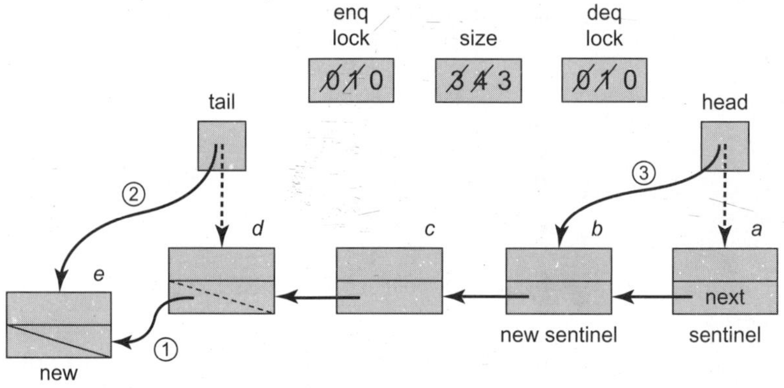

Figure 10.6 The enq() and deq() methods of the BoundedQueue with 4 slots. First a node is enqueued into the queue by acquiring the enqLock. The enq() checks that the size is 3 which is less than the bound. It then redirects the next field of the node referenced by the tail field (step 1), redirects tail to the new node (step 2), increments the size to 4, and releases the lock. Since size is now 4, any further calls to enq() will cause the threads to block until the notFullCondition is signalled by some deq(). Next, a node is dequeued from the queue by some thread. The deq() acquires the deqLock, reads the new value *b* from the successor of the node referenced by head (this node is the current sentinel), redirects head to this successor node (step 3), decrements the size to 3, and releases the lock. Before completing the deq(), because the size was 4 when it started, the thread acquires the enqLock and signals any enqueuers waiting on notFullCondition that they can proceed.

new item (the linearization point of the enq()), even if the enqueuer has not yet updated tail. For example, a thread can hold the enqLock and be in the process of inserting a new node. Suppose it has not yet redirected the tail field. A concurrent dequeuing thread could acquire the deqLock, read and return the new node's value, and redirect the head to the new node, all before the enqueuer redirects tail to the newly inserted node.

Once the dequeuer establishes that the queue is nonempty, the queue will remain nonempty for the duration of the deq() call, because all other dequeuers have been locked out. Consider the first nonsentinel node in the queue (i.e., the node referenced by the sentinel node's next field). The dequeuer reads this node's value field, and sets the queue's head to refer to it, making it the new sentinel node. The dequeuer then decrements size and releases deqLock. If the dequeuer found the former size was the queue capacity, then there may be enqueuers waiting on notEmptyCondition, so the dequeuer acquires enqLock, and signals all such threads to wake up.

One drawback of this implementation is that concurrent enq() and deq() calls interfere with each other, but not through locks. All method calls apply getAndIncrement() or getAndDecrement() calls to the size field. These methods are more expensive than ordinary reads–writes, and they could cause a sequential bottleneck.

One way to reduce such interactions is to split this field into two counters: enqSideSize is an integer field incremented by enq(), and deqSideSize is an integer field decremented by deq(). A thread calling enq() tests enqSideSize, and as long as it is less than the capacity, it proceeds. When the field reaches capacity, the thread locks deqLock, adds deqSize to EnqSize, and resets deqSideSize to 0. Instead of synchronizing on every method call, this technique synchronizes sporadically when the enqueuer's size estimate becomes too large.

10.4 An Unbounded Total Queue

We now describe a different kind of queue that can hold an unbounded number of items. The enq() method always enqueues its item, and deq() throws EmptyException if there is no item to dequeue. The representation is the same as the bounded queue, except there is no need to count the number of items in the queue, or to provide conditions on which to wait. As illustrated in Figs. 10.7 and 10.8, this algorithm is simpler than the bounded algorithm.

```
  public void enq(T x) {
    enqLock.lock();
    try {
      Node e = new Node(x);
      tail.next = e;
      tail = e;
    } finally {
      enqLock.unlock();
    }
  }
```

Figure 10.7 The UnboundedQueue<T> class: the enq() method.

```
public T deq() throws EmptyException {
    T result;
    deqLock.lock();
    try {
      if (head.next == null) {
        throw new EmptyException();
      }
      result = head.next.value;
      head = head.next;
    } finally {
      deqLock.unlock();
    }
    return result;
  }
```

Figure 10.8 The UnboundedQueue<T> class: the deq() method.

This queue cannot deadlock, because each method acquires only one lock, either `enqLock` or `deqLock`. A sentinel node alone in the queue will never be deleted, so each `enq()` call will succeed as soon as it acquires the lock. Of course, a `deq()` method may fail if the queue is empty (i.e., if `head.next` is *null*). As in the earlier queue implementations, an item is actually enqueued when the `enq()` call sets the last node's `next` field to the new node, even before `enq()` resets `tail` to refer to the new node. After that instant, the new item is reachable along a chain of the `next` references. As usual, the queue's actual head and tail are not necessarily the items referenced by `head` and `tail`. Instead, the actual head is the successor of the node referenced by `head`, and the actual tail is the last item reachable from the head. Both the `enq()` and `deq()` methods are total as they do not wait for the queue to become empty or full.

10.5 An Unbounded Lock-Free Queue

We now describe the `LockFreeQueue<T>` class, an unbounded lock-free queue implementation. This class, depicted in Figs. 10.9 through 10.11, is a natural

```
public class Node {
    public T value;
    public AtomicReference<Node> next;
    public Node(T value) {
      this.value = value;
      next  = new AtomicReference<Node>(null);
    }
  }
```

Figure 10.9 The `LockFreeQueue<T>` class: list node.

```
  public void enq(T value) {
    Node node = new Node(value);
    while (true) {
      Node last = tail.get();
      Node next = last.next.get();
      if (last == tail.get()) {
        if (next == null) {
          if (last.next.compareAndSet(next, node)) {
            tail.compareAndSet(last, node);
            return;
          }
        } else {
          tail.compareAndSet(last, next);
        }
      }
    }
  }
```

Figure 10.10 The `LockFreeQueue<T>` class: the `enq()` method.

```
26     public T deq() throws EmptyException {
27       while (true) {
28         Node first = head.get();
29         Node last = tail.get();
30         Node next = first.next.get();
31         if (first == head.get()) {
32           if (first == last) {
33             if (next == null) {
34               throw new EmptyException();
35             }
36             tail.compareAndSet(last, next);
37           } else {
38             T value = next.value;
39             if (head.compareAndSet(first, next))
40               return value;
41           }
42         }
43       }
44     }
```

Figure 10.11 The LockFreeQueue<T> class: the deq() method.

extension of the unbounded total queue of Section 10.4. Its implementation prevents method calls from starving by having the quicker threads help the slower threads.

As done earlier, we represent the queue as a list of nodes. However, as shown in Fig. 10.9, each node's `next` field is an `AtomicReference<Node>` that refers to the next node in the list. As can be seen in Fig. 10.12, the queue itself consists of two `AtomicReference<Node>` fields: `head` refers to the first node in the queue, and `tail` to the last. Again, the first node in the queue is a sentinel node, whose value is meaningless. The queue constructor sets both `head` and `tail` to refer to the sentinel.

An interesting aspect of the `enq()` method is that it is *lazy*: it takes place in two distinct steps. To make this method lock-free, threads may need to help one another. Fig. 10.12 illustrates these steps.

In the following description the line numbers refer to Figs. 10.9 through 10.11. Normally, the `enq()` method creates a new node (Line 10), locates the last node in the queue (Lines 12–13), and performs the following two steps:

1. It calls `compareAndSet()` to append the new node (Line 16), and
2. calls `compareAndSet()` to change the queue's `tail` field from the prior last node to the current last node (Line 17).

Because these two steps are not executed atomically, every other method call must be prepared to encounter a half-finished `enq()` call, and to finish the job. This is a real-world example of the "helping" technique we first saw in the universal construction of Chapter 6.

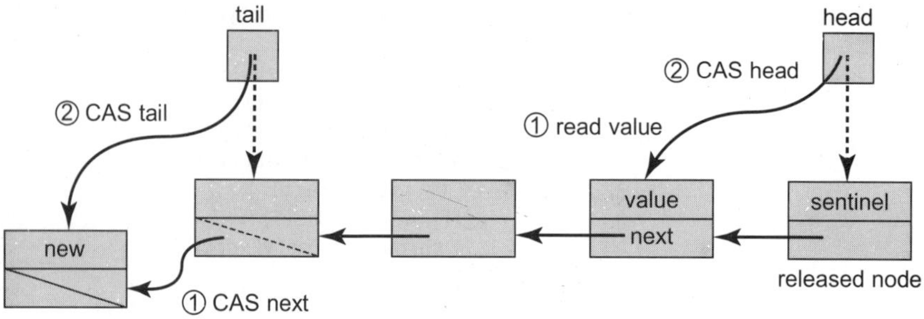

Figure 10.12 The lazy lock-free enq() and deq() methods of the LockFreeQueue. A node is inserted into the queue in two steps. First, a compareAndSet() call changes the next field of the node referenced by the queue's tail from null to the new node. Then a compareAndSet() call advances tail itself to refer to the new node. An item is removed from the queue in two steps. A compareAndSet() call reads the item from the node referred to by the sentinel node, and then redirects head from the current sentinel to the sentinel's next node, making the latter the new sentinel. Both enq() and deq() methods help complete unfinished tail updates.

We now review all the steps in detail. An enqueuer creates a new node with the new value to be enqueued (Line 10), reads tail, and finds the node that appears to be last (Lines 12–13). To verify that node is indeed last, it checks whether that node has a successor (Line 15). If so, the thread attempts to append the new node by calling compareAndSet() (Line 16). (A compareAndSet() is required because other threads may be trying the same thing.) If the compareAndSet() succeeds, the thread uses a second compareAndSet() to advance tail to the new node (Line 17). Even if this second compareAndSet() call fails, the thread can still return successfully because, as we will see, the call fails only if some other thread "helped" it by advancing tail. If the tail node has a successor (Line 20), then the method tries to "help" other threads by advancing tail to refer directly to the successor (Line 21) before trying again to insert its own node. This enq() is total, meaning that it never waits for a dequeuer. A successful enq() is linearized at the instant where the executing thread (or a concurrent helping thread) calls compareAndSet() to redirect the tail field to the new node at Line 21.

The deq() method is similar to its total counterpart from the UnboundedQueue. If the queue is nonempty, the dequeuer calls compareAndSet() to change head from the sentinel node to its successor, making the successor the new sentinel node. The deq() method makes sure that the queue is not empty in the same way as before: by checking that the next field of the head node is not *null*.

There is, however, a subtle issue in the lock-free case, depicted in Fig. 10.13: before advancing head one must make sure that tail is not left referring to the sentinel node which is about to be removed from the queue. To avoid this problem we add a test: if head equals tail (Line 32) and the (sentinel) node they refer to has a non-*null* next field (Line 33), then the tail is deemed to

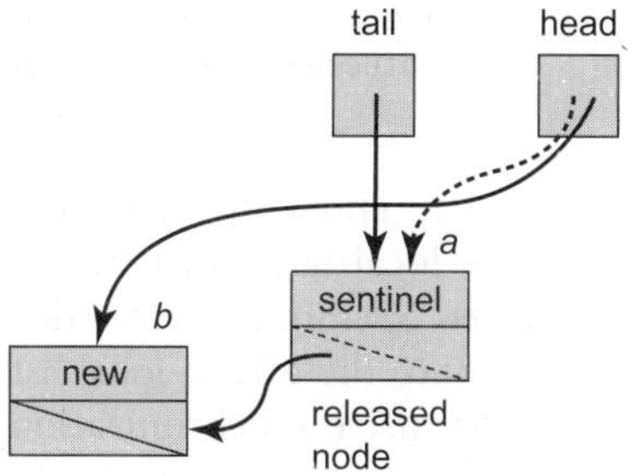

Figure 10.13 Why dequeuers must help advance `tail` in Line 36 of Fig. 10.11. Consider the scenario in which a thread enqueuing node *b* has redirected *a*'s `next` field to *b*, but has yet to redirect `tail` from *a* to *b*. If another thread starts dequeuing, it will read *b*'s value and redirect `head` from *a* to *b*, effectively removing *a* while `tail` still refers to it. To avoid this problem, the dequeuing thread must help advance `tail` from *a* to *b* before redirecting `head`.

be lagging behind. As in the `enq()` method, `deq()` then attempts to help make `tail` consistent by swinging it to the sentinel node's successor (Line 36), and only then updates `head` to remove the sentinel (Line 39). As in the partial queue, the value is read from the successor of the sentinel node (Line 38). If this method returns a value, then its linearization point occurs when it completes a successful `compareAndSet()` call at Line 39, and otherwise it is linearized at Line 33.

It is easy to check that the resulting queue is lock-free. Every method call first checks for an incomplete `enq()` call, and tries to complete it. In the worst case, all threads are trying to advance the queue's `tail` field, and one of them must succeed. A thread fails to enqueue or dequeue a node only if another thread's method call succeeds in changing the reference, so some method call always completes. As it turns out, being lock-free substantially enhances the performance of queue implementations, and the lock-free algorithms tend to outperform the most efficient blocking ones.

10.6 Memory Reclamation and the ABA Problem

Our queue implementations so far rely on the Java garbage collector to recycle nodes after they have been dequeued. What happens if we choose to do our own memory management? There are several reasons we might want to do this. Languages such as C or C++ do not provide garbage collection. Even if garbage collection is available, it is often more efficient for a class to do its own memory management, particularly if it creates and releases many small objects. Finally, if the garbage collection process is not lock-free, we might want to supply our own lock-free memory reclamation.

A natural way to recycle nodes in a lock-free manner is to have each thread maintain its own private *free list* of unused queue entries.

```
ThreadLocal<Node> freeList = new ThreadLocal<Node>() {
  protected Node initialValue() { return null; };
};
```

When an enqueuing thread needs a new node, it tries to remove one from the thread-local free list. If the free list is empty, it simply allocates a node using the **new** operator. When a dequeuing thread is ready to retire a node, it links it back onto the thread-local list. Because the list is thread-local, there is no need for expensive synchronization. This design works well, as long as each thread

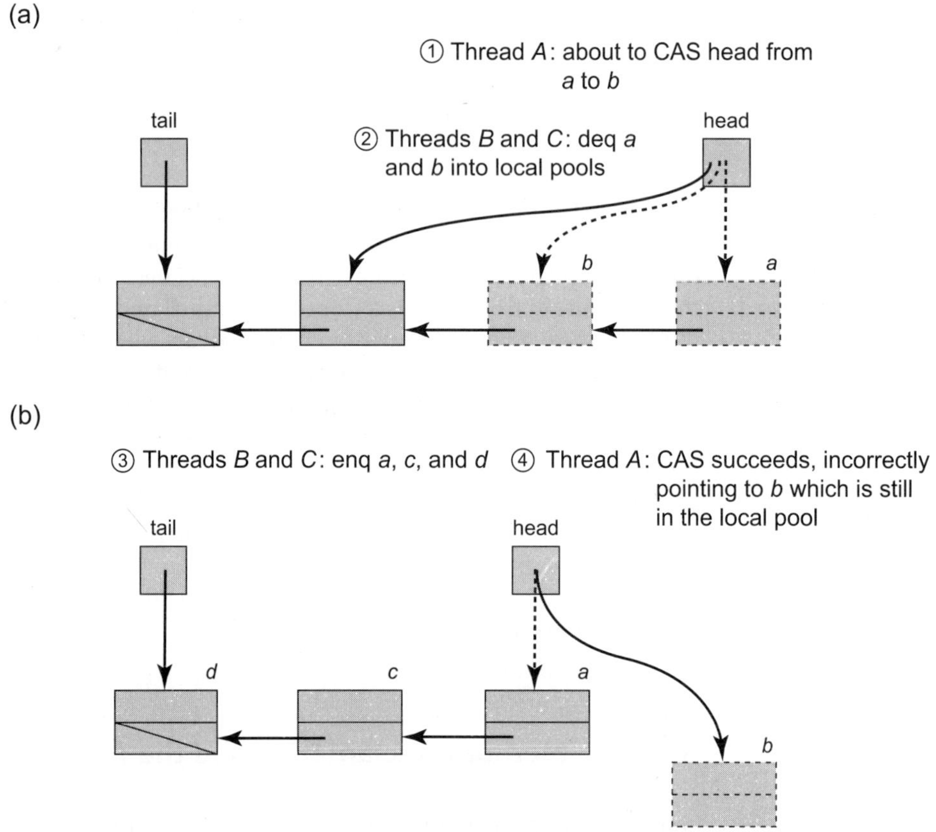

Figure 10.14 An ABA scenario: Assume that we use local pools of recycled nodes in our lock-free queue algorithm. In Part (a), the dequeuer thread *A* of Fig. 10.11 observes that the sentinel node is *a*, and next node is *b*. (Step 1) It then prepares to update `head` by applying a `compareAndSet()` with old value *a* and new value *b*. (Step 2) Suppose however, that before it takes another step, other threads dequeue *b*, then its successor, placing both *a* and *b* in the free pool. In Part (b) (Step 3) node *a* is reused, and eventually reappears as the sentinel node in the queue. (Step 4) thread *A* now wakes up, calls `compareAndSet()`, and succeeds in setting `head` to *b*, since the old value of `head` is indeed *a*. Now, `head` is incorrectly set to a recycled node.

performs roughly the same number of enqueues and dequeues. If there is an imbalance, then there may be a need for more complex techniques, such as periodically stealing nodes from other threads.

Surprisingly, perhaps, the lock-free queue will not work if nodes are recycled in the most straightforward way. Consider the scenario depicted in Fig. 10.14. In Part (a) of Fig. 10.14, the dequeuing thread A observes the sentinel node is *a*, and the next node is *b*. It then prepares to update `head` by applying a `compareAndSet()` with old value *a* and new value *b*. Before it takes another step, other threads dequeue *b* and its successor, placing both *a* and *b* in the free pool. Node *a* is recycled, and eventually reappears as the sentinel node in the queue, as depicted in Part (b) of Fig. 10.14. The thread now wakes up, calls `compareAndSet()`, and succeeds, since the old value of the `head` is indeed *a*. Unfortunately, it has redirected `head` to a recycled node!

This phenomenon is called the "ABA" problem. It shows up often, especially in dynamic memory algorithms that use conditional synchronization operations such as `compareAndSet()`. Typically, a reference about to be modified by a `compareAndSet()` changes from *a*, to *b*, and back to *a* again. As a result, the `compareAndSet()` call succeeds even though its effect on the data structure has changed, and no longer has the desired effect.

One straightforward way to fix this problem is to tag each atomic reference with a unique *stamp*. As described in detail in Pragma 10.6.1, an `AtomicStampedReference<T>` object encapsulates both a reference to an object of Type `T` and an integer `stamp`. These fields can be atomically updated either together or individually.

Pragma 10.6.1. The `AtomicStampedReference<T>` class encapsulates both a reference to an object of Type `T` and an integer *stamp*. It generalizes the `AtomicMarkableReference<T>` class (Pragma 9.8.1), replacing the Boolean *mark* with an integer stamp.

We usually use this stamp to avoid the ABA problem, incrementing the value of the stamp each time we modify the object, although sometimes, as in the `LockFreeExchanger` class of Chapter 11, we use the stamp to hold one of a finite set of states.

The stamp and reference fields can be updated atomically, either together or individually. For example, the `compareAndSet()` method tests expected reference and stamp values, and if both tests succeed, replaces them with updated reference and stamp values. As shorthand, the `attemptStamp()` method tests an expected reference value and if the test succeeds, replaces it with a new stamp value. The `get()` method has an unusual interface: it returns the object's reference value and stores the stamp value in an integer array argument. Fig. 10.15 illustrates the signatures for these methods.

```
public boolean compareAndSet(T expectedReference,
                             T newReference,
                             int expectedStamp,
                             int newStamp);
public T get(int[] stampHolder);
public void set(T newReference, int newStamp);
```

Figure 10.15 The `AtomicStampedReference<T>` class: the `compareAndSet()` and `get()` methods. The `compareAndSet()` method tests and updates both the stamp and reference fields, the `get()` method returns the encapsulated reference and stores the stamp at position 0 in the argument array, and `set()` updates the encapsulated reference and the stamp.

In a language like C or C++, one could provide this functionality efficiently in a 64-bit architecture by "stealing" bits from pointers, although a 32-bit architecture would probably require a level of indirection.

As shown in Fig. 10.16, each time through the loop, `deq()` reads both the reference and stamp values for the first, next, and last nodes (Lines 6–8). It uses `compareAndSet()` to compare both the reference and the stamp (Line 17).

```
1    public T deq() throws EmptyException {
2      int[] lastStamp = new int[1];
3      int[] firstStamp = new int[1];
4      int[] nextStamp = new int[1];
5      while (true) {
6        Node first = head.get(firstStamp);
7        Node last = tail.get(lastStamp);
8        Node next = first.next.get(nextStamp);
9          if (first == last) {
10           if (next == null) {
11             throw new EmptyException();
12           }
13           tail.compareAndSet(last, next,
14               lastStamp[0], lastStamp[0]+1);
15         } else {
16           T value = next.value;
17           if (head.compareAndSet(first, next, firstStamp[0],
                 firstStamp[0]+1)) {
18             free(first);
19             return value;
20           }
21         }
22     }
23   }
```

Figure 10.16 The `LockFreeQueueRecycle<T>` class: the `deq()` method uses stamps to avoid ABA.

It increments the stamp each time it uses `compareAndSet()` to update a reference (Lines 14 and 17).[1]

The ABA problem can occur in many synchronization scenarios, not just those involving conditional synchronization. For example, it can occur when using only loads and stores. Conditional synchronization operations such as *load-linked/store-conditional*, available on some architectures (see Appendix B), avoid ABA by testing not whether a value is the same at two points in time, but whether the value has ever changed between those points.

10.6.1 A Naïve Synchronous Queue

We now turn our attention to an even tighter kind of synchronization. One or more *producer* threads produce items to be removed, in first-in-first-out order, by one or more *consumer* threads. Here, however, producers and consumers *rendezvous* with one another: a producer that puts an item in the queue blocks until that item is removed by a consumer, and vice versa. Such rendezvous synchronization is built into languages such as CSP and Ada.

Fig. 10.17 illustrates the `SynchronousQueue<T>` class, a straightforward monitor-based synchronous queue implementation. It has the following fields: `item` is the first item waiting to be dequeued, `enqueuing` is a Boolean value used by enqueuers to synchronize among themselves, `lock` is the lock used for mutual exclusion, and `condition` is used to block partial methods. If the `enq()` method finds `enqueuing` to be *true* (Line 10) then another enqueuer has supplied an item and is waiting to rendezvous with a dequeuer, so the enqueuer repeatedly releases the lock, sleeps, and checks whether `enqueuing` has become *false* (Line 11). When this condition is satisfied, the enqueuer sets `enqueuing` to *true*, which locks out other enqueuers until the current rendezvous is complete, and sets `item` to refer to the new item (Lines 12–13). It then notifies any waiting threads (Line 14), and waits until `item` becomes *null* (Lines 15–16). When the wait is over, the rendezvous has occurred, so the enqueuer sets `enqueuing` to *false*, notifies any waiting threads, and returns (Lines 17 and 19).

The `deq()` method simply waits until `item` is non-*null* (Lines 26–27), records the item, sets the `item` field to *null*, and notifies any waiting threads before returning the item (Lines 28–31).

While the design of the queue is relatively simple, it incurs a high synchronization cost. At every point where one thread might wake up another, both enqueuers and dequeuers wake up all waiting threads, leading to a number of wakeups quadratic in the number of waiting threads. While it is possible to use condition objects to reduce the number of wakeups, it is still necessary to block on every call, which is expensive.

---

1 We ignore the remote possibility that the stamp could wrap around and cause an error.

```java
public class SynchronousQueue<T> {
  T item = null;
  boolean enqueuing;
  Lock lock;
  Condition condition;
  ...
  public void enq(T value) {
    lock.lock();
    try {
      while (enqueuing)
        condition.await();
      enqueuing = true;
      item = value;
      condition.signalAll();
      while (item != null)
        condition.await();
      enqueuing = false;
      condition.signalAll();
    } finally {
      lock.unlock();
    }
  }
  public T deq() {
    lock.lock();
    try {
      while (item == null)
        condition.await();
      T t = item;
      item = null;
      condition.signalAll();
      return t;
    } finally {
      lock.unlock();
    }
  }
}
```

Figure 10.17 The SynchronousQueue<T> class.

10.7 Dual Data Structures

To reduce the synchronization overheads of the synchronous queue, we consider an alternative synchronous queue implementation that splits enq() and deq() methods into two steps. Here is how a dequeuer tries to remove an item from an empty queue. In the first step, it puts a *reservation* object in the queue, indicating that the dequeuer is waiting for an enqueuer with which to rendezvous. The dequeuer then spins on a flag in the reservation. Later, when an enqueuer discovers the reservation, it *fulfills* the reservation by depositing an item and notifying the dequeuer by setting the reservation's flag. Similarly, an enqueuer can wait for a rendezvous partner by creating its own reservation, and spinning on the reservation's flag. At any time the queue itself contains either `enq()` reservations, `deq()` reservations, or it is empty.

This structure is called a *dual data structure*, since the methods take effect in two stages, reservation and fulfillment. It has a number of nice properties. First, waiting threads can spin on a locally cached flag, which we have seen is essential for scalability. Second, it ensures fairness in a natural way. Reservations are queued in the order they arrive, ensuring that requests are fulfilled in the same order. Note that this data structure is linearizable, since each partial method call can be ordered when it is fulfilled.

The queue is implemented as a list of nodes, where a node represents either an item waiting to be dequeued, or a reservation waiting to be fulfilled (Fig. 10.18). A node's `type` field indicates which. At any time, all queue nodes have the same type: either the queue consists entirely of items waiting to be dequeued, or entirely of reservations waiting to be fulfilled.

When an item is enqueued, the node's `item` field holds the item, which is reset to *null* when that item is dequeued. When a reservation is enqueued, the node's `item` field is *null*, and is reset to an item when fulfilled by an enqueuer.

Fig. 10.19 shows the `SynchronousDualQueue`'s constructor and `enq()` method. (The `deq()` method is symmetric.) Just like the earlier queues we have considered, the `head` field always refers to a *sentinel* node that serves as a place-holder, and whose actual value is unimportant. The queue is empty when `head` and `tail` agree. The constructor creates a sentinel node with an arbitrary value, referred to by both `head` and `tail`.

The `enq()` method first checks whether the queue is empty or whether it contains enqueued items waiting to be dequeued (Line 10). If so, then just as in the lock-free queue, the method reads the queue's `tail` field (Line 11), and checks that the values read are consistent (Line 12). If the `tail` field does not refer to the last node in the queue, then the method advances the `tail` field and starts over (Lines 13–14). Otherwise, the `enq()` method tries to append the new node to the end of the queue by resetting the tail node's `next` field to refer to the new

```
private enum NodeType {ITEM, RESERVATION};
private class Node {
  volatile NodeType type;
  volatile AtomicReference<T> item;
  volatile AtomicReference<Node> next;
  Node(T myItem, NodeType myType) {
    item = new AtomicReference<T>(myItem);
    next = new AtomicReference<Node>(null);
    type = myType;
  }
}
```

Figure 10.18 The `SynchronousDualQueue<T>` class: queue node.

```
1   public SynchronousDualQueue() {
2     Node sentinel = new Node(null, NodeType.ITEM);
3     head = new AtomicReference<Node>(sentinel);
4     tail = new AtomicReference<Node>(sentinel);
5   }
6   public void enq(T e) {
7     Node offer = new Node(e, NodeType.ITEM);
8     while (true) {
9       Node t = tail.get(), h = head.get();
10      if (h == t || t.type == NodeType.ITEM) {
11        Node n = t.next.get();
12        if (t == tail.get()) {
13          if (n != null) {
14            tail.compareAndSet(t, n);
15          } else if (t.next.compareAndSet(n, offer)) {
16            tail.compareAndSet(t, offer);
17            while (offer.item.get() == e);
18            h = head.get();
19            if (offer == h.next.get())
20              head.compareAndSet(h, offer);
21            return;
22          }
23        }
24      } else {
25        Node n = h.next.get();
26        if (t != tail.get() || h != head.get() || n == null) {
27          continue;
28        }
29        boolean success = n.item.compareAndSet(null, e);
30        head.compareAndSet(h, n);
31        if (success)
32          return;
33      }
34    }
35  }
```

Figure 10.19 The SynchronousDualQueue<T> class: enq() method and constructor.

node (Line 15). If it succeeds, it tries to advance the tail to the newly appended node (Line 16), and then spins, waiting for a dequeuer to announce that it has dequeued the item by setting the node's `item` field to *null*. Once the item is dequeued, the method tries to clean up by making its node the new sentinel. This last step serves only to enhance performance, because the implementation remains correct, whether or not the method advances the `head` reference.

If, however, the `enq()` method discovers that the queue contains dequeuers' reservations waiting to be fulfilled, then it tries to find a reservation to fulfill. Since the queue's `head` node is a sentinel with no meaningful value, `enq()` reads the head's successor (Line 25), checks that the values it has read are consistent (Lines 26–28), and tries to switch that node's `item` field from *null* to the item being enqueued. Whether or not this step succeeds, the method tries to advance head (Line 30). If the compareAndSet() call succeeds (Line 29), the method returns; otherwise it retries.

10.8 Chapter Notes

The partial queue employs a mixture of techniques adapted from Doug Lea [98] and from an algorithm by Maged Michael and Michael Scott [115]. The lock-free queue is a slightly simplified version of a queue algorithm by Maged Michael and Michael Scott [115]. The synchronous queue implementations are adapted from algorithms by Bill Scherer, Doug Lea, and Michael Scott [136].

10.9 Exercises

Exercise 119. Change the SynchronousDualQueue<T> class to work correctly with *null* items.

Exercise 120. Consider the simple lock-free queue for a single enqueuer and a single dequeuer, described earlier in Chapter 3. The queue is presented in Fig. 10.20.

```
class TwoThreadLockFreeQueue<T> {
  int head = 0, tail = 0;
  T[] items;
  public TwoThreadLockFreeQueue(int capacity) {
    head = 0; tail = 0;
    items = (T[]) new Object[capacity];
  }
  public void enq(T x) {
    while (tail - head == items.length) {};
    items[tail % items.length] = x;
    tail++;
  }
  public Object deq() {
    while (tail - head == 0) {};
    Object x = items[head % items.length];
    head++;
    return x;
  }
}
```

Figure 10.20 A Lock-free FIFO queue with blocking semantics for a single enqueuer and single dequeuer. The queue is implemented in an array. Initially the head and tail fields are equal and the queue is empty. If the head and tail differ by capacity, then the queue is full. The enq() method reads the head field, and if the queue is full, it repeatedly checks the head until the queue is no longer full. It then stores the object in the array, and increments the tail field. The deq() method works in a symmetric way.

This queue is blocking, that is, removing an item from an empty queue or inserting an item to a full one causes the threads to block (spin). The surprising thing about this queue is that it requires only loads and stores and not a more powerful read–modify–write synchronization operation. Does it however require the use of a memory barrier? If not, explain, and if so, where in the code is such a barrier needed and why?

Exercise 121. Design a bounded lock-based queue implementation using an array instead of a linked list.

1. Allow parallelism by using two separate locks for `head` and `tail`.
2. Try to transform your algorithm to be lock-free. Where do you run into difficulty?

Exercise 122. Consider the unbounded lock-based queue's `deq()` method in Fig. 10.8. Is it necessary to hold the lock when checking that the queue is not empty? Explain.

Exercise 123. In Dante's *Inferno*, he describes a visit to Hell. In a very recently discovered chapter, he encounters five people sitting at a table with a pot of stew in the middle. Although each one holds a spoon that reaches the pot, each spoon's handle is much longer than each person's arm, so no one can feed him- or herself. They are famished and desperate.

Dante then suggests "why do not you feed one another?"

The rest of the chapter is lost.

1. Write an algorithm to allow these unfortunates to feed one another. Two or more people may not feed the same person at the same time. Your algorithm must be, well, starvation-free.
2. Discuss the advantages and disadvantages of your algorithm. Is it centralized, decentralized, high or low in contention, deterministic or randomized?

Exercise 124. Consider the linearization points of the `enq()` and `deq()` methods of the lock-free queue:

1. Can we choose the point at which the returned value is read from a node as the linearization point of a successful `deq()`?
2. Can we choose the linearization point of the `enq()` method to be the point at which the `tail` field is updated, possibly by other threads (consider if it is within the `enq()`'s execution interval)? Argue your case.

Exercise 125. Consider the unbounded queue implementation shown in Fig. 10.21. This queue is blocking, meaning that the `deq()` method does not return until it has found an item to dequeue.

```
public class HWQueue<T> {
  AtomicReference<T>[] items;
  AtomicInteger tail;
  ...
  public void enq(T x) {
    int i = tail.getAndIncrement();
    items[i].set(x);
  }
  public T deq() {
    while (true) {
     int range = tail.get();
     for (int i = 0; i < range; i++) {
        T value = items[i].getAndSet(null);
        if (value != null) {
          return value;
        }
      }
    }
  }
}
```

Figure 10.21 Queue used in Exercise 125.

The queue has two fields: `items` is a very large array, and `tail` is the index of the next unused element in the array.

1. Are the enq() and deq() methods wait-free? If not, are they lock-free? Explain.
2. Identify the linearization points for enq() and deq(). (Careful! They may be execution-dependent.)

11 Concurrent Stacks and Elimination

11.1 Introduction

The Stack<T> class is a collection of items (of type T) that provides push() and pop() methods satisfying the *last-in-first-out* (LIFO) property: the last item pushed is the first popped. This chapter considers how to implement concurrent stacks. At first glance, stacks seem to provide little opportunity for concurrency, because push() and pop() calls seem to need to synchronize at the top of the stack.

Surprisingly, perhaps, stacks are not inherently sequential. In this chapter, we show how to implement concurrent stacks that can achieve a high degree of parallelism. As a first step, we consider how to build a lock-free stack in which pushes and pops synchronize at a single location.

11.2 An Unbounded Lock-Free Stack

Fig. 11.1 shows a concurrent LockFreeStack class, whose code appears in Figs. 11.2, 11.3 and 11.4. The lock-free stack is a linked list, where the top field points to the first node (or *null* if the stack is empty.) For simplicity, we usually assume it is illegal to add a *null* value to a stack.

A pop() call that tries to remove an item from an empty stack throws an exception. A push() method creates a new node (Line 13), and then calls tryPush() to try to swing the top reference from the current top-of-stack to its successor. If tryPush() succeeds, push() returns, and if not, the tryPush() attempt is repeated after backing off. The pop() method calls tryPop(), which uses compareAndSet() to try to remove the first node from the stack. If it succeeds, it returns the node, otherwise it returns *null*. (It throws an exception if the stack

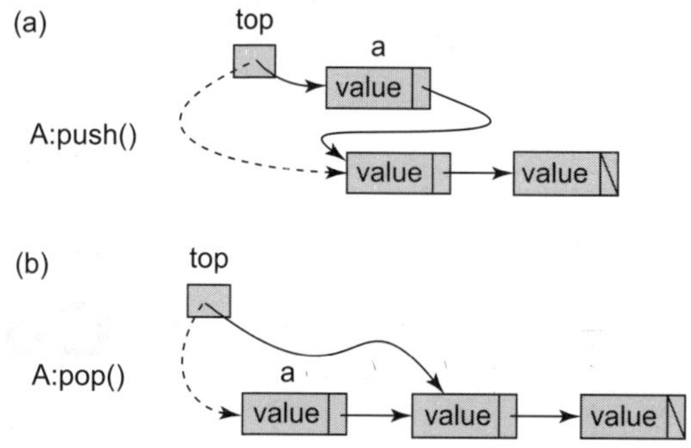

Figure 11.1 A Lock-free stack. In Part (a) a thread pushes value *a* into the stack by applying a `compareAndSet()` to the `top` field. In Part (b) a thread pops value *a* from the stack by applying a `compareAndSet()` to the `top` field.

```
public class LockFreeStack<T> {
  AtomicReference<Node> top = new AtomicReference<Node>(null);
  static final int MIN_DELAY = ...;
  static final int MAX_DELAY = ...;
  Backoff backoff = new Backoff(MIN_DELAY, MAX_DELAY);

  protected boolean tryPush(Node node){
    Node oldTop = top.get();
    node.next = oldTop;
    return(top.compareAndSet(oldTop, node));
  }
  public void push(T value) {
    Node node = new Node(value);
    while (true) {
      if (tryPush(node)) {
        return;
      } else {
        backoff.backoff();
      }
    }
  }
```

Figure 11.2 The `LockFreeStack<T>` class: in the `push()` method, threads alternate between trying to alter the `top` reference by calling `tryPush()`, and backing off using the `Backoff` class from Fig. 7.5 of Chapter 7.

is empty.) The `tryPop()` method is called until it succeeds, at which point `pop()` returns the value from the removed node.

As we have seen in Chapter 7, one can significantly reduce contention at the `top` field using exponential backoff (see Fig. 7.5 of Chapter 7). Accordingly, both

```
public class Node {
    public T value;
    public Node next;
    public Node(T value) {
      value = value;
      next = null;
    }
}
```

Figure 11.3 Lock-free stack list node.

```
1     protected Node tryPop() throws EmptyException {
2       Node oldTop = top.get();
3       if (oldTop == null) {
4         throw new EmptyException();
5       }
6       Node newTop = oldTop.next;
7       if (top.compareAndSet(oldTop, newTop)) {
8         return oldTop;
9       } else {
10        return null;
11      }
12    }
13    public T pop() throws EmptyException {
14      while (true) {
15        Node returnNode = tryPop();
16        if (returnNode != null) {
17          return returnNode.value;
18        } else {
19          backoff.backoff();
20        }
21      }
22    }
```

Figure 11.4 The LockFreeStack<T> class: The pop() method alternates between trying to change the top field and backing off.

the push() and pop() methods back off after an unsuccessful call to tryPush() or tryPop().

This implementation is lock-free because a thread fails to complete a push() or pop() method call only if there were infinitely many successful calls that modified the top of the stack. The linearization point of both the push() and the pop() methods is the successful compareAndSet(), or the throwing of the exception, in Line 3, in case of a pop() on an empty stack. Note that the compareAndSet() call by pop() does not have an ABA problem (see Chapter 10) because the Java garbage collector ensures that a node cannot be reused by one thread, as long as that node is accessible to another thread. Designing a lock-free stack that avoids the ABA problem without a garbage collector is left as an exercise.

11.3 Elimination

The LockFreeStack implementation scales poorly, not so much because the stack's top field is a source of *contention*, but primarily because it is a *sequential bottleneck*: method calls can proceed only one after the other, ordered by successful compareAndSet() calls applied to the stack's top field.

Although exponential backoff can significantly reduce contention, it does nothing to alleviate the sequential bottleneck. To make the stack parallel, we exploit this simple observation: if a push() is immediately followed by a pop(), the two operations cancel out, and the stack's state does not change. It is as if both operations never happened. If one could somehow cause concurrent pairs of pushes and pops to cancel, then threads calling push() could exchange values with threads calling pop(), without ever modifying the stack itself. These two calls would *eliminate* one another.

As depicted in Fig. 11.5, threads eliminate one another through an EliminationArray in which threads pick random array entries to try to meet complementary calls. Pairs of complementary push() and pop() calls exchange values and return. A thread whose call cannot be eliminated, either because it has failed to find a partner, or found a partner with the wrong kind of method call (such as a push() meeting a push()), can either try again to eliminate at a new location, or can access the shared LockFreeStack. The combined data structure, array, and shared stack, is linearizable because the shared stack is linearizable, and the eliminated calls can be ordered as if they happened at the point in which they exchanged values.

We can use the EliminationArray as a backoff scheme on a shared LockFreeStack. Each thread first accesses the LockFreeStack, and if it fails

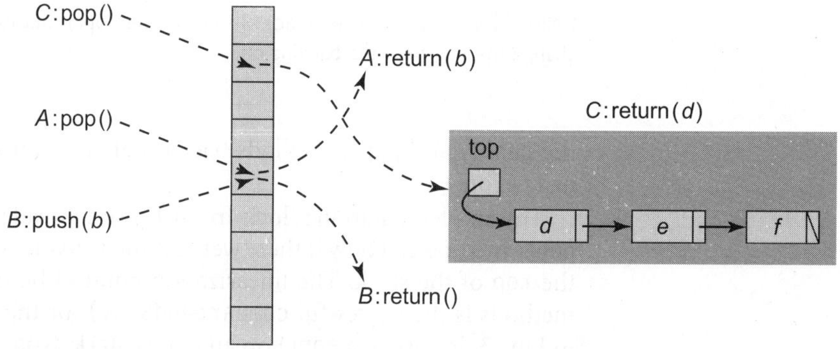

Figure 11.5 The EliminationBackoffStack<T> class. Each thread selects a random location in the array. If thread *A*'s pop() and *B*'s push() calls arrive at the same location at about the same time, then they exchange values without accessing the shared LockFreeStack. Thread *C* that does not meet another thread eventually pops the shared LockFreeStack.

to complete its call (that is, the `compareAndSet()` attempt fails), it attempts to eliminate its call using the array instead of simply backing off. If it fails to eliminate itself, it calls the `LockFreeStack` again, and so on. We call this structure an `EliminationBackoffStack`.

11.4 The Elimination Backoff Stack

Here is how to construct an `EliminationBackoffStack`, a lock-free linearizable stack implementation.

We are reminded of a story about two friends who are discussing politics on election day, each trying, to no avail, to convince the other to switch sides.

Finally, one says to the other: "Look, it's clear that we are unalterably opposed on every political issue. Our votes will surely cancel out. Why not save ourselves some time and both agree to not vote today?"

The other agrees enthusiastically and they part.

Shortly after that, a friend of the first one who had heard the conversation says, "That was a sporting offer you made."

"Not really," says the second. "This is the third time I've done this today."

The principle behind our construction is the same. We wish to allow threads with pushes and pops to coordinate and cancel out, but must avoid a situation in which a thread can make a sporting offer to more than one other thread. We do so by implementing the `EliminationArray` using coordination structures called *exchangers*, objects that allow exactly two threads (and no more) to rendezvous and exchange values.

We already saw how to exchange values using locks in the synchronous queue of Chapter 10. Here, we need a lock-free exchange, one in which threads spin rather than block, as we expect them to wait only for very short durations.

11.4.1 A Lock-Free Exchanger

A `LockFreeExchanger<T>` object permits two threads to exchange values of type `T`. If thread *A* calls the object's `exchange()` method with argument *a*, and *B* calls the same object's `exchange()` method with argument *b*, then *A*'s call will return value *b* and vice versa. On a high level, the exchanger works by having the first thread arrive to write its value, and spin until a second arrives. The second then detects that the first is waiting, reads its value, and signals the exchange. They each have now read the other's value, and can return. The first thread's call may timeout if the second does not show up, allowing it to proceed and leave the exchanger, if it is unable to exchange a value within a reasonable duration.

```
1  public class LockFreeExchanger<T> {
2    static final int EMPTY = ..., WAITING = ..., BUSY = ...;
3    AtomicStampedReference<T> slot = new AtomicStampedReference<T>(null, 0);
4    public T exchange(T myItem, long timeout, TimeUnit unit)
5      throws TimeoutException {
6      long nanos = unit.toNanos(timeout);
7      long timeBound = System.nanoTime() + nanos;
8      int[] stampHolder = {EMPTY};
9      while (true) {
10       if (System.nanoTime() > timeBound)
11         throw new TimeoutException();
12       T yrItem = slot.get(stampHolder);
13       int stamp = stampHolder[0];
14       switch(stamp) {
15       case EMPTY:
16         if (slot.compareAndSet(yrItem, myItem, EMPTY, WAITING)) {
17           while (System.nanoTime() < timeBound){
18             yrItem = slot.get(stampHolder);
19             if (stampHolder[0] == BUSY) {
20               slot.set(null, EMPTY);
21               return yrItem;
22             }
23           }
24           if (slot.compareAndSet(myItem, null, WAITING, EMPTY)) {
25             throw new TimeoutException();
26           } else {
27             yrItem = slot.get(stampHolder);
28             slot.set(null, EMPTY);
29             return yrItem;
30           }
31         }
32         break;
33       case WAITING:
34         if (slot.compareAndSet(yrItem, myItem, WAITING, BUSY))
35           return yrItem;
36         break;
37       case BUSY:
38         break;
39       default: // impossible
40         ...
41       }
42     }
43   }
44 }
```

Figure 11.6 The LockFreeExchanger<T> Class.

The LockFreeExchanger<T> class appears in Fig. 11.6. It has a single AtomicStampedReference<T> field,[1] slot. The exchanger has three possible states: EMPTY, BUSY, or WAITING. The reference's stamp records the exchanger's state (Line 14). The exchanger's main loop continues until the timeout limit

1 See Chapter 10, Pragma 10.6.1.

passes, when it throws an exception (Line 10). In the meantime, a thread reads the state of the `slot` (Line 12) and proceeds as follows:

- If the state is `EMPTY`, then the thread tries to place its item in the slot and set the state to `WAITING` using a `compareAndSet()` (Line 16). If it fails, then some other thread succeeds and it retries. If it was successful (Line 17), then its item is in the slot and the state is `WAITING`, so it spins, waiting for another thread to complete the exchange. If another thread shows up, it will take the item in the slot, replace it with its own, and set the state to `BUSY` (Line 19), indicating to the waiting thread that the exchange is complete. The waiting thread will consume the item and reset the state to `EMPTY`. Resetting to `EMPTY` can be done using a simple write because the waiting thread is the only one that can change the state from `BUSY` to `EMPTY` (Line 20). If no other thread shows up, the waiting thread needs to reset the state of the slot to `EMPTY`. This change requires a `compareAndSet()` because other threads might be attempting to exchange by setting the state from `WAITING` to `BUSY` (Line 24). If the call is successful, it raises a timeout exception. If, however, the call fails, some exchanging thread must have shown up, so the waiting thread completes the exchange (Line 26).
- If the state is `WAITING`, then some thread is waiting and the slot contains its item. The thread takes the item, and tries to replace it with its own by changing the state from `WAITING` to `BUSY` using a `compareAndSet()` (Line 34). It may fail if another thread succeeds, or the other thread resets the state to `EMPTY` following a timeout. If so, the thread must retry. If it does succeed changing the state to `BUSY`, then it can return the item.
- If the state is `BUSY` then two other threads are currently using the slot for an exchange and the thread must retry (Line 37).

Notice that the algorithm allows the inserted item to be *null*, something used later in the elimination array construction. There is no ABA problem because the `compareAndSet()` call that changes the state never inspects the item. A successful exchange's linearization point occurs when the second thread to arrive changes the state from `WAITING` to `BUSY` (Line 34). At this point both `exchange()` calls overlap, and the exchange is committed to being successful. An unsuccessful exchange's linearization point occurs when the timeout exception is thrown.

The algorithm is lock-free because overlapping `exchange()` calls with sufficient time to exchange will fail only if other exchanges are repeatedly succeeding. Clearly, too short an exchange time can cause a thread never to succeed, so care must be taken when choosing timeout durations.

11.4.2 The Elimination Array

An `EliminationArray` is implemented as an array of `Exchanger` objects of maximal size `capacity`. A thread attempting to perform an exchange picks an array entry at random, and calls that entry's `exchange()` method, providing

```
1  public class EliminationArray<T> {
2    private static final int duration = ...;
3    LockFreeExchanger<T>[] exchanger;
4    Random random;
5    public EliminationArray(int capacity) {
6      exchanger = (LockFreeExchanger<T>[]) new LockFreeExchanger[capacity];
7      for (int i = 0; i < capacity; i++) {
8        exchanger[i] = new LockFreeExchanger<T>();
9      }
10     random = new Random();
11   }
12   public T visit(T value, int range) throws TimeoutException {
13     int slot = random.nextInt(range);
14     return (exchanger[slot].exchange(value, duration,
15            TimeUnit.MILLISECONDS));
16   }
17 }
```

Figure 11.7 The `EliminationArray<T>` class: in each visit, a thread can choose dynamically the sub-range of the array from which it will will randomly select a slot.

its own input as an exchange value with another thread. The code for the `EliminationArray` appears in Fig. 11.7. The constructor takes as an argument the `capacity` of the array (the number of distinct exchangers). The `EliminationArray` class provides a single method, `visit()`, which takes timeout arguments. (Following the conventions used in the java.util.concurrent package, a timeout is expressed as a number and a time unit.) The `visit()` call takes a value of type `T` and either returns the value input by its exchange partner, or throws an exception if the timeout expires without exchanging a value with another thread. At any point in time, each thread will select a random location in a subrange of the array (Line 13). This subrange will be determined dynamically based on the load on the data structure, and will be passed as a parameter to the `visit()` method.

The `EliminationBackoffStack` is a subclass of `LockFreeStack` that overrides the `push()` and `pop()` methods, and adds an `EliminationArray` field. Figs. 11.8 and 11.9 show the new `push()` and `pop()` methods. Upon failure of a `tryPush()` or `tryPop()` attempt, instead of simply backing off, these methods try to use the `EliminationArray` to exchange values (Lines 15 and 34). A `push()` call calls `visit()` with its input value as argument, and a `pop()` call with *null* as argument. Both `push()` and `pop()` have a thread-local `RangePolicy` object that determines the `EliminationArray` subrange to be used.

When `push()` calls `visit()`, it selects a random array entry within its range and attempts to exchange a value with another thread. If the exchange is successful, the pushing thread checks whether the value was exchanged with a `pop()` method (Line 18) by testing if the value exchanged was *null*. (Recall that `pop()` always offers *null* to the exchanger while `push()` always offers a non-*null* value.) Symmetrically, when `pop()` calls `visit()`, it attempts an exchange, and if the

```java
public class EliminationBackoffStack<T> extends LockFreeStack<T> {
  static final int capacity = ...;
  EliminationArray<T> eliminationArray = new EliminationArray<T>(capacity);
  static ThreadLocal<RangePolicy> policy = new ThreadLocal<RangePolicy>() {
    protected synchronized RangePolicy initialValue() {
      return new RangePolicy();
    }

  public void push(T value) {
    RangePolicy rangePolicy = policy.get();
    Node node = new Node(value);
    while (true) {
      if (tryPush(node)) {
        return;
      } else try {
        T otherValue = eliminationArray.visit
                 (value, rangePolicy.getRange());
        if (otherValue == null) {
          rangePolicy.recordEliminationSuccess();
          return; // exchanged with pop
        }
      } catch (TimeoutException ex) {
        rangePolicy.recordEliminationTimeout();
      }
    }
  }
}
```

Figure 11.8 The `EliminationBackoffStack<T>` class: this `push()` method overrides the `LockFreeStack` `push()` method. Instead of using a simple `Backoff` class, it uses an `EliminationArray` and a dynamic `RangePolicy` to select the subrange of the array within which to eliminate.

```java
  public T pop() throws EmptyException {
    RangePolicy rangePolicy = policy.get();
    while (true) {
      Node returnNode = tryPop();
      if (returnNode != null) {
        return returnNode.value;
      } else try {
        T otherValue = eliminationArray.visit(null, rangePolicy.getRange());
        if (otherValue != null) {
          rangePolicy.recordEliminationSuccess();
          return otherValue;
        }
      } catch (TimeoutException ex) {
        rangePolicy.recordEliminationTimeout();
      }
    }
  }
```

Figure 11.9 The `EliminationBackoffStack<T>` class: this `pop()` method overrides the `LockFreeStack` `push()` method.

exchange is successful it checks (Line 36) whether the value was exchanged with a push() call by checking whether it is not *null*.

It is possible that the exchange will be unsuccessful, either because no exchange took place (the call to visit() timed out) or because the exchange was with the same type of operation (such as a pop() with a pop()). For brevity, we choose a simple approach to deal with such cases: we retry the tryPush() or tryPop() calls (Lines 13 and 31).

One important parameter is the range of the EliminationArray from which a thread selects an Exchanger location. A smaller range will allow a greater chance of a successful collision when there are few threads, while a larger range will lower the chances of threads waiting on a busy Exchanger (recall that an Exchanger can only handle one exchange at a time). Thus, if few threads access the array, they should choose smaller ranges, and as the number of threads increase, so should the range. One can control the range dynamically using a RangePolicy object that records both successful exchanges (as in Line 37) and timeout failures (Line 40). We ignore exchanges that fail because the operations do not match (such as push() with push()), because they account for a fixed fraction of the exchanges for any given distribution of push() and pop() calls. One simple policy is to shrink the range as the number of failures increases and vice versa.

There are many other possible policies. For example, one can devise a more elaborate range selection policy, vary the delays on the exchangers dynamically, add additional backoff delays before accessing the shared stack, and control whether to access the shared stack or the array dynamically. We leave these as exercises.

The EliminationBackoffStack is a linearizable stack: any successful push() or pop() call that completes by accessing the LockFreeStack can be linearized at the point of its LockFreeStack access. Any pair of eliminated push() and pop() calls can be linearized when they collide. As noted earlier, the method calls completed through elimination do not affect the linearizability of those completed in the LockFreeStack, because they could have taken effect in any state of the LockFreeStack, and having taken effect, the state of the LockFreeStack would not have changed.

Because the EliminationArray is effectively used as a backoff scheme, we expect it to deliver performance comparable to the LockFreeStack at low loads. Unlike the LockFreeStack, it has the potential to scale. As the load increases, the number of successful eliminations will grow, allowing many operations to complete in parallel. Moreover, contention at the LockFreeStack is reduced because eliminated operations never access the stack.

11.5 Chapter Notes

The LockFreeStack is credited to Treiber [145]. Actually it predates Treiber's report in 1986. It was probably invented in the early 1970s to motivate the

CAS operation on the IBM 370. The `EliminationBackoffStack` is due to Danny Hendler, Nir Shavit, and Lena Yerushalmi [57]. An efficient exchanger, which quite interestingly uses an elimination array, was introduced by Doug Lea, Michael Scott, and Bill Scherer [136]. A variant of this exchanger appears in the Java Concurrency Package. The `EliminationBackoffStack` we present here is modular, making use of exchangers, but somewhat inefficient. Mark Moir, Daniel Nussbaum, Ori Shalev, and Nir Shavit present a highly effective implementation of an `EliminationArray` [120].

11.6 Exercises

Exercise 126. Design an unbounded lock-based `Stack<T>` implementation based on a linked list.

Exercise 127. Design a bounded lock-based `Stack<T>` using an array.

1. Use a single lock and a bounded array.
2. Try to make your algorithm lock-free. Where do you run into difficulty?

Exercise 128. Modify the unbounded lock-free stack of Section 11.2 to work in the absence of a garbage collector. Create a thread-local pool of preallocated nodes and recycle them. To avoid the ABA problem, consider using the `AtomicStampedReference<T>` class from java.util.concurrent.atomic that encapsulates both a reference and an integer *stamp*.

Exercise 129. Discuss the backoff policies used in our implementation. Does it make sense to use the same shared `Backoff` object for both pushes and pops in our `LockFreeStack<T>` object? How else could we structure the backoff in space and time in the `EliminationBackoffStack<T>`?

Exercise 130. Implement a stack algorithm assuming there is a bound, in any state of the execution, on the total difference between the number of pushes and pops to the stack.

Exercise 131. Consider the problem of implementing a bounded stack using an array indexed by a `top` counter, initially zero. In the absence of concurrency, these methods are almost trivial. To push an item, increment `top` to reserve an array entry, and then store the item at that index. To pop an item, decrement `top`, and return the item at the previous `top` index.

Clearly, this strategy does not work for concurrent implementations, because one cannot make atomic changes to multiple memory locations. A single synchronization operation can either increment or decrement the `top` counter, but not both, and there is no way atomically to increment the counter and store a value.

Nevertheless, Bob D. Hacker decides to solve this problem. He decides to adapt the dual-data structure approach of Chapter 10 to implement a *dual* stack. His `DualStack<T>` class splits `push()` and `pop()` methods into *reservation* and *fulfillment* steps. Bob's implementation appears in Fig. 11.10.

The stack's top is indexed by the `top` field, an `AtomicInteger` manipulated only by `getAndIncrement()` and `getAndDecrement()` calls. Bob's `push()`

```
public class DualStack<T> {
  private class Slot {
    boolean full = false;
    volatile T value = null;
  }
  Slot[] stack;
  int capacity;
  private AtomicInteger top = new AtomicInteger(0); // array index
  public DualStack(int myCapacity) {
    capacity = myCapacity;
    stack = (Slot[]) new Object[capacity];
    for (int i = 0; i < capacity; i++) {
      stack[i] = new Slot();
    }
  }
  public T pop() throws EmptyException {
    while (true) {
      int i = top.getAndDecrement();
      if (i <= 0) { // is stack empty?
        throw new EmptyException();
       } else if (i-1 < capacity){
        while (!stack [i-1].full ) {};
        T value = stack[i-1].value;
        stack[i-1].full = false;
        return value ; //pop fulfilled
        }
     }
  }
  public T pop() throws EmptyException {
    while (true) {
      int i = top.getAndDecrement();
      if (i < 0) { // is stack empty?
        throw new EmptyException();
      } else if (i < capacity - 1) {
        while (!stack[i].full){};
        T value = stack[i].value;
        stack[i].full = false;
        return value; //pop fulfilled
      }
    }
  }
}
```

Figure 11.10 Bob's problematic dual stack.

method's reservation step reserves a slot by applying getAndIncrement() to top. Suppose the call returns index i. If i is in the range 0 ... capacity − 1, the reservation is complete. In the fulfillment phase, push(x) stores x at index i in the array, and raises the full flag to indicate that the value is ready to be read. The value field must be **volatile** to guarantee that once flag is raised, the value has already been written to index i of the array.

If the index returned from push()'s getAndIncrement() is less than 0, the push() method repeatedly retries getAndIncrement() until it returns an index greater than or equal to 0. The index could be less than 0 due to getAndDecrement() calls of failed pop() calls to an empty stack. Each such failed getAndDecrement() decrements the top by one more past the 0 array bound. If the index returned is greater than capacity −1, push() throws an exception because the stack is full.

The situation is symmetric for pop(). It checks that the index is within the bounds and removes an item by applying getAndDecrement() to top, returning index i. If i is in the range 0 ... capacity − 1, the reservation is complete. For the fulfillment phase, pop() spins on the full flag of array slot i, until it detects that the flag is true, indicating that the push() call is successful.

What is wrong with Bob's algorithm? Is this an inherent problem or can you think of a way to fix it?

Exercise 132. In Exercise 97 we ask you to implement the Rooms interface, reproduced in Fig. 11.11. The Rooms class manages a collection of *rooms*, indexed from 0 to m (where m is a known constant). Threads can enter or exit any room in that range. Each room can hold an arbitrary number of threads simultaneously, but only one room can be occupied at a time. The last thread to leave a room triggers an onEmpty() handler, which runs while all rooms are empty.

Fig. 11.12 shows an incorrect concurrent stack implementation.

1. Explain why this stack implementation does not work.
2. Fix it by adding calls to a two-room Rooms class: one room for pushing and one for popping.

```
public interface Rooms {
  public interface Handler {
    void onEmpty();
  }
  void enter(int i);
  boolean exit();
  public void setExitHandler(int i, Rooms.Handler h) ;
}
```

Figure 11.11 The Rooms interface.

```
public class Stack<T> {
  private AtomicInteger top;
  private T[] items;
  public Stack(int capacity) {
    top = new AtomicInteger();
    items = (T[]) new Object[capacity];
  }
  public void push(T x) throws FullException {
    int i = top.getAndIncrement();
    if (i >= items.length) { // stack is full
      top.getAndDecrement(); // restore state
      throw new FullException();
    }
    items[i] = x;
  }
  public T pop() throws EmptyException {
    int i = top.getAndDecrement() - 1;
    if (i < 0) {              // stack is empty
      top.getAndIncrement(); // restore state
      throw new EmptyException();
    }
    return items[i];
  }
}
```

Figure 11.12 Unsynchronized concurrent stack.

Exercise 133. This exercise is a follow-on to Exercise 132. Instead of having the push() method throw FullException, exploit the push room's exit handler to resize the array. Remember that no thread can be in any room when an exit handler is running, so (of course) only one exit handler can run at a time.

12 Counting, Sorting, and Distributed Coordination

12.1 Introduction

This chapter shows how some important problems that seem inherently sequential can be made highly parallel by "spreading out" coordination tasks among multiple parties. What does this spreading out buy us?

To answer this question, we need to understand how to measure the performance of a concurrent data structure. There are two measures that come to mind: *latency*, the time it takes an individual method call to complete, and *throughput*, the overall rate at which method calls complete. For example, real-time applications might care more about latency, and databases might care more about throughput.

In Chapter 11 we saw how to apply distributed coordination to the `EliminationBackoffStack` class. Here, we cover several useful patterns for distributed coordination: combining, counting, diffraction, and sampling. Some are deterministic, while others use randomization. We also cover two basic structures underlying these patterns: trees and combinatorial networks. Interestingly, for some data structures based on distributed coordination, high throughput does not necessarily mean low latency.

12.2 Shared Counting

We recall from Chapter 10 that a *pool* is a collection of items that provides `put()` and `get()` methods to insert and remove items (Fig. 10.1). Familiar classes such as stacks and queues can be viewed as pools that provide additional fairness guarantees.

One way to implement a pool is to use coarse-grained locking, perhaps making both `put()` and `get()` **`synchronized`** methods. The problem, of course, is that coarse-grained locking is too heavy-handed, because the lock itself creates both a *sequential bottleneck*, forcing all method calls to synchronize, as well as a *hot spot*, a source of memory contention. We would prefer to have `Pool` method calls work in parallel, with less synchronization and lower contention.

Let us consider the following alternative. The pool's items reside in a cyclic array, where each array entry contains either an item or *null*. We route threads through two counters. Threads calling `put()` increment one counter to choose an array index into which the new item should be placed. (If that entry is full, the thread waits until it becomes empty.) Similarly, threads calling `get()` increment another counter to choose an array index from which the new item should be removed. (If that entry is empty, the thread waits until it becomes full.)

This approach replaces one bottleneck: the lock, with two: the counters. Naturally, two bottlenecks are better than one (think about that claim for a second). We now explore the idea that shared counters need not be bottlenecks, and can be effectively parallelized. We face two challenges.

1. We must avoid *memory contention*, where too many threads try to access the same memory location, stressing the underlying communication network and cache coherence protocols.
2. We must achieve real parallelism. Is incrementing a counter an inherently sequential operation, or is it possible for n threads to increment a counter faster than it takes one thread to increment a counter n times?

We now look at several ways to build highly parallel counters through data structures that coordinate the distribution of counter indexes.

12.3 Software Combining

Here is a linearizable shared counter class using a pattern called *software combining*. A `CombiningTree` is a binary tree of *nodes*, where each node contains bookkeeping information. The counter's value is stored at the root. Each thread is assigned a leaf, and at most two threads share a leaf, so if there are p physical processors, then there are $p/2$ leaves. To increment the counter, a thread starts at its leaf, and works its way up the tree to the root. If two threads reach a node at approximately the same time, then they *combine* their increments by adding them together. One thread, the *active* thread, propagates their combined increments up the tree, while the other, the *passive* thread, waits for the active thread to complete their combined work. A thread may be active at one level and become passive at a higher level.

For example, suppose threads A and B share a leaf node. They start at the same time, and their increments are combined at their shared leaf. The first one, say, B, actively continues up to the next level, with the mission of adding 2 to the counter value, while the second, A, passively waits for B to return from the root with an acknowledgment that A's increment has occurred. At the next level in the tree, B may combine with another thread C, and advance with the renewed intention of adding 3 to the counter value.

When a thread reaches the root, it adds the sum of its combined increments to the counter's current value. The thread then moves back down the tree, notifying each waiting thread that the increments are now complete.

Combining trees have an inherent disadvantage with respect to locks: each increment has a higher latency, that is, the time it takes an individual method call to complete. With a lock, a `getAndIncrement()` call takes $O(1)$ time, while with a `CombiningTree`, it takes $O(\log p)$ time. Nevertheless, a `CombiningTree` is attractive because it promises far better throughput, that is, the overall rate at which method calls complete. For example, using a queue lock, p `getAndIncrement()` calls complete in $O(p)$ time, at best, while using a `CombiningTree`, under ideal conditions where all threads move up the tree together, p `getAndIncrement()` calls complete in $O(\log p)$ time, an exponential improvement. Of course, the actual performance is often less than ideal, a subject examined in detail later on. Still, the `CombiningTree` class, like other techniques we consider later, is intended to benefit throughput, not latency.

Combining trees are also attractive because they can be adapted to apply any commutative function, not just increment, to the value maintained by the tree.

12.3.1 Overview

Although the idea behind a `CombiningTree` is quite simple, the implementation is not. To keep the overall (simple) structure from being submerged in (not-so-simple) detail, we split the data structure into two classes: the `CombiningTree` class manages navigation within the tree, moving up and down the tree as needed, while the `Node` class manages each visit to a node. As you go through the algorithm's description, it might be a good idea to consult Fig. 12.3 that describes an example `CombiningTree` execution.

This algorithm uses two kinds of synchronization. Short-term synchronization is provided by synchronized methods of the `Node` class. Each method locks the node for the duration of the call to ensure that it can read–write node fields without interference from other threads. The algorithm also requires excluding threads from a node for durations longer than a single method call. Such long-term synchronization is provided by a Boolean `locked` field. When this field is *true*, no other thread is allowed to access the node.

Every tree node has a *combining status*, which defines whether the node is in the early, middle, or late stages of combining concurrent requests.

```
enum CStatus{FIRST, SECOND, RESULT, IDLE, ROOT};
```

These values have the following meanings:

- `IDLE`: This node is not in use.
- `FIRST`: One active thread has visited this node, and will return to check whether another passive thread has left a value with which to combine.
- `SECOND`: A second thread has visited this node and stored a value in the node's `value` field to be combined with the active thread's value, but the combined operation is not yet complete.

- `RESULT`: Both threads' operations have been combined and completed, and the second thread's result has been stored in the node's `result` field.
- `ROOT`: This value is a special case to indicate that the node is the root, and must be treated specially.

Fig. 12.1 shows the `Node` class's other fields.

To initialize the `CombiningTree` for p threads, we create a width $w \geqslant p/2$ array of `Node` objects. The root is `node[0]`, and for $0 < i < w$, the parent of `node[`i`]` is `node[`$(i-1)/2$`]`. The leaf nodes are the last $(w+1)/2$ nodes in the array, where thread i is assigned to leaf $i/2$. The root's initial combining state is `ROOT` and the other nodes combining state is `IDLE`. Fig. 12.2 shows the `CombiningTree` class constructor.

The `CombiningTree`'s `getAndIncrement()` method, shown in Fig. 12.4, has four phases. In the *precombining phase* (Lines 16 through 19), the `CombiningTree` class's `getAndIncrement()` method moves up the tree applying `precombine()` to

```
public class Node {
  enum CStatus{IDLE, FIRST, SECOND, RESULT, ROOT};
  boolean locked;
  CStatus cStatus;
  int firstValue, secondValue;
  int result;
  Node parent;
  public Node() {
    cStatus = CStatus.ROOT;
    locked = false;
  }
  public Node(Node myParent) {
    parent = myParent;
    cStatus = CStatus.IDLE;
    locked = false;
  }
  ...
}
```

Figure 12.1 The `Node` class: the constructors and fields.

```
  public CombiningTree(int width) {
    Node[] nodes = new Node[width - 1];
    nodes[0] = new Node();
    for (int i = 1; i < nodes.length; i++) {
      nodes[i] = new Node(nodes[(i-1)/2]);
    }
    leaf = new Node[(width + 1)/2];
    for (int i = 0; i < leaf.length; i++) {
      leaf[i] = nodes[nodes.length - i - 1];
    }
  }
```

Figure 12.2 The `CombiningTree` class: constructor.

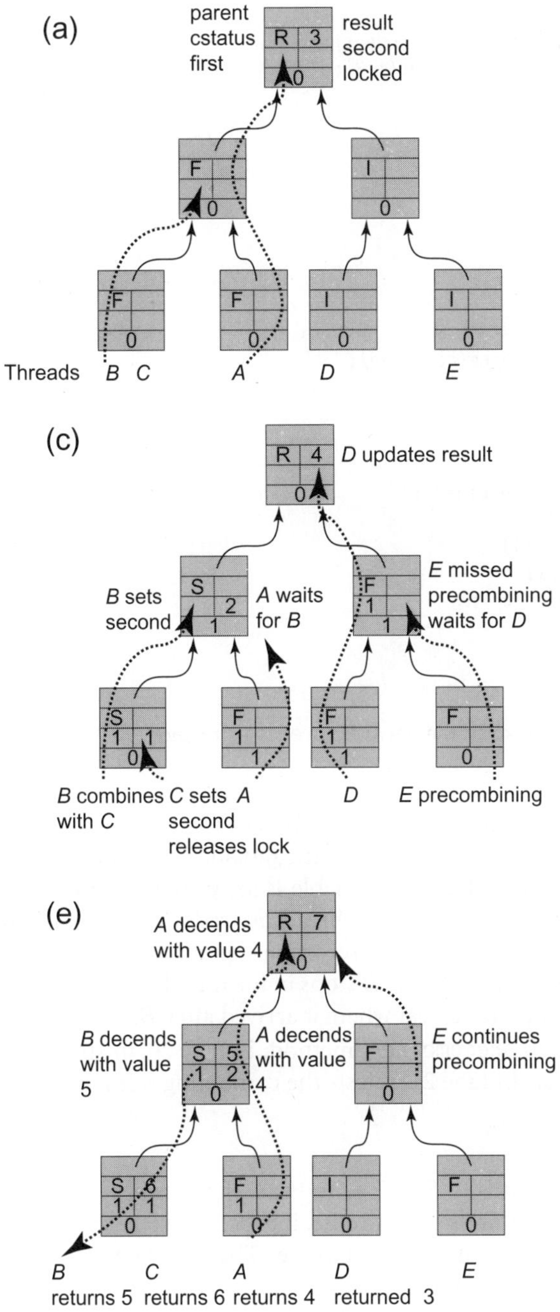

Figure 12.3 The concurrent traversal of a width 8 combining tree by 5 threads. The structure is initialized with all nodes unlocked, the root node having the CStatus ROOT and all other nodes having the CStatus IDLE.

```
  public int getAndIncrement() {
    Stack<Node> stack = new Stack<Node>();
    Node myLeaf = leaf[ThreadID.get()/2];
    Node node = myLeaf;
    // precombining phase
    while (node.precombine()) {
      node = node.parent;
    }
    Node stop = node;
    // combining phase
    node = myLeaf;
    int combined = 1;
    while (node != stop) {
      combined = node.combine(combined);
      stack.push(node);
      node = node.parent;
    }
    // operation phase
    int prior = stop.op(combined);
    // distribution phase
    while (!stack.empty()) {
      node = stack.pop();
      node.distribute(prior);
    }
    return prior;
  }
```

Figure 12.4 The `CombiningTree` class: the `getAndIncrement()` method.

each node. The `precombine()` method returns a Boolean indicating whether the thread was the first to arrive at the node. If so, the `getAndIncrement()` method continues moving up the tree. The `stop` variable is set to the last node visited, which is either the last node at which the thread arrived second, or the root. For example, Part (a) of Fig. 12.3 shows a precombining phase example. Thread A, which is fastest, stops at the root, while B stops in the middle-level node where it arrived after A, and C stops at the leaf where it arrived after B.

Fig. 12.5 shows the `Node`'s `precombine()` method. In Line 20, the thread waits until the locked field is false. In Line 21, it tests the combining status.

IDLE

The thread sets the node's status to `FIRST` to indicate that it will return to look for a value for combining. If it finds such a value, it proceeds as the active thread, and the thread that provided that value is passive. The call then returns *true*, instructing the thread to move up the tree.

FIRST

An earlier thread has recently visited this node, and will return to look for a value to combine. The thread instructs the thread to stop moving up the tree (by

```
19   synchronized boolean precombine() {
20     while (locked) wait();
21     switch (cStatus) {
22       case IDLE:
23         cStatus = CStatus.FIRST;
24         return true;
25       case FIRST:
26         locked = true;
27         cStatus = CStatus.SECOND;
28         return false;
29       case ROOT:
30         return false;
31       default:
32         throw new PanicException("unexpected Node state" + cStatus);
33     }
34   }
```

Figure 12.5 The Node class: the precombining phase.

returning *false*), and to start the next phase, computing the value to combine. Before it returns, the thread places a long-term lock on the node (by setting `locked` to *true*) to prevent the earlier visiting thread from proceeding without combining with the thread's value.

ROOT

If the thread has reached the root node, it instructs the thread to start the next phase.

Line 31 is a *default* case that is executed only if an unexpected status is encountered.

> *Pragma* 12.3.1. It is good programming practice always to provide an arm for every possible enumeration value, even if we know it cannot happen. If we are wrong, the program is easier to debug, and if we are right, the program may later be changed even by someone who does not know as much as we do. Always program defensively.

In the *combining phase*, (Fig. 12.4, Lines 21–28), the thread revisits the nodes it visited in the precombining phase, combining its value with values left by other threads. It stops when it arrives at the node `stop` where the precombining phase ended. Later on, we traverse these nodes in reverse order, so as we go we push the nodes we visit onto a stack.

The `Node` class's `combine()` method, shown in Fig. 12.6, adds any values left by a recently arrived passive process to the values combined so far. As before, the thread first waits until the `locked` field is *false*. It then sets a long-term lock on the node, to ensure that late-arriving threads do not expect to combine with it. If the status is `SECOND`, it adds the other thread's value to the accumulated value, otherwise it returns the value unchanged. In Part (c) of Fig. 12.3, thread *A* starts

```
35   synchronized int combine(int combined) {
36     while (locked) wait();
37     locked = true;
38     firstValue = combined;
39     switch (cStatus) {
40       case FIRST:
41         return firstValue;
42       case SECOND:
43         return firstValue + secondValue;
44       default:
45         throw new PanicException("unexpected Node state " + cStatus);
46     }
47   }
```

Figure 12.6 The Node class: the combining phase. This method applies addition to FirstValue and SecondValue, but any other commutative operation would work just as well.

```
48   synchronized int op(int combined) {
49     switch (cStatus) {
50       case ROOT:
51         int prior = result;
52         result += combined;
53         return prior;
54       case SECOND:
55         secondValue = combined;
56         locked = false;
57         notifyAll(); // wake up waiting threads
58         while (cStatus != CStatus.RESULT) wait();
59         locked = false;
60         notifyAll();
61         cStatus = CStatus.IDLE;
62         return result;
63       default:
64         throw new PanicException("unexpected Node state");
65     }
66   }
```

Figure 12.7 The Node class: applying the operation.

ascending the tree in the combining phase. It reaches the second level node locked by thread *B* and waits. In Part (d), *B* releases the lock on the second level node, and *A*, seeing that the node is in a SECOND combining state, locks the node and moves to the root with the combined value 3, the sum of the FirstValue and SecondValue fields written respectively by *A* and *B*.

At the start of the operation phase (Lines 29 and 30), the thread has now combined all method calls from lower-level nodes, and now examines the node where it stopped at the end of the precombining phase (Fig. 12.7). If the node is the root, as in Part (d) of Fig. 12.3, then the thread, in this case *A*, carries out the combined getAndIncrement() operations: it adds its accumulated value (3 in the example) to the result and returns the prior value. Otherwise, the thread unlocks the node, notifies any blocked thread, deposits its value as the

```
synchronized void distribute(int prior) {
   switch (cStatus) {
     case FIRST:
       cStatus = CStatus.IDLE;
       locked = false;
       break;
     case SECOND:
       result = prior + firstValue;
       cStatus = CStatus.RESULT;
       break;
     default:
       throw new PanicException("unexpected Node state");
   }
   notifyAll();
}
```

Figure 12.8 The Node class: the distribution phase.

SecondValue, and waits for the other thread to return a result after propagating the combined operations toward the root. For example, this is the sequence of actions taken by thread *B* in Parts (c) and (d) of Fig. 12.3.

When the result arrives, *A* enters the *distribution phase*, propagating the result down the tree. In this phase (Lines 31–36), the thread moves down the tree, releasing locks, and informing passive partners of the values they should report to their own passive partners, or to the caller (at the lowest level). The distribute method is shown in Fig. 12.8. If the state of the node is FIRST, no thread combines with the distributing thread, and it can reset the node to its initial state by releasing the lock and setting the state to IDLE. If, on the other hand, the state is SECOND, the distributing thread updates the result to be the sum of the prior value brought from higher up the tree, and the FIRST value. This reflects a situation in which the active thread at the node managed to perform its increment before the passive one. The passive thread waiting to get a value reads the result once the distributing thread sets the status to RESULT. For example, in Part (e) of Fig. 12.3, the active thread *A* executes its distribution phase in the middle level node, setting the result to 5, changing the state to RESULT, and descending down to the leaf, returning the value 4 as its output. The passive thread *B* awakes and sees that the middle-level node's state has changed, and reads result 5.

12.3.2 An Extended Example

Fig. 12.3 describes the various phases of a CombiningTree execution. There are five threads labeled *A* through *E*. Each node has six fields, as shown in Fig. 12.1. Initially, all nodes are unlocked and all but the root are in an IDLE combining state. The counter value in the initial state in Part (a) is 3, the result of an earlier computation. In Part (a), to perform a getAndIncrement(), threads *A* and *B* start the precombining phase. *A* ascends the tree, changing the nodes it visits from IDLE to FIRST, indicating that it will be the active thread in combining the values up the tree. Thread *B* is the active thread at its leaf node, but has not yet arrived at the second-level node shared with *A*. In Part (b), *B* arrives at the second-level node and stops, changing it from `FIRST` to `SECOND`, indicating that it will collect its combined values and wait here for *A* to proceed with them to the root. *B* locks the node (changing the `locked` field from *false* to *true*), preventing *A* from proceeding with the combining phase without *B*'s combined value. But *B* has not combined the values. Before it does so, *C* starts precombining, arrives at the leaf node, stops, and changes its state to `SECOND`. It also locks the node to prevent *B* from ascending without its input to the combining phase. Similarly, *D* starts precombining and successfully reaches the root node. Neither *A* nor *D* changes the root node state, and in fact it never changes. They simply mark it as the node where they stopped precombining. In Part (c) *A* starts up the tree in the combining phase. It locks the leaf so that any later thread will not be able to proceed in its precombining phase, and will wait until *A* completes its combining and distribution phases. It reaches the second-level node, locked by *B*, and waits. In the meantime, *C* starts combining, but since it stopped at the leaf node, it executes the `op()` method on this node, setting `SecondValue` to 1 and then releasing the lock. When *B* starts its combining phase, the leaf node is unlocked and marked `SECOND`, so *B* writes 1 to `FirstValue` and ascends to the second-level node with a combined value of 2, the result of adding the `FirstValue` and `SecondValue` fields.

When it reaches the second level node, the one at which it stopped in the precombining phase, it calls the `op()` method on this node, setting `SecondValue` to 2. *A* must wait until it releases the lock. Meanwhile, in the right-hand side of the tree, *D* executes its combining phase, locking nodes as it ascends. Because it meets no other threads with which to combine, it reads 3 in the `result` field in the root and updates it to 4. Thread *E* then starts precombining, but is late in meeting *D*. It cannot continue precombining as long as *D* locks the second-level node. In Part (d), *B* releases the lock on the second-level node, and *A*, seeing that the node is in state `SECOND`, locks the node and moves to the root with the combined value 3, the sum of the `FirstValue` and `SecondValue` fields written, respectively, by *A* and *B*. *A* is delayed while *D* completes updating the root. Once *D* is done, *A* reads 4 in the root's `result` field and updates it to 7. *D* descends the tree (by popping its local `Stack`), releasing the locks and returning the value 3 that it originally read in the root's `result` field. *E* now continues its ascent in the precombining phase. Finally, in Part (e), *A* executes its distribution phase. It returns to the middle-level node, setting `result` to 5, changing the state to `RESULT`, and descending to the leaf, returning the value 4 as its output. *B* awakens and sees the state of the middle-level node has changed, reads 5 as the `result`, and descends to its leaf where it sets the `result` field to 6 and the state to `RESULT`. *B* then returns 5 as its output. Finally, *C* awakens and observes that the leaf node state has changed, reads 6 as the `result`, which it returns as its output value. Threads *A* through *D* return values 3 to 6 which fit the root's `result` field value of 7. The linearization order of the `getAndIncrement()` method calls by the different threads is determined by their order in the tree during the precombining phase.

12.3.3 Performance and Robustness

Like all the algorithms described in this chapter, `CombiningTree` throughput depends in complex ways on the characteristics both of the application and of the underlying architecture. Nevertheless, it is worthwhile to review, in qualitative terms, some experimental results from the literature. Readers interested in detailed experimental results (mostly for obsolete architectures) may consult the chapter notes.

As a thought experiment, a `CombiningTree` should provide high throughput under ideal circumstances when each thread can combine its increment with another's. But it may provide poor throughput under worst-case circumstances, where many threads arrive late at a locked node, missing the chance to combine, and are forced to wait for the earlier request to ascend and descend the tree.

In practice, experimental evidence supports this informal analysis. The higher the contention, the greater the observed rate of combining, and the greater the observed speed-up. Worse is better. Combining trees are less attractive when concurrency is low. The combining rate decreases rapidly as the arrival rate of increment requests is reduced. Throughput is sensitive to the arrival rate of requests.

Because combining increases throughput, and failure to combine does not, it makes sense for a request arriving at a node to wait for a reasonable duration for another thread to arrive with a increment with which to combine. Not surprisingly, it makes sense to wait for a short time when the contention is low, and longer when contention is high. When contention is sufficiently high, unbounded waiting works very well.

An algorithm is *robust* if it performs well in the presence of large fluctuations in request arrival times. The literature suggests that the `CombiningTree` algorithm with a fixed waiting time is not robust, because high variance in request arrival rates seems to reduce the combining rate.

12.4 Quiescently Consistent Pools and Counters

> First shalt thou take out the Holy Pin. Then shalt thou count to three, no more, no less. Three shall be the number thou shalt count, and the number of the counting shall be three.... Once the number three, being the third number, be reached, then lobbest thou thy Holy Hand Grenade of Antioch towards thy foe, who, being naughty in my sight, shall snuff it.
>
> From *Monty Python and the Holy Grail.*

Not all applications require linearizable counting. Indeed, counter-based `Pool` implementations require only quiescently consistent[1] counting: all that matters is that the counters produce no duplicates and no omissions. It is enough that

1 See Chapter 3 for a detailed definition of quiescent consistency.

for every item placed by a put() in an array entry, another thread eventually executes a get() that accesses that entry, eventually matching put() and get() calls. (Wrap-around may still cause multiple put() calls or get() calls to compete for the same array entry.)

12.5 Counting Networks

Students of Tango know that the partners must be tightly coordinated: if they do not move together, the dance does not work, no matter how skilled the dancers may be as individuals. In the same way, combining trees must be tightly coordinated: if requests do not arrive together, the algorithm does not work efficiently, no matter how fast the individual processes.

In this chapter, we consider *counting networks*, which look less like Tango and more like a Rave: each participant moves at its own pace, but collectively the counter delivers a quiescently consistent set of indexes with high throughput.

Let us imagine that we replace the combining tree's single counter with multiple counters, each of which distributes a subset of indexes (see Fig. 12.9). We allocate w counters (in the figure $w = 4$), each of which distributes a set of unique indexes modulo w (in the figure, for example, the second counter distributes 2, 6, 10, $\ldots i \cdot w + 2$ for increasing i). The challenge is how to distribute the threads among the counters so that there are no duplications or omissions, and how to do so in a distributed and loosely coordinated style.

12.5.1 Networks That Count

A *balancer* is a simple switch with two input wires and two output wires, called the *top* and *bottom* wires (or sometimes the *north* and *south* wires). Tokens arrive on the balancer's input wires at arbitrary times, and emerge on their output wires, at some later time. A balancer can be viewed as a toggle: given a stream of input tokens, it sends one token to the top output wire, and the next to the bottom, and so on, effectively balancing the number of tokens between the two wires (see Fig. 12.10). More precisely, a balancer has two states: *up* and *down*. If

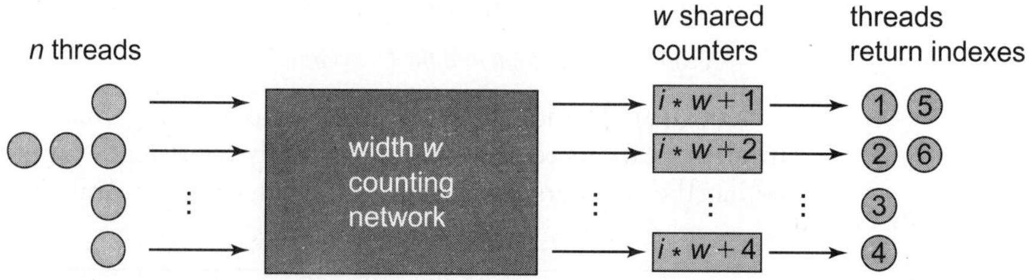

Figure 12.9 A quiescently consistent shared counter based on $w = 4$ counters preceded by a counting network. Threads traverse the counting network to choose which counters to access.

Figure 12.10 A balancer. Tokens arrive at arbitrary times on arbitrary input lines and are redirected to ensure that when all tokens have exited the balancer, there is at most one more token on the top wire than on the bottom one.

the state is *up*, the next token exits on the top wire, otherwise it exits on the bottom wire.

We use x_0 and x_1 to denote the number of tokens that respectively arrive on a balancer's top and bottom input wires, and y_0 and y_1 to denote the number that exit on the top and bottom output wires. A balancer never creates tokens: at all times.

$$x_0 + x_1 \geqslant y_0 + y_1.$$

A balancer is said to be *quiescent* if every token that arrived on an input wire has emerged on an output wire:

$$x_0 + x_1 = y_0 + y_1.$$

A *balancing network* is constructed by connecting some balancers' output wires to other balancers' input wires. A balancing network of width w has input wires $x_0, x_1, \ldots, x_{w-1}$ (not connected to output wires of balancers), and w output wires $y_0, y_1, \ldots, y_{w-1}$ (similarly unconnected). The balancing network's *depth* is the maximum number of balancers one can traverse starting from any input wire. We consider only balancing networks of finite depth (meaning the wires do not form a loop). Like balancers, balancing networks do not create tokens:

$$\sum x_i \geqslant \sum y_i.$$

(We usually drop indexes from summations when we sum over every element in a sequence.) A balancing network is *quiescent* if every token that arrived on an input wire has emerged on an output wire:

$$\sum x_i = \sum y_i.$$

So far, we have described balancing networks as if they were switches in a network. On a shared-memory multiprocessor, however, a balancing network can be implemented as an object in memory. Each balancer is an object, whose wires are references from one balancer to another. Each thread repeatedly traverses the object, starting on some input wire, and emerging at some output wire, effectively shepherding a token through the network.

Some balancing networks have interesting properties. The network shown in Fig. 12.11 has four input wires and four output wires. Initially, all balancers are *up*. We can check for ourselves that if any number of tokens enter the network, in any order, on any set of input wires, then they emerge in a regular pattern on the output wires. Informally, no matter how token arrivals are distributed among the

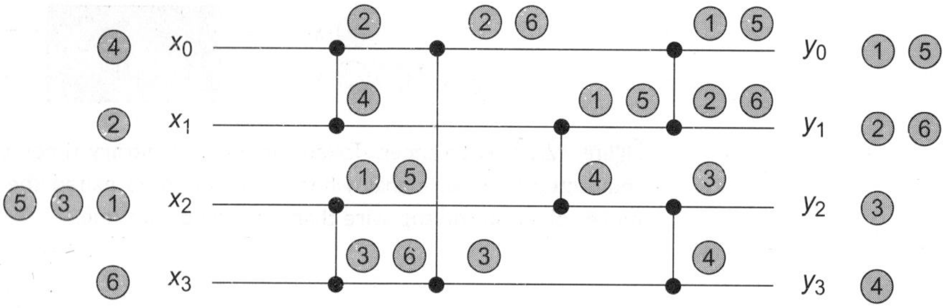

Figure 12.11 A sequential execution of a BITONIC [4] counting network. Each vertical line represents a balancer, and each balancer's two input and output wires are the horizontal lines it connects to at the dots. In this sequential execution, tokens pass through the network, one completely after the other in the order specified by the numbers on the tokens. We track every token as it passes through the balancers on the way to an output wire. For example, token number 3 enters on wire 2, goes down to wire 3, and ends up on wire 2. Notice how the step property is maintained in every balancer, and also in the network as a whole.

input wires, the output distribution is balanced across the output wires, where the top output wires are filled first. If the number of tokens n is a multiple of four (the network width), then the same number of tokens emerges from each wire. If there is one excess token, it emerges on output wire 0, if there are two, they emerge on output wires 0 and 1, and so on. In general, if

$$n = \sum x_i$$

then

$$y_i = (n/w) + (i \bmod w).$$

We call this property the *step property*.

Any balancing network that satisfies the step property is called a *counting network*, because it can easily be adapted to count the number of tokens that have traversed the network. Counting is done, as we described earlier in Fig. 12.9, by adding a local counter to each output wire i, so that tokens emerging on that wire are assigned consecutive numbers $i, i+w, \ldots, i+(y_i-1)w$.

The step property can be defined in a number of ways which we use interchangeably.

Lemma 12.5.1. If $y_0, \ldots, y_{w-1}$ is a sequence of nonnegative integers, the following statements are all equivalent:

1. For any $i < j$, $0 \leqslant y_i - y_j \leqslant 1$.
2. Either $y_i = y_j$ for all i, j, or there exists some c such that for any $i < c$ and $j \geqslant c$, $y_i - y_j = 1$.
3. If $m = \sum y_i$, $y_i = \left\lceil \frac{m-i}{w} \right\rceil$.

12.5.2 The Bitonic Counting Network

In this section we describe how to generalize the counting network of Fig. 12.11 to a counting network whose width is any power of 2. We give an inductive construction.

When describing counting networks, we do not care about when tokens arrive, we care only that when the network is quiescent, the number of tokens exiting on the output wires satisfies the step property. Define a width w *sequence* of inputs or outputs $x = x_0, \ldots, x_{w-1}$ to be a collection of tokens, partitioned into w subsets x_i. The x_i are the input tokens that arrive or leave on wire i.

We define the width-$2k$ balancing network MERGER $[2k]$ as follows. It has two input sequences of width k, x and x', and a single output sequence y of width $2k$. In any quiescent state, if x and x' both have the step property, then so does y. The MERGER $[2k]$ network is defined inductively (see Fig. 12.12). When k is equal to 1, the MERGER $[2k]$ network is a single balancer. For $k > 1$, we construct the MERGER $[2k]$ network with input sequences x and x' from two MERGER $[k]$ networks and k balancers. Using a MERGER $[k]$ network, we merge the even subsequence $x_0, x_2, \ldots, x_{k-2}$ of x with the odd subsequence $x'_1, x'_3, \ldots, x'_{k-1}$ of x' (that is, the sequence $x_0, \ldots, x_{k-2}, x'_1, \ldots, x'_{k-1}$ is the input to the MERGER $[k]$ network), while with a second MERGER $[k]$ network we merge the odd subsequence of x with the even subsequence of x'. We call the outputs of these two MERGER $[k]$ networks z and z'. The final stage of the network combines z and z' by sending each pair of wires z_i and z'_i into a balancer whose outputs yield y_{2i} and y_{2i+1}.

The MERGER $[2k]$ network consists of $\log 2k$ layers of k balancers each. It provides the step property for its outputs only when its two input sequences also have the step property, which we ensure by filtering the inputs through smaller balancing networks.

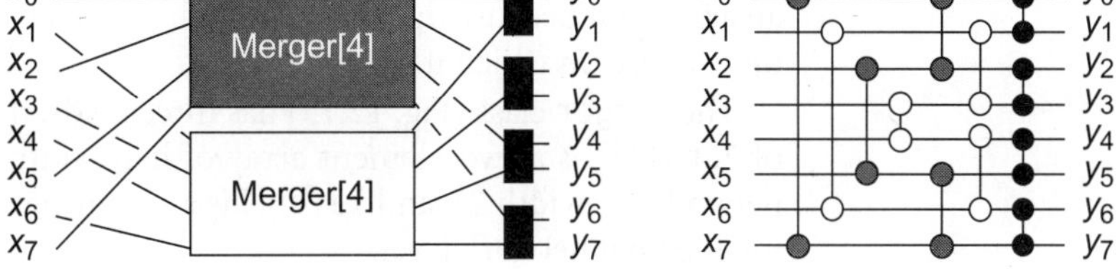

Figure 12.12 On the left-hand side we see the logical structure of a MERGER [8] network, into which feed two BITONIC [4] networks, as depicted in Fig. 12.11. The gray MERGER [4] network has as inputs the even wires coming out of the top BITONIC [4] network, and the odd ones from the lower BITONIC [4] network. In the lower MERGER [4] the situation is reversed. Once the wires exit the two MERGER [4] networks, each pair of identically numbered wires is combined by a balancer. On the right-hand side we see the physical layout of a MERGER [8] network. The different balancers are color coded to match the logical structure in the left-hand figure.

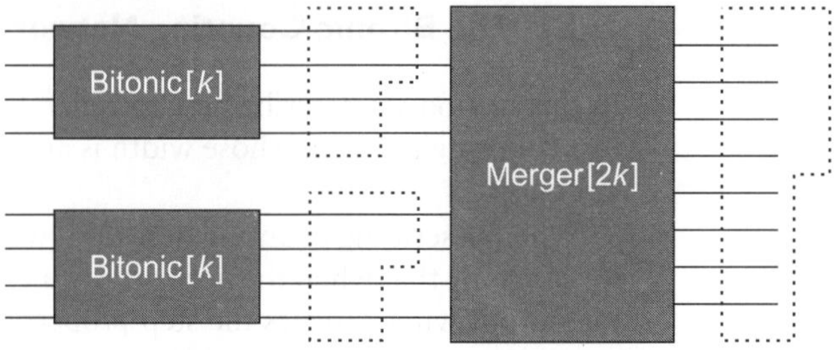

Figure 12.13 The recursive structure of a BITONIC [2k] Counting Network. Two BITONIC [k] counting networks feed into a MERGER [2k] balancing network.

The BITONIC $[2k]$ network is constructed by passing the outputs from two BITONIC $[k]$ networks into a MERGER $[2k]$ network, where the induction is grounded in the BITONIC $[2]$ network consisting of a single balancer, as depicted in Fig. 12.13. This construction gives us a network consisting of $\binom{\log 2k+1}{2}$ layers each consisting of k balancers.

A Software Bitonic Counting Network

So far, we have described counting networks as if they were switches in a network. On a shared-memory multiprocessor however, a balancing network can be implemented as an object in memory. Each balancer is an object, whose wires are references from one balancer to another. Each thread repeatedly traverses the object, starting on some input wire and emerging at some output wire, effectively shepherding a token through the network. Here, we show how to implement a BITONIC $[2]$ network as a shared-memory data structure.

The `Balancer` class (Fig. 12.14) has a single Boolean field: `toggle`. The synchronized `traverse()` method complements the `toggle` field and returns as output wire, either 0 or 1. The `Balancer` class's `traverse()` method does not need an argument because the wire on which a token exits a balancer does not depend on the wire on which it enters.

The `Merger` class (Fig. 12.15) has three fields: the `width` field must be a power of 2, `half[]` is a two-element array of half-width `Merger` objects (empty if the network has width 2), and `layer[]` is an array of `width/2` balancers implementing the final network layer.

The class provides a `traverse(`i`)` method, where i is the wire on which the token enters. (For merger networks, unlike balancers, a token's path depends on its input wire.) If the token entered on the lower `width/2` wires, then it passes through `half[0]`, otherwise `half[1]`. No matter which half-width merger network it traverses, a balancer that emerges on wire i is fed to the ith balancer at `layer[`i`]`.

The `Bitonic` class (Fig. 12.16) also has three fields: `width` is the width (a power of 2), `half[]` is a two-element array of half-width `Bitonic[]` objects,

```
public class Balancer {
  boolean toggle = true;
  public synchronized int traverse() {
    try {
      if (toggle) {
        return 0;
      } else {
        return 1;
      }
    } finally {
      toggle = !toggle;
    }
  }
}
```

Figure 12.14 The Balancer class: a **synchronized** implementation.

```
public class Merger {
  Merger[] half;  // two half-width merger networks
  Balancer[] layer; // final layer
  final int width;
  public Merger(int myWidth) {
    width = myWidth;
    layer = new Balancer[width / 2];
    for (int i = 0; i < width / 2; i++) {
      layer[i] = new Balancer();
    }
    if (width > 2) {
      half = new Merger[]{new Merger(width/2), new Merger(width/2)};
    }
  }
  public int traverse(int input) {
    int output = 0;
    if (input < width / 2) {
      output = half[input % 2].traverse(input / 2);
    } else {
      output = half[1 - (input % 2)].traverse(input / 2);
    return (2 * output) + layer[output].traverse();
  }
}
```

Figure 12.15 The Merger class.

and `merger` is a full width `Merger` network `width`. If the network has width 2, the `half[]` array is uninitialized. Otherwise, each element of `half[]` is initialized to a half-width `Bitonic[]` network.

The class provides a `traverse(i)` method. If the token entered on the lower `width`/2 wires, then it passes through `half[0]`, otherwise `half[1]`. A token that

```
public class Bitonic {
  Bitonic[] half; // two half-width bitonic networks
  Merger merger; // final merger layer
  final int width; // network width
  public Bitonic(int myWidth) {
    width = myWidth;
    merger = new Merger(width);
    if (width > 2) {
      half = new Bitonic[]{new Bitonic(width/2), new Bitonic(width/2)};
    }
  }
  public int traverse(int input) {
    int output = 0;
    if (width > 2) {
      output = half[input / (width / 2)].traverse(input / 2);
    }
    return merger.traverse((input >= (size / 2) ? (size / 2) : 0) + output);
  }
}
```

Figure 12.16 The `Bitonic[]` class.

emerges from the half-merger subnetwork on wire i then traverses the final merger network from input wire i.

Notice that this class uses a simple synchronized `Balancer` implementation, but that if the `Balancer` implementation were lock-free (or wait-free) the network implementation as a whole would be lock-free (or wait-free).

Proof of Correctness

We now show that BITONIC $[w]$ is a counting network. The proof proceeds as a progression of arguments about the token sequences passing through the network. Before examining the network itself, here are some simple lemmas about sequences with the step property.

Lemma 12.5.2. If a sequence has the step property, then so do all its subsequences.

Lemma 12.5.3. If $x_0, \ldots, x_{k-1}$ has the step property, then its even and odd subsequences satisfy:

$$\sum_{i=0}^{k/2-1} x_{2i} = \left\lceil \sum_{i=0}^{k-1} x_i/2 \right\rceil \quad \text{and} \quad \sum_{i=0}^{k/2-1} x_{2i+1} = \left\lfloor \sum_{i=0}^{k-1} x_i/2 \right\rfloor.$$

Proof: Either $x_{2i} = x_{2i+1}$ for $0 \leqslant i < k/2$, or by Lemma 12.5.1, there exists a unique j such that $x_{2j} = x_{2j+1} + 1$ and $x_{2i} = x_{2i+1}$ for all $i \neq j$, $0 \leqslant i < k/2$. In the first case, $\sum x_{2i} = \sum x_{2i+1} = \sum x_i/2$, and in the second case $\sum x_{2i} = \lceil \sum x_i/2 \rceil$ and $\sum x_{2i+1} = \lfloor \sum x_i/2 \rfloor$. □

Lemma 12.5.4. Let $x_0, \ldots, x_{k-1}$ and $y_0, \ldots, y_{k-1}$ be arbitrary sequences having the step property. If $\sum x_i = \sum y_i$, then $x_i = y_i$ for all $0 \leqslant i < k$.

Proof: Let $m = \sum x_i = \sum y_i$. By Lemma 12.5.1, $x_i = y_i = \left\lceil \frac{m-i}{k} \right\rceil$. □

Lemma 12.5.5. Let $x_0, \ldots, x_{k-1}$ and $y_0, \ldots, y_{k-1}$ be arbitrary sequences having the step property. If $\sum x_i = \sum y_i + 1$, then there exists a unique j, $0 \leqslant j < k$, such that $x_j = y_j + 1$, and $x_i = y_i$ for $i \neq j$, $0 \leqslant i < k$.

Proof: Let $m = \sum x_i = \sum y_i + 1$. By Lemma 12.5.1, $x_i = \left\lceil \frac{m-1}{k} \right\rceil$ and $y_i = \left\lceil \frac{m-1-i}{k} \right\rceil$. These two terms agree for all i, $0 \leqslant i < k$, except for the unique i such that $i = m - 1 \pmod{k}$. □

We now show that the MERGER $[w]$ network preserves the step property.

Lemma 12.5.6. If MERGER $[2k]$ is quiescent, and its inputs $x_0, \ldots, x_{k-1}$ and $x'_0, \ldots, x'_{k-1}$ both have the step property, then its outputs $y_0, \ldots, y_{2k-1}$ also have the step property.

Proof: We argue by induction on $\log k$. It may be worthwhile to consult Fig. 12.17 which shows an example of the proof structure for a MERGER [8] network.

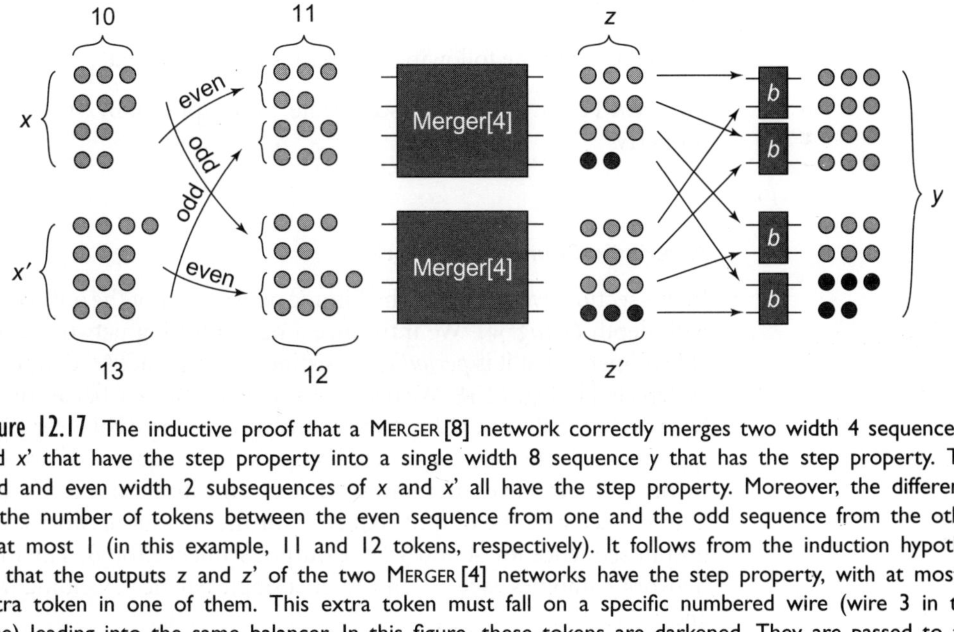

Figure 12.17 The inductive proof that a MERGER [8] network correctly merges two width 4 sequences x and x' that have the step property into a single width 8 sequence y that has the step property. The odd and even width 2 subsequences of x and x' all have the step property. Moreover, the difference in the number of tokens between the even sequence from one and the odd sequence from the other is at most 1 (in this example, 11 and 12 tokens, respectively). It follows from the induction hypothesis that the outputs z and z' of the two MERGER [4] networks have the step property, with at most 1 extra token in one of them. This extra token must fall on a specific numbered wire (wire 3 in this case) leading into the same balancer. In this figure, these tokens are darkened. They are passed to the southern-most balancer, and the extra token is pushed north, ensuring the final output has the step property.

If $2k = 2$, MERGER $[2k]$ is just a balancer, and its outputs are guaranteed to have the step property by the definition of a balancer.

If $2k > 2$, let $z_0, \ldots, z_{k-1}$ be the outputs of the first MERGER $[k]$ subnetwork which merges the even subsequence of x with the odd subsequence of x'. Let $z'_0, \ldots, z'_{k-1}$ be the outputs of the second MERGER $[k]$ subnetwork. Since x and x' have the step property by assumption, so do their even and odd subsequences (Lemma 12.5.2), and hence so do z and z' (induction hypothesis). Furthermore, $\sum z_i = \lceil \sum x_i/2 \rceil + \lfloor \sum x'_i/2 \rfloor$ and $\sum z'_i = \lfloor \sum x_i/2 \rfloor + \lceil \sum x'_i/2 \rceil$ (Lemma 12.5.3). A straightforward case analysis shows that $\sum z_i$ and $\sum z'_i$ can differ by at most 1.

We claim that $0 \leqslant y_i - y_j \leqslant 1$ for any $i < j$. If $\sum z_i = \sum z'_i$, then Lemma 12.5.4 implies that $z_i = z'_i$ for $0 \leqslant i < k/2$. After the final layer of balancers,

$$y_i - y_j = z_{\lfloor i/2 \rfloor} - z_{\lfloor j/2 \rfloor},$$

and the result follows because z has the step property.

Similarly, if $\sum z_i$ and $\sum z'_i$ differ by one, Lemma 12.5.5 implies that $z_i = z'_i$ for $0 \leqslant i < k/2$, except for a unique ℓ such that z_ℓ and z'_ℓ differ by one. Let $\max(z_\ell, z'_\ell) = x + 1$ and $\min(z_\ell, z'_\ell) = x$ for some nonnegative integer x. From the step property for z and z' we have, for all $i < \ell$, $z_i = z'_i = x + 1$ and for all $i > \ell$ $z_i = z'_i = x$. Since z_ℓ and z'_ℓ are joined by a balancer with outputs $y_{2\ell}$ and $y_{2\ell+1}$, it follows that $y_{2\ell} = x + 1$ and $y_{2\ell+1} = x$. Similarly, z_i and z'_i for $i \neq \ell$ are joined by the same balancer. Thus, for any $i < \ell$, $y_{2i} = y_{2i+1} = x + 1$ and for any $i > \ell$, $y_{2i} = y_{2i+1} = x$. The step property follows by choosing $c = 2\ell + 1$ and applying Lemma 12.5.1. □

The proof of the following theorem is now immediate.

***Theorem* 12.5.1.** In any quiescent state, the outputs of BITONIC $[w]$ have the step property.

A Periodic Counting Network

In this section, we show that the Bitonic network is not the only counting network with depth $O(log^2 w)$. We introduce a new counting network with the remarkable property that it is *periodic*, consisting of a sequence of identical subnetworks, as depicted in Fig. 12.18. We define the network BLOCK $[k]$ as follows. When k is equal to 2, the BLOCK $[k]$ network consists of a single balancer. The BLOCK $[2k]$ network for larger k is constructed recursively. We start with two BLOCK $[k]$ networks A and B. Given an input sequence x, the input to A is x^A, and the input to B is x^B. Let y be the output sequence for the two subnetworks, where y^A is the output sequence for A and y^B the output sequence for B. The final stage of the network combines each y_i^A and y_i^B in a single balancer, yielding final outputs z_{2i} and z_{2i+1}.

Fig. 12.19 describes the recursive construction of a BLOCK [8] network. The PERIODIC $[2k]$ network consists of $\log k$ BLOCK $[2k]$ networks joined so that

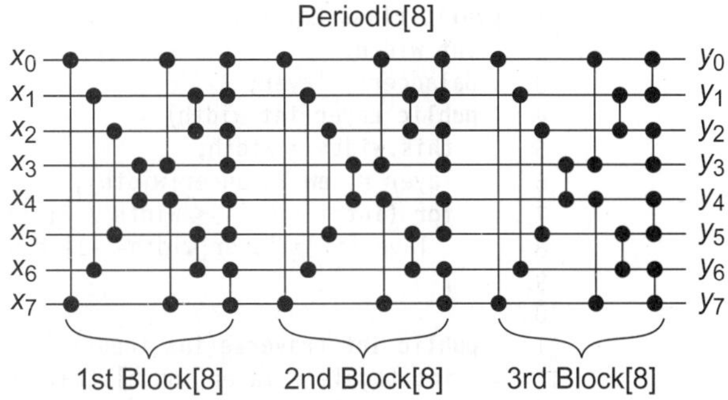

Figure 12.18 A PERIODIC [8] counting network constructed from 3 identical BLOCK [8] networks.

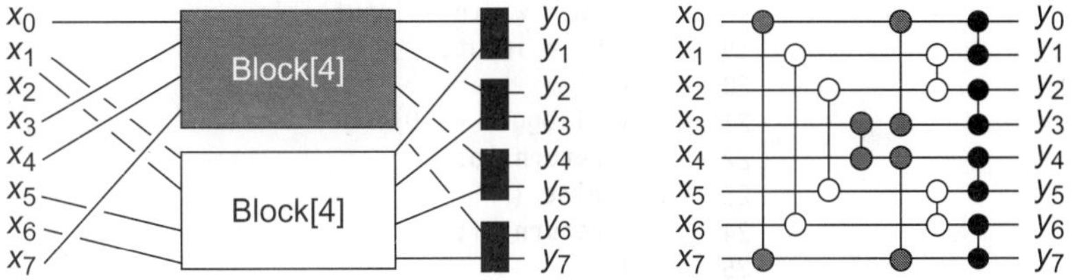

Figure 12.19 The left-hand side illustrates a BLOCK [8] network, into which feed two PERIODIC [4] networks. The right-hand illustrates the physical layout of a MERGER [8] network. The balancers are color-coded to match the logical structure in the left-hand figure.

the ith output wire of one is the ith wire of the next. Fig. 12.18 is a PERIODIC [8] counting network.[2]

A Software Periodic Counting Network

Here is how to implement the Periodic network in software. We reuse the `Balancer` class in Fig. 12.14. A single layer of a BLOCK $[w]$ network is implemented by the LAYER $[w]$ network (Fig. 12.20). A LAYER $[w]$ network joins input wires i and $w - i - 1$ to the same balancer.

In the BLOCK $[w]$ class (Fig. 12.21), after the token emerges from the initial LAYER $[w]$ network, it passes through one of two half-width BLOCK $[w/2]$ networks (called *north* and *south*).

The PERIODIC $[w]$ network (Fig. 12.22) is implemented as an array of $\log w$ BLOCK $[w]$ networks. Each token traverses each block in sequence, where the output wire taken on each block is the input wire for its successor. (The chapter notes cite the proof that the PERIODIC $[w]$ is a counting network.)

2 While the BLOCK $[2k]$ and MERGER $[2k]$ networks may look the same, they are not: there is no permutation of wires that yields one from the other.

```
public class Layer {
  int width;
  Balancer[] layer;
  public Layer(int width) {
    this.width = width;
    layer = new Balancer[width];
    for (int i = 0; i < width / 2; i++) {
      layer[i] = layer[width-i-1] = new Balancer();
    }
  }
  public int traverse(int input) {
    int toggle = layer[input].traverse();
    int hi, lo;
    if (input < width / 2) {
      lo = input;
      hi = width - input - 1;
    } else {
      lo = width - input - 1;
      hi = input;
    }
    if (toggle == 0) {
      return lo;
    } else {
      return hi;
    }
  }
}
```

Figure 12.20 The Layer network.

12.5.3 Performance and Pipelining

How does counting network throughput vary as a function of the number of threads and the network width? For a fixed network width, throughput rises with the number of threads up to a point, and then the network *saturates*, and throughput remains constant or declines. To understand these results, let us think of a counting network as a pipeline.

- If the number of tokens concurrently traversing the network is less than the number of balancers, then the pipeline is partly empty, and throughput suffers.
- If the number of concurrent tokens is greater than the number of balancers, then the pipeline becomes clogged because too many tokens arrive at each balancer at the same time, resulting in per-balancer contention.
- Throughput is maximized when the number of tokens is roughly equal to the number of balancers.

If an application needs a counting network, then the best size network to choose is one that ensures that the number of tokens traversing the balancer at any time is roughly equal to the number of balancers.

```
public class Block {
  Block north;
  Block south;
  Layer layer;
  int width;
  public Block(int width) {
    this.width = width;
    if (width > 2) {
      north = new Block(width / 2);
      south = new Block(width / 2);
    }
    layer = new Layer(width);
  }
  public int traverse(int input) {
    int wire = layer.traverse(input);
    if (width > 2) {
      if (wire < width / 2) {
        return north.traverse(wire);
      } else {
        return (width / 2) + south.traverse(wire - (width / 2));
      }
    } else {
      return wire;
    }
  }
}
```

Figure 12.21 The BLOCK [w] network.

```
public class Periodic {
  Block[] block;
  public Periodic(int width) {
    int logSize = 0;
    int myWidth = width;
    while (myWidth > 1) {
      logSize++;
      myWidth = myWidth / 2;
    }
    block = new Block[logSize];
    for (int i = 0; i < logSize; i++) {
      block[i] = new Block(width);
    }
  }
  public int traverse(int input) {
    int wire = input;
    for (Block b : block) {
      wire = b.traverse(wire);
    }
    return wire;
  }
}
```

Figure 12.22 The `Periodic` network.

12.6 Diffracting Trees

Counting networks provide a high degree of pipelining, so throughput is largely independent of network depth. Latency, however, does depend on network depth. Of the counting networks we have seen, the most shallow has depth $\Theta(\log^2 w)$. Can we design a logarithmic-depth counting network? The good news is yes, such networks exist, but the bad news is that for all known constructions, the constant factors involved render these constructions impractical.

Here is an alternative approach. Consider a set of balancers with a single input wire and two output wires, with the top and bottom labeled 0 and 1, respectively. The TREE $[w]$ network (depicted in Fig. 12.23) is a binary tree structured as follows. Let w be a power of two, and define TREE $[2k]$ inductively. When k is equal to 1, TREE $[2k]$ consists of a single balancer with output wires y_0 and y_1. For $k > 1$, construct TREE $[2k]$ from two TREE $[k]$ trees and one additional balancer. Make the input wire x of the single balancer the root of the tree and connect each of its output wires to the input wire of a tree of width k. Redesignate output wires $y_0, y_1, \ldots, y_{k-1}$ of the TREE $[k]$ subtree extending from the "0" output wire as the even output wires $y_0, y_2, \ldots, y_{2k-2}$ of the final TREE $[2k]$ network and the wires $y_0, y_1, \ldots, y_{k-1}$ of the TREE $[k]$ subtree extending from the balancer's "1" output wire as the odd output wires $y_1, y_3, \ldots, y_{2k-1}$ of final TREE $[2k]$ network.

To understand why the TREE $[2k]$ network has the step property in a quiescent state, let us assume inductively that a quiescent TREE $[k]$ has the step property. The root balancer passes at most one token more to the TREE $[k]$ subtree on its "0" (top) wire than on its"1" (bottom) wire. The tokens exiting the top TREE $[k]$ subtree have a step property differing from that of the bottom subtree at exactly one wire j among their k output wires. The TREE $[2k]$ outputs are a perfect shuffle of the wires leaving the two subtrees, and it follows that the two step-shaped token sequences of width k form a new step of width $2k$ where the possible single

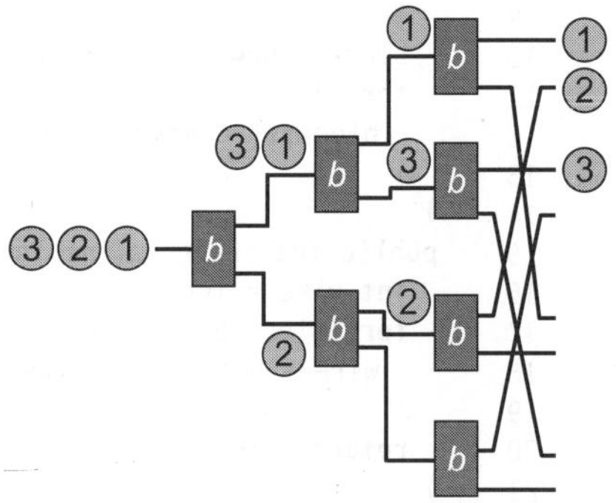

Figure 12.23 The TREE [8] class: a tree that counts. Notice how the network maintains the step property.

excess token appears at the higher of the two wires j, that is, the one from the top TREE $[k]$ tree.

The TREE $[w]$ network may be a counting network, but is it a *good* counting network? The good news is that it has shallow depth: while a BITONIC $[w]$ network has depth $\log^2 w$, the TREE $[w]$ network depth is just $\log w$. The bad news is contention: every token that enters the network passes through the same root balancer, causing that balancer to become a bottleneck. In general, the higher the balancer in the tree, the higher the contention.

We can reduce contention by exploiting a simple observation similar to one we made about the `EliminationBackoffStack` of Chapter 11:

> If an *even* number of tokens pass through a balancer, the outputs are evenly balanced on the top and bottom wires, but the balancer's state remains unchanged.

The basic idea behind *diffracting trees* is to place a `Prism` at each balancer, an out-of-band mechanism similar to the `EliminationArray` which allowed tokens (threads) accessing a stack to exchange items. The `Prism` allows tokens to pair off at random array locations and agree to diffract in different directions, that is, to exit on different wires without traversing the balancer's toggle bit or changing its state. A token traverses the balancer's toggle bit only if it is unable to pair off with another token within a reasonable period of time. If it did not manage to diffract, the token toggles the bit to determine which way to go. It follows that we can avoid excessive contention at balancers if the prism can pair off enough tokens without introducing too much contention.

A `Prism` is an array of `Exchanger<Integer>` objects, like the `EliminationArray`. An `Exchanger<T>` object permits two threads to exchange `T` values. If thread A calls the object's `exchange()` method with argument a, and B calls the same object's `exchange()` method with argument b, then A's call returns value b and vice versa. The first thread to arrive is blocked until the second arrives. The call includes a timeout argument allowing a thread to proceed if it is unable to exchange a value within a reasonable duration.

The `Prism` implementation appears in Fig. 12.24. Before thread A visits the balancer's toggle bit, it visits associated `Prism`. In the `Prism`, it picks an array entry at random, and calls that slot's `exchange()` method, providing its own thread ID as an exchange value. If it succeeds in exchanging ids with another thread, then the lower thread ID exits on wire 0, and the higher on wire 1.

Fig. 12.24 shows a `Prism` implementation. The constructor takes as an argument the capacity of the prism (the maximal number of distinct exchangers). The `Prism` class provides a single method, `visit()`, that chooses the random exchanger entry. The `visit()` call returns *true* if the caller should exit on the top wire, *false* if the bottom wire, and it throws a `TimeoutException` if the timeout expires without exchanging a value. The caller acquires its thread ID (Line 13), chooses a random entry in the array (Line 14), and tries to exchange its own ID with its partner's (Line 15). If it succeeds, it returns a Boolean value, and if it times out, it rethrows `TimeoutException`.

```java
public class Prism {
  private static final int duration = 100;
  Exchanger<Integer>[] exchanger;
  Random random;
  public Prism(int capacity) {
    exchanger = (Exchanger<Integer>[]) new Exchanger[capacity];
    for (int i = 0; i < capacity; i++) {
      exchanger[i] = new Exchanger<Integer>();
    }
    random = new Random();
  }
  public boolean visit() throws TimeoutException, InterruptedException {
    int me = ThreadID.get();
    int slot = random.nextInt(exchanger.length);
    int other = exchanger[slot].exchange(me, duration, TimeUnit.MILLISECONDS);
    return (me < other);
  }
}
```

Figure 12.24 The `Prism` class.

```java
public class DiffractingBalancer {
  Prism prism;
  Balancer toggle;
  public DiffractingBalancer(int capacity) {
    prism = new Prism(capacity);
    toggle = new Balancer();
  }
  public int traverse() {
    boolean direction = false;
    try{
      if (prism.visit())
        return 0;
      else
        return 1;
    } catch(TimeoutException ex) {
      return toggle.traverse();
    }
  }
}
```

Figure 12.25 The `DiffractingBalancer` class: if the caller pairs up with a concurrent caller through the prism, it does not need to traverse the balancer.

A `DiffractingBalancer` (Fig. 12.25), like a regular `Balancer`, provides a `traverse()` method whose return value alternates between 0 and 1. This class has two fields: `prism` is a `Prism`, and `toggle` is a `Balancer`. When a thread calls `traverse()`, it tries to find a partner through the `prism`. If it succeeds, then the partners return with distinct values, without creating contention at the `toggle`

```
1  public class DiffractingTree {
2    DiffractingBalancer root;
3    DiffractingTree[] child;
4    int size;
5    public DiffractingTree(int mySize) {
6      size = mySize;
7      root = new DiffractingBalancer(size);
8      if (size > 2) {
9        child = new DiffractingTree[]{
10         new DiffractingTree(size/2),
11         new DiffractingTree(size/2)};
12     }
13   }
14   public int traverse() {
15     int half = root.traverse();
16     if (size > 2) {
17       return (2 * (child[half].traverse()) + half);
18     } else {
19       return half;
20     }
21   }
22 }
```

Figure 12.26 The `DiffractingTree` class: fields, constructor, and `traverse()` method.

(Line 11). Otherwise, if the thread is unable to find a partner, it traverses (Line 16) the `toggle` (implemented as a balancer).

The `DiffractingTree` class (Fig. 12.26) has two fields. The `child` array is a two-element array of child trees. The `root` field is a `DiffractingBalancer` that alternates between forwarding calls to the left or right subtree. Each `DiffractingBalancer` has a capacity, which is actually the capacity of its internal prism. Initially this capacity is the size of the tree, and the capacity shrinks by half at each level.

As with the `EliminationBackoffStack`, `DiffractingTree` performance depends on two parameters: prism capacities and timeouts. If the prisms are too big, threads miss one another, causing excessive contention at the balancer. If the arrays are too small, then too many threads concurrently access each exchanger in a prism, resulting in excessive contention at the exchangers. If prism timeouts are too short, threads miss one another, and if they are too long, threads may be delayed unnecessarily. There are no hard-and-fast rules for choosing these values, since the optimal values depend on the load and the characteristics of the underlying multiprocessor architecture.

Nevertheless, experimental evidence suggests that it is sometimes possible to choose these values to outperform both the `CombiningTree` and `CountingNetwork` classes. Here are some heuristics that work well in practice. Because balancers higher in the tree have more contention, we use larger prisms near the top of the tree, and add the ability to dynamically shrink and grow the random range chosen. The best timeout interval choice depends on the load: if only a few threads are accessing the tree, then time spent waiting is mostly wasted, while if there are many threads, then time spent waiting pays off. Adaptive schemes are promising: lengthen the timeout while threads succeed in pairing off, and shorten it otherwise.

12.7 Parallel Sorting

Sorting is one of the most important computational tasks, dating back to Hollerith's Nineteenth-Century sorting machine, through the first electronic computer systems in the 1940s, and culminating today, when a high fraction of programs use sorting in some form or another. As most Computer Science undergraduates learn early on, the choice of sorting algorithm depends crucially on the number of items being sorted, the numerical properties of their keys, and whether the items reside in memory or in an external storage device. Parallel sorting algorithms can be classified in the same way.

We present two classes of sorting algorithms: *sorting networks*, which typically work well for small in-memory data sets, and *sample sorting algorithms*, which work well for large data sets in external memory. In our presentation, we sacrifice performance for simplicity. More complex techniques are cited in the chapter notes.

12.8 Sorting Networks

In much the same way that a counting network is a network of *balancers*, a sorting network is a network of *comparators*.[3] A comparator is a computing element with two input wires and two output wires, called the *top* and *bottom* wires. It receives two numbers on its input wires, and forwards the larger to its top wire and the smaller to its bottom wire. A comparator, unlike a balancer, is *synchronous*: it outputs values only when both inputs have arrived (see Fig. 12.27).

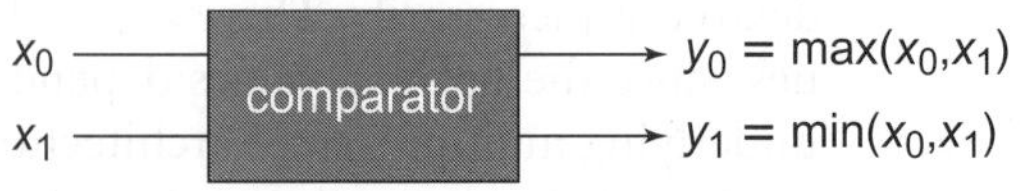

Figure 12.27 A comparator.

3 Historically sorting networks predate counting networks by several decades.

A *comparison network*, like a balancing network, is an acyclic network of comparators. An input value is placed on each of its w input lines. These values pass through each layer of comparators synchronously, finally leaving together on the network output wires.

A comparison network with input values x_i and output values y_i, $i \in \{0 \ldots 1\}$, each on wire i, is a valid *sorting network* if its output values are the input values sorted in descending order, that is, $y_{i-1} \geqslant y_i$.

The following classic theorem simplifies the process of proving that a given network sorts.

***Theorem* 12.8.1 (0-1-principle).** If a sorting network sorts every input sequence of 0s and 1s, then it sorts any sequence of input values.

12.8.1 Designing a Sorting Network

There is no need to design sorting networks, because we can recycle counting network layouts. A balancing network and a comparison network are *isomorphic* if one can be constructed from the other by replacing balancers with comparators, or vice versa.

***Theorem* 12.8.2.** If a balancing network counts, then its isomorphic comparison network sorts.

Proof: We construct a mapping from comparison network transitions to isomorphic balancing network transitions.

By Theorem 12.8.1, a comparison network which sorts all sequences of 0s and 1s is a sorting network. Take any arbitrary sequence of 0s and 1s as inputs to the comparison network, and for the balancing network place a token on each 1 input wire and no token on each 0 input wire. If we run both networks in lock-step, the balancing network simulates the comparison network.

The proof is by induction on the depth of the network. For level 0 the claim holds by construction. Assuming it holds for wires of a given level k, let us prove it holds for level $k+1$. On every comparator where two 1s meet in the comparison network, two tokens meet in the balancing network, so one 1 leaves on each wire in the comparison network on level $k + 1$, and one token leaves on each wire in the balancing network on level $k + 1$. On every comparator where two 0s meet in the comparison network, no tokens meet in the balancing network, so a 0 leaves on each level $k + 1$ wire in the comparison network, and no tokens leave in the balancing network. On every comparator where a 0 and 1 meet in the comparison network, the 1 leaves on the north (upper) wire and the 1 on the south (lower) wire on level $k + 1$, while in the balancing network the token leaves on the north wire, and no token leaves on the south wire.

If the balancing network is a counting network, that is, it has the step property on its output level wires, then the comparison network must have sorted the input sequence of 0s and 1s. □

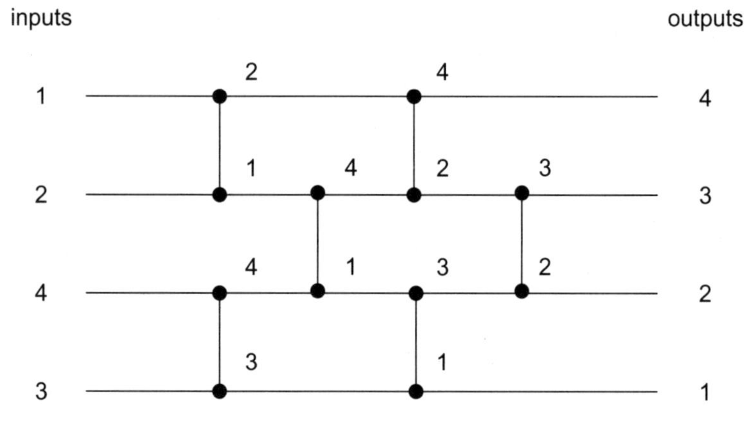

Figure 12.28 The `OddEven` sorting network.

The converse is false: not all sorting networks are counting networks. We leave it as an exercise to verify that the `OddEven` network in Fig. 12.28 is a sorting network but not a counting network.

***Corollary* 12.8.1.** Comparison networks isomorphic to BITONIC [] and PERIODIC [] networks are sorting networks.

Sorting a set of size w by comparisons requires $\Omega(w \log w)$ comparisons. A sorting network with w input wires has at most $O(w)$ comparators in each level, so its depth can be no smaller than $\Omega(\log w)$.

***Corollary* 12.8.2.** The depth of any counting network is at least $\Omega(\log w)$.

A Bitonic Sorting Algorithm

We can represent any width-w sorting network, such as BITONIC $[w]$, as a collection of d layers of $w/2$ balancers each. We can represent a sorting network layout as a table, where each entry is a pair that describes which two wires meet at that balancer at that layer. (E.g., in the BITONIC [4] network of Fig. 12.11, wires 0 and 1 meet at the first balancer in the first layer, and wires 0 and 3 meet at the first balancer of the second layer.) Let us assume, for simplicity, that we are given an unbounded table `bitonicTable`$[i][d][j]$, where each array entry contains the index of the associated north (0) or south (1) input wire to balancer i at depth d.

An *in-place* array-based sorting algorithm takes as input an array of items to be sorted (here we assume these items have unique integer keys) and returns the same array with the items sorted by key. Here is how we implement `BitonicSort`, an in-place array-based sorting algorithm based on a Bitonic sorting network. Let us assume that we wish to sort an array of $2 \cdot p \cdot s$ elements, where p is the number of threads (and typically also the maximal number of available processors on which the threads run) and $p \cdot s$ is a power of 2. The network has $p \cdot s$ comparators at every layer.

Each of the p threads emulates the work of s comparators. Unlike counting networks, which act like uncoordinated raves, sorting networks are synchronous: all inputs to a comparator must arrive before it can compute the outputs. The algorithm proceeds in rounds. In each round, a thread performs s comparisons in a layer of the network, switching the array entries of items if necessary, so that they are properly ordered. In each network layer, the comparators join different wires, so no two threads attempt to exchange the items of the same entry, avoiding the need to synchronize operations at any given layer.

To ensure that the comparisons of a given round (layer) are complete before proceeding to the next one, we use a synchronization construct called a `Barrier` (studied in more detail in Chapter 17). A barrier for p threads provides an `await()` method, whose call does not return until all p threads have called `await()`. The `BitonicSort` implementation appears in Fig. 12.29. Each thread proceeds through the layers of the network round by round. In each round, it awaits the arrival of the other threads (Line 12), ensuring that the `items` array contains the prior round's results. It then emulates the behavior of s balancers at that layer by comparing the items at the array positions corresponding to the

```
1  public class BitonicSort {
2    static final int[][][] bitonicTable = ...;
3    static final int width = ...; // counting network width
4    static final int depth = ...; // counting network depth
5    static final int p = ...;  // number of threads
6    static final int s = ...;  // a power of 2
7    Barrier barrier;
8    ...
9      public <T> void sort(Item<T>[] items) {
10       int i = ThreadID.get();
11       for (int d = 0; d < depth; d++) {
12         barrier.await();
13         for (int j = 0; j < s; j++) {
14           int north = bitonicTable[(i*s)+j][d][0];
15           int south = bitonicTable[(i*s)+j][d][1];
16           if (items[north].key < items[south].key) {
17             Item<T> temp = items[north];
18             items[north] = items[south];
19             items[south] = temp;
20           }
21         }
22       }
23     }
```

Figure 12.29 The `BitonicSort` class.

comparator's wires, and exchanging them if their keys are out of order (Lines 14 through 19).

The `BitonicSort` takes $O(s \log^2 p)$ time for p threads running on p processors, which, if s is constant, is $O(\log^2 p)$ time.

12.9 Sample Sorting

The `BitonicSort` is appropriate for small data sets that reside in memory. For larger data sets (where n, the number of items, is much larger than p, the number of threads), especially ones that reside on out-of-memory storage devices, we need a different approach. Because accessing a data item is expensive, we must maintain as much locality-of-reference as possible, so having a single thread sort items sequentially is cost-effective. A parallel sort like `BitonicSort`, where an item is accessed by multiple threads, is simply too expensive.

We attempt to minimize the number of threads that access a given item through randomization. This use of randomness differs from that in the `DiffractingTree`, where it was used to distribute memory accesses. Here we use randomness to guess the distribution of items in the data set to be sorted.

Since the data set to be sorted is large, we split it into buckets, throwing into each bucket the items that have keys within a given range. Each thread then sorts the items in one of the buckets using a sequential sorting algorithm, and the result is a sorted set (when viewed in the appropriate bucket order). This algorithm is a generalization of the well-known *quicksort* algorithm, but instead of having a single *splitter* key to divide the items into two subsets, we have $p - 1$ splitter keys that split the input set into p subsets.

The algorithm for n items and p threads involves three phases:

1. Threads choose $p - 1$ splitter keys to partition the data set into p buckets. The splitters are published so all threads can read them.
2. Each thread sequentially processes n/p items, moving each item to its bucket, where the appropriate bucket is determined by performing a binary search with the item's key among the splitter keys.
3. Each thread sequentially sorts the items in its bucket.

Barriers between the phases ensure that all threads have completed one phase before the next starts.

Before we consider Phase one, we look at the second and third phases.

The second phase's time complexity is $(n/p) \log p$, consisting of reading each item from memory, disk, or tape, followed by a binary search among p splitters cached locally, and finally adding the item into the appropriate bucket. The buckets into which the items are moved could be in memory, on disk, or on tape, so the dominating cost is that of the n/p accesses to the stored data items.

Let b be the number of items in a bucket. The time complexity of the third phase for a given thread is $O(b \log b)$, to sort the items using a sequential version of, say, *quicksort*.[4] This part has the highest cost because it consists of read–write phases that access relatively slow memory, such as disk or tape.

The time complexity of the algorithm is dominated by the thread with the most items in its bucket in the third phase. It is therefore important to choose the splitters to be as evenly distributed as possible, so each bucket receives approximately $n - p$ items in the second phase.

The key to choosing good splitters is to have each thread pick a set of *sample* splitters that represent its own $n - p$ size data set, and choose the final $p - 1$ splitters from among all the sample splitter sets of all threads. Each thread selects uniformly at random s keys from its data set of size $n - p$. (In practice, it suffices to choose s to be 32 or 64 keys.) Each thread then participates in running the parallel `BitonicSort` (Fig. 12.29) on the $s \cdot p$ sample keys selected by the p threads. Finally, each thread reads the $p - 1$ splitter keys in positions $s, 2s, \ldots, (p-1)s$ in the sorted set of splitters, and uses these as the splitters in the second phase. This choice of s samples, and the later choice of the final splitters from the sorted set of all samples, reduces the effects of an uneven key distribution among the $n - p$ size data sets accessed by the threads.

For example, a sample sort algorithm could choose to have each thread pick $p - 1$ splitters for its second phase from within its own n/p size data set, without ever communicating with other threads. The problem with this approach is that if the distribution of the data is uneven, the size of the buckets may differ greatly, and performance would suffer. For example, if the number of items in the largest bucket is doubled, so is the worst-case time complexity of sorting algorithm.

The first phase's complexity is s (a constant) to perform the random sampling, and $O(\log^2 p)$ for the parallel Bitonic sort. The overall time complexity of sample sort with a good splitter set (where every bucket gets $O(n/p)$ of the items) is

$$O(\log^2 p) + O((n/p)\log p) + O((n/p)\log(n/p))$$

which overall is $O((n/p)\log(n/p))$.

12.10 Distributed Coordination

This chapter covered several distributed coordination patterns. Some, such as combining trees, sorting networks, and sample sorting, have high parallelism and low overheads. All these algorithms contain synchronization bottlenecks, that is, points in the computation where threads must wait to rendezvous with others. In the combining trees, threads must synchronize to combine, and in sorting, when threads wait at barriers.

---

4 If the item's key size is known and fixed, one could use algorithms like *Radixsort*.

In other schemes, such as counting networks and diffracting trees, threads never wait for one another. (Although we implement balancers using **synchronized** methods, they could be implemented in a lock-free manner using compareAndSet().) Here, the distributed structures pass information from one thread to another, and while a rendezvous could prove advantageous (as in the Prism array), it is not necessary.

Randomization, which is useful in many places, helps to distribute work evenly. For diffracting trees, randomization distributes work over multiple memory locations, reducing the chance that too many threads simultaneously access the same location. For sample sort, randomization helps distribute work evenly among buckets, which threads later sort in parallel.

Finally, we saw that pipelining can ensure that some data structures can have high throughput, even though they have high latency.

Although we focus on shared-memory multiprocessors, it is worth mentioning that the distributed algorithms and structures considered in this chapter also work in message-passing architectures. The message-passing model might be implemented directly in hardware, as in a network of processors, or it could be provided on top of a shared-memory architecture through a software layer such as MPI.

In shared-memory architectures, switches (such as combining tree nodes or balancers) are naturally implemented as shared-memory counters. In message-passing architectures, switches are naturally implemented as processor-local data structures, where wires that link one processor to another also link one switch to another. When a processor receives a message, it atomically updates its local data structure and forwards messages to the processors managing other switches.

12.11 Chapter Notes

The idea behind combining trees is due to Allan Gottlieb, Ralph Grishman, Clyde Kruskal, Kevin McAuliffe, Larry Rudolph, and Marc Snir [47]. The software CombiningTree presented here is a adapted from an algorithm by PenChung Yew, Nian-Feng Tzeng, and Duncan Lawrie [151] with modifications by Maurice Herlihy, Beng-Hong Lim, and Nir Shavit [65], all based on an original proposal by James Goodman, Mary Vernon, and Philip Woest [45].

Counting networks were invented by Jim Aspnes, Maurice Herlihy, and Nir Shavit [16]. Counting networks are related to *sorting networks*, including the ground breaking Bitonic network of Kenneth Batcher [18], and the periodic network of Martin Dowd, Yehoshua Perl, Larry Rudolph, and Mike Saks [35]. Miklós Ajtai, János Komlós, and Endre Szemerédi discovered the AKS sorting network, an $O(\log w)$ depth sorting network [8]. (This asymptotic expression hides large constants which make networks based on AKS impractical.)

Mike Klugerman and Greg Plaxton [84, 85] were the first to provide an AKS-based counting network construction with $O(\log w)$ depth. The 0-1 principle for sorting networks is by Donald Knuth [86]. A similar set of rules for balancing networks is provided by Costas Busch and Marios Mavronicolas [25]. Diffracting trees were invented by Nir Shavit and Asaph Zemach [143].

Sample sorting was suggested by John Reif and Leslie Valiant [132] and by Huang and Chow [73]. The sequential Quicksort algorithm to which all sample sorting algorithms relate is due to Tony Hoare [70]. There are numerous parallel radix sort algorithms in the literature such as the one by Daniel Jiménez-González, Joseph Larriba-Pey, and Juan Navarro [82] or the one by Shin-Jae Lee and Minsoo Jeon and Dongseung Kim and Andrew Sohn [101].

Monty Python and the Holy Grail was written by Graham Chapman, John Cleese, Terry Gilliam, Eric Idle, Terry Jones, and Michael Palin and co-directed by Terry Gilliam and Terry Jones [27].

12.12 Exercises

Exercise 134. Prove Lemma 12.5.1.

Exercise 135. Implement a *trinary* `CombiningTree`, that is, one that allows up to three threads coming from three subtrees to combine at a given node. Can you estimate the advantages and disadvantages of such a tree when compared to a *binary* combining tree?

Exercise 136. Implement a `CombiningTree` using `Exchanger` objects to perform the coordination among threads ascending and descending the tree. What are the possible disadvantages of your construction when compared to the `CombiningTree` class presented in Section 12.3?

Exercise 137. Implement the cyclic array based shared pool described in Section 12.2 using two simple counters and a `ReentrantLock` per array entry.

Exercise 138. Provide an efficient lock-free implementation of a `Balancer`.

Exercise 139. (Hard) Provide an efficient wait-free implementation of a `Balancer` (i.e. not by using the universal construction).

Exercise 140. Prove that the TREE $[2k]$ balancing network constructed in Section 12.6 is a counting network, that is, that in any quiescent state, the sequences of tokens on its output wires have the step property.

Exercise 141. Let $\mathcal{B}$ be a width-w balancing network of depth d in a quiescent state s. Let $n = 2^d$. Prove that if n tokens enter the network on the same wire, pass through the network, and exit, then $\mathcal{B}$ will have the same state after the tokens exit as it did before they entered.

In the following exercises, a k*-smooth sequence* is a sequence $y_0, \ldots, y_{w-1}$ that satisfies

$$\text{if} \quad i < j \quad \text{then} \quad |y_i - y_j| \leqslant k.$$

Exercise 142. Let X and Y be k-smooth sequences of length w. A *matching* layer of balancers for X and Y is one where each element of X is joined by a balancer to an element of Y in a one-to-one correspondence.

Prove that if X and Y are each k-smooth, and Z is the result of matching X and Y, then Z is $(k+1)$-smooth.

Exercise 143. Consider a BLOCK $[k]$ network in which each balancer has been initialized to an arbitrary state (either *up* or *down*). Show that no matter what the input distribution is, the output distribution is $(\log k)$-smooth.

Hint: you may use the claim in Exercise 142.

Exercise 144. A *smoothing network* is a balancing network that ensures that in any quiescent state, the output sequence is 1-smooth.

Counting networks are smoothing networks, but not vice versa.

A Boolean sorting network is one in which all inputs are guaranteed to be Boolean. Define a *pseudo-sorting balancing network* to be a balancing network with a layout isomorphic to a Boolean sorting network.

Let $\mathcal{N}$ be the balancing network constructed by taking a smoothing network $\mathcal{S}$ of width w, a pseudo-sorting balancing network $\mathcal{P}$ also of width w, and joining the ith output wire of $\mathcal{S}$ to the ith input wire of $\mathcal{P}$.

Show that $\mathcal{N}$ is a counting network.

Exercise 145. A *3-balancer* is a balancer with three input lines and three output lines. Like its 2-line relative, its output sequences have the step property in any quiescent state. Construct a depth-3 counting network with 6 input and output lines from 2-balancers and 3-balancers. Explain why it works.

Exercise 146. Suggest ways to modify the `BitonicSort` class so that it will sort an input array of width w where w is not a power of 2.

Exercise 147. Consider the following w-thread counting algorithm. Each thread first uses a bitonic counting network of width w to take a counter value v. It then goes through a *waiting filter*, in which each thread waits for threads with lesser values to catch up.

The waiting filter is an array `filter[]` of w Boolean values. Define the phase function

$$\phi(v) = \lfloor (v/w) \rfloor \bmod 2.$$

A thread that exits with value v spins on `filter`$[(v-1) \bmod n]$ until that value is set to $\phi(v-1)$. The thread responds by setting `filter`$[v \bmod w]$ to $\phi(v)$, and then returns v.

1. Explain why this counter implementation is linearizable.
2. An exercise here shows that any linearizable counting network has depth at least w. Explain why the `filter[]` construction does not contradict this claim.
3. On a bus-based multiprocessor, would this `filter[]` construction have better throughput than a single variable protected by a spin lock? Explain.

Exercise 148. If a sequence $X = x_0, \ldots x_{w-1}$ is k-smooth, then the result of passing X through a balancing network is k-smooth.

Exercise 149. Prove that the `Bitonic`$[w]$ network has depth $(\log w)(1 + \log w)/2$ and uses $(w \log w)(1 + \log w)/4$ balancers.

Exercise 150. (Hard) Provide an implementation of a `DiffractingBalancer` that is lock-free.

Exercise 151. Add an adaptive timeout mechanism to the `Prism` of the `DiffractingBalancer`.

Exercise 152. Show that the `OddEven` network in Fig. 12.28 is a sorting network but not a counting network.

Exercise 153. Can counting networks do anything besides increments? Consider a new kind of token, called an *antitoken*, which we use for decrements. Recall that when a token visits a balancer, it executes a `getAndComplement()`: it atomically reads the toggle value and complements it, and then departs on the output wire indicated by the old toggle value. Instead, an antitoken complements the toggle value, and then departs on the output wire indicated by the new toggle value. Informally, an antitoken "cancels" the effect of the most recent token on the balancer's toggle state, and vice versa.

Instead of simply balancing the number of tokens that emerge on each wire, we assign a *weight* of $+1$ to each token and -1 to each antitoken. We generalize the step property to require that the sums of the weights of the tokens and antitokens that emerge on each wire have the step property. We call this property the *weighted step property*.

```java
public synchronized int antiTraverse() {
  try {
    if (toggle) {
      return 1;
    } else {
      return 0;
    }
  } finally {
    toggle = !toggle;
  }
}
```

Figure 12.30 The antiTraverse() method.

Fig. 12.30 shows how to implement an antiTraverse() method that moves an antitoken though a balancer. Adding an antiTraverse() method to the other networks is left as an exercise.

Let $\mathcal{B}$ be a width-w balancing network of depth d in a quiescent state s. Let $n = 2^d$. Show that if n tokens enter the network on the same wire, pass through the network, and exit, then $\mathcal{B}$ will have the same state after the tokens exit as it did before they entered.

Exercise 154. Let $\mathcal{B}$ be a balancing network in a quiescent state s, and suppose a token enters on wire i and passes through the network, leaving the network in state s'. Show that if an antitoken now enters on wire i and passes through the network, then the network goes back to state s.

Exercise 155. Show that if balancing network $\mathcal{B}$ is a counting network for tokens alone, then it is also a balancing network for tokens and antitokens.

Exercise 156. A *switching network* is a directed graph, where edges are called *wires* and node are called *switches.* Each thread shepherds a *token* through the network. Switches and tokens are allowed to have internal states. A token arrives at a switch via an input wire. In one atomic step, the switch absorbs the token, changes its state and possibly the token's state, and emits the token on an output wire. Here, for simplicity, switches have two input and output wires. Note that switching networks are more powerful than balancing networks, since switches can have arbitrary state (instead of a single bit) and tokens also have state.

An *adding network* is a switching network that allows threads to add (or subtract) arbitrary values.

We say that a token is *in front of* a switch if it is on one of the switch's input wires. Start with the network in a quiescent state q_0, where the next token to run will take value 0. Imagine we have one token t of weight a and n–1 tokens $t_1,\ldots,t_{n-1}$ all of weight b, where $b > a$, each on a distinct input wire. Denote by S the set of switches that t traverses if it traverses the network by starting in q_0.

Prove that if we run the $t_1, \ldots, t_{n-1}$ one at a time though the network, we can halt each t_i in front of a switch of $\mathcal{S}$.

At the end of this construction, $n - 1$ tokens are in front of switches of $\mathcal{S}$. Since switches have two input wires, it follows that t's path through the network encompasses at least $n - 1$ switches, so any adding network must have depth at least $n - 1$, where n is the maximum number of concurrent tokens. This bound is discouraging because it implies that the size of the network depends on the number of threads (also true for `CombiningTree`s, but not counting networks), and that the network has inherently high latency.

Exercise 157. Extend the proof of Exercise 156 to show that a *linearizable* counting network has depth at least n.

13 Concurrent Hashing and Natural Parallelism

13.1 Introduction

In earlier chapters, we studied how to extract parallelism from data structures like queues, stacks, and counters, that seemed to provide few opportunities for parallelism. In this chapter we take the opposite approach. We study *concurrent hashing*, a problem that seems to be "naturally parallelizable" or, using a more technical term, *disjoint–access–parallel*, meaning that concurrent method calls are likely to access disjoint locations, implying that there is little need for synchronization.

Hashing is a technique commonly used in sequential `Set` implementations to ensure that `contains()`, `add()`, and `remove()` calls take constant average time. The concurrent `Set` implementations studied in Chapter 9 required time linear in the size of the set. In this chapter, we study ways to make hashing concurrent, sometimes using locks and sometimes not. Even though hashing seems naturally parallelizable, devising an effective concurrent hash algorithm is far from trivial.

As in earlier chapters, the `Set` interface provides the following methods, which return Boolean values:

- `add(`x`)` adds x to the set. Returns *true* if x was absent, and *false* otherwise,
- `remove(`x`)` removes x from the set. Returns *true* if x was present, and *false* otherwise, and
- `contains(`x`)` returns *true* if x is present, and *false* otherwise.

When designing set implementations, we need to keep the following principle in mind: we can buy more memory, but we cannot buy more time. Given a choice between an algorithm that runs faster but consumes more memory, and a slower algorithm that consumes less memory, we tend to prefer the faster algorithm (within reason).

A *hash set* (sometimes called a *hash table*) is an efficient way to implement a set. A hash set is typically implemented as an array, called the *table*. Each table entry is a reference to one or more *items*. A *hash function* maps items to integers so that distinct items usually map to distinct values. (Java provides each object with a `hashCode()` method that serves this purpose.) To add, remove, or test an item for membership, apply the hash function to the item (modulo the table size) to identify the table entry associated with that item. (We call this step *hashing* the item.)

In some hash-based set algorithms, each table entry refers to a single item, an approach known as *open addressing*. In others, each table entry refers to a set of items, traditionally called a *bucket*, an approach known as *closed addressing*.

Any hash set algorithm must deal with *collisions*: what to do when two distinct items hash to the same table entry. Open-addressing algorithms typically resolve collisions by applying alternative hash functions to test alternative table entries. Closed-addressing algorithms place colliding items in the same bucket, until that bucket becomes too full. In both kinds of algorithms, it is sometimes necessary to *resize* the table. In open-addressing algorithms, the table may become too full to find alternative table entries, and in closed-addressing algorithms, buckets may become too large to search efficiently.

Anecdotal evidence suggests that in most applications, sets are subject to the following distribution of method calls: 90% `contains()`, 9% `add()`, and 1% `remove()` calls. As a practical matter, sets are more likely to grow than to shrink, so we focus here on *extensible hashing* in which hash sets only grow (shrinking them is a problem for the exercises).

It is easier to make closed-addressing hash set algorithms parallel, so we consider them first.

13.2 Closed-Address Hash Sets

Pragma 13.2.1. Here and elsewhere, we use the standard Java `List<T>` interface (in package **java.util.List**). A `List<T>` is an ordered collection of `T` objects, where `T` is a type. Here, we make use of the following List methods: `add`(x) appends x to the end of the list, `get`(i) returns (but does not remove) the item at position i, `contains`(x) returns *true* if the list contains x. There are many more.

The `List` interface can be implemented by a number of classes. Here, it is convenient to use the `ArrayList` class.

We start by defining a *base* hash set implementation common to all the concurrent closed-addressing hash sets we consider here. The `BaseHashSet<T>` class is an *abstract* class, that is, it does not implement all its methods. Later, we look at three alternative synchronization techniques: one using a single coarse-grained lock, one using a fixed-size array of locks, and one using a resizable array of locks.

```
1  public abstract class BaseHashSet<T> {
2    protected List<T>[] table;
3    protected int setSize;
4    public BaseHashSet(int capacity) {
5      setSize = 0;
6      table = (List<T>[]) new List[capacity];
7      for (int i = 0; i < capacity; i++) {
8        table[i] = new ArrayList<T>();
9      }
10   }
11   ...
12 }
```

Figure 13.1 BaseHashSet<T> class: fields and constructor.

Fig. 13.1 shows the base hash set's fields and constructor. The table[] field is an array of buckets, each of which is a set implemented as a list (Line 2). We use ArrayList<T> lists for convenience, supporting the standard sequential add(), remove(), and contains() methods. The setSize field is the number of items in the table (Line 3). We sometimes refer to the length of the table[] array, that is, the number of buckets in it, as its *capacity*.

The BaseHashSet<T> class does not implement the following *abstract* methods: acquire(x) acquires the locks necessary to manipulate item x, release(x) releases them, policy() decides whether to resize the set, and resize() doubles the capacity of the table[] array. The acquire(x) method must be *reentrant* (Chapter 8, Section 8.4), meaning that if a thread that has already called acquire(x) makes the same call, then it will proceed without deadlocking with itself.

Fig. 13.2 shows the contains(x) and add(x) methods of the BaseHashSet<T> class. Each method first calls acquire(x) to perform the necessary synchronization, then enters a **try** block whose **finally** block calls release(x). The contains(x) method simply tests whether x is present in the associated bucket (Line 17), while add(x) adds x to the list if it is not already present (Line 26).

How big should the bucket array be to ensure that method calls take constant expected time? Consider an add(x) call. The first step, hashing x, takes constant time. The second step, adding the item to the bucket, requires traversing a linked list. This traversal takes constant expected time only if the lists have constant expected length, so the table capacity should be proportional to the number of items in the table. This number may vary unpredictably over time, so to ensure that method call times remain (more-or-less) constant, we must *resize* the table every now and then to ensure that list lengths remain (more-or-less) constant.

We still need to decide *when* to resize the hash set, and how the resize() method synchronizes with the others. There are many reasonable alternatives. For closed-addressing algorithms, one simple strategy is to resize the set when the average bucket size exceeds a fixed threshold. An alternative policy employs two fixed integer quantities: the *bucket threshold* and the *global threshold*.

```
  public boolean contains(T x) {
    acquire(x);
    try {
      int myBucket = x.hashCode() % table.length;
      return table[myBucket].contains(x);
    } finally {
      release(x);
    }
  }
  public boolean add(T x) {
    boolean result = false;
    acquire(x);
    try {
      int myBucket = Math.abs(x.hashCode() % table.length);
      if (! table[myBucket].contains(x)) {
        table[myBucket].add(x);
        result = true;
        size++;
  }
    } finally {
      release(x);
    }
    if (policy())
      resize();
    return result;
  }
```

Figure 13.2 `BaseHashSet<T>` class: the `contains()` and `add()` methods hash the item to choose a bucket.

- If more than, say, 1/4 of the buckets exceed the bucket threshold, then double the table capacity, or
- If any single bucket exceeds the global threshold, then double the table capacity.

Both these strategies work well in practice, as do others. Open-addressing algorithms are slightly more complicated, and are discussed later.

13.2.1 A Coarse-Grained Hash Set

Fig. 13.3 shows the `CoarseHashSet<T>` class's fields, constructor, `acquire`(x), and `release`(x) methods. The constructor first initializes its superclass (Line 4). Synchronization is provided by a single reentrant lock (Line 2), acquired by `acquire`(x) (Line 8) and released by `release`(x) (Line 11).

Fig. 13.4 shows the `CoarseHashSet<T>` class's `policy()` and `resize()` methods. We use a simple policy: we resize when the average bucket length exceeds 4 (Line 16). The `resize()` method locks the set (Line 20), and checks that no other thread has resized the table in the meantime (Line 23). It then allocates and initializes a new table with double the capacity (Lines 25–29) and transfers items from the old to the new buckets (Lines 30–34). Finally, it unlocks the set (Line 36).

```
public class CoarseHashSet<T> extends BaseHashSet<T>{
  final Lock lock;
  CoarseHashSet(int capacity) {
    super(capacity);
    lock = new ReentrantLock();
  }
  public final void acquire(T x) {
    lock.lock();
  }
  public void release(T x) {
    lock.unlock();
  }
  ...
}
```

Figure 13.3 `CoarseHashSet<T>` class: fields, constructor, `acquire()`, and `release()` methods.

```
  public boolean policy() {
    return setSize / table.length > 4;
  }
  public void resize() {
    int oldCapacity = table.length;
    lock.lock();
    try {
      if (oldCapacity != table.length) {
        return; // someone beat us to it
      }
      int newCapacity = 2 * oldCapacity;
      List<T>[] oldTable = table;
      table = (List<T>[]) new List[newCapacity];
      for (int i = 0; i < newCapacity; i++)
        table[i] = new ArrayList<T>();
      for (List<T> bucket : oldTable) {
        for (T x : bucket) {
          table[x.hashCode() % table.length].add(x);
        }
      }
    } finally {
      lock.unlock();
    }
  }
```

Figure 13.4 `CoarseHashSet<T>` class: the `policy()` and `resize()` methods.

13.2.2 A Striped Hash Set

Like the coarse-grained list studied in Chapter 9, the coarse-grained hash set shown in the last section is easy to understand and easy to implement. Unfortunately, it is also a sequential bottleneck. Method calls take effect in a one-at-a-time order, even when there is no logical reason for them to do so.

We now present a closed address hash table with greater parallelism and less lock contention. Instead of using a single lock to synchronize the entire set, we split the set into independently synchronized pieces. We introduce a technique called *lock striping*, which will be useful for other data structures as well. Fig. 13.5 shows the fields and constructor for the `StripedHashSet<T>` class. The set is initialized with an array `locks[]` of L locks, and an array `table[]` of $N = L$ buckets, where each bucket is an unsynchronized `List<T>`. Although these arrays are initially of the same capacity, `table[]` will grow when the set is resized, but `lock[]` will not. Every now and then, we double the table capacity N without changing the lock array size L, so that lock i eventually protects each table entry j, where $j = i \pmod{L}$. The `acquire`(x) and `release`(x) methods use x's hash code to pick which lock to acquire or release. An example illustrating how a `StripedHashSet<T>` is resized appears in Fig. 13.6.

There are two reasons not to grow the lock array every time we grow the table:

- Associating a lock with every table entry could consume too much space, especially when tables are large and contention is low.
- While resizing the table is straightforward, resizing the lock array (while in use) is more complex, as discussed in Section 13.2.3.

Resizing a `StripedHashSet` (Fig. 13.7) is almost identical to resizing a `CoarseHashSet`. One difference is that `resize()` acquires the locks in `lock[]` in ascending order (Lines 18–20). It cannot deadlock with a `contains()`, `add()`, or `remove()` call because these methods acquire only a single lock. A `resize()` call cannot deadlock with another `resize()` call because both calls start without holding any locks, and acquire the locks in the same order. What if two or more threads try to resize at the same time? As in the `CoarseHashSet<T>`, when a thread starts to resize the table, it records the current table capacity. If, after it has acquired all the locks, it discovers that some other thread has changed the table

```
public class StripedHashSet<T> extends BaseHashSet<T>{
  final ReentrantLock[] locks;
  public StripedHashSet(int capacity) {
    super(capacity);
    locks = new Lock[capacity];
    for (int j = 0; j < locks.length; j++) {
      locks[j] = new ReentrantLock();
    }
  }
  public final void acquire(T x) {
    locks[x.hashCode() % locks.length].lock();
  }
  public void release(T x) {
    locks[x.hashCode() % locks.length].unlock();
  }
```

Figure 13.5 `StripedHashSet<T>` class: fields, constructor, `acquire()`, and `release()` methods.

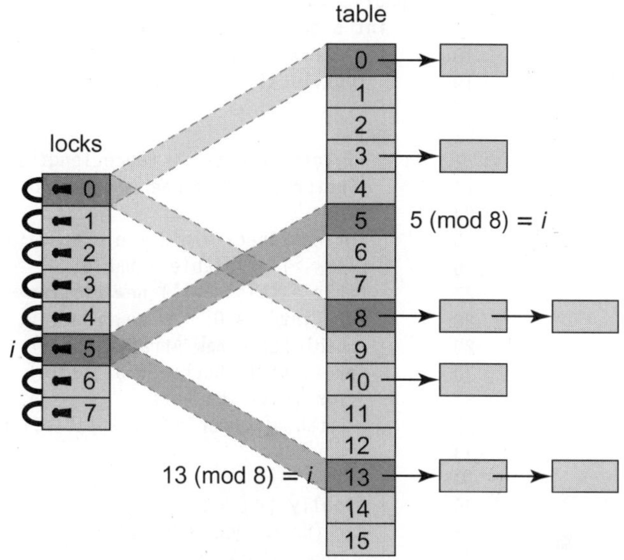

Figure 13.6 Resizing a `StripedHashSet` lock-based hash table. As the table grows, the striping is adjusted to ensure that each lock covers $2^{N/L}$ entries. In the figure above, $N=16$ and $L=8$. When N is doubled from 8 to 16, the memory is striped so that lock $i=5$ for example covers both locations that are equal to 5 modulo L.

capacity (Line 23), then it releases the locks and gives up. (It could just double the table size anyway, since it already holds all the locks.)

Otherwise, it creates a new `table[]` array with twice the capacity (Line 25), and transfer items from the old table to the new (Line 30). Finally, it releases the locks (Line 36). Because the `initializeFrom()` method calls `add()`, it may trigger nested calls to `resize()`. We leave it as an exercise to check that nested resizing works correctly in this and later hash set implementations.

To summarize, striped locking permits more concurrency than a single coarse-grained lock because method calls whose items hash to different locks can proceed in parallel. The `add()`, `contains()`, and `remove()` methods take constant expected time, but `resize()` takes linear time and is a "stop-the-world" operation: it halts all concurrent method calls while it increases the table's capacity.

13.2.3 A Refinable Hash Set

What if we want to refine the granularity of locking as the table size grows, so that the number of locations in a stripe does not continuously grow? Clearly, if we want to resize the lock array, then we need to rely on another form of synchronization. Resizing is rare, so our principal goal is to devise a way to permit the lock array to be resized without substantially increasing the cost of normal method calls.

```
  public void resize() {
    int oldCapacity = table.length;
    for (Lock lock : locks) {
      lock.lock();
    }
    try {
      if (oldCapacity != table.length) {
        return; // someone beat us to it
      }
      int newCapacity = 2 * oldCapacity;
      List<T>[] oldTable = table;
      table = (List<T>[]) new List[newCapacity];
      for (int i = 0; i < newCapacity; i++)
        table[i] = new ArrayList<T>();
      for (List<T> bucket : oldTable) {
        for (T x : bucket) {
          table[x.hashCode() % table.length].add(x);
        }
      }
    } finally {
      for (Lock lock : locks) {
        lock.unlock();
      }
    }
  }
```

Figure 13.7 `StripedHashSet<T>` class: to resize the set, lock each lock in order, then check that no other thread has resized the table in the meantime.

```
public class RefinableHashSet<T> extends BaseHashSet<T>{
  AtomicMarkableReference<Thread> owner;
  volatile ReentrantLock[] locks;
  public RefinableHashSet(int capacity) {
    super(capacity);
    locks = new ReentrantLock[capacity];
    for (int i = 0; i < capacity; i++) {
      locks[i] = new ReentrantLock();
    }
    owner = new AtomicMarkableReference<Thread>(null, false);
  }
  ...
}
```

Figure 13.8 `RefinableHashSet<T>` class: fields and constructor.

Fig. 13.8 shows the fields and constructor for the `RefinableHashSet<T>` class. To add a higher level of synchronization, we introduce a globally shared `owner` field that combines a Boolean value with a reference to a thread. Normally, the Boolean value is *false*, meaning that the set is not in the middle of resizing. While a resizing is in progress, however, the Boolean value is *true*, and the associated reference indicates the thread that is in charge of resizing. These two values are combined in an AtomicMarkableReference<Thread> to allow them to be modified atomically (see Pragma 9.8.1 in Chapter 9). We use the owner as a mutual exclusion flag between the resize() method and any of the add() methods, so that while resizing, there will be no successful updates, and while updating, there will be no successful resizes. Every add() call must read the owner field. Because resizing is rare, the value of owner should usually be cached.

Each method locks the bucket for *x* by calling acquire(*x*), shown in Fig. 13.9. It spins until no other thread is resizing the set (Lines 19–21), and then reads the lock array (Line 22). It then acquires the item's lock (Line 24), and checks again, this time while holding the locks (Line 26), to make sure no other thread is resizing, and that no resizing took place between Lines 21 and 26.

If it passes this test, the thread can proceed. Otherwise, the locks it has acquired could be out-of-date because of an ongoing update, so it releases them and starts over. When starting over, it will first spin until the current resize completes (Lines 19–21) before attempting to acquire the locks again. The release(*x*) method releases the locks acquired by acquire(*x*).

The resize() method is almost identical to the resize() method for the StripedHashSet class. The one difference appears on Line 46: instead of acquiring all the locks in lock[], the method calls quiesce() (Fig. 13.10) to ensure that no other thread is in the middle of an add(), remove(), or contains() call. The quiesce() method visits each lock and waits until it is unlocked.

```
14   public void acquire(T x) {
15     boolean[] mark = {true};
16     Thread me = Thread.currentThread();
17     Thread who;
18     while (true) {
19       do {
20         who = owner.get(mark);
21       } while (mark[0] && who != me);
22       ReentrantLock[] oldLocks = locks;
23       ReentrantLock oldLock = oldLocks[x.hashCode() % oldLocks.length];
24       oldLock.lock();
25       who = owner.get(mark);
26       if ((!mark[0] || who == me) && locks == oldLocks) {
27         return;
28       } else {
29         oldLock.unlock();
30       }
31     }
32   }
33   public void release(T x) {
34     locks[x.hashCode() % locks.length].unlock();
35   }
```

Figure 13.9 RefinableHashSet<T> class: acquire() and release() methods.

```
public void resize() {
  int oldCapacity = table.length;
  boolean[] mark = {false};
  int newCapacity = 2 * oldCapacity;
  Thread me = Thread.currentThread();
  if (owner.compareAndSet(null, me, false, true)) {
    try {
      if (table.length != oldCapacity) { // someone else resized first
        return;
      }
      quiesce();
      List<T>[] oldTable = table;
      table = (List<T>[]) new List[newCapacity];
      for (int i = 0; i < newCapacity; i++)
        table[i] = new ArrayList<T>();
      locks = new ReentrantLock[newCapacity];
      for (int j = 0; j < locks.length; j++) {
        locks[j] = new ReentrantLock();
      }
      initializeFrom(oldTable);
    } finally {
      owner.set(null, false);
    }
  }
}
```

Figure 13.10 `RefinableHashSet<T>` class: `resize()` method.

```
protected void quiesce() {
  for (ReentrantLock lock : locks) {
    while (lock.isLocked()) {}
  }
}
```

Figure 13.11 `RefinableHashSet<T>` class: `quiesce()` method.

The `acquire()` and the `resize()` methods guarantee mutually exclusive access via the flag principle using the `mark` field of the `owner` flag and the table's locks array: `acquire()` first acquires its locks and then reads the `mark` field, while `resize()` first sets `mark` and then reads the locks during the `quiesce()` call. This ordering ensures that any thread that acquires the locks after `quiesce()` has completed will see that the set is in the processes of being resized, and will back off until the resizing is complete. Similarly, `resize()` will first set the `mark` field, then read the locks, and will not proceed while any `add()`, `remove()`, or `contains()` call's lock is set.

To summarize, we have seen that one can design a hash table in which both the number of buckets and the number of locks can be continuously resized. One limitation of this algorithm is that threads cannot access the items in the table during a resize.

13.3 A Lock-Free Hash Set

The next step is to make the hash set implementation lock-free, and to make resizing *incremental*, meaning that each `add()` method call performs a small fraction of the work associated with resizing. This way, we do not need to "stop-the-world" to resize the table. Each of the `contains()`, `add()`, and `remove()` methods takes constant expected time.

To make resizable hashing lock-free, it is not enough to make the individual buckets lock-free, because resizing the table requires atomically moving entries from old buckets to new buckets. If the table doubles in capacity, then we must split the items in the old bucket between two new buckets. If this move is not done atomically, entries might be temporarily lost or duplicated.

Without locks, we must synchronize using atomic methods such as `compareAndSet()`. Unfortunately, these methods operate only on a single memory location, which makes it difficult to move a node atomically from one linked list to another.

13.3.1 Recursive Split-Ordering

We now describe a hash set implementation that works by flipping the conventional hashing structure on its head:

> Instead of moving the items among the buckets, move the buckets among the items.

More specifically, keep all items in a single lock-free linked list, similar to the `LockFreeList` class studied in Chapter 9. A bucket is just a reference into the list. As the list grows, we introduce additional bucket references so that no object is ever too far from the start of a bucket. This algorithm ensures that once an item is placed in the list, it is never moved, but it does require that items be inserted according to a *recursive split-order* algorithm that we describe shortly.

Part (b) of Fig. 13.12 illustrates a lock-free hash set implementation. It shows two components: a lock-free linked list, and an expanding array of references into the list. These references are *logical* buckets. Any item in the hash set can be reached by traversing the list from its head, while the bucket references provide short-cuts into the list to minimize the number of list nodes traversed when searching. The principal challenge is ensuring that the bucket references into the list remain well-distributed as the number of items in the set grows. Bucket references should be spaced evenly enough to allow constant-time access to any node. It follows that new buckets must be created and assigned to sparsely covered regions in the list.

As before, the capacity N of the hash set is always a power of two. The bucket array initially has Capacity 2 and all bucket references are *null*, except for the bucket at index 0, which refers to an empty list. We use the variable `bucketSize` to denote this changing capacity of the bucket structure. Each entry in the bucket

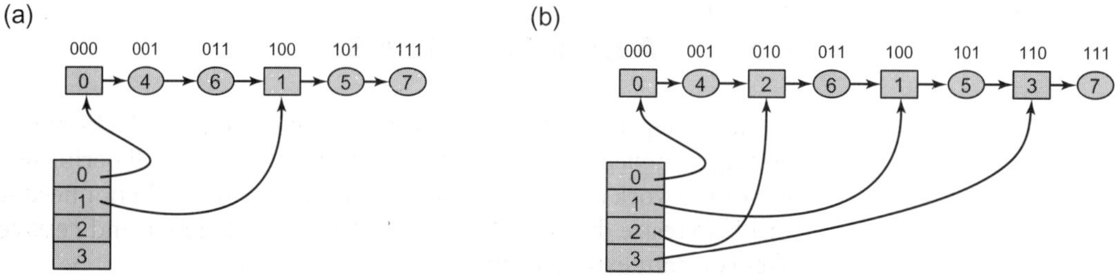

Figure 13.12 This figure explains the recursive nature of the split ordering. Part (a) shows a split-ordered list consisting of two buckets. The array of buckets refer into a single linked list. The split-ordered keys (above each node) are the reverse of the bitwise representation of the items' keys. The active bucket array entries 0 and 1 have special sentinel nodes within the list (square nodes), while other (ordinary) nodes are round. Items 4 (whose reverse bit order is "001") and 6 (whose reverse bit order is "011") are in Bucket 0 since the LSB of the original key, is "0." Items 5 and 7 (whose reverse bit orders are "101" and "111" respectively) are in Bucket 1, since the LSB of their original key is 1. Part (b) shows how each of the two buckets is split in half once the table capacity grows from 2 buckets to four. The reverse bit values of the two added Buckets 2 and 3 happen to perfectly split the Buckets 0 and 1.

array is initialized when first accessed, and subsequently refers to a node in the list.

When an item with hash code k is inserted, removed, or searched for, the hash set uses bucket index $k \pmod N$. As with earlier hash set implementations, we decide when to double the table capacity by consulting a `policy()` method. Here, however, the table is resized incrementally by the methods that modify it, so there is no explicit `resize()` method. If the table capacity is 2^i, then the bucket index is the integer represented by the key's i least significant bits (LSBs); in other words, each bucket b contains items each of whose hash code k satisfies $k = b \pmod{2^i}$.

Because the hash function depends on the table capacity, we must be careful when the table capacity changes. An item inserted before the table was resized must be accessible afterwards from both its previous and current buckets. When the capacity grows to 2^{i+1}, the items in bucket b are split between two buckets: those for which $k = b \pmod{2^{i+1}}$ remain in bucket b, while those for which $k = b + 2^i \pmod{2^{i+1}}$ migrate to bucket $b + 2^i$. Here is the key idea behind the algorithm: we ensure that these two groups of items are positioned one after the other in the list, so that splitting bucket b is achieved by simply setting bucket $b+2^i$ after the first group of items and before the second. This organization keeps each item in the second group accessible from bucket b.

As depicted in Fig. 13.12, items in the two groups are distinguished by their i^{th} binary digits (counting backwards, from least-significant to most-significant). Those with digit 0 belong to the first group, and those with 1 to the second. The next hash table doubling will cause each group to split again into two groups differentiated by the $(i + 1)^{st}$ bit, and so on. For example, the items 4 ("100" binary) and 6 ("110") share the same least significant bit. When the table capacity is 2^1, they are in the same bucket, but when it grows to 2^2, they will be in distinct buckets because their second bits differ.

This process induces a total order on items, which we call *recursive split-ordering*, as can be seen in Fig. 13.12. Given a key's hash code, its order is defined by its bit-reversed value.

To recapitulate: a *split-ordered hash set* is an array of buckets, where each bucket is a reference into a lock-free list where nodes are sorted by their bit-reversed hash codes. The number of buckets grows dynamically, and each new bucket is initialized when accessed for the first time.

To avoid an awkward "corner case" that arises when deleting a node referenced by a bucket reference, we add a *sentinel* node, which is never deleted, to the start of each bucket. Specifically, suppose the table capacity is 2^{i+1}. The first time that bucket $b + 2^i$ is accessed, a sentinel node is created with key $b + 2^i$. This node is inserted in the list via bucket b, the *parent* bucket of $b + 2^i$. Under split-ordering, $b + 2^i$ precedes all items of bucket $b + 2^i$, since those items must end with $(i + 1)$ bits forming the value $b + 2^i$. This value also comes after all the items of bucket b that do not belong to $b + 2^i$: they have identical LSBs, but their i^{th} bit is 0. Therefore, the new sentinel node is positioned in the exact list location that separates the items of the new bucket from the remaining items of bucket b. To distinguish sentinel items from ordinary items, we set the most significant bit (MSB) of ordinary items to 1, and leave the sentinel items with 0 at the MSB. Fig. 13.17 illustrates two methods: `makeOrdinaryKey()`, which generates a split-ordered key for an object, and `makeSentinelKey()`, which generates a split-ordered key for a bucket index.

Fig. 13.13 illustrates how inserting a new key into the set can cause a bucket to be initialized. The split-order key values are written above the nodes using 8-bit words. For instance, the split-order value of 3 is the bit-reverse of its binary representation, which is 11000000. The square nodes are the sentinel nodes corresponding to buckets with original keys that are 0,1, and 3 modulo 4 with their MSB being 0. The split-order keys of ordinary (round) nodes are exactly the bit-reversed images of the original keys after turning on their MSB. For example, items 9 and 13 are in the "1 mod 4" bucket, which can be recursively split in two by inserting a new node between them. The sequence of figures describes an object with hash code 10 being added when the table capacity is 4 and Buckets 0, 1, and 3 are already initialized.

The table is grown incrementally, that is, there is no explicit resize operation. Recall that each bucket is a linked list, with nodes ordered based on the split-ordered hash values. As mentioned earlier, the table resizing mechanism is independent of the policy used to decide when to resize. To keep the example concrete, we implement the following policy: we use a shared counter to allow `add()` calls to track the average bucket load. When the average load crosses a threshold, we double the table capacity.

To avoid technical distractions, we keep the array of buckets in a large, fixed-size array. We start out using only the first array entry, and use progressively more of the array as the set grows. When the `add()` method accesses an uninitialized bucket that should have been initialized given the current table capacity, it initializes it. While conceptually simple, this design is far from ideal,

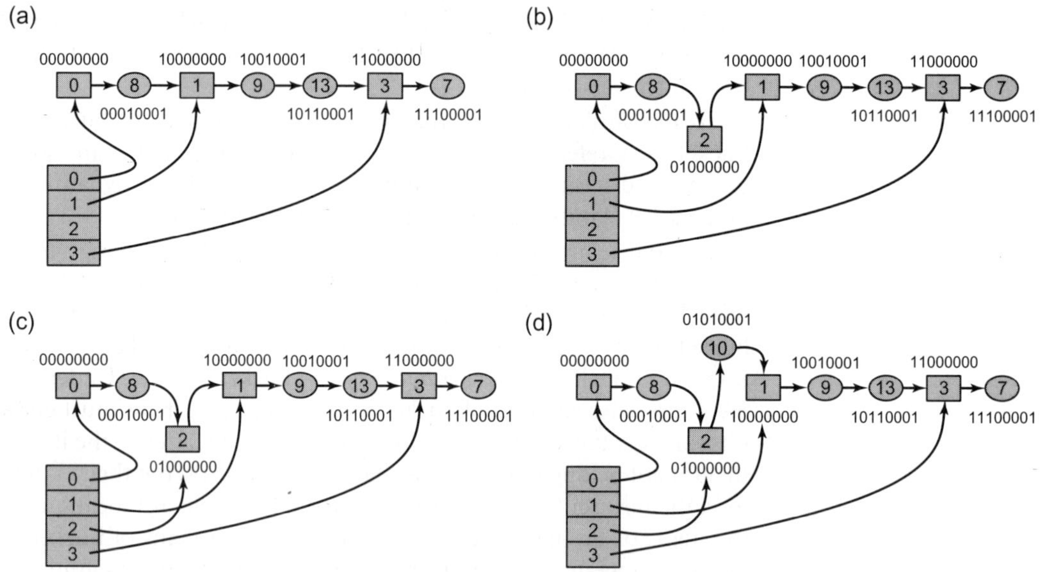

Figure 13.13 How the add() method places key 10 to the lock-free table. As in earlier figures, the split-order key values, expressed as 8-bit binary words, appear above the nodes. For example, the split-order value of 1 is the bit-wise reversal of its binary representation. In Step (a) Buckets 0, 1, and 3 are initialized, but Bucket 2 is uninitialized. In Step (b) an item with hash value 10 is inserted, causing Bucket 2 to be initialized. A new sentinel is inserted with split-order key 2. In Step (c) Bucket 2 is assigned a new sentinel. Finally, in Step (d), the split-order ordinary key 10 is added to Bucket 2.

since the fixed array size limits the ultimate number of buckets. In practice, it would be better to represent the buckets as a multilevel tree structure which would cover the machine's full memory size, a task we leave as an exercise.

13.3.2 The `BucketList` Class

Fig. 13.14 shows the fields, constructor, and some utility methods of the `BucketList class` that implements the lock-free list used by the split-ordered hash set. Although this class is essentially the same as the `LockFreeList` class, there are two important differences. The first is that items are sorted in recursive-split order, not simply by hash code. The `makeOrdinaryKey()` and `makeSentinelKey()` methods (Lines 10 and 14) show how we compute these split-ordered keys. (To ensure that reversed keys are positive, we use only the lower three bytes of the hash code.) Fig. 13.15 shows how the `contains()` method is modified to use the split-ordered key. (As in the `LockFreeList` class, the `find(`*x*`)` method returns a record containing the *x*'s node, if it exists, along with the immediately preceding and subsequent nodes.)

The second difference is that while the `LockFreeList` class uses only two sentinels, one at each end of the list, the `BucketList<T>` class places a sentinel

```
public class BucketList<T> implements Set<T> {
  static final int HI_MASK = 0x80000000;
  static final int MASK = 0x00FFFFFF;
  Node head;
  public BucketList() {
    head = new Node(0);
    head.next =
     new AtomicMarkableReference<Node>(new Node(Integer.MAX_VALUE), false);
  }
  public int makeOrdinaryKey(T x) {
    int code = x.hashCode() & MASK; // take 3 lowest bytes
    return reverse(code | HI_MASK);
  }
  private static int makeSentinelKey(int key) {
    return reverse(key & MASK);
  }
  ...
}
```

Figure 13.14 BucketList<T> class: fields, constructor, and utilities.

```
  public boolean contains(T x) {
    int key = makeOrdinaryKey(x);
    Window window = find(head, key);
    Node curr = window.curr;
    return (curr.key == key);
  }
```

Figure 13.15 BucketList<T> class: the contains() method.

at the start of each new bucket whenever the table is resized. It requires the ability to insert sentinels at intermediate positions within the list, and to traverse the list starting from such sentinels. The BucketList<T> class provides a getSentinel(x) method (Fig. 13.16) that takes a bucket index, finds the associated sentinel (inserting it if absent), and returns the tail of the BucketList<T> starting from that sentinel.

13.3.3 The LockFreeHashSet<T> Class

Fig. 13.17 shows the fields and constructor for the LockFreeHashSet<T> class. The set has the following mutable fields: bucket is an array of LockFreeHashSet<T> references into the list of items, bucketSize is an atomic integer that tracks how much of the bucket array is currently in use, and setSize is an atomic integer that tracks how many objects are in the set, used to decide when to resize.

Fig. 13.18 shows the LockFreeHashSet<T> class's add() method. If x has hash code k, add(x) retrieves bucket k (mod N), where N is the current table size, initializing it if necessary (Line 15). It then calls the BucketList<T>'s add(x) method. If x was not already present (Line 18) it increments setSize, and checks

```
  public BucketList<T> getSentinel(int index) {
    int key = makeSentinelKey(index);
    boolean splice;
    while (true) {
      Window window = find(head, key);
      Node pred = window.pred;
      Node curr = window.curr;
      if (curr.key == key) {
        return new BucketList<T>(curr);
      } else {
        Node node = new Node(key);
        node.next.set(pred.next.getReference(), false);
        splice = pred.next.compareAndSet(curr, node, false, false);
        if (splice)
          return new BucketList<T>(node);
        else
          continue;
      }
    }
  }
```

Figure 13.16 BucketList<T> class: getSentinel() method.

```
public class LockFreeHashSet<T> {
  protected BucketList<T>[] bucket;
  protected AtomicInteger bucketSize;
  protected AtomicInteger setSize;
  public LockFreeHashSet(int capacity) {
    bucket = (BucketList<T>[]) new BucketList[capacity];
    bucket[0] = new BucketList<T>();
    bucketSize = new AtomicInteger(2);
    setSize = new AtomicInteger(0);
  }
  ...
}
```

Figure 13.17 LockFreeHashSet<T> class: fields and constructor.

```
  public boolean add(T x) {
    int myBucket = BucketList.hashCode(x) % bucketSize.get();
    BucketList<T> b = getBucketList(myBucket);
    if (!b.add(x))
      return false;
    int setSizeNow = setSize.getAndIncrement();
    int bucketSizeNow = bucketSize.get();
    if (setSizeNow / bucketSizeNow > THRESHOLD)
      bucketSize.compareAndSet(bucketSizeNow, 2 * bucketSizeNow);
    return true;
  }
```

Figure 13.18 LockFreeHashSet<T> class: add() method.

```
24    private BucketList<T> getBucketList(int myBucket) {
25      if (bucket[myBucket] == null)
26        initializeBucket(myBucket);
27      return bucket[myBucket];
28    }
29    private void initializeBucket(int myBucket) {
30      int parent = getParent(myBucket);
31      if (bucket[parent] == null)
32        initializeBucket(parent);
33      BucketList<T> b = bucket[parent].getSentinel(myBucket);
34      if (b != null)
35        bucket[myBucket] = b;
36    }
37    private int getParent(int myBucket){
38      int parent = bucketSize.get();
39      do {
40        parent = parent >> 1;
41      } while (parent > myBucket);
42      parent = myBucket - parent;
43      return parent;
44    }
```

Figure 13.19 LockFreeHashSet<T> class: if a bucket is uninitialized, initialize it by adding a new sentinel. Initializing a bucket may require initializing its parent.

whether to increase `bucketSize`, the number of active buckets. The `contains`(x) and `remove`(x) methods work in much the same way.

Fig. 13.19 shows the `InitializeBucket()` method, whose role is to initialize the `bucket` array entry at a particular index, setting that entry to refer to a new sentinel node. The sentinel node is first created and added to an existing *parent* bucket, and then the array entry is assigned a reference to the sentinel. If the parent bucket is not initialized (Line 31), `InitializeBucket()` is applied recursively to the parent. To control the recursion we maintain the invariant that the parent index is less than the new bucket index. It is also prudent to choose the parent index as close as possible to the new bucket index, but still preceding it. We compute this index by unsetting the bucket index's most significant nonzero bit (Line 39).

The `add()`, `remove()`, and `contains()` methods require a constant expected number of steps to find a key (or determine that the key is absent). To initialize a bucket in a table of `bucketSize` N, the `InitializeBucket()` method may need to recursively initialize (i.e., split) as many as $O(\log N)$ of its parent buckets to allow the insertion of a new bucket. An example of this recursive initialization is shown in Fig. 13.20. In Part (a) the table has four buckets; only Bucket 0 is initialized. In Part (b) the item with key 7 is inserted. Bucket 3 now requires initialization, further requiring recursive initialization of Bucket 1. In Part (c) Bucket 1 is initialized. Finally, in Part (d), Bucket 3 is initialized. Although the total complexity in such a case is logarithmic, not constant, it can be shown that the *expected length* of any such recursive sequence of splits is constant, making the overall expected complexity of all the hash set operations constant.

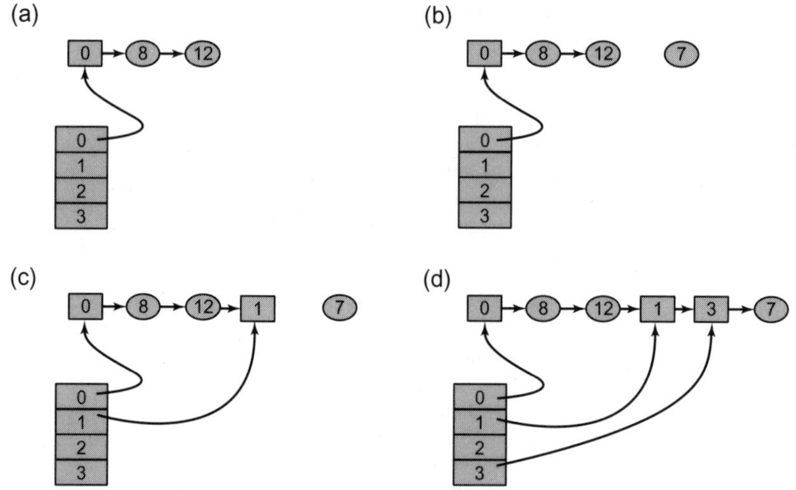

Figure 13.20 Recursive initialization of lock-free hash table buckets. (a) Table has four buckets; only bucket 0 is initialized. (b) We wish to insert the item with key 7. Bucket 3 now requires initialization, which in turn requires recursive initialization of Bucket 1. (c) Bucket 1 is initialized by first adding the 1 sentinel to the list, then setting the bucket to this sentinel. (d) Then Bucket 3 is initialized in a similar fashion, and finally 7 is added to the list. In the worst case, insertion of an item may require recursively initializing a number of buckets logarithmic in the table size, but it can be shown that the expected length of such a recursive sequence is constant.

13.4 An Open-Addressed Hash Set

We now turn our attention to a concurrent open hashing algorithm. Open hashing, in which each table entry holds a single item rather than a set, seems harder to make concurrent than closed hashing. We base our concurrent algorithm on a sequential algorithm known as Cuckoo Hashing.

13.4.1 Cuckoo Hashing

Cuckoo hashing is a (sequential) hashing algorithm in which a newly added item displaces any earlier item occupying the same slot.[1] For brevity, a *table* is a k-entry array of items. For a hash set of size $N = 2k$ we use a two-entry array `table[]` of tables,[2] and two independent hash functions,

$$h_0, h_1 : KeyRange \rightarrow 0, \ldots, k-1.$$

1 Cuckoos are a family of birds (not clocks) found in North America and Europe. Most species are nest parasites: they lay their eggs in other birds' nests. Cuckoo chicks hatch early, and quickly push the other eggs out of the nest.

2 This division of the table into two arrays will help in presenting the concurrent algorithm. There are sequential Cuckoo hashing algorithms that use, for the same number of hashed items, only a single array of size $2k$.

```
1  public boolean add(T x) {
2    if (contains(x)) {
3      return false;
4    }
5    for (int i = 0; i < LIMIT; i++) {
6      if ((x = swap(0, hash0(x), x)) == null) {
7        return true;
8      } else if ((x = swap(1, hash1(x), x)) == null) {
9        return true;
10     }
11   }
12   resize();
13   add(x);
14   }
```

Figure 13.21 Sequential Cuckoo Hashing: the add() method.

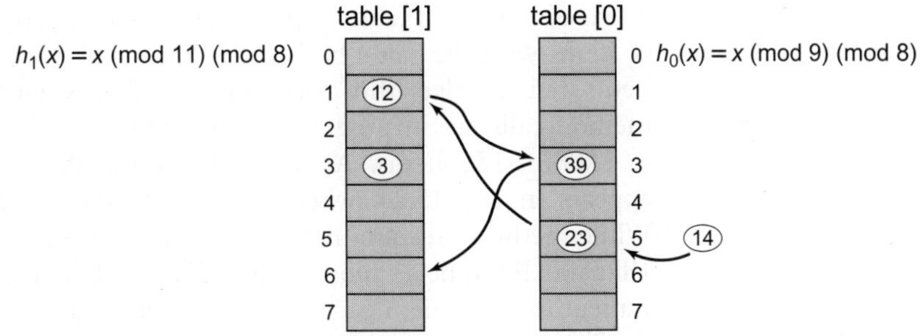

Figure 13.22 A sequence of displacements started when an item with key 14 finds both locations Table[0][h_0(14)] and Table[1][h_1(14)] taken by the values 3 and 23, and ends when the item with key 39 is successfully placed in Table[1][h_1(39)].

(denoted as `hash0()` and `hash1()` in the code) mapping the set of possible keys to entries in the array. To test whether a value x is in the set, `contains`(x) tests whether either `table`$[0][h_0(x)]$ or `table`$[1][h_1(x)]$ is equal to x. Similarly, `remove`(x) checks whether x is in either `table`$[0][h_0(x)]$ or `table`$[1][h_1(x)]$, and removes it if found.

The `add`(x) method (Fig. 13.21) is the most interesting. It successively "kicks out" conflicting items until every key has a slot. To add x, the method swaps x with y, the current occupant of `table`$[0][h_0(x)]$ (Line 6). If the prior value y was *null*, it is done (Line 7). Otherwise, it swaps the newly nest-less value y for the current occupant of `table`$[1][h_1(y)]$ in the same way (Line 8). As before, if the prior value was *null*, it is done. Otherwise, the method continues swapping entries (alternating tables) until it finds an empty slot. An example of such a sequence of displacements appears in Fig. 13.22.

We might not find an empty slot, either because the table is full, or because the sequence of displacements forms a cycle. We therefore need an upper limit on the number of successive displacements we are willing to undertake (Line 5). When this limit is exceeded, we resize the hash table, choose new hash functions (Line 12), and start over (Line 13).

Sequential cuckoo hashing is attractive for its simplicity. It provides constant-time contains() and remove() methods, and it can be shown that over time, the average number of displacements caused by each add() call will be constant. Experimental evidence shows that sequential Cuckoo hashing works well in practice.

13.4.2 Concurrent Cuckoo Hashing

The principal obstacle to making the sequential Cuckoo hashing algorithm concurrent is the add() method's need to perform a long sequence of swaps. To address this problem, we now define an alternative Cuckoo hashing algorithm, the PhasedCuckooHashSet<T> class. We break up each method call into a sequence of *phases*, where each phase adds, removes, or displaces a single item x.

Rather than organizing the set as a two-dimensional table of items, we use a two-dimensional table of *probe sets*, where a probe set is a constant-sized set of items with the same hash code. Each probe set holds at most PROBE_SIZE items, but the algorithm tries to ensure that when the set is quiescent (i.e., no method calls are in progress) each probe set holds no more than THRESHOLD < PROBE_SIZE items. An example of the PhasedCuckooHashSet structure appears in Fig. 13.24, where the PROBE_SIZE is 4 and the THRESHOLD is 2. While method calls are in-flight, a probe set may temporarily hold more than THRESHOLD but never more than PROBE_SIZE items. (In our examples, it is convenient to implement each probe set as a fixed-size List<T>.) Fig. 13.23 shows the PhasedCuckooHashSet<T>'s fields and constructor.

To postpone our discussion of synchronization, the PhasedCuckooHashSet<T> class is defined to be *abstract*, that is, it does not implement all its methods. The PhasedCuckooHashSet<T> class has the same abstract methods as the BaseHashSet<T> class: The acquire(x) method acquires all the locks necessary to manipulate item x, release(x) releases them, and resize() resizes the set. (As before, we require acquire(x) to be reentrant).

From a bird's eye view, the PhasedCuckooHashSet<T> works as follows. It adds and removes items by first locking the associated probe sets in both tables.

```
public abstract class PhasedCuckooHashSet<T> {
  volatile int capacity;
  volatile List<T>[][] table;
  public PhasedCuckooHashSet(int size) {
    capacity = size;
    table = (List<T>[][]) new java.util.ArrayList[2][capacity];
    for (int i = 0; i < 2; i++) {
      for (int j = 0; j < capacity; j++) {
        table[i][j] = new ArrayList<T>(PROBE_SIZE);
      }
    }
  }
  ...
}
```

Figure 13.23 PhasedCuckooHashSet<T> class: fields and constructor.

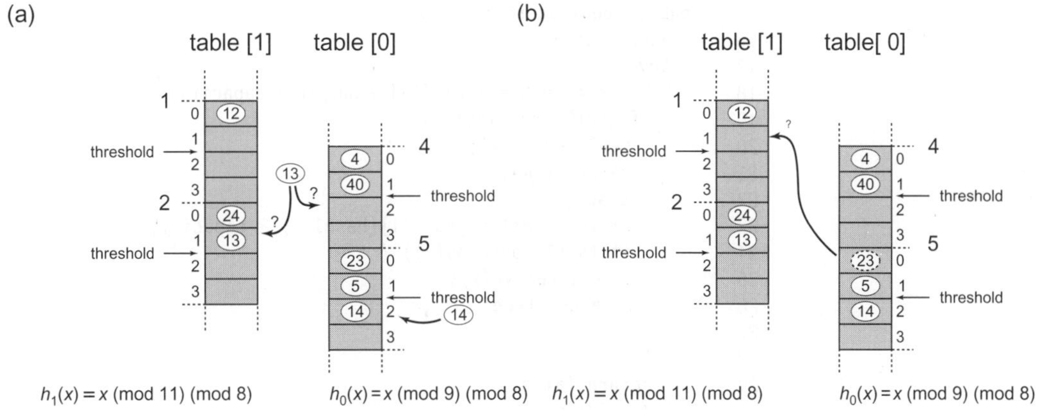

Figure 13.24 The PhasedCuckooHashSet<T> class: add() and relocate() methods. The figure shows the array segments consisting of 8 probe sets of size 4 each, with a threshold of 2. Shown are probe sets 4 and 5 of Table[0][] and 1 and 2 of Table[1][]. In Part (a) an item with key 13 finds Table[0][4] above threshold and Table[1][2] below threshold so it adds the item to the probe set Table[1][2]. The item with key 14 on the other hand finds that both of its probe sets are above threshold, so it adds its item to Table[0][5] and signals that the item should be relocated. In Part (b), the method tries to relocate the item with key 23, the oldest item in Table[0][5]. Since Table[1][1] is below threshold, the item is successfully relocated. If Table[1][1] were above threshold, the algorithm would attempt to relocate item 12 from Table[1][1], and if Table[1][1] were at the probe set's size limit of 4 items, it would attempt to relocate the item with key 5, the next oldest item, from Table[0][5].

To remove an item, it proceeds as in the sequential algorithm, checking if it is in one of the probe sets and removing it if so. To add an item, it attempts to add it to one of the probe sets. An item's probe sets serves as temporary overflow buffer for long sequences of consecutive displacements that might occur when adding an item to the table. The `THRESHOLD` value is essentially the size of the probe sets in a sequential algorithm. If the probe sets already has this many items, the item is added anyway to one of the `PROBE_SIZE–THRESHOLD` overflow slots. The algorithm then tries to relocate another item from the probe set. There are various policies one can use to choose which item to relocate. Here, we move the oldest items out first, until the probe set is below threshold. As in the sequential cuckoo hashing algorithm, one relocation may trigger another, and so on. Fig. 13.24 shows an example execution of the `PhasedCuckooHashSet<T>`.

Fig. 13.25 shows the `PhasedCuckooHashSet<T>` class's `remove(`x`)` method. It calls the abstract `acquire(`x`)` method to acquire the necessary locks, then enters a **`try`** block whose **`finally`** block calls `release(`x`)`. In the **`try`** block, the method simply checks whether x is present in Table$[0][h_0(x)]$ or Table$[1][h_1(x)]$. If so, it removes x and returns *true*, and otherwise returns *false*. The `contains(`x`)` method works in a similar way.

Fig. 13.26 illustrates the `add(`x`)` method. Like `remove()`, it calls `acquire(`x`)` to acquire the necessary locks, then enters a **`try`** block whose **`finally`** block calls `release(`x`)`. It returns *false* if the item is already present (Line 41). If either of

```
public boolean remove(T x) {
  acquire(x);
  try {
    List<T> set0 = table[0][hash0(x) % capacity];
    if (set0.contains(x)) {
      set0.remove(x);
      return true;
    } else {
      List<T> set1 = table[1][hash1(x) % capacity];
      if (set1.contains(x)) {
        set1.remove(x);
        return true;
      }
    }
    return false;
  } finally {
    release(x);
  }
}
```

Figure 13.25 PhasedCuckooHashSet<T> class: the remove() method.

```
public boolean add(T x) {
  T y = null;
  acquire(x);
  int h0 = hash0(x) % capacity, h1 = hash1(x) % capacity;
  int i = -1, h = -1;
  boolean mustResize = false;
  try {
    if (present(x)) return false;
    List<T> set0 = table[0][h0];
    List<T> set1 = table[1][h1];
    if (set0.size() < THRESHOLD) {
      set0.add(x); return true;
    } else if (set1.size() < THRESHOLD) {
      set1.add(x); return true;
    } else if (set0.size() < PROBE_SIZE) {
      set0.add(x); i = 0; h = h0;
    } else if (set1.size() < PROBE_SIZE) {
      set1.add(x); i = 1; h = h1;
    } else {
      mustResize = true;
    }
  } finally {
    release(x);
  }
  if (mustResize) {
    resize(); add(x);
  } else if (!relocate(i, h)) {
    resize();
  }
  return true; // x must have been present
}
```

Figure 13.26 PhasedCuckooHashSet<T> class: the add() method.

the item's probe sets is below threshold (Lines 44 and 46), it adds the item and returns. Otherwise, if either of the item's probe sets is above threshold but not full (Lines 48 and 50), it adds the item and makes a note to rebalance the probe set later. Finally, if both sets are full, it makes a note to resize the entire set (Line 53). It then releases the lock on *x* (Line 56).

If the method was unable to add *x* because both its probe sets were full, it resizes the hash set and tries again (Line 58). If the probe set at row *r* and column *c* was above threshold, it calls `relocate(r, c)` (described later) to rebalance probe set sizes. If the call returns *false*, indicating that it failed to rebalance the probe sets, then `add()` resizes the table.

The `relocate()` method appears in Fig. 13.27. It takes the row and column coordinates of a probe set observed to have more than `THRESHOLD` items, and

```
protected boolean relocate(int i, int hi) {
  int hj = 0;
  int j = 1 - i;
  for (int round = 0; round < LIMIT; round++) {
    List<T> iSet = table[i][hi];
    T y = iSet.get(0);
    switch (i) {
    case 0: hj = hash1(y) % capacity; break;
    case 1: hj = hash0(y) % capacity; break;
    }
    acquire(y);
    List<T> jSet = table[j][hj];
    try {
      if (iSet.remove(y)) {
        if (jSet.size() < THRESHOLD) {
          jSet.add(y);
          return true;
        } else if (jSet.size() < PROBE_SIZE) {
          jSet.add(y);
          i = 1 - i;
          hi = hj;
          j = 1 - j;
        } else {
          iSet.add(y);
          return false;
        }
      } else if (iSet.size() >= THRESHOLD) {
        continue;
      } else {
        return true;
      }
    } finally {
      release(y);
    }
  }
  return false;
}
```

Figure 13.27 PhasedCuckooHashSet<T> class: the `relocate()` method.

tries to reduce its size below threshold by moving items from this probe set to alternative probe sets.

This method makes a fixed number(LIMIT) of attempts before giving up. Each time around the loop, the following invariants hold: iSet is the probe set we are trying to shrink, *y* is the oldest item in iSet, and jSet is the other probe set where *y* could be. The loop identifies *y* (Line 70), locks both probe sets to which *y* could belong (Line 75), and tries to remove *y* from the probe set (Line 78). If it succeeds (another thread could have removed *y* between Lines 70 and 78), then it prepares to add *y* to jSet. If jSet is below threshold (Line 79), then the method adds *y* to jSet and returns *true* (no need to resize). If jSet is above threshold but not full (Line 82), then it tries to shrink jSet by swapping iSet and jSet (Lines 82–86) and resuming the loop. If jSet is full (Line 87), the method puts *y* back in iSet and returns *false* (triggering a resize). Otherwise it tries to shrink jSet by swapping iSet and jSet (Lines 82–86). If the method does not succeed in removing *y* at Line 78, then it rechecks the size of iSet. If it is still over threshold (Line 91), then the method resumes the loop and tries again to remove an item. Otherwise, iSet is below threshold, and the method returns *true* (no resize needed). Fig. 13.24 shows an example execution of the PhasedCuckooHashSet<T> where the item with key 14 causes a relocation of the oldest item 23 from the probe set table[0][5].

13.4.3 Striped Concurrent Cuckoo Hashing

We first consider a concurrent Cuckoo hash set implementation using lock striping (Chapter 13, Section 13.2.2). The StripedCuckooHashSet class extends PhasedCuckooHashSet, providing a fixed 2-by-L array of reentrant locks. As usual, lock[i][j] protects table[i][k], where $k \pmod{L} = j$. Fig. 13.28 shows the StripedCuckooHashSet class's fields and constructor. The constructor calls the PhasedCuckooHashSet<T> constructor (Line 4) and then initializes the lock array.

```
1  public class StripedCuckooHashSet<T> extends PhasedCuckooHashSet<T>{
2    final ReentrantLock[][] lock;
3    public StripedCuckooHashSet(int capacity) {
4      super(capacity);
5      lock = new ReentrantLock[2][capacity];
6      for (int i = 0; i < 2; i++) {
7        for (int j = 0; j < capacity; j++) {
8          lock[i][j] = new ReentrantLock();
9        }
10     }
11   }
12   ...
13 }
```

Figure 13.28 StripedCuckooHashSet class: fields and constructor.

The `StripedCuckooHashSet` class's `acquire`(x) method (Fig. 13.29) locks `lock[0]`[$h_0(x)$] and `lock[1]`[$h_1(x)$] in that order, to avoid deadlock. The `release`(x) method unlocks those locks.

The only difference between the `resize`() methods of `StripedCuckooHashSet` (Fig. 13.30) and `StripedHashSet` is that the latter acquires the locks in `lock[0]`

```
public final void acquire(T x) {
  lock[0][hash0(x) % lock[0].length].lock();
  lock[1][hash1(x) % lock[1].length].lock();
}
public final void release(T x) {
  lock[0][hash0(x) % lock[0].length].unlock();
  lock[1][hash1(x) % lock[1].length].unlock();
}
```

Figure 13.29 `StripedCuckooHashSet` class: `acquire()` and `release()`.

```
public void resize() {
  int oldCapacity = capacity;
  for (Lock aLock : lock[0]) {
    aLock.lock();
  }
  try {
    if (capacity != oldCapacity) {
      return;
    }
    List<T>[][] oldTable = table;
    capacity = 2 * capacity;
    table = (List<T>[][]) new List[2][capacity];
    for (List<T>[] row : table) {
      for (int i = 0; i < row.length; i++) {
        row[i] = new ArrayList<T>(PROBE_SIZE);
      }
    }
    for (List<T>[] row : oldTable) {
      for (List<T> set : row) {
        for (T z : set) {
          add(z);
        }
      }
    }
  } finally {
    for (Lock aLock : lock[0]) {
      aLock.unlock();
    }
  }
}
```

Figure 13.30 `StripedCuckooHashSet` class: the `resize()` method.

in ascending order (Line 24). Acquiring these locks in this order ensures that no other thread is in the middle of an `add()`, `remove()`, or `contains()` call, and avoids deadlocks with other concurrent `resize()` calls.

13.4.4 A Refinable Concurrent Cuckoo Hash Set

We can use the methods of Chapter 13, Section 13.2.3 to resize the lock arrays as well. This section introduces the `RefinableCuckooHashSet` class (Fig. 13.31). Just as for the `RefinableHashSet` class, we introduce an `owner` field of type `AtomicMarkableReference<Thread>` that combines a Boolean value with a reference to a thread. If the Boolean value is *true*, the set is resizing, and the reference indicates which thread is in charge of resizing.

Each phase locks the buckets for x by calling `acquire`(x), shown in Fig. 13.32. It reads the lock array (Line 24), and then spins until no other thread is resizing the set (Lines 21–23). It then acquires the item's two locks (Lines 27 and 28), and checks if the lock array is unchanged (Line 30). If the lock array has not changed between Lines 24 and 30, then the thread has acquired the locks it needs to proceed. Otherwise, the locks it has acquired are out of date, so it releases them and starts over. The `release`(x) method releases the locks acquired by `acquire`(x).

The `resize()` method in (Fig. 13.33) is almost identical to the `resize()` method for the `StripedCuckooHashSet` class. One difference is that the `locks[]` array has two dimensions.

The `quiesce()` method, like its counterpart in the `RefinableHashSet` class, visits each lock and waits until it is unlocked. The only difference is that it visits only the locks in `locks[0]`.

```
public class RefinableCuckooHashSet<T> extends PhasedCuckooHashSet<T>{
  AtomicMarkableReference<Thread> owner;
  volatile ReentrantLock[][] locks;
  public RefinableCuckooHashSet(int capacity) {
    super(capacity);
    locks = new ReentrantLock[2][capacity];
    for (int i = 0; i < 2; i++) {
      for (int j = 0; j < capacity; j++) {
        locks[i][j] = new ReentrantLock();
      }
    }
    owner = new AtomicMarkableReference<Thread>(null, false);
  }
  ...
}
```

Figure 13.31 `RefinableCuckooHashSet<T>`: fields and constructor.

```
public void acquire(T x) {
  boolean[] mark = {true};
  Thread me = Thread.currentThread();
  Thread who;
  while (true) {
    do { // wait until not resizing
      who = owner.get(mark);
    } while (mark[0] && who != me);
    ReentrantLock[][] oldLocks = locks;
    ReentrantLock oldLock0 = oldLocks[0][hash0(x) % oldLocks[0].length];
    ReentrantLock oldLock1 = oldLocks[1][hash1(x) % oldLocks[1].length];
    oldLock0.lock();
    oldLock1.lock();
    who = owner.get(mark);
    if ((!mark[0] || who == me) && locks == oldLocks) {
      return;
    } else {
      oldLock0.unlock();
      oldLock1.unlock();
    }
  }
}
public void release(T x) {
  locks[0][hash0(x)].unlock();
  locks[1][hash1(x)].unlock();
}
```

Figure 13.32 RefinableCuckooHashSet<T>: acquire() and release() methods.

13.5 Chapter Notes

The term *disjoint-access-parallelism* was coined by Amos Israeli and Lihu Rappoport [76]. Maged Michael [114] has shown that simple algorithms using a reader-writer lock [113] per bucket have reasonable performance without resizing. The lock-free hash set based on split-ordering described in Section 13.3.1 is by Ori Shalev and Nir Shavit [141]. The optimistic and fine-grained hash sets are adapted from a hash set implementation by Doug Lea [99], used in java.util.concurrent.

Other concurrent closed-addressing schemes include Meichun Hsu and Wei-Pang Yang [72], Vijay Kumar [87], Carla Schlatter Ellis [38], and Michael Greenwald [48]. Hui Gao, Jan Friso Groote, and Wim Hesselink [44] propose an almost wait-free extensible open-addressing hashing algorithm and Chris Purcell and Tim Harris [129] propose a concurrent non-blocking hash table with open addressing. Cuckoo hashing is credited to Rasmus Pagh and Flemming Rodler [122], and the concurrent version is by Maurice Herlihy, Nir Shavit, and Moran Tzafrir [68].

```
  public void resize() {
    int oldCapacity = capacity;
    Thread me = Thread.currentThread();
    if (owner.compareAndSet(null, me, false, true)) {
      try {
        if (capacity != oldCapacity) { // someone else resized first
          return;
        }
        quiesce();
        capacity = 2 * capacity;
        List<T>[][] oldTable = table;
        table = (List<T>[][]) new List[2][capacity];
        locks = new ReentrantLock[2][capacity];
        for (int i = 0; i < 2; i++) {
          for (int j = 0; j < capacity; j++) {
            locks[i][j] = new ReentrantLock();
          }
        }
        for (List<T>[] row : table) {
          for (int i = 0; i < row.length; i++) {
            row[i] = new ArrayList<T>(PROBE_SIZE);
          }
        }
        for (List<T>[] row : oldTable) {
          for (List<T> set : row) {
            for (T z : set) {
              add(z);
            }
          }
        }
      } finally {
        owner.set(null, false);
      }
    }
  }
```

Figure 13.33 `RefinableCuckooHashSet<T>`: the `resize()` method.

```
  protected void quiesce() {
    for (ReentrantLock lock : locks[0]) {
      while (lock.isLocked()) {}
    }
  }
```

Figure 13.34 `RefinableCuckooHashSet<T>`: the `quiesce()` method.

13.6 Exercises

Exercise 158. Modify the `StripedHashSet` to allow resizing of the range lock array using read/write locks.

Exercise 159. For the `LockFreeHashSet`, show an example of the problem that arises when deleting an entry pointed to by a bucket reference, if we do not add a *sentinel* entry, which is never deleted, to the start of each bucket.

Exercise 160. For the `LockFreeHashSet`, when an uninitialized bucket is accessed in a table of size N, it might be necessary to recursively initialize (i.e., split) as many as $O(\log N)$ of its parent buckets to allow the insertion of a new bucket. Show an example of such a scenario. Explain why the expected length of any such recursive sequence of splits is constant.

Exercise 161. For the `LockFreeHashSet`, design a lock-free data structure to replace the fixed-size bucket array. Your data structure should allow an arbitrary number of buckets.

Exercise 162. Outline correctness arguments for `LockFreeHashSet`'s `add()`, `remove()`, and `contains()` methods.

Hint: you may assume the `LockFreeList` algorithm's methods are correct.

14 Skiplists and Balanced Search

14.1 Introduction

We have seen several concurrent implementations of sets based on linked lists and on hash tables. We now turn our attention to concurrent search structures with logarithmic depth. There are many concurrent logarithmic search structures in the literature. Here, we are interested in search structures intended for in-memory data, as opposed to data residing on outside storage such as disks.

Many popular sequential search structures, such as red-black trees or AVL-trees, require periodic *rebalancing* to maintain the structure's logarithmic depth. Rebalancing works well for sequential tree-based search structures, but for concurrent structures, rebalancing may cause bottlenecks and contention. Instead, we focus here on concurrent implementations of a proven data structure that provides expected logarithmic time search without the need to rebalance: the `SkipList`. In the following sections we present two `SkipList` implementations. The `LazySkipList` class is a lock-based implementation, while the `LockFreeSkipList` class is not. In both algorithms, the typically most frequent method, `contains()`, which searches for an item, is wait-free. These constructions follow the design patterns outlined earlier in Chapter 9.

14.2 Sequential Skiplists

For simplicity we treat the list as a set, meaning that keys are unique. A `SkipList` is a collection of sorted linked lists, which mimics, in a subtle way, a balanced search tree. Nodes in a `SkipList` are ordered by key. Each node is linked into a subset of the lists. Each list has a *level*, ranging from 0 to a maximum. The bottom-level list contains all the nodes, and each higher-level list is a sublist of the lower-level lists. Fig. 14.1 shows a `SkipList` with integer keys. The higher-level lists are *shortcuts* into the lower-level lists, because, roughly speaking, each link

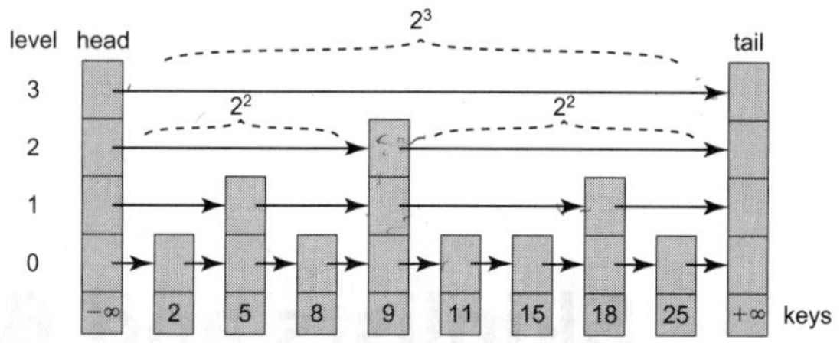

Figure 14.1 The `SkipList` class: this example has four levels of lists. Each node has a key, and the `head` and `tail` sentinels have $\pm\infty$ keys. The list at level i is a shortcut where each reference skips over 2^i nodes of the next lower level list. For example, at level 3, references skip 2^3 nodes, at level 2, 2^2 nodes, and so on.

at level i skips over about 2^i nodes in next lower-level list, (e.g., in the `SkipList` shown in Fig. 14.1, each reference at level 3 skips over 2^3 nodes.) Between any two nodes at a given level, the number of nodes in the level immediately below it is effectively constant, so the total height of the `SkipList` is roughly logarithmic in the number of nodes. One can find a node with a given key by searching first through the lists in higher levels, skipping over large numbers of lower nodes, and progressively descending until a node with the target key is found (or not) at the bottom level.

The `SkipList` is a *probabilistic* data structure. (No one knows how to provide this kind of performance without randomization.) Each node is created with a random top level (`topLevel`), and belongs to all lists up to that level. Top levels are chosen so that the expected number of nodes in each level's list decreases exponentially. Let $0 < p < 1$ be the conditional probability that a node at level i also appears at level $i + 1$. All nodes appear at level 0. The probability that a node at level 0 also appears at level $i > 0$ is p^i. For example, with $p = 1/2$, $1/2$ of the nodes are expected to appear at level 1, $1/4$ at level 2 and so on, providing a *balancing* property like the classical sequential tree-based search structures, except without the need for complex global restructuring.

We put `head` and `tail` sentinel nodes at the beginning and end of the lists with the maximum allowed height. Initially, when the `SkipList` is empty, the `head` (left sentinel) is the predecessor of the `tail` (right sentinel) at every level. The `head`'s key is less than any key that may be added to the set, and the `tail`'s key is greater.

Each `SkipList` node's `next` field is an array of references, one for each list to which it belongs and so finding a node means finding its predecessors and successors. Searching the `SkipList` always begins at the `head`. The `find()` method proceeds down the levels one after the other, and traverses each level as in the `LazyList` using references to a predecessor node `pred` and a current node `curr`. Whenever it finds a node with a greater or matching key, it records the `pred` and `curr` as the predecessor and successor of a node in arrays called `preds[]` and `succs[]`, and continues to the next lower level. The traversal ends at the bottom level. Fig. 14.2 (Part a) shows a sequential `find()` call.

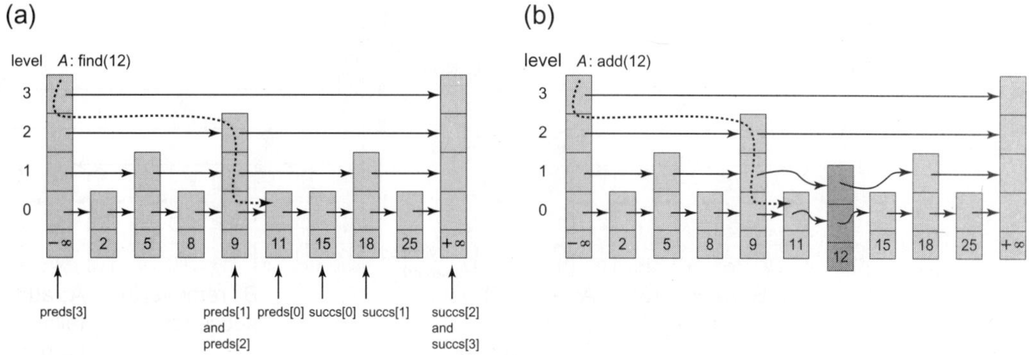

Figure 14.2 The `SkipList` class: `add()` and `find()` methods. In Part (a), `find()` traverses at each level, starting at the highest level, for as long as `curr` is less than or equal to the target key 12. Otherwise, it stores `pred` and `curr` in the `preds[]` and `succs[]` arrays at each level and descends to the next level. For example, the node with key 9 is `preds[2]` and `preds[1]`, while `tail` is `succs[2]` and the node with key 18 is `succs[1]`. Here, `find()` returns *false* since the node with key 12 was not found in the lowest-level list and so an `add(12)` call in Part (b) can proceed. In Part (b) a new node is created with a random `topLevel` = 2. The new node's `next` references are redirected to the corresponding `succs[]` nodes, and each predecessor node's `next` reference is redirected to the new node.

To add a node to a skiplist, a `find()` call fills in the `preds[]` and `succs[]` arrays. The new node is created and linked between its predecessors and successors. Fig. 14.2, Part (b) shows an `add(12)` call.

To remove a victim node from the skiplist, the `find()` method initializes the victim's `preds[]` and `succs[]` arrays. The victim is then removed from the list at all levels by redirecting each predecessor's `next` reference to the victim's successor.

14.3 A Lock-Based Concurrent Skiplist

We now describe the first concurrent skiplist design, the `LazySkipList` class. This class builds on the `LazyList` algorithm of Chapter 9: each level of the `SkipList` structure is a `LazyList`, and as in the `LazyList` algorithm, the `add()` and `remove()` methods use optimistic fine-grained locking, while the `contains()` method is wait-free.

14.3.1 A Bird's-Eye View

Here is a bird's-eye view of the `LazySkipList` class. Start with Fig. 14.3. As in the `LazyList` class, each node has its own lock and a `marked` field indicating whether it is in the abstract set, or has been logically removed. All along, the

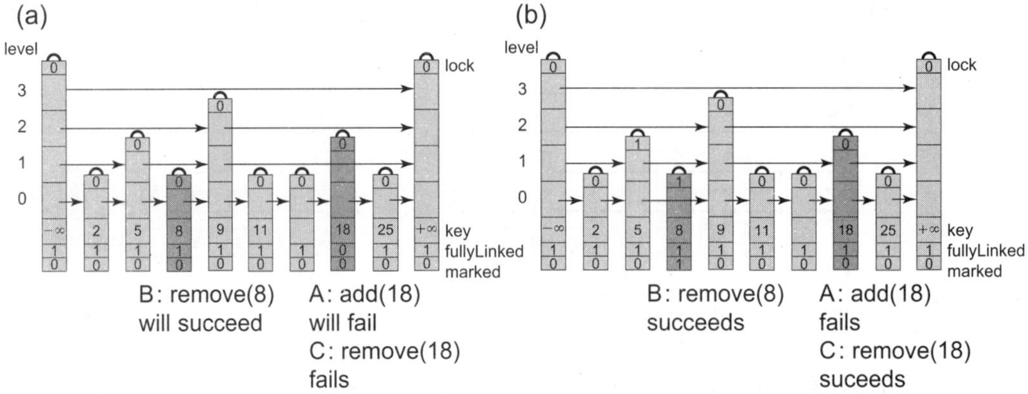

Figure 14.3 The `LazySkipList` class: failed and successful `add()` and `remove()` calls. In Part (a) the `add(18)` call finds the node with key 18 unmarked but not yet `fullyLinked`. It spins waiting for the node to become `fullyLinked` in Part (b), at which point it returns *false*. In Part (a) the `remove(8)` call finds the node with key 8 unmarked and fully linked, which means that it can acquire the node's lock in Part (b). It then sets the mark bit, and proceeds to lock the node's predecessors, in this case the node with key 5. Once the predecessor is locked, it physically removes the node from the list by redirecting the bottom-level reference of the node with key 5, completing the successful `remove()`. In Part (a) a `remove(18)` fails, because it found the node not fully linked. The same `remove(18)` call succeeds in Part (b) because it found that the node is fully linked.

algorithm maintains the *skiplist property*: higher-level lists are always contained in lower-level lists.

The skiplist property is maintained using locks to prevent structural changes in the vicinity of a node while it is being added or removed, and by delaying any access to a node until it has been inserted into all levels of the list.

To add a node, it must be linked into the list at several levels. Every `add()` call calls `find()`, which traverses the skiplist and returns the node's predecessors and successors at all levels. To prevent changes to the node's predecessors while the node is being added, `add()` locks the predecessors, validates that the locked predecessors still refer to their successors, then adds the node in a manner similar to the sequential `add()` shown in Fig. 14.2. To maintain the skiplist property, a node is not considered to be logically in the set until all references to it at all levels have been properly set. Each node has an additional flag, `fullyLinked`, set to *true* once it has been linked in all its levels. We do not allow access to a node until it is fully linked, so for example, the `add()` method, when trying to determine whether the node it wishes to add is already in the list, must spin waiting for it to become fully linked. Fig. 14.3 shows a call to `add(18)` that spins waiting until the node with key 18 becomes fully linked.

To remove a node from the list, `remove()` uses `find()` to check whether a victim node with the target key is already in the list. If so, it checks whether the victim is ready to be deleted, that is, is fully linked and unmarked. In Part (a) of Fig. 14.3, `remove(8)` finds the node with key 8 unmarked and fully linked, which means that it can remove it. The `remove(18)` call fails, because it found that the victim is not fully linked. The same `remove(18)` call succeeds in Part (b) because it found that the victim is fully linked.

If the victim can be removed, `remove()` logically removes it by setting its mark bit. It completes the physical deletion of the victim by locking its predecessors at all levels and then the victim node itself, validating that the predecessors are unmarked and still refer to the victim, and then splicing out the victim node one level at a time. To maintain the skiplist property, the victim is spliced out from top to bottom.

For example, in Part (b) of Fig. 14.3, `remove(8)` locks the predecessor node with key 5. Once this predecessor is locked, `remove()` physically removes the node from the list by redirecting the bottom-level reference of the node with key 5 to refer to the node with key 9.

In both the `add()` and `remove()` methods, if validation fails, `find()` is called again to find the newly changed set of predecessors, and the attempt to complete the method resumes.

The wait-free `contains()` method calls `find()` to locate the node containing the target key. If it finds a node, it determines whether the node is in the set by checking whether it is unmarked and fully linked. This method, like the `LazyList` class's `contains()`, is wait-free because it ignores any locks or concurrent changes in the `SkipList` structure.

To summarize, the `LazySkipList` class uses a technique familiar from earlier algorithms: it holds lock on all locations to be modified, validates that nothing important has changed, completes the modifications, and releases the locks (in this context, the `fullyLinked` flag acts like a lock).

14.3.2 The Algorithm

Fig. 14.4 shows the `LazySkipList`'s `Node` class. A key is in the set if, and only if the list contains an unmarked, fully linked node with that key. The key 8 in Part (a) of Fig. 14.3, is an example of such a key.

Fig. 14.5 shows the skiplist `find()` method. (The same method works in both the sequential and concurrent algorithms). The `find()` method returns −1 if the item is not found. It traverses the `SkipList` using `pred` and `curr` references starting at the `head` and at the highest level.[1] This highest level can be maintained dynamically to reflect the highest level actually in the `SkipList`, but for brevity, we do not do so here. The `find()` method goes down the levels one after the other. At each level it sets `curr` to be the `pred` node's successor. If it finds a node with a matching key, it records the level (Line 48). If it does not find a node with a matching key, then `find()` records the `pred` and `curr` as the predecessor and successor at that level in the `preds[]` and `succs[]` arrays (Lines 51–52), continuing to the next lower level starting from the current `pred` node. Part (a)

1 In Fig. 14.5 we make the `curr` field volatile to prevent compiler optimizations of the loop in Line 45. Recall that making the node array volatile does not make the array entries volatile.

```
public final class LazySkipList<T> {
  static final int MAX_LEVEL = ...;
  final Node<T> head = new Node<T>(Integer.MIN_VALUE);
  final Node<T> tail = new Node<T>(Integer.MAX_VALUE);
  public LazySkipList() {
    for (int i = 0; i < head.next.length; i++) {
      head.next[i] = tail;
    }
  }
  ...
  private static final class Node<T> {
    final Lock lock = new ReentrantLock();
    final T item;
    final int key;
    final Node<T>[] next;
    volatile boolean marked = false;
    volatile boolean fullyLinked = false;
    private int topLevel;
    public Node(int key) { // sentinel node constructor
      this.item = null;
      this.key = key;
      next = new Node[MAX_LEVEL + 1];
      topLevel = MAX_LEVEL;
    }
    public Node(T x, int height) {
      item = x;
      key = x.hashCode();
      next = new Node[height + 1];
      topLevel = height;
    }
    public void lock() {
      lock.lock();
    }
    public void unlock() {
      lock.unlock();
    }
  }
}
```

Figure 14.4 The `LazySkipList` class: constructor, fields, and `Node` class.

of Fig. 14.2 shows how `find()` traverses a `SkipList`. Part (b) shows how `find()` results would be used to `add()` a new item to a `SkipList`.

Because we start with `pred` at the `head` sentinel node and always advance the window only if `curr` is less than the target key, `pred` is always a predecessor of the target key, and never refers to the node with the key itself. The `find()` method returns the `preds[]` and `succs[]` arrays as well as the level at which the node with a matching key was found.

The `add(`k`)` method, shown in Fig. 14.6, uses `find()` (Fig. 14.5) to determine whether a node with the target key k is already in the list (Line 42). If an unmarked node with the key is found (Lines 62–67) then `add(`k`)` returns *false*,

```
int find(T x, Node<T>[] preds, Node<T>[] succs) {
  int key = x.hashCode();
  int lFound = -1;
  Node<T> pred = head;
  for (int level = MAX_LEVEL; level >= 0; level--) {
    volatile Node<T> curr = pred.next[level];
    while (key > curr.key) {
      pred = curr; curr = pred.next[level];
    }
    if (lFound == -1 && key == curr.key) {
      lFound = level;
    }
    preds[level] = pred;
    succs[level] = curr;
  }
  return lFound;
}
```

Figure 14.5 The `LazySkipList` class: the wait-free `find()` method. This algorithm is the same as in the sequential `SkipList` implementation. The `preds[]` and `succs[]` arrays are filled from the maximum level to level 0 with the predecessor and successor references for the given key.

indicating that the key k is already in the set. However, if that node is not yet fully linked (indicated by the `fullyLinked` field), then the thread waits until it is linked (because the key k is not in the abstract set until the node is fully linked). If the node found is marked, then some other thread is in the process of deleting it, so the `add()` call simply retries. Otherwise, it checks whether the node is unmarked and fully linked, indicating that the `add()` call should return *false.* It is safe to check if the node is unmarked before the node is fully linked, because `remove()` methods do not mark nodes unless they are fully linked. If a node is unmarked and not yet fully linked, it must become unmarked and fully linked before it can become marked (see Fig. 14.7). This step is the linearization point (Line 66) of an unsuccessful `add()` method call.

The `add()` method calls `find()` to initialize the `preds[]` and `succs[]` arrays to hold the ostensible predecessor and successor nodes of the node to be added. These references are unreliable, because they may no longer be accurate by the time the nodes are accessed. If no unmarked fully linked node was found with key k, then the thread proceeds to lock and validate each of the predecessors returned by `find()` from level 0 up to the `topLevel` of the new node (Lines 74–80). To avoid deadlocks, both `add()` and `remove()` acquire locks in ascending order. The `topLevel` value is determined at the very beginning of the `add()` method using the `randomLevel()` method.[2] The validation (Line 79) at each level checks that the predecessor is still adjacent to the successor and that neither is marked. If

2 The `randomLevel()` method is designed based on empirical measurements to maintain the `SkipList` property. For example, in the Java concurrency package, for a maximal `SkipList` level of 31, `randomLevel()` returns 0 with probability $\frac{3}{4}$, i with probability $2^{-(i+2)}$ for $i \in [1, 30]$, and 31 with probability 2^{-32}.

```
56   boolean add(T x) {
57     int topLevel = randomLevel();
58     Node<T>[] preds = (Node<T>[]) new Node[MAX_LEVEL + 1];
59     Node<T>[] succs = (Node<T>[]) new Node[MAX_LEVEL + 1];
60     while (true) {
61       int lFound = find(x, preds, succs);
62       if (lFound != -1) {
63         Node<T> nodeFound = succs[lFound];
64         if (!nodeFound.marked) {
65           while (!nodeFound.fullyLinked) {}
66           return false;
67         }
68         continue;
69       }
70       int highestLocked = -1;
71       try {
72         Node<T> pred, succ;
73         boolean valid = true;
74         for (int level = 0; valid && (level <= topLevel); level++) {
75           pred = preds[level];
76           succ = succs[level];
77           pred.lock.lock();
78           highestLocked = level;
79           valid = !pred.marked && !succ.marked && pred.next[level]==succ;
80         }
81         if (!valid) continue;
82         Node<T> newNode = new Node(x, topLevel);
83         for (int level = 0; level <= topLevel; level++)
84           newNode.next[level] = succs[level];
85         for (int level = 0; level <= topLevel; level++)
86           preds[level].next[level] = newNode;
87         newNode.fullyLinked = true; // successful add linearization point
88         return true;
89       } finally {
90         for (int level = 0; level <= highestLocked; level++)
91           preds[level].unlock();
92       }
93     }
94   }
```

Figure 14.6 The `LazySkipList` class: the `add()` method.

validation fails, the thread must have encountered the effects of a conflicting method, so it releases (in the **finally** block at Line 87) the locks it acquired and retries.

If the thread successfully locks and validates the results of `find()` up to the `topLevel` of the new node, then the `add()` call will succeed because the thread holds all the locks it needs. The thread then allocates a new node with the appropriate key and randomly chosen `topLevel`, links it in, and sets the new node's `fullyLinked` flag. Setting this flag is the linearization point of a successful `add()` method (Line 87). It then releases all its locks and returns *true* (Lines 89). The only time a thread modifies an unlocked node's `next` field is when it initializes the new node's `next` references (Line 83). This initialization is safe because it occurs before the new node is accessible.

The `remove()` method appears in Fig. 14.7. It calls `find()` to determine whether a node with the appropriate key is in the list. If so, the thread checks whether the

```
boolean remove(T x) {
  Node<T> victim = null; boolean isMarked = false; int topLevel = -1;
  Node<T>[] preds = (Node<T>[]) new Node[MAX_LEVEL + 1];
  Node<T>[] succs = (Node<T>[]) new Node[MAX_LEVEL + 1];
  while (true) {
    int lFound = find(x, preds, succs);
    if (lFound != -1) victim = succs[lFound];
    if (isMarked ||
        (lFound != -1 &&
        (victim.fullyLinked
        && victim.topLevel == lFound
        && !victim.marked))) {
      if (!isMarked) {
        topLevel = victim.topLevel;
        victim.lock.lock();
        if (victim.marked) {
          victim.lock.unlock();
          return false;
        }
        victim.marked = true;
        isMarked = true;
      }
      int highestLocked = -1;
      try {
        Node<T> pred, succ; boolean valid = true;
        for (int level = 0; valid && (level <= topLevel); level++) {
          pred = preds[level];
          pred.lock.lock();
          highestLocked = level;
          valid = !pred.marked && pred.next[level]==victim;
        }
        if (!valid) continue;
        for (int level = topLevel; level >= 0; level--) {
          preds[level].next[level] = victim.next[level];
        }
        victim.lock.unlock();
        return true;
      } finally {
        for (int i = 0; i <= highestLocked; i++) {
          preds[i].unlock();
        }
      }
    } else return false;
  }
}
```

Figure 14.7 The `LazySkipList` class: the `remove()` method.

node is ready to be deleted (Line 104): meaning it is fully linked, unmarked, and at its top level. A node found below its top level was either not yet fully linked (see the node with key 18 in Part (a) of Fig. 14.3), or marked and already partially unlinked by a concurrent `remove()` method call. (The `remove()` method could continue, but the subsequent validation would fail.)

If the node is ready to be deleted, the thread locks the node (Line 109) and verifies that it is still not marked. If it is still not marked, the thread marks the node, logically deleting that item. This step (Line 114), is the linearization point of a successful `remove()` call. If the node was marked, then the thread returns *false* since the node was already deleted. This step is one linearization point of an unsuccessful `remove()`. Another occurs when `find()` does not find a node with a matching key, or when the node with the matching key was marked, or not fully linked, or not found at its top level (Line 104).

The rest of the method completes the physical deletion of the `victim` node. To remove the victim from the list, the `remove()` method first locks (in ascending order, to avoid deadlock) the victim's predecessors at all levels up to the victim's `topLevel` (Lines 120–124). After locking each predecessor, it validates that the predecessor is still unmarked and still refers to the victim. It then splices out the victim one level at a time (Line 128). To maintain the `SkipList` property, that any node reachable at a given level is reachable at lower levels, the victim is spliced out from top to bottom. If the validation fails at any level, then the thread releases the locks for the predecessors (but not the victim) and calls `find()` to acquire the new set of predecessors. Because it has already set the victim's `isMarked` field, it does not try to mark the node again. After successfully removing the victim node from the list, the thread releases all its locks and returns *true*.

Finally, we recall that if no node was found, or the node found was marked, or not fully linked, or not found at its top level, then the method simply returns *false*. It is easy to see that it is correct to return *false* if the node is not marked, because for any key, there can at any time be at most one node with this key in the `SkipList` (i.e., reachable from the `head`). Moreover, once a node is entered into the list, (which must have occurred before it is found by `find()`), it cannot be removed until it is marked. It follows that if the node is not marked, and not all its links are in place, it must be in the process of being added into the `SkipList`, but the adding method has not reached the linearization point (see the node with key 18 in Part (a) of Fig. 14.3).

If the node is marked at the time it is found, it might not be in the list, and some unmarked node with the same key may be in the list. However, in that case, just like for the `LazyList` `remove()` method, there must have been some point during the `remove()` call when the key was not in the abstract set.

The wait-free `contains()` method (Fig. 14.8) calls `find()` to locate the node containing the target key. If it finds a node it checks whether it is unmarked and fully linked. This method, like that of the `LazyList` class of Chapter 9, is wait-free, ignoring any locks or concurrent changes in the `SkipList` list structure. A successful `contains()` call's linearization point occurs when the predecessor's `next` reference is traversed, having been observed to be unmarked and

```
boolean contains(T x) {
    Node<T>[] preds = (Node<T>[]) new Node[MAX_LEVEL + 1];
    Node<T>[] succs = (Node<T>[]) new Node[MAX_LEVEL + 1];
    int lFound = find(x, preds, succs);
    return (lFound != -1
        && succs[lFound].fullyLinked
        && !succs[lFound].marked);
}
```

Figure 14.8 The `LazySkipList` class: the wait-free `contains()` method.

fully linked. An unsuccessful `contains()` call, like the `remove()` call, occurs if the method finds a node that is marked. Care is needed, because at the time the node is found, it might not be in the list, while an unmarked node with the same key may be in the list. As with `remove()`, however, there must have been some point during the `contains()` call when the key was not in the abstract set.

14.4 A Lock-Free Concurrent Skiplist

The basis of our `LockFreeSkipList` implementation is the `LockFreeList` algorithm of Chapter 9: each level of the `SkipList` structure is a `LockFreeList`, each `next` reference in a node is an `AtomicMarkableReference<Node>`, and list manipulations are performed using `compareAndSet()`.

14.4.1 A Bird's-Eye View

Here is a bird's-eye view of the of the `LockFreeSkipList` class.

Because we cannot use locks to manipulate references at all levels at the same time, the `LockFreeSkipList` cannot maintain the `SkipList` property that each list is a sublist of the list at levels below it.

Since we cannot maintain the skiplist property, we take the approach that the abstract set is defined by the bottom-level list: a key is in the set if there is a node with that key whose `next` reference is unmarked in the bottom-level list. Nodes in higher-level lists in the skiplist serve only as shortcuts to the bottom level. There is no need for a `fullyLinked` flag as in the `LazySkipList`.

How do we add or remove a node? We treat each level of the list as a `LockFreeList`. We use `compareAndSet()` to insert a node at a given level, and we mark the `next` references of a node to remove it.

As in the `LockFreeList`, the `find()` method cleans up marked nodes. The method traverses the skiplist, proceeding down each list at each level. As in the `LockFreeList` class's `find()` method, it repeatedly snips out marked nodes as they are encountered, so that it never looks at a marked node's key. Unfortunately, this means that a node may be physically removed while it is in the process of being linked at the higher levels. A `find()` call that passes through a node's middle-level references may remove these references, so, as noted earlier, the `SkipList` property is not maintained.

The `add()` method calls `find()` to determine whether a node is already in the list, and to find its set of predecessors and successors. A new node is prepared with a randomly chosen `topLevel`, and its `next` references are directed to the potential successors returned by the `find()` call. The next step is to try to logically add the new node to the abstract set by linking it into the bottom-level list, using the same approach as in the `LockFreeList`. If the addition succeeds, the item is logically in the set. The `add()` call then links the node in at higher levels (up to its top level).

Fig. 14.9 shows the `LockFreeSkipList` class. In Part (a) `add(12)` calls `find(12)` while there are three ongoing `remove()` calls. Part (b) shows the results

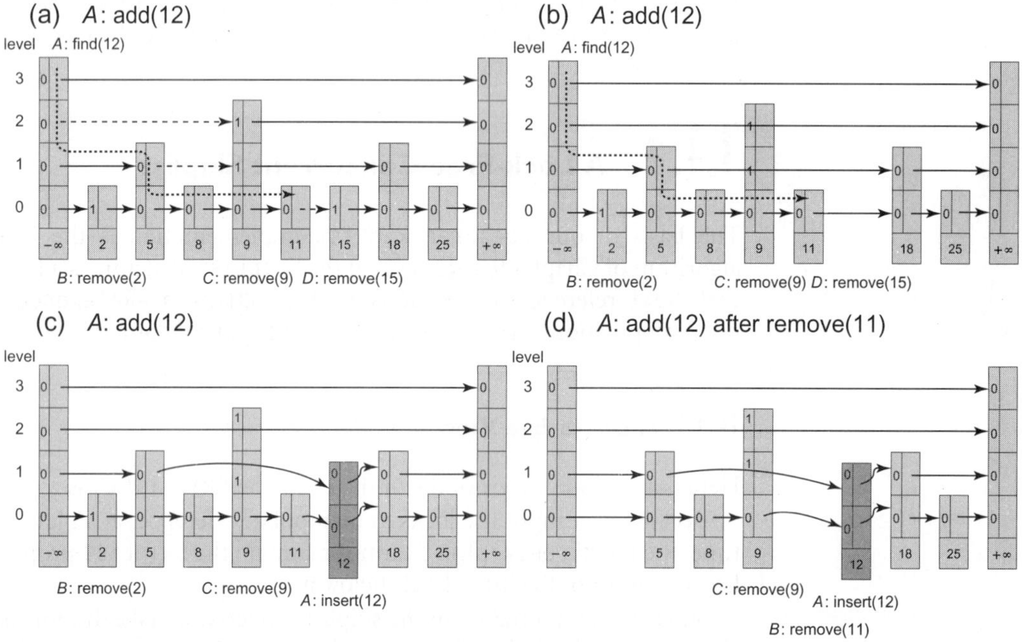

Figure 14.9 The `LockFreeSkipList` class: an `add()` call. Each node consists of links that are unmarked (a 0) or marked (a 1). In Part (a), `add(12)` calls `find(12)` while there are three ongoing `remove()` calls. The `find()` method "cleans" the marked links (denoted by 1s) as it traverses the skiplist. The traversal is not the same as a sequential `find(12)`, because marked nodes are unlinked whenever they are encountered. The path in the figure shows the nodes traversed by the `pred` reference, which always refers to unmarked nodes with keys less than the target key. Part (b) shows the result of redirecting the dashed links. We denote bypassing a node by placing the link in front of it. Node 15, whose bottom-level `next` reference was marked, is removed from the skiplist. Part (c) shows the subsequent addition of the new node with key 12. Part (d) shows an alternate addition scenario which would occur if the node with key 11 were removed before the addition of the node with key 12. The bottom-level `next` reference of the node with key 9 is not yet marked, and so the bottom-level predecessor node, whose `next` reference is marked, is redirected by the `add()` method to the new node. Once thread *C* completes marking this reference, the node with key 9 is removed and the node with key 5 becomes the immediate predecessor of the newly added node.

of redirecting the dashed links. Part (c) shows the subsequent addition of the new node with key 12. Part (d) shows an alternate addition scenario which would occur if the node with key 11 were removed before the addition of the node with key 12.

The remove() method calls find() to determine whether an unmarked node with the target key is in the bottom-level list. If an unmarked node is found, it is marked starting from the topLevel. All next references up to, but not including the bottom-level reference are logically removed from their appropriate level list by marking them. Once all levels but the bottom one have been marked, the method marks the bottom-level's next reference. This marking, if successful, removes the item from the abstract set. The physical removal of the node is the result of its physical removal from the lists at all levels by the remove() method itself and the find() methods of other threads that access it while traversing the skiplist. In both add() and remove(), if at any point a compareAndSet() fails, the set of predecessors and successors might have changed, and so find() must be called again.

The key to the interaction between the add(), remove(), and find() methods is the order in which list manipulations take place. The add() method sets its next references to the successors before it links the node into the bottom-level list, meaning that a node is ready to be removed from the moment it is logically added to the list. Similarly, the remove() method marks the next references top-down, so that once a node is logically removed, it is not traversed by a find() method call.

As noted, in most applications, calls to contains() usually outnumber calls to other methods. As a result contains() should not call find(). While it may be effective to have individual find() calls physically remove logically deleted nodes, contention results if too many concurrent find() calls try to clean up the same nodes at the same time. This kind of contention is much more likely with frequent contains() calls than with calls to the other methods.

However, contains() cannot use the approach taken by the LockFreeList's wait-free contains(): look at the keys of all reachable nodes independently of whether they are marked or not. The problem is that add() and remove() may violate the skiplist property. It is possible for a marked node to be reachable in a higher-level list after being physically deleted from the lowest-level list. Ignoring the mark could lead to skipping over nodes reachable in the lowest level.

Notice, however, that the find() method of the LockFreeSkipList is not subject to this problem because it never looks at keys of marked nodes, removing them instead. We will have the contains() method mimic this behavior, but without cleaning up marked nodes. Instead, contains() traverses the skiplist, ignoring the keys of marked nodes, and skipping over them instead of physically removing them. Avoiding the physical removal allows the method to be wait-free.

14.4.2 The Algorithm in Detail

As we present the algorithmic details, the reader should keep in mind that the abstract set is defined only by the bottom-level list. Nodes in the higher-level lists are used only as shortcuts into the bottom-level list. Fig. 14.10 shows the structure of the list's nodes.

The add() method, shown in Fig. 14.11, uses find(), shown in Fig. 14.13, to determine whether a node with key *k* is already in the list (Line 61). As in the LazySkipList, add() calls find() to initialize the preds[] and succs[] arrays to hold the new node's ostensible predecessors and successors.

If an unmarked node with the target key is found in the bottom-level list, find() returns *true* and the add() method returns *false*, indicating that the key is already in the set. The unsuccessful add()'s linearization point is the same as the successful find()'s (Line 42). If no node is found, then the next step is to try to add a new node with the key into the structure.

```
public final class LockFreeSkipList<T> {
  static final int MAX_LEVEL = ...;
  final Node<T> head = new Node<T>(Integer.MIN_VALUE);
  final Node<T> tail = new Node<T>(Integer.MAX_VALUE);
  public LockFreeSkipList() {
    for (int i = 0; i < head.next.length; i++) {
      head.next[i]
      = new AtomicMarkableReference<LockFreeSkipList.Node<T>>(tail, false);
    }
  }
  public static final class Node<T> {
    final T value; final int key;
    final AtomicMarkableReference<Node<T>>[] next;
    private int topLevel;
    // constructor for sentinel nodes
    public Node(int key) {
      value = null; key = key;
      next = (AtomicMarkableReference<Node<T>>[])
       new AtomicMarkableReference[MAX_LEVEL + 1];
      for (int i = 0; i < next.length; i++) {
        next[i] = new AtomicMarkableReference<Node<T>>(null,false);
      }
      topLevel = MAX_LEVEL;
    }
    // constructor for ordinary nodes
    public Node(T x, int height) {
      value = x;
      key = x.hashCode();
      next = (AtomicMarkableReference<Node<T>>[])
       new AtomicMarkableReference[height + 1];
      for (int i = 0; i < next.length; i++) {
        next[i] = new AtomicMarkableReference<Node<T>>(null,false);
      }
      topLevel = height;
    }
  }
```

Figure 14.10 The LockFreeSkipList class: fields and constructor.

A new node is created with a randomly chosen `topLevel`. The node's `next` references are unmarked and set to the successors returned by the `find()` method (Lines 46–49).

The next step is to try to add the new node by linking it into the bottom-level list between the `preds[0]` and `succs[0]` nodes returned by `find()`. As in the `LockFreeList`, we use `compareAndSet()` to set the reference while validating that these nodes still refer one to the other and have not been removed from the list (Line 54). If the `compareAndSet()` fails, something has changed and the call restarts. If the `compareAndSet()` succeeds, the item is added, and Line 54 is the call's linearization point.

The `add()` then links the node in at higher levels (Line 57). For each level, it attempts to splice the node in by setting the predecessor, if it refers to the valid

```
36    boolean add(T x) {
37      int topLevel = randomLevel();
38      int bottomLevel = 0;
39      Node<T>[] preds = (Node<T>[]) new Node[MAX_LEVEL + 1];
40      Node<T>[] succs = (Node<T>[]) new Node[MAX_LEVEL + 1];
41      while (true) {
42        boolean found = find(x, preds, succs);
43        if (found) {
44          return false;
45        } else {
46          Node<T> newNode = new Node(x, topLevel);
47          for (int level = bottomLevel; level <= topLevel; level++) {
48            Node<T> succ = succs[level];
49            newNode.next[level].set(succ, false);
50          }
51          Node<T> pred = preds[bottomLevel];
52          Node<T> succ = succs[bottomLevel];
53          if (!pred.next[bottomLevel].compareAndSet(succ, newNode,
54                                                   false, false)) {
55            continue;
56          }
57          for (int level = bottomLevel+1; level <= topLevel; level++) {
58            while (true) {
59              pred = preds[level];
60              succ = succs[level];
61              if (pred.next[level].compareAndSet(succ, newNode, false, false))
62                break;
63              find(x, preds, succs);
64            }
65          }
66          return true;
67        }
68      }
69    }
```

Figure 14.11 The `LockFreeSkipList` class: the `add()` method.

successor, to the new node (Line 61). If successful, it breaks and moves on to the next level. If unsuccessful, then the node referenced by the predecessor must have changed, and `find()` is called again to find a new valid set of predecessors and successors. We discard the result of calling `find()` (Line 63) because we care only about recomputing the ostensible predecessors and successors on the remaining unlinked levels. Once all levels are linked, the method returns *true* (Line 66).

The `remove()` method, shown in Fig. 14.12, calls `find()` to determine whether an unmarked node with a matching key is in the bottom-level list. If no node is found in the bottom-level list, or the node with a matching key is marked, the method returns *false*. The linearization point of the unsuccessful `remove()` is that of the `find()` method called in Line 76. If an unmarked node is found, then the method logically removes the associated key from the abstract set, and prepares

```
 70   boolean remove(T x) {
 71     int bottomLevel = 0;
 72     Node<T>[] preds = (Node<T>[]) new Node[MAX_LEVEL + 1];
 73     Node<T>[] succs = (Node<T>[]) new Node[MAX_LEVEL + 1];
 74     Node<T> succ;
 75     while (true) {
 76       boolean found = find(x, preds, succs);
 77       if (!found) {
 78         return false;
 79       } else {
 80         Node<T> nodeToRemove = succs[bottomLevel];
 81         for (int level = nodeToRemove.topLevel;
 82              level >= bottomLevel+1; level--) {
 83           boolean[] marked = {false};
 84           succ = nodeToRemove.next[level].get(marked);
 85           while (!marked[0]) {
 86             nodeToRemove.next[level].compareAndSet(succ, succ, false, true);
 87           succ = nodeToRemove.next[level].get(marked);
 88           }
 89         }
 90         boolean[] marked = {false};
 91         succ = nodeToRemove.next[bottomLevel].get(marked);
 92         while (true) {
 93           boolean iMarkedIt =
 94             nodeToRemove.next[bottomLevel].compareAndSet(succ, succ,
 95                                                           false, true);
 96           succ = succs[bottomLevel].next[bottomLevel].get(marked);
 97           if (iMarkedIt) {
 98             find(x, preds, succs);
 99             return true;
100           }
101           else if (marked[0]) return false;
102         }
103       }
104     }
105   }
```

Figure 14.12 The `LockFreeSkipList` class: the `remove()` method.

it for physical removal. This step uses the set of ostensible predecessors (stored by `find()` in `preds[]`) and the `nodeToRemove` (returned from `find()` in `succs[]`). First, starting from the `topLevel`, all links up to and not including the bottom-level link are marked (Lines 82–88) by repeatedly reading `next` and its mark and applying a `compareAndSet()`. If the link is found to be marked (either because it was already marked or because the attempt succeeded) the method moves on to the next-level link. Otherwise, the current level's link is reread since it must have been changed by another concurrent thread, so the marking attempt must be repeated. Once all levels but the bottom one have been marked, the method marks the bottom-level's `next` reference. This marking (Line 95), if successful, is the linearization point of a successful `remove()`. The `remove()` method tries to mark the `next` field using `compareAndSet()`. If successful, it can determine that it was the thread that changed the mark from *false* to *true*. Before returning *true*, the `find()` method is called again. This call is an optimization: as a side effect, `find()` physically removes all links to the node it is searching for if that node is already logically removed.

On the other hand, if the `compareAndSet()` call failed, but the `next` reference is marked, then another thread must have concurrently removed it, so `remove()` returns *false*. The linearization point of this unsuccessful `remove()` is the linearization point of the `remove()` method by the thread that successfully marked the `next` field. Notice that this linearization point must occur during the `remove()` call because the `find()` call found the node unmarked before it found it marked.

Finally, if the `compareAndSet()` fails and the node is unmarked, then the `next` node must have changed concurrently. Since the `nodeToRemove` is known, there is no need to call `find()` again, and `remove()` simply uses the new value read from `next` to retry the marking.

As noted, both the `add()` and `remove()` methods rely on `find()`. This method searches the `LockFreeSkipList`, returning *true* if and only if a node with the target key is in the set. It fills in the `preds[]` and `succs[]` arrays with the target node's ostensible predecessors and successors at each level. It maintains the following two properties:

- It never traverses a marked link. Instead, it removes the node referred to by a marked link from the list at that level.
- Every `preds[]` reference is to a node with a key strictly less than the target.

The `find()` method in Fig. 14.13 proceeds as follows. It starts traversing the `SkipList` from the `topLevel` of the `head` sentinel, which has the maximal allowed node level. It then proceeds in each level down the list, filling in `preds` and `succs` nodes that are repeatedly advanced until `pred` refers to a node with the largest value on that level that is strictly less than the target key (Lines 117–131). As in the `LockFreeList`, it repeatedly snips out marked nodes from the given level as they are encountered (Lines 119–125) using a `compareAndSet()`. Notice that the `compareAndSet()` validates that the `next` field of the predecessor references the current node. Once an unmarked `curr` is found (Line 126), it is tested to see if its key is less than the target key. If so, `pred` is advanced to `curr`.

```
106   boolean find(T x, Node<T>[] preds, Node<T>[] succs) {
107     int bottomLevel = 0;
108     int key = x.hashCode();
109     boolean[] marked = {false};
110     boolean snip;
111     Node<T> pred = null, curr = null, succ = null;
112     retry:
113       while (true) {
114         pred = head;
115         for (int level = MAX_LEVEL; level >= bottomLevel; level--) {
116           curr = pred.next[level].getReference();
117           while (true) {
118             succ = curr.next[level].get(marked);
119             while (marked[0]) {
120               snip = pred.next[level].compareAndSet(curr, succ,
121                                                     false, false);
122               if (!snip) continue retry;
123               curr = pred.next[level].getReference();
124               succ = curr.next[level].get(marked);
125             }
126             if (curr.key < key){
127               pred = curr; curr = succ;
128             } else {
129               break;
130             }
131           }
132           preds[level] = pred;
133           succs[level] = curr;
134         }
135         return (curr.key == key);
136       }
137   }
```

Figure 14.13 The LockFreeSkipList class: a more complex find() than in LazySkipList.

Otherwise, curr's key is greater than or equal to the target's, so the current value of pred is the target node's immediate predecessor. The find() method breaks out of the current level search loop, saving the current values of pred and curr (Line 132).

The find() method proceeds this way until it reaches the bottom level. Here is an important point: the traversal at each level maintains the two properties described earlier. In particular, if a node with the target key is in the list, it will be found at the bottom level even if traversed nodes are removed at higher levels. When the traversal stops, pred refers to a predecessor of the target node. The method descends to each next lower level without skipping over the target node. If the node is in the list, it will be found at the bottom level. Moreover, if the node is found, it cannot be marked because if it were marked, it would have been snipped out in Lines 119–125. Therefore, the test in Line 135 need only check if the key of curr is equal to the target key to determine if the target is in the set.

The linearization points of both successful and unsuccessful calls to the find() methods occur when the curr reference at the bottom-level list is set, at either

Line 116 or 123, for the last time before the `find()` call's success or failure is determined in Line 135. Fig. 14.9 shows how a node is successfully added to the `LockFreeSkipList`.

The wait-free `contains()` method appears in Fig. 14.14. It traverses the `SkipList` in the same way as the `find()` method, descending level-by-level from the `head`. Like `find()`, `contains()` ignores keys of marked nodes. Unlike `find()`, it does not try to remove marked nodes. Instead, it simply jumps over them (Line 147–150). For an example execution, see Fig. 14.15.

The method is correct because `contains()` preserves the same properties as `find()`, among them, that `pred`, in any level, never refers to an unmarked node whose key is greater than or equal to the target key. The `pred` variable arrives at the bottom-level list at a node before, and never after, the target node. If the node is added before the `contains()` method call starts, then it will be found. Moreover, recall that `add()` calls `find()`, which unlinks marked nodes from the bottom-level list before adding the new node. It follows that if `contains()` does not find the desired node, or finds the desired node at the bottom level but marked, then any concurrently added node that was not found must have been added to the bottom level after the start of the `contains()` call, so it is correct to return *false* in Line 159.

Fig. 14.16 shows an execution of the `contains()` method. In Part (a), a `contains(18)` call traverses the list starting from the top level of the `head` node. In Part (b) the `contains(18)` call traverses the list after the node with key 18 has been logically removed.

```
138   boolean contains(T x) {
139     int bottomLevel = 0;
140     int v = x.hashCode();
141     boolean[] marked = {false};
142     Node<T> pred = head, curr = null, succ = null;
143     for (int level = MAX_LEVEL; level >= bottomLevel; level--) {
144       curr = curr.next[level].getReference();
145       while (true) {
146         succ = curr.next[level].get(marked);
147         while (marked[0]) {
148           curr = pred.next[level].getReference();
149           succ = curr.next[level].get(marked);
150         }
151         if (curr.key < v){
152           pred = curr;
153           curr = succ;
154         } else {
155           break;
156         }
157       }
158     }
159     return (curr.key == v);
160   }
```

Figure 14.14 The `LockFreeSkipList` class: the wait-free `contains()` method.

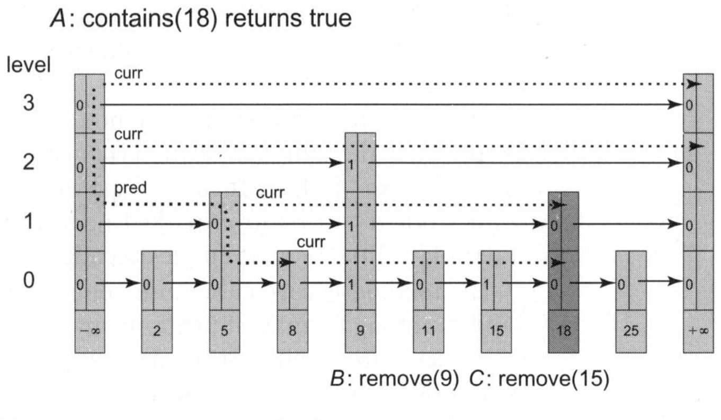

Figure 14.15 Thread *A* calls `contains(18)`, which traverses the list starting from the top level of the head node. The dotted line marks the traversal by the `pred` field, and the sparse dotted line marks the path of the `curr` field. The `curr` field is advanced to `tail` on level 3. Since its key is greater than 18, `pred` descends to level 2. The `curr` field advances past the marked reference in the node with key 9, again reaching `tail` which is greater than 18, so `pred` descends to level 1. Here `pred` is advanced to the unmarked node with key 5, and `curr` advances past the marked node with key 9 to reach the unmarked node with key 18, at which point `curr` is no longer advanced. Though 18 is the target key, the method continues to descend with `pred` to the bottom level, advancing `pred` to the node with key 8. From this point, `curr` traverses past marked Nodes 9 and 15 and Node 11 whose key is smaller than 18. Eventually `curr` reaches the unmarked node with key 18, returning *true*.

14.5 Concurrent Skiplists

We have seen two highly concurrent `SkipList` implementations, each providing logarithmic search without the need to rebalance. In the `LazySkipList` class, the `add()` and `remove()` methods use optimistic fine-grained locking, meaning that the method searches for its target node without locking, and acquires locks and validates only when it discovers the target. The `contains()` method, usually the most common, is wait-free. In the `LockFreeSkipList` class, the `add()` and `remove()` methods are lock-free, building on the `LockFreeList` class of Chapter 9. In this class too, the `contains()` method is wait-free.

In Chapter 15 we will see how one can build highly concurrent priority queues based on the concurrent `SkipList` we presented here.

14.6 Chapter Notes

Bill Pugh invented skiplists, both sequential [128] and concurrent [127]. The `LazySkipList` is by Yossi Lev, Maurice Herlihy, Victor Luchangco, and Nir Shavit [103]. The `LockFreeSkipList` presented here is credited to Maurice Herlihy,

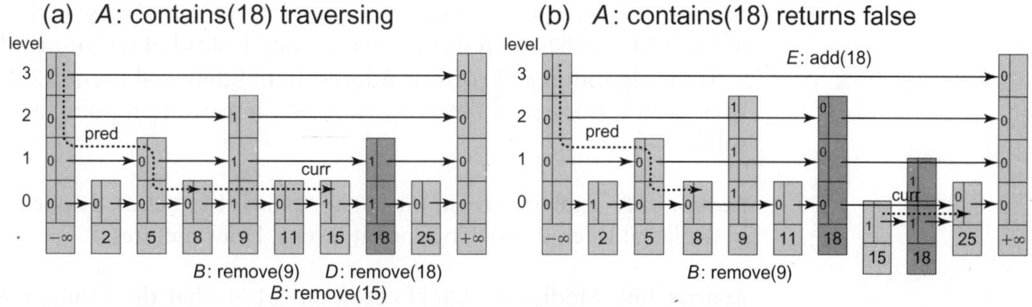

Figure 14.16 The `LockFreeSkipList` class: a `contains()` call. In Part (a), `contains(18)` traverses the list starting from the top level of the head node. The dotted line marks the traversal by the `pred` field. The `pred` field eventually reaches Node 8 at the bottom level and we show the path of `curr` from that point on using a sparser dotted line. The `curr` traverses past Node 9 and reaches the marked Node 15. In Part (b) a new node with key 18 is added to the list by a thread *E*. Thread *E*, as part of its `find(18)` call, physically removes the old nodes with keys 9, 15, and 18. Now thread *A* continues its traversal with the `curr` field from the removed node with key 15 (the nodes with keys 15 and 18 are not recycled since they are reachable by thread *A*). Thread *A* reaches the node with key 25 which is greater than 18, returning *false*. Even though at this point there is an unmarked node with key 18 in the `LockFreeSkipList`, this node was inserted by *E* concurrently with *A*'s traversal and is linearized after *A*'s `add(18)`.

Yossi Lev, and Nir Shavit [64]. It is partly based on an earlier lock-free `SkipList` algorithm developed by to Kier Fraser [42], a variant of which was incorporated into the Java Concurrency Package by Doug Lea [100].

14.7 Exercises

Exercise 163. Recall that a skiplist is a *probabilistic* data structure. Although the expected peformance of a `contains()` call is $O(\log n)$, where n is the number of items in the list, the worst-case peformance could be $O(n)$. Draw a picture of an 8-element skiplist with worst-case performance, and explain how it got that way.

Exercise 164. You are given a skiplist with probability p and `MAX_LEVEL` M. If the list contains N nodes, what is the expected number of nodes at each level from 0 to $M - 1$?

Exercise 165. Modify the `LazySkipList` class so `find()` starts at the level of the highest node currently in the structure, instead of the highest level possible (`MAX_LEVEL`).

Exercise 166. Modify the `LazySkipList` to support multiple items with the same key.

Exercise 167. Suppose we modify the `LockFreeSkipList` class so that at Line 101 of Fig. 14.12, `remove()` restarts the main loop instead of returning *false*.

Is the algorithm still correct? Address both safety and liveness issues. That is, what is an unsuccessful `remove()` call's new linearization point, and is the class still lock-free?

Exercise 168. Explain how, in the `LockFreeSkipList` class, a node might end up in the list at levels 0 and 2, but not at level 1. Draw pictures.

Exercise 169. Modify the `LockFreeSkipList` so that the `find()` method snips out a sequence of marked nodes with a single `compareAndSet()`. Explain why your implementation cannot remove a concurrently inserted unmarked node.

Exercise 170. Will the `add()` method of the `LockFreeSkipList` work even if the bottom level is linked and then all other levels are linked in some arbitrary order? Is the same true for the marking of the `next` references in the `remove()` method: the bottom level `next` reference is marked last, but references at all other levels are marked in an arbitrary order?

Exercise 171. (Hard) Modify the `LazySkipList` so that the list at each level is bidirectional, and allows threads to add and remove items in parallel by traversing from either the `head` or the `tail`.

Exercise 172. Fig. 14.17 shows a buggy `contains()` method for the `LockFreeSkipList` class. Give a scenario where this method returns a wrong answer. Hint: the reason this method is wrong is that it takes into account keys of nodes that have been removed.

```
boolean contains(T x) {
  int bottomLevel = 0;
  int key = x.hashCode();
  Node<T> pred = head;
  Node<T> curr = null;
  for (int level = MAX_LEVEL; level >= bottomLevel; level--) {
    curr = pred.next[level].getReference();
    while (curr.key < key ) {
      pred = curr;
      curr = pred.next[level].getReference();
    }
  }
  return curr.key == key;
}
```

Figure 14.17 The `LockFreeSkipList` class: an *incorrect* `contains()`.

15 Priority Queues

15.1 Introduction

A *priority queue* is a multiset of *items*, where each item has an associated *priority*, a score that indicates its importance (by convention, smaller scores are more important, indicating a higher priority). A priority queue typically provides an add() method to add an item to the set, and a removeMin() method to remove and return the item of minimal score (highest priority). Priority queues appear everywhere from high-level applications to low-level operating system kernels.

A *bounded-range* priority queue is one where each item's score is taken from a discrete set of items, while an *unbounded-range* priority queue is one where scores are taken from a very large set, say 32-bit integers, or floating-point values. Not surprisingly, bounded-range priority queues are generally more efficient, but many applications require unbounded ranges. Fig. 15.1 shows the priority queue interface.

15.1.1 Concurrent Priority Queues

In a concurrent setting, where add() and removeMin() method calls can overlap, what does it mean for an item to be in the set?

Here, we consider two alternative consistency conditions, both introduced in Chapter 3. The first is *linearizability*, which requires that each method call appear to take effect at some instant between its invocation and its response. The second is *quiescent consistency*, a weaker condition that requires that in any execution, at any point, if no additional method calls are introduced, then when all

```
public interface PQueue<T> {
  void add(T item, int score);
  T removeMin();
}
```

Figure 15.1 Priority Queue Interface.

pending method calls complete, the values they return are consistent with some valid sequential execution of the object. If an application does not require its priority queues to be linearizable, then it is usually more efficient to require them to be quiescently consistent. Careful thought is usually required to decide which approach is correct for a particular application.

15.2 An Array-Based Bounded Priority Queue

A bounded-range priority queue has *range m* if its priorities are taken from the range $0, \ldots, m-1$. For now, we consider bounded priority queue algorithms that use two component data structures: `Counter` and `Bin`. A `Counter` (see Chapter 12) holds an integer value, and supports `getAndIncrement()` and `getAndDecrement()` methods that atomically increment and decrement the counter value and return the counter's prior value. These methods may optionally be *bounded*, meaning they do not advance the counter value beyond some specified bound.

A `Bin` is a pool that holds arbitrary items, and supports a `put(`x`)` method for inserting an item x, and a `get()` method for removing and returning an arbitrary item, returning *null* if the bin is empty. Bins can be implemented using locks or in a lock-free manner using the stack algorithms of Chapter 11.

Fig. 15.2 shows the `SimpleLinear` class, which maintains an array of bins. To add an item with score i a thread simply places the item in the i-th bin. The

```
public class SimpleLinear<T> implements PQueue<T> {
  int range;
  Bin<T>[] pqueue;
  public SimpleLinear(int myRange) {
    range = myRange;
    pqueue = (Bin<T>[])new Bin[range];
    for (int i = 0; i < pqueue.length; i++){
      pqueue[i] = new Bin();
    }
  }
  public void add(T item, int key) {
    pqueue[key].put(item);
  }
  public T removeMin() {
    for (int i = 0; i < range; i++) {
       T item = pqueue[i].get();
       if (item != null) {
         return item;
       }
    }
    return null;
  }
}
```

Figure 15.2 The `SimpleLinear` class: `add()` and `removeMin()` methods.

removeMin() method scans the bins in decreasing priority and returns the first item it successfully removes. If no item is found it returns *null*. If the bins are quiescently consistent, so is SimpleLinear. The add() and removeMin() methods are lock-free if the Bin methods are lock-free.

15.3 A Tree-Based Bounded Priority Queue

The SimpleTree (Fig. 15.3) is a lock-free quiescently consistent bounded-range priority queue. It is a binary tree (Fig. 15.4) of treeNode objects (Fig. 15.5). As depicted in Fig. 15.3, the tree has m leaves where the i-th leaf node has a bin holding items of score i. There are $m - 1$ shared bounded counters in the tree's

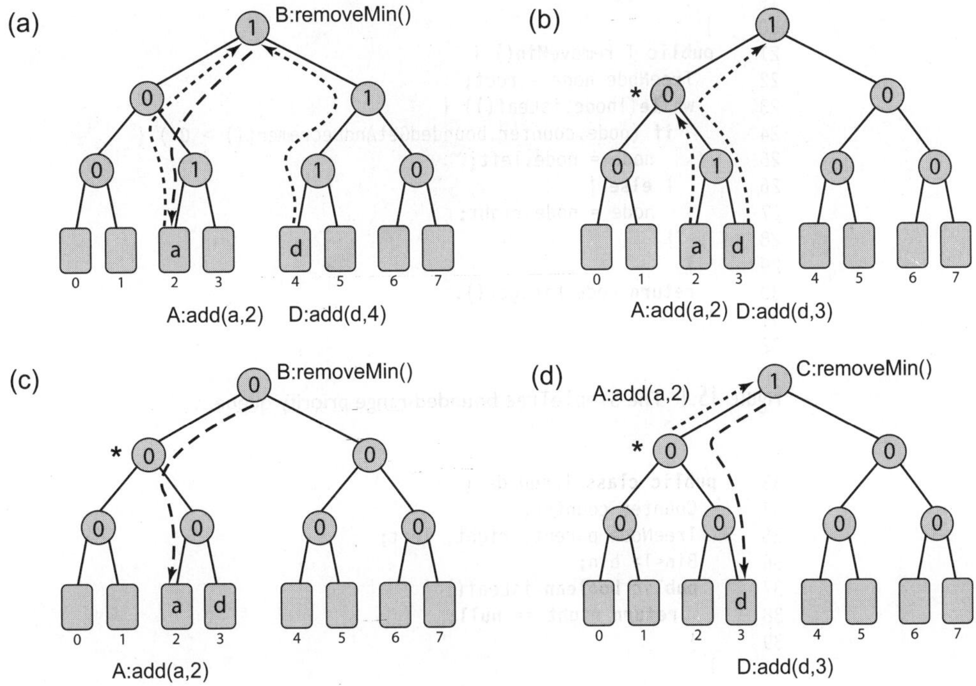

Figure 15.3 The SimpleTree priority queue is a tree of bounded counters. Items reside in bins at the leaves. Internal nodes hold the number of items in the subtree rooted at the node's left child. In Part (a) threads *A* and *D* add items by traversing up the tree, incrementing the counters in the nodes when they ascend from the left. Thread *B* follows the counters down the tree, descending left if the counter had a nonzero value (we do not show the effect of *B*'s decrements). Parts (b), (c), and (d) show a sequence in which concurrent threads *A* and *B* meet at the node marked by a star. In Part (b) thread *D* adds *d*, then *A* adds *a* and ascends to the starred node, incrementing a counter along the way. In Part (c) *B* traverses down the tree, decrementing counters to zero and popping *a*. In Part (d), *A* continues its ascent, incrementing the counter at the root even though *B* already removed any trace of *a* from the starred node down. Nevertheless, all is well, because the nonzero root counter correctly leads *C* to item *d*, the item with the highest priority.

```
public class SimpleTree<T> implements PQueue<T> {
  int range;
  List<TreeNode> leaves;
  TreeNode root;
  public SimpleTree(int logRange) {
    range = (1 << logRange);
    leaves = new ArrayList<TreeNode>(range);
    root = buildTree(logRange, 0);
  }
  public void add(T item, int score) {
    TreeNode node = leaves.get(score);
    node.bin.put(item);
    while(node != root) {
      TreeNode parent = node.parent;
      if (node == parent.left) {
        parent.counter.getAndIncrement();
      }
      node = parent;
    }
  }
  public T removeMin() {
    TreeNode node = root;
    while(!node.isLeaf()) {
      if (node.counter.boundedGetAndDecrement() > 0 ) {
        node = node.left;
      } else {
        node = node.right;
      }
    }
    return node.bin.get();
  }
}
```

Figure 15.4 The `SimpleTree` bounded-range priority queue.

```
  public class TreeNode {
    Counter counter;
    TreeNode parent, right, left;
    Bin<T> bin;
    public boolean isLeaf() {
      return right == null;
    }
  }
```

Figure 15.5 The `SimpleTree` class: the inner `treeNode` class.

internal nodes that keep track of the number of items in the leaves of the subtree rooted in each node's left (lower score/higher priority) child.

An `add`(x, k) call adds x to the bin at the kth leaf, and increments node counters in leaf-to-root order. The `removeMin()` method traverses the tree in root-to-leaf order. Starting from the root, it finds the leaf with highest priority whose bin is non empty. It examines each node's counter, going right if the counter is zero and decrementing it and going left otherwise (Line 24).

An `add()` traversal by a thread *A* moving up may meet a `removeMin()` traversal by a thread *B* moving down. As in the story of Hansel and Gretel, the descending thread *B* follows the trail of non-zero counters left by the ascending `add()` to locate and remove *A*'s item from its bin. Part (a) of Fig. 15.3 shows an execution of the `SimpleTree`.

One may be concerned about the following "Grimm" scenario. thread *A*, moving up, meets thread *B*, moving down, at a tree node marked by a star, as described in Fig. 15.3. Thread *B* moves down from the starred node to collect *A*'s item at the leaf, while *A* continues up the tree, incrementing counters until it reaches the root. What if another thread, *C*, starts to follow *A*'s path of nonzero counters from the root down to the starred node where *B* encountered *A*? When *C* reaches the starred node, it may be stranded there in the middle of the tree, and seeing no marks it would follow the right child branches to an empty `Bin`, even though there might be other items in the queue.

Fortunately, this scenario cannot happen. As depicted in Parts (b) through (d) of Fig. 15.3, the only way the descending thread *B* could meet the ascending thread *A* at the starred node is if another `add()` call by an earlier thread *D* incremented the same set of counters from the starred node to the root, allowing the descending thread *B* to reach the starred node in the first place. The ascending thread *A*, when incrementing counters from the starred node to the root, is simply completing the increment sequence leading to the item inserted by some other thread *D*. To summarize, if the item returned by some thread in Line 24 is *null*, then the priority queue is indeed empty.

The `SimpleTree` algorithm is not linearizable, since threads may overtake each other, but it is quiescently consistent. The `add()` and `removeMin()` methods are lock-free if the bins and counters are lock-free (the number of steps needed by `add()` is bounded by the tree depth and `removeMin()` can fail to complete only if items are continually being added and removed from the tree.) A typical insertion or deletion takes a number of steps logarithmic in the lowest priority (maximal score) in the range.

15.4 An Unbounded Heap-Based Priority Queue

This section presents a linearizable priority queue that supports priorities from an unbounded range. It uses fine-grained locking for synchronization.

A *heap* is a tree where each tree node contains an item and a score. If *b* is a child node of *a*, then *b*'s priority is no greater than *a*'s priority (i.e., items higher in the tree have lower scores and are more important). The `removeMin()` method removes and returns the root of the tree, and then rebalances the root's subtrees. Here, we consider binary trees, where there are only two subtrees to rebalance.

15.4.1 A Sequential Heap

Figs. 15.6 and 15.7 show a *sequential* heap implementation. An efficient way to represent a binary heap is as an array of nodes, where the tree's root is array entry 1, and the right and left children of array entry i are entries $2 \cdot i$ and $(2 \cdot i) + 1$, respectively. The `next` field is the index of the first unused node.

Each node has an `item` and a `score` field. To add an item, the `add()` method sets `child` to the index of the first empty array slot (Line 13). (For brevity, we omit code to resize a full array.) The method then initializes that node to hold the new item and score (Line 14). At this point, the heap property may be violated, because the new node, which is a leaf of the tree, may have higher priority (smaller score) than an ancestor. To restore the heap property, the new node "percolates up" the tree. We repeatedly compare the new node's priority with its parent's, swapping them if the parent's priority is lower (it has a larger score). When we encounter a parent with a higher priority, or we reach the root, the new node is correctly positioned, and the method returns.

To remove and return the highest-priority item, the `removeMin()` method records the root's item, which is the highest-priority item in the tree. (For brevity, we omit the code to deal with an empty heap.) It then moves a leaf entry up to replace the root (Lines 27–29). If the tree is empty, the method returns the recorded item (Line 30). Otherwise, the heap property may be violated, because

```
1  public class SequentialHeap<T> implements PQueue<T> {
2    private static final int ROOT = 1;
3    int next;
4    HeapNode<T>[] heap;
5    public SequentialHeap(int capacity) {
6      next = ROOT;
7      heap = (HeapNode<T>[]) new HeapNode[capacity + 1];
8      for (int i = 0; i < capacity + 1; i++) {
9        heap[i] = new HeapNode<T>();
10     }
11   }
12   public void add(T item, int score) {
13     int child = next++;
14     heap[child].init(item, score);
15     while (child > ROOT) {
16       int parent = child / 2;
17       int oldChild = child;
18       if (heap[child].score < heap[parent].score) {
19         swap(child, parent);
20         child = parent;
21       } else {
22         return;
23       }
24     }
25   }
```

Figure 15.6 The `SequentialHeap` class: inner node class and `add()` method.

```
26   public T removeMin() {
27     int bottom = --next;
28     T item = heap[ROOT].item;
29     heap[ROOT] = heap[bottom];
30     if (bottom == ROOT) {
31       return item;
32     }
33     int child = 0;
34     int parent = ROOT;
35     while (parent < heap.length / 2) {
36       int left = parent * 2; int right = (parent * 2) + 1;
37       if (left >= next) {
38         return item;
39       } else if (right >= next || heap[left].score < heap[right].score) {
40         child = left;
41       } else {
42         child = right;
43       }
44       if (heap[child].score < heap[parent].score) {
45         swap(parent, child);
46         parent = child;
47       } else {
48         return item;
49       }
50     }
51     return item;
52   }
53   ...
54 }
```

Figure 15.7 The `SequentialHeap` class: the `removeMin()` method.

the leaf node recently promoted to the root may have lower priority than some of its descendants. To restore the heap property, the new root "percolates down" the tree. If both children are empty, we are done (Line 37). If the right child is empty, or if the right child has lower priority than the left, then we examine the left child (Line 39). Otherwise, we examine the right child (Line 41). If the child has higher priority than the parent, then we swap the child and parent, and continue moving down the tree (Line 44). When both children have lower priorities, or we reach a leaf, the displaced node is correctly positioned, and the method returns.

15.4.2 A Concurrent Heap

Bird's-Eye View

The `FineGrainedHeap` class is mostly just a concurrent version of the `SequentialHeap` class. As in the sequential heap, `add()` creates a new leaf node, and percolates it up the tree until the heap property is restored. To allow concurrent calls to proceed in parallel, the `FineGrainedHeap` class percolates items up the tree as a sequence of discrete atomic steps that can be interleaved with other such steps. In the same way, `removeMin()` deletes the root node, moves a leaf node to the root, and percolates that node down the tree until the heap property is restored. The `FineGrainedHeap` class percolates items down the tree as a sequence of discrete atomic steps that can be interleaved with other such steps.

In Detail

Warning: The code presented here does *not* deal with heap overflow (adding an item when the heap is full) or underflow (removing an item when the heap is empty). Dealing with these cases makes the code longer, without adding much of interest.

The class uses a `heapLock` field to make short, atomic modifications to two or more fields (Fig. 15.8).

The `HeapNode` class (Fig. 15.9) provides the following fields. The `lock` field is a lock (Line 21) held for short-lived modifications, and also while the node is being percolated *down* the tree. For brevity, the class exports `lock()` and `unlock()` methods to lock and unlock the node directly. The `tag` field has one of the following states: `EMPTY` means the node is not in use, `AVAILABLE` means the node holds an item and a score, and `BUSY` means that the node is being percolated *up* the tree, and is not yet in its proper position. While the node is `BUSY`, the `owner` field holds the ID of the thread responsible for moving it. For brevity, the class provides an `amOwner` method that returns *true* if and only if the node's tag is `BUSY` and the owner is the current thread.

The asymmetry in synchronization between the `removeMin()` method, which percolates down the tree holding the lock, and the `add()` method (Fig. 15.10), which percolates up the tree with the `tag` field set to `BUSY`, ensures that a `removeMin()` call is not delayed if it encounters a node that is in the middle of being shepherded up the tree by an `add()` call. As a result, an `add()` call must be prepared to have its node swapped out from underneath it. If the node vanishes, the `add()` call simply moves up the tree. It is sure to encounter that node somewhere between its present position and the root.

```
public class FineGrainedHeap<T> implements PQueue<T> {
  private static int ROOT = 1;
  private static int NO_ONE = -1;
  private Lock heapLock;
  int next;
  HeapNode<T>[] heap;
  public FineGrainedHeap(int capacity) {
    heapLock = new ReentrantLock();
    next = ROOT;
    heap = (HeapNode<T>[]) new HeapNode[capacity + 1];
    for (int i = 0; i < capacity + 1; i++) {
      heap[i] = new HeapNode<T>();
    }
  }
```

Figure 15.8 The `FineGrainedHeap` class: fields.

```
  private static enum Status {EMPTY, AVAILABLE, BUSY};
  private static class HeapNode<S> {
    Status tag;
    int score;
    S item;
    int owner;
    Lock lock;
    public void init(S myItem, int myScore) {
      item = myItem;
      score = myScore;
      tag = Status.BUSY;
      owner = ThreadID.get();
    }
    public HeapNode() {
      tag = Status.EMPTY;
      lock = new ReentrantLock();
    }
    public void lock() {lock.lock();}
    ... // other methods omitted
}
```

Figure 15.9 The FineGrainedHeap class: inner HeapNode class.

The removeMin() method (Fig. 15.11) acquires the global heapLock, decrements the next field, returning the index of a leaf node, locks the first unused slot in the array, and releases heapLock (Lines 76–80). It then stores the root's item in a local variable to be returned later as the result of the call (Line 81). It marks the node as EMPTY and unowned, swaps it with the leaf node, and unlocks the (now empty) leaf (Lines 82–84).

At this point, the method has recorded its eventual result in a local variable, moved the leaf to the root, and marked the leaf's former position as EMPTY. It retains the lock on the root. If the heap had only one item, then the leaf and the root are the same, so the method checks whether the root has just been marked as EMPTY. If so, it unlocks the root and returns the item (Lines 85–89).

The new root node is now percolated down the tree until it reaches its proper position, following much the same logic as the sequential implementation. The node being percolated down is locked until it reaches its proper position. When we swap two nodes, we lock them both, and swap their fields. At each step, the method locks the node's right and left children (Line 96). If the left child is empty, we unlock both children and return (Line 98). If the right child is empty, but the left child has higher priority, then we unlock the right child and examine the left (Line 103). Otherwise, we unlock the left child and examine the right (Line 106).

If the child has higher priority, then we swap the parent and child, and unlock the parent (Line 111). Otherwise, we unlock the child and the parent and return.

The concurrent add() method acquires the heapLock, allocates, locks, initializes, and unlocks an empty leaf node (Lines 36–41). This leaf node has tag BUSY, and the owner is the calling thread. It then unlocks the leaf node.

It then proceeds to percolate that node up the tree, using the child variable to keep track of the node. It locks the parent, then the child (all locks are acquired in

```
35  public void add(T item, int score) {
36    heapLock.lock();
37    int child = next++;
38    heap[child].lock();
39    heap[child].init(item, score);
40    heapLock.unlock();
41    heap[child].unlock();
42
43    while (child > ROOT) {
44      int parent = child / 2;
45      heap[parent].lock();
46      heap[child].lock();
47      int oldChild = child;
48      try {
49        if (heap[parent].tag == Status.AVAILABLE && heap[child].amOwner()) {
50          if (heap[child].score < heap[parent].score) {
51            swap(child, parent);
52            child = parent;
53          } else {
54            heap[child].tag = Status.AVAILABLE;
55            heap[child].owner = NO_ONE;
56            return;
57          }
58        } else if (!heap[child].amOwner()) {
59          child = parent;
60        }
61      } finally {
62        heap[oldChild].unlock();
63        heap[parent].unlock();
64      }
65    }
66    if (child == ROOT) {
67      heap[ROOT].lock();
68      if (heap[ROOT].amOwner()) {
69        heap[ROOT].tag = Status.AVAILABLE;
70        heap[child].owner = NO_ONE;
71      }
72      heap[ROOT].unlock();
73    }
74  }
```

Figure 15.10 The `FineGrainedHeap` class: the `add()` method.

ascending order). If the parent is `AVAILABLE` and the child is owned by the caller, then it compares their priorities. If the child has higher priority, then the method swaps their fields, and moves up (Line 50). Otherwise the node is where it belongs, and it is marked `AVAILABLE` and unowned (Line 53). If the child is not owned by the caller, then the node must have been moved up by a concurrent `removeMin()` call so the method simply moves up the tree to search for its node (Line 58).

Fig. 15.12 shows an execution of the `FineGrainedHeap` class. In Part (a) the heap tree structure is depicted, with the priorities written in the nodes and the respective array entries above the nodes. The `next` field is set to 10, the next array

```
  public T removeMin() {
    heapLock.lock();
    int bottom = --next;
    heap[ROOT].lock();
    heap[bottom].lock();
    heapLock.unlock();
    T item = heap[ROOT].item;
    heap[ROOT].tag = Status.EMPTY;
    heap[ROOT].owner = NO_ONE;
    swap(bottom, ROOT);
    heap[bottom].unlock();
    if (heap[ROOT].tag == Status.EMPTY) {
      heap[ROOT].unlock();
      return item;
    }
    heap[ROOT].tag = Status.AVAILABLE;
    int child = 0;
    int parent = ROOT;
    while (parent < heap.length / 2) {
      int left = parent * 2;
      int right = (parent * 2) + 1;
      heap[left].lock();
      heap[right].lock();
      if (heap[left].tag == Status.EMPTY) {
        heap[right].unlock();
        heap[left].unlock();
        break;
      } else if (heap[right].tag == Status.EMPTY || heap[left].score
                                         < heap[right].score) {
        heap[right].unlock();
        child = left;
      } else {
        heap[left].unlock();
        child = right;
      }
      if (heap[child].score < heap[parent].score
       && heap[child].tag != Status.EMPTY) {
        swap(parent, child);
        heap[parent].unlock();
        parent = child;
      } else {
        heap[child].unlock();
        break;
      }
    }
    heap[parent].unlock();
    return item;
    }
    ...
  }
```

Figure 15.11 The FineGrainedHeap class: the removeMin() method.

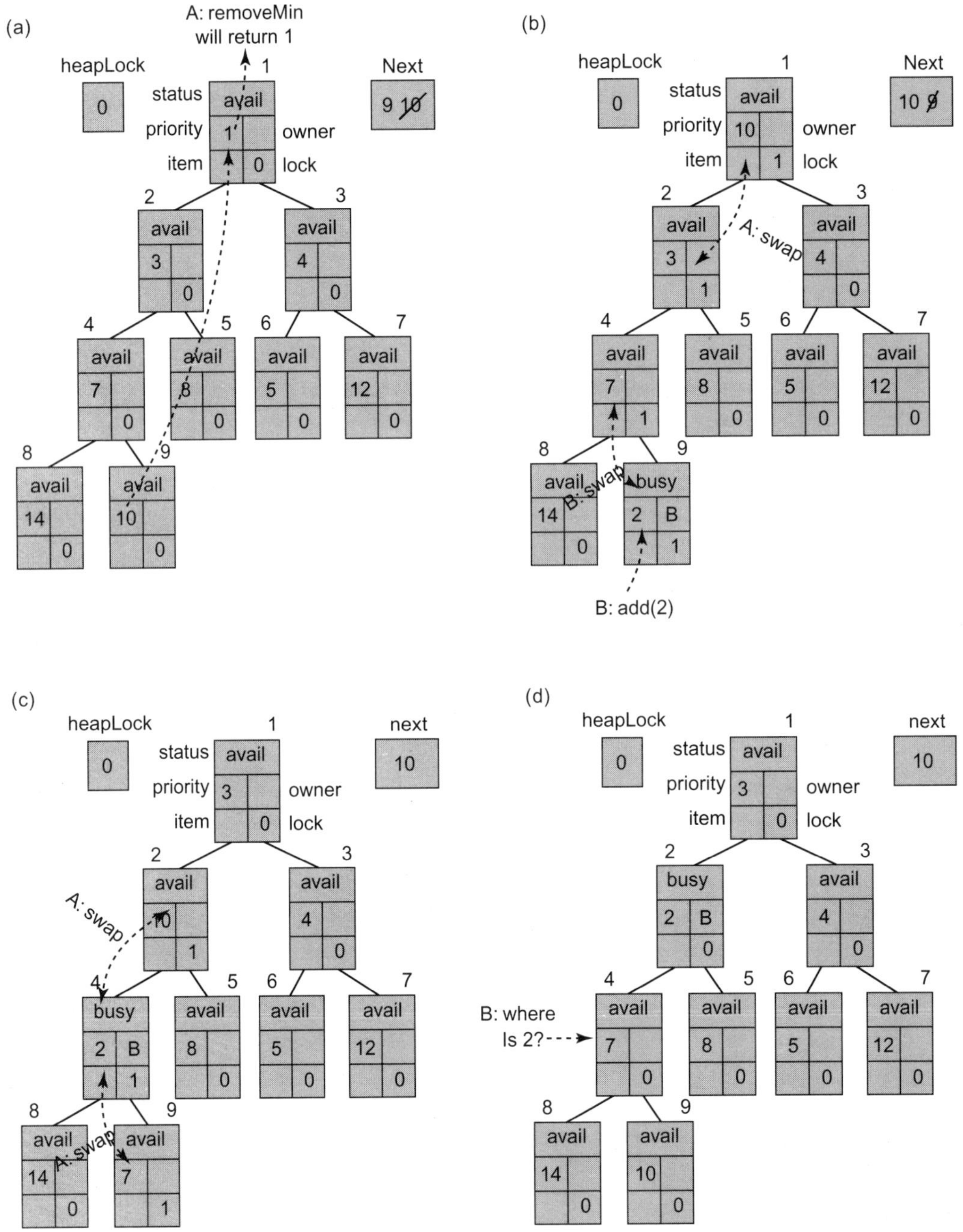

Figure 15.12 The `FineGrainedHeap` class: a heap-based priority queue.

entry into which a new item can be added. As can be seen, thread *A* starts a `removeMin()` method call, collecting the value 1 from the root as the one to be returned, moving the leaf node with score 10 to the root, and setting `next` back to 9. The `removeMin()` method checks whether 10 needs to be percolated down the heap. In Part (b) thread *A* percolates 10 down the heap, while thread *B* adds a new item with score 2 to the heap in the recently emptied array entry 9. The `owner` of the new node is *B*, and *B* starts to percolate 2 up the heap, swapping it with its parent node of score 7. After this swap, it releases the locks on the nodes. At the same time *A* swaps the node with scores 10 and 3. In Part (c), *A*, ignoring the busy state of 2, swaps 10 and 2 and then 10 and 7 using hand-over-hand locking. It has thus swapped 2, which was not locked, from under thread *B*. In Part (d), when *B* moves to the parent node in array entry 4, it finds that the busy node with score 2 it was percolating up has disappeared. However, it continues up the heap and locates the node with 2 as it ascends, moving it to its correct position in the heap.

15.5 A Skiplist-Based Unbounded Priority Queue

One drawback of the `FineGrainedHeap` priority queue algorithm is that the underlying heap structure requires complex, coordinated rebalancing. In this section, we examine an alternative that requires no rebalancing.

Recall from Chapter 14 that a skiplist is a collection of ordered lists. Each list is a sequence of *nodes*, and each node contains an *item*. Each node belongs to a subset of the lists, and nodes in each list are sorted by their hash values. Each list has a *level*, ranging from 0 to a maximum. The bottom-level list contains all the nodes, and each higher-level list is a sublist of the lower-level lists. Each list contains about half the nodes of the next lower-level list. As a result, inserting or removing a node from a skiplist containing k items takes expected time $O(\log k)$.

In Chapter 14 we used skiplists to implement sets of items. Here, we adapt skiplists to implement a priority queue of items tagged with priorities. We describe a `PrioritySkipList` class that provides the basic functionality needed to implement an efficient priority queue. We base the `PrioritySkipList` (Figs. 15.13 and 15.14) class on the `LockFreeSkipList` class of Chapter 14, though we could just as easily have based it on the `LazySkipList` class. Later, we describe a `SkipQueue` wrapper to cover some of the `PrioritySkipList<T>` class's rough edges.

Here is a bird's-eye view of the algorithm. The `PrioritySkipList` class sorts items by priority instead of by hash value, ensuring that high-priority items (the ones we want to remove first) appear at the front of the list. Fig. 15.15 shows such a `PrioritySkipList` structure. Removing the item with highest priority is done *lazily* (See Chapter 9). A node is *logically* removed by marking it as removed, and is later *physically removed* by unlinking it from the list. The `removeMin()` method works in two steps: first, it scans through the bottom-level

```
public final class PrioritySkipList<T> {
  public static final class Node<T> {
    final T item;
    final int score;
    AtomicBoolean marked;
    final AtomicMarkableReference<Node<T>>[] next;
    // sentinel node constructor
    public Node(int myPriority) { ... }
    // ordinary node constructor
    public Node(T x, int myPriority) { ... }
  }
  boolean add(Node node) { ... }
  boolean remove(Node<T> node) { ... }
  public Node<T> findAndMarkMin() {
    Node<T> curr = null;
    curr = head.next[0].getReference();
    while (curr != tail) {
      if (!curr.marked.get()) {
        if (curr.marked.compareAndSet(false, true))
          return curr;
        } else {
          curr = curr.next[0].getReference();
        }
      }
    }
    return null; // no unmarked nodes
  }
```

Figure 15.13 The PrioritySkipList<T> class: inner Node<T> class.

```
public class SkipQueue<T> {
  PrioritySkipList<T> skiplist;
  public SkipQueue() {
    skiplist = new PrioritySkipList<T>();
  }
  public boolean add(T item, int score) {
    Node<T> node = (Node<T>)new Node(item, score);
    return skiplist.add(node);
  }
  public T removeMin() {
    Node<T> node = skiplist.findAndMarkMin();
    if (node != null) {
      skiplist.remove(node);
      return node.item;
    } else{
      return null;
    }
  }
}
```

Figure 15.14 The SkipQueue<T> class.

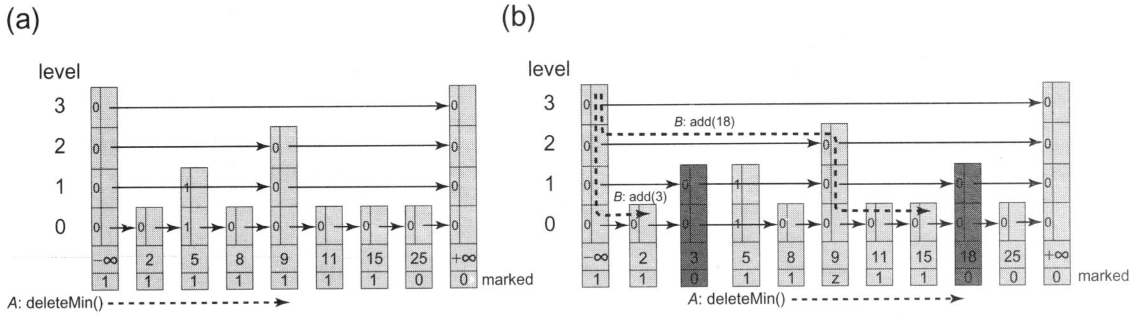

Figure 15.15 The SkipQueue priority queue: an execution that is quiescently consistent but not linearizable. In Part (a) thread *A* starts a removeMin() method call. It traverses the lowest-level list in the PrioritySkipList to find and logically remove the first unmarked node. It traverses over all marked nodes, even ones like the node with score 5 which is in the process of being physically removed from the SkipList. In Part (b) while *A* is visiting the node with score 9, thread *B* adds a node with score 3, and then adds a node with score 18. Thread *A* marks and returns the node with score 18. A linearizable execution could not return an item with score 18 before the item with score 3 is returned.

list for the first unmarked node. When it finds one, it tries to mark it. If it fails, it continues scanning down the list, but if it succeeds, then removeMin() calls the PrioritySkipList class's logarithmic-time remove() method to physically remove the marked node.

We now turn our attention to the algorithm details. Fig. 15.13 shows an outline of the the PrioritySkipList class, a modified version of the LockFreeSkipList class of Chapter 14. It is convenient to have the add() and remove() calls take skiplist nodes instead of items as arguments and results. These methods are straightforward adaptations of the corresponding LockFreeSkipList methods, and are left as exercises. This class's nodes differ from LockFreeSkipList nodes in two fields: an integer score field (Line 4), and an AtomicBoolean marked field used for logical deletion from the priority queue (not from the skiplist) (Line 5). The findAndMarkMin() method scans the lowest-level list until it finds a node whose marked field is *false*, and then atomically tries to set that field to *true* (Line 19). If it fails, it tries again. When it succeeds, it returns the newly marked node to the caller (Line 20).

Fig. 15.14 shows the SkipQueue<T> class. This class is just a wrapper for a PrioritySkipList<T>. The add(x, p) method adds item x with score p by creating a node to hold both values, and passing that node to the PrioritySkipList class's add() method. The removeMin() method calls the PrioritySkipList class's findAndMarkMin() method to mark a node as logically deleted, and then calls remove() to physically remove that node.

The SkipQueue class is quiescently consistent: if an item x was present before the start of a removeMin() call, then the item returned will have a score less than or equal to that of x. This class is not linearizable: a thread might add a higher priority (lower score) item and then a lower priority item, and the traversing thread might find and return the later inserted lower priority item, violating linearizability. This behavior is quiescently consistent, however, because one can reorder add() calls concurrent with any removeMin() to be consistent with a sequential priority queue.

The SkipQueue class is lock-free. A thread traversing the lowest level of the SkipList might always be beaten to the next logically undeleted node by another call, but it can fail repeatedly only if other threads repeatedly succeed.

In general, the quiescently consistent SkipQueue tends to outperform the linearizable heap-based queue. If there are n threads, then the first logically undeleted node is always among the first n nodes in the bottom-level list. Once a node has been logically deleted, then it will be physically deleted in worst-case $O(\log k)$ steps, where k is the size of the list. In practice, a node will probably be deleted much more quickly, since that node is likely to be close to the start of the list.

There are, however, several sources of contention in the algorithm that affect its performance and require the use of backoff and tuning. Contention could occur if several threads concurrently try to mark a node, where the losers proceed together to try to mark the next node, and so on. Contention can also arise when physically removing an item from the skiplist. All nodes to be removed are likely to be neighbors at the start of the skiplist, so chances are high that they share predecessors, which could cause repeated compareAndSet() failures when attempting to snip out references to the nodes.

15.6 Chapter Notes

The FineGrainedHeap priority queue is by Galen Hunt, Maged Michael, Srinivasan Parthasarathy, and Michael Scott [74]. The SimpleLinear and SimpleTree priority queues are credited to Nir Shavit and Asaph Zemach [143]. The SkipQueue is by Itai Lotan and Nir Shavit [107] who also present a linearizable version of the algorithm.

15.7 Exercises

Exercise 173. Give an example of a quiescently consistent priority queue execution that is not linearizable.

Exercise 174. Implement a quiescently consistent Counter with a lock-free implementation of the boundedGetAndIncrement() and boundedGetAndDecrement() methods using a counting network or diffracting tree.

Exercise 175. In the SimpleTree algorithm, what would happen if the boundedGetAndDecrement() method were replaced with a regular getAndDecrement()?

Exercise 176. Devise a SimpleTree algorithm with bounded capacity using boundedGetAndIncrement() methods in treeNode counters.

Exercise 177. In the `SimpleTree` class, what would happen if `add()`, after placing an item in the appropriate `Bin`, incremented counters in the same *top-down* manner as in the `removeMin()` method? Give a detailed example.

Exercise 178. Prove that the `SimpleTree` is a quiescently consistent priority queue implementation.

Exercise 179. Modify `FineGrainedHeap` to allocate new heap nodes dynamically. What are the performance limitations of this approach?

Exercise 180. Fig. 15.16 shows a *bit-reversed* counter. We could use the bit-reversed counter to manage the `next` field of the `FineGrainedHeap` class. Prove

```
public class BitReversedCounter {
  int counter, reverse, highBit;
  BitReversedCounter(int initialValue) {
    counter = initialValue;
    reverse = 0;
    highBit = -1;
  }
  public int reverseIncrement() {
    if (counter++ == 0) {
      reverse = highBit = 1;
      return reverse;
    }
    int bit = highBit >> 1;
    while (bit != 0) {
      reverse ^= bit;
      if ((reverse & bit) != 0) break;
      bit >>= 1;
    }
    if (bit == 0)
      reverse = highBit <<= 1;
    return reverse;
  }
  public int reverseDecrement() {
    counter--;
    int bit = highBit >> 1;
    while (bit != 0) {
      reverse ^= bit;
      if ((reverse & bit) == 0) {
        break;
      }
      bit >>= 1;
    }
    if (bit == 0) {
      reverse = counter;
      highBit >>= 1;
    }
    return reverse;
  }
}
```

Figure 15.16 A bit-reversed counter.

the following: for any two consecutive insertions, the two paths from the leaves to the root have no common nodes other than the root. Why is this a useful property for the FineGrainedHeap?

Exercise 181. Provide the code for the PrioritySkipList class's add() and remove() methods.

Exercise 182. The PrioritySkipList class used in this chapter is based on the LockFreeSkipList class. Write another PrioritySkipList class based on the LazySkipList class.

Exercise 183. Describe a scenario in the SkipQueue implementation in which contention would arise from multiple concurrent removeMin() method calls.

Exercise 184. The SkipQueue class is quiescently consistent but not linearizable. Here is one way to make this class linearizable by adding a simple time-stamping mechanism. After a node is completely inserted into the SkipQueue, it acquires a timestamp. A thread performing a removeMin() notes the time at which it starts its traversal of the lower level of the SkipQueue, and only considers nodes whose timestamp is earlier than the time at which it started its traversal, effectively ignoring nodes inserted during its traversal. Implement this class and justify why it works.

16 Futures, Scheduling, and Work Distribution

16.1 Introduction

In this chapter we show how to decompose certain kinds of problems into components that can be executed in parallel. Some applications break down naturally into parallel threads. For example, when a request arrives at a web server, the server can just create a thread (or assign an existing thread) to handle the request. Applications that can be structured as producers and consumers also tend to be easily parallelizable. In this chapter, however, we look at applications that have inherent parallelism, but where it is not obvious how to take advantage of it.

Let us start by thinking about how to multiply two matrices in parallel. Recall that if a_{ij} is the value at position (i, j) of matrix A, then the product C of two $n \times n$ matrices A and B is given by:

$$c_{ij} = \sum_{k=0}^{n-1} a_{ik} \cdot b_{kj}$$

As a first step, we could put one thread in charge of computing each c_{ij}. Fig. 16.1 shows a matrix multiplication program that creates an $n \times n$ array of `Worker` threads (Fig. 16.2), where the worker thread in position (i, j) computes c_{ij}. The program starts each task, and waits for them all to finish.[1]

In principle, this might seem like an ideal design. The program is highly parallel, and the threads do not even have to synchronize. In practice, however, while this design might perform well for small matrices, it would perform very poorly for matrices large enough to be interesting. Here is why: threads require memory for stacks and other bookkeeping information. Creating, scheduling, and destroying threads takes a substantial amount of computation. Creating lots of short-lived threads is an inefficient way to organize a multi-threaded computation.

1 In real code, you should check that all the dimensions agree. Here we omit most safety checks for brevity.

```
class MMThread {
  double[][] a, b, c;
  int n;
  public MMThread(double[][] myA, double[][] myB) {
    n = myA.length;
    a = myA;
    b = myB;
    c = new double[n][n];
  }
  void multiply() {
    Worker[][] worker = new Worker[n][n];
    for (int row = 0; row < n; row++)
      for (int col = 0; col < n; col++)
        worker[row][col] = new Worker(row,col);
    for (int row = 0; row < n; row++)
      for (int col = 0; col < n; col++)
        worker[row][col].start();
    for (int row = 0; row < n; row++)
      for (int col = 0; col < n; col++)
        worker[row][col].join();
  }
```

Figure 16.1 The `MMThread` task: matrix multiplication using threads.

```
  class Worker extends Thread {
    int row, col;
    Worker(int myRow, int myCol) {
      row = myRow; col = myCol;
    }
    public void run() {
      double dotProduct = 0.0;
      for (int i = 0; i < n; i++)
        dotProduct += a[row][i] * b[i][col];
      c[row][col] = dotProduct;
    }
  }
}
```

Figure 16.2 The `MMThread` task: inner `Worker` thread class.

A more effective way to organize such a program is to create a *pool* of long-lived threads. Each thread in the pool repeatedly waits until it is assigned a *task*, a short-lived unit of computation. When a thread is assigned a task, it executes that task, and then rejoins the pool to await its next assignment. Thread pools can be platform-dependent: it makes sense for large-scale multiprocessors to provide large pools, and vice versa. Thread pools avoid the cost of creating and destroying threads in response to short-lived fluctuations in demand.

In addition to performance benefits, thread pools have another equally important, but less obvious advantage: they insulate the application programmer from platform-specific details such as the number of concurrent threads that can be scheduled efficiently. Thread pools make it possible to write a single program that runs equally well on a uniprocessor, a small-scale multiprocessor, and a large-scale multiprocessor. They provide a simple interface that hides complex, platform-dependent engineering trade-offs.

In Java, a thread pool is called an *executor service* (interface java.util.ExecutorService). It provides the ability to submit a task, the ability to wait for a set of submitted tasks to complete, and the ability to cancel uncompleted tasks. A task that does not return a result is usually represented as a `Runnable` object, where the work is performed by a `run()` method that takes no arguments and returns no results. A task that returns a value of type `T` is usually represented as a `Callable<T>` object, where the result is returned by a `call()` with the `T` method that takes no arguments.

When a `Callable<T>` object is submitted to an executor service, the service returns an object implementing the `Future<T>` interface. A `Future<T>` is a *promise* to deliver the result of an asynchronous computation, when it is ready. It provides a `get()` method that returns the result, blocking if necessary until the result is ready. (It also provides methods for canceling uncompleted computations, and for testing whether the computation is complete.) Submitting a `Runnable` task also returns a future. Unlike the future returned for a `Callable<T>` object, this future does not return a value, but the caller can use that future's `get()` method to block until the computation finishes. A future that does not return an interesting value is declared to have class `Future<?>`.

It is important to understand that creating a future does not guarantee that any computations actually happen in parallel. Instead, these methods are *advisory*: they tell an underlying executor service that it may execute these methods in parallel.

We now consider how to implement parallel matrix operations using an executor service. Fig. 16.3 shows a `Matrix` class that provides `put()` and `get()` methods to access matrix elements, along with a constant-time `split()` method that splits an n-by-n matrix into four $(n/2)$-by-$(n/2)$ submatrices. In Java terminology, the four submatrices are *backed* by the original matrix, meaning that changes to the submatrices are reflected in the original, and vice versa.

Our job is to devise a `MatrixTask` class that provides parallel methods to add and multiply matrices. This class has one static field, an executor service called `exec`, and two static methods to add and multiply matrices.

For simplicity, we consider matrices whose dimension n is a power of 2. Any such matrix can be decomposed into four submatrices:

$$A = \begin{pmatrix} A_{00} & A_{01} \\ A_{10} & A_{11} \end{pmatrix}$$

Matrix addition $C = A + B$ can be decomposed as follows:

$$\begin{pmatrix} C_{00} & C_{01} \\ C_{10} & C_{11} \end{pmatrix} = \begin{pmatrix} A_{00} & A_{01} \\ A_{10} & A_{11} \end{pmatrix} + \begin{pmatrix} B_{00} & B_{01} \\ B_{10} & B_{11} \end{pmatrix}$$

$$= \begin{pmatrix} A_{00} + B_{00} & A_{01} + B_{01} \\ A_{10} + B_{10} & A_{11} + B_{11} \end{pmatrix}$$

```
public class Matrix {
  int dim;
  double[][] data;
  int rowDisplace, colDisplace;
  public Matrix(int d) {
    dim = d;
    rowDisplace = colDisplace = 0;
    data = new double[d][d];
  }
  private Matrix(double[][] matrix, int x, int y, int d) {
    data = matrix;
    rowDisplace = x;
    colDisplace = y;
    dim = d;
  }
  public double get(int row, int col) {
    return data[row+rowDisplace][col+colDisplace];
  }
  public void set(int row, int col, double value) {
    data[row+rowDisplace][col+colDisplace] = value;
  }
  public int getDim() {
    return dim;
  }
  Matrix[][] split() {
    Matrix[][] result = new Matrix[2][2];
    int newDim = dim / 2;
    result[0][0] =
      new Matrix(data, rowDisplace, colDisplace, newDim);
    result[0][1] =
      new Matrix(data, rowDisplace, colDisplace + newDim, newDim);
    result[1][0] =
      new Matrix(data, rowDisplace + newDim, colDisplace, newDim);
    result[1][1] =
      new Matrix(data, rowDisplace + newDim, colDisplace + newDim, newDim);
    return result;
  }
}
```

Figure 16.3 The `Matrix` class.

These four sums can be done in parallel.

The code for multithreaded matrix addition appears in Fig. 16.4. The `AddTask` class has three fields, initialized by the constructor: `a` and `b` are the matrices to be summed, and `c` is the result, which is updated in place. Each task does the following. At the bottom of the recursion, it simply adds the two scalar values (Line 20 of Fig. 16.4).[2] Otherwise, it splits each of its arguments into four sub-matrices

2 In practice, it is usually more efficient to stop the recursion well before reaching a matrix size of one. The best size will be platform-dependent.

```
1  public class MatrixTask {
2    static ExecutorService exec = Executors.newCachedThreadPool();
3    ...
4    static Matrix add(Matrix a, Matrix b) throws ExecutionException {
5      int n = a.getDim();
6      Matrix c = new Matrix(n);
7      Future<?> future = exec.submit(new AddTask(a, b, c));
8      future.get();
9      return c;
10   }
11   static class AddTask implements Runnable {
12     Matrix a, b, c;
13     public AddTask(Matrix myA, Matrix myB, Matrix myC) {
14       a = myA; b = myB; c = myC;
15     }
16     public void run() {
17       try {
18         int n = a.getDim();
19         if (n == 1) {
20           c.set(0, 0, a.get(0,0) + b.get(0,0));
21         } else {
22           Matrix[][] aa = a.split(), bb = b.split(), cc = c.split();
23           Future<?>[][] future = (Future<?>[][]) new Future[2][2];
24           for (int i = 0; i < 2; i++)
25             for (int j = 0; j < 2; j++)
26               future[i][j] =
27                 exec.submit(new AddTask(aa[i][j], bb[i][j], cc[i][j]));
28           for (int i = 0; i < 2; i++)
29             for (int j = 0; j < 2; j++)
30               future[i][j].get();
31         }
32       } catch (Exception ex) {
33         ex.printStackTrace();
34       }
35     }
36   }
37 }
```

Figure 16.4 The MatrixTask class: parallel matrix addition.

(Line 22), and launches a new task for each sub-matrix (Lines 24–27). Then, it waits until all futures can be evaluated, meaning that the sub-computations have finished (Lines 28–30). At that point, the task simply returns, the result of the computation having been stored in the result matrix. Matrix multiplication $C = A \cdot B$ can be decomposed as follows:

$$\begin{pmatrix} C_{00} & C_{01} \\ C_{10} & C_{11} \end{pmatrix} = \begin{pmatrix} A_{00} & A_{01} \\ A_{10} & A_{11} \end{pmatrix} \cdot \begin{pmatrix} B_{00} & B_{01} \\ B_{10} & B_{11} \end{pmatrix}$$

$$= \begin{pmatrix} A_{00} \cdot B_{00} + A_{01} \cdot B_{10} & A_{00} \cdot B_{01} + A_{01} \cdot B_{11} \\ A_{10} \cdot B_{00} + A_{11} \cdot B_{10} & A_{10} \cdot B_{01} + A_{11} \cdot B_{11} \end{pmatrix}$$

The eight product terms can be computed in parallel, and when those computations are done, the four sums can then be computed in parallel.

Fig. 16.5 shows the code for the parallel matrix multiplication task. Matrix multiplication is structured in a similar way to addition. The `MulTask` class creates two scratch arrays to hold the matrix product terms (Line 42). It splits all five matrices (Line 50), submits tasks to compute the eight product terms in parallel (Line 56), and waits for them to complete (Line 60). Once they are complete, the thread submits tasks to compute the four sums in parallel (Line 64), and waits for them to complete (Line 65).

The matrix example uses futures only to signal when a task is complete. Futures can also be used to pass values from completed tasks. To illustrate this use of futures, we consider how to decompose the well-known Fibonacci

```
38    static class MulTask implements Runnable {
39      Matrix a, b, c, lhs, rhs;
40      public MulTask(Matrix myA, Matrix myB, Matrix myC) {
41        a   = myA; b = myB; c = myC;
42        lhs = new Matrix(a.getDim());
43        rhs = new Matrix(a.getDim());
44      }
45      public void run() {
46        try {
47          if (a.getDim() == 1) {
48            c.set(0, 0, a.get(0,0) * b.get(0,0));
49          } else {
50            Matrix[][] aa = a.split(), bb = b.split(), cc = c.split();
51            Matrix[][] ll = lhs.split(), rr = rhs.split();
52            Future<?>[][][] future = (Future<?>[][][]) new Future[2][2][2];
53            for (int i = 0; i < 2; i++)
54              for (int j = 0; j < 2; j++) {
55                future[i][j][0] =
56                  exec.submit(new MulTask(aa[i][0], bb[0][i], ll[i][j]));
57                future[i][j][1] =
58                  exec.submit(new MulTask(aa[1][i], bb[i][1], rr[i][j]));
59              }
60            for (int i = 0; i < 2; i++)
61              for (int j = 0; j < 2; j++)
62                for (int k = 0; k < 2; k++)
63                  future[i][j][k].get();
64            Future<?> done = exec.submit(new AddTask(lhs, rhs, c));
65            done.get();
66          }
67        } catch (Exception ex) {
68          ex.printStackTrace();
69        }
70      }
71    }
72    ...
73  }
```

Figure 16.5 The `MatrixTask` class: parallel matrix multiplication.

```java
class FibTask implements Callable<Integer> {
  static ExecutorService exec = Executors.newCachedThreadPool();
  int arg;
  public FibTask(int n) {
    arg = n;
  }
  public Integer call() {
    if (arg >= 2) {
      Future<Integer> left = exec.submit(new FibTask(arg-1));
      Future<Integer> right = exec.submit(new FibTask(arg-2));
      return left.get() + right.get();
    } else {
      return 1;
    }
  }
}
```

Figure 16.6 The FibTask class: a Fibonacci task with futures.

function into a multithreaded program. Recall that the Fibonacci sequence is defined as follows:

$$F(n) = \begin{cases} 1 & \text{if } n = 0, \\ 1 & \text{if } n = 1, \\ F(n-1) + F(n-2) & \text{if } n > 1, \end{cases}$$

Fig. 16.6 shows one way to compute Fibonacci numbers in parallel. This implementation is very inefficient, but we use it here to illustrate multithreaded dependencies. The `call()` method creates two futures, one that computes $F(n-2)$ and another that computes $F(n-1)$, and then sums them. On a multiprocessor, time spent blocking on the future for $F(n-1)$ can be used to compute $F(n-2)$.

16.2 Analyzing Parallelism

Think of a multithreaded computation as a *directed acyclic graph* (DAG), where each node represents a task, and each directed edge links a *predecessor* task to a *successor* task, where the successor depends on the predecessor's result. For example, a conventional thread is just a chain of nodes where each node depends on its predecessor. By contrast, a node that creates a future has two successors: one node is its successor in the same thread, and the other is the first node in the future's computation. There is also an edge in the other direction, from child to parent, that occurs when a thread that has created a future calls that future's `get()` method, waiting for the child computation to complete. Fig. 16.7 shows the DAG corresponding to a short Fibonacci execution.

Some computations are inherently more parallel than others. Let us make this notion precise. Assume that all individual computation steps take the same amount of time, which constitutes our basic measuring unit. Let T_P be

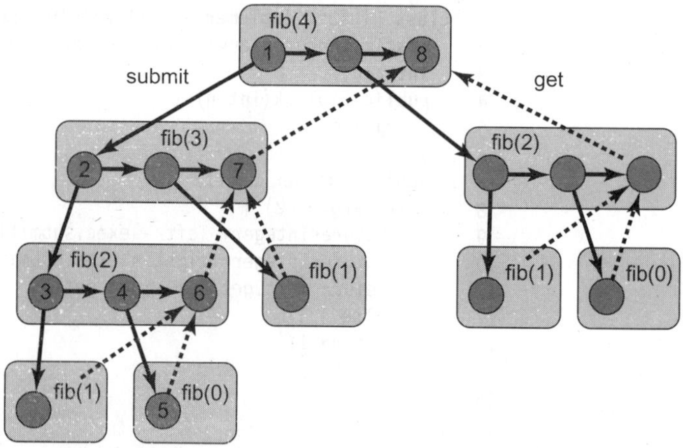

Figure 16.7 The DAG created by a multithreaded Fibonacci execution. The caller creates a FibTask(4) task, which in turn creates FibTask(3) and FibTask(2) tasks. The round nodes represent computation steps and the arrows between the nodes represent dependencies. For example, there are arrows pointing from the first two nodes in FibTask(4) to the first nodes in FibTask(3) and FibTask(2) respectively, representing `submit()` calls, and arrows from the last nodes in FibTask(3) and FibTask(2) to the last node in FibTask(4) representing `get()` calls. The computation's critical path has length 8 and is marked by numbered nodes.

the minimum time (measured in computation steps) needed to execute a multithreaded program on a system of P dedicated processors. T_P is thus the program's *latency*, the time it would take it to run from start to finish, as measured by an outside observer. We emphasize that T_P is an idealized measure: it may not always be possible for every processor to find steps to execute, and actual computation time may be limited by other concerns, such as memory usage. Nevertheless, T_P is clearly a lower bound on how much parallelism one can extract from a multithreaded computation.

Some values of T are important enough that they have special names. T_1, the number of steps needed to execute the program on a single processor, is called the computation's *work*. Work is also the total number of steps in the entire computation. In one time step (of the outside observer), P processors can execute at most P computation steps, so

$$T_P \geqslant T_1/P.$$

The other extreme is also of special importance: T_∞, the number of steps to execute the program on an unlimited number of processors, is called the *critical-path length*. Because finite resources cannot do better than infinite resources,

$$T_P \geqslant T_\infty.$$

The *speedup* on P processors is the ratio:

$$T_1/T_P$$

We say a computation has *linear speedup* if $T_1/T_P = \Theta(P)$. Finally, a computation's *parallelism* is the maximum possible speedup: T_1/T_∞. A computation's parallelism is also the *average* amount of work available at each step along the critical path, and so provides a good estimate of the number of processors one should devote to a computation. In particular, it makes little sense to use substantially more than that number of processors.

To illustrate these concepts, we now revisit the concurrent matrix add and multiply implementations introduced in Section 16.1.

Let $A_P(n)$ be the number of steps needed to add two $n \times n$ matrices on P processors. Recall that matrix addition requires four half-size matrix additions, plus a constant amount of work to split the matrices. The work $A_1(n)$ is given by the recurrence:

$$\begin{aligned} A_1(n) &= 4A_1(n/2) + \Theta(1) \\ &= \Theta(n^2). \end{aligned}$$

This program has the same work as the conventional doubly-nested loop implementation.

Because the half-size additions can be done in parallel, the critical path length is given by the following formula.

$$\begin{aligned} A_\infty(n) &= A_\infty(n/2) + \Theta(1) \\ &= \Theta(\log n) \end{aligned}$$

Let $M_P(n)$ be the number of steps needed to multiply two $n \times n$ matrices on P processors. Recall that matrix multiplication requires eight half-size matrix multiplications and four matrix additions. The work $M_1(n)$ is given by the recurrence:

$$\begin{aligned} M_1(n) &= 8M_1(n/2) + 4A_1(n) \\ M_1(n) &= 8M_1(n/2) + \Theta(n^2) \\ &= \Theta(n^3). \end{aligned}$$

This work is also the same as the conventional triply-nested loop implementation. The half-size multiplications can be done in parallel, and so can the additions, but the additions must wait for the multiplications to complete. The critical path length is given by the following formula:

$$\begin{aligned} M_\infty(n) &= M_\infty(n/2) + A_\infty(n) \\ &= M_\infty(n/2) + \Theta(\log n) \\ &= \Theta(log^2 n) \end{aligned}$$

The parallelism for matrix multiplication is given by:

$$M_1(n)/M_\infty(n) = \Theta(n^3/\log^2 n),$$

which is pretty high. For example, suppose we want to multiply two 1000-by-1000 matrices. Here, $n^3 = 10^9$, and $\log n = \log 1000 \approx 10$ (logs are base two), so the parallelism is approximately $10^9/10^2 = 10^7$. Roughly speaking, this instance of matrix multiplication could, in principle, keep roughly a million processors busy well beyond the powers of any multiprocessor we are likely to see in the immediate future.

We should understand that the parallelism in the computation given here is a highly idealized upper bound on the performance of any multithreaded matrix multiplication program. For example, when there are idle threads, it may not be easy to assign those threads to idle processors. Moreover, a program that displays less parallelism but consumes less memory may perform better because it encounters fewer page faults. The actual performance of a multithreaded computation remains a complex engineering problem, but the kind of analysis presented in this chapter is an indispensable first step in understanding the degree to which a problem can be solved in parallel.

16.3 Realistic Multiprocessor Scheduling

Our analysis so far has been based on the assumption that each multithreaded program has P dedicated processors. This assumption, unfortunately, is not realistic. Multiprocessors typically run a mix of jobs, where jobs come and go dynamically. One might start, say, a matrix multiplication application on P processors. At some point, the operating system may decide to download a new software upgrade, preempting one processor, and the application then runs on $P - 1$ processors. The upgrade program pauses waiting for a disk read or write to complete, and in the interim the matrix application has P processors again.

Modern operating systems provide user-level *threads* that encompass a program counter and a stack. (A thread that includes its own address space is often called a *process*.) The operating system kernel includes a *scheduler* that runs threads on physical processors. The application, however, typically has no control over the mapping between threads and processors, and so cannot control when threads are scheduled.

As we have seen, one way to bridge the gap between user-level threads and operating system-level processors is to provide the software developer with a three-level model. At the top level, multithreaded programs (such as matrix multiplication) decompose an application into a dynamically-varying number of short-lived *tasks*. At the middle level, a user-level *scheduler* maps these tasks to a fixed number of *threads*. At the bottom level, the *kernel* maps these threads onto hardware *processors*, whose availability may vary dynamically. This last level of mapping is not under the application's control: applications cannot tell the kernel how to schedule threads (especially because commercially available operating systems kernels are hidden from users).

Assume for simplicity that the kernel works in discrete steps: at step i, the kernel chooses an arbitrary subset of $0 \leqslant p_i \leqslant P$ user-level threads to run for one step. The *processor average* P_A over T steps is defined to be:

$$P_A = \frac{1}{T}\sum_{i=0}^{T-1} p_i. \tag{16.3.1}$$

Instead of designing a user-level schedule to achieve a P-fold speedup, we can try to achieve a P_A-fold speedup. A schedule is *greedy* if the number of program steps executed at each time step is the minimum of p_i, the number of available processors, and the number of ready nodes (ones whose associated step is ready to be executed) in the program DAG. In other words, it executes as many of the ready nodes as possible, given the number of available processors.

***Theorem* 16.3.1.** Consider a multithreaded program with work T_1, critical-path length T_∞, and P user-level threads. We claim that any greedy execution has length T which is at most

$$\frac{T_1}{P_A} + \frac{T_\infty(P-1)}{P_A}.$$

Proof: Equation 16.3.1 implies that:

$$T = \frac{1}{P_A}\sum_{i=0}^{T-1} p_i.$$

We bound T by bounding the sum of the p_i. At each kernel-level step i, let us imagine getting a token for each thread that was assigned a processor. We can place these tokens in one of two buckets. For each user-level thread that executes a node at step i, we place a token in a *work bucket*, and for each thread that remains idle at that step (that is, it was assigned to a processor but was not ready to execute because the node associated with its next step had dependencies that force it to wait for some other threads), we place a token in an *idle bucket*. After the last step, the work bucket contains T_1 tokens, one for each node of the computation DAG. How many tokens does the idle bucket contain?

We define an *idle step* as one in which some thread places a token in the idle bucket. Because the application is still running, at least one node is ready for execution in each step. Because the scheduler is greedy, at least one node will be executed, so at least one processor is not idle. Thus, of the p_i threads scheduled at step i, at most $p_i - 1 \leqslant P - 1$ can be idle.

How many idle steps could there be? Let G_i be a sub-DAG of the computation consisting of the nodes that have not been executed at the end of step i. Every node that does not have incoming edges (apart from its predecessor in program order) in G_{i-1} (such as the last node of FibTask(2) at the end of step 6) was ready at the start of step i. There must be fewer than p_i such nodes, because otherwise the greedy schedule could execute p_i of them, and the step i would not be idle. Thus, the scheduler must have executed this step. It follows that the longest directed path in G_i is one shorter than the longest directed path in G_{i-1}. The longest directed path before step 0 is T_∞, so the greedy schedule can have at most T_∞ idle steps. Combining these observations we deduce that at most T_∞ idle steps are executed with at most $(P-1)$ tokens added in each, so the idle bucket contains at most $T_\infty(P-1)$ tokens.

The total number of tokens in both buckets is therefore

$$\sum_{i=0}^{T-1} p_i \leqslant T_1 + T_\infty(P-1),$$

yielding the desired bound. □

It turns out that this bound is within a factor of two of optimal. Actually, achieving an optimal schedule is NP-complete, so greedy schedules are a simple and practical way to achieve performance that is reasonably close to optimal.

16.4 Work Distribution

We now understand that the key to achieving a good speedup is to keep user-level threads supplied with tasks, so that the resulting schedule is as greedy as possible. Multithreaded computations, however, create and destroy tasks dynamically, sometimes in unpredictable ways. A *work distribution* algorithm is needed to assign ready tasks to idle threads as efficiently as possible.

One simple approach to work distribution is *work dealing*: an overloaded thread tries to offload tasks to other, less heavily loaded threads. This approach may seem sensible, but it has a basic flaw: if most threads are overloaded, then they waste effort in a futile attempt to exchange tasks. Instead, we first consider *work stealing*, in which a thread that runs out of work tries to "steal" work from others. An advantage of work stealing is that if all threads are already busy, then they do not waste time trying to offload work on one another.

16.4.1 Work Stealing

Each thread keeps a pool of tasks waiting to be executed in the form of a *double-ended queue* (`DEQueue`), providing `pushBottom()`, `popBottom()`, and `popTop()` methods (there is no need for a `pushTop()` method). When a thread creates a new task, it calls `pushBottom()` to push that task onto its `DEQueue`. When a thread needs a task to work on, it calls `popBottom()` to remove a task from its own `DEQueue`. If the thread discovers its queue is empty, then it becomes a *thief*: it chooses a *victim* thread at random, and calls that thread's `DEQueue`'s `popTop()` method to "steal" a task for itself.

```
1  public class WorkStealingThread {
2    DEQueue[] queue;
3    Random random;
4    public WorkStealingThread(DEQueue[] myQueue) {
5      queue = myQueue;
6      random = new Random();
7    }
8    public void run() {
9      int me = ThreadID.get();
10     Runnable task = queue[me].popBottom();
11     while (true) {
12       while (task != null) {
13         task.run();
14         task = queue[me].popBottom();
15       }
16       while (task == null) {
17         Thread.yield();
18         int victim = random.nextInt(queue.length);
19         if (!queue[victim].isEmpty()) {
20           task = queue[victim].popTop();
21         }
22       }
23     }
24   }
25 }
```

Figure 16.8 The `WorkStealingThread` class: a simplified work stealing executer pool.

In Section 16.5 we devise an efficient linearizable implementation of a `DEQueue`. Fig. 16.8 shows one possible way to implement a thread used by a work-stealing executor service. The threads share an array of `DEQueues` (Line 2), one for each thread. Each thread repeatedly removes a task from its own `DEQueue` and runs it (Lines 12–15). If it runs out, then it repeatedly chooses a victim thread at random and tries to steal a task from the top of the victim's `DEQueue` (Lines 16–22). To avoid code clutter, we ignore the possibility that stealing may trigger an exception.

This simplified executer pool may keep trying to steal forever, long after all work in all queues has been completed. To prevent threads from endlessly searching for nonexistent work, we can use a termination-detecting barrier of the kind described in Chapter 17, Section 17.6.

16.4.2 Yielding and Multiprogramming

As noted earlier, multiprocessors provide a three-level model of computation: short-lived *tasks* are executed by system-level *threads*, which are scheduled by the operating system on a fixed number of *processors*. A *multiprogrammed environment* is one in which there are more threads than processors, implying that not all threads can run at the same time, and that any thread can be preemptively suspended at any time. To guarantee progress, we must ensure that threads that have work to do are not unreasonably delayed by (*thief*) threads which are idle except for task-stealing. To prevent this situation, we have each thief call `Thread.yield()` immediately before trying to steal a task (Line 17 in Fig. 16.8). This call yields the thief's processor to another thread, allowing descheduled threads to regain a processor and make progress. (We note that calling `yield()` has no effect if there are no descheduled threads capable of running.)

16.5 Work-Stealing Dequeues

Here is how to implement a work-stealing `DEQueue`. Ideally, a work-stealing algorithm should provide a linearizable implementation whose pop methods always return a task if one is available. In practice, however, we can settle for something weaker, allowing a `popTop()` call to return *null* if it conflicts with a concurrent `popTop()` call. Though we could have the unsuccessful thief simply try again, it makes more sense in this context to have a thread retry the `popTop()` operation on a different, randomly chosen `DEQueue` each time. To support such a retry, a `popTop()` call may return *null* if it conflicts with a concurrent `popTop()` call.

We now describe two implementations of the work-stealing `DEQueue`. The first is simpler, because it has bounded capacity. The second is somewhat more complex, but virtually unbounded in its capacity; that is, it does not suffer from the possibility of overflow.

16.5.1 A Bounded Work-Stealing Dequeue

For the executer pool `DEQueue`, the common case is for a thread to push and pop a task from its own queue, calling `pushBottom()` and `popBottom()`. The uncommon case is to steal a task from another thread's `DEQueue` by calling `popTop()`. Naturally, it makes sense to optimize the common case. The idea behind the `BoundedDEQueue` in Figs. 16.9 and 16.10 is thus to have the `pushBottom()` and `popBottom()` methods use only reads–writes in the common case. The `BoundedDEQueue` consists of an array of `tasks` indexed by `bottom` and `top` fields that reference the bottom and top of the dequeue, and depicted in Fig. 16.11. The `pushBottom()` and `popBottom()` methods use reads–writes to manipulate the `bottom` reference. However, once the `top` and `bottom` fields are close (there might be only a single item in the array), `popBottom()` switches to `compareAndSet()` calls to coordinate with potential `popTop()` calls.

Let us describe the algorithm in more detail. The `BoundedDEQueue` algorithm is ingenious in the way it avoids the use of costly `compareAndSet()` calls. This elegance comes at a cost: it is delicate and the order among instructions is crucial. We suggest the reader take time to understand how method interactions among methods are determined by the order in which reads-writes and `compareAndSet()` calls occur.

```
1  public class BDEQueue {
2    Runnable[] tasks;
3    volatile int bottom;
4    AtomicStampedReference<Integer> top;
5    public BDEQueue(int capacity) {
6      tasks = new Runnable[capacity];
7      top = new AtomicStampedReference<Integer>(0, 0);
8      bottom = 0;
9    }
10   public void pushBottom(Runnable r){
11     tasks[bottom] = r;
12     bottom++;
13   }
14   // called by thieves to determine whether to try to steal
15   boolean isEmpty() {
16     int localTop = top.getReference();
17     int localBottom = bottom;
18     return localBottom <= localTop;
19   }
20 }
21 }
```

Figure 16.9 The BoundedDEQueue class: fields, constructor, pushBottom() and isEmpty() methods.

The BoundedDEQueue class has three fields: tasks, bottom, and top (Fig. 16.9, Lines 2–4). The tasks field is an array of Runnable tasks that holds the tasks in the queue, bottom is the index of the first empty slot in tasks, and top is an AtomicStampedReference<Integer>.[3] The top field encompasses two logical fields; the *reference* is the index of the first task in the queue, and the *stamp* is a counter incremented each time the reference is changed. The stamp is needed to avoid an "ABA" problem of the type that often arises when using compareAndSet(). Suppose thread *A* tries to steal a task from index 3. *A* reads a reference to the task at that position, and tries to steal it by calling compareAndSet() to set the index to 4. It is delayed before making the call, and in the meantime, thread *B* removes all the tasks and inserts three new tasks. When *A* awakens, its compareAndSet() call will succeed in changing the index from 3 to 4, but it will have stolen a task that has already been completed, and removed a task that will never be completed. The stamp ensures that *A*'s compareAndSet() call will fail because the stamps no longer match.

The popTop() method (Fig. 16.10) checks whether the BoundedDEQueue is empty, and if not, tries to steal the top element by calling compareAndSet() to increment top. If the compareAndSet() succeeds, the theft is successful, and otherwise the method simply returns *null*. This method is nondeterministic: returning *null* does not necessarily mean that the queue is empty.

3 See Chapter 10, Pragma 10.6.1.

```
1   public Runnable popTop() {
2     int[] stamp = new int[1];
3     int oldTop = top.get(stamp), newTop = oldTop + 1;
4     int oldStamp = stamp[0], newStamp = oldStamp + 1;
5     if (bottom <= oldTop)
6       return null;
7     Runnable r = tasks[oldTop];
8     if (top.compareAndSet(oldTop, newTop, oldStamp, newStamp))
9       return r;
10    return null;
11  }
12  public Runnable popBottom() {
13    if (bottom == 0)
14      return null;
15    bottom--;
16    Runnable r = tasks[bottom];
17    int[] stamp = new int[1];
18    int oldTop = top.get(stamp), newTop = 0;
19    int oldStamp = stamp[0], newStamp = oldStamp + 1;
20    if (bottom > oldTop)
21      return r;
22    if (bottom == oldTop) {
23      bottom = 0;
24      if (top.compareAndSet(oldTop, newTop, oldStamp, newStamp))
25        return r;
26    }
27    top.set(newTop,newStamp);
28    bottom = 0;
29    return null;
30  }
```

Figure 16.10 The BoundedDEQueue class: popTop() and popBottom() methods.

As we noted earlier, we optimize for the common case where each thread pushes and pops from its own local `BoundedDEQueue`. Most of the time, a thread can push and pop tasks on and off its own `BoundedDEQueue` object, simply by loading and storing the `bottom` index. If there is only one task in the queue, then the caller might encounter interference from a thief trying to steal that task. So if `bottom` is close to `top`, the calling thread switches to using `compareAndSet()` to pop tasks.

The `pushBottom()` method (Fig. 16.9, Line 10) simply stores the new task at the `bottom` queue location and increments `bottom`.

The `popBottom()` method (Fig. 16.10) is more complex. If the queue is empty, the method returns immediately (Line 13), and otherwise, it decrements `bottom`, claiming a task (Line 15). Here is a subtle but important point. If the claimed task was the last in the queue, then it is important that thieves notice that the `BoundedDEQueue` is empty (Line 5). But, because `popBottom()`'s decrement is neither atomic nor synchronized, the Java memory model does not guarantee that the decrement will be observed right away by concurrent thieves. To ensure

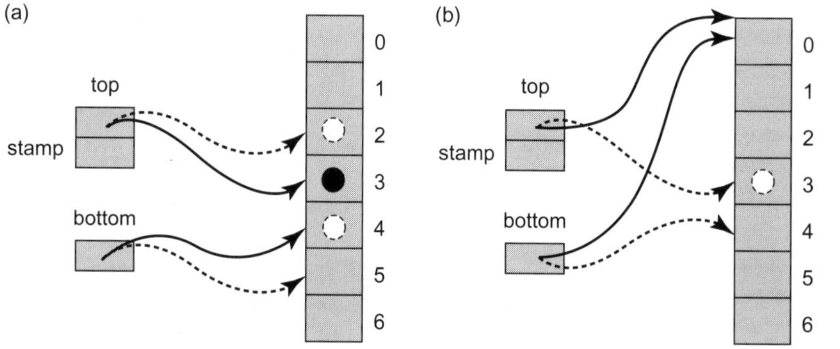

Figure 16.11 The BoundedDEQueue implementation. In Part (a) popTop() and popBottom() are called concurrently while there is more than one task in the BoundedDEQueue. The popTop() method reads the element in entry 2 and calls compareAndSet() to redirect the top reference to entry 3. The popBottom() method redirects the bottom reference from 5 to 4 using a simple store and then, after checking that bottom is greater than top it removes the task in entry 4. In Part (b) there is only a single task. When popBottom() detects that after redirecting from 4 to 3 top and bottom are equal, it attempts to redirect top with a compareAndSet(). Before doing so it redirects bottom to 0 because this last task will be removed by one of the two popping methods. If popTop() detects that top and bottom are equal it gives up, and otherwise it tries to advance top using compareAndSet(). If both methods apply compareAndSet() to the top, one wins and removes the task. In any case, win or lose, popBottom() resets top to 0 since the BoundedDEQueue is empty.

that thieves can recognize an empty BoundedDEQueue, the bottom field must be declared **volatile**.[4]

After the decrement, the caller reads the task at the new bottom index (Line 16), and tests whether the current top field refers to a higher index. If so, the caller cannot conflict with a thief, and the method returns (Line 20). Otherwise, if the top and bottom fields are equal, then there is only one task left in the BoundedDEQueue, but there is a danger that the caller conflicts with a thief. The caller resets bottom to 0 (Line 23). (Either the caller will succeed in claiming the task, or a thief will steal it first.) The caller resolves the potential conflict by calling compareAndSet() to reset top to 0, matching bottom (Line 22). If this compareAndSet() succeeds, the top has been reset to 0, and the task has been claimed by the caller, so the method returns. Otherwise the queue must be empty because a thief succeeded, but this means that top points to some entry greater than bottom which was set to 0 earlier. So before the caller returns *null*, it resets top to 0 (Line 27).

As noted, an attractive aspect of this design is that an expensive compareAndSet() call is needed only rarely when the BoundedDEQueue is almost empty.

---

4 In a C or C++ implementation you would need to introduce a write barrier as described in Appendix B.

We linearize each unsuccessful popTop() call at the point where it detects that the BoundedDEQueue is empty, or at a failed compareAndSet(). Successful popTop() calls are linearized at the point when a successful compareAndSet() took place. We linearize pushBottom() calls when bottom is incremented, and popBottom() calls when bottom is decremented or set to 0, though the outcome of popBottom() in the latter case is determined by the success or failure of the compareAndSet() that follows.

The isEmpty() method (Fig. 16.10) first reads top, then bottom, checking whether bottom is less than or equal to top (Line 4). The order is important for linearizability, because top never decreases unless bottom is first reset to 0, and so if a thread reads bottom after top and sees it is no greater, the queue is indeed empty because a concurrent modification of top could only have increased top. On the other hand, if bottom is greater than top, then even if top is increased after it was read and before bottom is read (and the queue becomes empty), it is still true that the BoundedDEQueue must not have been empty when top was read. The only alternative is that bottom is reset to 0 and then top is reset to 0, so reading top and then bottom will correctly return empty. It follows that the isEmpty() method is linearizable.

16.5.2 An Unbounded Work-Stealing DEQueue

A limitation of the BoundedDEQueue class is that the queue has a fixed size. For some applications, it may be difficult to predict this size, especially if some threads create significantly more tasks than others. Assigning each thread its own BoundedDEQueue of maximal capacity wastes space.

To address these limitations, we now consider an *unbounded double-ended queue* UnboundedDEQueue class that dynamically resizes itself as needed.

We implement the UnboundedDEQueue in a cyclic array, with top and bottom fields as in the BoundedDEQueue (except indexed modulo the array's capacity). As before, if bottom is less than or equal to top, the UnboundedDEQueue is empty. Using a cyclic array eliminates the need to reset bottom and top to 0. Moreover, it permits top to be incremented but never decremented, eliminating the need for top to be an AtomicStampedReference. Moreover, in the UnboundedDEQueue algorithm, if pushBottom() discovers that the current circular array is full, it can resize (enlarge) it, copying the tasks into a bigger array, and pushing the new task into the new (larger) array. Because the array is indexed modulo its capacity, there is no need to update the top or bottom fields when moving the elements into a bigger array (although the actual array indexes where the elements are stored might change).

The CircularArray() class is depicted in Fig. 16.12. It provides get() and put() methods that add and remove tasks, and a resize() method that allocates a new circular array and copies the old array's contents into the new array. The use of modular arithmetic ensures that even though the array has changed size

```
class CircularArray {
    private int logCapacity;
    private Runnable[] currentTasks;
    CircularArray(int myLogCapacity) {
      logCapacity = myLogCapacity;
      currentTasks = new Runnable[1 << logCapacity];
    }
    int capacity() {
      return 1 << logCapacity;
    }
    Runnable get(int i) {
      return currentTasks[i % capacity()];
    }
    void put(int i, Runnable task) {
      currentTasks[i % capacity()] = task;
    }
    CircularArray resize(int bottom, int top) {
      CircularArray newTasks =
          new CircularArray(logCapacity+1);
      for (int i = top; i < bottom; i++) {
        newTasks.put(i, get(i));
      }
      return newTasks;
    }
  }
```

Figure 16.12 The UnboundedDEQueue class: the circular task array.

and the tasks may have shifted positions, thieves can still use the top field to find the next task to steal.

The UnboundedDEQueue class has three fields: tasks, bottom, and top (Fig. 16.13, Lines 3–5). The popBottom() (Fig. 16.13) and popTop() methods (Fig. 16.14) are almost the same as those of the BoundedDEQueue, with one key difference: the use of modular arithmetic to compute indexes means the top index need never be decremented. As noted, there is no need for a timestamp to prevent ABA problems. Both methods, when competing for the last task, steal it by incrementing top. To reset the UnboundedDEQueue to empty, simply increment the bottom field to equal top. In the code, popBottom(), immediately after the compareAndSet() in Line 25, sets bottom to equal top+1 whether or not the compareAndSet() succeeds, because, even if it failed, a concurrent thief must have stolen the last task. Storing top+1 into bottom makes top and bottom equal, resetting the UnboundedDEQueue object to an empty state.

The isEmpty() method (Fig. 16.13) first reads top, then bottom, checking whether bottom is less than or equal to top (Line 4). The order is important because top never decreases, and so if a thread reads bottom after top and sees it is no greater, the queue is indeed empty because a concurrent modification of top could only have increased the top value. The same principle applies in the popTop() method call. An example execution is provided in Fig. 16.15.

```
1  public class UnboundedDEQueue {
2    private final static int LOG_CAPACITY = 4;
3    private volatile CircularArray tasks;
4    volatile int bottom;
5    AtomicInteger top;
6    public UnboundedDEQueue(int LOG_CAPACITY) {
7      tasks = new CircularArray(LOG_CAPACITY);
8      top = new AtomicInteger(0);
9      bottom = 0;
10   }
11   boolean isEmpty() {
12     int localTop = top.get();
13     int localBottom = bottom;
14     return (localBottom <= localTop);
15   }
16
17   public void pushBottom(Runnable r) {
18     int oldBottom = bottom;
19     int oldTop = top.get();
20     int size = oldBottom - oldTop;
21     if (size >= currentTasks.capacity()-1) {
22       currentTasks = currentTasks.resize(oldBottom, oldTop);
23       tasks = currentTasks;
24     }
25     tasks.put(oldBottom, r);
26     bottom = oldBottom + 1;
27   }
```

Figure 16.13 The `UnboundedDEQueue` class: fields, constructor, `pushBottom()`, and `isEmpty()` methods.

The `pushBottom()` method (Fig. 16.13) is almost the same as that of the `BoundedDEQueue`. One difference is that the method must enlarge the circular array if the current push is about to cause it to exceed its capacity. Another is that `popTop()` does not need to manipulate a timestamp. The ability to resize carries a price: every call must read `top` (Line 20) to determine if a resize is necessary, possibly causing more cache misses because `top` is modified by all processes. We can reduce this overhead by having threads save a local value of `top` and using it to compute the size of the `UnboundedDEQueue` object. A thread reads the `top` field only when this bound is exceeded, indicating that a `resize()` may be necessary. Even though the local copy may become outdated because of changes to the shared `top`, `top` is never decremented, so the real size of the `UnboundedDEQueue` object can only be smaller than the one calculated using the local variable.

In summary, we have seen two ways to design a nonblocking linearizable `DEQueue` class. We can get away with using only loads and stores in the most common manipulations of the `DEQueue`, but at the price of having more complex algorithms. Such algorithms are justifiable for an application such as an executer pool whose performance may be critical to a concurrent multithreaded system.

```
public Runnable popTop() {
  int oldTop = top.get();
  int newTop = oldTop + 1;
  int oldBottom = bottom;
  int size = oldBottom - oldTop;
  if (size <= 0) return null;
  Runnable r = tasks.get(oldTop);
  if (top.compareAndSet(oldTop, newTop))
    return r;
  return null;
}

public Runnable popBottom() {
  bottom--;
  int oldTop = top.get();
  int newTop = oldTop + 1;
  int size = bottom - oldTop;
  if (size < 0) {
    bottom = oldTop;
    return null;
  }
  Runnable r = tasks.get(bottom);
  if (size > 0)
    return r;
  if (!top.compareAndSet(oldTop, newTop))
    r = null;
  bottom = oldTop + 1;
  return r;
}
```

Figure 16.14 The UnboundedDEQueue class: popTop() and popBottom() methods.

16.5.3 Work Balancing

We have seen that in work-stealing algorithms, idle threads steal tasks from others. An alternative approach is to have each thread periodically *balance* its workloads with a randomly chosen partner. To ensure that heavily loaded threads do not waste effort trying to rebalance, we make lightly-loaded threads more likely to initiate rebalancing. More precisely, each thread periodically flips a biased coin to decide whether to balance with another. The thread's probability of balancing is inversely proportional to the number of tasks in the thread's queue. In other words, threads with few tasks are likely to rebalance, and threads with nothing to do are certain to rebalance. A thread rebalances by selecting a victim uniformly at random, and, if the difference between its workload and the victim's exceeds a predefined threshold, they transfer tasks until their queues contain the same number of tasks. It can be shown that this algorithm provides strong fairness guarantees: the expected length of each thread's task queue is pretty close to the average. One advantage of this approach is that the balancing operation moves multiple tasks at each exchange. A second advantage occurs if one thread has

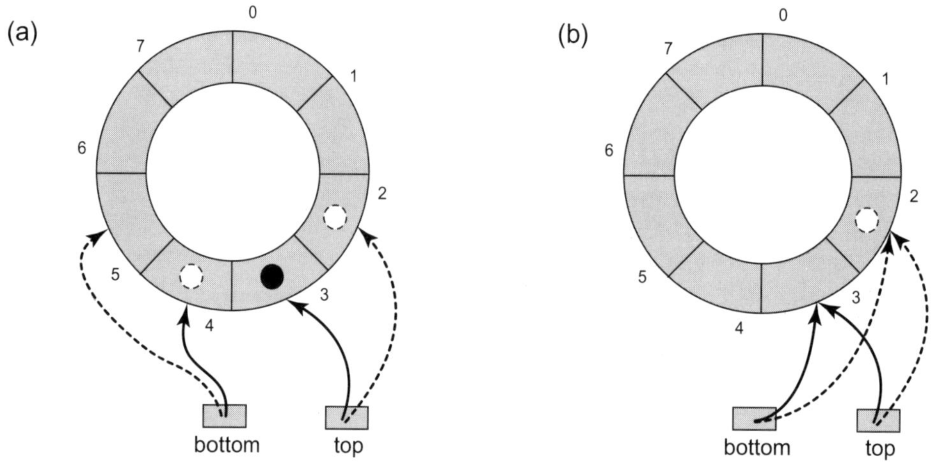

Figure 16.15 The `UnboundedDEQueue` class implementation. In Part (a) `popTop()` and `popBottom()` are executed concurrently while there is more than one task in the `UnboundedDEQueue` object. In Part (b) there is only a single task, and initially `bottom` refers to Entry 3 and `top` to 2. The `popBottom()` method first decrements `bottom` from 3 to 2 (we denote this change by a dashed line pointing to Entry 2 since it will change again soon). Then, when `popBottom()` detects that the gap between the newly-set `bottom` and `top` is 0, it attempts to increment `top` by 1 (rather than reset it to 0 as in the `BoundedDEQueue`). The `popTop()` method attempts to do the same. The `top` field is incremented by one of them, and the winner takes the last task. Finally, the `popBottom()` method sets `bottom` back to Entry 3, which is equal to `top`.

much more work than the others, especially if tasks require approximately equal computation. In the work-stealing algorithm presented here, contention could occur if many threads try to steal individual tasks from the overloaded thread.

In such a case, in the work-stealing executer pool, if some thread has a lot of work, chances are that that other threads will have to repeatedly compete on the same local task queue in an attempt to steal at most a single task each time. On the other hand, in the work-sharing executer pool, balancing multiple tasks at a time means that work will quickly be spread out among tasks, and there will not be a synchronization overhead per individual task.

Fig. 16.16 illustrates a work-sharing executor. Each thread has its own queue of tasks, kept in an array shared by all threads (Line 2). Each thread repeatedly dequeues the next task from its queue (Line 12). If the queue was empty, the `deq()` call returns *null*, and otherwise, the thread runs the task (Line 13). At this point, the thread decides whether to rebalance. If the thread's task queue has size s, then the thread decides to rebalance with probability $1/(s+1)$ (Line 15). To rebalance, the thread chooses a *victim* thread uniformly at random. The thread locks both queues (Lines 17–20), in thread ID order (to avoid deadlock). If the difference in queue sizes exceeds a threshold, it evens out the queue sizes. (Fig. 16.16, Lines 27–35).

```
public class WorkSharingThread {
  Queue[] queue;
  Random random;
  private static final int THRESHOLD = ...;
  public WorkSharingThread(Queue[] myQueue) {
    queue = myQueue;
    random = new Random();
  }
  public void run() {
    int me = ThreadID.get();
    while (true) {
      Runnable task = queue[me].deq();
      if (task != null) task.run();
      int size = queue[me].size();
      if (random.nextInt(size+1) == size) {
        int victim = random.nextInt(queue.length);
        int min = (victim <= me) ? victim : me;
        int max = (victim <= me) ? me : victim;
        synchronized (queue[min]) {
          synchronized (queue[max]) {
            balance(queue[min], queue[max]);
          }
        }
      }
    }
  }
  private void balance(Queue q0, Queue q1) {
    Queue qMin = (q0.size() < q1.size()) ? q0 : q1;
    Queue qMax = (q0.size() < q1.size()) ? q1 : q0;
    int diff = qMax.size() - qMin.size();
    if (diff > THRESHOLD)
      while (qMax.size() > qMin.size())
        qMin.enq(qMax.deq());
  }
}
```

Figure 16.16 The `WorkSharingThread` class: a simplified work sharing executer pool.

16.6 Chapter Notes

The DAG-based model for analysis of multithreaded computation was introduced by Robert Blumofe and Charles Leiserson [20]. They also gave the first deque-based implementation of work stealing. Some of the examples in this chapter were adapted from a tutorial by Charles Leiserson and Harald Prokop [102]. The bounded lock-free dequeue algorithm is credited to Anish Arora, Robert Blumofe, and Greg Plaxton [15]. The unbounded timestamps used in this algorithm can be made bounded using a technique due to Mark Moir [117]. The unbounded dequeue algorithm is credited to David Chase and Yossi Lev [28]. Theorem 16.3.1 and its proof are by Anish Arora, Robert Blumofe, and

Greg Plaxton [15]. The work-sharing algorithm is by Larry Rudolph, Tali Slivkin-Allaluf, and Eli Upfal [134]. The algorithm of Anish Arora, Robert Blumofe, and Greg Plaxton [15] was later improved by Danny Hendler and Nir Shavit [56] to include the ability to steal half of the items in a dequeue.

16.7 Exercises

Exercise 185. Consider the following code for an in-place merge-sort:

```
void mergeSort(int[] A, int lo, int hi) {
  if (hi > lo) {
    int mid = (hi - lo)/2;
    executor.submit(new mergeSort(A, lo, mid));
    executor.submit(new mergeSort(A, mid+1, hi));
    awaitTermination();
    merge(A, lo, mid, hi);
}
```

Assuming that the merge method has no internal parallelism, give the work, critical path length, and parallelism of this algorithm. Give your answers both as recurrences and as $\Theta(f(n))$, for some function f.

Exercise 186. You may assume that the actual running time of a parallel program on a dedicated P-processor machine is

$$T_P = T_1/P + T_\infty.$$

Your research group has produced two chess programs, a simple one and an optimized one. The simple one has $T_1 = 2048$ seconds and $T_\infty = 1$ second. When you run it on your 32-processor machine, sure enough, the running time is 65 steps. Your students then produce an "optimized" version with $T_1' = 1024$ seconds and $T_\infty' = 8$ seconds. Why is it optimized? When you run it on your 32-processor machine, the running time is 40 seconds, as predicted by our formula.

Which program will scale better to a 512-processor machine?

Exercise 187. Write a class, `ArraySum` that provides a method

```
static public int sum(int[] a)
```

that uses divide-and-conquer to sum the elements of the array argument in parallel.

Exercise 188. Professor Jones takes some measurements of his (deterministic) multithreaded program, which is scheduled using a greedy scheduler, and finds that $T_4 = 80$ seconds and $T_{64} = 10$ seconds. What is the fastest that the professor's computation could possibly run on 10 processors? Use the following inequalities and the bounds implied by them to derive your answer. Note that P is the number of processors.

$$T_P \geqslant \frac{T_1}{P}$$

$$T_P \geqslant T_\infty$$

$$T_P \leqslant \frac{(T_1 - T_\infty)}{P} + T_\infty$$

(The last inequality holds on a greedy scheduler.)

Exercise 189. Give an implementation of the `Matrix` class used in this chapter. Make sure your `split()` method takes constant time.

Exercise 190. Let $P(x) = \sum_{i=0}^{d} p_i x^i$ and $Q(x) = \sum_{i=0}^{d} q_i x^i$ be polynomials of degree d, where d is a power of 2. We can write

$$P(x) = P_0(x) + (P_1(x) \cdot x^{d/2})$$

$$Q(x) = Q_0(x) + (Q_1(x) \cdot x^{d/2})$$

where $P_0(x), P_1(x), Q_0(x)$, and $Q_1(x)$ are polynomials of degree $d/2$.

The `Polynomial` class shown in Fig. 16.17 provides `put()` and `get()` methods to access coefficients and it provides a constant-time `split()` method that splits a d-degree polynomial $P(x)$ into the two $(d/2)$-degree polynomials $P_0(x)$ and $P_1(x)$ defined above, where changes to the split polynomials are reflected in the original, and vice versa.

Your task is to devise parallel addition and multiplication algorithms for this polynomial class.

1. The *sum* of $P(x)$ and $Q(x)$ can be decomposed as follows:

$$P(x) + Q(x) = (P_0(x) + Q_0(x)) + (P_1(x) + Q_1(x)) \cdot x^{d/2}.$$

   a) Use this decomposition to construct a task-based concurrent polynomial addition algorithm in the manner of Fig. 16.13.
   b) Compute the work and critical path length of this algorithm.

2. The *product* of $P(x)$ and $Q(x)$ can be decomposed as follows:

$$P(x) \cdot Q(x) = (P_0(x) \cdot Q_0(x)) + (P_0(x) \cdot Q_1(x) + P_1(x) \cdot Q_0(x)) \cdot x^{d/2} + (P_1(x) \cdot Q_1(x))$$

   a) Use this decomposition to construct a task-based concurrent polynomial multiplication algorithm in the manner of Fig. 16.4
   b) Compute the work and critical path length of this algorithm.

```
public class Polynomial {
  int[] coefficients; // possibly shared by several polynomials
  int first;  // index of my constant coefficient
  int degree; // number of coefficients that are mine
  public Polynomial(int d) {
    coefficients = new int[d];
    degree = d;
    first = 0;
  }
  private Polynomial(int[] myCoefficients, int myFirst, int myDegree) {
    coefficients = myCoefficients;
    first = myFirst;
    degree = myDegree;
  }
  public int get(int index) {
    return coefficients[first + index];
  }
  public void set(int index, int value) {
    coefficients[first + index] = value;
  }
  public int getDegree() {
    return degree;
  }
  public Polynomial[] split() {
    Polynomial[] result = new Polynomial[2];
    int newDegree = degree / 2;
    result[0] = new Polynomial(coefficients, first, newDegree);
    result[1] = new Polynomial(coefficients, first + newDegree, newDegree);
    return result;
  }
}
```

Figure 16.17 The `Polynomial` class.

```
    Queue qMin = (q0.size() < q1.size()) ? q0 : q1;
    Queue qMax = (q0.size() < q1.size()) ? q1 : q0;
    synchronized (qMin) {
      synchronized (qMax) {
        int diff = qMax.size() - qMin.size();
        if (diff > THRESHOLD)
          while (qMax.size() > qMin.size())
            qMin.enq(qMax.deq());
      }
    }
```

Figure 16.18 Alternate rebalancing code.

Exercise 191. Give an efficient and highly parallel multithreaded algorithm for multiplying an $n \times n$ matrix A by a length-n vector x that achieves work $\Theta(n^2)$ and critical path $\Theta(\log n)$. Analyze the work and critical-path length of your implementation, and give the parallelism.

Exercise 192. Fig. 16.18 shows an alternate way of rebalancing two work queues: first, lock the smaller queue, then lock the larger queue, and rebalance if their difference exceeds a threshold. What is wrong with this code?

Exercise 193.

1. In the `popBottom()` method of Fig. 16.10, the `bottom` field is volatile to assure that in `popBottom()` the decrement at Line 15 is immediately visible. Describe a scenario that explains what could go wrong if `bottom` were not declared as volatile.
2. Why should we attempt to reset the `bottom` field to zero as early as possible in the `popBottom()` method? Which line is the earliest in which this reset can be done safely? Can our `BoundedDEQueue`overflow anyway? Describe how.

Exercise 194.

- In `popTop()`, if the `compareAndSet()` in Line 8 succeeds, it returns the element it read right before the successful `compareAndSet()` operation. Why is it important to read the element from the array before we do the `compareAndSet()`?
- Can we use `isEmpty()` in Line 6 of `popTop()`?

Exercise 195. What are the linearization points of the `UnboundedDEQueue` methods? Justify your answers.

Exercise 196. Modify the `popTop()` method of the linearizable `BoundedDEQueue` implementation so it will return null only if there are no tasks in the queue. Notice that you may need to make its implementation blocking.

Exercise 197. Do you expect that the `isEmpty()` method call of a `BoundedDEQueue` in the executer pool code will actually improve its performance?

17 Barriers

17.1 Introduction

Imagine you are writing the graphical display for a computer game. Your program prepares a sequence of *frames* to be displayed by a graphics package (perhaps a hardware coprocessor). This kind of program is sometimes called a *soft real-time* application: real-time because it must display at least 35 frames per second to be effective, and soft because occasional failure is not catastrophic. On a single-threaded machine, you might write a loop like this:

```
while (true) {
  frame.prepare();
  frame.display();
  }
```

If, instead, you have n parallel threads available, then it makes sense to split the frame into n disjoint parts, and to have each thread prepare its own part in parallel with the others.

```
int me = ThreadID.get();
while (true) {
  frame[me].prepare();
  frame[me].display();
}
```

The problem with this approach is that different threads will require different amounts of time to prepare and display their portions of the frame. Some threads might start displaying the ith frame before others have finished the $(i-1)^{st}$.

To avoid such synchronization problems, we can organize computations such as this as a sequence of *phases*, where no thread should start the ith phase until the others have finished the $(i-1)^{st}$. We have already seen this phased computation pattern before. In Chapter 12, the sorting network algorithms required each comparison phase to be separate from the others. Similarly, in the sample sorting

```
public interface Barrier {
  public void await();
}
```

Figure 17.1 The `Barrier` interface.

```
private Barrier b;
 ...
 while (true) {
    frame[my].prepare();
    b.await();
    frame[my].display();
 }
```

Figure 17.2 Using a barrier to synchronize concurrent displays.

algorithm, each phase had to make sure that prior phases had completed before proceeding.

The mechanism for enforcing this kind of synchronization is called a *barrier* (Fig. 17.1). A barrier is a way of forcing asynchronous threads to act almost as if they were synchronous. When a thread finishing phase i calls the barrier's `await()` method, it is blocked until all n threads have also finished that phase. Fig. 17.2 shows how one could use a barrier to make the parallel rendering program work correctly. After preparing frame i, all threads synchronize at a barrier before starting to display that frame. This structure ensures that all threads concurrently displaying a frame display the same frame.

Barrier implementations raise many of the same performance issues as spin locks in Chapter 7, as well as some new issues. Clearly, barriers should be fast, in the sense that we want to minimize the duration between when the last thread reaches the barrier and when the last thread leaves the barrier. It is also important that threads leave the barrier at roughly the same time. A thread's *notification time* is the interval between when some thread has detected that all threads have reached the barrier, and when that specific thread leaves the barrier. Having uniform notification times is important for many soft real-time applications. For example, picture quality is enhanced if all portions of the frame are updated at more-or-less the same time.

17.2 Barrier Implementations

Fig. 17.3 shows the `SimpleBarrier` class, which creates an `AtomicInteger` counter initialized to n, the barrier size. Each thread applies `getAndDecrement()` to lower the counter. If the call returns 1 (Line 10), then that thread is the last to reach the barrier, so it resets the counter for the next use (Line 11). Otherwise,

```
1  public class SimpleBarrier implements Barrier {
2    AtomicInteger count;
3    int size;
4    public SimpleBarrier(int n){
5      count = new AtomicInteger(n);
6      size = n;
7    }
8    public void await() {
9      int position = count.getAndDecrement();
10     if (position == 1) {
11       count.set(size);
12     } else {
13       while (count.get() != 0){};
14     }
15   }
16 }
```

Figure 17.3 The SimpleBarrier class.

the thread spins on the counter, waiting for the value to fall to zero (Line 13). This barrier class may look like it works, but it does not.

Unfortunately, the attempt to make the barrier reusable causes it to break (see Fig. 17.2). Suppose there are only two threads. Thread *A* applies getAndDecrement() to the counter, discovers it is not the last thread to reach the barrier, and spins waiting for the counter value to reach zero. When *B* arrives, it discovers it is the last thread to arrive, so it resets the counter to *n* in this case 2. It finishes the next phase and calls await(). Meanwhile, *A* continues to spin, and the counter never reaches zero. Eventually, *A* is waiting for phase 0 to finish, while *B* is waiting for phase 1 to finish, and the two threads starve.

Perhaps the simplest way to fix this problem is just to alternate between two barriers, using one for even-numbered phases, and another for odd-numbered ones. However, such an approach wastes space, and requires too much bookkeeping from applications.

17.3 Sense-Reversing Barrier

A *sense-reversing* barrier is a more elegant and practical solution to the problem of reusing barriers. As depicted in Fig. 17.4, a phase's *sense* is a Boolean value: *true* for even-numbered phases and *false* otherwise. Each SenseBarrier object has a Boolean sense field indicating the sense of the currently executing phase. Each thread keeps its current sense as a thread-local object (see Pragma 17.3.1). Initially the barrier's sense is the complement of the local sense of all the threads. When a thread calls await(), it checks whether it is the last thread to decrement the counter. If so, it reverses the barrier's sense and continues.

```
1  public SenseBarrier(int n) {
2    count = new AtomicInteger(n);
3    size = n;
4    sense = false;
5    threadSense = new ThreadLocal<Boolean>() {
6      protected Boolean initialValue() { return !sense; };
7    };
8  }
9  public void await() {
10   boolean mySense = threadSense.get();
11   int position = count.getAndDecrement();
12   if (position == 1) {
13     count.set(size);
14     sense = mySense;
15   } else {
16     while (sense != mySense) {}
17   }
18   threadSense.set(!mySense);
19 }
```

Figure 17.4 The `SenseBarrier` class: a sense-reversing barrier.

Otherwise, it spins waiting for the barrier's `sense` field to change to match its own local sense.

Decrementing the shared counter may cause memory contention, since all the threads are trying to access the counter at about the same time. Once the counter has been decremented, each thread spins on the `sense` field. This implementation is well suited for cache-coherent architectures, since threads spin on locally cached copies of the field, and the field is modified only when threads are ready to leave the barrier. The `sense` field is an excellent way of maintaining a uniform notification time on symmetric cache-coherent multiprocessors.

> *Pragma* 17.3.1. The constructor code for the sense-reversing barrier, shown in Fig. 17.4, is mostly straightforward. The one exception occurs on lines 5 and 6, where we initialize the thread-local `threadSense` field. This somewhat complicated syntax defines a thread-local Boolean value whose initial value is the complement of the `sense` field's initial value. See Appendix A.2.4 for a more complete explanation of thread-local objects in Java.

17.4 Combining Tree Barrier

One way to reduce memory contention (at the cost of increased latency) is to use the combining paradigm of Chapter 12. Split a large barrier into a tree of smaller

```
public class TreeBarrier implements Barrier {
  int radix;
  Node[] leaf;
  ThreadLocal<Boolean> threadSense;
  ...
  public void await() {
    int me = ThreadID.get();
    Node myLeaf = leaf[me / radix];
    myLeaf.await();
  }
  ...
}
```

Figure 17.5 The `TreeBarrier` class: each thread indexes into an array of leaf nodes and calls that leaf's `await()` method.

barriers, and have threads combine requests going up the tree and distribute notifications going down the tree. As shown in Fig. 17.5, a *tree barrier* is characterized by a *size* n, the total number of threads, and a *radix* r, each node's number of children. For convenience, we assume there are exactly $n = r^{d+1}$ threads, where d is the depth of the tree.

Specifically, the combining tree barrier is a tree of *nodes*, where each node has a counter and a sense, just as in the sense-reversing barrier. A node's implementation is shown in Fig. 17.6. Thread i starts at leaf node $\lfloor i/r \rfloor$. The node's `await()` method is similar to the sense-reversing barrier's `await()`, the principal difference being that the last thread to arrive, the one that completes the barrier, visits the parent barrier before waking up the other threads. When r threads have arrived at the root, the barrier is complete, and the sense is reversed. As before, thread-local Boolean sense values allow the barrier to be reused without reinitialization.

The tree-structured barrier reduces memory contention by spreading memory accesses across multiple barriers. It may or may not reduce latency, depending on whether it is faster to decrement a single location or to visit a logarithmic number of barriers.

The root node, once its barrier is complete, lets notifications percolate down the tree. This approach may be good for a NUMA architecture, but it may cause nonuniform notification times. Because threads visit an unpredictable sequence of locations as they move up the tree, this approach may not work well on cacheless NUMA architectures.

Pragma 17.4.1. Tree nodes are declared as an *inner class* of the tree barrier class, so nodes are not accessible outside the class. As shown in Fig. 17.7, the tree is initialized by a recursive `build()` method. The method takes a parent node and a depth. If the depth is nonzero, it creates *radix* children, and recursively creates the children's children. If the depth is zero, it places

```
private class Node {
  AtomicInteger count;
  Node parent;
  volatile boolean sense;
  public Node() {
    sense = false;
    parent = null;
    count = new AtomicInteger(radix);
  }
  public Node(Node myParent) {
    this();
    parent = myParent;
  }
  public void await() {
    boolean mySense = threadSense.get();
    int position = count.getAndDecrement();
    if (position == 1) {  // I'm last
      if (parent != null) { // Am I root?
        parent.await();
      }
      count.set(radix);
      sense = mySense;
    } else {
      while (sense != mySense) {};
    }
    threadSense.set(!mySense);
  }
 }
}
```

Figure 17.6 The `TreeBarrier` class: internal tree node.

each node in a `leaf[]` array. When a thread enters the barrier, it uses this array to choose a leaf to start from. See Appendix A.2.1 for a more complete discussion of inner classes in Java.

17.5 Static Tree Barrier

The barriers seen so far either suffer from contention (the simple and sense-reversing barriers) or have excessive communication (the combining-tree barrier). In the last barrier, threads traverse an unpredictable sequence of nodes, which makes it difficult to lay out the barriers on cacheless NUMA architectures. Surprisingly, there is another simple barrier that allows both static layout and low contention.

```
public class TreeBarrier implements Barrier {
  int radix;
  Node[] leaf;
  int leaves;
  ThreadLocal<Boolean> threadSense;
  public TreeBarrier(int n, int r) {
    radix = r;
    leaves = 0;
    leaf = new Node[n / r];
    int depth = 0;
    threadSense = new ThreadLocal<Boolean>() {
      protected Boolean initialValue() { return true; };
    };
    // compute tree depth
    while (n > 1) {
      depth++;
      n = n / r;
    }
    Node root = new Node();
    build(root, depth - 1);
  }
  // recursive tree constructor
  void build(Node parent, int depth) {
    if (depth == 0) {
      leaf[leaves++] = parent;
    } else {
      for (int i = 0; i < radix; i++) {
        Node child = new Node(parent);
        build(child, depth - 1);
      }
    }
  }
  ...
}
```

Figure 17.7 The `TreeBarrier` class: initializing a combining tree barrier. The `build()` method creates *r* children for each node, and then recursively creates the children's children. At the bottom, it places leaves in an array.

The static tree barrier of Fig. 17.8 works as follows. Each thread is assigned to a node in a tree (see Fig. 17.9). The thread at a node waits until all nodes below it in the tree have finished, and then informs its parent. It then spins waiting for the global sense bit to change. Once the root learns that its children are done, it toggles the global sense bit to notify the waiting threads that all threads are done. On a cache-coherent multiprocessor, completing the barrier requires $\log(n)$ steps moving up the tree, while notification simply requires changing the global sense, which is propagated by the cache-coherence mechanism. On machines without coherent caches threads propagate notification down the tree as in the combining barrier we saw earlier.

```
public class StaticTreeBarrier implements Barrier {
  int radix;
  boolean sense;
  Node[] node;
  ThreadLocal<Boolean> threadSense;
  int nodes;
  public StaticTreeBarrier(int size, int myRadix) {
    radix = myRadix;
    nodes = 0;
    node = new Node[size];
    int depth = 0;
    while (size > 1) {
      depth++;
      size = size / radix;
    }
    build(null, depth);
    sense = false;
    threadSense = new ThreadLocal<Boolean>() {
      protected Boolean initialValue() { return !sense; };
    };
  }
  // recursive tree constructor
  void build(Node parent, int depth) {
    if (depth == 0) {
      node[nodes++] = new Node(parent, 0);
    } else {
      Node myNode = new Node(parent, radix);
      node[nodes++] = myNode;
      for (int i = 0; i < radix; i++) {
        build(myNode, depth - 1);
      }
    }
  }
  public void await() {
    node[ThreadID.get()].await();
  }
}
```

Figure 17.8 The `StaticTreeBarrier` class: each thread indexes into a statically assigned tree node and calls that node's `await()` method.

17.6 Termination Detecting Barriers

All the barriers considered so far were directed at computations organized in phases, where each thread finishes the work for a phase, reaches the barrier, and then starts a new phase.

There is, however, another interesting class of programs, in which each thread finishes its own part of the computation, only to be put to work again when another thread generates new work. An example of such a program is the

```
    public Node(Node myParent, int count) {
      children = count;
      childCount = new AtomicInteger(count);
      parent = myParent;
    }
    public void await() {
      boolean mySense = threadSense.get();
      while (childCount.get() > 0) {};
      childCount.set(children);
      if (parent != null) {
        parent.childDone();
        while (sense != mySense) {};
      } else {
        sense = !sense;
      }
      threadSense.set(!mySense);
    }
    public void childDone() {
      childCount.getAndDecrement();
    }
```

Figure 17.9 The StaticTreeBarrier class: internal Node class.

simplified work stealing executer pool from Chapter 16 (see Fig. 17.10). Here, once a thread exhausts the tasks in its local queue, it tries to steal work from other threads' queues. The execute() method itself may push new tasks onto the calling thread's local queue. Once all threads have exhausted all tasks in their queues, the threads will run forever while repeatedly attempting to steal items. Instead, we would like to devise a *termination detection* barrier so that these threads can all terminate once they have finished all their tasks.

Each thread is either *active* (it has a task to execute) or *inactive* (it has none). Note that any inactive thread may become active as long as some other thread is active, since an inactive thread may steal a task from an active one. Once all threads have become inactive, then no thread will ever become active again. Detecting that the computation as a whole has terminated is the problem of determining that at some instant in time there are no longer any active threads.

None of the barrier algorithms studied so far can solve this problem. Termination cannot be detected by having each thread announce that it has become inactive, and simply count how many have done so, because threads may repeatedly change from inactive to active and back. For example, consider threads A, B, and C running as shown in Fig. 17.10, and assume that each has a Boolean value indicating whether it is active or inactive. When A becomes inactive, it may then observe that B is also inactive, and then observe that C is inactive. Nevertheless, A cannot conclude that the overall computation has completed; as B might have stolen work from C after A checked B, but before it checked C.

```
public class WorkStealingThread {
  DEQueue[] queue;
  int size;
  Random random;
  public WorkStealingThread(int n) {
    queue = new DEQueue[n];
    size = n;
    random = new Random();
    for (int i = 0; i < n; i++) {
      queue[i] = new DEQueue();
    }
  }
  public void run() {
    int me = ThreadID.get();
    Runnable task = queue[me].popBottom();
    while (true) {
      while (task != null) {
        task.run();
        task = queue[me].popBottom();
      }
      while (task == null) {
        int victim = random.nextInt() % size;
        if (!queue[victim].isEmpty()) {
          task = queue[victim].popTop();
        }
      }
    }
  }
}
```

Figure 17.10 Work stealing executer pool revisited.

```
public interface TDBarrier {
  void setActive(boolean state);
  boolean isTerminated();
}
```

Figure 17.11 Termination detection barrier interface.

A *termination-detection* barrier (Fig. 17.11) provides methods `setActive`(*v*) and `isTerminated`(). Each thread calls `setActive`(*true*) to notify the barrier when it becomes active, and `setActive`(*false*) to notify the barrier when it becomes inactive. The `isTerminated`() method returns *true* if and only if all threads had become inactive at some earlier instant. Fig. 17.12 shows a simple implementation of a termination-detection barrier.

The barrier encompasses an `AtomicInteger` initialized to 0. Each thread that becomes active increments the counter (Line 8) and each thread that becomes inactive decrements it (Line 10). The computation is deemed to have terminated when the counter reaches zero (Line 14).

```
public class SimpleTDBarrier implements TDBarrier {
  AtomicInteger count;
  public SimpleTDBarrier(int n){
    count = new AtomicInteger(n);
  }
  public void setActive(boolean active) {
    if (active) {
      count.getAndIncrement();
    } else {
      count.getAndDecrement();
    }
  }
  public boolean isTerminated() {
    return count.get() == 0;
  }
}
```

Figure 17.12 A simple termination detecting barrier.

```
1    public void run() {
2      int me = ThreadID.get();
3      tdBarrier.setActive(true);
4      Runnable task = queue[me].popBottom();
5      while (true) {
6        while (task != null) {
7          task.run();
8          task = queue[me].popBottom();
9        }
10       tdBarrier.setActive(false);
11       while (task == null) {
12         int victim = random.nextInt() % queue.length;
13         if (!queue[victim].isEmpty()) {
14           tdBarrier.setActive(true);
15           task = queue[victim].popTop();
16           if (task == null) {
17             tdBarrier.setActive(false);
18           }
19         }
20         if (tdBarrier.isTerminated()) {
21           return;
22         }
23       }
24     }
25   }
26 }
```

Figure 17.13 Work-stealing executer pool: the run() method with termination.

The termination-detection barrier works only if used correctly. Fig. 17.13 shows how to modify the work-stealing thread's run() method to return when the computation has terminated. Initially, every thread registers as active (Line 3). Once a thread has exhausted its local queue, it registers as inactive (Line 10).

Before it tries to steal a new task, however, it must register as active (Line 14). If the theft fails, it registers as inactive again (Line 17).

Notice that a thread sets its state to active before stealing a task. Otherwise, if a thread were to steal a task while inactive, then the thread whose task was stolen might also declare itself inactive, resulting in a computation where all threads declare themselves inactive while the computation continues.

Here is a subtle point. A thread tests whether the queue is empty (Line 13) before it attempts to steal a task. This way, it avoids declaring itself active if there is no chance the theft will succeed. Without this precaution, it is possible that the threads will not detect termination because each one repeatedly switches to an active state before a steal attempt that is doomed to fail.

Correct use of the termination-detection barrier must satisfy both a safety and a liveness property. The safety property is that if `isTerminated()` returns *true*, then the computation really has terminated. Safety requires that no active thread ever declare itself inactive, because it could trigger an incorrect termination detection. For example, the work-stealing thread of Fig. 17.13 would be incorrect if the thread declared itself to be active only after successfully stealing a task. By contrast, it is safe for an inactive thread to declare itself active, which may occur if the thread is unsuccessful in stealing work at Line 15.

The liveness property is that if the computation terminates, then `isTerminated()` eventually returns *true*. (It is not necessary that termination be detected instantly.) While safety is not jeopardized if an inactive thread declares itself active, liveness will be violated if a thread that does not succeed in stealing work fails to declare itself inactive again (Line 15), because termination will not be detected when it occurs.

17.7 Chapter Notes

John Mellor–Crummey and Michael Scott [113] provide a survey of several barrier algorithms, though the performance numbers they provide should be viewed from a historical perspective. The combining tree barrier is based on code due to John Mellor–Crummey and Michael Scott [113], which is in turn based on the combining tree algorithm of Pen-Chung Yew, Nian-Feng Tzeng, and Duncan Lawrie [151]. The dissemination barrier is credited to Debra Hensgen, Raphael Finkel, and Udi Manber [59]. The tournament tree barrier used in the exercises is credited to John Mellor–Crummey and Michael Scott [113]. The simple barriers and the static tree barrier are most likely folklore. We learned of the static tree barrier from Beng-Hong Lim. The termination detection barrier and its application to an executer pool are based on a variation suggested by Peter Kessler to an algorithm by Dave Detlefs, Christine Flood, Nir Shavit, and Xiolan Zhang [41].

17.8 Exercises

Exercise 198. Fig. 17.14 shows how to use barriers to make a parallel prefix computation work on an asynchronous architecture.

A *parallel prefix* computation, given a sequence $a_0, \ldots, a_{m-1}$, of numbers, computes in parallel the partial sums:

$$b_i = \sum_{j=0}^{i} a_j.$$

In a synchronous system, where all threads take steps at the same time, there are simple, well-known algorithms for m threads to compute the partial sums in $\log m$ steps. The computation proceeds in a sequence of rounds, starting at round zero. In round r, if $i \geqslant 2^r$, thread i reads the value at $a[i-2^r]$ into a local variable. Next, it adds that value to $a[i]$. Rounds continue until $2^r \geqslant m$. It is not hard to see that after $\log_2(m)$ rounds, the array a contains the partial sums.

1. What could go wrong if we executed the parallel prefix on $n > m$ threads?
2. Modify this program, adding one or more barriers, to make it work properly in a concurrent setting with n threads. What is the minimum number of barriers that are necessary?

Exercise 199. Change the sense-reversing barrier implementation so that waiting threads call `wait()` instead of spinning.

```
class Prefix extends java.lang.Thread {
  private int[] a;
  private int i;
  public Prefix(int[] myA, int myI) {
    a = myA;
    i = myI;
  }
  public void run() {
    int d = 1, sum = 0;
    while (d < m) {
      if (i >= d)
        sum = a[i-d];
      if (i >= d)
        a[i] += sum;
      d = d * 2;
    }
  }
}
```

Figure 17.14 Parallel prefix computation.

- Give an example of a situation where suspending threads is better than spinning.
- Give an example of a situation where the other choice is better.

Exercise 200. Change the tree barrier implementation so that it takes a `Runnable` object whose `run()` method is called once after the last thread arrives at the barrier, but before any thread leaves the barrier.

Exercise 201. Modify the combining tree barrier so that nodes can use any barrier implementation, not just the sense-reversing barrier.

Exercise 202. A *tournament tree barrier* (Class `TourBarrier` in Fig. 17.15) is an alternative tree-structured barrier. Assume there are n threads, where n is a power of 2. The tree is a binary tree consisting of $2n - 1$ nodes. Each leaf is owned by a single, statically determined thread. Each node's two children are linked as *partners.* One partner is statically designated as *active*, and the other as *passive.* Fig. 17.16 illustrates the tree structure.

```
private class Node {
 volatile boolean flag;    // signal when done
 boolean active;           // active or passive?
 Node parent;              // parent node
 Node partner;             // partner node
 // create passive node
 Node() {
   flag    = false;
   active = false;
   partner = null;
   parent  = null;
 }
 // create active node
 Node(Node myParent) {
   this();
   parent = myParent;
   active = true;
 }
 void await(boolean sense) {
   if (active) { // I'm active
    while (flag != sense) {};                      // wait for partner
    if (parent != null) {parent.await(sense};      // wait for parent
    partner.flag = sense;                          // tell partner
    } else {                     // I'm passive
      partner.flag = sense;      // tell partner
      while (flag != sense) {};  // wait for partner
   }
 }
}
```

Figure 17.15 The `TourBarrier` class.

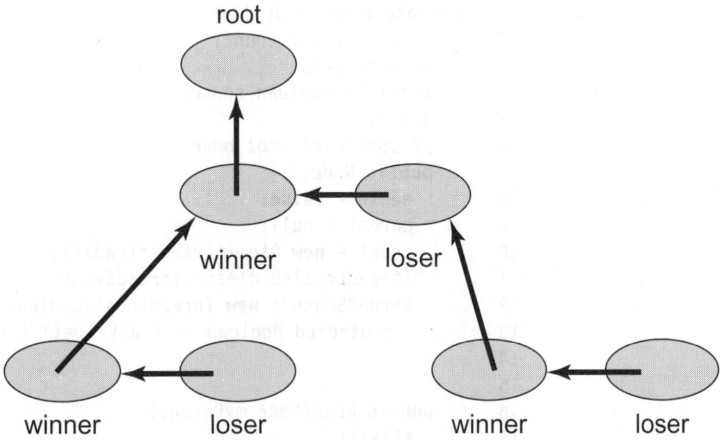

Figure 17.16 The `TourBarrier` class: information flow. Nodes are paired statically in active/passive pairs. Threads start at the leaves. Each thread in an active node waits for its passive partner to show up; then it proceeds up the tree. Each passive thread waits for its active partner for notification of completion. Once an active thread reaches the root, all threads have arrived, and notifications flow down the tree in the reverse order.

Each thread keeps track of the current sense in a thread-local variable. When a thread arrives at a passive node, it sets its active partner's `sense` field to the current sense, and spins on its own `sense` field until its partner changes that field's value to the current sense. When a thread arrives at an active node, it spins on its `sense` field until its passive partner sets it to the current sense. When the field changes, that particular barrier is complete, and the active thread follows the `parent` reference to its parent node. Note that an active thread at one level may become passive at the next level. When the root node barrier is complete, notifications percolate down the tree. Each thread moves back down the tree setting its partner's `sense` field to the current sense.

This barrier improves a little on the combining tree barrier of Fig. 17.5. Explain how.

The tournament barrier code uses `parent` and `partner` references to navigate the tree. We could save space by eliminating these fields and keeping all the nodes in a single array with the root at index 0, the root's children at indexes 1 and 2, the grandchildren at indexes 3–6, and so on. Re-implement the tournament barrier to use indexing arithmetic instead of references to navigate the tree.

Exercise 203. The combining tree barrier uses a single thread-local sense field for the entire barrier. Suppose instead we were to associate a thread-local sense with each node as in Fig. 17.8. Either:

- Explain why this implementation is equivalent to the other one, except that it consumes more memory, or.
- Give a counterexample showing that this implementation is incorrect.

```
private class Node {
  AtomicInteger count;
  Node parent;
  volatile boolean sense;
  int d;
  // construct root node
  public Node() {
    sense = false;
    parent = null;
    count = new AtomicInteger(radix);
    ThreadLocal<Boolean> threadSense;
    threadSense = new ThreadLocal<Boolean>() {
      protected Boolean initialValue() { return true; };
  };
  }
  public Node(Node myParent) {
    this();
    parent = myParent;
  }
  public void await() {
    boolean mySense = threadSense.get();
    int position = count.getAndDecrement();
    if (position == 1) {     // I'm last
      if (parent != null) { // root?
        parent.await();
      }
      count.set(radix);   // reset counter
      sense = mySense;
    } else {
      while (sense != mySense) {};
    }
    threadSense.set(!mySense);
  }
}
```

Figure 17.17 Thread-local tree barrier.

Exercise 204. The tree barrier works "bottom-up," in the sense that barrier completion moves from the leaves up to the root, while wake-up information moves from the root back down to the leaves. Figs. 17.18 and 17.19 show an alternative design, called a *reverse tree barrier*, which works just like a tree barrier except for the fact that barrier completion starts at the root and moves down to the leaves. Either:

- Sketch an argument why this is correct, perhaps by reduction to the standard tree barrier, or
- Give a counterexample showing why it is incorrect.

Exercise 205. Implement an n-thread reusable barrier from an n-wire counting network and a single Boolean variable. Sketch a proof that the barrier works.

```
public class RevBarrier implements Barrier {
  int radix;
  ThreadLocal<Boolean> threadSense;
  int leaves;
  Node[] leaf;
  public RevBarrier(int mySize, int myRadix) {
    radix = myRadix;
    leaves = 0;
    leaf = new Node[mySize / myRadix];
    int depth = 0;
    threadSense = new ThreadLocal<Boolean>() {
      protected Boolean initialValue() { return true; };
    };
    // compute tree depth
    while (mySize > 1) {
      depth++;
      mySize = mySize / myRadix;
    }
    Node root = new Node();
    root.d = depth;
    build(root, depth - 1);
  }
  // recursive tree constructor
  void build(Node parent, int depth) {
    // are we at a leaf node?
    if (depth == 0) {
      leaf[leaves++] = parent;
    } else {
      for (int i = 0; i < radix; i++) {
        Node child = new Node(parent);
        child.d = depth;
        build(child, depth - 1);
      }
    }
  }
```

Figure 17.18 Reverse tree barrier Part 1.

Exercise 206. Can you devise a "distributed" termination detection algorithm for the executer pool in which threads do not repeatedly update or test a central location for termination, but rather use only local uncontended variables? Variables may be unbounded, but state changes should take constant time, (so you cannot parallelize the shared counter).

Hint: adapt the atomic snapshot algorithm from Chapter 4.

Exercise 207. A *dissemination barrier* is a symmetric barrier implementation in which threads spin on statically-assigned locally-cached locations using only loads and stores. As illustrated in Fig. 17.20, the algorithm runs in a series of rounds. At round r, thread i notifies thread $i + 2^r \pmod n$, (where n is the number of threads) and waits for notification from thread $i - 2^r \pmod n$.

```
  public void await() {
    int me = ThreadInfo.getIndex();
    Node myLeaf = leaf[me / radix];
    myLeaf.await(me);
  }
  private class Node {
    AtomicInteger count;
    Node parent;
    volatile boolean sense;
    int d;
    // construct root node
    public Node() {
      sense = false;
      parent = null;
      count = new AtomicInteger(radix);
    }
    public Node(Node myParent) {
      this();
      parent = myParent;
    }
    public void await(int me) {
      boolean mySense = threadSense.get();
      // visit parent first
      if ((me % radix) == 0) {
        if (parent != null) { // root?
          parent.await(me / radix);
        }
      }
      int position = count.getAndDecrement();
      if (position == 1) {  // I'm last
        count.set(radix);   // reset counter
        sense = mySense;
      } else {
        while (sense != mySense) {};
      }
      threadSense.set(!mySense);
    }
  }
}
```

Figure 17.19 Reverse tree barrier Part 2: correct or not?

For how many rounds must this protocol run to implement a barrier? What if n is not a power of 2? Justify your answers.

Exercise 208. Give a reusable implementation of a dissemination barrier in Java.

Hint: you may want to keep track of both the parity and the sense of the current phase.

Exercise 209. Create a table that summarizes the total number of operations in the static tree, combining tree, and dissemination barriers.

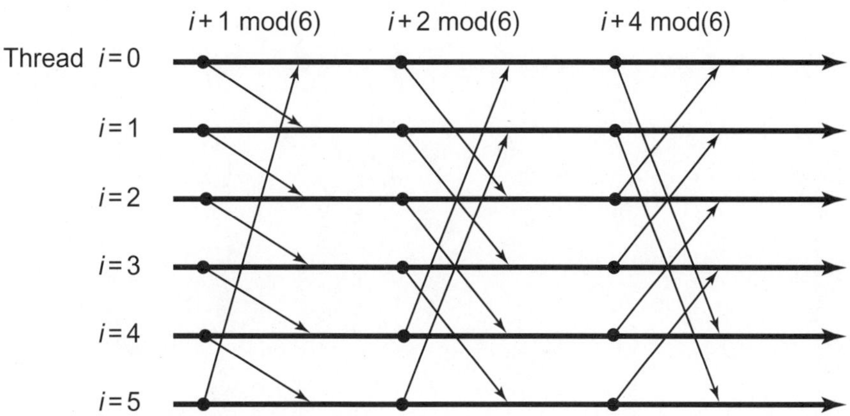

Figure 17.20 Communication in the dissemination barrier. In each round r a thread i communicates with thread $i+2^r (\text{mod } n)$.

Exercise 210. In the termination detection barrier, the state is set to active before stealing the task; otherwise the stealing thread could be declared inactive; then it would steal a task, and before setting its state back to active, the thread it stole from could become inactive. This would lead to an undesirable situation in which all threads are declared inactive yet the computation continues. Can you devise a terminating executer pool in which the state is set to active only *after* successfully stealing a task?

18 Transactional Memory

18.1 Introduction

We now turn our attention from devising data structures and algorithms to critiquing the tools we use to solve these problems. These tools are the synchronization primitives provided by today's architectures, encompassing various kinds of locking, both spinning and blocking, and atomic operations such as `compareAndSet()` and its relatives. They have mostly served us well. We, the community of multiprocessor programmers, have been able to construct many useful and elegant data structures. Nevertheless, everyone knows that *the tools are flawed.* In this chapter, we review and analyze the strengths and weaknesses of the standard synchronization primitives, and describe some emerging alternatives that are likely to extend, and perhaps even to displace many of today's standard primitives.

18.1.1 What is Wrong with Locking?

Locking, as a synchronization discipline, has many pitfalls for the inexperienced programmer. *Priority inversion* occurs when a lower-priority thread is preempted while holding a lock needed by higher-priority threads. *Convoying* occurs when a thread holding a lock is descheduled, perhaps by exhausting its scheduling quantum by a page fault, or by some other kind of interrupt. While the thread holding the lock is inactive, other threads that require that lock will queue up, unable to progress. Even after the lock is released, it may take some time to drain the queue, in much the same way that an accident can slow traffic even after the debris has been cleared away. *Deadlock* can occur if threads attempt to lock the same objects in different orders. Deadlock avoidance can be awkward if threads must lock many objects, particularly if the set of objects is not known in advance. In the past, when highly scalable applications were rare and valuable,

```
/*
 * When a locked buffer is visible to the I/O layer BH_Launder
 * is set. This means before unlocking we must clear BH_Launder,
 * mb() on alpha and then clear BH_Lock, so no reader can see
 * BH_Launder set on an unlocked buffer and then risk to deadlock.
 */
```

Figure 18.1 Synchronization by convention: a typical comment from the Linux kernel.

these hazards were avoided by deploying teams of dedicated expert programmers. Today, when highly scalable applications are becoming commonplace, the conventional approach is just too expensive.

The heart of the problem is that no one really knows how to organize and maintain large systems that rely on locking. The association between locks and data is established mostly by convention. Ultimately, it exists only in the mind of the programmer, and may be documented only in comments. Fig. 18.1 shows a typical comment from a Linux header file[1] describing the conventions governing the use of a particular kind of buffer. Over time, interpreting and observing many such conventions spelled out in this way may complicate code maintenance.

18.1.2 What is Wrong with `compareAndSet()`?

One way to bypass the problems of locking is to rely on atomic primitives like `compareAndSet()`. Algorithms that use `compareAndSet()` and its relatives are often hard to devise, and sometimes, though not always, have a high overhead. The principal difficulty is that nearly all synchronization primitives, whether reading, writing, or applying an atomic `compareAndSet()`, operate only on a single word. This restriction often forces a complex and unnatural structure on algorithms.

Let us review the lock-free queue of Chapter 10 (reproduced in Fig. 18.2), this time with an eye toward the underlying synchronization primitives.

A complication arises between Lines 12 and 13. The `enq()` method calls `compareAndSet()` to change both the `tail` node's `next` field and the `tail` field itself to the new node. Ideally, we would like to atomically combine both `compareAndSet()` calls, but because these calls occur one-at-a-time both `enq()` and `deq()` must be prepared to encounter a half-finished `enq()` (Line 12). One way to address this problem is to introduce a `multiCompareAndSet()` primitive, as shown in Fig. 18.3. This method takes as arguments an array of `AtomicReference<T>` objects, an array of expected `T` values, and an array of `T`-values used for updates. It performs a simultaneous `compareAndSet()` on all

1 Kernel v2.4.19 `/fs/buffer.c`

```
1  public class LockFreeQueue<T> {
2    private AtomicReference<Node> head;
3    private AtomicReference<Node> tail;
4    ...
5    public void enq(T item) {
6      Node node = new Node(item);
7      while (true) {
8        Node last = tail.get();
9        Node next = last.next.get();
10       if (last == tail.get()) {
11         if (next == null) {
12           if (last.next.compareAndSet(next, node)) {
13             tail.compareAndSet(last, node);
14             return;
15           }
16         } else {
17           tail.compareAndSet(last, next);
18         }
19       }
20     }
21   }
22 }
```

Figure 18.2 The LockFreeQueue class: the enq() method.

```
<T> boolean multiCompareAndSet(
    AtomicReference<T>[] target,
    T[] expected,
    T[] update) {
  atomic {
    for (int i = 0; i < target.length)
      if (!target[i].get().equals(expected[i].get()))
        return false;
    for (int i = 0; i < target.length)
      target[i].set(update[i].get);
    return true;
  }
}
```

Figure 18.3 Pseudocode for multiCompareAndSet(). This code is executed atomically.

array elements, and if any one fails, they all do. In more detail: if, for all i, the value of target[i] is expected[i], then set target[i]'s value to update[i] and return *true*. Otherwise leave target[i] unchanged, and return *false*.

Note that there is no obvious way to implement multiCompareAndSet() on conventional architectures. If there were, comparing the LockFreeQueue implementations in Figs. 18.2 and 18.4 illustrates how multiCompareAndSet() simplifies concurrent data structures. The complex logic of Lines 11–12 is replaced by a call to a single multiCompareAndSet() call.

```
public void enq(T item) {
  Node node = new Node(item);
  while (true) {
    Node last = tail.get();
    Node next = last.next.get();
    if (last == tail.get()) {
      AtomicReference[] target = {last.next, tail};
      T[] expect = {next, last};
      T[] update = {node, node};
      if (multiCompareAndSet(target, expect, update)) return;
    }
  }
}
```

Figure 18.4 The `LockFreeQueue` class: simplified `enq()` method with `multiCompareAndSet()`.

While multi-word extensions such as `multiCompareAndSet()` might be useful, they do not help with another serious flaw, discussed in Section 18.1.3.

18.1.3 What is Wrong with Compositionality?

All the synchronization mechanisms we have considered so far, with or without locks, have a major drawback: they cannot easily be *composed*. Let us imagine that we want to dequeue an item x from queue `q0` and enqueue it at another, `q1`. The transfer must be *atomic*: no concurrent thread should observe either that x has vanished, or that it is present in both queues. In `Queue` implementations based on monitors, each method acquires the lock internally, so it is essentially impossible to combine two method calls in this way.

Failure to compose is not restricted to mutual exclusion. Let us consider a bounded queue class whose `deq()` method blocks as long as the queue is empty (using either `wait/notify` or explicit condition objects). We imagine that we have two such queues, and we want to dequeue an item from *either* queue. If both queues are empty, then we want to block until an item shows up in either one. In `Queue` implementations based on monitors, each method provides its own conditional waiting, so it is essentially impossible to wait on two conditions in this way.

Naturally, there are always *ad hoc* solutions. For the atomic transfer, we could introduce a lock to be acquired by any thread attempting an atomic modification to both `q0` and `q1`. But such a lock would be a concurrency bottleneck (no concurrent transfers) and it requires knowing in advance the identities of the two queues. Or, the queues themselves might export their synchronization state, (say, via `lock()` and `unlock()` methods), and rely on the caller to manage multi-object synchronization. Exposing synchronization state in this way would have a devastating effect on modularity, complicating interfaces, and relying on callers to follow complicated conventions. Also, this approach simply would not work for nonblocking queue implementations.

18.1.4 What can We Do about It?

We can summarize the problems with conventional synchronization primitives as follows.

- Locks are hard to manage effectively, especially in large systems.
- Atomic primitives such as `compareAndSet()` operate on only one word at a time, resulting in complex algorithms.
- It is difficult to compose multiple calls to multiple objects into atomic units.

In Section 18.2, we introduce *transactional memory*, an emerging programming model that proposes a solution to each of these problems.

18.2 Transactions and Atomicity

A *transaction* is a sequence of steps executed by a single thread. Transactions must be *serializable*, meaning that they appear to execute sequentially, in a one-at-a-time order. Serializability is a kind of coarse-grained version of linearizability. Linearizability defined atomicity of individual objects by requiring that each method call of a given object appear to take effect instantaneously between its invocation and response, Serializability, on the other hand, defines atomicity for entire transactions, that is, blocks of code that may include calls to multiple objects. It ensures that a transaction appears to take effect between the invocation of its first call and the response to its last call.[2] Properly implemented, transactions do not deadlock or livelock.

We now describe some simple programming language extensions to Java that support a transactional model of synchronization. These extensions are not currently part of Java, but they illustrate the model. The features described here are a kind of average of features provided by contemporary transactional memory systems. Not all systems provide all these features: some provide weaker guarantees, some stronger. Nevertheless, understanding these features will go a long way toward understanding modern transactional memory models.

The **`atomic`** keyword delimits a transaction in much the same way the **`synchronized`** keyword delimits a critical section. While **`synchronized`** blocks acquire a specific lock, and are atomic only with respect to other **`synchronized`** blocks that acquire the same lock, an **`atomic`** block is atomic with respect to all

2 Some definitions of serializability in the literature do not require transactions to be serialized in an order compatible with their real-time precedence order.

```
public class TransactionalQueue<T> {
  private Node head;
  private Node tail;
  public TransactionalQueue() {
    Node sentinel = new Node(null);
    head = sentinel;
    tail = sentinel;
  }
  public void enq(T item) {
    atomic {
      Node node = new Node(item);
      tail.next = node;
      tail = node;
    }
  }
```

Figure 18.5 An unbounded transactional queue: the `enq()` method.

other **`atomic`** blocks. Nested **`synchronized`** blocks can deadlock if they acquire locks in opposite orders, while nested **`atomic`** blocks cannot.

Because transactions allow atomic updates to multiple locations, they eliminate the need for `multiCompareAndSet()`. Fig. 18.5 shows the `enq()` method for a transactional queue. Let us compare this code with the lock-free code of Fig. 18.2: there is no need for `AtomicReference` fields, `compareAndSet()` calls, or retry loops. Here, the code is essentially sequential code bracketed by **`atomic`** blocks.

To explain how transactions are used to write concurrent programs, it is convenient to say something about how they are implemented. Transactions are executed *speculatively*: as a transaction executes, it makes *tentative* changes to objects. If it completes without encountering a synchronization conflict, then it *commits* (the tentative changes become permanent) or it *aborts* (the tentative changes are discarded).

Transactions can be nested. Transactions must be nested for simple modularity: one method should be able to start a transaction and then call another method without caring whether the nested call starts a transaction. Nested transactions are especially useful if a nested transaction can abort without aborting its parent. This property will be important when we discuss conditional synchronization later on.

Recall that atomically transferring an item from one queue to another was essentially impossible with objects that use internal monitor locks. With transactions, composing such atomic method calls is almost trivial. Fig. 18.7 shows how to compose a `deq()` call that dequeues an item x from a queue `q0` and an `enq(`x`)` call that enqueues that item to another queue `q1`.

What about conditional synchronization? Fig. 18.6 shows the `enq()` method for a bounded buffer. The method enters an **`atomic`** block (Line 2), and tests whether the buffer is full (Line 3). If so, it calls `retry` (Line 4), which rolls

```
public void enq(T x) {
  atomic {
    if (count == items.length)
      retry;
    items[tail] = x;
    if (++tail == items.length)
      tail = 0;
    ++count;
  }
}
```

Figure 18.6 A bounded transactional queue: the `enq()` method with `retry`.

```
atomic {
  x = q0.deq();
  q1.enq(x);
}
```

Figure 18.7 Composing atomic method calls.

```
1 atomic {
2   x = q0.deq();
3 } orElse {
4   x = q1.deq();
5 }
```

Figure 18.8 The `orElse` statement: waiting on multiple conditions.

back the enclosing transaction, pauses it, and restarts it when the object state has changed. Conditional synchronization is one reason it may be convenient to roll back a nested transaction without rolling back the parent. Unlike the `wait()` method or explicit condition variables, `retry` does not easily lend itself to lost wake-up bugs.

Recall that waiting for one of several conditions to become *true* was impossible using objects with internal monitor condition variables. A novel aspect of `retry` is that such composition becomes easy. Fig. 18.8 shows a code snippet illustrating the `orElse` statement, which joins two or more code blocks. Here, the thread executes the first block (Line 2). If that block calls `retry`, then that subtransaction is rolled back, and the thread executes the second block (Line 4). If that block also calls `retry`, then the `orElse` as a whole pauses, and later reruns each of the blocks (when something changes) until one completes.

In the rest of this chapter, we examine techniques for implementing transactional memory. Transactional synchronization can be implemented in hardware (*HTM*), in software (*STM*), or both. In the following sections, we examine STM implementations.

18.3 Software Transactional Memory

Unfortunately, the language support sketched in Section 18.2 is not currently available. Instead, this section describes how to support transactional synchronization using a software library. We present `TinyTM`, a simple Software Transactional Memory package that could be the target of the language extensions described in Section 18.2. For brevity, we ignore such important issues as nested transactions, `retry`, and `orElse`. There are two elements to a software transactional memory construction: the threads that run the transactions, and the objects that they access.

We illustrate these concepts by walking though part of a concurrent `SkipList` implementation, like those found in Chapter 14. This class uses a skiplist to implement a *set* providing the usual methods: `add`(x) adds x to the set, `remove`(x) removes x from the set, and `contains`(x) returns *true* if, and only if x is in the set.

Recall that a skiplist is a collection of linked lists. Each node in the list contains an `item` field (an element of the set), a `key` field (the item's hash code), and a `next` field, which is an array of references to successor nodes in the list. Array slot zero refers to the very next node in the list, and higher-numbered slots refer to successively later successors. To find a given key, search first though higher levels, moving to a lower level each time a search overshoots. In this way, one can find an item in time logarithmic in the length of the list. (Refer to Chapter 14 for a more complete description of skiplists.)

Using `TinyTM`, threads communicate via shared *atomic objects*, which provide *synchronization*, ensuring that transactions cannot see one another's uncommitted effects, and *recovery*, undoing the effects of aborted transactions. Fields of atomic objects are not directly accessible. Instead, they are accessed indirectly through *getter* and *setter* methods. For example, the getter method for the `key` field has the form

```
int getKey();
```

while the matching setter method has the form

```
void setKey(int value);
```

Accessing fields through getters and setters provides the ability to interpose transactional synchronization and recovery on each field access. Fig. 18.9 shows the complete `SkipNode` interface.

In a similar vein, the transactional `SkipList` implementation cannot use a standard array, because `TinyTM` cannot intercept access to the array. Instead, `TinyTM` provides an `AtomicArray<T>` class that serves the same functionality as a regular array.

Fig. 18.10 shows the fields and constructor for the `SkipListSet` class, and Fig. 18.11 shows the code for the `add()` method. Except for the syntactic clutter

```
public interface SkipNode<T> {
  public int getKey();
  public void setKey(int value);
  public T getItem();
  public void setItem(T value);
  public AtomicArray<SkipNode<T>> getNext();
  public void setNext(AtomicArray<SkipNode<T>> value);
}
```

Figure 18.9 The SkipNode interface.

```

public final class SkipListSet<T> {
  final SkipNode<T> head;
  final SkipNode<T> tail;
  public SkipListSet() {
    head = new TSkipNode<T>(MAX_HEIGHT, Integer.MIN_VALUE, null);
    tail = new TSkipNode<T>(0, Integer.MAX_VALUE, null);
    AtomicArray<SkipNode<T>> next = head.getNext();
    for (int i = 0; i < next.length; i++) {
      next.set(i, tail);
    }
  }
  ...
```

Figure 18.10 The SkipListSet class: fields and constructor.

```
14    public boolean add(T v) {
15      int topLevel = randomLevel();
16      SkipNode<T>[] preds = (SkipNode<T>[]) new SkipNode[MAX_HEIGHT];
17      SkipNode<T>[] succs = (SkipNode<T>[]) new SkipNode[MAX_HEIGHT];
18      if (find(v, preds, succs) != -1) {
19        return false;
20      }
21      SkipNode<T> newNode = new TSkipNode<T>(topLevel+1, v);
22      for (int level = 0; level <= topLevel; level++) {
23        newNode.getNext().set(level, succs[level]);
24        preds[level].getNext().set(level, newNode);
25      }
26      return true;
27    }
```

Figure 18.11 The SkipListSet class: the add() method.

caused by the getters and setters, this code is almost identical to that of a sequential implementation. (The getter and setter calls could be generated by a compiler or preprocessor, but here we will make the calls explicit.) In Line 21 we create a new TSkipNode (transactional skip node) implementing the SkipNode interface. We will examine this class later on.

```
public class TThread extends java.lang.Thread {
  static Runnable onAbort = ...;
  static Runnable onCommit = ...;
  static Callable<Boolean> onValidate = ...;
  public static <T> T doIt(Callable<T> xaction) throws Exception {
    T result = null;
    while (true) {
      Transaction me = new Transaction();
      Transaction.setLocal(me);
      try {
        result = xaction.call();
      } catch (AbortedException e) {
      } catch (Exception e) {
        throw new PanicException(e);
      }
      if (onValidate.call()) {
        if (me.commit()) {
          onCommit.run(); return result;
        }
      }
      me.abort();
      onAbort.run();
    }
  }
}
```

Figure 18.12 The TThread class.

```
SkipListSet<Integer> list = new SkipListSet<Integer>();
for (int i = 0; i < 100; i++) {
    result = TThread.doIt( new Callable<Boolean>() {
                              public Boolean call() {
                                  return list.add(i);
                              }
                          });
}
```

Figure 18.13 Adding items to an integer list.

A transaction that returns a value of type T is implemented by a Callable<T> object (see Chapter 16) where the code to be executed is encapsulated in the object's call() method.

A *transactional thread* (class TThread) is a thread capable of running transactions. A TThread (Fig. 18.12) runs a transaction by calling the doIt() method with the Callable<T> object as an argument. Fig. 18.13 shows a code snippet in which a transactional thread inserts a sequence of values into a skiplist tree. The list variable is a skiplist shared by multiple transactional threads. Here, the argument to doIt() is an *anonymous inner class*, a Java construct that allows short-lived classes to be declared in-line. The result variable is a Boolean indicating whether the value was already present in the list.

We now describe the TinyTM implementation in detail. In Section 18.3.1, we describe the transactional thread implementation, and then we describe how to implement transactional atomic objects.

18.3.1 Transactions and Transactional Threads

A transaction's status is encapsulated in a thread-local `Transaction` object (Fig. 18.14) which can assume one of three states: `ACTIVE`, `ABORTED`, or `COMMITTED` (Line 2). When a transaction is created, its default status is `ACTIVE` (Line 11). It is convenient to define a constant `Transaction.COMMITTED` transaction object for threads that are not currently executing within a transaction (Line 3). The `Transaction` class also keeps track of each thread's current transaction through a thread-local field `local` (Lines 5–8).

The `commit()` method tries to change the transaction state from `ACTIVE` to `COMMITTED` (Line 19), and the `abort()` method from `ACTIVE` to `ABORTED`

```
1  public class Transaction {
2    public enum Status {ABORTED, ACTIVE, COMMITTED};
3    public static Transaction COMMITTED = new Transaction(Status.COMMITTED);
4    private final AtomicReference<Status> status;
5    static ThreadLocal<Transaction> local = new ThreadLocal<Transaction>() {
6      protected Transaction initialValue() {
7        return new Transaction(Status.COMMITTED);
8      }
9    };
10   public Transaction() {
11     status = new AtomicReference<Status>(Status.ACTIVE);
12   }
13   private Transaction(Transaction.Status myStatus) {
14     status = new AtomicReference<Status>(myStatus);
15   }
16   public Status getStatus() {
17     return status.get();
18   }
19   public boolean commit() {
20     return status.compareAndSet(Status.ACTIVE, Status.COMMITTED);
21   }
22   public boolean abort() {
23     return status.compareAndSet(Status.ACTIVE, Status.ABORTED);
24   }
25   public static Transaction getLocal() {
26     return local.get();
27   }
28   public static void setLocal(Transaction transaction) {
29     local.set(transaction);
30   }
31 }
```

Figure 18.14 The `Transaction` class.

(Line 22). A thread can test its current transaction state by calling `getStatus()` (Line 16). If a thread discovers that its current transaction has been aborted, it throws `AbortedException`. A thread can get and set its current transaction by calling static `getLocal()` or `setLocal()` methods.

The `TThread` (transactional thread) class is a subclass of the standard Java `Thread` class. Each transactional thread has several associated *handlers*. The `onCommit` and `onAbort` handlers are called when a transaction commits or aborts, and the *validation* handler is called when a transaction is about to commit. It returns a `Boolean` indicating whether the thread's current transaction should try to commit. These handlers can be defined at run-time. Later, we will see how these handlers can be used to implement different techniques for transaction synchronization and recovery.

The `doIt()` method (Line 5 of Fig. 18.12) takes a `Callable<T>` object and executes its `call()` method as a transaction. It creates a new `ACTIVE` transaction (Line 8), and calls the transaction's `call()` method. If that method throws `AbortedException` (Line 12), then the `doIt()` method simply retries the loop. Any other exception means the application has made an error (Line 13), and (for simplicity) the method throws `PanicException`, which prints an error message and shuts down everything. If the transaction returns, then `doIt()` calls the validation handler to test whether to commit (Line 16), and if the validation succeeds, then it tries to commit the transaction (Line 17). If the commit succeeds, then it runs the commit hander and returns (Line 18). Otherwise, if validation fails, it explicitly aborts the transaction. If commit fails for any reason, it runs the abort handler before retrying (Line 22).

18.3.2 Zombies and Consistency

Synchronization conflicts cause transactions to abort, but it is not always possible to halt a transaction's thread immediately after the conflict occurs. Instead, such *zombie*[3] transactions may continue to run even after it has become impossible for them to commit. This prospect raises another important design issue: how to prevent zombie transactions from seeing inconsistent states.

Here is how an inconsistent state could arise. An object has two fields x and y, initially 1 and 2. Each transaction preserves the invariant that y is always equal to $2x$. Transaction Z reads y, and sees value 2. Transaction A changes x and y to 2 and 4, respectively, and commits. Z is now a zombie, since it keeps running, but will never commit. Z later reads x, and sees the value 2, which is inconsistent with the value it read for y.

One approach is to deny that inconsistent states are a problem. Since zombie transactions must eventually abort, their updates will be discarded, so why should we care what they observe? Unfortunately, a zombie can cause problems,

3 A *zombie* is a reanimated human corpse. Stories of zombies originated in the Afro-Caribbean spiritual belief system of Vodou.

even if its updates never take effect. In the scenario described earlier, where $y = 2x$ in every consistent state, but Z has read the inconsistent value 2 for both x and y, if Z evaluates the expression

```
1/(x-y)
```

it will throw an "impossible" divide-by-zero exception, halting the thread, and possibly crashing the application. For the same reason, if Z now executes the loop

```
int i = x + 1;  // i is 3
while (i++ != y) {  // y is actually 2, should be 4
  ...
}
```

it would never terminate.

There is no practical way to avoid "impossible" exceptions and infinite loops in a programming model where invariants cannot be relied on. As a result, TinyTM guarantees that all transactions, even zombies, see consistent states.

18.3.3 Atomic Objects

As mentioned earlier, concurrent transactions communicate through shared *atomic objects*. As we have seen (Fig. 18.9), access to an atomic object is provided by a stylized interface that provides a set of matching getter and setter methods. The AtomicObject interface appears in Fig. 18.15.

We will need to construct two classes that implement this interface: a *sequential* implementation that provides no synchronization or recovery, and a *transactional* implementation that does. Here too, these classes could easily be generated by a compiler, but we will do these constructions by hand.

The sequential implementation is straightforward. For each matching getter–setter pair, for example:

```
T getItem();
void setItem(T value);
```

```
public abstract class AtomicObject <T extends Copyable<T>> {
  protected Class<T> internalClass;
  protected T internalInit;
  public AtomicObject(T init) {
    internalInit = init;
    internalClass = (Class<T>) init.getClass();
  }
  public abstract T openRead();
  public abstract T openWrite();
  public abstract boolean validate();
}
```

Figure 18.15 The AtomicObject<T> abstract class.

the sequential implementation defines a private field `item` of type `T`. We also require the sequential implementation to satisfy a simple `Copyable<T>` interface that provides a `copyTo()` method that copies the fields of one object to another (Fig. 18.16). As a technical matter, we also require the type to provide a no-argument constructor. For brevity, we use the term *version* to refer to an instance of a sequential, `Copyable<T>` implementation of an atomic object interface.

Fig. 18.17 shows the `SSkipNode` class, a sequential implementation of the `SkipNode` interface. This class has three parts. The class must provide a no-argument constructor for use by atomic object implementations (as described later), and may provide any other constructors convenient to the class. Second, it provides the getters and setters defined by the interface, where each getter or setter simply reads or writes its associated field. Finally, the class also implements the `Copyable` interface, which provides a `copyTo()` method that initializes one

```
public interface Copyable<T> {
  void copyTo(T target);
}
```

Figure 18.16 The `Copyable<T>` interface.

```
public class SSkipNode<T>
 implements SkipNode<T>, Copyable<SSkipNode<T>> {
  AtomicArray<SkipNode<T>> next;
  int key;
  T item;
  public SSkipNode() {}
  public SSkipNode(int level) {
    next = new AtomicArray<SkipNode<T>>(SkipNode.class, level);
  }
  public SSkipNode(int level, int myKey, T myItem) {
    this(level); key = myKey; item = myItem;
  }
  public AtomicArray<SkipNode<T>> getNext() {return next;}
  public void setNext(AtomicArray<SkipNode<T>> value) {next = value;}
  public int getKey() {return key;}
  public void setKey(int value) {key = value;}
  public T getItem() {return item;}
  public void setItem(T value) {item = value;}

  public void copyTo(SSkipNode<T> target) {
    target.next = next;
    target.key  = key;
    target.item = item;
  }
}
```

Figure 18.17 The `SSkipNode` class: a sequential `SkipNode` implementation.

object's fields from another's. This method is needed to make back-up copies of the sequential object.

18.3.4 Dependent or Independent Progress?

One goal of transactional memory is to free the programmer from worrying about starvation, deadlock, and "the thousand natural shocks" that locking is heir to. Nevertheless, those who implement STMs must decide which progress condition to meet.

We recall from Chapter 3 that implementations that meet strong independent progress conditions such as wait-freedom or lock-freedom guarantee that a thread always makes progress. While it is possible to design wait-free or lock-free STM systems, no one knows how to make them efficient enough to be practical.

Instead, research on nonblocking STMs has focused on weaker dependent progress conditions. There are two approaches that promise good performance: nonblocking STMs that are obstruction-free, and blocking, lock-based STMs that are deadlock-free. Like the other nonblocking conditions, obstruction-freedom ensures that not all threads can be blocked by delays or failures of other threads. This property is weaker than lock-free synchronization, because it does not guarantee progress when two or more conflicting threads are executing concurrently.

The deadlock-free property does not guarantee progress if threads halt in critical sections. Fortunately, as with many of the lock-based data structures we saw earlier, scheduling in modern operating systems can minimize the possibility of threads getting swapped out in the middle of a transaction. Like obstruction-freedom, deadlock-freedom does not guarantee progress when two or more conflicting threads are executing concurrently.

For both the nonblocking obstruction-free and blocking deadlock-free STMs, progress for conflicting transactions is guaranteed by a *contention manager*, a mechanism that decides when to delay contending threads, through spinning or yielding, so that some thread can always make progress.

18.3.5 Contention Managers

In TinyTM, as in many other STMs, a transaction can detect when it is about to cause a synchronization conflict. The *requester* transaction then consults a *contention manager*. The contention manager serves as an oracle,[4] advising the transaction whether to abort the *other* transaction immediately, or stall to allow the other a chance to complete. Naturally, no transaction should stall forever waiting for another.

4 Dating back to 1400 BC, Pythia, the Oracle of Delphi, provided advice and predictions about crops and wars.

```
1  public abstract class ContentionManager {
2    static ThreadLocal<ContentionManager> local
3     = new ThreadLocal<ContentionManager>() {
4      protected ContentionManager initialValue() {
5        try {
6          return (ContentionManager) Defaults.MANAGER.newInstance();
7        } catch (Exception ex) {
8          throw new PanicException(ex);
9        }
10     }
11   };
12   public abstract void resolve(Transaction me, Transaction other);
13   public static ContentionManager getLocal() {
14     return local.get();
15   }
16   public static void setLocal(ContentionManager m) {
17     local.set(m);
18   }
19 }
```

Figure 18.18 Contention manager base class.

Fig. 18.18 shows a simplified base class for contention managers. It provides a single method, `resolve()` (Line 12), that takes two transactions, the requester's and the other's, and either pauses the requester, or aborts the other. It also keeps track of each thread's local contention manager (Line 2), accessible by `getLocal()` and `setLocal()` methods (Lines 16 and 13).

The `ContentionManager` class is *abstract* because it does not implement any conflict resolution policy. Here are some possible contention manager policies. Suppose transaction *A* is about to conflict with transaction *B*.

- *Backoff: A* repeatedly backs off for a random duration, doubling the expected time up to some limit. When that limit is reached, it aborts *B*.
- *Priority:* Each transaction takes a timestamp when it starts. If *A* has an older timestamp than *B*, it aborts *B*, and otherwise it waits. A transaction that restarts after an abort keeps its old timestamp, ensuring that every transaction eventually completes.
- *Greedy:* Each transaction takes a timestamp when it starts. *A* aborts *B* if either *A* has an older timestamp than *B*, or *B* is waiting for another transaction. This strategy eliminates chains of waiting transactions. As in the priority policy, every transaction eventually completes.
- *Karma:* Each transaction keeps track of how much work it has accomplished, and the transaction that has accomplished more has priority.

Fig. 18.19 shows a contention manager implementation that uses the back-off policy. The manager imposes minimum and maximum delays (Lines 2–3). The `resolve()` method checks whether this is the first time it has encountered the other thread (Line 8). If so, it resets its delay to the minimum, and otherwise it uses its current delay. If the current delay is less than the maximum, the thread

```
1  public class BackoffManager extends ContentionManager {
2    private static final int MIN_DELAY = ...;
3    private static final int MAX_DELAY = ...;
4    Random random = new Random();
5    Transaction previous = null;
6    int delay = MIN_DELAY;
7    public void resolve(Transaction me, Transaction other) {
8      if (other != previous) {
9        previous = other;
10       delay = MIN_DELAY;
11     }
12     if (delay < MAX_DELAY) {
13       Thread.sleep(random.nextInt(delay));
14       delay = 2 * delay;
15     } else {
16       other.abort();
17       delay = MIN_DELAY;
18     }
19   }
20 }
```

Figure 18.19 A simple contention manager implementation.

sleeps for a random duration bounded by the delay (Line 13), and doubles the next delay. If the current delay exceeds the maximum, the caller aborts the other transaction (Line 16).

18.3.6 Implementing Atomic Objects

Linearizability requires that individual method calls appear to take place atomically. We now consider how to guarantee serializability: that multiple atomic calls have the same property.

A *transactional* implementation of an atomic object must provide getter and setter methods that invoke transactional synchronization and recovery. We review two alternative approaches to synchronization and recovery: the `FreeObject` class is obstruction-free, while the `LockObject` class uses locking for synchronization. These alternatives are implementations of the abstract `AtomicObject` class, shown in Fig. 18.15. The `init()` method takes the atomic object's class as argument and records it for later use. The `openRead()` method returns a version suitable for reading (that is, one can call its getter methods only), while the `openWrite()` method returns a version that may be written (that is, one can call both getters and setters).

The `validate()` method returns *true* if and only if the value to be returned is guaranteed to be consistent. It is necessary to call `validate()` before returning any information extracted from an atomic object. The `openRead()`, `openWrite()`, and `validate()` methods are all abstract.

Fig. 18.20 shows the `TSkipNode` class a transactional `SkipNode` implementation. This class uses the `LockObject` atomic object implementation for synchronization and recovery (Line 8).

```
public class TSkipNode<T> implements SkipNode<T> {
  AtomicObject<SSkipNode<T>> atomic;
  public TSkipNode(int level) {
    atomic = new LockObject<SSkipNode<T>>(new SSkipNode<T>(level));
  }
  public TSkipNode(int level, int key, T item){
    atomic =
      new LockObject<SSkipNode<T>>(new SSkipNode<T>(level, key, item));
  }
  public TSkipNode(int level, T item){
    atomic = new LockObject<SSkipNode<T>>(new SSkipNode<T>(level,
        item.hashCode(), item));
  }
  public AtomicArray<SkipNode<T>> getNext() {
    AtomicArray<SkipNode<T>> forward = atomic.openRead().getNext();
    if (!atomic.validate())
      throw new AbortedException();
    return forward;
  }
  public void setNext(AtomicArray<SkipNode<T>> value) {
    atomic.openWrite().setNext(value);
  }
  // getKey, setKey, getItem, and setItem omitted ...
}
```

Figure 18.20 The `TSkipNode` class: a transactional `SkipNode` implementation.

This class has a single `AtomicObject<SSkipNode>` field. The constructor takes as argument values to initialize the `AtomicObject<SSkipNode>` field. Each getter performs the following sequence of steps.

1. It calls `openRead()` to extract a version.
2. It calls the version's getter to extract the field value, which it stores in a local variable.
3. It calls `validate()` to ensure the value read is consistent.

The last step is needed to ensure that the object did not change between the first and second step, and that the value recorded in the second step is consistent with all the other values observed by that transaction.

Setters are implemented in a symmetric way, calling the setter in the second step.

We now have two alternative atomic object implementations. The implementations will be relatively unoptimized to simplify the presentation.

18.3.7 An Obstruction-Free Atomic Object

Recall that an algorithm is *obstruction-free* if any thread that runs by itself for long enough makes progress. In practice, this condition means that a thread makes progress if it runs for long enough without a synchronization conflict from a concurrent thread. Here, we describe an obstruction-free implementation of `AtomicObject`.

Bird's-Eye View

Each object has three logical fields: an *owner* field, an *old* version, and a *new* version. (We call them *logical* fields because they may not be implemented as fields.) The owner is the last transaction to access the object. The old version is the object state before that transaction arrived, and the new version reflects that transaction's updates, if any. If owner is `COMMITTED`, then the new version is the current object state, while if it is `ABORTED`, then the old version is current. If the owner is `ACTIVE`, there is no current version, and the future current version depends on whether the owner commits or aborts.

When a transaction starts, it creates a `Transaction` object to hold the transaction's status, initially `ACTIVE`. If that transaction commits, it sets the status to `COMMITTED`, and if it is aborted by another transaction, the other transaction sets the status to `ABORTED`.

Each time transaction *A* accesses an object it first *opens* that object, possibly resetting the owner, old value, and new value fields. Let *B* be the object's prior owner.

1. If *B* was `COMMITTED`, then the new version is current. *A* installs itself as the object's current owner, sets the old version to the prior new version, and the new version to a copy of the prior new version (if the call is a setter), or to the new version itself (if the call is a getter).
2. Symmetrically, if *B* was `ABORTED`, then the old version is current. *A* installs itself as the object's current owner, sets the old version to the prior old version, and the new version to a copy of the prior old version (if the call is a setter), or to the old version itself (if the call is a getter).
3. If *B* is still `ACTIVE`, then *A* and *B* conflict, so *A* consults the contention manager for advice whether to abort *B*, or to pause, giving *B* a chance to finish. One transaction aborts another by successfully calling `compareAndSet()` to change the victim's status to `ABORTED`.

We leave it to the readers to extend this algorithm to allow concurrent readers.

After opening the object, the getter reads the version's field into a local variable. Before returning that value, it calls `validate()` to check that the calling transaction has not been aborted. If all is well, it returns the field value to the caller. (Setters work symmetrically).

When it is time for *A* to commit, it calls `compareAndSet()` to change its status to `COMMITTED`. If it succeeds, the commit is complete. The next transaction to access an object owned by *A* will observe that *A* has committed, and will treat the object's new version (the one installed by *A*) as current. If it fails, it has been aborted by another transaction. The next transaction to access an object updated by *A* will observe that *A* has been aborted, and will treat the object's old version (the one prior to *A*) as current. Fig. 18.21 shows an example execution.

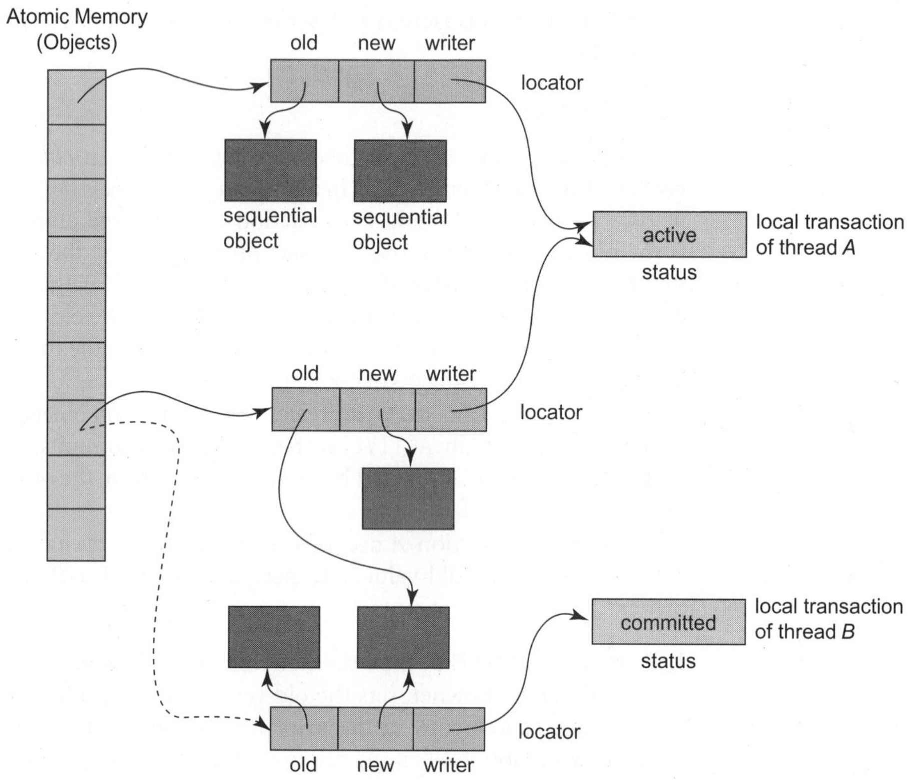

Figure 18.21 The FreeObject class: an obstruction-free atomic object implementation. Thread *A* has completed the writing of one object and is in the process of switching a copy of the second object that was last written by thread *B*. It prepares a new locator with a fresh new copy of the object and an old object field that refers to the new field of thread *B*'s locator. It then uses a compareAndSet() to switch the object to refer to the newly created locator.

Why It Works

Here is why every transaction observes a consistent state. When a transaction *A* calls a getter method to read an object field, it opens the object, installing itself as the object's owner. If the object already had an active owner, *B*, then *A* aborts *B*. *A* then reads the field value into a local variable. Before the getter returns that value to the application, however, it calls validate() to check that the value is consistent. If another transaction *C* displaced *A* as owner of any object, then *C* aborted *A*, and *A*'s validation fails. It follows that if a setter returns a value, that value is consistent.

Here is why transactions are serializable. If a transaction *A* successfully changes its status from ACTIVE to COMMITTED, then it must still be owner of all the objects it accessed, because any transaction that usurps *A*'s ownership must abort *A* first. It follows that none of the objects it read or wrote have changed since *A* accessed them, so *A* is effectively updating a snapshot of the objects it accessed.

In Detail

Opening an object requires changing multiple fields atomically, modifying the owner, old version, and new version fields. Without locks, the only way to accomplish this atomic multi-field update is to introduce a level of indirection. As shown in Fig. 18.22, the `FreeObject` class has a single field, `start`, that is an `AtomicReference` to a `Locator` object (Line 3), which holds the object's current transaction, old version, and new version (Lines 5–7).

Recall that an object field is modified in the following steps: (1) call `openWrite()` to acquire an object version, (2) tentatively modify that version, and (3) call `validate()` to ensure the version is still good. Fig. 18.23 shows the `FreeObject` class's `openWrite()` method. First, the thread tests its own transactional state (Line 14). If that state is committed, then the thread is not running in a transaction, and updates the object directly (Line 15). If that state is aborted, then the thread immediately throws an `AbortedException` exception (Line 16). Finally, if the transaction is active, then the thread reads the current locator and checks whether it has already opened this object for writing, returning immediately if so (Line 19). Otherwise, it enters a loop (Line 22) where it repeatedly initializes and tries to install a new locator. To determine the object's current value, the thread checks the status of the last transaction to write the object (Line 25), using the new version if the owner is committed (Line 27) and the old version if it is `ABORTED` (Line 30). If the owner is still active (Line 30), there there is a synchronization conflict, and the thread calls the contention manager module to resolve the conflict. In the absence of conflict, the thread creates and initializes a new version (Lines 37–39). Finally, the thread calls `compareAndSet()` to replace the old locator with the new, returning if it succeeds, and retrying if it fails.

The `openRead()` method (not shown) works in the same way, except that it does not need to make a copy of the old version.

The `FreeObject` class's `validate()` method (not shown) simply checks that current thread's transaction status is `ACTIVE`.

```
1  public class FreeObject<T extends Copyable<T>>
2                               extends TinyTM.AtomicObject<T> {
3    AtomicReference<Locator> start;
4    private class Locator {
5      Transaction owner;
6      T oldVersion;
7      T newVersion;
8      ...
9     }
10   ...
11 }
```

Figure 18.22 The `FreeObject` class: the inner `Locator` class.

```
  public T openWrite() {
    Transaction me = Transaction.getLocal();
    switch (me.getStatus()) {
      case COMMITTED: return openSequential();
      case ABORTED: throw new AbortedException();
      case ACTIVE:
        Locator locator = start.get();
        if (locator.owner == me)
          return locator.newVersion;
        Locator newLocator = new Locator();
        while (!Thread.currentThread().isInterrupted()) {
          Locator oldLocator = start.get();
          Transaction owner = oldLocator.owner;
          switch (owner.getStatus()) {
            case COMMITTED:
              newLocator.oldVersion = oldLocator.newVersion;
              break;
            case ABORTED:
              newLocator.oldVersion = oldLocator.oldVersion;
              break;
            case ACTIVE:
              ContentionManager.getLocal().resolve(me, owner);
              continue;
          }
          try {
            newLocator.newVersion = (T) _class.newInstance();
          } catch (Exception ex) {throw new PanicException(ex);}
          newLocator.oldVersion.copyTo(newLocator.newVersion);;
          if (start.compareAndSet(oldLocator, newLocator))
            return newLocator.newVersion;
        }
        me.abort();
        throw new AbortedException();
      default: throw new PanicException("Unexpected transaction state");
    }
  }
```

Figure 18.23 The `FreeObject` class: the `openWrite()` method.

18.3.8 A Lock-Based Atomic Object

The obstruction-free implementation is somewhat inefficient because writes continually allocate locators and versions and reads must go through two levels of indirection (two references) to reach the actual data to be read. In this section, we present a more efficient atomic object implementation that uses short critical sections to eliminate the need for a locator and to remove a level of indirection.

A lock-based STM could lock each object as it is read or written. Many applications, however, follow the 80/20 rule: roughly 80% of accesses are reads and roughly 20% are writes. Locking an object is expensive, since it requires a `compareAndSet()` call, which seems excessive when read/write conflicts are expected to be infrequent. Is it really necessary to lock objects for reading? The answer is *no*.

Bird's-Eye View

The lock-based atomic object implementation reads objects optimistically, and later checks for conflicts. It detects conflicts using a global *version clock*, a counter shared by all transactions and incremented each time a transaction commits. When a transaction starts, it records the current version clock value in a thread-local *read stamp*.

Each object has the following fields: the *stamp* field is the read stamp of the last transaction to write to that object, the *version* field is an instance of the sequential object, and the *lock* field is a lock. As explained earlier, the sequential type must implement the `Copyable` interface, and provide a no-argument constructor.

The transaction *virtually* executes a sequence of read and write accesses to objects. By "virtually", we mean that no objects are actually modified. Instead, the transaction uses a thread-local *read set* to keep track of the objects it has read, and a thread-local *write set* to keep track of the objects it intends to modify, and their tentative new versions.

When a transaction calls a getter to return a field value, the `LockObject`'s `openRead()` method first checks whether the object already appears in the write set. If so, it returns the tentative new version. Otherwise, it checks whether the object is locked. If so, there is a synchronization conflict, and the transaction aborts. If not, `openRead()` adds the object to the read set and returns its version.

The `openWrite()` method is similar. If the object is not found in the write set, the method creates a new, tentative version, adds the tentative version to the write set, and returns that version.

The `validate()` method checks that the object's stamp is not greater than the transaction's read stamp. If so, a conflict exists, and the transaction aborts. If not, the getter returns the value read in the previous step.

It is important to understand that the `LockObject`'s `validate()` method guarantees only that the value is consistent. It does not guarantee that the caller is not a zombie transaction. Instead, a transaction must take the following steps to commit.

1. It locks each of the objects in its write set, in any convenient order, using timeouts to avoid deadlock.
2. It uses `compareAndSet()` to increment the global version clock, storing the result in a thread-local write stamp. If the transaction commits, this is the point where it is serialized.
3. The transaction checks that each object in its read set is not locked by another thread, and that each object's stamp is not greater than the transaction's read stamp. If this validation succeeds, the transaction commits. (In the special case where the transaction's write stamp is one more than its read stamp, there is

no need to validate the read set, because no concurrent modification could have happened.)

4. The transaction updates the stamp field of each object in its write set. Once the stamps are updated, the transaction releases its locks.

If any of these tests fails, the transaction aborts, discards its read and write sets, and releases any locks it is holding.

Fig. 18.24 shows an example execution.

Why It Works

Transactions are serializable in the order they increment the global version clock. Here is why every transaction observes a consistent state. If A, with read stamp r, observes that the object is not locked, then this version will have the latest stamp not exceeding r. Any transaction that modifies the object at a later time locks the object, increments the global version clock, and sets that object's stamp to the new version clock value, which exceeds r. If A observes the object is not locked, then A cannot miss an update with a stamp less than or equal to r. A also checks

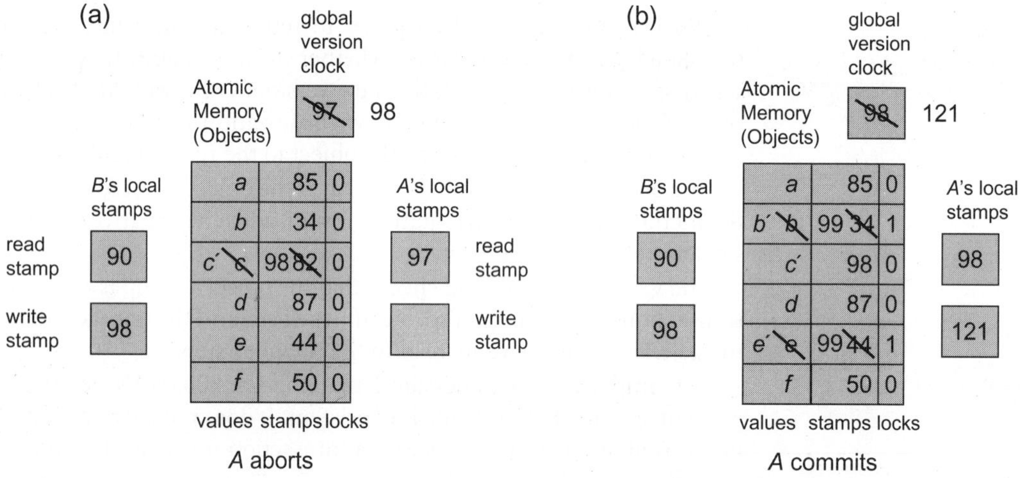

Figure 18.24 The `LockObject` class: A lock-based transactional memory implementation. In Part (a) thread *A* starts its transaction, setting its read stamp rs to 97, the global version clock value. Before *A* starts reading and writing objects, thread *B* commits: it increments the global version clock to 98, records 98 in its local write stamp ws field, and after a successful validation writes a new value c' with *stamp* 98. (*B*'s acquisition and release of the object locks is not shown.) When *A* reads the object with stamp 98, it detects thread *B*'s modification because its read stamp is less than 98, so *A* aborts. In Part (b) on the other hand, *A* starts its transaction after *B* completed, and reads a read stamp value of 98, and does not abort when reading c'. *A* creates read–write sets, and increments the global version clock. (Notice that other threads have incremented the clock to 120.). It locks the objects it intends to modify, and successfully validates. It then updates the values and stamps of these objects based on the write stamp value. In the figure, we do not show *A*'s final release of the locks on the written objects.

that the object's stamp does not exceed r by reading and testing the stamp after it reads the field.

Here is why transactions are serializable. We claim that if A reads x and A later commits, then x could not have changed between the time A first reads x and the time A increments the global version clock. As noted earlier, if A with read stamp r observes x is unlocked at time t, then any subsequent modifications to x will give x a stamp larger than r. If a transaction B commits before A, and modifies an object read by A, then A's validation handler will either observe that x is locked by B, or that x's stamp is greater than r, and will abort either way.

In Detail

Before we describe the algorithm, we describe the basic data structures. Fig. 18.25 shows the `WriteSet` class used by the locking implementation. This class is essentially a map from objects to versions, sending each object written by

```
public class WriteSet {
  static ThreadLocal<Map<LockObject<?>, Object>> map
    = new ThreadLocal<Map<LockObject<?>,Object>>() {
    protected synchronized Map<LockObject<?>, Object> initialValue() {
      return new HashMap();
    }
  };
  public static Object get(LockObject<?> x) {
    return map.get().get(x);
  }
  public static void put(LockObject<?> x, Object y) {
    map.get().put(x, y);
  }
  public static boolean tryLock(long timeout, TimeUnit timeUnit) {
    Stack<LockObject<?>> stack = new Stack<LockObject<?>>();
    for (LockObject<?> x : map.get().keySet()) {
      if (!x.tryLock(timeout, timeUnit)) {
        for (LockObject<?> y : stack) {
          y.unlock();
        }
        throw new AbortedException();
      }
    }
    return true;
  }
  public static void unlock() {
    for (LockObject<?> x : map.get().keySet()) {
      x.unlock();
    }
  }
  ...
}
```

Figure 18.25 The `LockObject` class: the inner `WriteSet` class.

the transaction to its tentative new version. In addition to the `get()` and `set()` methods, the class also includes methods to lock and unlock each object in the table. The `ReadSet` class (not shown) is just a set of objects.

Fig. 18.26 shows the version clock. All fields and methods are static. The class manages a singe global version counter, and a set of thread-local read stamps. The `getWriteStamp()` method returns the current global version and `setWriteStamp()` advances it by one. The `getReadStamp()` method returns the caller's thread-local read stamp, and `setReadStamp()` sets the thread-local read stamp to the current global clock value.

The `LockObject` class (Fig. 18.27) has three fields: the object's lock, its read stamp, and the object's actual data. Fig. 18.28 shows how to open an object for reading. If a copy of the object is not already in the transaction's write set (Line 13), then it places the object in the transaction's read set. If, however, the object is locked, then it is in the middle of an update by a concurrent transaction, and

```
public class VersionClock {
  // global clock read and advanced by all
  static AtomicLong global = new AtomicLong();
  // thread-local cached copy of global clock
  static ThreadLocal<Long> local = new ThreadLocal<Long>() {
    protected Long initialValue() {
      return 0L;
    }
  };
  public static void setReadStamp() {
    local.set(global.get());
  }
  public static long getReadStamp() {
    return local.get();
  }
  public static void setWriteStamp() {
    local.set(global.incrementAndGet());
  }
  public static long getWriteStamp() {
    return local.get();
  }
}
```

Figure 18.26 The `VersionClock` class.

```
public class LockObject<T extends Copyable<T>> extends AtomicObject<T> {
  ReentrantLock lock;
  volatile long stamp;
  T version;
  ...
```

Figure 18.27 The `LockObject` class: fields.

```
6    public T openRead() {
7      ReadSet readSet = ReadSet.getLocal();
8      switch (Transaction.getLocal().getStatus()) {
9        case COMMITTED:
10         return version;
11       case ACTIVE:
12         WriteSet writeSet = WriteSet.getLocal();
13         if (writeSet.get(this) == null) {
14           if (lock.isLocked()) {
15             throw new AbortedException();
16           }
17           readSet.add(this);
18           return version;
19         } else {
20           T scratch = (T)writeSet.get(this);
21           return scratch;
22         }
23       case ABORTED:
24         throw new AbortedException();
25       default:
26         throw new PanicException("unexpected transaction state");
27     }
28   }
```

Figure 18.28 The `LockObject` class: the openRead() method.

the reader aborts (Line 15). If the object has a tentative version in the write set, it returns that version (Line 19).

Fig. 18.29 shows the `LockObject` class's `openWrite()` method. If the call occurs outside a transaction (Line 31), it simply returns the object's current version. If the transaction is active (Line 33), it tests whether the object is in its write set (Line 35). If so, it returns that version. If not, the caller aborts if the object is locked (Line 37). Otherwise it creates a new, tentative version using the type's no-argument constructor (Line 39), initializes it by copying the old version (Line 40), puts it in the write set (Line 41), and returns the tentative version.

The `validate()` method simply checks whether the object's read stamp is less than or equal to the transaction's read stamp (Line 56).

We now look at how a transaction commits. Recall that `TinyTM` allows users to register handlers to be executed on validation, commit, and abort. Fig. 18.31 shows how the locking TM validates transactions. It first locks each object in the write set (Line 66). If the lock acquisition times out, there may be a deadlock, so the method returns *false*, meaning the transaction should not commit. It then validates the read set. For each object, it checks that it is not locked by another transaction (Line 70) and that the object's stamp does not exceed the transaction's read stamp (Line 72).

If validation succeeds, the transaction may now commit. Fig. 18.32 shows the `onCommit()` handler. It increments the version clock (Line 83), copies the tentative versions from the write set back to the original objects (Lines 86–89) and

```
29   public T openWrite() {
30     switch (Transaction.getLocal().getStatus()) {
31       case COMMITTED:
32         return version;
33       case ACTIVE:
34         WriteSet writeSet = WriteSet.getLocal();
35         T scratch = (T) writeSet.get(this);
36         if (scratch == null) {
37           if (lock.isLocked())
38             throw new AbortedException();
39           scratch = myClass.newInstance();
40           version.copyTo(scratch);
41           writeSet.put(this, scratch);
42         }
43         return scratch;
44       case ABORTED:
45         throw new AbortedException();
46       default:
47         throw new PanicException("unexpected transaction state");
48     }
49   }
```

Figure 18.29 The `LockObject` class: the `openWrite()` method.

```
50    public boolean validate() {
51     Transaction.Status status = Transaction.getLocal().getStatus();
52     switch (status) {
53       case COMMITTED:
54         return true;
55       case ACTIVE:
56         return stamp <= VersionClock.getReadStamp(); ;
57       case ABORTED:
58         return false;
59     }
60   }
61 }
```

Figure 18.30 The `LockObject` class: the `validate()` method.

sets each object's stamp to the newly incremented version clock value (Line 90). Finally, it releases the locks, and clears the thread-local read–write sets for the next transaction.

What have we learned so far? We have seen how a single transactional memory framework can support two substantially different kinds of synchronization mechanisms: one obstruction-free, and one employing short-lived locking. Each of these implementations, by itself, provides weak progress guarantees, so we rely on a separate contention manager to ensure progress.

```
public class OnValidate implements Callable<Boolean>{
  public Boolean call() throws Exception {
    WriteSet writeSet = WriteSet.getLocal();
    ReadSet readSet = ReadSet.getLocal();
    if (!writeSet.tryLock(TIMEOUT, TimeUnit.MILLISECONDS)) {
      return false;
    }
    for (LockObject x : readSet) {
      if (x.lock.isLocked() && !x.lock.isHeldByCurrentThread())
        return false;
      if (stamp > VersionClock.getReadStamp()) {
        return false;
      }
    }
    return true;
  }
}
```

Figure 18.31 The LockObject class: the onValidate() hander.

```
public class OnCommit implements Runnable {
  public void run() {
    WriteSet writeSet = WriteSet.getLocal();
    ReadSet readSet = ReadSet.getLocal();
    VersionClock.setWriteStamp();
    long writeVersion = VersionClock.getWriteStamp();
    for (Map.Entry<LockObject<?>, Object> entry : writeSet) {
      LockObject<?> key = (LockObject<?>) entry.getKey();
      Copyable destin = (Copyable) key.openRead();
      Copyable source = (Copyable) entry.getValue();
      source.copyTo(destin);
      key.stamp = writeVersion;
    }
    writeSet.unlock();
    writeSet.clear();
    readSet.clear();
  }
}
```

Figure 18.32 The LockObject class: the onCommit() handler.

18.4 Hardware Transactional Memory

We now describe how a standard hardware architecture can be augmented to support short, small transactions directly in hardware. The HTM design presented here is high-level and simplified, but it covers the principal aspects of HTM design. Readers unfamiliar with cache coherence protocols may consult Appendix B.

The basic idea behind HTM is that modern cache-coherence protocols already do most of what we need to do to implement transactions. They already detect and resolve synchronization conflicts between writers, and between readers and writers, and they already buffer tentative changes instead of updating memory directly. We need change only a few details.

18.4.1 Cache Coherence

In most modern multiprocessors, each processor has an attached *cache*, a small, high-speed memory used to avoid communicating with large and slow main memory. Each cache entry holds a group of neighboring words called a *line*, and has some way of mapping addresses to lines. Consider a simple architecture in which processors and memory communicate over a shared broadcast medium called a *bus*. Each cache line has a *tag*, which encodes state information. We start with the standard *MESI* protocol, in which each cache line is marked with one of the following states:

- *Modified*: the line in the cache has been modified, and must eventually be written back to memory. No other processor has this line cached.
- *Exclusive*: the line has not been modified, but no other processor has this line cached. (A line is typically loaded in exclusive mode before being modified.)
- *Shared*: the line has not been modified, and other processors may have this line cached.
- *Invalid*: the line does not contain meaningful data.

The *cache coherence* protocol detects synchronization conflicts among individual loads and stores, and ensures that different processors agree on the state of the shared memory. When a processor loads or stores a memory address a, it broadcasts the request on the bus, and the other processors and memory listen in (sometimes called *snooping*).

A full description of a cache coherence protocol can be complex, but here are the principal transitions of interest to us.

- When a processor requests to load a line in exclusive mode, the other processors invalidate any copies of that line. Any processor with a modified copy of that line must write the line back to memory before the load can be fulfilled.
- When a processor requests to load a line into its cache in shared mode, any processor with an exclusive copy must change its state to shared, and any processor with a modified copy must write that line back to memory before the load can be fulfilled.

- If the cache becomes full, it may be necessary to *evict* a line. If the line is shared or exclusive, it can simply be discarded, but if it is modified, it must be written back to memory.

We now show how to adapt this protocol to support transactions.

18.4.2 Transactional Cache Coherence

We keep the same MESI protocol as before, except that we add a *transactional* bit to each cache line's tag. Normally, this bit is unset. When a value is placed in the cache line on behalf of a transaction, this bit is set, and we say the entry is *transactional*. We only need to ensure that modified transactional lines cannot be written back to memory, and that invalidating a transactional line aborts the transaction.

Here are the rules in more detail.

- If the MESI protocol invalidates a transactional entry, then that transaction is aborted. Such an invalidation represents a synchronization conflict, either between two stores, or a load and a store.
- If a modified transactional line is invalidated or evicted, its value is discarded instead of being written to memory. Because any transactionally written value is tentative, we cannot let it "escape" while the transaction is active. Instead, we must abort the transaction.
- If the cache evicts a transactional line, then that transaction must be aborted, because once the line is no longer in the cache, then the cache-coherence protocol cannot detect synchronization conflicts.

If, when a transaction finishes, none of its transactional lines have been invalidated or evicted, then it can commit, clearing the transactional bits in its cache lines. If an invalidation or eviction causes the transaction to abort, its transactional cache lines are invalidated. These rules ensure that commit and abort are processor-local steps.

18.4.3 Enhancements

Although the scheme correctly implements a transactional memory in hardware, it has a number of flaws and limitations. One limitation, common to nearly all HTM proposals, is that the size of the transaction is limited by the size of the cache. Most operating systems clean out the cache when a thread is descheduled, so the duration of the transaction may be limited by the length of the platform's scheduling quantum. It follows that HTM is best suited for short, small transactions. Applications that need longer transactions should use STM, or a combination of HTM and STM. When a transaction aborts, however, it is important that the hardware return a condition code indicating whether the abort was due to a synchronization conflict (so the transaction should be retried), or whether it was due to resource exhaustion (so there is no point in retrying the transaction).

This particular design, however, has some additional drawbacks. Many caches are *direct-mapped*, meaning that an address a maps to exactly one cache line. Any transaction that accesses two addresses that map to the same cache line is doomed to fail, because the second access will evict the first, aborting the transaction. Some caches are *set-associative*, mapping each address to a set of k lines. Any transaction that accesses $k+1$ addresses that map to the same set is doomed to fail. Few caches are *fully-associative*, mapping each address to any line in the cache.

There are several ways to alleviate this problem by splitting the cache. One is to split the cache into a large, direct-mapped *main cache* and a small fully associated *victim cache* used to hold entries that overflow from the main cache. Another is to split the cache into a large set-associated *non-transactional* cache, and a small fully-associative *transactional cache* for transactional lines. Either way, the cache coherence protocol must be adapted to handle coherence between the split caches.

Another flaw is the absence of contention management, which means that transactions can starve one another. Transaction A loads address a in exclusive mode, then transaction B loads a in exclusive mode, aborting A. A immediately restarts, aborting B, and so on. This problem could be addressed at the level of the coherence protocol, allowing a processor to refuse or delay an invalidation request, or it could be addressed at the software level, perhaps by having aborted transactions execute exponential backoff in software.

Readers interested in addressing these issues in depth may consult the chapter notes.

18.5 Chapter Notes

Maurice Herlihy and Eliot Moss [67] were the first to propose hardware transactional memory as a general-purpose programming model for multiprocessors. Nir Shavit and Dan Touitou [142] proposed the first software transactional memory. The `retry` and `orElse` constructs are credited to Tim Harris, Simon Marlowe, Simon Peyton-Jones, and Maurice Herlihy [54]. Many papers, both earlier and later, have contributed to this area. Larus and Rajwar [97] provide the authoritative survey of both the technical issues and the literature.

The Karma contention manager is taken from William Scherer and Michael Scott [137], and the Greedy contention manager from Rachid Guerraoui, Maurice Herlihy, and Bastian Pochon [49]. The obstruction-free STM is based on the *Dynamic Software Transactional Memory* algorithm of Maurice Herlihy, Victor Luchangco, Mark Moir, and Bill Scherer [66]. The lock-based STM is based on the *Transactional Locking 2* algorithm of Dave Dice, Ori Shalev, and Nir Shavit [32].

18.6 Exercises

Exercise 211. Implement the *Priority*, *Greedy*, and *Karma* contention managers.

Exercise 212. Describe the meaning of `orElse` without mentioning transaction roll-back.

Exercise 213. In `TinyTM`, implement the `openRead()` method of the `FreeObject` class. Notice that the order in which the `Locator` fields are read is important. Argue why your implementation provides a serializable read of an object.

Exercise 214. Invent a way to reduce the contention on the global version clock in `TinyTM`.

Exercise 215. Extend the `LockObject` class to support concurrent readers.

Exercise 216. In `TinyTM`, the `LockObject` class's `onCommit()` handler first checks whether the object is locked by another transaction, and then whether its stamp is less than or equal to the transaction's read stamp.

- Give an example showing why it is necessary to check whether the object is locked.
- Is it possible that the object could be locked by the committing transaction?
- Give an example showing why it is necessary to check whether the object is locked *before* checking the version number.

Exercise 217. Design an `AtomicArray<T>` implementation optimized for small arrays such as used in a skiplist.

Exercise 218. Design an `AtomicArray<T>` implementation optimized for large arrays in which transactions access disjoint regions within the array.

Appendix

A Software Basics

A.1 Introduction

This appendix describes the basic programming language constructs needed to understand our examples and to write your own concurrent programs. Mostly, we use Java, but the same ideas could be equally well expressed in other high-level languages and libraries. Here, we review the basic software concepts needed to understand this text, first in Java, and then in other important models such as C# or the Pthreads library for C and C++. Unfortunately, our discussion here must be incomplete: if in doubt, consult the current documentation for the language or library of interest.

A.2 Java

The Java programming language uses a concurrency model in which threads and objects are separate entities.[1] Threads manipulate objects by calling the objects' methods, coordinating these possibly concurrent calls using various language and library constructs. We begin by explaining the basic Java constructs used in this text.

A.2.1 Threads

A *thread* executes a single, sequential program. In Java, a thread is usually a subclass of `java.lang.Thread`, which provides methods for creating threads, starting them, suspending them, and waiting for them to finish.

1 Technically, threads are objects.

First, create a class that implements the Runnable interface. The class's run() method does all the work. For example, here is a simple thread that prints a string.

```
public class HelloWorld implements Runnable {
  String message;
  public HelloWorld(String m) {
    message = m;
  }
  public void run() {
    System.out.println(message);
  }
}
```

A Runnable object can be turned into a thread by calling the Thread class constructor that takes a Runnable object as its argument, like this:

```
String m = "Hello World from Thread" + i;
Thread thread = new Thread(new HelloWorld(m));
```

Java provides a syntactic shortcut, called an *anonymous inner class*, that allows you to avoid defining an explicit HelloWorld class:

```
final String m = "Hello world from thread" + i;
thread = new Thread(new Runnable() {
   public void run() {
     System.out.println(m);
   }
 });
```

This snippet creates an anonymous class implementing the Runnable interface, whose run() method behaves as shown.

After a thread has been created, it must be *started*:

```
thread.start();
```

This method causes the thread to run. The thread that calls this method returns immediately. If the caller wants to wait for the thread to finish, it must *join* the thread:

```
thread.join();
```

The caller is blocked until the thread's run() method returns.

Fig. A.1 shows a method that initializes multiple threads, starts them, waits for them to finish, and then prints out a message. The method creates an array of threads, and initializes them in Lines 2–10, using the anonymous inner class syntax. At the end of this loop, it has created an array of dormant threads. In Lines 11–13, it starts the threads, and each thread executes its run() method, displaying its message. Finally, in Lines 14–16, it waits for each thread to finish, and displays a message when they are done.

```
public static void main(String[] args) {
  Thread[] thread = new Thread[8];
  for (int i = 0; i < thread.length; i++) {
    final String message = "Hello world from thread" + i;
    thread[i] = new Thread(new Runnable() {
      public void run() {
        System.out.println(message);
      }
    });
  }
  for (int i = 0; i < thread.length; i++) {
    thread[i].start();
  }
  for (int i = 0; i < thread.length; i++) {
    thread[i].join();
  }
}
```

Figure A.1 This method initializes a number of Java threads, starts them, and then waits for them to finish.

A.2.2 Monitors

Java provides a number of ways to synchronize access to shared data, both built-in and through packages. Here we describe the built-in model, called the *monitor* model, which is the simplest and most commonly used approach. We discuss monitors in Chapter 8.

Imagine you are in charge of software for a call center. During peak hours, calls arrive faster than they can be answered. When a call arrives, your switchboard software places that call in a queue, and it plays a recorded announcement assuring the caller that you consider this call to be very important, and that calls will be answered in the order received. An employee in charge of answering a call is called an *operator*. Each operator dispatches an *operator thread* to dequeue and answer the next call. When an operator has finished with one call, he or she dequeues the next call from the queue and answers it.

Fig. A.2 is a simple (but incorrect) queue class. The calls are kept in an array `calls`, where `head` is the index of the next call to remove, and `tail` is the index of the next free slot in the array.

It is easy to see that this class does not work correctly if two operators try to dequeue a call at the same time. The expression

```
return calls[(head++) % QSIZE]
```

does not happen as an indivisible, *atomic* step. Instead, the compiler produces code that looks something like this:

```
int temp0 = head;
head = temp0 + 1;
int temp1 = (temp0 % QSIZE);
return calls[temp1];
```

```
1   class CallQueue {
2     final static int QSIZE = 100; // arbitrary size
3     int head = 0;                 // next item to dequeue
4     int tail = 0;                 // next empty slot
5     Call[] calls = new Call[QSIZE];
6     public enq(Call x) {          // called by switchboard
7       calls[(tail++) % QSIZE] = x;
8     }
9     public Call deq() {           // called by operators
10      return calls[(head++) % QSIZE]
11    }
12  }
```

Figure A.2 An *incorrect* queue class.

Two operators might execute these statements together: they execute Line 1 at the same time, then Line 2, and so on. In the end, both operators dequeue and answer the same call, possibly annoying the customer.

To make this queue work correctly, we must ensure that only one operator at a time can dequeue the next call, a property called *mutual exclusion.* Java provides a useful built-in mechanism to support mutual exclusion. Each object has an (implicit) *lock.* If a thread *A acquires* the object's lock (or, equivalently, *locks* that object), then no other thread can acquire that lock until *A releases* the lock (or, equivalently, until it *unlocks* that object). If a class declares a method to be **synchronized**, then that method implicitly acquires the lock when it is called, and releases it when it returns.

Here is one way to ensure mutual exclusion for the enq() and deq() methods:

```
public synchronized T deq() {
  return call[(head++) % QSIZE]
}
public synchronized enq(T x) {
  call[(tail++) % QSIZE] = x;
}
```

Once a call to a synchronized method has acquired the object's lock, any call to another synchronized method for that object is blocked until the lock is released. (Calls to other objects, subject to other locks, are not blocked.) The body of a synchronized method is often called a *critical section.*

There is more to synchronization than mutual exclusion. What should an operator do if he or she tries to dequeue a call, but there are no calls waiting in the queue? The call might throw an exception or return *null*, but what could the operator do then, other than try again? Instead, it makes sense for the operator to *wait* for a call to appear. Here is a first attempt at a solution:

```
public synchronized T deq() {
  while (head == tail) {}; // spin while empty
  call[(head++) % QSIZE];
}
```

This solution is not just wrong, it is disastrously wrong. The dequeuing thread waits inside a synchronized method, locking out every other thread, including the switchboard thread that could be trying to enqueue a call. This is a *deadlock*: the dequeuing thread holds the lock waiting for an enqueuing thread, while the enqueuing thread waits for the dequeuing thread to release the lock. Nothing will ever happen.

From this we learn that if a thread executing a synchronized method needs to wait for something to happen, then it must *unlock* the object while it waits. The waiting thread should periodically reacquire the lock to test whether it can proceed. If so, it proceeds, and if not, it releases the lock and goes back to waiting.

In Java, each object provides a `wait()` method that unlocks the object and suspends the caller. While that thread is waiting, another thread can lock and change the object. Later, when the suspended thread resumes, it locks the object again before it returns from the `wait()` call. Here is a revised (but still not correct) dequeue method[2]

```
public synchronized T deq() {
  while (head == tail) {wait();}
  return call[(head++) % QSIZE];
}
```

Here, each operator thread, seeking a call to answer, repeatedly tests whether the queue is empty. If so, it releases the lock and waits, and if not, it removes and returns the item. In a similar way, an enqueuing thread checks whether the buffer is full.

When does a waiting thread wake up? It is the programmer's responsibility to *notify* waiting threads when something significant happens. The `notify()` method wakes up one waiting thread, eventually, chosen arbitrarily from the set of waiting threads. When that thread awakens, it competes for the lock like any other thread. When that thread reacquires the lock, it returns from its `wait()` call. You cannot control which waiting thread is chosen. By contrast, the `notifyAll()` method wakes up all waiting threads, eventually. Each time the object is unlocked, one of these newly awakened threads will reacquire the lock and return from its `wait()` call. You cannot control the order in which the threads reacquire the lock.

In the call center example, there are multiple operators and one switchboard. Suppose the switchboard software decides to optimize its use of `notify()` as follows. If it adds a call to an empty queue, then it should notify only one blocked dequeuer, since there is only one call to consume. While this optimization may seem reasonable, it is flawed. Suppose the operator threads *A* and *B* discover the queue is empty, and block waiting for calls to answer. The switchboard thread

---

2 This program will not compile because the `wait()` call can throw `InterruptedException`, which must be caught or rethrown. As discussed in Pragma 8.3 in Chapter 8, we often ignore such exceptions to make the examples easier to read.

S puts a call in the queue, and calls `notify()` to wake up one operator thread. Because the notification is asynchronous, however, there is a delay. *S* then returns and places another call in the queue, and because the queue already had a waiting call, it does not notify other threads. The switchboard's `notify()` finally takes effect, waking up *A*, but not *B*, even though there is a call for *B* to answer. This pitfall is called the *lost wakeup* problem: one or more waiting threads fail to be notified that the condition for which they are waiting has become true. See Section 8.2.2 (Chapter 8) for a more detailed discussion.

A.2.3 Yielding and Sleeping

In addition to the `wait()` method, which allows a thread holding a lock to release the lock and pause, Java provides other ways for a thread that does not hold a lock to pause. A `yield()` call pauses the thread, asking the schedule to run something else. The scheduler decides whether to pause the thread, and when to restart it. If there are no other threads to run, the schedule may ignore the `yield()` call. Section 16.4.1 in Chapter 16 describes how yielding can be an effective way to prevent livelock. A call to `sleep(`*t*`)`, where *t* is a time value, instructs the scheduler not to run that thread for that duration. The scheduler is free to restart the thread at any later time.

A.2.4 Thread-Local Objects

Often it is useful for each thread to have its own private instance of a variable. Java supports such *thread-local* objects through the `ThreadLocal<T>` class, which manages a collection of objects of type `T`, one for each thread. Because thread-local variables were not built into Java, they have a somewhat complicated and awkward interface. Nevertheless, they are extremely useful, and we use them often, so we review how to use them here.

The `ThreadLocal<T>` class provides `get()` and `set()` methods that read and update the thread's local value. The `initialValue()` method is called the first time a thread tries to get the value of a thread-local object. We cannot use the `ThreadLocal<T>` class directly. Instead, we must define a thread-local variable as a *subclass* of `ThreadLocal<T>` that overrides the parent's `initialValue()` method to initialize each thread's object appropriately.

This mechanism is best illustrated by an example. In many of our algorithms, we assume that each of n concurrent threads has a unique thread-local identifier between 0 and $n - 1$. To provide such an identifier, we show how to define a `ThreadID` class with a single static method: `get()` returns the calling thread's identifier. When a thread calls `get()` for the first time, it is assigned the next unused identifier. Each subsequent call by that thread returns that thread's identifier.

Fig. A.3 shows the simplest way to use a thread-local object to implement this useful class. Line 2 declares an integer `nextID` field that holds the next identifier to

```
1  public class ThreadID {
2    private static volatile int nextID = 0;
3    private static class ThreadLocalID extends ThreadLocal<Integer> {
4      protected synchronized Integer initialValue() {
5        return nextID++;
6      }
7    }
8    private static ThreadLocalID threadID = new ThreadLocalID();
9    public static int get() {
10     return threadID.get();
11   }
12   public static void set(int index) {
13     threadID.set(index);
14 }
```

Figure A.3 The `ThreadID` class: give each thread a unique identifier.

be issued. Lines 3 through 7 define an *inner class* accessible only within the body of the enclosing `ThreadID` class. This inner class manages the thread's identifier. It is a subclass of `ThreadLocal<Integer>` that overrides the `initialValue()` method to assign the next unused identifier to the current thread.

Because the inner `ThreadLocalID` class is used exactly once, it makes little sense to give it a name (for the same reason that it makes little sense to name your Thanks-giving turkey). Instead, it is more common to use an anonymous class as described earlier.

Here is an example how the `ThreadID` class might be used:

```
thread = new Thread(new Runnable() {
  public void run() {
    System.out.println("Hello world from thread" + ThreadID.get());
  }
});
```

Pragma A.2.1. In the type expression `ThreadLocal<Integer>`, you must use `Integer` instead of **`int`** because **`int`** is a primitive type, while `Integer` is a reference type, and only reference types are allowed in angle brackets. Since Java 1.5, a feature called *auto-boxing* allows you to use **`int`** and `Integer` values more-or-less interchangeably, for example:

```
Integer x = 5;
int y = 6;
Integer z = x + y;
```

Consult your Java reference manual for complete details.

A.3 C#

C# is a Java-like language that runs on Microsoft's .Net platform.

A.3.1 Threads

C# provides a threading model similar to Java's. C# threads are implemented by the `System.Threading.Thread` class. When you create a thread, you tell it what to do by passing it a `ThreadStart` *delegate*, a kind of pointer to the method you want to call. For example, here is a method that prints a simple message:

```
void HelloWorld()
  {
    Console.WriteLine("Hello World");
  }
```

We then turn this method into a `ThreadStart` delegate, and pass that delegate to the thread constructor.

```
ThreadStart hello = new ThreadStart(HelloWorld);
Thread thread = new Thread(hello);
```

C# provides a syntactic shortcut, called an *anonymous method*, that allows you to define a delegate directly, for example, by combining the previous steps into a single expression:

```
Thread thread = new Thread(delegate()
  {
     Console.WriteLine("Hello World");
  });
```

As in Java, after a thread has been created, it must be *started*:

```
thread.Start();
```

This call causes the thread to run, while the caller returns immediately. If the caller wants to wait for the thread to finish, it must *join* the thread:

```
thread.Join();
```

The caller is blocked until the thread's method returns.

Fig. A.4 shows a method that initializes a number of threads, starts them, waits for them to finish, and then prints out a message. The method creates an array of threads, initializing each thread with its own `ThreadStart` delegate. We then start the threads, and each thread executes its delegate, displaying its message. Finally, we wait for each thread to finish, and display a message when they are

```
static void Main(string[] args)
{
    Thread[] thread = new Thread[8];
    // create threads
    for (int i = 0; i < thread.Length; i++)
    {
        String message = "Hello world from thread" + i;
        ThreadStart hello = delegate()
        {
            Console.WriteLine(message);
        };
        thread[i] = new Thread(hello);
    }
    // start threads
    for (int i = 0; i < thread.Length; i++)
    {
        thread[i].Start();
    }
    // wait for them to finish
    for (int i = 0; i < thread.Length; i++)
    {
        thread[i].Join();
    }
    Console.WriteLine("done!");
}
```

Figure A.4 This method initializes a number of C# threads, starts them, waits for them to finish, and then prints out a message.

all done. Except for minor syntactic differences, this code is similar to what you would write in Java.

A.3.2 Monitors

For simple mutual exclusion, C# provides the ability to *lock* an object much like the **synchronized** modifier in Java:

```
int GetAndIncrement()
{
    lock (this)
    {
        return value++;
    }
}
```

Unlike Java, C# does not allow you to use a `lock` statement to modify a method directly. Instead, the `lock` statement is used to enclose the method body.

Concurrent data structures require more than mutual exclusion: they also require the ability to wait and signal conditions. Unlike in Java, where every object is an implicit monitor, in C# you must explicitly create the monitor associated with an object. To acquire a monitor lock, call `Monitor.Enter(this)`, and to release the lock, call `Monitor.Exit(this)`. Each monitor has a single implicit condition, which is waited upon by `Monitor.Wait(this)`, and signaled by `Monitor.Pulse(this)` or `Monitor.PulseAll(this)`, which respectively wake up one or all sleeping threads. Figs. A.5 and A.6 show how to implement a simple bounded queue using C# monitor calls.

A.3.3 Thread-Local Objects

C# provides a very simple way to make a static field thread-local: simply prefix the field declaration with the attribute `[ThreadStatic]`.

```
[ThreadStatic]
static int value;
```

Do not provide an initial value for a `[ThreadStatic]` field, because the initialization happens once, not once per thread. Instead, each thread will find the field

```
class Queue<T>
{
    int head, tail;
    T[] call;
    public Queue(int capacity)
    {
        call = new T[capacity];
        head = tail = 0;
    }
    public void Enq(T x)
    {
        Monitor.Enter(this);
        try
        {
            while (tail - head == call.Length)
            {
                Monitor.Wait(this); // queue is full
            }
            calls[(tail++) % call.Length] = x;
            Monitor.Pulse(this);  // notify waiting dequeuers
        }
        finally
        {
            Monitor.Exit(this);
        }
     }
    }
}
```

Figure A.5 A bounded Queue class: fields and enq() method.

```
public T Deq()
    {
        Monitor.Enter(this);
        try
        {
            while (tail == head)
            {
                Monitor.Wait(this); // queue is empty
            }
            T y = calls[(head++) % call.Length];
            Monitor.Pulse(this);  // notify waiting enqueuers
            return y;
        }
        finally
        {
            Monitor.Exit(this);
        }
    }
}
```

Figure A.6 A bounded Queue class: the deq() method.

```
class ThreadID
{
    [ThreadStatic] static int myID;
    static int counter;
    public static int get()
    {
        if (myID == 0)
        {
            myID = Interlocked.Increment(ref counter);
        }
        return myID - 1;
    }
}
```

Figure A.7 The `ThreadID` class provides each thread a unique identifier implemented using `[ThreadStatic]`.

initially has that type's default value: zero for integers, *null* for references, and so on.

Fig. A.7 shows how to implement the `ThreadID` class (Java version in Fig. A.3). There is one point about this program that may require comment. The first time a thread inspects its `[ThreadStatic]` identifier, that field will be zero, the default value for integers. To distinguish between an uninitialized zero and a thread ID zero, this field holds the thread ID displaced by one: thread 0 has field value 1, and so on.

A.4 Pthreads

Pthreads provides much of the same functionality for C or C++. Programs that use Pthreads must import the include file:

```
#include <pthread.h>
```

The following function creates and starts a thread:

```
int pthread_create (
  pthread_t* thread_id,
  const pthread_attr_t* attributes,
  void* (*thread_function)(void*),
  void* argument);
```

The first argument is a pointer to the thread itself. The second allows you to specify various aspects of the thread, the third is a pointer to the code the thread is to run (in C# this would be a delegate, and in Java a `Runnable` object), and the fourth is the argument to the thread function. Unlike Java or C#, a single call both creates and starts a thread.

A thread terminates when the function returns or calls `pthread_exit()`. Threads can also join by the call:

```
int pthread_join (pthread_t thread, void** status_ptr);
```

The exit status is stored in the last argument. For example, the following program prints out a simple per-thread message.

```
#include <pthread.h>
#define NUM_THREADS 8
void* hello(void* arg) {
  printf("Hello from thread %i\n", (int)arg);
}
int main() {
  pthread_t thread[NUM_THREADS];
  int status;
  int i;
  for (i = 0; i < NUM_THREADS; i++) {
    if ( pthread_create(&thread[i], NULL, hello, (void*)i) != 0 ) {
      printf("pthread_create() error");
      exit();
    }
  }
  for (i = 0; i < NUM_THREADS; i++) {
    pthread_join(thread[i], NULL);
  }
}
```

The Pthreads library calls locks *mutexes*. A mutex is created by calling

```
int pthread_mutex_init (pthread_mutex_t* mutex,
                        const pthread_mutexattr_t* attr);
```

A mutex can be locked:

```
int pthread_mutex_lock (pthread_mutex_t* mutex);
```

and unlocked:

```
int pthread_mutex_unlock (pthread_mutex_t* mutex);
```

Like a Java lock, it is possible to return immediately if a mutex is busy:

```
int pthread_mutex_trylock (pthread_mutex_t* mutex);
```

The Pthreads library provides condition variables, which can be created by calling:

```
int pthread_cond_init (pthread_cond_t* cond, pthread_condattr_t* attr);
```

As usual, the second argument sets attributes to nondefault values. Unlike in Java or C#, the association between a lock and a condition variable is explicit, not implicit. The following call releases a lock and waits on a condition variable:

```
int pthread_cond_wait (pthread_cond_t* cond, pthread_mutex_t* mutex);
```

(Just as in the other languages, when a thread awakens, there is no guarantee that the condition it is awaiting holds, so it must be checked explicitly.) It is also possible to wait with a timeout.

The following call is similar to Java's `notify()`, awakening at least one suspended thread:

```
int pthread_cond_signal (pthread_cond_t *cond);
```

The following is like Java's `notifyAll()`, awakening all suspended threads:

```
int pthread_cond_broadcast (pthread_cond_t* cond);
```

Because C is not garbage collected, threads, locks, and condition variables all provide `destroy()` functions that allow their resources to be reclaimed.

Figs. A.8 and A.9 illustrate a simple concurrent FIFO queue. Call are kept in an array, and `head` and `tail` fields count the number of call enqueued and dequeued. Unlike the Java implementation, it uses two different condition variables to wait for the buffer to become either not full or not empty.

A.4.1 Thread-Local Storage

Fig. A.10 illustrates how Pthreads manages thread-local storage. The Pthreads library associates a thread-specific *value* with a *key*, which is declared at Line 1 and initialized at Line 6. The value is a pointer, initially *null*. A thread acquires an ID by calling `threadID_get()`. This method looks up the thread-local value bound to the key (Line 10). On the first call, that value is *null* (Line 11), so the thread must take a new unique ID by incrementing the `counter` variable. Here, we use a mutex to synchronize access to a counter (Lines 12–16).

```
#include <pthread.h>
#define QSIZE 16
typedef struct {
  int buf[QSIZE];
  long head, tail;
  pthread_mutex_t *mutex;
  pthread_cond_t *notFull, *notEmpty;
} queue;
void queue_enq(queue* q, int item) {
  // lock object
  pthread_mutex_lock (q->mutex);
  // wait while full
  while (q->tail - q->head == QSIZE) {
    pthread_cond_wait (q->notFull, q->mutex);
  }
  q->buf[q->tail % QSIZE] = item;
  q->tail++;
  // release lock
  pthread_mutex_unlock (q->mutex);
  // inform waiting dequeuers
  pthread_cond_signal (q->notEmpty);
}
queue *queue_init (void) {
  queue *q;
  q = (queue*)malloc (sizeof (queue));
  if (q == NULL) return (NULL);
  q->head = 0;
  q->tail = 0;
  q->mutex = (pthread_mutex_t*) malloc (sizeof (pthread_mutex_t));
  pthread_mutex_init (q->mutex, NULL);
  q->notFull = (pthread_cond_t*) malloc (sizeof (pthread_cond_t));
  pthread_cond_init (q->notFull, NULL);
  q->notEmpty = (pthread_cond_t*) malloc (sizeof (pthread_cond_t));
  pthread_cond_init (q->notEmpty, NULL);
  return (q);
}
```

Figure A.8 Initialization and Enqueue methods of a concurrent FIFO Queue using Pthreads.

A.5 Chapter Notes

The Java programming language was created by James Gosling [46]. Dennis Ritchie is credited with creating C. Pthreads was invented as part of the IEEE Posix package. The basic monitor model is credited to Tony Hoare [71] and Per Brinch Hansen [52], although they used different mechanisms for waiting and notification. The mechanisms used by Java (and later by C#) were originally proposed by Butler Lampson and David Redell [96].

```
int queue_deq(queue* q) {
  int result;
  // lock object
  pthread_mutex_lock (q->mutex);
  // wait while full
  while (q->tail == q->head) {
    pthread_cond_wait (q->notEmpty, q->mutex);
  }
  result = q->buf[q->head % QSIZE];
  q->head++;
  // release lock
  pthread_mutex_unlock (q->mutex);
  // inform waiting dequeuers
  pthread_cond_signal (q->notFull);
  return result;
}
void queue_delete (queue* q) {
  pthread_mutex_destroy (q->mutex);
  free (q->mutex);
  pthread_cond_destroy (q->notFull);
  free (q->notFull);
  pthread_cond_destroy (q->notEmpty);
  free (q->notEmpty);
  free (q);
}
```

Figure A.9 Pthreads: a concurrent FIFO queue's dequeue and delete methods.

```
pthread_key_t key;      /* key */
int counter;            /* generates unique value */
pthread_mutex_t mutex;    /* synchronizes counter */
threadID_init() {
  pthread_mutex_init(&mutex, NULL);
  pthread_key_create(&key, NULL);
  counter = 0;
}
int threadID_get() {
  int* id = (int*)pthread_getspecific(key);
  if (id == NULL) {   /* first time? */
    id = (int*)malloc(sizeof(int));
    pthread_mutex_lock(&mutex);
    *id = counter++;
    pthread_setspecific(key, id);
    pthread_mutex_unlock(&mutex);
  }
  return *id;
}
```

Figure A.10 This program provides each thread a unique identifier using Pthreads thread-local storage management calls.

Hardware Basics

> A novice was trying to fix a broken Lisp machine by turning the power off and on. Knight, seeing what the student was doing spoke sternly: "You cannot fix a machine just by power-cycling it with no understanding of what is going wrong." Knight turned the machine off and on. The machine worked.

(From "AI Koans", a collection of jokes popular at MIT in the 1980s).

B.1 Introduction (and a Puzzle)

You cannot program a multiprocessor effectively unless you know what a multiprocessor *is.* You can do a pretty good job of programming a uniprocessor without understanding much about computer architecture, but the same is not true of multiprocessors. We will illustrate this point by a puzzle. We will consider two programs that are logically equivalent, except that one is much less efficient than the other. Ominously, the simpler program is the inefficient one. This discrepancy cannot be explained, nor the danger avoided, without a basic understanding of modern multiprocessor architectures.

Here is the background to the puzzle. Suppose two threads share a resource that can be used by only one thread at a time. To prevent concurrent use, each thread must *lock* the resource before using it, and *unlock* it afterward. We will study many ways to implement locks in Chapter 7. For the puzzle, we consider two simple implementations in which the lock is a single Boolean field. If the field is *false*, the lock is free, and otherwise it is in use. We manipulate the lock with the `getAndSet(`*v*`)` method, which atomically swaps its argument *v* with the field value. To acquire the lock, a thread calls `getAndSet(`*true*`)`. If the call returns *false*, then the lock was free, and the caller succeeded in locking the object. Otherwise, the object was already locked, and the thread must try again later. A thread releases a lock simply by storing *false* into the Boolean field.

In Fig. B.1, the *test-and-set* (`TASLock`) lock repeatedly calls `getAndSet(`*true*`)` (Line 4) until it returns *false*. By contrast, in Fig. B.2, the *test-and-test-and-set* lock (`TTASLock`) repeatedly reads the lock field (by calling `state.get()` at

```
public class TASLock implements Lock {
  ...
  public void lock() {
    while (state.getAndSet(true)) {} // spin
  }
  ...
}
```

Figure B.1 The `TASLock` class.

```
1  public class TTASLock implements Lock {
2    ...
3    public void lock() {
4      while (true) {
5        while (state.get()) {}; // spin
6        if (!state.getAndSet(true))
7          return;
8      }
9    }
10   ...
11 }
```

Figure B.2 The `TTASLock` class.

Line 5) until it returns *false*, and only then calls `getAndSet()` (Line 6). It is important to understand that reading the lock value is atomic, and applying `getAndSet()` to the lock value is atomic, but the combination is not atomic: between the time a thread reads the lock value and the time it calls `getAndSet()`, the lock value may have changed.

Before you proceed, you should convince yourself that the `TASLock` and `TTASLock` algorithms are logically the same. The reason is simple: in the `TTASLock` algorithm, reading that the lock is free does not guarantee that the next call to `getAndSet()` will succeed, because some other thread may have acquired the lock in the interval between reading the lock and trying to acquire it. So why bother reading the lock before trying to acquire it?

Here is the puzzle. While the two lock implementations may be logically equivalent, they perform very differently. In a classic 1989 experiment, Anderson measured the time needed to execute a simple test program on several contemporary multiprocessors. He measured the elapsed time for *n* threads to execute a short critical section one million times. Fig. B.3 shows how long each lock takes, plotted as a function of the number of threads. In a perfect world, both the `TASLock` and `TTASLock` curves would be as flat as the ideal curve on the bottom, since each run does the same number of increments. Instead, we see that both curves slope up, indicating that lock-induced delay increases with the number of threads. Curiously, however, the `TASLock` is much slower than the `TTASLock` lock, especially as the number of threads increases. Why?

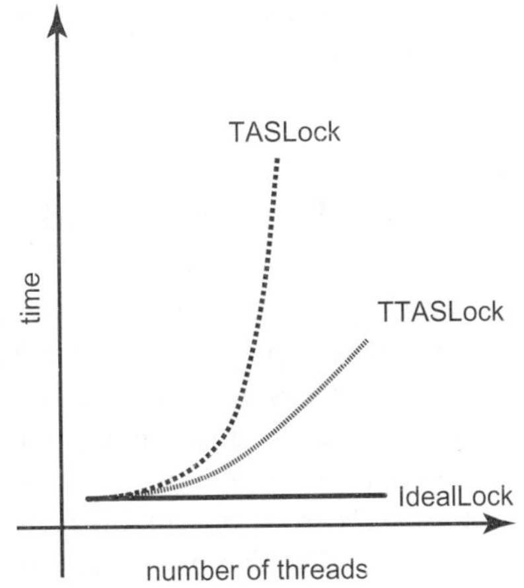

Figure B.3 Schematic performance of a TASLock, a TTASLock, and an ideal lock.

This chapter covers much of what you need to know about multiprocessor architecture to write efficient concurrent algorithms and data structures. (Along the way, we will explain the divergent curves in Fig. B.3.)

We will be concerned with the following components:

- The *processors* are hardware devices that execute software *threads*. There are typically more threads than processors, and each processor runs a thread for a while, sets it aside, and turns its attention to another thread.
- The *interconnect* is a communication medium that links processors to processors and processors to memory.
- The *memory* is actually a hierarchy of components that store data, ranging from one or more levels of small, fast *caches* to a large and relatively slow *main memory*. Understanding how these levels interact is essential to understanding the actual performance of many concurrent algorithms.

From our point of view, one architectural principle drives everything else: *processors and main memory are far apart.* It takes a long time for a processor to read a value from memory. It also takes a long time for a processor to write a value to memory, and longer still for the processor to be sure that value has actually been installed in memory. Accessing memory is more like mailing a letter than making a phone call. Almost everything we examine in this chapter is the result of trying to alleviate the long time it takes ("high latency") to access memory.

Both processor and memory speed change over time, but their *relative* performance changes slowly. Let us consider the following analogy. We imagine that it is 1980, and you are in charge of a messenger service in mid-town Manhattan. While cars outperform bicycles on the open road, bicycles outperform cars in heavy traffic, so you choose to use bicycles. Even though the technology behind both bicycles and cars has advanced, the *architectural* comparison remains the same. Then as now, if you are designing an urban messenger service, you should use bicycles, not cars.

B.2 Processors and Threads

A multiprocessor consists of multiple hardware *processors*, each of which executes a sequential program. When discussing multiprocessor architectures, the basic unit of time is the *cycle*: the time it takes a processor to fetch and execute a single instruction. In absolute terms, cycle times change as technology advances (from about 10 million cycles per second in 1980 to about 3000 million in 2005), and they vary from one platform to another (processors that control toasters have longer cycles than processors that control web servers). Nevertheless, the relative cost of instructions such as memory access changes slowly when expressed in terms of cycles.

A *thread* is a sequential program. While a processor is a hardware device, a thread is a software construct. A processor can run a thread for a while and then set it aside and run another thread, an event known as a *context switch.* A processor may set aside a thread, or *deschedule* it, for a variety of reasons. Perhaps the thread has issued a memory request that will take some time to satisfy, or perhaps that thread has simply run long enough, and it is time for another thread to make progress. When a thread is descheduled, it may resume execution on another processor.

B.3 Interconnect

The *interconnect* is the medium by which processors communicate with the memory and with other processors. There are essentially two kinds of interconnect architectures in use: *SMP* (symmetric multiprocessing) and *NUMA* (nonuniform memory access).

In an SMP architecture, processors and memory are linked by a *bus* interconnect, a broadcast medium that acts like a tiny Ethernet. Both processors and the main memory have *bus controller* units in charge of sending and listening for messages broadcast on the bus. (Listening is sometimes called *snooping*). Today, SMP architectures are the most common, because they are the easiest to build, but they are not scalable to large numbers of processors because eventually the bus becomes overloaded.

In a NUMA architecture, a collection of *nodes* are linked by a point-to-point network, like a tiny local area network. Each node contains one or more processors and a local memory. One node's local memory is accessible to the other nodes, and together, the nodes' memories form a global memory shared by all processors. The NUMA name reflects the fact that a processor can access memory

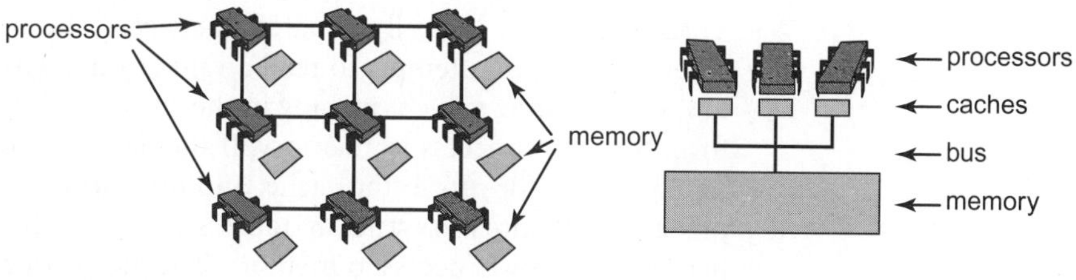

Figure B.4 An SMP architecture with caches on the right and a cacheless NUMA architecture on the left.

residing on its own node faster than it can access memory residing on other nodes. Networks are more complex than buses, and require more elaborate protocols, but they scale better than buses to large numbers of processors.

The division between SMP and NUMA architectures is a bit of a simplification: one could design hybrid architectures, where processors within a cluster communicate over a bus, but processors in different clusters communicate over a network.

From the programmer's point of view, it may not seem important whether the underlying platform is based on a bus, a network, or a hybrid interconnect. It is important, however, to realize that the interconnect is a finite resource shared among the processors. If one processor uses too much of the interconnect's bandwidth, then the others may be delayed.

B.4 Memory

Processors share a *main memory*, which is a large array of *words*, indexed by *address*. Depending on the platform, a word is typically either 32 or 64 bits, and so is an address. Simplifying somewhat, a processor reads a value from memory by sending a message containing the desired address to memory. The response message contains the associated *data*, that is, the contents of memory at that address. A processor writes a value by sending the address and the new data to memory, and the memory sends back an acknowledgment when the new data has been installed.

B.5 Caches

Unfortunately, on modern architectures a main memory access may take hundreds of cycles, so there is a real danger that a processor may spend much of its time just waiting for the memory to respond to requests. We can alleviate this problem by introducing one or more *caches*: small memories that are situated closer to the processors and are therefore much faster than main memory.

These caches are logically situated "between" the processor and the memory: when a processor attempts to read a value from a given memory address, it first looks to see if the value is already in the cache, and if so, it does not need to perform the slower access to memory. If the desired address's value was found, we say the processor *hits* in the cache, and otherwise it *misses.* In a similar way, if a processor attempts to write an address that is in the cache, it does not need to perform the slower access to memory. The proportion of requests satisfied in the cache is called the cache *hit ratio* (or *hit rate*).

Caches are effective because most programs display a high degree of *locality*: if a processor reads or writes a memory address (also called a memory location), then it is likely to read or write the same location again soon. Moreover, if a processor reads or writes a memory location, then it is also likely to read or write *nearby* locations soon. To exploit this second observation, caches typically operate at a *granularity* larger than a single word: a cache holds a group of neighboring words called *cache lines* (sometimes called *cache blocks*).

In practice, most processors have two levels of caches, called the *L*1 and *L*2 caches. The L1 cache typically resides on the same chip as the processor, and takes one or two cycles to access. The L2 cache may reside either on or off-chip, and may take tens of cycles to access. Both are significantly faster than the hundreds of cycles required to access the memory. Of course, these times vary from platform to platform, and many multiprocessors have even more elaborate cache structures.

The original proposals for NUMA architectures did not include caches because it was felt that local memory was enough. Later, however, commercial NUMA architectures did include caches. Sometimes the term cc-NUMA (for *cache-coherent NUMA*) is used to mean NUMA architectures with caches. Here, to avoid ambiguity, we use NUMA to include cache-coherence unless we explicitly state otherwise.

Caches are expensive to build and therefore significantly smaller than the memory: only a fraction of the memory locations will fit in a cache at the same time. We would therefore like the cache to maintain values of the most highly used locations. This implies that when a location needs to be cached and the cache is full, it is necessary to *evict* a line, discarding it if it has not been modified, and writing it back to main memory if it has. A *replacement policy* determines which cache line to replace to make room for a given new location. If the replacement policy is free to replace any line then we say the cache is *fully associative.* If, on the other hand, there is only one line that can be replaced then we say the cache is *direct mapped.* If we split the difference, allowing any line from a *set* of size k to be replaced to make room for a given line, then we say the cache is k*-way set associative.*

B.5.1 Coherence

Sharing (or, less politely, *memory contention*), occurs when one processor reads or writes a memory address that is cached by another. If both processors are reading the data without modifying it, then the data can be cached at both processors. If, however, one processor tries to update the shared cache line, then the other's copy must be *invalidated* to ensure that it does not read an out-of-date value.

In its most general form, this problem is called *cache coherence.* The literature contains a variety of very complex and clever cache coherence protocols. Here we review one of the most commonly used, called the *MESI* protocol (pronounced "messy") after the names of possible cache line states. This protocol has been used in the Pentium and PowerPC processors. Here are the cache line states.

- *Modified*: the line has been modified in the cache, and it must eventually be written back to main memory. No other processor has this line cached.
- *Exclusive*: the line has not been modified, and no other processor has this line cached.
- *Shared*: the line has not been modified, and other processors may have this line cached.
- *Invalid*: the line does not contain meaningful data.

We illustrate this protocol by a short example depicted in Fig. B.5. For simplicity, we assume processors and memory are linked by a bus.

Processor *A* reads data from address *a*, and stores the data in its cache in the *exclusive* state. When processor *B* attempts to read from the same address, *A* detects the address conflict, and responds with the associated data. Now *a* is

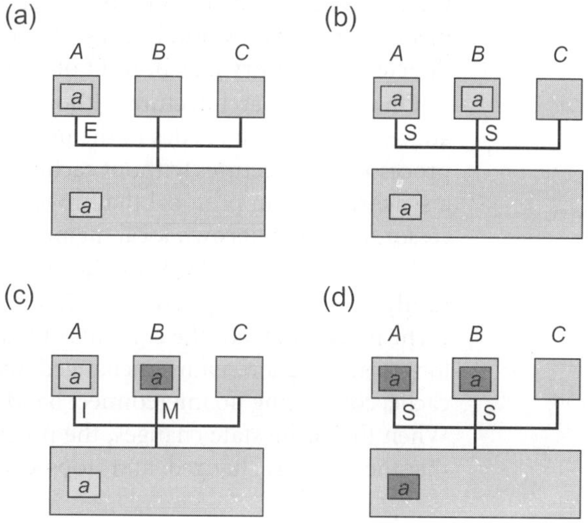

Figure B.5 Example of the MESI cache coherence protocol's state transitions. (a) Processor *A* reads data from address *a*, and stores the data in its cache in the *exclusive* state. (b) When processor *B* attempts to read from the same address, *A* detects the address conflict, and responds with the associated data. Now *a* is cached at both *A* and *B* in the *shared* state. (c) If *B* writes to the shared address *a*, it changes its state to *modified*, and broadcasts a message warning *A* (and any other processor that might have that data cached) to set its cache line state to *invalid.* (d) If *A* then reads from *a*, it broadcasts a request, and *B* responds by sending the modified data both to *A* and to the main memory, leaving both copies in the *shared* state.

cached at both A and B in the *shared* state. If B writes to the shared address a, it changes its state to *modified*, and broadcasts a message warning A (and any other processor that might have that data cached) to set its cache line state to *invalid*. If A then reads from a, it broadcasts a request, and B responds by sending the modified data both to A and to the main memory, leaving both copies in the *shared* state.

False sharing occurs when processors that are accessing logically distinct data nevertheless conflict because the locations they are accessing lie on the same cache line. This observation illustrates a difficult tradeoff: large cache lines are good for locality, but they increase the likelihood of false sharing. The likelihood of false sharing can be reduced by ensuring that data objects that might be accessed concurrently by independent threads lie far enough apart in memory. For example, having multiple threads share a byte array invites false sharing, but having them share an array of double-precision integers is less dangerous.

B.5.2 Spinning

A processor is *spinning* if it is repeatedly testing some word in memory, waiting for another processor to change it. Depending on the architecture, spinning can have a dramatic effect on overall system performance.

On an SMP architecture without caches, spinning is a very bad idea. Each time the processor reads the memory, it consumes bus bandwidth without accomplishing any useful work. Because the bus is a broadcast medium, these requests directed to memory may prevent other processors from making progress.

On a NUMA architecture without caches, spinning may be acceptable if the address in question resides in the processor's local memory. Even though multiprocessor architectures without caches are rare, we will still ask when we consider a synchronization protocol that involves spinning, whether it permits each processor to spin on its own local memory.

On an SMP or NUMA architecture with caches, spinning consumes significantly fewer resources. The first time the processor reads the address, it takes a cache miss, and loads the contents of that address into a cache line. Thereafter, as long as that data remains unchanged, the processor simply rereads from its own cache, consuming no interconnect bandwidth, a process known as *local spinning*. When the cache state changes, the processor takes a single cache miss, observes that the data has changed, and stops spinning.

B.6 Cache-Conscious Programming, or the Puzzle Solved

We now know enough to explain why the `TTASLock` examined in Section B.1 outperforms the `TASLock`. Each time the `TASLock` applies `getAndSet`(*true*) to the lock, it sends a message on the interconnect causing a substantial amount of traffic. In an SMP architecture, the resulting traffic may be enough to saturate the interconnect, delaying all threads, including a thread trying to release the lock, or even threads not contending for the lock. By contrast, while the lock is busy, the `TTASLock` spins, reading a locally cached copy of the lock, and producing no interconnect traffic, explaining its improved performance.

The `TTASLock` is itself however far from ideal. When the lock is released, all its cached copies are invalidated, and all waiting threads call `getAndSet`(*true*), resulting in a burst of traffic, smaller than that of the `TASLock`, but nevertheless significant.

We will further discuss the interactions of caches with locking in Chapter 7. In the meantime, here are some simple ways to structure data to avoid false sharing. Some of these techniques are easier to carry out in languages like C or C++ that provide finer-grained control over memory use than Java.

- Objects or fields that are accessed independently should be aligned and padded so that they end up on different cache lines.
- Keep read-only data separate from data that is modified frequently. For example, consider a list whose structure is constant, but whose elements' value fields change frequently. To ensure that modifications do not slow down list traversals, one could align and pad the value fields so that each one fills up a cache line.
- When possible, split an object into thread-local pieces. For example, a counter used for statistics could be split into an array of counters, one per thread, each one residing on a different cache line. While a shared counter would cause invalidation traffic, the split counter allows each thread to update its own replica without causing coherence traffic.
- If a lock protects data that is frequently modified, then keep the lock and the data on distinct cache lines, so that threads trying to acquire the lock do not interfere with the lock-holder's access to the data.
- If a lock protects data that is frequently uncontended, then try to keep the lock and the data on the same cache lines, so that acquiring the lock will also load some of the data into the cache.

B.7 Multi-Core and Multi-Threaded Architectures

In a *multi-core* architecture, as in Fig. B.6, multiple processors are placed on the same chip. Each processor on that chip typically has its own L1 cache, but they share a common L2 cache. Processors can communicate efficiently through the shared L2 cache, avoiding the need to go through memory, and to invoke the cumbersome cache coherence protocol.

In a *multi-threaded* architecture, a single processor may execute two or more threads at once. Many modern processors have substantial internal parallelism. They can execute instructions out of order, or in parallel (e.g., keeping both fixed and floating-point units busy), or even execute instructions speculatively

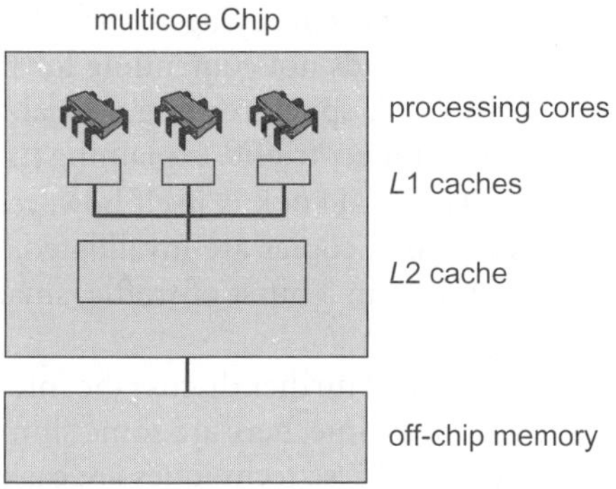

Figure B.6 A multi-core SMP architecture. The *L*2 cache is on chip and shared by all processors while the memory is off-chip.

before branches or data have been computed. To keep hardware units busy, multi-threaded processors can mix instructions from multiple streams.

Modern processor architectures combine multi-core with multi-threading, where multiple individually multi-threaded cores may reside on the same chip. The context switches on some multi-core chips are inexpensive and are performed at a very fine granularity, essentially context switching on every instruction. Thus, multi-threading serves to hide the high latency of accessing memory: whenever a thread accesses memory, the processor allows another thread to execute.

B.7.1 Relaxed Memory Consistency

When a processor writes a value to memory, that value is kept in the cache and marked as *dirty*, meaning that it must eventually be written back to main memory. On most modern processors, write requests are not applied to memory when they are issued. Rather, they are collected in a hardware queue, called a *write buffer* (or *store buffer*), and applied to memory together at a later time. A write buffer provides two benefits. First, it is often more efficient to issue a number of requests all at once, a phenomenon called *batching*. Second, if a thread writes to an address more than once, the earlier request can be discarded, saving a trip to memory, a phenomenon called *write absorption*.

The use of write buffers has a very important consequence: the order in which reads–writes are issued to memory is not necessarily the order in which they occur in the program. For example, recall the flag principle of Chapter 1 which was crucial to the correctness of mutual exclusion: if two processors each first write their own flag and then read the other's flag location, then one of them will see the other's newly written flag value. Using write buffers this is no longer true, both may write, each in its respective write buffer, but the buffers may both be written only after both processors each read the other's flag location in memory. Thus, neither reads the other's flag.

Compilers make matters even worse. They are very good at optimizing performance on single-processor architectures. Often, this optimization requires *reordering* an individual thread's reads–writes to memory. Such reordering is invisible for single-threaded programs, but it can have unexpected consequences for multi-threaded programs in which threads may observe the order in which writes occur. For example, if one thread fills a buffer with data and then sets an indicator to mark the buffer as full, then concurrent threads may see the indicator set before they see the new data, causing them to read stale values. The erroneous *double-checked locking* pattern described in Chapter 3 is an example of a pitfall produced by unintuitive aspects of the Java memory model.

Different architectures provide different guarantees about the extent to which memory reads–writes can be reordered. As a rule, it is better not to rely on such guarantees, and to use more expensive techniques, described in the following paragraph, to prevent such reordering.

All architectures allow you to force your writes to take place in the order they are issued, but at a price. A *memory barrier* instruction (sometimes called a *fence*) flushes write buffers, ensuring that all writes issued before the barrier become visible to the processor that issued the barrier. Memory barriers are often inserted transparently by atomic read-modify-write operations such as `getAndSet()`, or by standard concurrency libraries. Thus, explicit use of memory barriers is needed only when processors perform read–write instructions on shared variables outside of critical sections.

On the one hand, memory barriers are expensive (100s of cycles, maybe more), and should be used only when necessary. On the other, synchronization bugs can be very difficult to track down, so memory barriers should be used liberally, rather than relying on complex platform-specific guarantees about limits to memory instruction reordering.

The Java language itself allows reads–writes to object fields to be reordered if they occur outside **`synchronized`** methods or blocks. Java provides a **`volatile`** keyword that ensures that reads–writes to a **`volatile`** object field that occur outside **`synchronized`** blocks or methods are not reordered. Using this keyword can be expensive, so it should be used only when necessary. We notice that in principle, one could use volatile fields to make double-checked locking work correctly, but there would not be much point, since accessing volatile variables requires synchronization anyway.

Here ends our primer on multiprocessor hardware. We will continue to discuss these architectural concepts in the context of specific data structures and algorithms. A pattern will emerge: the performance of multiprocessor programs is highly dependent on synergy with the underlying hardware.

B.8 Hardware Synchronization Instructions

As discussed in Chapter 5, any modern multiprocessor architecture must support powerful synchronization primitives to be universal, that is, provide concurrent computation's equivalent of a Universal Turing machine. It is therefore not surprising that the implementation of the Java language relies on such specialized hardware instructions (also called hardware primitives) in implementing synchronization, from spin-locks and monitors to the most complex lock-free structures.

Modern architectures typically provide one of two kinds of universal synchronization primitives. The *compare-and-swap* (CAS) instruction is supported in architectures by AMD, Intel, and Sun. It takes three arguments: an address a in memory, an *expected* value e, and an *update* value v. It returns a Boolean. It *atomically* executes the following steps:

- If the memory at address a contains the expected value e,
- write the update value v to that address and return *true*,
- otherwise leave the memory unchanged and return *false*.

On Intel and AMD architectures, CAS is called `CMPXCHG`, while on SPARC™ it is called `CAS`.[1] Java's `java.util.concurrent.atomic` library provides atomic Boolean, integer, and reference classes that implement CAS by a `compareAndSet()` method. (Because our examples are mostly in Java, we refer to `compareAndSet()` instead of CAS everywhere else.) C# provides the same functionality with the `Interlocked.CompareExchange` method.

The CAS instruction has one pitfall. Perhaps the most common use of CAS is the following. An application reads value a from a given memory address, and computes a new value c for that location. It intends to store c, but only if the value a in the address has not changed since it was read. One might think that applying a CAS with expected value a and update value c would accomplish this goal. There is a problem: a thread could have overwritten the value a with another value b, and later written a again to the address. The *compare-and-swap* will replace a with c, but the application may not have done what it was intended to do (for example, if the address stores a pointer, the new value a may be the address of a recycled object). The CAS call will replace e with v, but the application may not have done what it was intended to do. This problem is known as the *ABA* problem, discussed in detail in Chapter 10.

Another hardware synchronization primitive is a pair of instructions: *load-linked* and *store-conditional* (LL/SC). The LL instruction reads from an address a. A later SC instruction to a attempts to store a new value at that address. The instruction succeeds if the contents of address a are unchanged since that thread issued the earlier LL instruction to a. It fails if the contents of that address has changed in the interval.

The LL and SC instructions are supported by a number of architectures: Alpha AXP (`ldl_l`/`stl_c`), IBM PowerPC (`lwarx`/`stwcx`) MIPS `ll`/`sc`, and ARM (`ldrex`/`strex`). LL/SC does not suffer from the ABA problem, but in practice there are often severe restrictions on what a thread can do between a LL and the

---

1 Instead of a Boolean, CAS on Sparc returns the location's prior value, which can be used to retry an unsuccessful CAS. CMPXCHG on Intel's Pentium effectively returns both a Boolean and the prior value.

matching SC. A context switch, another LL, or another load or store instruction may cause the SC to fail.

It is good idea to use atomic fields and their associated methods sparingly because they are often based on CAS or LL/SC. A CAS or LL/SC instruction takes significantly more cycles to complete than a load or store: it includes a memory barrier and prevents out-of-order execution and various compiler optimizations. The precise cost depends on many factors, and varies not only from one architecture to the next, but also from one application of the instruction to the next within the same architecture. It suffices to say that CAS or LL/SC can be an order of magnitude slower than a simple load or store.

B.9 Chapter Notes

John Hennessy and David Patterson [58] give a comprehensive treatment of computer architecture. The MESI protocol is used by Intel's Pentium processor [75]. The tips on cache-conscious programming are adapted from Benjamin Gamsa, Orran Krieger, Eric Parsons, and Michael Stumm [43]. Sarita Adve and Karosh Gharachorloo [1] give an excellent survey of memory consistency models.

B.10 Exercises

Exercise 219. Thread A must wait for a thread on another processor to change a flag bit in memory. The scheduler can either allow A to spin, repeatedly retesting the flag, or it can deschedule A, allowing some other thread to run. Suppose it takes a total of 10 milliseconds for the operationg system to switch a processor from one thread to another. If the operating system deschedules thread A and immediately reschedules it, then it wastes 20 milliseconds. If, instead, A starts spinning at time t_0, and the flag changes at t_1, then the operating system will have wasted $t_1 - t_0$ time doing unproductive work.

A *prescient* scheduler is one that can predict the future. If it foresees that the flag will change in less than 20 milliseconds, it makes sense to have A spin, wasting less than 20 milliseconds, because descheduling and rescheduling A wastes 20 milliseconds. If, on the other hand, it takes more than 20 milliseconds for the flag to change, it makes sense to replace A with another thread, wasting no more than 20 milliseconds.

Your assignment is to implement a scheduler that never wastes more than *twice* the time a prescient scheduler would have wasted under the same circumstances.

Exercise 220. Imagine you are a lawyer, paid to make the best case you can for a particular point of view. How would you argue the following claim: if context switches took negligible time, then processors would not need caches, at least for applications that encompass large numbers of threads.

Extra credit: critique your argument.

Exercise 221. Consider a direct-mapped cache with 16 cache lines, indexed 0 to 15, where each cache line encompasses 32 words.

- Explain how to map an address a to a cache line in terms of bit shifting and masking operations. Assume for this question that addresses refer to words, not bytes: address 7 refers to the 7th word in memory.
- Compute the best and worst possible hit ratios for a program that loops 4 times through an array of 64 words.
- Compute the best and worst possible hit ratios for a program that loops 4 times through an array of 512 words.

Exercise 222. Consider a direct-mapped cache with 16 cache lines, indexed 0 to 15, where each cache line encompasses 32 words.

Consider a two-dimensional, 32×32 array of words a. This array is laid out in memory so that $a[0,0]$ is next to $a[0,1]$, and so on. Assume the cache is initially empty, but that $a[0,0]$ maps to the first word of cache line 0.

Consider the following *column-first* traversal:

```
int sum = 0;
for (int i = 0; i < 32; i++) {
  for (int j = 0; j < 32; j++) {
    sum += a[i,j];  // 2nd dim changes fastest
  }
}
```

and the following *row-first* traversal:

```
int sum = 0;
for (int i = 0; i < 32; i++) {
  for (int j = 0; j < 32; j++) {
    sum += a[j,i];  // 1st dim changes fastest
  }
}
```

Compare the number of cache misses produced by the two traversals, assuming the oldest cache line is evicted first.

Exercise 223. In the MESI cache-coherence protocol, what is the advantage of distinguishing between exclusive and modified modes?

What is the advantage of distinguishing between exclusive and shared modes?

Exercise 224. Implement the test-and-set and test-and-test-and-set locks shown in Figs. B.1 and B.2, test their relative performance on a multiprocessor, and analyze the results.

Bibliography

[1] S. V. Adve and K. Gharachorloo. Shared memory consistency models: A tutorial. *Computer*, 29(12):66–76, 1996.

[2] Y. Afek, H. Attiya, D. Dolev, E. Gafni, M. Merritt, and N. Shavit. Atomic snapshots of shared memory. *Journal of the ACM (JACM)*, 40(4):873–890, 1993.

[3] Y. Afek, D. Dauber, and D. Touitou. Wait-free made fast. In *STOC '95: Proc. of the Twenty-seventh Annual ACM Symposium on Theory of Computing*, pp. 538–547, NY, USA, 1995, ACM Press.

[4] Y. Afek, G. Stupp, and D. Touitou. Long-lived and adaptive atomic snapshot and immediate snapshot (extended abstract). In *PODC '00: Proc. of the Nineteenth Annual ACM Symposium on Principles of Distributed Computing*, Portland, Oregon, USA, pp. 71–80, NY, USA, 2000, ACM Press.

[5] Y. Afek, E. Weisberger, and H. Weisman. A completeness theorem for a class of synchronization objects. In *PODC '93: Proc. of the Twelfth Annual ACM Symposium on Principles of Distributed Computing*, pp. 159–170, NY, USA, 1993, ACM Press.

[6] A. Agarwal and M. Cherian. Adaptive backoff synchronization techniques. In *Proc. of the Sixteenth International Symposium on Computer Architecture*, pp. 396–406, May 1989.

[7] O. Agesen, D. Detlefs, A. Garthwaite, R. Knippel, Y. S. Ramakrishna, and D. White. An efficient meta-lock for implementing ubiquitous synchronization. *ACM SIGPLAN Notices*, 34(10):207–222, 1999.

[8] M. Ajtai, J. Komlós, and E. Szemerédi. An $O(n \log n)$ sorting network. *Combinatorica*, 3(1):1–19, 1983.

[9] G. M. Amdahl. Validity of the single-processor approach to achieving large scale computing capabilities. In *AFIPS Conference Proceedings*, pp. 483–485, Atlantic City, NJ, April 1967, Reston, VA, USA, AFIPS Press.

[10] J. H. Anderson. Composite registers. *Distributed Computing*, 6(3):141–154, 1993.

[11] J. H. Anderson and M. Moir. Universal constructions for multi-object operations. In *PODC '95: Proc. of the Fourteenth Annual ACM Symposium on Principles of Distributed Computing*, pp. 184–193, NY, USA, 1995, ACM Press.

[12] J. H. Anderson, M. G. Gouda, and A. K. Singh. The elusive atomic register. Technical Report TR 86.29, University of Texas at Austin, 1986.

[13] J. H. Anderson, M. G. Gouda, and A. K. Singh. The elusive atomic register. *Journal of the ACM*, 41(2):311–339, 1994.

[14] T. E. Anderson. The performance of spin lock alternatives for shared-memory multiprocessors. *IEEE Transactions on Parallel and Distributed Systems*, 1(1):6–16, 1990.

[15] N. S. Arora, R. D. Blumofe, and C. G. Plaxton. Thread scheduling for multiprogrammed multiprocessors. In *Proc. of the Tenth Annual ACM Symposium on Parallel Algorithms and Architectures*, pp. 119–129, NY, USA, 1998, ACM Press.

[16] J. Aspnes, M. Herlihy, and N. Shavit. Counting networks. *Journal of the ACM*, 41(5):1020–1048, 1994.

[17] D. F. Bacon, R. B. Konuru, C. Murthy, and M. J. Serrano. Thin locks: Featherweight synchronization for Java. In *PLDI '98: Proc. of the ACM SIGPLAN 1998 conference on Programming Language Design and Implementation*, Montreal, Quebec, Canada, pp. 258–268, NY, USA, 1998, ACM Press.

[18] K. Batcher. Sorting Networks and Their Applications. In *Proc. of the AFIPS Spring Joint Computer Conference*, 32:307–314, Reston, VA, USA, 1968.

[19] R. Bayer and M. Schkolnick. Concurrency of operations on B-trees. *Acta Informatica*, 9:1–21, 1977.

[20] R. D. Blumofe and C. E. Leiserson. Scheduling multithreaded computations by work stealing. *Journal of the ACM (JACM)*, 46(5):720–748, 1999.

[21] H. J. Boehm. Threads cannot be implemented as a library. In *PLDI '05: Proc. of the 2005 ACM SIGPLAN Conference on Programming Language Design and Implementation*, pp. 261–268, NY, USA, 2005, ACM Press.

[22] E. Borowsky and E. Gafni. Immediate atomic snapshots and fast renaming. In *PODC '93: Proc. of the Twelfth Annual ACM Symposium on Principles of Distributed Computing*, pp. 41–51, NY, USA, 1993, ACM Press.

[23] J. E. Burns and N. A. Lynch. Bounds on shared memory for mutual exclusion. *Information and Computation*, 107(2):171–184, December 1993.

[24] J. E. Burns and G. L. Peterson. Constructing multi-reader atomic values from non-atomic values. In *PODC '87: Proc. of the Sixth Annual ACM Symposium on Principles of Distributed Computing*, pp. 222–231, NY, USA, 1987, ACM Press.

[25] C. Busch and M. Mavronicolas. A combinatorial treatment of balancing networks. *Journal of the ACM*, 43(5):794–839, 1996.

[26] T. D. Chandra, P. Jayanti, and K. Tan. A polylog time wait-free construction for closed objects. In *PODC '98: Proc. of the Seventeenth Annual ACM Symposium on Principles of Distributed Computing*, pp. 287–296, NY, USA, 1998, ACM Press.

[27] G. Chapman, J. Cleese, T. Gilliam, E. Idle, T. Jones, and M. Palin. Monty phyton and the holy grail, Motion Picture, Michael White Productions, Released 10 May 1975, USA.

[28] D. Chase and Y. Lev. Dynamic circular work-stealing deque. In *SPAA '05: Proc. of the Seventeenth Annual ACM Symposium on Parallelism in Algorithms and Architectures*, pp. 21–28, NY, USA, 2005, ACM Press.

[29] A. Church. A note on the entscheidungs problem. *Journal of Symbolic Logic*, 1936.

[30] T. Craig. Building FIFO and priority-queueing spin locks from atomic swap. Technical Report TR 93-02-02, University of Washington, Department of Computer Science, February 1993.

[31] D. Dice. Implementing fast Java monitors with relaxed-locks. *Proc. of the JavaTM Virtual Machine Research and Technology Symposium on JavaTM Virtual Machine Research and Technology Symposium*, Monterey, California, p. 13, April 23–24, 2001.

[32] D. Dice, O. Shalev, and N. Shavit. Transactional locking II. *Proc. of the Twentieth International Symposium on Distributed Computing (DISC 2006)*, Stockholm, Sweden, pp. 194–208, 2006.

[33] E. W. Dijkstra. The structure of the THE multiprogramming system. *Communications of the ACM*, 11(5):341–346, NY, USA, 1968, ACM Press.

[34] D. Dolev and N. Shavit. Bounded concurrent time-stamping. *SIAM Journal of Computing*, 26(2):418–455, 1997.

[35] M. Dowd, Y. Perl, L. Rudolph, and M. Saks. The periodic balanced sorting network. *Journal of the ACM*, 36(4):738–757, 1989.

[36] A. C. Doyle. *A Study in Scarlet and the Sign of Four*. Berkley Publishing Group, NY, 1994. ISBN: 0425102408.

[37] C. Dwork and O. Waarts. Simple and efficient bounded concurrent timestamping and the traceable use abstraction. *Journal of the ACM (JACM)*, 46(5):633–666, 1999.

[38] C. Ellis. Concurrency in linear hashing. *ACM Transactions on Database Systems (TODS)*, 12(2):195–217, 1987.

[39] F. E. Fich, D. Hendler, and N. Shavit. On the inherent weakness of conditional primitives. *Distributed Computing*, 18(4):267–277, 2006.

[40] M. J. Fischer, N. A. Lynch, and M. S. Paterson. Impossibility of distributed consensus with one faulty process. *Journal of the ACM (JACM)*, 32(2):374–382, 1985.

[41] C. H. Flood, D. Detlefs, N. Shavit, and X. Zhang. Parallel garbage collection for shared memory multiprocessors. In *JVM '01 Proc. of the JavaTM Virtual Machine Research and Technology Symposium on JavaTM Virtual Machine Research and Technology Symposium*, Monterey, California, 2001. Berkelay, CA, USA, USENIX Association.

[42] K. Fraser. *Practical Lock-Freedom.* Ph.D. dissertation, Kings College, University of Cambridge, Cambridge, England, September 2003.

[43] B. Gamsa, O. Kreiger, E. W. Parsons, and M. Stumm. Performance issues for multiprocessor operating systems. Technical report, Computer Systems Research Institute, University of Toronto, 1995.

[44] H. Gao, J. F. Groote, and W. H. Hesselink. Lock-free dynamic hash tables with open addressing. *Distributed Computing*, 18(1):21–42, 2005.

[45] J. R. Goodman, M. K. Vernon, and P. J. Woest. Efficient synchronization primitives for large-scale cache-coherent multiprocessors. In *Proc. of the Third International Conference on Architectural support for Programming Languages and Operating Systems*, pp. 64–75, 1989, ACM Press.

[46] J. Gosling, B. Joy, G. L. Steele Jr., and G. Bracha. *The Java Language Specification*, Prentice Hall PTR, third edition, Upper Saddle River, New Jersey, USA, 2005. ISBN: 0321246780.

[47] A. Gottlieb, R. Grishman, C. P. Kruskal, K. P. McAuliffe, L. Rudolph, and M. Snir. The NYU ultracomputer-designing an MIMD parallel computer. *IEEE Transactions on Computers*, C-32(2):175–189, February 1984.

[48] M. Greenwald. Two-handed emulation: How to build non-blocking implementations of complex data-structures using DCAS. In *PODC '02: Proc. of the Twenty-first Annual Symposium on Principles of Distributed Computing*, Monterey, California, pp. 260–269, NY, USA, July 2002, ACM Press.

[49] R. Guerraoui, M. Herlihy, and B. Pochon. Toward a theory of transactional contention managers. In *PODC '05: Proc. of the Twenty-fourth Annual ACM Symposium on Principles of Distributed Computing*, pp. 258–264, Las Vegas, NY, USA, 2005, ACM Press.

[50] S. Haldar and K. Vidyasankar. Constructing 1-writer multireader multivalued atomic variables from regular variables. *Journal of the ACM*, 42(1):186–203, 1995.

[51] S. Haldar and P. Vitányi. Bounded concurrent timestamp systems using vector clocks. *Journal of the ACM (JACM)*, 49(1):101–126, 2002.

[52] P. B. Hansen. Structured multi-programming. *Communications of the ACM*, 15(7):574–578, 1972.

[53] T. Harris. A pragmatic implementation of non-blocking linked-lists. In *Proc. of Fifteenth International Symposium on Distributed Computing (DISC 2001), Lisbon, Portugal*, volume 2180 of *Lecture Notes in Computer Science*, pp. 300–314, October 2001, Springer-Verlag.

[54] T. Harris, S. Marlowe, S. Peyton-Jones, and M. Herlihy. Composable memory transactions. In *PPoPP '05: Proc. of the Tenth ACM SIGPLAN Symposium on Principles and Practice of Parallel Programming*, Chicago, IL, USA, pp. 48–60, NY, USA, 2005, ACM Press.

[55] S. Heller, M. Herlihy, V. Luchangco, M. Moir, W. N. Scherer III, and N. Shavit. A Lazy Concurrent List-Based Set Algorithm. *Proc. of the Ninth International Conference on Principles of Distributed Systems (OPODIS 2005)*, Pisa, Italy, pp. 3–16, 2005.

[56] D. Hendler and N. Shavit. Non-blocking Steal-half Work Queues. In *Proc. of the Twenty-first Annual ACM Symposium on Principles of Distributed Computing (PODC)*, Monterey, California, pp. 280–289, 2002, ACM Press.

[57] D. Hendler, N. Shavit, and L. Yerushalmi. A scalable lock-free stack algorithm. In *SPAA '04: Proc. of the Sixteenth Annual ACM Symposium on Parallelism in Algorithms and Architectures*, pp. 206–215, NY, USA, 2004, ACM Press.

[58] J. L. Hennessy and D. A. Patterson. *Computer Architecture: A Quantitative Approach.* Morgan Kaufmann Publishers, 1995.

[59] D. Hensgen, R. Finkel, and U. Manber. Two algorithms for barrier synchronization. *International Journal of Parallel Programming*, 17(1): 1–17, 0885-7458 1988.

[60] M. Herlihy. A methodology for implementing highly concurrent data objects. *ACM Transactions on Programming Languages and Systems*, 15(5):745–770, November 1993.

[61] M. Herlihy, V. Luchangco, and M. Moir. Obstruction-Free Synchronization: Double-Ended Queues as an Example. In *ICDCS '03: Proc. of the Twenty-third International Conference on Distributed Computing Systems*, p. 522, Washington, DC, USA, 2003. IEEE Computer Society.

[62] M. Herlihy. Wait-free synchronization. *ACM Transactions on Programming Languages and Systems (TOPLAS)*, 13(1):124–149, 1991.

[63] M. Herlihy and N. Shavit. On the nature of progress. In *Principles of Distributed Systems—15th International Conference, OPODIS 2011*, Toulouse, France, pp. 313–328, December 13–16, 2011.

[64] M. Herlihy, Y. Lev, and N. Shavit. A lock-free concurrent skiplist with wait-free search. Unpublished Manuscript, Sun Microsystems Laboratories, Burlington, Massachusetts, 2007.

[65] M. Herlihy, B.-H. Lim, and N. Shavit. Scalable concurrent counting. *ACM Transactions on Computer Systems*, 13(4):343–364, 1995.

[66] M. Herlihy, V. Luchangco, M. Moir, and W. N. Scherer III. Software transactional memory for dynamic-sized data structures. In *PODC '03, Proc. of the Twenty-second Annual Symposium on Principles of Distributed Computing*, Boston, Massachusetts, pp. 92–101, NY, USA, 2003, ACM Press.

[67] M. Herlihy and J. E. B. Moss. Transactional memory: architectural support for lock-free data structures. In *Proc. of the Twentieth Annual International Symposium on Computer Architecture*, pp. 289–300, San Diego, California, 1993, ACM Press.

[68] M. Herlihy, N. Shavit, and M. Tzafrir. Concurrent cuckoo hashing. Technical report, Providence RI, Brown University, 2007.

[69] M. Herlihy and J. M. Wing. Linearizability: a correctness condition for concurrent objects. *ACM Transactions on Programming Languages and Systems (TOPLAS)*, 12(3):463–492, 1990.

[70] C. A. R. Hoare. "partition: Algorithm 63," "quicksort: Algorithm 64," and "find: Algorithm 65." *Communications of the ACM*, 4(7):321–322, 1961.

[71] C. A. R. Hoare. Monitors: an operating system structuring concept. *Communications of the ACM*, 17(10):549–557, 1974.

[72] M. Hsu and W. P. Yang. Concurrent operations in extendible hashing. In *Symposium on Very Large Data Bases*, pp. 241–247, San Francisco, CA, USA, 1986. Morgan Kaufmann Publishers Inc.

[73] J. S. Huang and Y. C. Chow. Parallel sorting and data partitioning by sampling. In *Proc. of the IEEE Computer Society's Seventh International Computer Software and Applications Conference*, pp. 627–631, 1983.

[74] G. C. Hunt, M. M. Michael, S. Parthasarathy, and M. L. Scott. An efficient algorithm for concurrent priority queue heaps. *Inf. Process. Lett.*, 60(3):151–157, 1996.

[75] Intel Corporation. *Pentium Processor User's Manual.* Intel Books, 1993. ISBN: 1555121934.

[76] A. Israeli and L. Rappaport. Disjoint-access-parallel implementations of strong shared memory primitives. In *PODC '94: Proc. of the Thirteenth Annual ACM Symposium on Principles of Distributed Computing*, Los Angeles, California, United States, pp. 151–160, NY, USA, August 14–17 1994, ACM Press.

[77] A. Israeli and M. Li. Bounded time stamps. *Distributed Computing*, 6(5): 205–209, 1993.

[78] A. Israeli and A. Shaham. Optimal multi-writer multi-reader atomic register. In *PODC '92: Proc. of the Eleventh Annual ACM Symposium on Principles of Distributed Computing*, Vancouver, British Columbia, Canada, pp. 71–82, NY, USA, 1992, ACM Press.

[79] P. Jayanti. Robust wait-free hierarchies. *Journal of the ACM*, 44(4):592–614, 1997.

[80] P. Jayanti. A lower bound on the local time complexity of universal constructions. In *PODC '98: Proc. of the Seventeenth Annual ACM Symposium on Principles of Distributed Computing*, pp. 183–192, NY, USA, 1998, ACM Press.

[81] P. Jayanti and S. Toueg. Some results on the impossibility, universality, and decidability of consensus. In *WDAG '92: Proc. of the Sixth International Workshop on Distributed Algorithms*, pp. 69–84, London, UK, 1992. Springer-Verlag.

[82] D. Jiménez-González, J. Larriba-Pey, and J. Navarro. CC-Radix: A cache conscious sorting based on Radix sort. In *Proc. Eleventh Euromicro Conference on Parallel, Distributed, and Network-Based Processing*, pp. 101–108, 2003. ISBN: 0769518753.

[83] L. M. Kirousis, P. G. Spirakis, and P. Tsigas. Reading many variables in one atomic operation: Solutions with linear or sublinear complexity. In *IEEE Trans. Parallel Distributed System*, 5(7): 688–696, Piscataway, NJ, USA, 1994, IEEE Press.

[84] M. R. Klugerman. Small-depth counting networks and related topics. Technical Report MIT/LCS/TR-643, MIT Laboratory for Computer Science, 1994.

[85] M. Klugerman and C. Greg Plaxton. Small-depth counting networks. In *STOC '92: Proc. of the Twenty-fourth Annual ACM Symposium on Theory of Computing*, pp. 417–428, NY, USA, 1992, ACM Press.

[86] D. E. Knuth. *The Art of Computer Programming: Second Ed. (Addison-Wesley Series in Computer Science and Information)*. Boston, MA, USA, 1978 Addison-Wesley Longman Publishing Co., Inc.

[87] V. Kumar. Concurrent operations on extendible hashing and its performance. *Communications of the ACM*, 33(6):681–694, 1990.

[88] L. Lamport. A new solution of Dijkstra's concurrent programming problem. *Communications of the ACM*, 17(5):543–545, 1974.

[89] L. Lamport. Time, clocks, and the ordering of events. *Communications of the ACM*, 21(7):558–565, July 1978.

[90] L. Lamport. How to make a multiprocessor computer that correctly executes multiprocess programs. *IEEE Transactions on Computers*, C-28(9):690, September 1979.

[91] L. Lamport. Specifying concurrent program modules. *ACM Transactions on Programming Languages and Systems*, 5(2):190–222, 1983.

[92] L. Lamport. Invited address: Solved problems, unsolved problems and non-problems in concurrency. In *Proc. of the Third Annual ACM Symposium on Principles of Distributed Computing*, pp. 1–11, 1984, ACM Press.

[93] L. Lamport. The mutual exclusion problem—Part I: A theory of interprocess communication. *Journal of the ACM (JACM)*, 33(2):313–326, 1986, ACM Press.

[94] L. Lamport. The mutual exclusion problem—Part II: Statement and solutions. *Journal of the ACM (JACM)*, 33(2):327–348, 1986.

[95] L. Lamport. A fast mutual exclusion algorithm. *ACM Trans. Comput. Syst.*, 5(1):1–11, 1987.

[96] B. Lampson and D. Redell. Experience with processes and monitors in mesa. *Communications of the ACM*, 2(23):105–117, 1980.

[97] J. R. Larus and R. Rajwar. *Transactional Memory*. Morgan and Claypool, San Francisco, 2006.

[98] D. Lea. Java community process, JSR 166, concurrency utilities. `http://gee.cs.oswego.edu/dl/concurrency-interest/index.html`, 2003.

[99] D. Lea. Concurrent hash map in JSR 166 concurrency utilities. `http://gee.cs.oswego.edu/dl/concurrency-interest/index.html`. Dec 2007.

[100] D. Lea, Personal Communication, 2007.

[101] S.-J. Lee, M. Jeon, D. Kim, and A. Sohn. Partitioned parallel radix sort. *J. Parallel Distributed Computing*, 62(4):656–668, 2002.

[102] C. E. Leiserson and H. Prokop. A minicourse on multithreaded programming, Massachusetts Institute of Technology, Available on the Internet from `http://theory.lcs.mit.edu/~click, 1998. citeseer.ist.psu.edu/leiserson98minicourse.html`.

[103] Y. Lev, M. Herlihy, V. Luchangco, and N. Shavit. A Simple Optimistic Skiplist Algorithm. Fourteenth Colloquium on structural information and

communication complexity (SIROCCO) 2007 pp. 124–138, June 5–8, 2007, Castiglioncello (LI), Italy.

[104] M. Li, J. Tromp, and P. M. B. Vitányi. How to share concurrent wait-free variables. *Journal of the ACM*, 43(4):723–746, 1996.

[105] B.-H. Lim. Personal Communication, Cambridge, Massachusetts. 1995.

[106] W.-K. Lo and V. Hadzilacos. All of us are smarter than any of us: wait-free hierarchies are not robust. In *STOC '97: Proc. of the Twenty-ninth Annual ACM Symposium on Theory of Computing*, pp. 579–588, NY, USA, 1997, ACM Press.

[107] I. Lotan and N. Shavit. Skiplist-based concurrent priority queues. In *Proc. of the Fourteenth International Parallel and Distributed Processing Symposium (IPDPS)*, pp. 263–268, Cancun, Mexico, 2000.

[108] M. Loui and H. Abu-Amara. Memory requirements for agreement among unreliable asynchronous processes. In F. P. Preparata, editor, *Advances in Computing Research*, volume 4, pages 163–183. JAI Press, Greenwich, CT, 1987.

[109] V. Luchangco, D. Nussbaum, and N. Shavit. A Hierarchical CLH Queue Lock. In *Proc. of the European Conference on Parallel Computing (EuroPar 2006)*, pp. 801–810, Dresdan, Germany, 2006.

[110] P. Magnussen, A. Landin, and E. Hagersten. Queue locks on cache coherent multiprocessors. In *Proc. of the Eighth International Symposium on Parallel Processing (IPPS)*, pp. 165–171, April 1994. IEEE Computer Society, April 1994. Vancouver, British Columbia, Canada, NY, USA, 1987, ACM Press.

[111] J. Manson, W. Pugh, and S. V. Adve. The Java memory model. In *POPL '05: Proc. of the Thirty-second ACM SIGPLAN-SIGACT Symposium on Principles of Programming Languages*, pp. 378–391, NY, USA, 2005, ACM Press.

[112] P. E. McKenney. Selecting locking primitives for parallel programming. *Communications of the ACM*, 39(10):75–82, 1996.

[113] J. Mellor-Crummey and M. L. Scott. Algorithms for scalable synchronization on shared-memory multiprocessors. *ACM Transactions on Computer Systems*, 9(1):21–65, 1991.

[114] M. M. Michael. High performance dynamic lock-free hash tables and list-based sets. In *SPAA '02: Proc. of the Fourteenth Annual ACM Symposium on Parallel Algorithms and Architectures*, pp. 73–82. Winnipeg, Manitoba, Canada, NY, USA, 2002, ACM Press.

[115] M. M. Michael and M. L. Scott. Simple, fast, and practical non-blocking and blocking concurrent queue algorithms. In *Proc. of the Fifteenth Annual ACM Symposium on Principles of Distributed Computing*, pp. 267–275, 1996, ACM Press.

[116] J. Misra. Axioms for memory access in asynchronous hardware systems. *ACM Transactions on Programming Languages and Systems (TOPLAS)*, 8(1):142–153, 1986.

[117] M. Moir. Practical implementations of non-blocking synchronization primitives. In *PODC '97: Proc. of the Sixteenth Annual ACM Symposium*

on Principles of Distributed Computing, pp. 219–228, NY, USA, 1997, ACM Press.

[118] M. Moir. Laziness pays! Using lazy synchronization mechanisms to improve non-blocking constructions. In *PODC '00: Proc. of the Nineteenth Annual ACM Symposium on Principles of Distributed Computing*, pp. 61–70, NY, USA, 2000, ACM Press.

[119] M. Moir, D. Nussbaum, O. Shalev, and N. Shavit. Using elimination to implement scalable and lock-free fifo queues. In *SPAA '05: Proc. of the Seventeenth Annual ACM Symposium on Parallelism in Algorithms and Architectures*, pp. 253–262, NY, USA, 2005, ACM Press.

[120] M. Moir V. Marathe and N. Shavit. Composite abortable locks. In *Proc. of the 20th IEEE International Parallel & Distributed Processing Symposium (IPDPS)*, pages 1–10, 2006.

[121] I. Newton, I. B. Cohen (Translator), and A. Whitman (Translator). *The Principia: Mathematical Principles of Natural Philosophy*. University of California Press, CA, USA, 1999.

[122] R. Pagh and F. F. Rodler. Cuckoo hashing. *J. Algorithms*, 51(2):122–144, 2004.

[123] C. H. Papadimitriou. The serializability of concurrent database updates. *Journal of the ACM (JACM)*, 26(4):631–653, 1979.

[124] G. Peterson. Myths about the mutual exclusion problem. *Information Processing Letters*, 12(3):115–116, June 1981.

[125] G. L. Peterson. Concurrent reading while writing. *ACM Trans. Program. Lang. Syst.*, 5(1):46–55, 1983.

[126] S. A. Plotkin. Sticky bits and universality of consensus. In *PODC '89: Proc. of the Eighth Annual ACM Symposium on Principles of Distributed Computing*, pp. 159–175, NY, USA, 1989, ACM Press.

[127] W. Pugh. Concurrent maintenance of skip lists. Technical Report CS-TR-2222.1, Institute for Advanced Computer Studies, Department of Computer Science, University of Maryland, 1989.

[128] W. Pugh. Skip lists: a probabilistic alternative to balanced trees. *ACM Transactions on Database Systems*, 33(6):668–676, 1990.

[129] C. Purcell and T. Harris. Non-blocking hashtables with open addressing. Lecture Notes in Computer Science. Distributed Computing. In *DISC*, Springer Berlin/Heidelberg, pp. 108–121, 2005.

[130] Z. Radović and E. Hagersten. Hierarchical Backoff Locks for Nonuniform Communication Architectures. In *Ninth International Symposium on High Performance Computer Architecture*, pp. 241–252, Anaheim, California, USA, February 2003.

[131] M. Raynal. *Algorithms for Mutual Exclusion*. The MIT Press, Cambridge, MA, 1986.

[132] J. H. Reif and L. G. Valiant. A logarithmic time sort for linear size networks. *Journal of the ACM*, 34(1):60–76, 1987.

[133] L. Rudolph and Z. Segall. Dynamic decentralized cache schemes for mimd parallel processors. In *Proceedings of the 11th Annual International*

Symposium on Computer Architecture, ISCA '84, pp. 340–347. ACM, New York, NY, USA, 1984.

[134] L. Rudolph, M. Slivkin-Allalouf, and E. Upfal. A simple load balancing scheme for task allocation in parallel machines. In *Proc. of the Third Annual ACM Symposium on Parallel Algorithms and Architectures*, pp. 237–245, July 1991, ACM Press.

[135] M. Saks, N. Shavit, and H. Woll. Optimal time randomized consensus—making resilient algorithms fast in practice. In *SODA '91: Proc. of the Second Annual ACM-SIAM Symposium on Discrete Algorithms*, pp. 351–362, Philadelphia, PA, USA, 1991. Society for Industrial and Applied Mathematics.

[136] W. N. Scherer III, D. Lea, and M. L. Scott. Scalable synchronous queues. In *PPoPP '06: Proc. of the Eleventh ACM SIGPLAN Symposium on Principles and Practice of Parallel Programming*, pp. 147–156, NY, USA, 2006, ACM Press.

[137] W. N. Scherer III and M. L. Scott. Advanced contention management for dynamic software transactional memory. In *PODC '05: Proc. of the Twenty-fourth Annual ACM Symposium on Principles of Distributed Computing*, pp. 240–248, NY, USA, 2005, ACM Press.

[138] M. L. Scott. Non-blocking timeout in scalable queue-based spin locks. In *PODC '02: Proc. of the Twenty-first Annual Symposium on Principles of Distributed Computing*, pp. 31–40, NY, USA, 2002, ACM Press.

[139] M. L. Scott and W. N. Scherer III. Scalable queue-based spin locks with timeout. *ACM SIGPLAN Notices*, 36(7):44–52, 2001.

[140] M. Sendak. *Where the Wild Things Are.* Publisher: HarperCollins, NY, USA, 1988. ISBN: 0060254920.

[141] O. Shalev and N. Shavit. Split-ordered lists: lock-free extensible hash tables. In *Journal of the ACM*, 53(3):379–405, NY, USA, 2006, ACM Press.

[142] N. Shavit and D. Touitou. Software transactional memory. In *Distributed Computing*, Special Issue 10(2):99–116, 1997.

[143] N. Shavit and A. Zemach. Diffracting trees. *ACM Trans. Comput. Syst.*, 14(4):385–428, 1996.

[144] E. Shenk. The consensus hierarchy is not robust. In *PODC '97: Proc. of the Sixteenth Annual ACM Symposium on Principles of Distributed Computing*, p. 279, NY, USA, 1997, ACM Press.

[145] R. K. Treiber. Systems programming: Coping with parallelism. Technical Report RJ 5118, IBM Almaden Research Center, April 1986. San Jose, CA.

[146] A. Turing. On computable numbers, with an application to the entscheidungs problem. *Proc. Lond. Math. Soc*, Historical document, 1937.

[147] J. D. Valois. Lock-free linked lists using compare-and-swap. In *PODC '95: Proc. of the Fourteenth Annual ACM Symposium on Principles of Distributed Computing*, pp. 214–222. Ottowa, Ontario, Canada, NY, USA, 1995, ACM Press.

[148] P. Vitányi and B. Awerbuch. Atomic shared register access by asynchronous hardware. In *Twenty-seventh Annual Symposium on Foundations*

of Computer Science, pp. 233–243, Los Angeles, CA, USA, October 1986, IEEE Computer Society Press.

[149] W. E. Weihl. Local atomicity properties: modular concurrency control for abstract data types. *ACM Transactions on Programming Languages and Systems (TOPLAS)*, 11(2):249–282, 1989.

[150] R. N. Wolfe. A protocol for wait-free, atomic, multi-reader shared variables. In *PODC '87: Proc. of the Sixth Annual ACM Symposium on Principles of Distributed Computing*, pp. 232–248, NY, USA, 1987, ACM Press.

[151] P. Yew, N. Tzeng, and D. Lawrie. Distributing hot-spot addressing in large-scale multiprocessors. *IEEE Transactions on Computers*, C-36(4):388–395, April 1987.

Index